Thoughts and Utterances

For Vlad

Thoughts and Utterances

The Pragmatics of Explicit Communication

ROBYN CARSTON

Blackwell Publishing

350 Main Street, Malden, MA 02148-5018, USA
108 Cowley Road, Oxford OX4 1JF, UK
550 Swanston Street, Carlton, Victoria 3053, Australia
Kurfürstendamm 57, 10707 Berlin, Germany

First published 2002 by Blackwell Publishers Ltd, a Blackwell Publishing company

Library of Congress Cataloging-in-Publication Data

Carston, Robyn.
Thoughts and utterances : the pragmatics of explicit communication / Robyn Carston.
p. cm.
Includes bibliographical references and index.
ISBN 0-631-17891-0 (alk. paper)—ISBN 0-631-21488-7 (pbk. : alk. paper)
1. Pragmatics. 2. Semantics. 3. Communication—Philosophy. I. Title.
P99.4.P72 C37 2002
306.44—dc21

2002066420

A catalogue record for this title is available from the British Library.

Set in 10 on 12pt Sabon
by SNP Best-set Typesetter Ltd, Hong Kong
Printed and bound in the United Kingdom
by MPG Books Ltd, Bodmin, Cornwall

For further information on
Blackwell Publishing, visit our website:
http://www.blackwellpublishing.com

Contents

99.4
.P72
C37
2002

Acknowledgements

My greatest intellectual debt, as evident throughout this book, is to Dan Sperber and Deirdre Wilson, the founders of Relevance Theory, and I am deeply grateful to them.

Noel Burton-Roberts's meticulous comments on the first complete draft were an enormous help to me in the long process of reworking what was a PhD thesis into this book. Special thanks also to Corinne Iten, Deirdre Wilson and Vladimir Žegarac who have been very generous in reading and commenting on my work. Discussions with Diane Blakemore, Bob Borsley, Richard Breheny, Billy Clark, Carmen Curcó, Annabel Cormack, Marjolein Groefsema, Richard Horsey, Ruth Kempson, Adrian Pilkington, George Powell, Villy Rouchota, Neil Smith, Rosa Vega-Moreno and Tim Wharton have been illuminating and energizing.

I have benefited greatly from communication with a number of philosophers, whose incisive thinking has been an inspiration: Martin Davies, Steven Davis, Marcus Giaquinto, Sam Guttenplan, Andreas Kemmerling, Barry Lee, Barry Smith, Rob Stainton, Jason Stanley and, especially, Kent Bach and François Recanati, whose work in semantics and pragmatics is an ongoing rich source of ideas and intellectual pleasure.

Throughout the writing of this book, as always, my parents, Norma Carston and Cecil Carston, and my sisters, Linda Vassar and Kay Carston, have been a constant source of care and support. I am deeply grateful to my dear friends: Tony Bellette, Diane Blakemore, Lynn Coleman, Judith Dale, Marcus Giaquinto, Valérie Hazan, Corinne Iten, Dinah Murray, Neil Smith, Deirdre Wilson, Chrysoula Worrall and, especially, Diana Woollard, bringer of light during my long hours in the academic tunnel. Across the language barrier, Mile Žegarac and Ljubica Šuput-Žegarac have communicated their unstinting encouragement and support. Above all, the constant companionship of Vladimir Žegarac has given me the peace and security which has made it possible to think and write.

Many thanks to the production team at Blackwell Publishing, who were efficient and helpful. I'm especially grateful to Philip Carpenter for his humour and kindness over many years, and to Valery Rose whose calm clarity soothed away many worries.

The final stages of this work were greatly enabled by the support of a research fellowship from the Leverhulme Trust (RF&G/1/9900510).

I acknowledge Curtis Brown (Aust.), Sydney, for copyright permission to quote the passage at the beginning of chapter 2, taken from Janet Frame's short story 'Keel and Kool'.

Introduction

Could mortal lip divine
The undeveloped Freight
Of a delivered syllable
'Twould crumble with the weight.
(Emily Dickinson, 1894)

Some formidably able minds have maintained that a pragmatic theory is not possible, that communication and interpretation are not topics which submit to
scientific study. Donald Davidson (1986) observes that 'the interpreter' includes
everything that people might know and are capable of doing, so nothing sensible
can be said about it. Noam Chomsky (1992a) endorses this view, seeing the wish
for a theory of the interpreter as tantamount to a 'demand for a theory of everything', the pursuit of which will lead to a theory of nothing. By a theory of 'the
interpreter', both Chomsky and Davidson mean something very much like a pragmatic theory: 'The interpreter, presented with an utterance and a situation, assigns
some interpretation to what is being said by a person in this situation.' But this, the
topic of successful communication, 'is far too complex and obscure to merit attention in empirical inquiry' (Chomsky 1992a: 120); it would seem to be a mystery, in
Chomsky's terms, rather than a tractable intellectual problem.

Jerry Fodor (1983, 1986, 1987b) holds a similar position. Understanding an utterance involves arriving at a confirmed hypothesis about what the speaker meant;
that is, it is one kind of belief fixation and fixing beliefs is the function of the holistic inference processes of the central systems of the mind. While the peripheral input
and output systems, which mediate perception (including language perception) and
execute motor routines, are fast, automatic processors, oblivious to much potentially relevant information, the central systems are intelligent and reflective, they
look around and consider the options. Precisely because these central thought
processes are domain-general, with no architectural constraints on the information

that may be consulted in arriving at their decisions, they are very unlikely, in Fodor's view, to yield to scientific investigation. He formulates this as his First Law of the Non-existence of Cognitive Science: 'the more global a cognitive process is, the less anybody understands it'. His pet case is scientific hypothesis formation and confirmation, but, clearly, utterance interpretation is also a global process, albeit a much quicker, more spontaneous one, than scientific theorizing; in principle, information from virtually anywhere about virtually anything might have a bearing on the interpretation of an utterance.[1] So, in Fodor's (and Chomsky's) view, among the full range of processes involved in verbal understanding, we may come to have some systematic understanding of just those that deliver the logical forms of linguistic expressions, since they are fully determined by a system of autonomous domain-specific principles responsive to the acoustic properties of speech, that is, they are context-independent. There is going to be no science of human communication; we have to turn to the arts, to novelists and playwrights, in order to get some (inevitably unsystematic and anecdotal) insights into communication and interpretation.

The relevance-theoretic framework developed in the 1980s by Dan Sperber and Deirdre Wilson can be seen as a response to the challenge presented by these sceptics. Their work lies squarely within the wider Fodorian view of mind: it assumes that the mind is, at least in part, a system of (subsystems of) representations which have syntactic and semantic properties, and that mental processes are computations driven by the formal (syntactic) properties of these representations, it recognizes a conceptual language of thought which is distinct from any particular natural language, and it adopts the view that the mind is to some extent modular in structure. Assuming this Fodorian basis, Sperber and Wilson (1986a/1995b) set out to give an account of how hearers (interpreters) reach the intended interpretation of an utterance quickly and with relative certainty, despite the fact that there are, in principle, indefinitely many possible interpretations, all compatible with the linguistically encoded content. The question that has to be addressed is how it is that hearers do not get into ever lengthier chains of inference, searching for more and more possible interpretations and comparing them, in a bid to find the 'right' one or the 'best' one.

Sperber and Wilson point out that fixing a belief about a speaker's informative intention differs from scientific theorizing and also from quite mundane human decision-making processes in two ways. First, it typically involves a much shorter time-scale than scientific theorizing and is also generally quicker than much non-scientific decision-making (what to buy mother for Christmas, whether to accept a job offer, where to go for a relaxing summer holiday, etc.). Utterance interpretation is very rapid and, however much evidence might, in principle, be taken into account, only a very small range is usually considered, in practice. Second, while the data for scientific theorizing comes from impassive nature, which is not actively involved in helping scientists build correct theories, the data for utterance interpretation comes from a helpful source: speakers generally want their informative intentions to be fulfilled and so shape their communicative stimuli accordingly.

These two factors – the time pressure inherent in on-line processing and the speaker's responsibility for the quality of the stimulus she produces – are reflected in the concept of 'optimal relevance' which is the key notion in the theory. (It is discussed here in a fairly intuitive sort of way; see 'presumption of optimal relevance' in appendix 1 for a little more precision, and chapter 2 for exemplification.) By virtue of the overt demand for attention, hence for expenditure of processing resources, that an utterance (or any other ostensive communicative behaviour) makes on an addressee, he is entitled to expect it to yield an interpretation which has a worthwhile range of cognitive effects for him and to require no gratuitous expenditure of effort on his part in deriving these effects; an interpretation which meets this expectation is 'optimally relevant'. Given this way of viewing the mental interaction of speaker and hearer, 'the very fact that an element of interpretation comes first to [the hearer's] mind is an argument in its favour' (Sperber 2000: 132). This is, clearly, a major factor in overcoming the alleged 'all things considered', inferentially unconstrained nature of the interpretive processes. The claim, then, is that hearers construct and test interpretive hypotheses in order of their accessibility, and once they have found an interpretation which satisfies their expectation of relevance they stop.

This construal of pragmatics, as a cognitive account of the processes involved in understanding utterances, is clearly a quite different matter from the 'pragmatic turn' taken within the philosophy of language in the 1950s, which has, nevertheless, exerted an important influence on all subsequent pragmatic theorizing whether philosophical, linguistic or of this cognitive psychological sort. The so-called 'ordinary language' philosophers (J. L. Austin, Peter Strawson, the later Wittgenstein and, in many ways, H. P. Grice) concentrated their conceptual analytical efforts on describing natural language meaning as used by ordinary people, both in their one-to-one interactions and in the context of social institutions. They were reacting to the focus on 'ideal' logical languages, which dominated the first half of the twentieth century (associated with, among others, Gottlob Frege and Bertrand Russell), where the primary aim was to make quite explicit which inferences were logically valid and which were not, and so to pin down the logical commitments of expressing a particular proposition or making a particular statement. Naturally enough, extrapolation from the properties of fully explicit, content-invariant logical languages to the properties of natural language had led to a gross underestimation of the context-sensitivity of natural language utterances, a lack of interest in the nuances of non-logical word meaning and a sidelining of all sentence types other than declaratives. The ordinary language philosophers, and the ensuing speech act tradition, redressed that imbalance and, under the influence of Grice, in particular, the two approaches were largely reconciled as complementary endeavours – the one, semantics, concerned with 'what the words say'; the other, pragmatics, with 'what the speaker means' – rather than as rival approaches to linguistic meaning. (See Recanati (1994, 1998) for a more detailed account of the development of pragmatics within the philosophy of language.)

A primary motivation for Grice's interest in the conditions or norms governing conversation, or discourse more generally, was that he saw them as providing a means for preserving some of the important parallels between logical languages and natural language semantics, which had been established by Russell, Frege and other logicians, and which were under threat from the meaning analyses of some of the ordinary language philosophers (see Grice 1975: 41–3). These included the position that the meaning of certain natural language connectives, such as 'and', 'or' and 'if', is identical to the truth-functional semantics of their apparent counterparts in the predicate calculus and that Russell's quantificational theory of descriptions provides a fully adequate semantics for definite descriptions in natural language. Grice's system of norms or maxims governing the communicative use of language was employed to account for the various divergences between the meanings these words have in ordinary use and the semantics predicted by the logical analyses. In this way the logical semantic core of the linguistic elements at issue could be maintained and the 'extra' meaning acquired in use understood as pragmatic (conversational) implications of a certain sort. Following Grice, an interest in a pragmatic account of some aspect of utterance meaning has often been fuelled by a concern to avoid multiple lexical ambiguities or to solve some other problem in natural language semantics.

The advent of cognitive pragmatics, specifically of the relevance-theoretic approach, has brought a rather different orientation: 'pragmatics' is a capacity of the mind, a kind of information-processing system, a system for interpreting a particular phenomenon in the world, namely human ostensive communicative behaviour. It is a proper object of study in itself, no longer to be seen as simply an adjunct to natural language semantics, though it clearly continues to have an essential interaction with semantics, as will be evident in every chapter of this book. Set within a cognitive scientific framework, this kind of pragmatic theorizing is answerable to different sources of evidence and criteria of adequacy from that of any philosophical analytical investigation. For instance, evidence from children's communicative development, from people with specific communicative and interpretive difficulties or deficits and from certain psycholinguistic experiments on comprehension may well have a bearing on an account of how the pragmatic system works, as may facts about the functioning and architecture of other mental capacities which interact with the utterance comprehension system, such as the language faculty and the so-called 'theory of mind' mechanism for interpreting people's behaviour in terms of certain of their mental states (beliefs, desires, intentions).[2]

Within current philosophical and cognitive scientific approaches to the study of the mind, there is a variety of different kinds and levels of explanation. I'll consider some of these briefly, with a view to assessing which of them may apply to the relevance-theoretic approach to pragmatics. The great nineteenth-century psychologist, William James, believed there were only two levels in discussing the human mind/brain: the phenomenological and the neurological. He conducted most of his psychological work at the upper level (the level of the whole person, the intentional, the conscious), this being, of the two, the specifically *psychological* level of inquiry. Among current philosophers of mind, John Searle appears to hold the same position; in his view, the only properly *mental* states are those which are conscious (or potentially conscious); the rest are a matter for physiology. (See Searle 1983, 1992, and some discussion in chapter 1.) However, the current dominant cognitive science paradigm works at a quite different level, which can be thought of as situated between the other two. This is the symbolic, computational level, which, it is claimed, is a genuine psychological level, a level of mental states and processes, many of which are unconscious and not accessible to consciousness even in principle. The main impetus for this view came from Alan Turing's fundamental insight that mental processes can be thought of as changes of mental states that are governed by the syntactic or formal properties of mental representations just like the symbol manipulations performed by (unconscious) computing machines. The assumed tacit nature of the knowledge and processes entails a need for methods of *scientific* enquiry, additional to the intense introspection and philosophical analysis that have been applied to understanding the conscious mind. Among the central commitments of this kind of theorizing about the mind are: *materialism* (since everything that has causal powers ultimately owes those powers to physical properties of some sort, all mental phenomena must be realized in physical material), *non-reductionism* (there is, nonetheless, an autonomous level of psychological description, explanation and generalization, which is not reducible to the physiological/neurological or the behavioural), and *methodological naturalism*, according to which the methods of investigation into human cognitive capacities are those that typify any inquiry in the natural sciences (physiology, chemistry, geology, astronomy, etc.), as opposed to the assumption that when it comes to the human mind some other kind of inquiry must be conducted ('methodological dualism', see Chomsky 1994, 1995).

As a strong proponent of the sort of approach to human cognition just outlined, Chomsky stresses the importance of distinguishing those components, of the complex of systems involved in any human state or action, which might prove tractable to scientific study, from those that won't. In his discussions of language use and interpretation (Chomsky 1992a, 1992b, 1995), he singles out as components which may be amenable to empirical inquiry what he calls 'I-language' (the internal computational procedure which interfaces with the phonetic system, on the one hand, and the conceptual system, on the other) and some performance systems, such as the parser. He points out that, while such systems play a crucial role in human linguistic communication, it would be an error to attribute to them, or to a complex of them, the achievements of 'referring' or of 'understanding':

> People . . . pronounce words, refer to cats, speak their thoughts, understand what others say, play chess, or whatever; their brains don't and computer programs don't . . . just as it is persons who take a walk, not their feet.   (Chomsky 1992b: 213)

I think that the distinction Chomsky is drawing here is (or bears a close relation to) the philosophical distinction between the 'personal' and the 'sub-personal' levels of explanation, first introduced by Daniel Dennett (1969). Persons are conscious thinking agents, who engage in actions (voluntary behaviours) which can be explained in terms of reasons, that is, in terms of commonsense psychological attributions of beliefs, desires and practical inferences that would normally lead to such actions. A mundane example of such personal-level explanation is the following: X picked up her umbrella before she went out of doors because she believed it was going to rain and she wanted to stay dry. This intentional (belief/desire) explanation makes her action reasonable or justified, makes it an intelligible behaviour. The hallmark of this sort of explanation is that it is normative, it is given in terms of what *ought* to be the case; we find someone intelligible as a person by interpreting her actions in terms of what she ought to be doing if she is rational. For instance, we might explain what a speaker meant by her utterance in terms of what it would be rational for her to have meant given the words she used in the particular context. Sub-personal explanation, on the other hand, deals in entities and properties that can be shown to play a *causal role* in the action or behaviour, without necessarily standing in rational or normative relations to it. A physiological account in terms of the neuronal activity in the brain which accompanies the production, or the understanding, of an utterance would have nothing to do with considerations of people as agents with reasons and would be an obvious instance of a sub-personal explanation. However, given the current cognitive scientific case for an autonomous level of unconscious syntactically-driven mental computation, there is plainly another level of sub-personal explanation, one which is, arguably, not reducible to the neurological. In the following discussion, talk of the sub-personal level of explanation is directed at this psychological level of information-processing mechanisms.

If I understand him right, what Chomsky is saying is that, while we can never come to a full scientific understanding of a personal-level state or activity, we may be able to get some grip on some of the sub-personal components that play a causal role in the activities described at the level of the person, such as seeing, referring and understanding utterances. So, for instance, the information-processing algorithms which, according to David Marr (1982), deliver a 3-D model representation from an input of retinal stimulation, are crucial elements contributing to what might be described at the personal level as 'seeing a tree' or 'recognizing a certain building'; similarly, the computational I-language system is an essential enabling component of the personal-level abilities of speaking and understanding utterances. Accounts pitched at the sub-personal level offer partial explanations for whatever personal-level ability we are focusing on. The personal level is not primarily a level of scientific description and explanation, but is more a matter for the philosophy of mind and, perhaps, for a kind of speculative psychology; it is not directly amenable to empirical study. Hypotheses framed at the personal level are testable only in so far as they can be broken down into some sub-personal-level components, which can be examined scientifically (that is, naturalistically).[3]

On the assumption that this is a distinction which has useful application to all areas of mental theorizing (something that might be questioned), let us consider how it stands for the case of pragmatics. At which level is an account of utterance interpretation (to be) conducted, the personal or the sub-personal (or both)? Discussion of pragmatics within the philosophy of language is most often conducted at the level of the person (the hearer/interpreter as person reasoning about the speaker/actor as person). For instance, François Recanati (2002) presents the Gricean view of pragmatics as follows: 'It [pragmatic interpretation] is not concerned with language *per se*, but with human action. When someone acts, whether linguistically or otherwise, there is a reason why she does what she does. To provide an interpretation for that action is to find that reason, that is, to ascribe the agent a particular intention in terms of which we can make sense of the action. . . . Pragmatic interpretation is possible only if we presuppose that the agent is *rational*.' On this view of pragmatics, one which Recanati very largely endorses, pragmatic interpretation is a personal-level activity: the hearer's interpretation of the speaker's linguistic behaviour rests on the assumption that the speaker is a rational agent acting in accordance with certain norms (truthfulness, an appropriate degree of informativeness, etc.) and he attributes to her beliefs and desires that provide reasons for her to have spoken as she did. The Gricean schema for figuring out a speaker's conversational implicature(s) from what she has said is a pure piece of such personal-level practical belief/desire reasoning; it is conscious, rational and normative (see Grice 1975: 50).

The relevance-theoretic approach, on the other hand, embedded as it is within the assumptions and methods of current cognitive science, aims at a causal mechanistic account, an account in terms of interacting sub-personal systems. Certain components of the theory are clearly of this sort. In addition to the decoding system (the language module), there is the deductive device, the inferential system which blindly performs its computations on the input it is given, using the logical elimination rules which constitute its proprietary database. The treatment of background knowledge, which plays an essential role in comprehension, as lodged in cross-referenced encyclopaedic entries attached to particular conceptual addresses looks amenable, in principle, to modelling as a complex sub-personal system. As noted above, the concept of 'accessibility', and degrees of it, plays an important role in the account, the degree of accessibility of contextual assumptions being a crucial factor in the effort required to process an utterance or other ostensive stimulus. Supposing that it could be modelled to a reasonable extent, then the question would be 'accessible to who or what?' We generally talk about accessibility to 'the hearer', and about 'the speaker' shaping her utterance in accordance with judgements she has made about the hearer's accessible assumptions. This is personal-level talk, but the assumption is that it can be recast in terms of 'accessibility to the ostension understanding system', a sub-personal system.

In recent years, the relevance-theoretic account has moved more clearly in the direction of a mechanistic sub-personal theory by proposing that the comprehension system is a mental *module*: it is fast and automatic, and, more crucial to the position, it is domain-specific, in that it is activated exclusively by ostensive stimuli and employs its own proprietary concepts and processing strategies and routines (see Sperber 1994b, 1996; Sperber and Wilson 2002). This move constitutes a leap across the Fodorian modular/non-modular divide. Fodor's persistent claim, backed by argument and some empirical support, is that while input and output systems are domain-specific, encapsulated systems, that is, modules, the central conceptual systems are architecturally unstructured and holistic, that is, non-modular. If the move to modular conceptual systems can be sustained (and Fodor, 2000a, argues that it cannot), one of his main arguments against the possibility of serious empirical work in pragmatics (a central belief-fixing activity) is directly undermined, since it is precisely the modular systems of the mind that he claims have the properties that make it possible to tackle them scientifically. Alan Leslie and others are making the modularity claim for another central interpretive system, known as the 'theory of mind' mechanism (ToMM) (see, for instance, Scholl and Leslie 1999). The two systems are closely related; the theory of mind system interprets the behaviour of others by attributing to them such intentional (that is, world-representing) mental states as beliefs, desires and intentions, and the pragmatic comprehension system interprets communicative behaviour in terms of an intention on the part of the speaker to bring about a certain intentional mental state in the addressee. Sperber (2000: 133) suggests that the latter may be a sub-system of the former, that is, that the relevance-based comprehension module may be a sub-module of the more general mental-state attributing module.

Although detailed discussion of these interesting developments is beyond my limited concerns here, it may be worth pointing out that the crossing of the Fodorian divide brings certain complications with it. First, it is not clear that the original conception of a module as a dumb, reflex-like, rigidly informationally encapsulated system can be carried over intact to these central conceptual systems; if some reconceptualization of modularity is required, as seems likely, it may constitute a step forward in our understanding of human cognition. The second point bears on the personal/sub-personal distinction, which is that the explanatory vocabulary in these (sub-personal-level) accounts of how we interpret each other's behaviour (whether it is communicative or non-communicative) includes the propositional attitude terminology ('intention', 'belief', etc.) which is typical of explanation at the level of the person. In effect, the 'theory of mind' mechanism is a sub-personal system which, in a presumably limited, unconscious and automatic way, computes interpretations which are a counterpart to those of the philosopher or psychologist who develops personal-level explanations of human actions. Some of the mental states which might be cited as *reasons* for a particular action by a personal-level theorist, intent on making a person's behaviour intelligible, are given a sub-personal *causal* status in the workings of the 'theory of mind' mechanism. So, for instance, an explanation along the lines of 'he *believes* the bus is about to arrive, and he *wants* to get on it and . . .' for someone's behaviour of running towards a bus stop might occur as part of a rationalizing personal-level explanation or as an interpretive output of the theory of mind mechanism. Much the same confluence of personal-level explanation and output of a sub-personal mechanism appears to hold for utterance interpretation; a personal-level explanation might have the form 'her reason for saying that it is late is that she wants her addressee to believe that it is time to leave' and this might be matched in the sub-personal comprehension mechanism by an input representation, 'she has said it is late', and an output representation, 'she intends me to believe that (she wants me to believe that) it is time to leave' (see Sperber 1994a for discussion of the multi-level metarepresentation here). Of course, the unconscious inferential processes, mediating input and output representations, internal to the modular mental systems are very likely to be quite distinct from the conscious, normative rationalizations of the personal-level theorist.[4]

The intentional ('about the world') nature of the representations that feature in pragmatic theory (as distinct from, say, the phonological or syntactic representations of the language module and the primal sketches, etc., of the visual module) may appear to present a problem for the kind of explanation typical of the sub-personal level. As it is often put, sub-personal explanation deals with syntactic engines, while it is personal-level explanation that deals in propositional contents, that is, in the semantic, the intentional. So, if the intentionality (aboutness) of mental representations is not a feature of the sub-personal level, it might seem reasonable to conclude that explanation at that level is not going to yield us much in the fields of semantics and pragmatics. But this line of thought can be quickly defused. We need only recall that, assuming Fodor's language of thought hypothesis is right, the mental representations which are the objects of such attitudes as 'believe', 'want' and 'intend' have syntactic as well as semantic properties (and these syntactic properties mirror, to an important extent, the semantic ones) and that the account of interpretation aimed at in cognitive pragmatics is a computational one. In other words, the transitions from one set of representational mental states to another and, finally, to those that constitute the interpretation of the utterance are accounted for entirely in terms of inferential processes that are responsive to their formal (syntactic) properties; for instance, given a [Q if P]-shaped representation and given a [P]-shaped representation, the system will deliver a [Q]-shaped representation.

As for the concern that nothing of interest can be said at the sub-personal level about semantics, it may well be true of 'real world' referential semantics. But semantics of that sort needs to be distinguished from the idea of a semantic 'representation', that is, a structured (presumably conceptual) mental representation into which a phonetic representation is mapped by the linguistic system; if fully propositional, that representation itself has a semantics of the 'out there in the world' sort. Chomsky and Fodor part company on the possibility of any sort of externalist truth-based semantics of thought and/or of language, Chomsky being against and Fodor for (see, for instance, Chomsky 1995; Fodor 2000b). While arguing against any scientifically viable conception of externalist semantics, Chomsky seems to endorse pragmatics: 'insofar as we understand language use, the argument for a reference-based semantics (apart from an internalist syntactic version) seems to me weak. It is possible that natural language has only syntax and pragmatics' (Chomsky 1995: 26). Given his general scepticism about the feasibility of a theory of interpretation, it is not clear that what he means by 'pragmatics' here is what most current pragmatists mean by it. The point, however, is that pragmatics, both on his conception, whatever it is, and on the relevance-theoretic conception, comes together with his account of natural language syntax (I-language) in that both are utterly internalist, formal endeavours. The interface of the two systems can be thought of as a 'semantic' representation, some appropriate notion of logical form, computed by linguistic decoding processes. The entire set of processes, from phonetic input to full and relevant interpretation, fall squarely within the domain of syntactic (computational) engines, that is, the machinery of the sub-personal level.

The personal/sub-personal distinction seems to entail a distinction between different, albeit often intimately related (as component part to whole), phenomena, which by their very nature require one or the other kind of explanation; for instance, seeing (experiencing) a landscape, on the one hand, and forming 3-D mental models of objects, on the other hand, or understanding some behaviour of another person, on the one hand, and forming mental representations of some underlying causal component of that behaviour, on the other. When we focus on those cognitive systems amenable to scientific study, that is, sub-personal (infra-individual) systems, there are other taxonomies of explanatory levels, or levels of organization of the systems, which are presented as different ways of talking about one and the same phenomenon. The best known of these is probably Marr's (1982) three-way vertical distinction between (a) the abstract computational theory level, which provides a specification of the nature of the ability or task at issue, (b) the representation-and-algorithm level, at which the actual representations and operating principles and procedures are made explicit, and (c) the implementational or physical level, at which details of the hardware or neurology are given. The idea is that there are different generalizations at each of the three levels and that for a complete understanding of a cognitive system we need to understand it at all three levels (though, in Marr's view, the ordering from (a) to (c) reflects an order of priority in scientific understanding).

Then, at any one level, there may be different *kinds* of sub-personal system implicated in a full account of a given cognitive capacity, for instance, the human language faculty. Chomsky's *competence/performance* distinction can be understood in this way: both the generative procedure which constitutes the system of (tacit) linguistic knowledge (a competence) and the parsing performance system, which deploys the competence system in assigning a syntactic structure to a linguistic stimulus, can be given abstract computational characterizations (and characterizations at any of the other explanatory levels).[5] The question now is whether cognitive pragmatics (the comprehension faculty) is to be viewed as a competence system, a performance mechanism or a capacity which requires both kinds of system.

In one of his few statements bearing on this issue, Chomsky (1980) speaks of 'pragmatic competence' as a component of the mental state of 'knowing a language', that is, as part of linguistic competence. He distinguishes the following: (a) *grammatical competence*: the computational aspects of language, that constitute knowledge of form and meaning, and (b) *pragmatic competence*: knowledge of the conditions for appropriate use, of how to use grammatical and conceptual resources to achieve certain ends or purposes (Chomsky 1980: 224–5). It seems to follow from the logic of this position that there must be some sorts of pragmatic performance mechanisms which put this pragmatic knowledge system to use. One of the few people to pursue this view of pragmatics as a competence system, a body of knowledge about language use, is Asa Kasher. One of his conclusions is that 'pragmatic competence, as such, is independent of communication' (Kasher 1991a: 135), parallel with the position that grammatical competence is independent of communication. If this is so, then the pragmatics he is pursuing is something quite other than that developed within relevance theory, whose domain precisely is ostensive-inferential communication. I very much doubt that there is any such pragmatic competence system and Kasher's own work gives backing to these doubts. Despite talking of competences (bodies of knowledge), he ends up distinguishing different types of pragmatic system, one for basic speech act assignment, another for fixing the referents of indexicals, another for generating conversational implicatures, in terms of Fodorian performance systems (modular input processors and non-modular central processors) (see Kasher 1991b, 1991c).

Relevance-theoretic pragmatics doesn't postulate a pragmatic competence in Chomsky's sense, a body of knowledge of how to use language, which would then have to be accessed by that system, whatever it might be, that actually does the interpretive work. The relevance-driven comprehension system is a mechanism, a doer, which operates within the constraints of real-time, on-line processing. In short, it is a performance system, with its own concepts and procedures, though, unlike the parser, it is not a specifically *linguistic* performance system, in that its domain is ostensive stimuli generally.

A plausible view of the semantics/pragmatics distinction, understood as an internalist cognitive distinction, is that it is a manifestation, at the level of meaning, of the competence/performance distinction (see, for instance, Larson and Segal 1995, chapter 1). According to this position, semantic knowledge is a component of linguistic knowledge, while utterance interpretation is a performance which employs this knowledge together with a range of other competences (knowledge of logical rules, for instance), general world knowledge, and specific communicative principles. Within relevance theory, however, the semantics/pragmatics distinction is discussed as a distinction which correlates closely with two types of cognitive process: decoding and inference, so that it, in fact, has more the flavour of a distinction between two types of cognitive performance. The relationship between linguistic competence (including semantic competence, if there is such a subsystem) and pragmatic performance is indirect. The point of contact between the language faculty and the pragmatics module is a 'semantic' representation (that is, a conceptual representation of some sort), which is either the output of the parser or of some further performance system interfacing between parser and pragmatics.[6]

So, summing up, if we are willing to endorse the various distinctions outlined here and to make the required choices among the options they present, it looks as if cognitive pragmatics, specifically the relevance-theoretic approach, is to be characterized as a sub-personal-level explanatory account of a specific performance mechanism conducted at the level of representations-and-procedures (to slightly adapt Marr's second level). No doubt, as naturalistic cognitive science progresses, different distinctions will emerge, perhaps better suited to characterizing work in pragmatics and other domain-specific interpretive capacities of the conceptual central systems.

In the chapters that follow I shall often consider different accounts of what seems to be a single semantic or pragmatic phenomenon, but given the different questions, distinctions and kinds of explanation appropriate to different approaches, whether within philosophically-oriented or more cognitive-scientific frameworks, comparisons and assessments need to be approached with caution. Assessing the validity of a particular philosophical distinction on its own terms, say a distinction between semantic information and broader pragmatic context, is one thing; consideration of its utility in an empirical account of on-line utterance processing is quite another. Similarly, within the broad field of cognitive science, two accounts may be either complementary or in competition depending on the level of explanation at which they are pitched and on whether they aim to characterize knowledge (competence) or to model some aspect of performance.

In chapter 1, I start by making a fairly uncontroversial and intuitive distinction between linguistic meaning and speaker meaning, and then move on to develop a more contentious distinction, within speaker meaning, between what the speaker communicates explicitly and what she communicates implicitly. Conducted within the relevance-theoretic framework, the approach is entirely in terms of the mental representations and processes involved in a cognitive account of utterance understanding. The primary focus is on the relation between encoded linguistic meaning and proposition(s) explicitly communicated (explicatures) and the main claim is that a variety of pragmatic processes, some of which receive no mandate from linguistic elements, play a major role in mediating the two. I argue in chapter 2 that there is no role in *this sort of account* for any other intermediate semantically oriented notion of 'what is said' or the 'minimal' proposition expressed (that is, minimal in its departures from the meaning given by the linguistic expression type). It is here that the cross-disciplinary assessments are at their most delicate and debatable. In the following two chapters, I survey existing accounts of the semantics and pragmatics of 'and'-conjunction and negation, ending in each case with a relevance-theoretic account according to which the manifest pragmatic element of the interpretation contributes to the proposition(s) explicitly communicated. In the fifth and final chapter, it is argued that processes of pragmatic narrowing and broadening of encoded lexical meaning are the norm in understanding utterances, so that the relation between sentence meaning and proposition(s) explicitly communicated is frequently quite a distant one.

NOTES

1   The big problem for the processes of belief fixation, of which utterance interpretation is one kind, is the Frame Problem, or 'the problem of the holism of reasoning', or, as Fodor sometimes calls it, Hamlet's Problem: there is no non-arbitrary way to exclude in advance any fact or belief from the set of those that may be relevant in confirming or disconfirming the hypothesis currently under consideration. This problem manifests itself most vividly in Artificial Intelligence, where attempts to programme machines to perform the sort of decision-making and belief-updating activities that human intelligence performs apparently effortlessly run into seemingly insoluble difficulties (see Fodor 1983, 1987b; Pylyshyn 1987).

   Sperber and Wilson (1996) argue that Fodor has an idealized view of the 'rationality' of human processes of belief fixation. These processes never access *all* the relevant available evidence; considerations of processing costs and cognitive benefits enter into all 'rational' mental activity. Processing of newly impinging information stops when a criterion of satisfactory integration with the existing information system has been met, or when the effort expended passes a certain threshold and is written off as sunk costs.

2   The relevance-theoretic approach has probably the strongest cognitive *processing* orientation of all the various post-Gricean strands of pragmatic work. Within the philosophy of language, Jay Atlas and Kent Bach have generally adopted Grice's principles and his analytic approach in their semantic and pragmatic theorizing, though both have argued for significant changes to his distinction between what is said and what is implicated. François Recanati has argued for two quite distinct kinds of pragmatic processes, subpropositional associative primary processes, driven solely by cognitive effort considerations, and properly inferential propositional secondary processes, guided by the standard Gricean maxims and not obviously explainable at a sub-personal computational level. Among more linguistically oriented pragmatists, such as Larry Horn and Stephen Levinson, the focus has been on pragmatic inferences that seem to be of a general or default nature, since these interact more closely with lexical and structural semantic concerns; the essence of the Gricean maxims has been retained (truthfulness, informativeness, relevance), while the role of cognitive effort (on both sides, speaker and hearer) has

been given new prominence. Reinhard Blutner, Bart Geurts and others are currently developing an 'optimality'-theoretic approach, according to which the 'correct' (= optimal) interpretation of an utterance emerges from the interaction of a set of competing ranked pragmatic constraints (concerning informativeness and efficiency); for a useful general discussion of this approach, see Blutner (2000). Although most of these accounts work with some notion of cognitive effort or cost, they vary considerably in their degree of abstraction from actual on-line cognitive processes.

3   The personal/sub-personal distinction has been widely discussed since Dennett introduced it in 1969, and has evolved in several, somewhat divergent, directions. Some take it to be a categorical distinction, so that explanation at the one level does not interact with or affect explanation at the other level, while others believe that the empirical facts about how human beings are constructed, sub-personal matters, place constraints on analyses at the personal level. See Elton (2000) for a short introduction to the distinction and see Davies (2000a, 2000b) for helpful discussion of the way in which it can be construed within the current cognitive science paradigm, where apparently personal-level concepts such as representations, rules and knowledge are employed at the sub-personal level of (unconscious) information-processing mechanisms. The other papers in the special issue of *Philosophical Explorations* (volume 3 (1), January 2000) on the personal/sub-personal distinction assess it from a range of points of view.

A similar distinction is made by Sperber (1997b) in his discussion of two construals of 'methodological individualism', the one turning on the 'strong' conception of the individual as *person* (a partially social construct), acting voluntarily and out of reasons, and the other on the 'weak' conception of the individual as *organism* and locus of causally efficacious, unconscious infra-individual entities and properties. Sperber's primary concern in this paper is to make a case for the role of the latter in explanations of social-cultural (supra-individual) phenomena; the specific entities he has in mind are mental representations of many kinds, which form causal chains with each other and with public representations, within and across individuals. His programme for providing a naturalistic account of social facts is in terms of an epidemiology of such representations (Sperber 1996), a programme within which a cognitive account of communication and interpretation clearly has a central part to play.

4   A further difference arises when modularity, and sub-personal theorizing more generally, is extended from peripheral systems to central interpretive capacities of the mind, such as pragmatics, and this concerns the issue of consciousness. Consciousness is generally taken to be an attribute of the person, not of the underlying sub-personal machinery. With regard to the standard Fodorian modules, such as the perceptual input systems, both their internal processes and their output representations (3-D models, logical forms, etc.) are inaccessible to consciousness. However, in the cases of the theory of mind and pragmatics modules, while their inner workings seem to be unconscious, the results of their interpretive activities, outputs such as 'she means that we should leave now', for instance, are, arguably, accessible to consciousness. For some discussion, see Recanati (1993, section 13.4, and 2002).

5   It has been assumed by some that Chomsky's distinction between competence and performance can be assimilated to Marr's distinction between the level of computational theory and the level of representation and algorithm; that is, that a competence theory and a performance model are different levels of explanation of essentially the one phenomenon. However, Patterson (1996, 1998) argues very persuasively that this view is mistaken. Marr's computational theories (level 1) and representation-and-algorithm models (level 2) are accounts of the *same system*, couched at different levels of abstraction. Competence models and performance models are theories of *different things*: the aim of an

account of a cognitive competence is to describe and explain an internal (tacit) knowl-edge system (such as I-language); the aim of an account of a performance mechanism is to describe and explain how it operates in real time, including how it calls on the knowl-edge in certain competence systems. Both competence and performance systems could, in principle, be explained at Marr's two levels (and, of course, also at his third level, the physical level).

(Note that the 'performance' part of the competence/performance distinction is some-times understood a bit differently from its construal here as a kind of mental system or mechanism. The idea, put crudely, is that performance contaminates and masks competence. Linguistic performances, such as speaking, comprehending utterances, and making linguistic judgements (say, of grammaticality), may be affected by any of a great variety of 'performance factors', such as tiredness, emotional stress, limitations on memory or processing capacity, and distractions of one sort or another, so that perfor-mance data are seldom a straightforward reflection of underlying linguistic competence and, therefore, their use as evidence for or against a particular account of competence is not a straightforward matter (see Chomsky 1965: 3–4).)

6 For discussions of the relation between the competence/performance and semantics/pragmatics distinctions, see Green and Morgan (1981), Horn (1988), Prince (1988), Kasher (1991a), Sinclair (1995) and Carston (2000a). For consideration of some of the different ways in which the semantics/pragmatics distinction has been drawn, see Bach (1997/99a) and Carston (1999b).

1

Pragmatics and Linguistic Underdeterminacy

It is astonishing what language can do. With a few syllables it can express an incalculable number of thoughts, so that even a thought grasped by a terrestrial being for the very first time can be put into a form of words which will be understood by someone to whom the thought is entirely new.

(Frege 1923/77: 55)

all that is required is that the properties of the ostensive stimulus [utterance] should set the inferential process on the right track; to do this they need not represent or encode the communicator's informative intention in any great detail.

(Sperber and Wilson 1986a/95b: 254)

1.1 Saying and Meaning

It is widely observed that there is often a divergence between what a person says and what she means, between the meaning of the linguistic expression she uses and the meaning she seeks to communicate by using it. Some distinction or other of this sort is made by virtually everyone working in pragmatics and its reality is confirmed by our daily experience as speakers and hearers. I aim to do the following in this chapter: first, to chart the extent of this gap between the meaning of the linguistic forms we use and what we mean on occasions of our use of them; second, to examine why there should be such a gap and whether it is a contingent or necessary property of verbal communication; third, briefly to consider whether there is any analogous discrepancy between thought representations and their content.

Let us start with some phenomena which are obviously part of what is meant by the speaker but not part of what her linguistic string means, and move towards instances where the distinction is not so clear. The textbook case is irony and its standard characterization is that of saying one thing while meaning the opposite.

Though this is certainly an inadequate characterization, it is good enough for the immediate point. So a speaker may utter (1), when what she intends to communicate is that Joan has a very poor sense of direction, that she is bound to get lost and that it is laughable to expect her to arrive on time:

(1)   With her excellent spatial sense, Joan is sure to find a shortcut and be the first to arrive.

Tropes, or figurative uses of language, in general, tend to exemplify clearly the saying/meaning distinction. So metaphor, metonymy and hyperbole, for instance, all involve saying one thing in order to communicate something else. All of these can be, and standardly are, viewed as cases where what is said is not even a part of what is meant, but is merely a vehicle for conveying what is meant.

There is another class of cases, where what is said is included in what is meant, but constitutes only a small part of what is meant and is, at least in some instances, not the main point of the utterance. Similes, understatements, and indirect answers provide such examples, so the speaker of (2) or (3B) means what she says, but she means a great deal more as well:

(2)   Bill behaves like a three-year-old child whose teddy-bear has been taken away.

(3)   A: Did you enjoy the evening at Bob and Sue's?
       B: I'm not much of a party person.

The speaker in each case intends her utterance to be taken literally, but she also intends her addressee to draw certain further implications from it: in (2), implications regarding Bill's behaviour and character, and, in (3B), a rather negative answer to A's question and other implications concerning her own preferences and dispositions.

A property that both of these classes of saying/meaning divergences may exhibit is a kind of open-endedness in what is meant, while what is said is usually felt to be determinate and singular. So in (4), a metaphorical case, where the speaker does not mean (at least part of) what she says, what she communicates is an impression of the sort of behaviour, demeanour and psychological state typical of Mary when she is crossed.

(4)   When she doesn't get her own way Mary becomes a raging inferno.

It would be difficult to formulate this in terms of a small definitive set of propositions and there is room for differences across hearers as to the specific implications they entertain as part of their understanding of the utterance. A similar point can be made about the more mundane example in (5), where the speaker does mean what she says, but would also standardly communicate a range of implications about her ability to function today, her readiness to get on with work, her improved state of mind, etc.

(5) I'm feeling better today.

Utterances which employ a subsentential linguistic expression are another sort of case again. The utterance in (6) employs just a prepositional phrase and the one in (7) just an adjective, but what is meant by a speaker in both cases is something sentence-shaped (propositional), presumably quite obvious in the context.

(6) On the top shelf.

(7) Higher.

When (6) is uttered by a speaker who realizes that the hearer, making his breakfast, is looking for the marmalade, it communicates 'the marmalade is on the top shelf'. From there on, the example is just like those of the second set above in that it may well have various further intended implications: the marmalade does not belong on the bottom shelf, I have moved it to its proper place, I am not trying to hide it from you, etc.

What these examples demonstrate is that, in addition to a speaker standardly meaning more or other than she says, the 'what is said' of the utterance may itself involve more than the meaning of the linguistic expressions used. So it looks as if we have to distinguish two notions which, in these preliminary observations, have been run together: there is linguistic meaning, the information encoded in the particular lexical-syntactic form employed, and there is the thought or proposition which it is being used to express, that is, what is said. While there is a fair amount of variation in how the term 'what is said' is construed, it is generally agreed to be something fully propositional, that is, semantically complete, and so truth-evaluable.[1] It is this disparity, between linguistic meaning and the proposition expressed, that I want to concentrate on in what follows in this chapter. That other major symptom of the disparity between linguistic content and what a speaker means, the intended implications (the implicatures or implicit import) of an utterance, will be taken up again in chapter 2.

While subsentential utterances are typical of much ordinary conversation among familiars, most of those linguistic productions that have the status of discourses or texts are supersentential, that is, they generally consist of more than a single sentence. There is a range of relations which may be understood to hold between sequences of sentences uttered in a discourse and these too are frequently not encoded by the linguistic expressions used:

(8) a. He mistook his wife for a hat-stand; he wasn't wearing his glasses.
     b. Her life was in a mess. Her lover had left her and her electric toothbrush wasn't working.

In an utterance of (8a), the second sentence would be understood as giving an explanation for the state of affairs described in the first. In an utterance of (8b), the second sentence would be understood as elaborating on or exemplifying the statement in the first. An utterance of a single sentence which consists of more than one clause may also be understood as communicating a stronger relationship between the states of affairs described than is encoded by the element that connects the clauses:

(9) a. He wasn't wearing his glasses and he mistook his wife for a hat-stand.
     b. When she saw Mrs Simpson coming down the aisle she hid behind the breakfast cereals.

In both of these cases, a cause–consequence relation is understood to hold between the states of affairs described, though neither of the clausal connectives, 'and' and 'when', nor any other linguistic element in the utterances, encodes this. Whether these communicated relationships are part of what the speaker has said (the proposition she has expressed) or are merely implications of the utterance will be considered in chapter 3.

Before looking more closely at ways in which encoded linguistic meaning falls short of determining the proposition expressed or 'what is said', there is another sort of case of the coming apart of speaker meaning and linguistic meaning which should be mentioned, if only to set it aside for the moment. This is the phenomenon of linguistic mistakes and misuses. Speakers believe that the linguistic forms they employ in an utterance have a meaning (or encode some information) and that knowledge of this form–meaning correlation is shared among competent users of the form. They generally intend these meanings encoded by their utterance to be recovered by their addressees and used by them, in conjunction with their pragmatic abilities, in the derivation of the intended content. This holds for all the examples discussed so far, including those where what is said is not part of what is meant. So, although the speaker of (1) did not intend her hearer to take her to be endorsing the view that Joan has excellent powers of spatial orientation, she nevertheless did intend her hearer to access those very concepts (encoded in the linguistic expression she used) in the process of arriving at the intended interpretation. When certain sorts of misuse occur, however, it seems that some specific element of the meaning encoded in the linguistic form the speaker employs falls outside any intention she has in producing the utterance. Consider the case of a speaker who uses the sentence in (10) with the intention of communicating that Mary is a member of the upper class, believing that 'hoi polloi' encodes the concept UPPER CLASS:

(10) Mary is one of the hoi polloi.

The concept COMMON FOLK which is 'actually' encoded by 'hoi polloi' (in the public language system) falls under no intention the speaker has in uttering (10). She may, nonetheless, succeed in her communicative intention, if one or other of two special conditions pertain. Either the hearer is also 'mistaken', and in the same way as the speaker, in his understanding of the expression 'hoi polloi' (perhaps through a sound association with 'hoity toity'); or the hearer, whose lexical form 'hoi polloi' maps 'correctly' to a conceptual address for [COMMON FOLK], recognizes the disparity between its meaning and the speaker's intention and, charitably, makes the appropriate adjustment.[2] There are many types of mistake, each with its own particular properties, to which these general remarks apply, including malapropisms, so-called Freudian slips, and various articulatory errors, such as spoonerisms, which are temporary malfunctions of the system, brought on by performance factors such as tiredness or emotional strain.

What is the proposition expressed by an utterance of (10) in this situation? What has been said? Some might say that, strictly and literally, it is that Mary is one of the common people, although this is quite different from what is meant, and a rather poor vehicle for (non-ironically) communicating what is meant. Others might say that the proposition expressed is that Mary is a member of the upper class, just as the speaker intended, although the concept decoded from the form 'hoi polloi' is quite different. Clearly, much depends on our conception of 'what is said' or 'the proposition expressed' by an utterance, how close it is taken to be to linguistic meaning, the extent to which, if at all, speaker intentions play a role in its determination. These issues are addressed in the next chapter.

One might reasonably feel that the very fact that these are errors, that what is encoded in a case like (10) (and, on some construals, therefore, 'what is said') falls right outside the speaker's intentions, makes them special and marginal. Certainly, they bring an unclarity into the concept of what is said, since up to now we have been assuming that what a speaker says by an utterance is not at odds with what the words she uses mean, even if she doesn't in fact intend to be taken as meaning what they mean. However, while such cases can be safely ignored by a semantic theory (concerned with explicating linguistic meaning), an adequate pragmatic theory, whose mission is to explain how utterances are interpreted, does have to attend to them; in particular, it has to account for how such encoding disparities between speakers and addressees can, sometimes at least, be cases of successful communication.

1.2 The Underdeterminacy Thesis

From the discussion above, three levels of utterance meaning have emerged, which, although quite distinct, remain in need of considerable clarification: linguistic meaning, what is said and what is meant. I started out by treating the first two as if they were the same, distinguishing them from what is meant, but it soon became clear that what is said has to be distinguished from linguistic meaning. As a result, we have three possible underdeterminacy theses:

(a)   Linguistic meaning underdetermines what is meant.
(b)   What is said underdetermines what is meant.
(c)   Linguistic meaning underdetermines what is said.

I do not think that anyone, apart, perhaps, from a rabid 'language is all' social semiotician, would dispute the first two. I want to examine the third one, which I will call the linguistic underdeterminacy thesis or the semantic underdeterminacy thesis or just *the* underdeterminacy thesis. What is meant by this is that the linguistic semantics of the utterance, that is, the meaning encoded in the linguistic expressions used, the relatively stable meanings in a linguistic system, meanings which are widely shared across a community of users of the system, underdetermines the proposition expressed (what is said). The hearer has to undertake processes of pragmatic inference in order to work out not only what the speaker is implicating but also what proposition she is directly expressing. My purpose here is twofold: (a) to demonstrate the vast extent of this phenomenon, and (b) to prepare the way for an investigation in the next chapter of the various notions of explicitness found in the semantic and pragmatic literature, including 'saying' and 'what is said', 'making as if to say', 'proposition expressed', 'propositional form of the utterance', 'truth-conditional content', 'explicature' and, unlikely though it may sound in a discussion of explicitness, 'impli*citure*'. All of these lie on one side of a divide, on the other side of which is 'implicature', the standard term for the implicit content of an utterance.

Before looking at some of the sources of linguistic underdeterminacy, I'll make a brief terminological digression. Perhaps it is sufficiently clear from what has been said so far that the two terms '*under*determinacy' and '*in*determinacy', are not synonymous, but let's try to be explicit about this. 'Indeterminacy' seems to be used with reference to several different phenomena. First, it is sometimes used in a contrast with ambiguity. Linguists tend to reserve the term 'ambiguity' for those random and arbitrary coincidences of bits of linguistic form which encode two or more distinct concepts, such as 'bank' and 'visiting relatives'. Indeterminacy, then, is used of some of the other sources of the linguistic underdeterminacy of propositional form, so we see 'referential indeterminacy' used of indexicals and definite descriptions which require contextual considerations for the determination of their reference; regarded as formal types within a linguistic system, they have no determinate reference. The term could be similarly used in 'predicational indeterminacy' or 'conceptual indeterminacy', though here we more often find the expressions 'vagueness' and/or 'generality of sense', a matter of practice rather than principle.

Then, stepping outside the linguistic underdeterminacy thesis and considering the implicit content of utterances, there is the indeterminacy of implicature mentioned by Grice (1975/89b: 40) and given theoretical flesh by Sperber and Wilson's (1986a/95b: 195–200) concept of weak implicature, to be discussed in chapter 2. Examples (4) and (5) above are cases where the particular implicatures derived by an addressee may not have been specifically intended by the speaker; that is, there is indeterminacy regarding which implications within a range of possibilities fall within the speaker's informative intention. Finally, of course, there is the much touted 'indeterminacy of translation/interpretation' thesis of Quine: according to this, there just is no fact of the matter concerning which of several hypotheses about the meaning of a linguistic expression or its translation into another language is correct; all of them may be compatible with the available evidence (the evidence allowed by Quine being restricted to observable features of the behaviour of the users of the linguistic expression). The common feature of these various uses of the term 'indeterminacy' is, I think, captured by the phrase 'no fact of the matter'; no conclusion can be drawn because there is none to be drawn. Linguistic 'underdeterminacy', by comparison, does not entail that there is no fact of the matter as regards the proposition expressed, but rather that it cannot be determined by linguistic meaning alone. It may be that the proposition expressed by an utterance can also exhibit the property of 'indeterminacy' (a possibility considered in chapter 5), but that is a quite separate matter from the current focus on its linguistic underdeterminacy. That's the end of this terminological digression.

1.2.1   Sources of linguistic underdeterminacy

Now to some of the ways in which a linguistic expression may underdetermine the proposition expressed, or, in other words, ways in which content is context-sensitive. First, there are linguistic ambiguities to be resolved and indexical expressions whose referents must be assigned. These two pragmatic processes are widely acknowledged, even by those who want to keep the gap between linguistic meaning and 'what is said' to a minimum; for instance, they are the two processes singled out by Grice (1975/89b: 25)[3] as necessary additions to conventional content in identifying what is said. Those semanticists who aim to give natural language sentences a truth-conditional (hence propositional) semantics are, of course, not concerned with how ambiguities or referential indeterminacies are resolved but, nevertheless, have to accommodate both indexicality and ambiguity in their accounts. One semantic approach to indexicality is demonstrated in the two (roughly equivalent) versions of a truth-statement for the sentence 'this is green' in (11), where the statement quantifies over *utterances* of an indexical *sentence*, thereby abstracting away from particular contexts and so particular referential resolutions:

(11)   a.   An utterance of 'this is green' is true just in case the entity that the speaker refers to with 'this' is green.
       b. $(u)(x)$ [If u is an utterance of 'this is green' and 'this' refers to x, then u is true just in case x is green]

This truth-conditional treatment of indexicality is taken up again briefly in section 1.5, where I consider the general feasibility and appropriateness of a truth-conditional approach to the semantics of natural language expressions.

The way ambiguity (lexical and syntactic) is reflected in truth-conditional theories highlights the difference between this sort of semantic theory and the cognitive processing account of utterance understanding that I am working towards. A semantics for an *n*-ways ambiguous natural language string is complete once it has provided *n* different T(ruth)-sentences in the metalanguage, one for each sense of the natural language string.[4] This is obviously not a trivial undertaking, but the point is that the *n* different sentences are distinguished in advance of their treatment by the truth theory. What the pragmatic theory must confront is the very different issue of how the hearer recognizes (or 'alights on') the one (or, on the occasion of a pun, two) of these *n* possibilities the speaker intends on a particular occasion of use.

Although Grice acknowledges that reference assignment and disambiguation are necessary for a full identification of what the speaker has said, he does not say anything about how these processes are achieved. It seems reasonable to surmise from the omission of any reference to conversational maxims at this point (in a lecture/article which is primarily focused on these maxims and the work they do in communication; Grice 1975/89b: 22–40) that he did not think they played a role in disambiguation and reference assignment, a point to be considered more thoroughly in chapter 2. On the more cognitively oriented approach of relevance theory, the communicative principle responsible for deriving conversational implicatures is also instrumental in identifying the intended sense of an ambiguous linguistic form and the intended referent of an indexical.

The third way in which linguistic content underdetermines what is said arises when the expression employed does not determine a full proposition even after all necessary reference assignments and disambiguations have taken place. Phrasal and lexical utterances, such as those in (6) and (7), are the obvious cases here. However, there are also fully sentential utterances whose encoded meaning does not seem to determine a fully propositional representation, that is, one which, in principle at least, could be assigned a truth value:

(12) a. Paracetamol is better.　[than what?]
　　　b. It's the same.　　　　 [as what?]
　　　c. She's leaving.　　　　 [from where?]
　　　d. He is too young.　　　 [for what?]
　　　e. It is raining.　　　　 [where?]

As the bracketed questions indicate, these examples require completion before they can be judged as true or false of a state of affairs. What they determine (given reference assignment, etc.) has been described as a subpropositional logical form (Sperber and Wilson 1986a/95b: 188), or a propositional radical, or a fragment of a proposition (Bach 1994a: 269). The missing constituent which will bring them up to full propositionhood has to be supplied pragmatically. These sorts of cases were not described by Grice so we cannot know for sure what he would have said about them. Since he seems to have conceived of 'what is said' as fully propositional (the truth-conditional content of an utterance) he might have agreed that a completion process was necessary and that the missing material would be readily contextually determined, again most likely without any role for conversational maxims (but see discussion in section 2.2.2).

It is appropriate at this point to mention a principle that has been held fairly widely by philosophers, but which is questionable in the light of the previous considerations. This is the **Isomorphism Principle**. As Frege puts it (in the continuation of the quotation at the beginning of this chapter): 'we [are] able to distinguish parts in the thought corresponding to the parts of a sentence, so that the structure of the sentence serves as the image of the structure of the thought' (Frege 1923/77: 55). A more recent formulation, from Fodor and Lepore (1991), is: 'If a sentence S expresses the proposition P, then syntactic constituents of S express the constituents of P.' They describe this isomorphism as a perfectly universal feature of natural language, but acknowledge (in a footnote) that there is an issue to be addressed: 'Suppose, for example, that you hold that (in a null discourse) the sentence "it's raining" expresses the proposition that it's raining in the context of utterance. Then

either you must say that "it's raining" has more constituents than appear on its
surface or that the isomorphism principle can be violated by pragmatically carried
information' (Fodor and Lepore 1991: 333, note 2; and see Fodor 2001, for a fuller
recognition of violations of the principle).

For those who want to preserve the principle, there are, in fact, two quite different directions that could be taken. The first is, as Fodor and Lepore note, to insist
that, contrary to appearances, there are hidden unarticulated linguistic constituents,
such as a covert location indexical in the sentence 'it's raining', which, like overt
indexicals, call for the contextual provision of a value. This position, currently taken
by Stanley (2000) among others, is discussed in section 2.7 in the next chapter. The
second approach, taken by Bach (1994a, 1994b), generally eschews hidden linguistic
elements but involves such a strict and delimited sense of 'what is said' that the Isomorphism Principle is observed. For instance, what is said by a speaker who utters
'it's raining' does not include anything concerning a location of the instance of
raining. It follows from this stance that what is said in cases such as those in (12)
is subpropositional and so cannot be evaluated for truth. The third approach to
these examples, which I support, allows that pragmatic processes can supply constituents to what is said solely on communicative grounds, without any linguistic
pointer, in which case the Isomorphism Principle does not hold. This is demonstrated in the next chapter (section 2.3.4).

Consider now some cases which are fully sentential and which, given reference
assignment, seem to be fully propositional and so not to require any further contextual supplementation in identifying the proposition expressed:

(13)   a.   Bob is well groomed.
       b.   This fruit is green.
       c.   That is difficult.
       d.   It is serviceable.

Surely, one might think, Bob is either well groomed or he is not; the particular fruit
in question is green or it is not; that is, these are truth-evaluable as they stand, once
we know the referents of the subject terms. In fact, as pointed out by Gross (1998,
chapter 1), from whom the examples are taken, the adjectival predicates here exhibit
four different kinds of context-sensitivity, hence four further ways in which linguistic
meaning may underdetermine the proposition a speaker expresses. In (13a), the
adjective is 'scalar', by which he means it allows for comparison between things
with respect to the degree with which they have the property concerned. For
instance, Bob may be well groomed for your average graduate student, but not for
a candidate for a job in a city bank; he may be well groomed for him (that is, compared with his usual appearance) but not for the sort of man Mary likes to be seen
with. The colour predicate in (13b) is what Gross calls 'part-dependent', since on
different occasions of use it may apply to different parts or aspects of the thing it
is being predicated of. For instance, (13b) may be judged true in a particular context
provided its peel is green even though its interior is white and its stem is brown,
while in a different circumstance (say, fruits are being separated into the ripe and
the unripe), the proposition expressed will be evaluated according to whether or

not the interior is green, the colour of the skin being irrelevant. The adjective 'difficult' in (13c) demonstrates the context-sensitive property of 'relativity', that is, its applicability is relative to something else; for instance, a problem might be difficult relative to my abilities but not relative to yours. Finally, there is the property of 'vagueness', where there is no clear boundary between things of which the adjective is true and things of which it is false, and the standards of precision may vary across contexts, so that in one context an object has the property, in another it doesn't, and in yet another it is borderline. Probably all the examples in (13) have this property. Gross gives (13d) as a case where all four kinds of context-sensitivity are present, so that the proposition expressed by a particular utterance of it could look something like the following:

(14) This program is serviceable, according to such and such a standard, compared to other programs for such and such a task, for beginners in computing.

These sources of context-sensitivity are not peculiar to adjectives but carry over to many other linguistic elements too (verbs, adverbs, etc.). Again, someone wanting to maintain the Isomorphism Principle has the options given above: (a) to posit hidden linguistic constituents corresponding to each of these pragmatically inferred elements, or (b) to deny that they are part of what is said (in which case 'what is said' is not truth-evaluable and the inferred elements arise at some other representational level). According to the 'free pragmatic enrichment' approach, which I will pursue in the next chapter, these elements do contribute to the proposition expressed (what is said) and their recovery is not only effected pragmatically but is also motivated pragmatically (rather than linguistically).

Most theorists, though not all (for instance, Bach), would agree that the processes discussed so far are necessary supplements to the linguistically encoded information for arriving at what the speaker has said (the proposition expressed). However, there are, at least, three more groups of cases about which there is little consensus. First, there are examples which raise some tricky questions about the semantics of particular elements of the language. Let's briefly take the case of negation.

(15) a. Everyone isn't hungry.
      b. She didn't butter the toast in the bathroom with a knife.
      c. The local witch didn't put a spell on us.
      d. Bill didn't eat some of the cakes; he ate all of them.

In (15a), there are two possible interpretations: 'not everyone is hungry' and 'no one is hungry', which are truth-conditionally distinct. This is usually described as a scope ambiguity: either the negation takes scope over the universal quantifier or vice versa. This may be taken as a linguistic ambiguity such that the grammar gives the sentence two logical forms and a truth-conditional semantics for the sentence would assign it two T-sentences. Or it may be that the linguistic system gives the negation operator wide scope over the whole of the rest of the sentence and that, on occasion, a pragmatic process of logical strengthening eventuates in the stronger interpretation 'no one is hungry'; then there would be but one T-sentence specifying the truth-conditions of the *sentence*. Or the linguistic system may dictate nothing at all about the relation between the quantifier and the negation, so it is left to pragmatics to fix that relation; on such a conception it seems unlikely that any truth-conditional specification could be given for the sentence (an issue to be taken up below). At least these three positions have been supported at different times. On the first position, this example would simply present the pragmatic system with another ambiguity to resolve, a choice between two possible logical forms. On the third one, a pragmatic process of scope fixing would be obligatory; that is, there would be no fully propositional representation until that process took place. The second position gives rise to an interesting situation: once the intended domain of the quantifier has been inferred and reference fixed, we seem to have a fully propositional representation, say 'not everyone at the party is hungry', but in some contexts this would not be the proposition the speaker intended to express; it would be weaker than the truth-conditional content she intended the hearer to understand, namely 'no one at the party is hungry'. This is just one of a set of contentious cases where the proposition derived through the essential processes required to complete the encoded logical form is, arguably, not the proposition the speaker expresses.

Other ambiguities have been claimed for negation. Example (15b) has six or seven interpretations depending on which constituent the negation is taken to apply to (e.g. 'in the bathroom', 'the toast', etc.). In spoken utterances, these would typically be distinguished by the pattern of accentuation, but in written form, the ambiguity has to be resolved entirely pragmatically. Example (15c) has been taken by some to be ambiguous between an understanding on which the negation operator is presupposition-preserving (that is, the entailment of the corresponding positive sentence, 'there is a local witch', is maintained in the negative sentence) and an understanding (less immediately obvious) on which negation is presupposition-cancelling, since this sentence has a reading on which it is compatible with a following utterance denying that there is a local witch: 'the local witch didn't put a spell on us; there is no witch around here.' Finally, the negation in (15d) has been supposed by some to express a rejection of a previous utterance of the corresponding positive sentence, rather than to function in the logical truth-value-reversing way that it does in (15a): the use of the quantifier 'some' is rejected, not because it gives rise to falsehood, but because what it expresses is too weak, as the follow-up clause makes explicit. All, none or some of these various different interpretations of utterances of negative sentences might be a function of the language system itself, that is, different meanings encoded by the word 'not'. Those that are not encoded have to be accounted for pragmatically and would appear to be further strong candidates for pragmatic contributions to the proposition expressed ('what is said') by an utterance. The wide range of semantic and pragmatic analyses of negation that have been entertained are surveyed in chapter 4, and a particular account, within the precepts of a relevance-based cognitive view of pragmatics, is proposed and defended.

Some of the same issues arise for the analysis of 'and'-conjunctions where it seems that a variety of relations between the conjuncts may be understood (including the cause–consequence connection in (9a) above). There are various rich semantic accounts which might be proposed to explain this, and there are more minimalist semantic accounts which leave it to pragmatics to supply stronger connections, thereby raising the question of whether these connections are aspects of the proposition expressed or distinct implicated assumptions. Other cases are scalar terms, which can have at least two different interpretations in a context – for instance, 'some' may be understood as 'some and possibly all' or 'some but not all' – and descriptions (definite and indefinite), which may have a range of interpretations, including the famous attributive or referential understandings. These cases (negation, conjunction, scalars, descriptions) are quite different from that of, say, pronouns, which patently do not encode either their referents or uniquely identifying descriptions of their referents, so that the role of pragmatics in determining their referents is indisputable.[5] It is not obvious with the phenomena just surveyed whether they do or do not encode the interpretations they may have in different contexts; they may encode several senses, or a single strong sense, or a single weak sense. In such a situation, semantic and pragmatic analyses have to be developed together.

There is a second set of cases for which a pragmatic process is required to arrive at the proposition intended by the speaker, even though the representation recovered without this process is fully propositional and could, therefore, be argued to constitute what is said by the utterance.

(16)   a.   Mending this fault will take time.
        b.   The north island is some distance from the south island.
        c.   Something has happened.
        d.   I haven't eaten lunch.
        e.   I haven't eaten frogs' legs.
        f.   There's nothing on telly tonight.

Given reference fixing, each of (16a)–(16c) expresses a trivial obvious truth: any activity takes place over a period of time; there is some distance or other between any two islands; at any moment in time something or other has happened. The point is, of course, that these dull truisms are virtually never what a speaker has intended to express; there is hardly any context in which they will be relevant. So some pragmatic process of enriching or adding conceptual material is necessary in order to arrive at what the speaker intended to express: perhaps, 'mending this fault will take a longer period of time than such fault-mendings standardly take', 'the north island is further from the south island than you think', 'something bad has happened on the day of utterance [to x]'. It's worth noting the negative flavour of these enrichments; the relevance of these utterances lies in their alerting the hearer to a state of affairs that runs against his prevailing hopes or expectations.

Some sort of temporal span has to be assigned to (16d) and (16e) and the point of interest here is the difference that the object ('lunch', 'frogs' legs') makes in each case to the understanding of the identical verbs, both with the perfect aspect (have + en): in (16d), the most likely interpretation, across a wide range of contexts of utterances, is that the time-span to which the not-having-eaten-lunch applies is the day of utterance, while in (16e) it is probably the speaker's lifetime. Arguably, (16f) expresses a proposition (given reference fixing for 'tonight') and one which would be standardly false (there's always something on telly, however dire) and obviously so to the interlocutors. In order to arrive at the proposition intended by the speaker, the domain over which 'nothing' operates has to be narrowed down to something like 'programmes worth watching', and then it may well be true. If these assessments of the proposition expressed ('what is said') by the speaker of these examples are correct, then we have another group of cases where pragmatic inference must augment linguistic encoding, even though it is not strictly necessary for the derivation of a fully propositional form. However, for the examples involving a quantifier like 'something' or 'nothing', it might be claimed that there is an implicit (hidden) variable in the linguistic form marking the requirement that a quantifier domain be contextually supplied. If that is so, these examples do not express a proposition until that variable is contextually filled, so the pragmatic process does not, after all, take us from one proposition to another. As with all such claims, this one is contentious: Stanley and Szabo (2000a) favour it; Bach (2000a) and Neale (2000) oppose it (see brief discussion in the next chapter, section 2.7).

The third set of cases also demonstrates the enrichment of one proposition to give another, but differs from the previous sets in that the pragmatic process required seems to involve, not the adding of conceptual constituents, but rather adjustments to linguistically encoded concepts. Here are some possible cases of this:

(17) a. I'm tired.
      b. Ann wants to meet a bachelor.
      c. The path is uneven.

(18) a. Her face is oblong.
      b. The steak is raw.
      c. The room was silent.

The idea here is that, in certain contexts, utterances of the examples in (17) involve narrowings or strengthenings of the concepts encoded by 'tired', 'bachelor' and 'uneven'. For instance, in an utterance of (17a), the relevant degree of tiredness might vary from a mild form to a much stronger condition which prevents the speaker from doing a range of mundane household tasks; in an utterance of (17b), the sort of 'bachelor' Ann is understood as wanting to meet may belong just to a particular subset of the set of bachelors, the subset of those who are heterosexual, youngish, interested in marriage, etc. The examples in (18) are intended potentially to involve an opposite process of loosening or widening of a lexically encoded concept. For instance, an utterance of (18a) requires a relaxing of the concept 'oblong' since her face is not likely to be literally oblong; in (18b) the concept 'raw' (encoding 'not cooked') may be adjusted so as to be applicable to foods that have had some, but grossly insufficient, cooking. An interesting possibility to consider with regard to these examples is that the lexically encoded concept in the logical form of the utterance is replaced by an *ad hoc* concept, pragmatically derived from the lexical one, and that this new non-lexicalized concept is a constituent of the proposition expressed by the speaker of the utterance. This is more controversial in the case of the examples in (18) than in those in (17), since there it effectively involves the loss of some linguistic content; for instance, the *ad hoc* concept that replaces the concept encoded by 'raw' does not analytically imply [uncookedness]. I will argue for this position in chapter 5.

These last three sets of cases all involve a pragmatic process whose result is not necessary in order to secure full propositionality, but seems to be required if we are interested in finding that proposition which it is rational to assume the speaker intended to express. A natural-language semanticist interested in giving a truth-conditional specification of these examples could feel quite justified in ignoring these pragmatic adjustments in a way that he cannot with ambiguity, indexicality and other features of a sentence that leave it subpropositional (semantically incomplete). These then are the most interesting and contentious cases when it comes to giving an account of 'what is said' (the proposition explicitly expressed) by a speaker, especially if this is equated with the truth-conditional content of the utterance, as it standardly is. Some would opt to rule these pragmatic developments out of any concept of 'what is said' and treat them at some other level of utterance understanding; others would prefer a concept of 'what is said' which incorporates the result of all these processes and so would have to argue that the concept of the truth-conditional content of an *utterance* is quite distinct from the concept of the minimal truth-conditional content which is to be assigned to a natural-language *sentence*.

It can be seen that considerable work in clarifying the concept of 'what is said', or the proposition expressed by an utterance, remains to be done; this is tackled in the next chapter. All I have tried to do in this section is to give examples of the range of ways in which encoded linguistic meaning may underdetermine the proposition a speaker expresses by her utterance of a particular linguistic string. These can be summarized in the following short taxonomy:

1 multiple encodings (i.e. ambiguities)
2 indexical references
3 missing constituents
4 unspecified scope of elements
5 underspecificity or weakness of encoded conceptual content
6 overspecificity or narrowness of encoded conceptual content

1.2.2 Underdeterminacy: essential or merely convenient?

The question which arises now and which the following sections will venture towards answering is: is the linguistic underdeterminacy of the proposition (or thought) expressed a necessary or contingent matter? It is presumably not *logically* necessary, since there seems to be no reason to suppose that there simply could not be a language system of some sort capable of fully encoding propositions (or Fregean thoughts) including all those that a communicator could want to express. The question must be: does linguistic underdeterminacy follow inevitably from the sort of linguistic systems that human mind/brains naturally develop, or is it a feature of utterances which comes from some other source, say, a convention of linguistic usage or the outcome of some natural drive towards communicative efficiency? There are at least the following views on this question:

1   The *'convenient abbreviation' view*: while the linguistic expression employed in an utterance does, more often than not, underdetermine the proposition or thought expressed, this is merely a matter of effort-saving convenience for speakers and another sentence which fully encodes the proposition/thought *could* always be supplied.
2   The *essentialist view*: underdeterminacy is an essential feature of the relation between linguistic expressions and the propositions (thoughts) they are used to express; generally, for any given proposition/thought, there is no sentence which fully encodes it. There are weaker and stronger versions of essentialism:
    (a)   Underdeterminacy is widespread, but there are some (few) sentences which do fully encode the propositions they are used to express.
    (b)   Underdeterminacy is universal and no sentence ever fully encodes the thought or proposition it is used to express.

On the 'convenience' view, for every underdetermining sentence (or subsentential expression), there is another sentence provided by the language system which does fully encode the proposition which the incomplete one, uttered in a particular context, was used to express. These proposition-determining, context-insensitive sentences are called 'eternal' sentences, a term which is fairly transparent, but, anyway, will be explained in the next section. So for any (non-eternal) linguistic string which expresses a proposition when uttered in a given context, there is an eternal (context-free) counterpart which expresses that proposition. For instance, for each of the (a) members of the examples in (19)–(21), which underdetermine the proposition expressed in one or more of the ways described in the previous section, there is a fully encoding counterpart. A possible candidate for this in each case is given in the corresponding (b) examples:

(19)   a.   He went to the bank.
       b.   Simon Lewis went to a financial institution situated at 32 Totten-ham Court Road in London between 2.00 and 2.30 on 18 May 1999.

(20)   a.   It's the same.
       b.   Ibuprofen is the same in chemical composition as Nurofen.

(21)   a.   On the top shelf.
       b.   The thick-cut orange and ginger marmalade is on the top shelf of the cupboard facing the door in the kitchen of the attic flat at 57 Sunnyside Road, London N19.

Putative eternal sentences are usually longer and more complex than the under-determining (non-eternal) linguistic expressions standardly used by speakers, as the (b) examples show; one might think here also of the terrible convolutions of many legal documents where the aim is full encoding. So speakers standardly choose to save themselves the mental effort of formulating (and the physical effort of articu-lating) eternal sentences, which fully encode the propositions they want to express. They know they can rely on the hearer's inferential powers to map the non-eternal sentence or phrase they have uttered on to a mental representation of the intended proposition, or on to the eternal sentence in the language which maps on to that mental representation (if there is a distinction between the two on this view of language and thought).

On the essentialist view, however, while the (b) examples come closer to encod-ing the proposition expressed by the speaker than the corresponding (a) examples, they are still underdetermining and, no matter how hard one tries to be fully explicit, by elaborating descriptions so that they may pick out unique entities and proper-ties, one is doomed to failure, at least in the vast majority of cases, according to the weak essentialist view, and across the board, according to the strong view. On the weaker view, the following sentences, which are not context-sensitive in any obvious way, might be eternal sentences, but they are the exception rather than the rule in the linguistic system:

(22) a. Lions are animals.
      b. The earth goes round the sun.
      c. Two plus two is four.

I shall argue against the 'underdeterminacy as convenience' view and in favour of the essentialist views, inclining toward the stronger of the two, despite the more immediate plausibility, perhaps, of the weaker one. I think that public-language systems are intrinsically underdetermining of complete (semantically evaluable) thoughts because they evolved on the back, as it were, of an already well-developed cognitive capacity for forming hypotheses about the thoughts and intentions of others on the basis of their behaviour. Formulating natural-language sentences of a progressively more determining sort may approach ever closer to a full encoding of propositions expressed, but the progression is asymptotic. Before trying to make this case, I'll consider the concept of eternal sentences and the 'convenience' view of non-eternal sentences in a little more detail.

1.3 Eternal Sentences and Effability

In the previous section, I implicitly equated thoughts and propositions, which seemed harmless on a Fregean notion of thought (as the sense of a proposition). However, there is a more fine-grained psychological notion of thought, on which thought and proposition may come apart. The propositional content of two thoughts, 'the meeting begins now' (occurring at 3 p.m.) and 'the meeting begins at

3 p.m.', might be identical, but the former may move me to act while the latter does not (if I do not know that it is now 3 p.m.). Similarly, an utterance by X addressed to Y of 'I would like to shake your hand' might lead Y to extend his hand to the person speaking to him, while an utterance by the same speaker to the same addressee of 'X would like to shake your hand' might not (if Y doesn't realize that the speaker is X), even though both express the same proposition. The thought expressed by a speaker of the indexical sentence and grasped by the addressee appears to have some property that distinguishes it from the proposition expressed (say, 'X would like to shake Y's hand at 2.30 a.m. on 27 June 2001'). (For extensive discussion, see Perry (1979, 1997), from whom these examples are borrowed.) In the next sections, talk of 'thoughts' will generally be of the individualist psychological sort (which, of course, includes a wide range for which thought expressed and proposition expressed are the same).

For the moment I am assuming that thoughts, whether expressed by utterances or not, are semantically complete, that is, that they are truth-evaluable in and of themselves, without any need of contextual completion or specification. In other words, whether or not there is a sentence in the public language that fully encodes them, they themselves are 'eternal': if a thought is true/false at this moment, it has always been true/false and always will be true/false. This assumption will be questioned in section 1.7, where I briefly consider the possibility of the underdeterminacy of thought.

1.3.1   Eternal sentences and Platonism

Now let us consider the concept of an 'eternal sentence', where by 'sentence' I mean a natural-language sentence, one of those syntactically complete entities which has phonological, syntactic and semantic properties, and which can be used by human beings to make their thoughts known to others. If we take thoughts to be semantically complete, then eternal sentences are 'complete formulations' of thoughts, as Wettstein (1979: 92) puts it; the truth value of an eternal sentence stays fixed through time and from speaker to speaker (see Hookway 1997). On the 'convenience' view of linguistic underdeterminacy, when a non-eternal linguistic expression is uttered (i.e. an incomplete formulation), what is expressed thereby can, in every case, be completely formulated by some eternal sentence. This position was held by Frege (1918a), and was more recently and fully presented by Quine (1960: 193–4). Katz (1972, 1977, 1978, 1981) endorses Quine's view:

> Quine's idea is that a [non-eternal sentence] . . . can be expanded on the basis of the information in the context to provide another sentence that expresses a proposition that always makes the statement in question, no matter what the context of utterance. The expansion consists of replacing each indexical element by an expression that has the same reference as the indexical element it replaces but whose referent stays fixed with variations in time, place, speaker, etc. The usual indexical tense indicator will be replaced by such a referentially unique time designation, devised with respect to some

appropriate calendar and clock; indexical nominal elements like 'I', 'he', 'it' and 'John' will be replaced by precise specifications of the individuals or objects that include whatever information about their vital statistics is required to make the specifications resist changes in reference.   (Katz 1972: 126)

In other words, the infinite set of sentences that a linguistic system generates can be partitioned into two infinite subsets, one consisting of the underdetermining non-eternal sentences, which speakers find a very convenient effort-saving means for communicating their thoughts, and the other consisting of the infinite set of fully determining (i.e. proposition-encoding) eternal sentences, which can be employed when total explicitness, leaving no room for interpretive manoeuvre, is called for. The relation between the shorthand-type sentences and the eternal ones must be a many-to-many mapping, a particular mapping in any given instance being determined by the context within which the convenient abbreviation is uttered. Katz concludes his discussion of the view that languages provide a large stock of eternal sentences as follows:

> The only alternative to [this view] is . . . a form of mysticism that claims that some things to which we can refer by the use of indexical elements are, in principle, beyond the range of unique description.   (Katz 1972: 127)

He has maintained this position over the years as he has developed his Platonist view of language (Katz 1981), within which it sits comfortably. According to the Platonist view, languages (hence sentences) are abstract objects whose properties can and should be investigated independently of their instantiations in human minds. The analogy is with systems of mathematics (hence numbers) and logic (hence propositions), whose properties have been extensively investigated independently of the mathematical or logical knowledge represented in human mind/brains. The contrast is with Chomsky's conceptualist (mentalist) view, according to which language is a natural object, the only reality it has being in the form of a, largely genetically programmed, system of knowledge, one component of a much more complex natural object, the human mind/brain.[6] Katz (1981) presents some interesting arguments for the Platonist view; however, it would be too great a digression for me here to review these or the various counterattacks that have been launched (see Fodor 1981a; Chomsky 1986; and, for a recent sustained defence of a 'naturalistic' and 'internalist' approach to language, Chomsky 1995). Suffice it to say at this point, it probably makes better sense within a Platonist conception of language than within any other to posit the view that sentences, one kind of abstract object, map directly on to another kind of abstract object, namely propositions.[7]

1.3.2   Effability principles

The property of 'effability' or 'expressibility' concerns the extent to which it is possible, through the use of a public language system, for us to make our thoughts available to others. The most general formulation of a principle of effability is along the following lines: 'each proposition or thought can be expressed by some sentence in any natural language'. Much hangs on what is meant by 'expressed' here. In the previous sections, when I have talked of a proposition or thought expressed, I have not assumed this meant that it was 'encoded', or fully formulated, by a linguistic expression, quite the contrary in fact. But, as used by Katz (1978, 1981), 'can be expressed by some sentence' would seem to mean 'can be encoded by some sentence'. So there are at least the following two, very different, possible principles to be considered:

First Principle of Effability: 'Each proposition or thought can be expressed (= conveyed) by some utterance of some sentence in any natural language.'

Second Principle of Effability: 'Each proposition or thought can be expressed (= encoded) by some sentence in any natural language.'

Note that while the second of these entails the existence of eternal sentences in the language (one for each proposition or thought), the first does not. The first principle is quite weak and seems largely unobjectionable. It refers to utterances in context rather than to abstract sentences and makes no stipulations about what the linguistic expression used must encode; it leaves open the possibility that much of the determining of the precise conceptual content of the thought is effected by means other than linguistic coding. Given no arbitrary limits on the richness of contexts or on ways in which contextually available material can be used to supplement encoded material, this effability principle does not raise too many problems. Of course, an individual speaker may not have the ability to express verbally a particular thought she has, but that does not touch on the claim, provided the thought *could* be expressed (by a more able speaker) in some context.

The second principle is considerably stronger and open to the following objection:

> It seems plausible that in our internal language we often fix time and space references not in terms of universal coordinates, but in terms of a private logbook and an ego-centred map; furthermore, most kinds of reference – to people and events for instance – can be fixed in terms of these private time and space coordinates. Thoughts which contain such private references could not be *encoded* in natural language but could only be incompletely represented.   (Sperber and Wilson 1986a/95b: 192)

Clearly, the conception of 'thought' here is finer than that of 'proposition expressed' or Fregean thought; it is the individualist psychological notion of thought mentioned at the beginning of this section and it, indeed, does not seem amenable to natural language encoding. The force of this point is perhaps most vividly felt by considering thoughts one has about oneself; how I represent myself to myself must inevitably be quite different from the way you or anyone else represents me, and so it must be for all of us. The same holds for the way I mentally represent my spatial and temporal location at any given instant, that which I might express by the words 'here' and 'now'; your representation of my here and now is likely to be very different from mine and my representation of your here and now is likely to be very different from yours. This is a function of the 'ego-centred map' referred to in the quote and it extends far beyond these self-references. My mental representation of the woman who is my mother is doubtless a private one, probably not even shared with my siblings. This can be extended step by step to all of the people I have encountered in my life, and to all the activities and events I have taken part in or observed. My mental representation of the cup of coffee in front of me on my desk at this moment is determined by its relation to me, and it is that representation that enters into my current thoughts about it; it would be differently represented by another person sitting elsewhere in the room and, to that extent at least, the thoughts he might have about it would differ from mine.

Recanati (1993, 1994) endorses this line of argument. In his terminology, a *de re* thought (that is, a thought about a particular object) involves a particular 'mode of presentation' of that object and that particular mode of presentation may be entirely private, that is, peculiar to a given individual.[8] So the *de re* thoughts of two people predicating the same property of the same object are generally distinct from each other and may also be entirely private.[9] These sorts of differences in representations of an object are not, and cannot be, encoded in natural-language sentences. Imagine for a moment that they could be, perhaps by rapidly making up new audible or visible signals for each different psychological mode of presentation (assuming we have sufficient awareness of these). Such a process would be totally counterproductive since these signals could not be used for the very communicative purpose for which they were supposedly being invented; my public sign for the cup of coffee (which would have to change as my mental representations of it changed) would be meaningless to you; your sounds expressive of your mental representations of the people around you would be meaningless to me. These 'signals' could not be used in the way that natural-language referring expressions are used; they present an unsolvable coordination problem. So they would not in fact be 'linguistic' symbols, properly speaking; they could not acquire that status as they would have no hope of settling into the language system.

Recanati (1994: 157) considers (but does not endorse) another effability principle:

> **Third Principle of Effability:** 'For every statement that can be made using a context-sensitive sentence in a given context, there is an eternal sentence that can be used to make the same statement in any context.'

For the purposes of the discussion to follow, I shall assume that there is no crucial difference between 'statement made' and 'proposition expressed', and, therefore, that this principle could be reformulated using the latter term. Though it is clearly stronger than the first principle in which expressibility is equated with communicability, this third principle is not as strong as the second one. The shift from 'thought' (on an individualist interpretation) to 'statement made' (or 'proposition expressed') secures this principle against the objection just considered. There are *de re* statements (and propositions), that is, statements (or propositions) which predicate a property of an entity, but these are different from *de re* thoughts in at least one essential respect: they do not contain private (psychological) modes of presentation of the object they are about. As Recanati (1994: 157–8) puts it, 'a *de re* statement corresponds to a class of [*de re*] thoughts, each involving a particular (and, perhaps, private) mode of presentation of the object referred to. . . . statements are public objects at a more abstract level than thoughts, and as such do not contain private modes of presentation.' So the possibility of eternalization of statements made (propositions expressed) needs to be given separate consideration.

This third effability principle seems to be implicit in the quote in the previous section from Katz (1972: 126), where the focus is on eternal sentences which encode *statements* made. This carries through to his subsequent Platonist position on which 'Every proposition is a sense of some sentence in each natural language' (Katz 1978: 216), where propositions are to be understood as the abstract entities themselves, rather than as mental representations of them. If this principle is correct, then it is not out of necessity that speakers use non-eternal (context-sensitive) means of expressing propositions, but it must be for some other reason. It comes as no surprise, then, to find that Katz takes the convenience view of linguistic underdeterminacy: 'it [underdeterminacy] allows speakers to make use of contextual features to speak far more concisely than otherwise. . . . Pragmatics saves us from . . . wasteful verbosity' (Katz 1977: 19–20). Thus our capacity for pragmatic inference, on this view, is a useful add-on to our language capacity, not strictly essential in making possible the sort of expressive and communicative powers we have.

In the rest of this section, I present evidence against this third effability position, drawing on arguments from Wettstein (1979) and Recanati (1987b, 1994). Then, in section 1.4, I will outline a view of pragmatic interpretation and of the cognitive capacities that underpin it (the relevance-theoretic view), from which, I believe, the essential nature of linguistic underdeterminacy follows. The picture is the opposite of Katz's in every respect: only the first principle holds (on which effability = communicability), there are no eternal sentences, and pragmatic inference is fundamental.

Wettstein (1979) specifically addresses Katz (1972) and argues against his view that, for any statement made (proposition expressed) by the use of a non-eternal sentence in a particular context, there is an eternal sentence that can be used to make the same statement (express the same proposition) across contexts (or in the hypothetical absence of any context). A crucial part of the process of 'eternalizing' a non-eternal sentence is the replacement of each indexical expression by a non-indexical expression which picks out, in all contexts, for all time, the object that was referred to by the given use of the indexical in a particular context. According to Frege, Quine and Katz, what achieves this is a uniquely denoting description. Wettstein points out that the object concerned can be picked out by a range of *non-synonymous* descriptions. For instance, the pronoun 'she' in an utterance of (23a) can be replaced by a variety of descriptions, including those given in (23b)–(23d). Assuming, as Wettstein does, that there are such things as uniquely denoting descriptions and that these are likely candidates, each of them may denote the woman in question. (I haven't attempted to eternalize the predicates.)

(23) a. She left in a hurry.
       b. The woman who spoke to Tony Blair at t_1 left in a hurry.
       c. The woman in the red velvet dress who was in the Islington Town Hall between t_1 and t_2 left in a hurry.
       d. The middle-aged lady who organized the anti-junk-food campaign in June 1999 left in a hurry.

But these cannot all be part of the complete formulation of the statement the speaker made, and it is not clear that any one of them rather than any other, or indeed that any of them at all, does in fact figure in the statement made by the speaker of the original indexical sentence. As Wettstein (1979: 94) says, 'Since these descriptions are not synonymous, it would seem that each of the resulting eternal sentences formulates a *different* proposition. The genuine eternal sentence counterpart will be the one that actually formulates the proposition the speaker asserted. But is there clearly one of these eternal sentences that, as opposed to the others, actually formulates what was asserted?' He argues that there is no basis for thinking that any one among the several non-synonymous eternal sentences is the one that corresponds to the proposition expressed by the indexical utterance, and that this is because, in fact, none of them does.[10]

The point carries over equally to attempts to eternalize patently incomplete definite descriptions like 'the table', 'the child', 'the government', etc., whether used attributively or referentially. There are many possible completions all of which may uniquely denote the entity picked out in context by the original non-uniquely denoting description, but no one of which is *the* eternalized version of the incomplete description (see Wettstein 1981). The point also extends in an obvious way to certain subsentential utterances. Suppose two people are talking at a party and one of them, looking in the direction of a man near the door, says 'Tom's father'. As Stainton (1994) has shown, a speaker can use 'Tom's father' to assert of a certain man that he is, say, the father of Tom Adams. But, of course, the search for the 'right' eternal sentence to encode what is asserted here is fairly unconstrained; either of the following, or any number of others, might do:

(24) a. The man wearing a pink tie and drinking a martini at t_1 is the father of Tom Adams.
       b. The nervous-looking man standing in the doorway of the kitchen of Tom Adams's flat at t_1 is the father of Tom Adams.

As Wettstein would doubtless say about this example, it is not clear that any particular one of these eternal sentences, as opposed to any other, 'actually formulates what was asserted'. The issue cannot be resolved by referring to the speaker's intention, since very often she will have no determinate intention; if asked which of the various possible eternal sentences correctly formulates the statement she intended to make she will be unable to answer. Indexical reference (and unarticulated reference, as in this last case) appears to be irrevocably context-bound; it is not reformulable in terms of a uniquely denoting description, but depends on the addressee's capacity to identify the intended entity by some means which is non-linguistic or, at least, not wholly linguistic.

This argument effectively undermines the third effability principle, held by Frege, Quine and Katz, and so supports an essentialist view of linguistic underdeterminacy. The absence from the language of any eternal sentence which encodes the proposition expressed by an indexical sentence (uttered in a context) is sufficient to achieve this, even if there are, in fact, some eternal sentences in the language. Wettstein seems to assume that there *are* such things as eternal sentences and that the elaborated sentences given above are candidates; similarly, Sayward (1968), who also shows that there is no eternal sentence equivalent for a range of indexical utterances, assumes that, nonetheless, there are some eternal sentences in the language. On this view, there is generally no mapping between indexical sentences (uttered in a context) and eternal sentences; rather, they are complementary in their expressive powers.

So the essentialist position established is the weaker one, which is good enough for my purposes. However, the head-on attack against the strong effability principles (the second and third) would be to deny the existence of eternal sentences altogether, as Recanati (1994) does. His discussion extends beyond the usual concentration on referring expressions to some consideration of predicates, quantifiers and tense. I will take a brief look in the next two subsections just at his arguments against the existence of eternal referring expressions and of eternal predicates.

1.3.3 Eternal reference?

Although Wettstein establishes that any process of substitution of an indexical by a complete description leads to a difference in the proposition expressed (and statement made), he doesn't question the existence of uniquely denoting descriptions. In fact, he speaks of a continuum of descriptions, from the patently incomplete 'the table', to more complete but still indefinite definite descriptions, and, finally, to a uniquely denoting description, usually containing proper names and precise temporal specifications, such as 'the table in room 209 of Camden Hall at t_1', where t_1 is, presumably, to be replaced by some eternal natural-language phrase (Wettstein 1981: 253–4).

Recanati (1987b, 1994, 1995) suggests that there simply cannot be reference (or unique denotation) without a context, that reference is always a pragmatic context-dependent matter. To establish this very broad claim, the case has to be made for proper names and for complete definite descriptions (whether used attributively or in the strongly referential way discussed by Donnellan 1966/91). It would take some considerable time and space to do this in anything approaching a conclusive fashion, given the vast range of work in the philosophy of language on proper names and descriptions. I shall not attempt that here. As regards proper names, the approach which treats them as a variety of indexical is intuitively appealing: just like pronouns, one and the same proper name may refer to different individuals in different contexts. Note that Katz (following Frege and Quine) included them in the class of cases which are to be replaced by a uniquely denoting description in the process of formulating an eternal sentence. In my view, the analysis of the linguistic meaning of a proper name as some sort of rule requiring that it refers to a bearer of the name seems to be on the right track. This position is defended by Bach (1987) and Recanati (1993, chapters 8–9). Whether it turns out to be correct or not, proper names are not eternal, any more than any other indexical, so nor are descriptions that contain them.

Recanati (1987b) goes on to consider apparently complete descriptions like 'the prime minister of Britain in 1999'. Of course, the names of countries and nations like 'Britain' are not essentially different in their semantics from the names of persons (although multiple use of these names is more studiously avoided for practical reasons), so they are also indexical and any description containing them is non-eternal. However, Recanati takes up a different line of argument: he sets out to show that the reference of a definite description, even one with no indexical element, always depends on the 'domain of discourse', what Fauconnier (1985) terms a 'mental space' and Barwise and Perry (1983) call a 'resource situation'. The domain of discourse is 'that with respect to which the speaker presents his or her utterance as true' (Recanati 1987b: 62). Possible domains of discourse are the actual world, a fragment of the actual world (say, the current political situation in Britain), someone's belief-world, a fictional world, a fragment of some counterfactual world.

He discusses the following sort of case: you and I know that Lucinda wrongly believes that Peter Mandelson is the prime minister of Britain in 1999. Knowing that Mandelson is in the next room, I utter (25) to you (in 1999):

(25)   Lucinda will be delighted to find that the current prime minister of Britain is in the next room.

I am here using the definite description to refer to Mandelson rather than the actual prime minster (Tony Blair), because I intend it to be interpreted with respect to Lucinda's belief-world, within which Mandelson is the British prime minister. Of course, this example has a metarepresentational flavour, involving as it does an implicit attribution to Lucinda of a particular belief, and it could be argued that this somehow takes it outside the realm of the cases under discussion. I don't think any such objection can be sustained, since this sort of use is utterly commonplace and merely reflects the fundamental point that the linguistic system is a tool, which does not have fixed communicative content but can be used in a range of ways by human communicators. The proposition expressed by the given utterance of (25) includes as a constituent (a concept of) someone who, on a different utterance of the same sentence in 1999, would not be picked out by the description 'the current prime minister of Britain'; the same holds for the arguably more complete description, 'the prime minister of Britain in 1999'.[11]

This relativity of reference to the domain of discourse extends to those complete descriptions which have seemed the least likely to yield to the general context-dependence thesis. These are cases of so-called rigid descriptions where the semantic value of the description is the same across all possible worlds, for instance 'the cube root of 27'. While 3 is the cube root of 27 in all possible worlds, it is not so in all domains of discourse, since Lucinda might believe that 9 is the cube-root of

27, and, as we have seen, Lucinda's belief-world is a possible domain of discourse. Recanati (1987b: 64–5) goes on to show that when a domain-indicator like 'Lucinda thinks that . . .' or 'According to Lucinda . . .' is given explicitly, as a constituent of the sentence uttered, its own interpretation is relative to a domain of discourse, which may or may not be the actual world, and which has to be pragmatically inferred, for instance, 'In Paul's story, Lucinda believes that . . .'. So there is an unavoidably context-dependent dimension in understanding any utterance. Even the 'normal' (some would say 'literal') understanding, where the description is interpreted with respect to the actual world, is a pragmatic matter, as it is dependent on the identification of the domain of discourse as the actual world. On this basis, even the best candidates for eternal sentences, for instance those in (22), are, in fact, context-dependent.

Not all subject noun phrases involve reference to particular entities; quantified noun phrase subjects like 'everybody', 'some students', 'most films', etc., are not referential. Of course, to be correctly understood these require a domain of quantification (e.g. 'some students doing the BA Linguistics at University College London in 1998/9') which is supplied contextually. Could the domain be explicitly described, that is, could the quantified phrase be made eternal? Again, this seems highly improbable because of the indexical nature of elements in the domain specification. Recanati (1994) argues further that, even if the quantificational domain could be given fully explicitly, the correct interpretation of it could only be made relative to the intended domain of discourse (mental space). Consider in this regard the phrase 'some of the spin doctors of the prime minister of Britain in 1999', interpreted relative to Lucinda's belief-world as described above. So it looks as if no quantificational sentence is eternal either.

If natural language predicates can also be shown to be non-eternal, then that will be yet another source of underdeterminacy in the descriptions that are supposed to replace indexicals and achieve a timelessly fixed specification.

1.3.4   Eternal predication?

The *in*effability of reference provides perhaps the clearest argument against eternal sentences and those principles of effability which entail the complete linguistic encodability of the proposition expressed by an utterance. However, the case can be extended to include the predication function of language, the assigning of properties and relations to the entities picked out by referring expressions. That this is so has been shown in some detail by Travis (1981, 1985, 1991), Lahav (1989, 1993) and Gross (1998). Travis considers simple examples like the following:

(26)   a.   The kettle is black.
       b.   The table was covered with butter.
       c.   Hugo is a sailor.

Discussing what is meant by the predicate 'black' in (26a), he outlines a range of possible circumstances in each of which it has a different interpretation:

> Suppose the kettle is normal aluminum, but soot covered; normal aluminum but painted; cast iron, but glowing from heat; cast iron but enamelled white on the inside; on the outside; cast iron with a lot of brown grease stains on the outside; etc. (Compare a postage stamp, black on one side – a black stamp?, a 'yellow' labrador retriever painted to look like a black one – is the dog black? a 'black' narcissus, with a green stem; the North Sea [look at it from the deck on a normal North Sea day, then pull up a bucket of it and look at that].)   (Travis 1985: 197)

His point is that the sentence in (26a), like virtually all sentences, may be used to say any of indefinitely many distinct things, each of which is true under different conditions. The bearer of truth is not the sentence but the proposition the speaker uses the sentence to express on the given occasion of utterance. One of the sources of these propositional differences in (26a) is the property communicated by the adjectival predicate 'black', both what property that is (clearly visible black, a wider colour spectrum taking in various dark browns, invisible black) and what exactly it is taken to apply to (the whole kettle, the inside, the outside, most of the outside, etc.). The same issues arise for (26b) and (26c); Travis spins numerous possible ways in which butter might be conceived of as covering a table and Hugo might be conceived of as a sailor (that is, different sets of truth conditions for different occasions of use of the sentence). This has interesting implications for the project of formulating a truth-conditional semantics for natural-language *sentences*, some of which are discussed in section 1.5.1; the context-sensitivity of predicates, in fact, proves to be a greater problem for the T-sentence approach than the context-sensitivity of reference.

Consider the following example, discussed by Sperber and Wilson (1997/98a: 192–5), where the concept communicated by a predicate is more specific than the concept it encodes:

(27)   A: Do you want to go to the cinema?
      B: I'm tired.

Most of us are tired to some degree or other most of the time; what B communicates by the predicate 'tired' in this context is something much more specific than that, something stronger perhaps than the sort of tiredness that makes an undemanding evening out quite agreeable, but not as strong as the sort of tiredness that necessitates going to bed immediately. Just how narrowed down this *ad hoc* concept of tiredness is will depend on other contextually available information, perhaps concerning B's general energy levels, her liking for the cinema, etc. The prospects for finding another lexical item or even a lengthy description which fully encodes the concept of tiredness communicated here, and still others that encode the innumerable other concepts of tiredness that may be communicated in other contexts, look dim. In other words, as well as not uniquely determining the objects they can be used to refer to, natural language expressions seem to be intrinsically underdetermining of the properties and relations they may be used to predicate of an object.

Following the well-known example of Austin (1962), there is a range of examples which can be described as cases where the concept communicated (as opposed to the one encoded) depends on the standard of precision relevant in the particular context:

(28) a. France is hexagonal.
      b. This steak is raw.
      c. The fridge is empty.

These are cases where, arguably, the predicate is clearly defined and the definition is part of the native speaker's knowledge of the language; for instance, 'a hexagon is a geometric figure with six equal sides', 'something is raw if and only if it has received no cooking', etc. However, the proposition expressed on particular occasions of use might vary considerably depending on the degree of looseness the context allows or calls for.[12] The addition of modifiers such as 'approximately', 'to some extent', 'more or less' will make it explicit that the following predicate is not being used strictly but, clearly, they will not effect a full encoding of the intended concept of hexagonalness, rawness, etc. Eternalization does not look like a possibility here.[13] In fact, as I will suggest in chapter 5, the proposition expressed (what is said) by these cases may in some instances be indeterminate; there may be no absolute fact of the matter; speaker and hearer may diverge somewhat in the propositional form they entertain, though in ways that are quite innocuous as regards the success of the communicative interaction.

It is worth noting that Recanati's concept of a 'domain of discourse' needs to be applied with care in these predication cases. Consider a situation in which we know that Lucinda believes that cats are primates. On an application parallel to the case of the denotation of 'the prime minister of Britain' in the previous section, I could say to you, of my ancient tabby, 'Dear old Fleabag is a primate', where the domain of discourse pertaining to my use of the predicate 'primate' is Lucinda's belief world. Or consider the case of a young child who calls all four-legged animals of a certain size 'dogs', leading me to say to you 'Fleabag is a nice dog', where 'dog' must be understood relative to the child's belief world. But these seem to be different in an important way from the reference cases in that both Lucinda and the child are talking a different language from the one that you and I know; they assign a different ('wrong') sense to the words 'primate' and 'dog'. As far as I can see, the interpretations you would recover from these utterances are 'Lucinda thinks Fleabag is a primate', 'The child thinks Fleabag is a dog', where you would understand 'primate' and 'dog' in accordance with your knowledge of the language and not as communicating some different (wider) concept. In the reference cases, recognition of the relevant domain of discourse plays a crucial role in picking out an intended referent despite the fact that the description used for the purpose does not apply to him/her in the actual world. In that case, the belief world called upon involves idiosyncratic beliefs about entities in the world (e.g. that Mandelson is the prime minister of Britain) rather than idiosyncratic linguistic encodings. As I understand it, the idea of varying 'domains of discourse' concerns distinct belief worlds in which, nonetheless, the language has the same meaning. So there is an important difference here between reference and predication, no doubt just one manifestation of a more general asymmetry between the two phenomena.

To conclude, I should note that although I've concentrated on utterances of declarative sentences, the points made carry over to all the other sentence types: interrogatives, imperatives, optatives, hortatives, subjunctives, etc. On the whole, the advocates of eternal sentences, generally logicians or philosophers of language who put a premium on the statement-making function of language, especially the stating of scientific truths, have not been much interested in interrogatives and even less in sentences in the other moods. Katz, as a semanticist of natural language, does not confine his interest in this way; it is clear from Katz (1977), where he explores the semantics of sentences used to express a range of illocutionary forces, that he intends his effability principle to apply across the board. A belief that indexicals can be replaced by uniquely denoting non-indexicals must apply to sentences of all mood types, and so too a belief that vague or open-textured predicates can be replaced by well-defined ones. It follows then that the arguments against the existence of eternal declarative sentences apply equally against the existence of eternal imperatives and interrogatives.[14]

Summing up: the position I've been arguing for is that there are no eternal sentences in natural languages (that is, no sentences which encode a proposition or thought which is constant across all contexts), from which it follows that the linguistic underdeterminacy of the proposition expressed by an utterance is an essential feature of natural language. Neither of the strong principles of effability (the second or the third) applies to the semantic structures provided by natural languages. This is not to say, of course, that linguistic expressions, though inevitably non-eternal, cannot be used in appropriate contexts to communicate most, if not all, the propositions which humans are capable of instantiating in thought. This may well be so. In the next section, I will try to sketch a view of the human mind from which both this unbounded communicability of thought *and* the absence of eternal sentences in natural language follow, if not necessarily, very naturally.

1.4 Metarepresentation, Relevance and Pragmatic Inference

1.4.1 Mind-reading and ostension

Dan Sperber has emphasized the following fact about human cognition: while observed behaviour can, in principle, be conceptualized both in purely physical terms and in mentalistic (intentional) terms, we almost inevitably go for the latter (Sperber 1994a, 1996). Imagine observing a scene in which a man slowly lowers himself, head and arms first, down into a hole in the ground while another man holds on to his legs. Very few observers will represent this scene to themselves as I have just described it and leave it at that; most of us will look for some plausible beliefs, desires and/or intentions that we can attribute to these two men, some set of mental states which will explain their behaviour. For instance, we may attribute to both men a *belief* that there is something worth retrieving down in that hole, to the first man an *intention* to retrieve it, to the second man a *belief* that the first may fall into the hole and hurt himself if his legs are not held, etc.

We can't help doing this sort of thing, that is, we can't help attributing beliefs, desires and intentions, with quite specific content, to others; it seems to be built in to our cognitive system for interpreting the behaviour of our fellow humans. This capacity is more intelligent than one that simply assumes that every observed outcome of human action is an intended outcome; it is able to consider the sorts of beliefs and intentions people are likely to have and those they are not likely to have. So if the second man loses his grip on the first man's legs and the first man emerges some time later covered in slime, we will recognize these physical happenings as undesirable to the men and so not to be explained in terms of any intentions they had. Or, if there is some desirable outcome to their behaviour but which the men could not reasonably be expected to have foreseen, we will not try to explain it in terms of their beliefs or intentions. This capacity is not confined to one or two levels of attribution nor to attributions which involve but a single cognizer: you can attribute to *me* an *intention* to get *you* to *believe* that some *third person* does not *want* to go to a party. The mental faculty responsible for this is known as the 'theory of mind' or 'mind-reading' capacity and there is now a huge psychological literature on its nature, its place in our overall cognitive architecture, how it develops in infancy, its impairment in certain pathological conditions, such as autism, and its rudimentary manifestation in some other primates (see, for example, Astington, Harris and Olson 1988; Premack 1988; Baron-Cohen 1995; Smith and Tsimpli 1995, 1996; Scholl and Leslie 1999).

On the representational/computational view of the mind (which is assumed throughout this book), having a cognitive mental state like a belief or an intention involves being in a relation to a mental representation (a conceptual sentence in the language of thought, perhaps; see Fodor 1978, 1980). For instance, my believing that Felix is a cat involves my being in a belief relation to the representation 'FELIX IS A CAT' (or, as it is sometimes put, having a token of this representation in my belief box). Given this general picture, it can be seen that a crucial feature enabling the attribution of a mental state to someone, which may itself involve the attribution of a mental state, is a capacity for *meta*representation, that is, an ability to represent not just states of the external physical world but also other representations, and representations of still further representations, etc., up to several orders of complexity. This capacity makes it possible for us to reflect on our own mental states; for instance, to recall our former cognitive selves as consisting of beliefs, desires and hopes that may have been superseded. It makes it possible for us to hold reflective beliefs, that is, beliefs embedded in attributive phrases (such as 'The wise elders say that . . .'), which may be at odds with basic factual beliefs which we hold, or which may duplicate the content of factual beliefs; for instance, certain religious or mythical beliefs, on the one hand, and certain scientific or theory-embedded beliefs, on the other (see Sperber 1982/85, 1997a). Most important in the current context, the metarepresentational capacity makes possible the kind of communication which appears to be unique to humans: ostensive-inferential communication. Sperber (1994a) claims that adult communicators employ at least fourth-order metarepresentations, and that the interpretation of utterances and other ostensive behaviours requires inferential processes involving premises of several metarepresentational levels, which hearers perform with ease.

Continuing the scenario from above: suppose the second man, who is holding the legs of the first, swivels his eyes leftwards in our direction and starts to jerk his head quite violently from left to right. It is likely that we'll take him to be communicating something to us, that we'll take the head movement to be, not some involuntary tic he developed upon seeing us, but rather a movement designed to make it evident to us that he wants our attention and has something to tell us. We might even hazard a guess at (infer) what the intended message is, something like 'I want you to help me' perhaps. Note that this is achieved *without any element of encoding* whatsoever; the same type of head movement would be interpreted in quite different ways in different situations. Ostensive behaviour of this sort is explained by the attribution to their originators of a particular sort of intention, which Sperber and Wilson (1986a/95b: 50–64) call a 'communicative intention'. This is an intrinsically higher-order mental state, hence requires metarepresentation, as it is an intention to make manifest (or evident) an intention to inform someone of something (that is, to say, tell, ask, make known something). (See appendix 1 for a stricter definition of a communicative intention.) For instance, in the given example, the man who is making the ostensive head movements intends thereby to make it manifest to us that he intends us to recognize that he wants us to help him.[15]

Sperber (2000) argues in favour of a comprehension system whose domain is specifically utterances and other ostensive stimuli. This is a metarepresentational system and may be a submodule of the theory of mind (or 'metapsychological') system, to which it is clearly intimately related. The main argument for the claim that it is a distinct mental module hinges on the fact that the comprehension process requires a particular pattern of inference which distinguishes it from the inferential processes involved in interpreting non-ostensive behaviour. Someone observing the activities of the two men described above can impute to them certain intentions on the basis of an observed desirable outcome of their behaviour (e.g. the retrieval of a diamond ring). But in interpreting an instance of ostensive behaviour, the desirable effect (which is that the addressee grasp the communicator's meaning) cannot be achieved without the addressee's prior recognition of the communicator's intention to achieve that effect. That is, the standard pattern of inference from behaviour to identification of desirable outcome and then to intention is not available to the process of understanding acts of overt communication. Relevance theory makes a specific proposal about the particular computational strategy employed by a dedicated ostension comprehension module.[16] I turn to that in the next section.

1.4.2 Relevance and utterance understanding

According to Sperber and Wilson's (1986a/95b) framework, relevance is a property of the inputs to cognitive processes (whether perceptual or higher-level conceptual); it is a positive function of cognitive effects and a negative function of the processing effort expended in deriving those effects. Cognitive effects (or contextual effects) include the strengthening of existing assumptions of the system, by providing further evidence for them, the elimination of assumptions that appear to be false, in the light of the new evidence, and the derivation of new assumptions ('contextual implications') through the interaction of the new information with existing assumptions. A basic principle of the framework is the **Cognitive Principle of Relevance** according to which the human cognitive system as a whole is oriented towards the maximization of relevance. That is, the various subsystems involved, in effect, conspire together in a bid to achieve the greatest number of cognitive effects for the least processing effort overall. The perceptual input systems have evolved in such a way that they generally respond automatically to stimuli which are very likely to have cognitive effects, quickly converting them into the sort of representational formats that are appropriate inputs to the conceptual inferential systems; these systems then integrate them, as efficiently as possible, with some accessible subset of existing representations to achieve as many cognitive effects as possible.

What distinguishes ostensive behaviour (including verbal utterances) from nonostensive behaviour (and, all the more so, from observed events that are not the result of volitional behaviour at all) is that it raises an expectation of a particular level of relevance in the relevance-seeking cognitive system of the addressee. A speaker (or more generally, an ostensive communicator) overtly requests an expenditure of mental effort from an addressee (an outlay of attentional and inferential resources) and that licenses an expectation of a worthwhile yield of cognitive effects with no gratuitous expenditure of effort. This is captured by the **Communicative Principle of Relevance**: every act of ostension communicates a presumption of its own *optimal relevance*; that is, a presumption that it will be at least relevant enough to warrant the addressee's attention and, moreover, as relevant as is compatible with the communicator's competence and her personal goals and preferences. The specific procedure employed by the comprehension system, on the basis of the presumption of optimal relevance, is given in (29):

(29) Check interpretive hypotheses in order of their accessibility, that is, follow a path of least effort, until an interpretation which satisfies the expectation of relevance is found; then stop.

The least-effort strategy follows from the presumption of optimal relevance in that the speaker is expected to have found a vehicle for the communication of her thoughts which minimizes the hearer's effort (within the parameters set by the speaker's own abilities and goals/preferences); the justification for the addressee stopping processing as soon as an interpretation satisfies his expectation of relevance follows similarly, in that any other interpretation that might also achieve the requisite level of effects will be less accessible and so incur greater processing costs.[17]

The operation of this procedure, peculiar to the processing of ostensive behaviour, provides a solution to the apparent problem, mentioned in the previous section, that the desirable outcome (the grasping of the communicator's meaning) is dependent on a prior recognition of the communicator's intention. Processing by the addressee's pragmatic system employing the strategy in (29) is automatically triggered by an ostensive stimulus, irrespective of the actual intentions of the producer of the stimulus, and this strategy provides a reliable, though by no means foolproof, means of inferring a speaker's meaning. In fact, there are three distinct ways the general strategy may be implemented, depending on the precise nature of the 'expectation of relevance' which an interpretive hypothesis must satisfy if it is to be accepted. With each of these three sorts of expectation there come differences in the complexity of the (meta)representational manipulations involved in the comprehension process.

The simplest case is an expectation of actual optimal relevance, which depends on assuming complete competence and good will on the part of the speaker; a more sophisticated expectation allows for speaker fallibility (for instance, gaps in her knowledge which make her unable to assess accurately what is relevant to the addressee at the particular time) and the most advanced expectation drops the assumption of inevitable speaker benevolence (after all, it might not be in the speaker's own interests to give relevant information to the addressee). Assuming an utterance with content P and assuming communicative success, on the most straightforward strategy (probably the default case), the result of comprehension is a second-order metarepresentation: she intends me to believe that P. In its most sophisticated version, the expectation is merely one of purported relevance so that the strategy is geared to finding, not the first sufficiently relevant interpretation, but the first one that the speaker could have thought would *seem* relevant enough to the addressee. This results in a fourth-order metarepresentation: 'She intends me to believe that she intends me to believe that P.' (For much more detailed exposition with worked examples, see Sperber 1994a.)

Expectations of relevance may also vary in their specificity. For instance, in the case of a conversation initiated by a stranger who happens to be sitting beside you on an aeroplane, you may have only quite a general expectation, while, in the case of an utterance made by a close friend in response to a question you've just asked, your expectation will be quite specific (that is, that she will give the information you asked for). The role of expectations of relevance of different degrees of specificity is explored in chapter 2 (section 2.3.4), where the relevance-based procedure is seen at work in the interpretation of some cases of verbal utterances.

Recall that, although Katz (1977) recognizes that, as a matter of fact, speakers rely on hearers' capacities to infer their informative intentions, his view is that this is just to save speakers the effort of (a) finding the natural-language sentence that fully encodes the proposition they want to express, and of (b) having to work their articulatory apparatus unnecessarily. According to this view, there is nothing fundamental about pragmatic inference. However, in the previous section, I made the case that the language system does not have the resources to encode the propositions speakers succeed in expressing, and what I am suggesting here is that there is a very good reason for this: that sort of expressive power is redundant. A powerful 'mind-reading' capacity is employed in the interpretation of human behaviour quite generally, with a specialized subsystem for dealing with ostensive behaviour including instances involving no coded element (such as various ostensive movements of parts of the face or body). The wide application of this capacity in human cognitive activity and its presence in a rudimentary form in apes, who lack a linguistic system, make it reasonable to suppose that the linguistic code evolved later than the general capacity to attribute mental states and also later than, or in step with, the more specific capacity to attribute communicative intentions. If it had been in place in the absence of an ability to attribute beliefs and intentions, it would have been largely functionally inert, at least for communicative purposes.[18]

If these somewhat speculative thoughts are on the right track, it seems that nature designed (speaking metaphorically, as we do) a linguistic code that has just the expressive resources that are needed to supplement an already pretty effective interpretive system. A linguistic system is undeniably enabling; it allows us to achieve a degree of explicitness, clarity and abstractness not possible in non-verbal communication (try communicating the proposition just expressed without using a language), but it is not essential for the basic function of referring, and the predicates it offers are but a tiny subset of the properties and relations that humans can think about and communicate.[19]

Within the bounds of her competence and her personal concerns and preferences, a speaker's choice of linguistic form takes account of the hearer's immediately accessible assumptions, encoding just what seems to be necessary to direct the hearer's inferential processes to the intended interpretation; what the coded bits of an utterance do is 'set the inferential process on the right track'. A (very) rough non-psychological analogy might be with a constructed system of banks and trenches, which channel the inevitable downhill flow of a river in certain directions, diverting it from others it might go in if left to its own devices. Verbal communication, on this view, is not a means of thought duplication; the thought(s) that the speaker seeks to communicate are seldom, if ever, perfectly replicated in the mind of the audience; communication is deemed successful (that is, good enough) when the interpretation derived by the addressee sufficiently resembles the thoughts the speaker intended to communicate. That communication is often successful in this sense is due partly to the channelling provided by the linguistic code, partly to our innate ability to attribute beliefs and intentions to each other and, crucially, given our constant cognitive bid for relevance, to the prevailing presumption of optimal relevance carried by utterances (and ostensive stimuli generally).

Recall Katz's charge, quoted in the previous section, that the only alternative to the availability of 'eternal' sentences is some kind of mysticism. I believe the cognitive picture just outlined provides an alternative of a non-mystical sort; it is a solid empirical hypothesis about the nature of human communication, one that is rather well supported by what is currently known about human cognitive capacities. Part of the motivation for Katz's formulation of an effability principle was to try to capture the essence of natural language, that which distinguishes it from artificial languages, on the one hand, and from animal communication systems, on the other. There are, doubtless, properties of natural human language, such as the complexity and recursiveness of its syntax, which distinguish it from animal signal systems, but the sort of uniqueness that concerned Katz, the 'expressive power of natural languages', seems to follow not from the linguistic system itself, but from its recruitment by the distinct capacity for ostensive communicative behaviour, itself dependent on a highly developed metarepresentational ability for instantiating and attributing intentional states of several orders of complexity.[20]

1.5   Underdeterminacy, Truth Conditions and the Semantics/Pragmatics Distinction

> if you just take a bunch of sentences . . . impeccably formulated in some language or other, there can be no question of sorting them out into those that are true and those that are false; for . . . the question of truth and falsehood does not turn only on what a sentence *is*, nor yet on what it *means*, but on, speaking very broadly, the circum-stances in which it is uttered. Sentences are not *as such* either true or false.   (Austin 1962: 110–11)

This quote from one of the most famous of the ordinary-language philosophers is, in effect, a statement of the underdeterminacy thesis. The designation 'ordinary-language' is to distinguish the focus of these philosophers from that of preceding generations of philosophers whose energies had been engaged in the construction of 'formal' logical languages (Austin's specific targets here are Carnap and Ayer). The aim of the formalists, I think, was to achieve the precise expression of scientific truths in a representation system which would wear its logic on its face, its logical implications following transparently from its form, as is the case with the predicate calculus, for instance. Non-natural formal languages are set up so as to be free from all those features that make natural languages underdetermining of propositions: they contain no indexicals, no ambiguous or vague predicates, no operators with unspecified scope, and no unarticulated or hidden constituents. On a given inter-pretation of the language, each of its well-formed formulas has context-free truth conditions and is either true or false, regardless of the context in which it appears.

However, it seems quite clear that if these formal languages were for some reason pressed into use by normally functioning human beings, in ordinary communicative situations, they would soon appear to lose their well-definedness. They would be used to communicate all sorts of propositions that, as originally constructed at least, they did not encode, that lay beyond their intrinsic (context-free) power of expres-sion. Then, over time, if employed in this way, they would probably lose their origi-nal characteristic of being uniquely denoting: names would become indexical and many predicates would lose their univocality or would become very much more general in meaning. Why should this be so? It is communicatively convenient (that is, it makes for savings in the overall cognitive economy) to have forms that cause several senses to spring to mind or which have a quite general and open-textured sense. At least, it is convenient given the pragmatic inferential capacities of humans, which are acutely responsive to contextual considerations, enabling them easily and rapidly to choose among senses and to home in on more specific interpretations of a general sense.[21] Note that this answer is, in effect, the reverse of the 'pragmatic inference as convenient shortcut', which I have rejected in the previous sections. Even if the integrity of the original, precisely defined system could be somehow (arti-ficially) preserved, the basic pragmatic fact about natural languages would carry over to the use of the formal language: communicators would succeed in express-ing, and being understood as expressing, propositions that this language did not encode.

The linguistic underdeterminacy view is now fairly widely endorsed by philosophers of language and pragmatists, in some form or other, to varying degrees and for different reasons. The outstanding exception to this is Grice, who appears to want to keep 'what is said' as close as possible to conventional (encoded) sentence meaning (conceding only indexicality). His reasons for this are explored in the next chapter. As we have seen, Travis (1981, 1985, 1991, 1997) and Recanati (1989b/91, 1993, 1994, 1995) hold strong essentialist positions on underdeterminacy, as do relevance theorists. Searle (1978/79, 1983, 1992) holds a radical underdeterminacy thesis which applies not only to language but to all intentional mental states (beliefs, intentions, thoughts); I will look at this in section 1.6.

Jay Atlas (1977, 1984, 1989) makes remarks that indicate support for the underdeterminacy view, albeit from the fairly restricted perspective of particular semantic analyses:

> Meanings [of sentences] might be identified with mappings from points of reference into propositions, but not with the propositions themselves. If semantic representations represent meaning, they are not propositions or [Russellian] logical forms, though which propositions can be literally expressed by a sentence is determined by its semantic representation.   (Atlas 1977: 332–3)

> The sense-generality of a sentence radically underdetermines (independently of indexicality) the truth-conditional contents of its utterances.   (Atlas 1989: 31)

His specific interest is in establishing his 'sense generality' thesis, as against appeals to ambiguity (multiplicity of sense), in the semantic analysis of several key areas of language, in particular negation (this is discussed in chapter 4 of this book). Kempson and Cormack (1981, 1982) and Bach (1982) have taken a similar line on sentences with several quantifiers (that is, that sentence meaning is neutral as regards their relative scopes). It follows from this semantic nonspecificity that sentence meaning is not fully propositional and there is an obligatory pragmatic process of scope fixing.

Within more linguistically oriented pragmatics, underdeterminacy has been noted by several authors (for instance, Fauconnier (1975, 1978, 1985), Dascal (1981), Green and Morgan (1981), Levinson (1988, 2000)), though not in the strong form I am advocating, that is, that linguistically encoded meaning *never* fully determines the intended proposition expressed. Levinson presents a huge range of data illustrating what he calls 'pragmatic intrusion' into the truth-conditional content of utterances. He finds this problematic since, in his view, it undermines the autonomy of semantics, which, following Gazdar (1979), he equates with truth conditions. It gives rise to an allegedly problematic circle because a crucial input to pragmatic inference is the semantic representation of the utterance, but pragmatic inference is necessary in order to establish that very semantic (truth-conditional) content (for disambiguation, reference assignment, supplying of unarticulated constituents, enrichment, etc.). I shall suggest below and in the next chapter that the problem comes from an implicit equation of sentence meaning with 'what is said' (= truth-conditional content) and an accompanying assumption that all pragmatic inference gives rise to implicatures.

1.5.1 A truth-conditional semantics for natural language?

The semantics of a formal logical language is typically given in terms of a truth theory for the language, which assigns to each sentential formula conditions on its truth; the propositionality and context-independence of the sentences of the language are important factors in making this feasible. The context-sensitivity and non-propositionality of natural-language sentences raises the question of how their semantics is to be characterized. A dominant view is that, notwithstanding indexicality, vagueness and incompleteness, sentence meaning *must* be given in terms of truth conditions. As is well known, the Tarskian 'normal form' for the statements of truth conditions (that is, the T-sentences, which are theorems of the truth theory for the language), alternative formulations of which are shown in (30), cannot be applied directly to the context-sensitive sentences of natural language.

(30)   a.   S is true if and only if p
        b.   'S' is true if and only if S

If the p in (30a) is replaced by a context-insensitive clause, as it is in (31a) below, then the resulting T-sentence is false for the vast bulk of the occurrences of the object sentence, for instance, 'I am happy' when uttered by Bill Clinton, or by Madonna, or by you. If, on the other hand, the transparently disquotational form in (30b) is instantiated, as in (31b), then the whole T-sentence is context-sensitive. Either we have to find some way of capturing the different interpretations it has in different contexts, or we have to take it as relativized to one particular context, in which case, again, the sentence 'I am happy' will be assigned non-variable truth conditions which will be false on many occasions of use. The widely adopted solution is to employ a different kind of schema, one which quantifies over *utterances* and contextual features. An instance of this is given in (31c), where a single contextual factor, that of the speaker of the utterance, is incorporated.

(31)   a.   'I am happy' is true iff Robyn Carston is happy.
        b.   'I am happy' is true iff I am happy.
        c.   If u is an utterance of 'I am happy', and x is the speaker of u, then [u is true iff x is happy].

So the 'modified normal form' for the statement of the truth conditions of natural language sentences is the conditional schema shown in (32). The truth-statement itself is given in the consequent (shown in square brackets in (32)), but is conditional on the various contextual parameters enumerated in the antecedent. This schema provides a means of meeting the requirement of giving context-variable truth conditions for a sentence without getting embroiled in the details of particular contexts:

(32)   If u is an utterance of sentence S, and $uR(x, y \ldots z)$, then [u is true iff $F(x, y, \ldots z)$]

The questions to be addressed briefly here are: (a) Can an account in terms of conditional truth-conditional statements capture the full range of encoded linguistic meaning? (b) Do these statements provide an appropriate input to the pragmatic processes involved in the recovery of full utterance meaning (that is, what is communicated)? In considering these matters, I refer principally to the framework of Higginbotham (1986, 1988, 1994), who advocates the application of the conditional truth-conditional approach, initiated by Davidson (1967) and Burge (1974), to the project of describing the semantic knowledge (competence) of native speakers. This work is taken to complement accounts of the phonological and syntactic knowledge of native speakers, each of these being distinct components within the generative grammar enterprise of characterizing native speakers' linguistic competence.

Higginbotham (1988) discusses the application of the approach to demonstratives and other elements used in referring. Consider, for instance, the accommodation of the context-sensitive expressions 'this', 'she' and 'that woman' by the following conditional T-statements:

(33) a. If u is an utterance of 'this is green', and the speaker of u refers with 'this' to x, then [u is true iff x is green].
  b. If u is an utterance of 'she is happy', and the speaker of u refers with 'she' to x, and x is female, then [u is true iff x is happy].
  c. If u is an utterance of 'that woman is happy', and the speaker of u refers with 'that woman' to x, and x is a woman, then [u is true iff x is happy].

The linguistic meaning of 'I' in (31c), 'this', 'she' and 'that woman' in (33), which consists of constraints on what they can be used to refer to, occurs in the antecedent among the conditions that must be fulfilled for the T-statement in the consequent to hold. This sort of truth-conditional account thereby succeeds in capturing the semantic contribution of these linguistic elements whose meaning does not enter into the truth conditions themselves.

The approach is extended to 'incomplete' definite descriptions, such as 'the ginger cat', 'the murderer', on both their attributive and referential uses.[22] On the attributive use, the descriptive content occurs in the consequent of the conditional statement as an essential element of the truth conditions. However, a second-order variable is introduced into the antecedent in order to indicate the contextual requirement that the domain of the description be appropriately restricted (Higginbotham 1988: 39):

(34) a. The murderer (whoever s/he is) is insane.
  b. If u is an utterance of (34a), and the speaker of u confines the domain of 'murderer' to entities x such that X_x, then [u is true iff $(ix$: murderer(x) and $X_x)$ (x is insane)].

The requirement of a contextually supplied domain restriction extends to quantifiers quite generally, e.g. 'Every student [in such and such a domain] must write a dissertation', and to tense and time-reference, e.g. 'We worked hard [at times t within such and such a period of time]'. So the underdeterminacy (context-sensitivity) of a range of referring and quantificational expressions is represented as part of speakers' semantic knowledge; certain pragmatic requirements (to find particular contextual instantiations on particular occasions of use) are marked out in the antecedent of these conditional semantic statements.

This approach raises a number of interesting issues. First, Higginbotham himself (1993b: 2), in discussing demonstrative cases such as (33a), says 'the speaker's perspective on what she speaks about – the object x – is wholly left out of account, so if we cannot be said to have understood the utterance without knowing that perspective then there will be aspects of understanding not covered by semantic rules'. In the current context of the strong underdeterminacy view, this comes as no surprise and does not strike home as a major worry; on this view, there are numerous aspects of the understanding of an utterance that are not encoded (either as truth-conditional content or as constraints on truth-conditional content) in the linguistic system, but are supplied on wholly pragmatic grounds.

Of more concern here is the fact that there are linguistic elements whose semantic contribution does not seem to be captured by this approach. Higginbotham (1994: 98) discusses the case of the 'specific indefinite' description, 'a certain F', which he compares with the simple indefinite description, 'an F', in examples such as the following:

(35)   a.   A politician rang me yesterday.
       b.   A certain politician rang me yesterday.

While there seems to be no truth-conditional difference between (35a) and (35b), hence no difference in their T-sentence specifications, there clearly is one when the simple sentence is embedded:

(36)   a.   If a politician rings today, tell him I'm out.
       b.   If a certain politician rings us today, tell him I'm out.

Similarly, as observed by Gazdar (1979: 166–7) and Seuren (2000), different patterns of what is called the topic-comment, or presupposition-focus, structure of a sentence are truth-conditionally inert in simple sentences, such as those in (37) and (38), but make themselves felt when embedded in certain other structures, such as those in (39) and (40):

(37)   a.   Jane gave ME the tickets.
       b.   Jane gave me the TICKETS.

(38)   a.   It was Sam who won the champagne.
       b.   It was the champagne that Sam won.

(39)   a.   Jane gave ME the tickets by mistake.
       b.   Jane gave me the TICKETS by mistake.

(40)   a.   Mary was annoyed that it was Sam who won the champagne.
       b.   Mary was annoyed that it was the champagne that Sam won.

The adverbial 'by mistake' in (39) is understood as pertaining just to the element highlighted by contrastive stress in each case, and the attitudinal verb in (40) as applying just to the element in the focus of the cleft construction.

Finally, there is a category of elements, noted by Segal (1994: 112) and Larson and Segal (1995: 44), whose encoded content seems to make no contribution to truth conditions or to constraints on truth conditions, in either simple or embedded sentences:

(41)   a.   Luke likes Sam and Hank loves Rob.
       b.   Luke likes Sam but Hank loves Rob.
       c.   I am surprised that Luke likes Sam and Hank loves Rob.
       d.   I am surprised that Luke likes Sam but Hank loves Rob.

The crucial element here is the much discussed 'but', whose truth-conditional contribution seems to be identical to that of 'and', although its inherent meaning clearly incorporates another feature (of 'contrast', roughly speaking). There are numerous other cases of this sort (often labelled devices of 'conventional implicature'), for instance, 'although', 'however', 'nevertheless', 'moreover', 'anyway', 'whereas', 'after all', 'even', 'yet', 'still', 'besides', and on certain uses, 'so', 'therefore', 'since', and 'while'.

In his discussion of the specific indefinite description, 'a certain F', Higginbotham (1994: 99–100) suggests the following adjustment to the conception of a semantic theory: 'Suppose that the theory of knowledge of meaning gives us, not quite the truth conditions (or conditional truth conditions) of an utterance, but rather what a person who used the utterance to make an assertion would represent himself as believing.' Very often, truth conditions and what a person represents herself as believing coincide, but on occasion they do not. In the case of an assertion of (35a), the speaker represents herself as believing that some politician or other rang her yesterday, that is, $(Ex)[F(x) \& G(x)]$, while in the case of an assertion of (35b), she represents herself as having in mind a particular person and believing of him that he is a politician and that he rang her yesterday, that is, $F(\alpha) \& G(\alpha)$, where α is some individual concept or sense. Although these are clearly distinct beliefs, the hearer gets the same information in the two cases about how things must be if the world is as the speaker says it is. Higginbotham believes that a move of this sort will mop up most, perhaps all, cases of implicature and presupposition which are directly triggered by linguistic form. Although he does not specifically address the stress and focus cases in (37)–(40), I see no reason, in principle, why the idea shouldn't extend to them as well. But what conclusion are we to draw from this about the nature of semantic description? According to Higginbotham, despite this 'concession' concerning the limits of truth-conditional semantics, truth conditions (and reference more generally) remain fundamental, since it is only they that have the properties needed for a systematic compositional semantic theory (Higginbotham 1994: 97,100).

Finally, let us consider the adequacy of the conditional truth-conditional approach in accommodating cases of predicate context-sensitivity. Here I closely follow Gross (1998, chapter 3) and focus on what he calls the 'part' context-sensitivity of adjectival predicates, as exemplified in the following:

(42) a. The book is green.
      b. This fruit is smooth.
      c. Mr Jones is hairy.

As discussed earlier, the truth conditions of particular utterances of these sentences vary according to that part of the subject referent that is contextually relevant; in other words, the proposition expressed is linguistically underdetermined as regards the part to which the property is attributed. In the case of (42a), it could be the cover of the book which is the relevant part and so that to which greenness is being attributed, or it could be just a dominant part of a design on the cover, or just the spine (when one is scanning a shelf of books) or, in a less typical circumstance, the pages inside, and so on.[23] As a first try at capturing this kind of underdeterminacy, we might take the earlier treatments of referring expressions as a model and quantify over contextually relevant parts of the subject of predication, thereby registering that the pragmatic determination of the relevant part is an essential contribution to the truth conditions of an utterance of the sentence:

(43) If u is an utterance of 'a is green', and x is the contextually relevant part of a, then [u is true iff a is green-at-x]

As Gross points out, this raises a pressing question: what is it to be green-at-x? Among the answers he considers are the following:

(44) a. a is green-at-x iff x is green
      b. a is green-at-x iff x is wholly green

The problem with (44a) is obvious: the right-hand side is context-sensitive, and in just the same way as the original sentence, 'a is green', whose truth conditions we are trying to specify. For instance, suppose 'green' is predicated of a book and the contextually salient part is its cover, then it is the cover that must be green. But what part of the cover – the whole of it, or all of it except the white lettering, or the background only, against which there is a gold and black design, or . . . ? The next suggestion is (44b), where, let us suppose, 'wholly' is not context-sensitive, so the right-hand side yields context-free truth conditions for each occurrence of the sentence (given a contextual value for x). The problem now, though, is that the truth conditions are wrong for a number of cases: suppose the utterance is 'the apple is green', and the contextually relevant part is the peel of the apple, which is indeed green except for a tiny patch of yellow near the stem. In such a case, the claim that the apple is green might be true even though it does not meet the requirement of being 'wholly green'.

Gross considers a number of further variants of this general approach of treating the part context-sensitivity of predicates as a matter of referential indeterminacy. Then, since these are unsuccessful, he tries locating the context-sensitivity elsewhere, that is, directly in the property expressed by the predicate. So the conditional T-sentence features a variable for the different properties the predicate can contribute to the truth conditions of different utterances of the sentence:

(45)   If u is an utterance of 'a is green', and 'green' expresses property G, then [u is true iff a is G]

The trouble with this is that, as it stands, replacement of 'green' by 'red', or by any other colour term, will result in the same T-statement. In fact, not only will the truth conditions provided for all colour terms be the same, but they will be the same for all predicates which are part context-sensitive (e.g. 'smooth', 'hairy', 'spotted', 'soft', etc.). This is clearly unsatisfactory for a theory which aims at a comprehensive description of speakers' semantic knowledge. One might look to impose some sort of constraints on the property that a given predicate can express, comparable to the constraints imposed by referring expressions like 'she' (the referent is female) or 'that man' (the referent is a man). The problem becomes one of finding sufficiently restrictive constraints coined in a vocabulary which does not introduce yet further context-sensitivity. For instance, in the case of 'green', the restriction might be something like 'having to do with the colour of a certain part and not being red or blue, or . . .', but 'not red' is just as context-sensitive as 'green' itself.

Gross concludes the discussion by considering the possible stance that it is not, after all, up to the truth-theoretic account to distinguish these predicates, that its purpose is just to characterize the type of semantic value assigned to linguistic categories (indexicals, demonstratives, names, classes of predicates) and to the different modes of combination allowed by the language. However, if limited in this way, the truth-conditional approach provides, at best, a very incomplete description of speakers' semantic competence, and has to be complemented by some other account which captures speakers' knowledge of the distinct meanings of different predicates.

Let's return now to the two questions that were asked at the beginning of this section: (a) Can the truth-conditional approach account for the native speaker's knowledge of linguistic meaning? (b) Do T-statements provide an appropriate input to the processes of pragmatic comprehension? In order to give a definitive answer to the first question, much more assessment is needed (including investigation of other truth-conditional frameworks), but the considerations gathered together in this section seem to indicate a negative conclusion. Several distinct aspects of encoded linguistic meaning looked at here do not seem to be amenable to the truth-conditional treatment. And, as the discussion in the following chapters will show, there are numerous other ways in which the proposition expressed by an utterance is linguistically underdetermined, some of which provide further challenges to the truth-conditional approach.

Clearly, the apparent shortfall in accounting for speakers' semantic knowledge bears directly on the second question too; the elements not accounted for (for instance, the focus cases and the so-called conventional implicature examples), play a significant role in shaping the interpretation of the utterance that the hearer will recover, not only in the complex cases, where they may affect truth conditions, but also in the simple cases where they do not. Their semantics is a crucial input to the processes of pragmatic interpretation. Recall Higginbotham's suggestion prompted by these cases: perhaps the account of semantic knowledge gives us, rather than truth conditions, what a person who assertively utters a sentence represents herself as believing. He sets the idea aside, since it doesn't seem to have the properties that a semantic theory needs (systematicity, amenability to combinatorial rules, etc.). I have to set it aside, because it seems quite remote from my concern for a linguistic semantics which can serve as appropriate input to an inferential processing account of utterance interpretation. What his suggestion highlights for me is how distinct the two overall approaches to linguistic meaning are; the difference is at least one of explanatory levels – the one concerned with characterizing a system of knowledge (a *competence*) in quite abstract terms, the other with finding a repre-sentational level (or levels) which enters into an account of a particular kind of mental *performance*, that of comprehending the intended meaning of a linguistic utterance. At the least, there would seem to have to be the mediating work of another performance system, the *parser*, which might access and deploy elements of both the syntactic and semantic competence systems in building a representation usable by the comprehension performance system. The relationship between the account of the on-line processes of utterance interpretation and the theory of knowl-edge of meaning is probably not a simple one; the components of neither one of them may translate into or correlate with, in any direct way, the components of the other.

Although they acknowledge the insufficiency of the truth-conditional approach, Higginbotham (1994) and Segal (1994) maintain that 'knowledge of conditions on reference and truth is the backbone of a theory of meaning'. Higginbotham makes no claim for the incorporation of the T-statements of semantic theory into an account of utterance processing, but Segal (1994: 112) and Larson and Segal (1995: 20–2) appear to do so. They locate the T-theory within a wider (modular) view of interacting mental systems and see certain of these systems as taking the output of the T-theory, that is, the T-sentences, and employing them (together with other sources of information) in such linguistic performances as understanding utterances and making judgements of meaning. So, unlike many truth-conditionalists, they are claiming that the truth theory for a language plays a direct role in the performance theory of verbal comprehension. The statements of the T-theory seem to me to be at one (or several) remove(s) from an account which will actually run, as it were, an account in terms of representations and processes (computations). However, even if they do play a more direct role in these processes than I envisage, they will have to be supplemented by a distinct account of the semantic contribution of the non-truth-conditional elements in the sentence (or phrase) uttered.

1.5.2   A translational semantics for natural language?

I turn now to the relevance-theoretic conception of linguistic semantics and its role in the cognitive account of utterance interpretation. The distinction between linguistic semantics and pragmatics is seen in performance terms, as closely tied to a distinction between two types of processes involved in understanding utterances: linguistic decoding and pragmatic inference (see Sperber and Wilson 1986a/95b). The decoding process is performed by an autonomous linguistic system, the parser or language perception module. Having identified a particular acoustic (or visual) stimulus as linguistic, this system executes a series of deterministic grammatical computations, or mappings, resulting in an output representation, which is the semantic representation, or logical form, of the sentence or phrase employed in the utterance. It is a structured string of concepts, with certain logical and causal properties, but it is seldom, if ever, fully propositional. It is a kind of template or schema for a range of possible propositions, rather than itself being a particular proposition. As a 'schema', it is a formula that contains slots to be filled; what may go into a given slot may be partially constrained by a procedure which specifies how to go about filling it. Such a formula necessarily requires the second type of cognitive process, pragmatic inference, to develop it into the proposition the speaker intended to express.

On this construal, a characterization of an individual's linguistic semantics consists of a systematic description of the elements of meaning that the linguistic forms making up that individual's language encode. It will give an account of which conceptual representations, in what syntactic configurations, are activated in the mind, by which bits of phonological (or graphological) form. It will also include entries for all those linguistic forms that have been set aside by truth-conditionalists as cases of (non-truth-conditional) conventional implicature or presupposition. Interestingly, in the relevance-theoretic account, the distinction between the truth-conditional and the non-truth-conditional is largely reflected in a distinction between two types of cognitive information that a linguistic form may map on to: concepts, which are constituents of mental representations, and procedures, which do not enter into representations, but rather constrain the processes of pragmatic inference involved in deriving particular conceptual constituents of representations. This distinction within linguistic semantics is discussed in the next chapter (section 2.3.7).

Now, in the view of many truth-conditional semanticists, we are simply not going to be saying anything of semantic interest if our characterization of the meaning of sentences is not in terms of truth and reference. The familiar charge is that accounts which give the semantics of linguistic expressions in terms of a logical, or some other, notation are merely translating one kind of representation into another kind of representation, and you can go on doing that sort of thing *ad infinitum* without ever getting any closer to the essence of semantics, which is that it concerns a relation between representations and the non-representational external world they represent. The classic statement of this position is by David Lewis, in a critique of the approach of Katz and Postal (1964), who gave 'semantic' representations of natural-language sentences in terms of a system of what they called 'semantic markers'. Lewis says: 'But we can know the Markerese translation of an English sentence without knowing the first thing about the meaning of the English sentence: namely, the conditions under which it would be true. . . . Markerese semantics [does not deal] with the relations between symbols and the world of non-symbols – that is, with genuinely semantic relations' (Lewis 1970: 18).[24] If we substitute 'Mentalese' (the conceptual thought representation system) for 'Markerese', Lewis's objection would appear to carry over directly to the position being advocated here, so what response do we have?

We can agree that, by giving an account of the encoded meaning of natural language sentences, we are essentially performing a translation into another system of representations, but resist the charge that this is a vacuous enterprise by insisting that it is this latter representational system which is given a 'real' semantics, that is, is related to the objects and states of affairs in the world which it represents. This, in essence, is the view of Jerry Fodor:

> It's entirely natural to run a computational story about the attitudes [beliefs, intentions and other kinds of thought] together with a translation story about language comprehension; and there's no reason to doubt, so far at least, that the sort of translation that's required is an exhaustively syntactic operation.
>
>   ... Syntax is about what's in your head, but semantics is about how your head is connected to the world. Syntax is part of the story about the mental representation of sentences, but semantics isn't.   (Fodor 1989/90: 187)

See also Fodor (1975, 1981b, 1990). This position has been expressed often in the relevance-theoretic literature in talk of 'two types of semantics': (1) a translational linguistic semantics, which could be described in statements of the form '*abc*' *means (= encodes) 'ijk'*, where 'abc' is a public-language form and 'ijk' is a Mentalese form (most likely an incomplete, schematic Mentalese form); (2) a 'real' semantics, which explicates the relation between our mental representations and that which they represent (so it must be 'disquotational') and whose statements may take the form '*hijk*' *means (= is true iff) such-and-such*. There are, no doubt, various qualifications called for here. For instance, the translational schema given in (1) involves the quoting (that is, the mention rather than use) of forms in the two distinct representational systems, and if this were the format of the mentally represented translations of each element of linguistic meaning, a process of disquoting would be essential at some stage in the compositional construction of the conceptual representation of the proposition expressed. As manifest in the minds of speakers/hearers, the translation process is better characterized as a direct mapping from a natural-language form to a Mentalese form, such that with the recognition of a particular linguistic element, for instance, the morpheme 'cat', comes the activation of a particular concept, say CAT.[25] What the translation process does is effect an interface between two distinct processing systems: the linguistic and the pragmatic.

Although this is the merest sketch of a picture, it would appear, at least in principle, to meet Lewis's objection: translation stops, truth conditions enter the account and the connection with the world is made. In fact, on an account of this sort, we could construe at least some natural-language expressions as having a 'real' truth-conditional semantics by inheritance; that is, given that they map on to parts of propositional thought representations, they can be thought of as having the truth-conditional (referential) content that those parts of the thought representations have. For instance, assuming the word 'cat' maps to the concept CAT and the concept CAT refers to (is true of) cats, then 'cat' inherits this referential semantics from CAT. Fodor (1975, 1998) argues that there is largely a one-to-one mapping of this sort between words (or morphemes) and concepts. To the extent that this is the case, the construction of a truth-conditional semantics for natural language (really a (partial) truth-conditional semantics for thought) could proceed in parallel with the translational account advocated here. After all, we have a much better grip on the components of natural language than we have on those of Mentalese (assuming there is such a thing) so, given the putative one-to-one mapping, we might as well take the former as the domain of the truth-theory. Then the translational 'semantics' can be thought of as the complementary enterprise of showing how phonetic forms are transformed (translated) into a representational format usable by the utterance comprehension system. The computational processes of this system have to integrate information from a range of sources – language, immediate perception, memory – so they must all be in, or be translatable into, a single common language that these processes can operate over.

However, given that natural language sentences (understood as expression *types*) quite generally underdetermine propositional thoughts, there won't be any wholesale straightforward inheritance by *sentences* of natural language of a truth-based semantics of thought. Recall, for instance, the example 'The book is green', discussed in the previous section; this sentence can express myriad different propositions in different contexts and, despite employing the conditional T-schema, it seemed impossible to give it a context-free truth-conditional statement, so that inheritance by this English sentence of a truth-conditional semantics from that assigned to Mentalese sentences looks highly unlikely. Perhaps, then, the 'semantics by inheritance' idea works just at the *word* level, at least for those words that encode concepts (as opposed to inferential procedures), like 'cat', 'eat', 'clever'. After some detailed discussion of particular cases in the intervening chapters, I will suggest in the final chapter (section 5.4) that even this quite modest claim for the truth-based properties of natural language is doubtful. Word meaning may be of such an abstract and schematic nature that even at this most basic level of linguistic expressions there is no direct inheritance of the referential semantics of components of thoughts, that is, concepts.

I'll move on now to say a little more about the sort of linguistic semantics (internalist, translational) that a cognitive account of utterance interpretation such as relevance theory requires. Here I follow Sperber and Wilson (1986a) and Wilson and Sperber (1993a). Take a simple sentence: 'She hasn't called.' On any normal occasion of use, this will be understood as expressing a complete proposition in which it is predicated of a particular female that it is not the case that she has called (in some specific sense of 'call') some other particular person within some relevantly delimited time span up to the time of utterance. However, the sentence form itself encodes something much less specific, a non-propositional (non-truth-evaluable) logico-conceptual structure, an 'assumption schema', which functions as a template for the construction of fully propositional (truth-evaluable) logico-conceptual structures. It is this schematic logical form that the initial (purely linguistic) phase of understanding delivers and which is the input to the pragmatic processes aimed at constructing the propositional form intended by the speaker, or one similar enough to it to have the intended effects.

Exactly how to represent the encoded logical form (or assumption schema) remains an open question with a number of subsidiary issues to be resolved, including how to represent the encoded meaning of indexicals like 'she' and what the syntactic structure of a logical form looks like.[26] Here is one, undoubtedly wrong, possibility, which might at least give the flavour of the idea (upper case indicating concepts):

(46)   NOT [t_i {past} [CALL$_1$ (X{singular, female})]]

Much explanation is in order: (a) 'CALL$_1$' is one of the conceptual encodings of the ambiguous verb form 'call'; strictly speaking, then, the surface sentence form 'she hasn't called' may map on to several logical forms depending on how many lexical items of the form 'call' there are; (b) there may be an unarticulated 'object-of-the-calling' constituent here as well, which would be recovered pragmatically; this may be marked in the logical form as a further open slot, Y, in the second argument position if the concept 'CALL$_1$'; (c) although the scope of the negation operator is shown as maximally wide, it might be that all scope specifications are left to pragmatics and the operator is scope-neutral in logical form (these possibilities are discussed in chapter 4); (d) the somewhat mysterious '{singular, female}' is intended to indicate that the encoded linguistic meaning, or character, of the pronoun 'she' does not enter into the logical form as a conceptual constituent but is instead a procedural indication to the pragmatic processor of the sort of entity being referred to; (e) the same goes for '{past}', which is a constraint, contributed by the tense marking on the verb. Once the hearer has accessed the referents involved (a concept of an individual and a temporal-span concept), those concepts fill the slots marked in the logical form by X and t_i, and the procedural features disappear, having served their purpose. As argued by Wilson and Sperber (1993a), this distinction between procedural and conceptual encodings is a cognitive processing correlate of the character/content distinction made by Kaplan (1977/89a) (though there are also some differences, which I won't go into here). I hope this example gives at least some idea of the schematic nature of the semantic representation envisaged as the result of linguistic encoding. This is not a truth-conditional entity. It is fully propositional conceptual representations, rather than sentences, or even utterances of sentences, that are the primary bearers of truth conditions. Intuitions about the truth conditions of utterances are intuitions about the truth conditions of the proposition(s) the speaker intended to express.

The objection that decoding or translation into Mentalese is not semantics is widely made, not only by natural-language semanticists, but also from within pragmatics. Levinson (1988, 1989) contends that the position of relevance-theorists (and of those generative grammarians who investigate a syntactically determined level of logical form (LF), and Katz and Jackendoff, whose 'semantic' representations are similar in the crucial syntactic respect) is one of 'semantic retreat' and constitutes 'throwing in the sponge' (Levinson 1988: 59). He starts with a (perfectly accurate) characterization of the relevance-theoretic conception of linguistic semantics as follows: it consists of the algorithmic extraction of a semantic representation from a syntactic representation; the result of this is an extremely impoverished level of representation with scope of operators undecided, metavariables for pronouns, etc. His concern seems to be that, if this is how semantics is construed, most of the well-established aims of a semantic theory cannot be realized: specifically, traditional sense relations, such as entailment, synonymy, contradiction cannot be captured at this level of semantic representation (or logical form) and truth conditions cannot be assigned.[27] This is right, but merely indicates that if a statement of sense properties and relations is considered desirable, it will have to be formulated over some other level (conceptual representations, perhaps). At most, there might be a case for a terminological change here. The term 'semantics' could be reserved for the account of the relation between fully propositional forms and the states of affairs they represent ('real' semantics). The output of decoding, which is the input to pragmatic inference, could be called something else: logical form, the level of conceptual interface, the semantically relevant level of syntax, a linguistically determined partial Mentalese representation, or whatever. Once we know what we are talking about this is a matter of little interest; as is sometimes said of this sort of wrangle, it is merely a matter of semantics (in yet another use of the term).

I would like to consider a final objection to the relevance-theoretic stance on linguistic semantics, specifically to its conception of the logical form of sentences as non-propositional. According to this objection, it is simply false that the vast array of natural language sentences do not encode propositions. This is a disagreement from within the overall project, since it is held by people who are generally sympathetic with the decoding (translational) approach to linguistic semantics, and to the role it is assumed to play within the wider cognitive account of utterance comprehension. Someone holding this propositional view (let's call him Leon)[28] grants that a sentence seldom, if ever, encodes, or fully determines, the very proposition that a speaker expresses by uttering it on a particular occasion, and that its logical form functions as a template for the pragmatic construction of the more specific proposition expressed by the speaker. As Leon points out, quite rightly, it does not follow from this that the sentence does not encode any proposition at all. He then goes on to argue that, in fact, sentences do encode propositions and that a proposition (or assumption) schema must itself be propositional because a genuinely inferential process must proceed from one propositional form to another. It is over these latter claims that we differ.

Leon's propositional view comes in two versions. According to the first version, the indexical sentences in (47) encode generic propositions, which are (inevitably, roughly) represented by the natural-language sentences in (48):

(47) a. She carried it in her hand.
    b. Paul's book is there.
    c. It's raining.

(48) a. Some female entity carried at some past time something in some female entity's hand.
    b. Some unique book that is in some relation to somebody called Paul is somewhere.
    c. Raining occurs somewhere at some time.

The procedure which takes us from a sentence in (47) to the corresponding one in (48) is simple enough: wherever you find an indexical you put in a phrase which spells out the encoded constraint (the character of the indexical) in conceptual terms and wherever you spot an unarticulated constituent you use an appropriate member of the family of 'some'-indefinites (*something, somewhere, sometime*, etc.) to make it visible. The first problem with this is the assumption that the pairs are truth-conditionally synonymous; in the case of (47a) and (48a), this seems clearly false. Any of the well-developed truth-conditional theories around, such as that of Higginbotham discussed above, would certainly assign quite different T-sentences to these. So (47a) would receive a conditional T-sentence along the lines of (49a), omitting several details, such as those to do with tense, and the likely anaphoric nature of 'her', while (48a) would receive a simple (non-conditional) T-sentence since it has no referential elements:

(49)   a. $(u)(x)(y)(z)$[If u is an utterance of 'she held it in her hand', and the speaker of u refers to x with her use of 'she', and to y with her use of 'it' and to z with her use of 'her' and, x is female and z is female, then (u is true iff x held y in z's hand)]

         b.   'Some female entity carried something in some female entity's hand' is true iff $ExEyEz$ (x held y in z's hand)

The statement in (49a) makes it clear that no truth condition (hence no proposition) is forthcoming until contextual values are supplied to the variables x, y and z; the statement in (49b), on the other hand, makes it clear that no such fixing of referential values is required before the sentence/utterance can be assigned a determinate truth condition.

Second, each of the propositional representations in (48) cannot but be true (I don't mean that they are necessary truths, but given the way the world is they are bound to be true). Take any book you like. It will be in some relation or other with some person by the name of Paul in the world (in fact, it will be in *some* relation with *every* person by the name of Paul); for instance, the book may be in the relation of being 62.34 miles north-north-east of my friend Paul Johnson, and it will, inevitably, be located somewhere. Since (48b) is allegedly encoded by (or synonymous with) (47b), we would expect (47b) to have the same property, that is, to be inevitably true. So, let me ask you, is the sentence 'Paul's book is there' true (or is it false)? I'm afraid you may not seek clarification as to who is meant by Paul, or which book, or place, is being referred to. What's under discussion here is a *sentence*, not a use of the sentence. The answer to the question surely is that the sentence is neither true nor false, that it is not the sort of thing that can be true or false, it is not truth-evaluable, it doesn't encode a proposition, not even a very general one.

The second version of Leon's view claims that, while the sentences in (47a)–(47c) may not encode the respective propositions represented in (48a)–(48c), they do entail them. For instance, the semantic representation of the sentence 'she carried it in her hand' entails the propositional form 'some female individual carried at some past time something in some female individual's hand', and, since entailment is a relation between propositional forms, it follows that the sentence itself must encode a proposition. This line of reasoning has a plausible look to it (the sentences/

propositions in (48) do seem to follow from the sentences in (47)), although note that it is now not at all clear just what proposition it is that is encoded by the indexical sentence.

In fact, much depends here on how one understands the logical relation of 'entailment'. One line of resistance would be to deny that the entailment relation holds only between propositional entities; I won't try that here (but see Sperber and Wilson 1986a/95b: 73, on the logical properties of non-propositional logical forms). Another is to deny that, contrary to appearances, there really is an entailment relation here. I don't believe that the relation here is one of entailment as that notion is standardly understood, which is as a relation between two truth-evaluable (propositional) entities such that from the truth of the first the truth of the second inevitably (necessarily) follows. First, as argued above, the indexical sentence (abstracted from any occasion of utterance) is not truth-evaluable (hence is not propositional). Second, the undoubted inference to the 'some female entity carried . . .' proposition can be explained as arising from consideration of the incomplete conceptual representation together with the referential constraints encoded by the indexicals. That is, on the basis of knowing the meaning of all the parts of the sentence in (47a), we are able to infer that, for any given *utterance* of the sentence, if/when the required contextual/pragmatic work of finding referents for the indexicals has been done, the resulting proposition will entail (48a). If this is right, the second version of the propositional view does not succeed in establishing that indexical sentences (or sentences whose use involves the recovery of an unarticulated constituent) encode propositions.[29,30]

A final consideration here, that crosscuts both versions of Leon's propositional view, concerns utterances such as 'Tom's father', or 'on the top shelf'. These phrasal utterances encode a semantic representation (a logical form), which provides the pragmatic processor with a template for the construction of the proposition expressed by the utterance. On some occurrences, these will be ellipsed versions of complete sentences (for instance, when they are produced as answers to questions, such as 'Who's the guy by the door?', etc.), but they need not be (see Stainton 1994, 1997; Elugardo and Stainton forthcoming b; and the discussion in the next chapter – section 2.3.5). There is a genuine and rather commonplace phenomenon of non-elliptical subsentential utterances, and what they encode simply cannot be propositional. Leon could respond to this that he is only concerned with sentential utterances. But recall that one of the main factors motivating his propositional view is his assumption that all inferential processes must operate over fully propositional forms. From this, it follows that the input to the (non-demonstrative) inferential process of developing the logical form of an utterance into that proposition which the speaker actually expressed must itself be propositional. But this consequence of the assumption, and so the assumption itself, is utterly undermined by the subsentential cases, which show that the pragmatic processor *can* take as input a non-propositional logical form and enrich it into a fully propositional form. There is no compelling reason to suppose that the story goes differently for the sentential cases. I conclude that the claim that sentences encode propositions has not been upheld and that there is not even any particular reason to view propositionality as a desirable property for sentences to have.

Summing up this section, the first stage of interpreting an utterance involves decoding the linguistic expression employed. The result of this is a (generally non-propositional) logical form which is in a format usable by the pragmatic processor. This logical form is a syntactically structured string of concepts with some slots, or free variables, indicating where certain contextual values (in the form of concepts) must be supplied; the nature of the contextual value may be constrained by procedural information (as in the case of certain indexicals). So, on this sort of account, linguistic semantics specifies mappings (translations) between lexical forms and concepts or procedures, and between surface syntactic structures and their underlying logical structure.

1.6   Radical Underdeterminacy and the Background

Perhaps what is inexpressible (what I find mysterious and am not able to express) is the background against which whatever I could express has its meaning.

(Wittgenstein 1931/80: 16e)

1.6.1   The Background

John Searle (1978, 1980, 1983, 1992, 1996) is a strong advocate of the underdeterminacy thesis:

> The literal meaning of a sentence only determines a set of truth conditions given a set of background practices and assumptions. Relative to one set of practices and assumptions, a sentence may determine one set of truth conditions; relative to another set of practices and assumptions, another set; and if some sets of assumptions and practices are given, the literal meaning of a sentence may not determine a definite set of truth conditions at all.   (Searle 1980: 227)

Searle believes that existing discussions barely scratch the surface of the phenomenon of the linguistic underdeterminacy of propositions expressed (see Searle 1992: 181; 1996: 131). In his view, the issue that needs highlighting is that of the Background (with a capital 'B'); this is fundamental to meaning and understanding, there is no literal meaning without it, there is nothing truth-evaluable without it. The force of his position is best appreciated by considering some of the examples he discusses, although it should be borne in mind that the kind of underdeterminacy that is a result of the Background is not a characteristic of just some groups of linguistic expressions, but is a property of linguistic meaning quite generally.

He shows how the literal use of common verbs, like 'cut', 'open', 'close', 'clean', 'mend', 'play', 'bring', 'take' and 'make', determines different truth conditions as a result of different relevant parts of the Background coming into play. For instance, let's take several substitution instances of 'X opened Y', restricting ourselves to human agents, concrete objects and a strictly literal use of 'open':

(50) a. Jane opened the window.
      b. Bill opened his mouth.
      c. Sally opened her book to page 56.
      d. Mike opened his briefcase.
      e. Pat opened the curtains.
      f. The child opened the package.
      g. The carpenter opened the wall.
      h. The surgeon opened the wound.

                          (adapted from Searle 1983: 145)

Though the semantics (the encoded meaning) of the word 'open' is the same in these examples, it is understood differently in each case; the contribution it makes to the truth conditions of quite literal utterances varies with the sentential context it occurs in. What constitutes opening a book is very different from what constitutes opening one's mouth, which is quite different again from what constitutes opening a package, etc. Importantly, although it looks as if it is the meaning of the expressions we substitute for 'X' and 'Y', particularly 'Y', that determines the interpretation of 'open', this is only so given a Background of assumptions concerning what is involved in an X opening a Y. That is, we could imagine a situation in which, say, a mouth had been stitched closed for some reason (to prevent some disease, or to stop an obese person from eating, etc.), and then the process of opening would be quite different from the one we assume given our standard assumptions about people and their mouths.

Furthermore, given our current Background we are unable to understand (assign truth-conditional content to) the following:

(51) a. Bob opened the grass.
      b. Chris opened the fork.
      c. Jane opened a hair.

This is because, although we understand each word in these sentences and their syntax is unproblematic, our Background does not supply us with any know-how concerning opening grass or forks or hairs.

Searle also considers some cases which are among the most likely counterexamples to the generality of the thesis of the Background, that is, plausible candidates for eternal sentencehood, such as the following:

(52) a. Four plus five is nine.
      b. Snow is white.

The claim is that even these only determine a set of truth conditions against a Background of practices and assumptions, which are so deeply entrenched that we do not notice them. If arithmetic practices changed, in the one case, or if some fundamental alteration to the course of nature took place and our Background assumptions with it, in the other, these sentences might determine different truth conditions from those they currently do, or perhaps determine none at all (Searle 1980: 229–31).

Before locating the Background within Searle's wider account of intentionality, I want to mention two points which arise within the present narrower context of utterance interpretation. First, it seems that for Searle there is no distinction between utterance meaning and sentence meaning when the speaker means what she says; he takes it that the speaker's knowing of literal meaning that it applies only against a particular Background is part of her linguistic (semantic) competence. So there is no sharp distinction between a speaker's semantic competence and her (background) knowledge of the world (Searle 1978/79: 134). This may ultimately prove to be the case (it has some formidable supporters (see note 7 of this chapter)), but I don't think we have to accept it as a foregone conclusion on the basis of the facts about interpretation just considered. I find an equivocation in the way Searle talks of 'literal meaning'. On the one hand, he says 'the *same literal meaning* will determine different truth conditions given different Backgrounds' (Searle 1983: 145), and, on the other, he talks of the dependence of literal (sentence) meaning on context/ background (Searle 1978/79: 134–5). That is, on the one hand, 'open' has the same literal meaning in each of the examples above, and, on the other, its literal meaning depends on context and so is different in each case. The first way of talking of 'literal meaning' leaves open the possibility that it can be given its own Background-free characterization, though it cannot be applied (used, understood) except in relation to a body of Background assumptions/practices. In short, a principled semantic/pragmatic distinction is not ruled out by accepting, as I do, the fundamental and pervasive role of the Background.

Second, for anyone interested in an account of utterance interpretation, that is, an account of the hearer's interpretive processes and the representations he recovers, there is a pressing question here. I have suggested above that hearers recover unarticulated constituents of the proposition expressed by an utterance. So the question is: how much of this great mass of contextual/background material goes into the proposition expressed? How do we distinguish between what the hearer must infer and build into his representation of the speaker's informative intention and what is left in the Background?

Recanati (1993: 260) quotes one of Searle's more grotesque scenarios in which he discusses the example 'I have had breakfast' from Sperber and Wilson (1986a/95b: 189–90). In addition to the narrowing down of the temporal specification (in most instances, to the day of utterance), which they give as an example of a pragmatic contribution to the proposition expressed, Searle points out that 'having breakfast' is interpreted as '*eating*' breakfast and 'eating' breakfast is taken to mean putting it in one's mouth, chewing it, swallowing it, etc., as opposed to stuffing it into one's ears or digesting it through the soles of one's feet, though none of this is encoded in the phrase itself. Recanati agrees with Searle about this and concludes from it 'that "what is said" – the situation our utterance intends to describe – necessarily involves unarticulated constituents. No proposition could be expressed without *some* unarticulated constituents being contextually provided' (Recanati 1993: 260). This statement is surely right, but it is a rather lame conclusion in this context, since it runs together the deepest taken-for-granted unrepresented aspects of meaning (e.g. what's involved in eating) and other much less general, context-particular, features of understanding that a hearer will have to infer and represent if he is to recover the speaker's intended message. I will return briefly to this question in chapter 3 (section 3.7.1), in the context of a discussion of the pragmatics of 'and'-conjunctions, where I consider whether we can distinguish which among the many unarticulated aspects of meaning must be recovered and mentally represented.

Searle's thesis of the Background should be situated within his overall view of the mind, which I will now indicate, in a very sketchy but, I hope, accurate way. We have intentional (representational) states, such as beliefs, desires, intentions; these are real, they are properties of human biology; that is, they are not convenient fictions and they are not reducible to something else, although they are, of course, caused by neurological processes in the brain; linguistic meaning is (one instantiation of) derived intentionality, that is, it is grounded in the more basic intentionality which is an intrinsic property of the mind/brain; consciousness (like intentionality) is an intrinsic and ineliminable feature of the human mind/brain; some, but not all, conscious states are intentional in that they represent something beyond themselves; some, but not all, of one's intentional states are conscious at any given moment, but all are capable, in principle, of being brought to consciousness; without consciousness there is no intentionality (in fact, for a state to count as mental it must be potentially conscious);[31] the workings of the (holistic) system of intentional states are wholly dependent on a massive set of capabilities, dispositions, know-how, that are not themselves intentional, that is, the Background.

Searle makes a distinction between features of the Background that are common to all human beings and features that are culture-specific. So, for instance, the basic know-how involved in walking and eating are aspects of the 'deep Background' while specific aspects of, say, appropriate conduct at meals, or the sitting and standing conventions at public gatherings would be elements of the 'local Background'. He makes a further distinction between knowing *how to do* things and knowing *how things are*; for example, we know how to walk and one aspect of our knowing how things are with the world is our taking it for granted that the ground won't shift around beneath our feet.

Searle admits that there is some obscurity in the concept of the Background, but he finds its existence an inescapable matter of fact and has a range of arguments for it, some of which, pertaining specifically to language understanding, have been alluded to above. I do not doubt the existence of some such body of capacities and assumptions, but I would like to try to think about it in a way that will mesh better with the relevance-theoretic approach to utterance understanding that I am employing. It is crucial to Searle that the Background set of assumptions/practices is not itself 'intentional', since it is what makes intentionality (the 'aboutness' of our beliefs and of the meanings of our utterances, etc.) possible; it is that without which intentional states would be indeterminate. The Background is, however, not to be construed as actual objects or states of affairs in the world; it is mental ('in the head' – Searle 1991: 291). I suggest that the concept of 'manifestness' as characterized by Sperber and Wilson (1986a/95b: 38–42) is helpful here: an assumption is manifest to an individual at a given time if and only if he or she is capable at that time of representing it mentally and accepting its representation as true or probably true. They then define the concept of an individual's 'cognitive environment' as the set of assumptions that are manifest to him or her at a particular moment. Thinking of the Background as a set of (merely) manifest assumptions seems to answer to Searle's broad requirements that the Background does not consist of states of affairs in the world, on the one hand, nor of intentional states (representing the world), on the other, but is mental insofar as it is dependent on – would not exist without – the mind/brain.

There are several features of the concepts of manifestness and cognitive environment that are relevant in applying them to the Background: (a) manifestness is a matter of degree, and the degree of manifestness of a given assumption in an individual's cognitive environment may shift from moment to moment depending on features of the external physical environment and on his/her internal cognitive states (for instance, where attention is focused); (b) some assumptions are such that once they are manifest to an individual they remain so thereafter, as stable elements of his or her cognitive environment, and others are temporary and may be very short-lived, a function of where one happens to be, who one happens to be with, etc., at a particular moment; (c) an individual's cognitive environment overlaps to a greater or lesser extent with every other individual's cognitive environment: assumptions that are common to human existence (e.g. 'objects are solid and permanent', 'the earth does not recede beneath one's feet', etc.) are part of everyone's cognitive environment; other assumptions are shared by largish subsets of cognitive environments, such as those pertaining to practices and conventions taken for granted in a particular culture; close friends share a huge further range derived from their shared experiences, verbal and non-verbal. Some shared manifest assumptions are in fact mutually manifest, that is, it is manifest to the sharers that they share those assumptions and with whom they share them.

We might usefully think of the Background as a set of assumptions and practices that maintain a fairly steady degree of not very high manifestness, across time, in an individual's cognitive environment. A subset of the Background consists in assumptions/practices which make up the mutual cognitive environment of all (non-pathological) human beings – the deep Background; other subsets are the mutual cognitive environments of what can be loosely termed culturally defined groups of human beings – local Backgrounds). Most, perhaps all, Background assumptions and practices figure in some mutual cognitive environment or other. Some of these assumptions might be occasionally actually represented by the individual when he or she is confronted with 'strange' situations, situations with features which contradict some feature of the Background and so make that feature highly manifest to him or her, situations of shock. For the most part, though, the Background keeps its place, in the background, unrepresented, an essential foundation for thinking and understanding and, though not discussed here, action.[32]

This way of thinking of the Background may or may not do full justice to Searle's conception; I suspect that I have not succeeded in fully capturing its bedrock nature. Some of the capacities, the know-how, the *savoir-faire*, that Searle refers to, do not seem appropriately thought of as sets of *assumptions*. However, I do not see any glaring problem in extending the concept of manifestness to a broader array of dispositional sorts of structures, like procedures, action schemas and processing schemas; these seem better suited than assumptions to be the vehicles of such aspects of the Background as how to eat, how to walk, what's involved in behaving normally in a shop/classroom/someone else's house/at home, etc. Constituents of these schemas could, in principle at least, be represented by an individual and held as true, for instance, 'in order to eat x, one places x in one's mouth'. Anyway, given the rather limited use to which I will be putting the Background in what follows, I think a characterization in terms of manifest assumptions and procedures will suffice.

1.6.2 Radical underdeterminacy and 'expressibility'

Let's return briefly to the issue of linguistic (in)effability. Recall that Searle was mentioned, along with Katz and Frege, as one of those espousing a strong principle of effability, though his is labelled the principle of 'expressibility': 'whatever can be meant can be said' (Searle 1969: 19–21). It might seem that anyone holding as strong an underdeterminacy thesis as is entailed by the thesis of the Background must be a supporter of the anti-effability view I took in the previous section. So is Searle being inconsistent? Did his development of the idea of the Background put paid to his earlier advocacy of Expressibility? The answer to the second question is certainly 'no':

> there is nothing in the thesis of the relativity of literal meaning [to the Background] which is inconsistent with the Principle of Expressibility, the principle that whatever can be meant can be said. It is not part of, nor a consequence of, my argument for the relativity of literal meaning [to the Background] that there are meanings that are inherently inexpressible.   (Searle 1978/79: 134)

This emphatic denial is all we get from Searle on the issue. One way of trying to convince oneself that the two theses are consistent would be to reason as follows. The principle Searle endorses must be quite different from that of Katz and Frege who claim that, for each indexical sentence paired with a context, natural language affords an eternal sentence, which fully encodes the proposition expressed by the first. Searle's principle must be the innocuous truth that the human interpretive capacities are set up so that for any propositional content that a person might want to communicate, there is some linguistic expression or other (perhaps several) that she could use to express that propositional content in a given context. An essential part of those interpretive capacities is, of course, the Background; another is a pragmatic inferential system. This position would be equivalent to the unobjectionable first principle of effability, given in section 1.3.2. However, a look at the actual formulation of the Principle of Expressibility shows that this is not the way out:

> For any meaning X and any speaker S whenever S means (intends to convey, wishes to communicate in an utterance, etc.) X then it is possible that there is some expression E such that E is an exact expression of or formulation of X. Symbolically: (S)(X)(S means X $\rightarrow$ P($\exists$ E)(E is an expression of X)).   (Searle 1969: 20)

Clearly, by 'said' he intends 'encoded' (that is, 'an exact expression of or formulation of meaning X'), making this principle more like the second principle of effability discussed earlier. It seems, then, that the explanation for the apparent coexistence of this principle with the Background must lie with the concept of 'what is meant'. Just as what we say is relative to the Background, so is what we mean, what we intend to convey, what we think, etc. Essential though they are to interpretation, I take it that elements of the Background do not fall within the scope of our communicative intentions (they cannot, since they are non-intentional). Then the fact that they do not enter into what is said (= 'encoded' here) does not threaten Expressibility. The non-representational Background underlies both the said and the meant, and so is not the source of any disparity between them. Thus there is no inconsistency in maintaining both the Principle of Expressibility and the thesis of the Background. This does not, of course, touch the arguments in section 1.3, on the basis of which Searle's Principle of Expressibility, like Katz's Principle of Effability, must be wrong.[33]

1.6.3   Radical underdeterminacy and semantic compositionality

Having considered the Isomorphism Principle briefly and the Effability Principle lengthily, I come now to a third principle, perhaps the most cherished of all by philosophers of language. This is the **Principle of Semantic Compositionality**: 'The semantic value (meaning) of an expression is determined by the semantic value (meaning) of its constituents and the manner in which they are combined.' This is usually attributed to Frege but is maintained, in variant forms, by most semanticists. The principle is taken to hold for every type or level of semantics, so, for Frege, who distinguished between sense/content and reference/extension, the principle holds for both these types of entity,[34] and, for those who make further distinctions between linguistic meaning or character, and propositional (truth-conditional) content, it holds also at this third (or fourth) level: the linguistic meaning encoded by an expression is determined by the encoded meaning of its constituent parts and their manner of combination.

Compositionality is generally deemed essential in explaining the learnability, productivity and systematicity of the human language capacity, that is, in explaining how it is that the finite human mind is able to produce and understand indefinitely many novel sentences, which is itself a factor in accounting for the unbounded expressive and communicative power of human utterances (see, for example, Fodor 1987a; Fodor and Pylyshyn 1988, section 3; Butler 1995a). But the Principle of Semantic Compositionality imposes a stronger constraint than is entailed by these considerations; it embodies a determinacy requirement: the semantic value of a complex expression E must be 'completely determined by the constituent expressions $e_1 \ldots e_i \ldots e_n$ of which it is composed. That is, any semantic property with which the complex expression is endowed, must be traceable to one of the constituent elements, or to the construction itself' (Welsh 1986: 553–4).

As Searle (1980) points out, given the role of the Background, the Compositionality Principle (CP) does not hold for the view that the meaning of a sentence is to be given as a specification of its truth conditions. The truth conditions of a completely literal use of a sentence, such as 'I have had breakfast' or the various examples in (50) above, involving the verb 'open', seem not to be fully determined by the contribution of their constituent parts and their mode of combination, but to be profoundly affected by a body of Background assumptions that inevitably permeates meaning/understanding.

Some of the other sources of linguistic underdeterminacy, discussed in sections 1.2 and 1.3, also make trouble for the CP if the meaning of a sentence is taken to be the proposition it expresses:

(53) a. It's raining.
      b. The book is green.
      c. He handed her the key and she opened the door.
      d. She insulted him and he left the room.

In understanding each of these, we seem to supply a component of meaning that is not determined by any of the lexical constituents or introduced by the syntactic composition process: a location component for (53a), a salient-part component for (53b), an instrument component for (53c) (she opened the door *with the key he gave her*), and a cause-consequence component for (53d).

Pelletier (1994) discusses another set of cases, all of which involve an ambiguity that does not seem to be traceable to any syntactic or lexical feature of the sentence:

(54) a. Every linguist knows two languages.
      b. The philosophers lifted the piano.
      c. When Alice rode a bicycle, she went to school.

Each of these sentences can be understood in two ways (that is, has two distinct propositional meanings, hence two distinct semantic values): in (54a), the two readings involve different scope relations between the two quantifiers; in (54b), there is a distributive/collective ambiguity concerning whether it was all of the philosophers together who lifted the piano or whether they each did it separately; in (54c), there is an understanding on which each of the instances of bicycle riding is an instance of going to school, and an understanding on which Alice's bike-riding days were back when she was a schoolgirl. I agree with Pelletier that it is not very plausible that any of these originates from a lexical ambiguity or from two distinct *syntactic* analyses; rather, there are some additional factors (of a pragmatic inferential sort) which interact with the single linguistic meaning to give the two distinct understandings for each case.

Jackendoff (1997: 51–67) discusses a range of examples that he considers problematic for any 'syntactically transparent' notion of semantic composition, including the following:

(55)   a.   Mary finished the novel.
     b.   Mary finished the beer.
     c.   The ham sandwich in the corner wants some coffee.
     d.   I'm parked out back.

The truth-conditional content of (55a) and (55b) seems to involve the finishing of quite different processes in the two cases, content that arises from general, rather than linguistic, knowledge: one reads (or writes) a novel, one drinks a beer. The next two examples are cases of 'reference transfer': the subject of (55c) is understood as a customer who has ordered, or who is eating, a ham sandwich, and the subject of (55d) is understood as the speaker's car. Jackendoff points out that the inferred referent in these cases can enter into grammatical binding relations, so that it seems impossible to argue that the result of the pragmatic transfer does not fall within the compositional process.

Each of the three authors has a different response to these problems (and others that they discuss) for the Principle of Semantic Compositionality. Pelletier opts for the abandonment of the principle. Jackendoff accepts that 'one cannot "do semantic composition first and pragmatics later"' and moves in the direction of developing a concept of 'enriched compositionality'; this allows the compositional process to incorporate a measure of pragmatic inference together with the linguistically encoded meaning of the constituent parts, in order to arrive at the meaning of sentences such as those in (55) (see Jackendoff 1997: 49–55). Searle's (1980) solution to the relativity of truth conditions to the Background is to drop the assumption that the literal meaning of a sentence is a set of truth conditions, a move that has been advocated throughout this chapter.

However, neither the examples just cited, nor Searle's points about the Background, affect the validity of the CP as applied to linguistic semantics construed as an account of encoded meaning (the translational, as opposed to truth-conditional, approach). As discussed in section 1.5, on this approach, the semantic representation of a sentence is an incomplete conceptual structure, with some empty slots marking the need for further conceptual material, that is, it is a schema for proposition construction. The arrangement of conceptual constituents and slots reflects the relations encoded by the syntax (the combinatorics) of the natural-language expression used, or in some instances, such as the scope of negation and quantifiers perhaps, leaves those relations to be fixed pragmatically. That the CP holds at this level is perhaps trivially true. The 'semantic' representation (logical form) of a sentence cannot but conform to the CP, since it just is a product of the linguistic semantics of each word/morpheme making it up and the semantic relations imposed by the syntactic structure of the sentence, and of nothing else. That simply follows from the modular view of linguistic processing. It should be noted, in passing, that this 'semantic' entity may never be mentally represented as such by a hearer processing an utterance. By the time the last word of an utterance is processed, the earlier parts of the string are already buried within the pragmatically supplied flesh of a fully propositional thought. As the utterance is processed millisecond by millisecond (left to right, as it were), pragmatic processes come into play; indexical references are resolved, disambiguations performed, unarticulated constituents supplied and decoded concepts enriched, as soon as they can be. Standardly, that is before the whole utterance is heard and, certainly, before the decoding processes have delivered the whole sentential semantic representation.

Paul Horwich, who has written extensively on semantic compositionality (see Horwich 1997, forthcoming), says the following:

> the content of SEM [= the meaning of a complex linguistic expression] is determined by the contents of its parts . . . but this can be explained trivially – in a way that has nothing to do with truth conditions. It suffices to suppose that *understanding* a complex expression (i.e. implicitly knowing its meaning) is, by definition, nothing over and above understanding its parts and appreciating how they have been combined. If this is so, then the property in virtue of which a sentence possesses its particular content is simply the property of its being constructed in a certain manner from primitives with certain meanings.   (Horwich forthcoming: 20–1)

Although Horwich's own approach to linguistic meaning is quite different from those discussed in this chapter (it is in terms of conceptual roles), this statement reflects rather closely the way in which compositionality applies to the translational approach to linguistic semantics.

It could be objected at this point that, while the CP clearly does hold of sentence meanings (logical forms), as construed here, if this is all there is to be said for it, the interest of the CP is greatly reduced. The linguistically determined logical form is, some might argue, essentially pre-semantic; it is not communicated, but is merely a vehicle for what is communicated, it is not knowingly 'grasped' by addressees, it is not phenomenologically salient. What we are really interested in is the propositional thought expressed, perhaps communicated, by an uttered sentence, and this is what the CP has been generally supposed to apply to. I have some sympathy with this dissatisfaction. The conclusion reached above is a bit of a comedown for the CP, although its applicability just to abstract encoded linguistic meaning is probably quite sufficient to answer to the observations concerning the productivity and systematicity of language. There just is no escaping the fact that the propositions that may be expressed by sentences in use are a function, not only of linguistic meaning, but also of pragmatic inference. Perhaps this marks the demise of an *interesting* principle of semantic compositionality, or perhaps it points to the possible development of a different sort of compositionality principle, one that can accommodate an interaction of decoded and pragmatically inferred meaning in the determination of the proposition expressed (a principle of semantic/pragmatic compositionality).[35]

Finally, Searle's observations raise the further question of whether a truth-conditional semantics of sentences in *Mentalese* conforms with the CP. Assuming, as I do, that the question is meaningful (that there are such things as structured sentences of Mentalese, and that it makes sense to assign them truth conditions), it seems that the thesis of the Background must lead to a negative answer here too. The syntactic (compositional) nature of sentences in the language of thought might explain their productivity and systematicity, but the truth conditions of a thought are dependent, not only on the referential properties of basic constituents (concepts) and their compositional relations to one another, but also on the Background. Whether they are also subject to (some of) the other sources of truth-conditional underdeterminacy which are typical of natural language sentences is briefly considered in the next section.

1.7 Underdeterminacy of Thought?

I follow Jerry Fodor's view that having a thought with a particular content P involves the occurrence (the mental 'tokening', as it is often put) of a sentence of the language of thought (Mentalese) which means that P. I take it that Mentalese is distinct from any particular natural language, that it has a compositional syntax and semantics, but no phonology, and its syntax consists of a single level (as opposed to the multiple levels often assumed in syntactic theories of natural language). A Mentalese sentence has truth conditions, that is, there is a specifiable state of affairs which, if it is the case, makes the sentence true. The basic constituents of Mentalese sentences are concepts, such as CAT and SMILE, and there are no dummy elements, that is, elements with no semantics (like expletive 'it', or the copula 'is', in some of its manifestations in English). These representations stand in certain causal relations with each other, relations that constitute inference of a sort; for instance, the belief that Hugo is a spaniel causes the belief that Hugo is a dog. See Fodor (1975, 1978, 1987a) for detailed arguments supporting the existence of such a 'language of thought' and Lycan (1990) for succinct characterizations of various versions of the Mentalese view.

In the previous sections of this chapter, much has been made of the context-sensitivity of linguistic utterances, that is, of their having content (expressing a proposition) which is not fully encoded, content which is underdetermined by the natural-language sentence employed in the utterance. So the question here, by analogy, is 'Are there aspects of the (truth-conditional) content of a thought that are not encoded in the Mentalese representation which occurs in having the thought; that is, are Mentalese sentences context-sensitive?' I'll do no more than skim the surface of this large (and, probably, insufficiently articulated) question in the next two subsections.

1.7.1 Mentalese, pragmatics and compositional semantics

Mentalese is the medium of thought. Given the computational view of mental states and processes, it follows that, for every feature of content that a thought process is sensitive to, there must be a formal element present in the Mentalese representation of that content. So, for instance, if my train of thought moves from recalling that the Smith family have two cats to the conclusion that some of my neighbours have pets, then the relation between the properties *the Smith family* and *neighbours of mine* and between *having cats* and *having pets* must be reflected in the form (the symbols) of those Mentalese representations which enter into the (computational) thinking process. A consequence of this 'formality condition' is that once the sensory perception systems have delivered their representations of the external world to central thought processes, the external world has no further influence on the thinking that follows. That is then a matter of what is present in the form of those representations and of other representations within the system that the processes have access to. This is reflected in the well-known assumption in cognitive psychology of a strategy of 'methodological solipsism', that is, of proceeding in the study of mental states and processes as if nothing outside the mind existed (see Fodor 1980).

This view seems to indicate an immediate answer to our underdeterminacy question with regard to thought: Mentalese sentences do not underdetermine their truth-conditional content, they are not context-sensitive, they are eternal. Given the formality constraint, Mentalese sentences and phrases must be unambiguous; that is, there are no elements of form which have several distinct semantic values, as do 'bank' and 'visiting relatives' in English. Otherwise, a 'bank' thought, for instance, would be simultaneously a thought about a financial institution and a thought about the side of a river; you could never have one without the other and every 'bank' thought would send you off on two wildly divergent inferential tracks. Similar considerations would seem to apply to indexicals. For instance, take the thought of a person who, if she wanted to express it, might utter the English sentence 'That one is better than that one', while pointing first at one object, then at another (say, two cars). The English sentence contains identical elements for referring to the two cars, but the Mentalese sentence must contain distinct components. If it did not, that thought would be indistinguishable from a nonsensical one in which a person predicates of an object that it is better than itself. In fact, the issue is wider than this example makes it seem; it doesn't arise just for utterances involving *multiple* uses of an indexical. A thought about a particular object, say a vase I am looking at, which could be expressed by an utterance of 'That's beautiful', must surely involve a formal component that distinguishes it from those thoughts I have about other objects which could also be expressed by the utterance of a 'that' sentence. Otherwise, we could not keep track (to the quite considerable extent that we do) of distinct objects in our environment. The question of what form these object-distinguishing constituents of Mentalese sentences might take is discussed in the next section.

What about the other symptoms of linguistic underdeterminacy, such as subsentential representation, unarticulated constituents, generality of sense, vagueness and polysemy, which are so characteristic of natural-language utterances? Surely these are not possible features of thoughts. After all, the process of understanding *utterances* with these properties is one of, as it were, recovering the missing bits, so as to discern the *thoughts* being expressed. Recall the following sorts of example:

(56) a. On the top shelf.
      b. Nurofen is better.   [than what, and for what purpose?]
      c. It's raining.   [where?]

While (56a) is a subsentential element of English and the other two are fully sentential, their Mentalese counterparts are all subsentential elements of that representational system; that is, they are all semantically incomplete, and so not truth-evaluable. For any utterance of one of the strings in (56), the thought expressed is complete and so incorporates a constituent whose content is not encoded in the linguistic expression, but is pragmatically derived.

Another sort of case, canvassed earlier, involves the use of a word to communicate a concept which differs from that encoded by the word:

(57)   a.   I am happy.
       b.   The house was silent.

In the case of (57a), the idea here is that different concepts of 'happy' are communicated in different contexts, from a mild sense of acceptance of life to a feeling of joyous delight; supposing the word meaning is general enough for all these different senses to fall within its domain, then any more specific concept has to be pragmatically inferred. The example in (57b) might go the other way, that is, from the absolute concept of noiselessness putatively encoded, looser notions of 'silent' might have to be inferred in understanding the utterance (for instance, the inhabitants of the house may be asleep, so there is the sound of their breathing, as well as the various creakings, crackings and drippings of the fabric of the house). The particular concept is a component of the thought the speaker seeks to communicate (a 'word' of the Mentalese sentence tokened) and, if communication is successful, of the thought recovered by the addressee. On this view, Mentalese must have a large stock of concepts that are not encoded by any element of natural-language form. This idea is pursued in more detail in chapter 5.

What bridges the gap between the underdetermining encoding of a natural-language utterance and the thought(s) expressed is a powerful pragmatic inferential mechanism, whose job it is to figure out the informative intention behind a linguistic utterance (or any other act of ostension). Having thoughts is a strikingly different kind of mental activity from comprehending utterances. We do not have to undergo a process of *comprehending* occurrences (tokenings) of our thoughts (hence Mentalese sentences), as we must comprehend occurrences of linguistic utterances. Thoughts are, in effect, an end-product: they are the *result* of utterance comprehension processes, or are prompted by the deliverances of our sensory-perceptual systems, or are generated from within the central thought system itself (in ways that remain largely mysterious). A thought token is not ostensive, it is not a communicative act, it doesn't involve an interaction of speaker and addressee, it doesn't come with a presumption of optimal relevance, which warrants a particular expectation of effect and effort and so a particular pattern of processing geared to satisfying that expectation. There surely cannot be a 'pragmatics of thought', in the sense of pragmatics at issue here.[36] Furthermore, as Butler (1995b: 14) says, 'Since mental representation is presupposed by communication, it cannot, and obviously does not, involve communication itself (on pain of regress).'

In accordance with these observations about the nature of thoughts, and setting aside issues of the Background for the moment, it looks as if a Principle of Semantic Compositionality should hold for Mentalese: the semantic value of a sentence is fully determined by the semantic value of its constituents and their syntactic combination. Assuming that the 'semantics' at issue here is truth-conditional, what the principle says is that the truth conditions of a Mentalese sentence are fully determined by the semantic entities that its constituents refer to and the way in which they are related according to the structure of the sentence. For instance, the thought that it is raining encodes a location constituent, LOC_x, so that it is true iff it is raining at LOC_x (at such and such a time); the thought that Mary is happy encodes a particular concept of happiness, HAPPY*, so that it is true iff the property denoted by HAPPY* applies to Mary (at such and such a time). It's worth noting differences in the application of this principle to natural languages and to thought: while the semantics of thought is compositional, this is not a semantics that thinkers know (in the way in which truth-conditional semanticists envisage speakers knowing the semantics of their natural language system) and there is no compositional *process* of understanding it as there is in understanding linguistic utterances, because there is no process of understanding it at all. (For relevant discussion of the compositionality of language and of thought, and of the issue of understanding sentences in the two kinds of representational system, see Fodor and Lepore 1999.)

Butler (1995a, 1995b) discusses a range of cases of alleged context-sensitivity of mental representation, which have been taken to threaten the compositionality of thought. The cases in question are extrapolated from the *linguistic* context-sensitivity of examples such as the following:

(58) a. The apple is red.   [on its peel]
      b. The watermelon is red.   [in its flesh]
      c. Mary finished the novel. [finished reading or writing]
      d. Mary finished the beer.   [finished drinking]

He concludes: 'What we find . . . is *not* a context-sensitivity of mental *semantics*, but a context-sensitivity of the *deployment* of mental representations' (Butler 1995b: 13). What he means by this is that the occurrence of the mental representation that corresponds (roughly) to 'red on most of the peel', or 'red on the inside flesh', in the cases of (58a) and (58b), is sensitive to other elements of the sentential representation of which it is a constituent, that is, whether redness is being predicated of an apple, a watermelon, or something else. He confines his attention to sentence-internal context-sensitivity: 'red' predicated of 'the apple', 'finished' predicated of 'the novel', etc., but this statement about the deployment (occurrence) of a particular conceptual representation applies to a wider notion of context-sensitivity. Although the interpretation he assumes for the examples given in (58a) and (58b) is a kind of default, predicating a colour of either of those (or of any other object) could give rise to a quite different mental representation. Suppose, for instance, that a chemical test for the presence of a particular bacterium in apples turns their flesh red when there is a positive result; then, obviously, in such a context, an occurrence of a thought that a particular apple is red will involve the deployment of a mental representation with a different part constituent from the default case.

The old idea that communication is a matter of a speaker encoding her thoughts and a hearer decoding them has been completely undermined by, on the one hand, the linguistic underdeterminacy facts, and, on the other, the presence in human cognitive architecture of an inferential device dedicated to recognizing the informative intentions that lie behind ostensive communicative acts. These considerations do not seem to carry over to thoughts; a conception of them as fully encoding their truth-conditional content seems to make very good sense. However, consider the following remark by Kent Bach: 'Since the contents of thoughts cannot be conceptually incomplete, the conceptual representations that comprise them cannot be semantically underdeterminate *in the way* that sentences can be' (Bach 1994b: 157; my emphasis). There is an implication here that thoughts can perhaps be semantically underdeterminate *in some way*, even if not in the way that natural language utterances are. What Bach is allowing for here is a kind of indexicality within thought, specifically within what are known as singular or *de re* thoughts (that is, thoughts about particular objects). And, in fact, the philosophical literature abounds with papers on indexical (egocentric or demonstrative) thought. (See, for instance, Castañeda 1966, 1967, 1990; Burge 1977; Perry 1977, 1979, 1993; Kaplan 1977/89a; Stalnaker 1981; McGinn 1982; and Recanati 1990, 1993). This needs some consideration since, if it is right, the view of thoughts as involving occurrences of Mentalese sentences that fully encode their content, and so are eternal, has to be modified. Just as indexicality in natural language ensures the context-dependence of the truth-conditional content of linguistic utterances, so too for thoughts: if they can be indexical, then their truth conditions are context-dependent. I move now to a short discussion of mental indexicals.

1.7.2 Mental indexicals and the mind–world connection

In order to understand someone's use of a natural-language singular term (such as a name, a pronoun, a demonstrative or a definite description), we have to figure out (by considering the context) what it is he is referring to. Our *thoughts* about objects are, clearly, not like that; there is no such process of 'understanding' to be undertaken. Suppose you have a thought which, if you chose to, you might express by uttering the English sentence in (59):

(59)   That's beautiful.

The Mentalese sentence that you token in having the thought does not involve you in figuring out the referent; it is part and parcel of having the thought that you think of the referent and, in accordance with the 'formality' constraint, the thought constituent which corresponds to the utterance of the word 'that' should be distinct from your mental representations of other objects if your thinking about the world is not to go wrong. So, if there are mental indexicals, they must be different in some fundamental way from natural language indexicals. Let's consider some views on the nature of the mental symbol that occupies the position in your thought that 'that' occupies in your utterance of (59).

An obvious first idea about this is that Mentalese (unlike natural languages) provides uniquely denoting descriptions and that, in thinking the thought that you might express by (59), you token a Mentalese sentence with such a descriptive singular term in subject position; for instance, a conceptually complete, hence eternal, version of 'The curving glass vase in Nawab's gift shop . . .'. However, a number of authors have made it clear that this cannot be right (see, for instance, Bach 1986, 1987; Levine 1988; Elugardo and Stainton forthcoming a). Levine (1988: 226) points out various problems for the description view. First, a person may be entirely unaware of any definite description under which she thinks of the object and although she might acknowledge, if asked, that the object she has proclaimed beautiful is indeed the curving glass vase in . . . , still there is no clear sense in which she had that description in mind when she uttered (59). Second, for any description of the form 'The F' that might be proposed as the one that represents the object, the sentence 'That is the F' seems to express something informative, that is, not something equivalent to 'The F is the F'. Third, for any description under which a person might think of the object, she could turn out to be mistaken in thinking the object satisfies the description (for instance, the vase is not made of glass but of perspex) and yet she has, nonetheless, had a thought about that very object.

Bach (1986: 188) makes a more general point against any wholesale descriptivist account of thought:

> If *all* your thoughts about things could only be descriptive, your total conception of the world would be merely qualitative. You would never be related in thought to anything in particular. . . . Since the object of a descriptive thought is determined *satisfactionally*, the fact that the thought is of that object does not require any connection between thought and object. However, the object of a *de re* thought [i.e. a thought of that object] is determined *relationally*. For something to be the object of a *de re* thought, it must stand in a certain kind of [real, natural] relation to that very thought.

The clearest case of this sort of directly world-connected thought is one that involves an object currently perceived, as in the thought about the vase occasioned by seeing it in a shop. The relation between the object and the thought about it is a causal one: the object causes a pattern of activation on a sensory receptor, which, in turn, causes the formation of a certain percept, which eventuates in the tokening of a symbol in a Mentalese sentence, which is a thought about the object.

At this stage, we can approach the symbol question with some constraints in place. One is that the mental demonstrative element does not specify (and is not an abbreviation for) an individuating description of the object in question; rather, it must be 'directly referential', that is, it must reflect the causal relation between the object and the occurrence of the mental symbol. Another constraint follows from the fact that it is possible to think of the same object in different ways without realizing that it is the same object. For instance, you might think of an object that you can see, that it is a candlestick, and of an object that you can hear, that it is a flute (so not a candlestick), without realizing that they are one and the same object, so the mental symbols representing the object in the two thoughts must be distinct. One of the attractions of the description view is that it can meet this second requirement ('the long wooden object with a flute-like shape is . . .'; 'the instrument making a sweet breathy sound is . . .'), but this possibility is no longer in the running.

Simplifying somewhat, the proposal is that the mental symbol concerned is either a percept of the object, that is, a way in which a physical object can appear to a perceiver (Bach 1986, 1987), or a mental pointer to a percept (Levine 1988).[37] So your thought about the vase that it is beautiful is represented as 'BEAUTIFUL ([→ α])', where '[→ α]' is a Mentalese pointer and 'α' is your percept of the vase. My thought about the two cars, expressed verbally as 'this one is better than this one', is represented as 'BETTER THAN ([→ β], [→ γ])', where 'β' is my percept of the first car referred to and 'γ' is my percept of the second one, and the two thoughts about the flute are 'CANDLESTICK ([→ Ω])' and 'FLUTE ([→ Δ])', where 'Ω' and 'Δ' are different percepts of the one object. So Mentalese has at its disposal a category of symbols not present in natural language, symbols that denote an object without being descriptive of it, while, nonetheless, reflecting the uniqueness of that object for the thinker at that moment.

The perceptual component in the Mentalese sentences given in the previous paragraph functions as a mental indexical: its semantic value (its referent) is determined, not via the 'satisfaction' of any conceptual conditions, but by an appropriate perceptual causal relation between an object in the context and that mental token. So thoughts in which these symbols occur are not eternal propositions; that is, their truth conditions are context-dependent. This is not a problem for the Compositionality Principle which requires only that the semantic value of the sentence be determined by the semantic value of its parts (and the combinatorial structure). Indexicals are parts of Mentalese sentences and their semantic values (the entities in the external word that caused their occurrence), together with the semantic values of the descriptive conceptual content of the sentences, play the role required by the principle.

There is nothing in these Mentalese symbols that makes them about one particular object as opposed to another except for their causal histories; that is, one and the same indexical symbol can pick out different objects in different contexts. This last point could, perhaps, do with some elaboration (see, especially, Burge 1977; Bach 1986, 1987), but the following simple illustration, adapted from Bach (1987: 22), may suffice here. I am looking at a tomato and I have a thought of the form 'RIPE ([→ #])', where '#' is my percept of the tomato; I look away for a moment, then glance back and think again 'RIPE ([→ #])', and perhaps resolve to buy the tomato (= '[→ #]'). However, in the brief moment that my attention was elsewhere, the tomato I had seen first was removed and another, very similar, put in its place. As regards the object mentally demonstrated the two thought tokens are identical in form, and so, by the formality constraint, must play one and the same role in my thought processes, but they are truth-conditionally distinct: the first one is true iff the first tomato is ripe and the second one is true iff the second tomato is ripe. Another way of seeing the point is to envisage the possibility of two individuals, one in the context just given, the other in some other tomato-involving context, each of whom tokens 'RIPE ([→ #])'. On a narrow (psychological) construal of thought content, the thoughts of these individuals are the same because the percepts are type-identical, but on a 'wide' (truth-conditional) construal of content, their thoughts are different because they are about different things (the token percepts have different causal histories).[38]

Bach (1986, 1987) extends his account of *de re* thought, from perception-based thoughts about objects, to memory-based and communication-based ones. Each of these involves a different, more complex, relation between a thinker and the object thought about than in the perceptual case, but, in both cases, a crucial feature of the account is the ultimate causal connection between the object in the world and the representation(s) of it in the mind. Levine (1988; 239, note 20) sees no reason to limit the type of representation mentally demonstrated to percepts; so, for instance, recalling a day last week when I quarrelled with a friend and then missed my train, I may have a thought which could be verbally expressed by 'That was a bad day', where the representation mentally pointed to is some complex of memory traces. The details and full range of possibilities do not matter for the limited point I want to make here, which concerns the indexical (context-dependent) nature of thought.

There are, clearly, many more mental indexicals than there are linguistic indexicals (any percept is potentially a mental indexical), and the two types of indexical belong to quite different sorts of representational systems. Linguistic indexicals are communicative vehicles *par excellence*; they encode a procedure, or rule for use (in the case of 'that', something like 'is used to refer to a salient entity'). Mental indexicals can be thought of as possible cognitive correlates of particular uses of a linguistic indexical on particular occasions, though, of course, many occurrences of mental indexicals are never verbally expressed. What these two kinds of element have in common is their intrinsic context-sensitivity; their semantic value (a Mentalese symbol in the case of a linguistic indexical, an object in the world in the case of a mental indexical) is determined contextually. However, just as there are important differences in the functioning of the two kinds of representational systems, public language and Mentalese, and in their respective semantics, translational for linguistic sentences, truth-conditional for Mentalese sentences, so the appropriate notion of context is different in the two cases. The processes involved in understanding a verbal utterance lie within the solipsistic psychological system of representations and computations, so the 'context' that addressees employ in understanding an utterance (in disambiguating, in assigning referents to indexicals, in recovering unarticulated constituents, etc.) is a set of mental representations. The context of thought, on the other hand, is external to the system, it is the world of objects and states of affairs within which the thinker is situated and parts of which he mentally represents. The context for utterance interpretation (a set of mentally represented assumptions) can be called an I-context ('I' for internal, individual, interpretative), as opposed to the E-context of the semantics of thought ('E' for external, environmental). As McGinn (1982: 209) puts it, the object which a mental indexical is about 'is determined by the occurrence of a representation *in* a context, not by way of a representation *of* the context.' The relation between objects in the E-context and mental representations of those objects is not itself mentally represented and so is not a matter for a (solipsistic) cognitive psychology; rather, it is the domain of a 'real' semantics, whose concern is to articulate the relation between mental representations and the features of the outside world that are represented.

This brief discussion of mental indexicals has focused on thoughts about individuals and objects other than oneself. Thoughts about oneself (first-person thoughts), such as the thought that one might express verbally by 'I am tired', seem to be special in certain ways; they issue 'from within', as it were, they are not perception-based in quite the way that thoughts about others are, and, while one can be wrong about the identity of the referent of one's thoughts about other individuals and objects, one's 'I'-thoughts are immune to that sort of error (I am acquainted with the object of my thought 'I am tired' in a way that I am not acquainted with any other object). Similar points apply to thinking of a place as 'here', or of a time as 'now'. Each of these involves a special source of information: information about a person acquired through being that person, information about a place or a moment in time gained from occupying the space and time that one does. These and many other facets of such thoughts, which I cannot pursue here, are investigated in detail by Recanati (1993). Some similar observations regarding tensed thoughts (as opposed to tenseless ones that specify a time descriptively) are made by Higginbotham (1995); such thoughts involve a mental indexical element of a temporal sort (for the present, the past, the future).

Consider the following pairs of thoughts, which, let us assume, are truth-conditionally equivalent, so that the first two refer to the same person and the second two (taken from Higginbotham 1995: 22) refer to the same moment in time:

(60) a. My child is crying.
      b. The child in the next room is crying.

(61) a. My root canal operation is over.
      b. My root canal operation is over as of 4 p.m., 31 October 1994.

The thought represented by (60a) may set in train certain further thoughts and cause me to take action (for instance, to go and pick the child up) in a way that the thought represented by (60b) might not if, for some reason, I am unaware that the child in the next room is, in fact, my child. Similarly, the thought represented by (61a) might bring with it a feeling of deep relief, while the thought in (61b) would not occasion a sense of relief, unless I know of the time at which I have the thought that it is, or is later than, 4 p.m., 31 October 1994. In short, indexical thoughts have a range of causal properties that distinguish them from any truth-conditionally equivalent descriptive thoughts.

Summing up, while occurrences of Mentalese sentences are free from many of the sources of truth-conditional underdeterminacy that are typical of natural-language utterances, they are not, in general, eternal either. Recall Katz's (1972, 1981) position that for every context-dependent, non-eternal sentence there is an eternal, hence context-independent, sentence, so for every occurrence of an indexical, there is a descriptive expression 'that has the same reference as the indexical element it replaces but whose referent stays fixed with variations in time, place, etc.' As we've seen, this is not true for natural-language sentences. As regards Mentalese sentences, even if mental indexicals can be replaced by mental representations whose reference is eternal, a thought which involves tokening a mental indexical and a thought with the corresponding eternal representation would be different thoughts, playing different roles in thought and feeling, and leading to different behaviours on the part of the thinker.

As discussed in section 1.6, according to Searle, the content of thoughts (and intentional states generally) determines conditions of truth only against a Background. If this is correct (see note 32), then thoughts share the property of under-determinacy with natural-language utterances to the extent that it is an effect of the Background. In addition, as we've seen, indexicality of a sort is a common feature of thoughts. But, whatever properties of context-dependence and truth-conditional incompleteness our thoughts may have, the encoded content of natural-language sentences takes underdeterminacy to a different level, in both quantity and type.[39]

1.8 Summary

To end this long chapter I will briefly and baldly state its main claims, which are assumed in the rest of the book:

1 Linguistically encoded meaning underdetermines the proposition expressed by an utterance (its truth-conditional content).
2 Linguistic underdeterminacy is an essential feature of natural languages because there are no eternal sentences in natural languages.
3 The primary mental capacity underlying the communicative and interpretive powers of humans is the capacity to infer the mental states of others, and this runs to several orders of attribution.
4 The pragmatic inferential capacity, whose specific domain is utterances and other communicative acts, employs a particular interpretive strategy, distinct from that of the more general capacity of mental state attribution, and warranted by the presumption of optimal relevance that is automatically conveyed by such stimuli.
5 All intentionality (mental and linguistic) is dependent on a massive Background of weakly manifest (taken-for-granted) unrepresented assumptions and practices.
6 Linguistically encoded meaning is, then, doubly underdetermining of utterance meaning; as well as its own inherent underdeterminacy it inherits the under-determinacy of the representational states it is used to express.

Finally, I should mention that in the chapters that follow I will sometimes try to give some sort of representation of the proposition expressed by an utterance, and this will often look like some attempt at finding an eternal natural-language sentence. This will not be the intention. In fact, in most cases the given representation would fail miserably as a candidate for an eternal sentence for the sorts of reasons surveyed in section 1.3; the point will usually be to alert the reader to those aspects of the proposition expressed that have been *pragmatically* supplied, so points of difference from the semantic representation encoded by the linguistic expression will be highlighted. Precisely because of the non-existence of eternal sentences, the propositional representations may contain numbers and other symbols (like the hopelessly inadequate but suggestive 't's for temporal reference) in a bid to repre-sent elements of meaning that natural-language sentences cannot represent.

NOTES

1 However, Kent Bach is an exception to this. He ties 'what is said' as closely to linguis-tic meaning as one can without equating the two, so that for him 'what is said' need

not be propositional (Bach 1994a, 1994b, 1997/99a, 2001). His views are discussed in chapter 2, section 2.5.

2 Talk of linguistic error and misuse raises some quite fundamental questions about the nature of language. It seems to presuppose the existence of a common public language which is used by a particular population of individuals, some of whom have a less complete grasp of it than others. However, on an internalist and 'idiolectal' view (such as Chomsky's – see any of his writings) there is really no issue of 'correctness' or of what is 'actually', as opposed to 'mistakenly', encoded by a linguistic form (hence my scare quotes in the text). An individual's linguistic knowledge (including form/meaning mappings) simply is her language and its utility for communication with another individual depends on its degree of similarity to the language (idiolect) of the other. Nevertheless, whether we individuate languages as social entities or, much more finely, as individualistic entities, the issue for a cognitive pragmatic account of utterance interpretation remains the same: both communication failures due to disparate encodings, and communication which is successful only because either the speaker or the hearer recognizes such a disparity and adjusts for it, are real phenomena and have to be accounted for.

   For discussion of so-called language misuses, in the context of different conceptions of 'language', see Davidson (1986), Chomsky (1987; 1992a; 1995) and Chng (1999).

3 All page references to articles by Grice are to the reprintings in Grice (1989b).

4 According to this approach to ambiguity, there are, strictly speaking, no ambiguous lexical items, phrases or sentences, but rather distinct lexical items (e.g. 'bank$_1$' and 'bank$_2$') that happen to have the same phonological form, and distinct phrases/sentences (e.g. 'I went to the bank$_1$' and 'I went to the bank$_2$', '[visiting relatives]$_{NP}$' and '[(e)$_{NP}$ [visiting relatives]$_{VP}$]$_S$'), each making a distinct contribution to truth-conditional content. In accordance with this, context is said to play a 'pre-semantic' role in distinguishing ambiguous forms (see Perry 1997, 1998). That is, disambiguation is a process of figuring out from the context which of several lexical items or phrases with the same surface perceptual properties has been uttered, that is, which semantic entity we are dealing with.

   However, earlier work in the application of truth theory to the semantics of natural language did not allow itself this sorting of perceptually identical forms into distinct linguistic entities and, as a result, ambiguity presented a problem. Davidson (1967, 1970) tried out the following two possibilities:

   (i)   For any a, 'is a bank' is true of a in English if and only if a is a bank.
   (ii) 'John went to the bank' is true for an English speaker x at time t if and only if either John went to the financial institution and the circumstances surrounding x at t meet condition C, or John went to the wall of the river channel before t and the circumstances surrounding x at t meet condition D.

   In the first of these, the idea is that, provided one can translate the ambiguity in the object language into an ambiguity in the metalanguage, truth will be preserved. This turns out not to work (see Parsons 1973). In the second attempt, the idea is that the theory should specify a single T-sentence with a disjunction of truth conditions, together with reference to different contextual conditions for each disjunct. This too is problematic (for discussion, see Parsons 1973; Lycan 1984, chapter 2; and Cohen 1985).

5 This is not to say that the semantics of pronouns is a cut-and-dried matter; it is not. The point here is that we do not need to get the semantics of pronouns straight in order to convince ourselves that understanding utterances of them presents a task for pragmatics.

6 Katz was led to abandon the Chomskyan psychological conception of language, of which he had been a staunch supporter, by his philosophical interest in necessary truths and his belief that they are expressible in natural language. He claims that Chomsky's mentalism denies the possibility of genuine necessary truth in natural languages, since the most it can offer is the concept of something's being necessary *relative to human cognitive capacities* (Katz 1981: 4–6).

7 Katz (1981) notes conceptualist scepticism about the possibility of doing semantics; here is one of the examples he quotes: 'It seems that other cognitive systems – in particular our system of beliefs concerning things in the world and their behaviour – play an essential part in our judgements of meaning [sense] and reference, in an extremely intricate manner, and it is not at all clear that much will remain if we try to separate the purely linguistic components of what in informal usage or even in technical discussions we call the "meaning of a linguistic expression". I doubt that one can separate semantic representation from beliefs and knowledge about the world' (Chomsky 1979: 142). The same position is reiterated in more recent work, for example Chomsky (1995: 26). Little wonder then that Katz, the prime mover in developing the 'semantic component' of a grammar, prefers a Platonist conception. Recall Chomsky's scepticism regarding a theory of utterance interpretation, pointed out in the introduction; the current quote indicates a deeper, more thoroughgoing, scepticism about the prospects for theories of meaning of even quite a narrow sort.

8 Searle (1992: 131, 155) too emphasizes that every intentional (i.e. representational) state has an 'aspectual shape', by which he means to emphasize the first-person perspective we cannot but have on the objects we perceive and think about. I take it that 'aspectual shape' is another term for 'mode of presentation'.

9 As Perry (1977) notes, Frege's view that each thought is the sense of some sentence (though there are sentence senses which are not thoughts because they are incomplete) was severely tested by indexicals like 'here', 'now' and 'I'. Having recognized the 'special and primitive way in which we each present ourselves to ourselves' (Frege 1918a/77: 12–13), he could not but accept that there are incommunicable senses. So it seems that even those most drawn to it cannot hold the Effability Principle in its strongest form.

10 Clearly, the point depends on the assumption that the conceptual content of the description is a crucial component of the proposition expressed (or statement made), so that differences in descriptive content entail differences in proposition expressed (or statement made), as is most clearly the case on attributive (as opposed to referential) uses of descriptions, in the sense of Donnellan (1966/91). This is indeed Wettstein's assumption, since the main purpose of his 1979 paper is to argue against the Fregean view that indexical expressions (names, pronouns, demonstratives), uttered in a particular context, acquire a particular sense or descriptive content, which they contribute to the proposition expressed by the utterance. He favours the direct reference view of names and other indexicals, associated with Mill, Kripke and Donnellan, according to which the context in which the indexical sentence is uttered 'reveals *which item* is in question' rather than providing 'some unique characterisation' of it (Wettstein 1979: 96). So his argument against the possibility of finding that one among a number of eternal descriptions which is the very one that enters into the proposition expressed by an utterance of an indexical sentence is ultimately directed towards this bigger theoretical end. It seems to me that the directly referential view of indexicals is incompatible with the strong effability positions.

11 It might be objected that, in fact, the dependence of the intended reference on the domain of discourse does not affect the proposition expressed but comes in at some other level

altogether, perhaps as an implicature. This is a standard Gricean kind of gambit which we will see more of in chapter 2. The result here would be that 'what is said' is that the prime minister of Britain, whoever that actually is, (i.e. Tony Blair) is in the next room and 'what is implicated' would be that the prime minister of Britain, according to Lucinda, (i.e. Peter Mandelson) is in the next room. This runs counter to a quite robust intuition that what the speaker of (25) said (that is, the proposition she expressed) was that Lucinda will be delighted to find that the person who she believes to be the current prime minister of Britain is in the next room. If the speaker in the same set of circumstances were to add: 'Of course, the prime minister is not, in fact, the prime minister', she would not be understood as contradicting herself, but as expressing the proposition that the person whom Lucinda thinks is the prime minister is not in fact the prime minister.

   Furthermore, as Recanati (1987b: 68–72) points out, different elements in a sentence may be interpreted relative to different domains of discourse, so in the current example while 'the prime minister of Britain' is interpreted relative to Lucinda's belief world, the predicate 'is in the next room' is interpreted relative to another domain (the actual world). In principle, there could be several different discourse domains relative to which different parts of an utterance are to be interpreted. Recanati suggests that, at the level of sentence meaning, every predicate comes with a variable ranging over domains of discourse, so that, for any utterance, these variables have to be contextually determined in the process of deriving what is said (the proposition expressed, the truth-conditional content of the utterance). If this is right, it follows that every sentence is intrinsically context-dependent and non-eternal.

12   Dan Sperber, Deirdre Wilson and I have discussed a range of other cases where processes of pragmatic adjustment of a lexical concept eventuate in an *ad hoc* concept in the proposition expressed, a concept which may be narrower than the original one, as in the example in (27), or wider as in the examples in (28), or a combination of the two. See, for instance, Sperber and Wilson (1997/98a), Wilson (1995), and Carston (1996b/97a). *Ad hoc* concept formation and its role in the proposition expressed is the subject of chapter 5 of this book.

13   An obvious (Gricean) sort of response here would be to say that the proposition expressed (what is said) by the utterance does contain within it the precise linguistically encoded concept, even though what is meant is something looser. On this view, the speaker does not endorse (that is, 'mean' or communicate) the proposition expressed and in most cases that proposition is clearly false (e.g. France has six equal sides). The broader concept which is communicated is registered at some other level of utterance meaning (the implicature level). This is also the standard relevance-theoretic position (Sperber and Wilson 1986a/95b: 232–5). In chapter 5 I argue for a different relevance-theoretic account.

14   I am ignoring here crucial questions about what the interrogative and other moods actually encode. It does look very much as if a proper analysis of moods will reveal another area of intrinsic underdeterminacy in natural language (see Gazdar 1981; Wilson and Sperber 1988a, 1988b; Clark 1991, 1993a).

15   Wilson (1999b/2000) provides an illuminating exposition of how psychological research on the 'theory of mind' capacity and work within the broadly Gricean inferential pragmatic tradition interrelate, and how both of these bear on the more general mental ability for metarepresentation. She also brings in a third strand of research on metarepresentation, one which focuses on the various ways in which metarepresentational elements may occur within the content of utterances; for instance, cases of quotation, direct or indirect, and of allusions to, and echoes of, other people's thoughts and utterances. Some cases of such 'meta*linguistic* use' are discussed in chapter 4.

16   The issues of how exactly the mind-reading ability and the system for interpreting ostensive stimuli are related, what it means to think of them as mental modules, and how
they are situated in our overall cognitive architecture are far from settled. Sperber and
Wilson (1986a/95b) and Wilson and Sperber (1986b) adopted Fodor's (1983) distinction between modular systems of perception and motor output, on the one hand, and
non-modular central systems, on the other, and they took pragmatics to belong at the
non-modular centre (along with other apparently context-sensitive reasoning systems).
However, in more recent work, Sperber (1994b, 1996) has made a case, largely based
on evolutionary considerations, for a thoroughgoing modularity of mind, within which
central inferential systems are also modular, including those systems that manipulate
metarepresentations, such as the theory of mind (or metapsychological) system and the
pragmatic (or ostension comprehension) system. Smith and Tsimpli (1996) suggest that
a concept of 'quasi'-modularity is more appropriate in the case of these and other systems
dealing in conceptual representations. Carston (1997b) discusses, in a preliminary way,
the idea of a pragmatics module.

17   I am not giving a fully comprehensive outline of relevance theory in this book, although
many of the main concepts and distinctions of the pragmatic theory developed within
the broader framework are introduced and discussed in chapter 2 (section 2.3), and there
is a glossary of terms in appendix 1. For introductions to the framework, see Wilson
and Sperber (1986b; 1986c), Blakemore (1992), Wilson (1994; 1999), Noh (1998b,
2000, chapter 2). For more advanced accounts, see Sperber and Wilson (1986a/95b),
Sperber and Wilson (1987) and Sperber and Wilson (1995a).

18   Premack (1990) presents arguments for the coevolution of the human linguistic system
and 'social modules', including the theory of mind, and Sperber (1990) gives a succinct
demonstration that a linguistic system has adaptive value only for a species already able
to engage in ostensive-inferential communication. These ideas are further developed in
Sperber (2000) and Origgi and Sperber (2000). Given the assumption that the language
faculty and the metarepresentational capacity coevolved in humans, Sperber considers
the question 'which of these two, the linguistic or the metarepresentational, might have
developed first to a degree sufficient to bootstrap the coevolutionary process.' He considers both possibilities (language first, or metarepresentations first) and concludes that
the more plausible scenario is that a metarepresentational capacity first developed in a
social environment involving both competitive and cooperative interactions, that that
capacity made possible ostensive communication, perhaps as a side effect, and 'the
beneficial character of this side effect turned it into a function of metarepresentations,
and created a favorable environment for the evolution of a new adaptation, a linguistic
ability' (Sperber 2000: 127).

19   The issue of the language (or languages) of thought is clearly relevant here. Carruthers
(1996) and Horwich (forthcoming) support an account of language and thought in
which a person's Mentalese just is their natural public language. Fodor (1975, 1987a)
is well known for his view that the medium of thought, though syntactic like natural
language, is distinct from (and precedes, and enables, the acquisition of) a person's public
language; however, he seems to assume a more or less one-to-one mapping between
words and the basic constituents of thought, that is, concepts (see Fodor 1975: 152–6,
and Fodor and Lepore 1991: 333). Both views are incompatible with the essential underdeterminacy thesis. While any settled answers to questions about the nature of thought
are a long way off, I suggest that the arguments presented in this chapter against strong
effability (the linguistic encodability of thoughts and propositions expressed) are just
as much arguments against the view that thought consists either of public-language
sentences or of representations whose constituents are in a one-to-one relation with the

constituents of natural-language sentences. For discussion of the implications of linguistic underdeterminacy for the view of thought as 'inner speech', see Elugardo and Stainton (forthcoming a).

20   The property of 'coherence and appropriateness to situations', which Chomsky frequently mentions as one of the features that makes natural language unique (along with 'unboundedness' and 'freedom from stimulus control'), strikes me as also explained by these wider cognitive capacities involved in ostensive communication (that is, language use) rather than as a property of the language system (competence) *per se*. (See, for instance, Chomsky 1966: 4–5; 1988: 5.)

21   Gross (1998, chapter 1) makes (and elaborates on) three claims for the 'utility of context-sensitivity': (i) it is essential for various aspects of the learning of language; for instance, the learning of many predicates depends on exposure to exemplars in the environment; (ii) it makes for a considerable increase in the efficiency of communication, since appropriate exploitation of shared knowledge and circumstances reduces the effort and time needed in both production and comprehension; (iii) it bestows a greater flexibility on language, making it fit for a much wider range of purposes than it would otherwise have. He goes on to endorse the view that context-sensitivity is not eliminable, even in principle, from natural language use, that is, in the terms of section 1.2.2 of this book, underdeterminacy is an essential feature of language.

22   Higginbotham's (1988) treatment of the referential use of definite descriptions parallels that of the other referential cases (pronouns, demonstrative descriptions) and captures the specific contribution of the definite article in terms of conditions enumerated in the antecedent of the conditional T-statement:

   (i)   If *u* is an utterance of 'The dog is hungry', and the speaker of *u* refers with
         'the dog' to *x*, and (a) the speaker does not refer to anything else with 'the
         dog'; (b) *x* is a dog; (c) *x* is obvious or familiar, then [*u* is true iff *x* is hungry].

The assumption that the referential use of a definite description is a matter of linguistic semantics is highly debatable. A currently popular view is that the referential use is pragmatically inferred (see Recanati 1993; Bezuidenhout 1997b; Rouchota 1992, 1994b; Powell 1999), on the basis of a radically underdetermining linguistic semantics for 'The F'. If this proves to be correct, then there is no T-statement of this sort for definite description sentences.

23   In addition to applying the modified truth-conditional approach to these cases, Gross (1998, chapter 3) considers two other possible ways of handling them, which can be dubbed the implicature approach (or the Gricean gambit) and the ambiguity approach. According to the first of these, there is no part context-sensitivity of predicates and the sentence 'The book is green' simply expresses a false proposition if the book has some other colours on it, though it may implicate (via considerations of relevance) the true proposition that a certain part of the book is green. According to the other line of thought, there is not a single univocal sentence of the form 'The book is green' that is uttered across the different contexts expressing different propositions. Rather, there are a large number of sentences of this form, to each of which the truth-theory must assign a distinct T-statement, for instance:

   (i)   'The book is green$_1$' is true iff the cover of the book is green.
   (ii)   'The book is green$_2$' is true iff the spine of the book is green.
   (iii) 'The book is green$_3$' is true iff the whole cover and spine apart from the
          lettering are green.

Gross provides a range of good arguments against both of these attempts to deny the part context-sensitivity of certain predicates.

24   In a response to this argument of Lewis, Harman (1974) observes that just as we can know how to translate between two languages without knowing the meaning of the expressions in either, so we can have knowledge of truth conditions without having knowledge of meaning: 'there is a sense in which we can know the truth conditions of an English sentence without knowing the first thing about the meaning of the English sentence'. When we first come upon the sentence 'All mimsy were the borogoves' in Lewis Carroll's *Through the Looking Glass*, we know the following:

(i)   'All mimsy were the borogoves' is true iff all mimsy were the borogoves.

Harman's claim is that we can know this without knowing the meaning of the sentence 'All mimsy were the borogoves'. For interesting discussion of this general issue and a deflation of Harman's point, see Higginbotham (1989). On the relative merits and short-comings of translational approaches to semantics, see Lepore and Loewer (1981) and Lepore (1996).

25   For further discussion of the relevance-theoretic view of these two kinds of semantics, see Sperber and Wilson (1986a/95b, chapter 4), Blakemore (1987, chapter 1), Carston (1988: 175–8), Wilson and Sperber (1988b: 134), Sperber and Wilson (1995a: 257–8), Carston (1999b).

26   Unfortunately, different uses of the term 'logical form' abound. There are so-called 'regimented' notions of logical form, such as those of Frege or Russell, which are intended to replace the ambiguous, vague and context-sensitive sentences of natural language, in the interest of expressing scientific propositions in a way that makes their logical properties transparent and, perhaps also, makes their relation to the external world transparent. Stanley (2000: 391–2) distinguishes this '*revisionary* conception of logical form' from the '*descriptive* conception of logical form, [according to which] the logical form of a sentence is something like the "real structure" of that sentence'. Clearly, linguists' notions of logical form, such as Chomsky's LF ('the level of linguistic representation at which all grammatical structure relevant to semantic interpretation is provided' – Hornstein 1995: 3), and the relevance-theoretic notion belong to the descriptive conception. These have in common a concern to specify the (underlying) structure of a sentence (or phrase) in such a way as to reflect its semantic properties, its meaning, as opposed to its surface syntactic structure, but they appear to diverge in a range of ways that have yet to be properly explored and assessed. For interesting discussion of some of the 'descriptively' conceived notions of logical form within current linguistics and philosophy, see Higginbotham (1993a), Neale (1994) and Larson and Segal (1995: 100–5).

27   Levinson (1988, 1989, 2000) seems to be of the view that if you do not assign something of a fully propositional nature (thereby admitting of truth conditions and the description of sense relations) to natural-language sentences, you simply cannot say anything of interest about linguistic semantics. In fact, although a full account of the conceptual and procedural encodings of natural-language words and sentences does not exist (yet), the programme for giving such an account is clear enough and relevance theorists have made many concrete proposals concerning the semantics of particular natural-language expressions. See, for example, Blakemore (1987, 1988, 1989b, 1990, 1997b), Blass (1990), Breheny (1999), Carston (1988/91, 1993, 1994a, 1994b/96a), Clark (1993a, 1993b), Groefsema (1995a, 1995b), Iten (1998, 2000), Papafragou (1998a, 1998b, 1998c), Powell (1999), Rouchota (1994a, 1994b, 1996), Žegarac (1991, 1993). Work in other frameworks also shows that giving an account of natural-language seman-

tics in terms of an intermediate (conceptually oriented) system of representations is very much a live option (see Katz 1972; Jackendoff 1983, 1990).

28   For the most part, I have encountered this propositional view in discussion and in some unpublished work, and can give only one reference to it in available written form: Chng (1999). NoeL Burton-Roberts has defended the position strongly on several occasions in discussion; I think he would stand by the second version I give in the text.

29   A very similar sort of argument would be endorsed by those direct reference theorists who, following Kaplan (1977/89a), make a distinction between the semantic character of indexicals (roughly their encoded linguistic meaning) and their semantic content, that is, their truth-conditional contribution in a particular context. On this view, although (i) and (ii) are universal truths of some sort, they are not necessary truths:

    (i)   If she is kind some female is kind.
    (ii) If that spy is clever then someone is a spy.

Although there is no entailment between the contents of the antecedent and the consequent in either of these cases, the appearance (illusion) of an entailment is explained in terms of the semantic character of the pronoun 'she' and of the complex demonstrative 'that spy'. The character of 'she' is such that on any proper use it will deliver as its content someone who is, in fact, female; the character of 'that spy' is such that on any proper use it will deliver as its content someone who is a spy. See Kaplan (1989b) for a discussion of such logical truths that are not necessary truths, and Braun (1994) for an application of the idea to complex demonstratives, such as 'that spy'.

30   There are other manifestations of the view that the meaning of any natural-language sentence (including indexical sentences) is a proposition. These are usually of a highly abstract sort, for instance, the 'diagonal proposition' of Stalnaker (1978), the 'external proposition' discussed by Recanati (1993: 289–91) and, perhaps, the 'created proposition' of Perry (1988). What each of these concepts is designed to capture is the context-invariant conditions which must be met by *any* utterance of a sentence for it to express a true proposition. For example, the diagonal proposition associated with the sentence S 'I am happy' is the proposition that there is an x such that x utters S and x is happy. As Recanati (1989a: 237) puts it, in a very useful discussion, 'the diagonal proposition globally indicates the conditions under which the utterance expresses a true proposition, but it does not tell us which of these conditions are contextual conditions, i.e. conditions which must be contextually satisfied for the sentence to express a definite proposition, and which are truth conditions proper, i.e. conditions which must be satisfied for the proposition expressed to be true'. In other words, no distinction is made between conceptual aspects of sentence meaning, which enter into the proposition expressed, and procedural constraints, that do not. This extraction of a very general proposition can obviously be done and may be useful for certain purposes; for instance, Stalnaker (1978) suggests that if for some reason an addressee cannot figure out what proposition has been expressed by a particular utterance, he can at least add the diagonal proposition to the common ground (or set of contextual assumptions). However, it is clearly not the sort of representation of linguistic meaning which can function as input to the pragmatic process of figuring out what proposition has been expressed, because it erases the distinction between two kinds of linguistic meaning, a distinction which plays an essential role in guiding those processes.

31   This is what he calls the **Connection Principle**: an essential property of *mental* features of brain states (as opposed to *non-mental* features, such as axon myelination, for instance) is that they are either conscious or potentially conscious (see Searle 1992:

155–61). From this follows his repudiation of an assumption held in current cognitive science: that we can have unconscious knowledge which is, in principle, inaccessible to consciousness (Searle 1992: 197–248), an assumption behind the Chomskyan account of language, for instance. Both Searle and, following him, Nagel (1993) maintain that neither language nor visual perception are strictly speaking psychological; they each simply involve some physical (hardware) mechanism that functions in certain constrained ways. Chomsky (1994: 197–201) presents compelling considerations against the Connection Principle, the mind–body dualism it entails and the alleged non-mental nature of language. I cannot pursue this debate here, but I believe it is possible to take on board the thesis of the Background, or something closely akin to Searle's conception of it, without automatically having to accept these further claims.

32   It is not perfectly clear to me whether Searle intends his 'Connection Principle' to apply to everything he is prepared to call mental or just to intentional states (and, of course, qualitative states such as pain). The mental and the intentional are not coextensive on his conception, since the Background is mental though not intentional (Searle 1991: 290). As I've pointed out, it does seem that at least some elements of the Background can become intentional states when, for some reason or other, something hitherto 'taken for granted' becomes apprehended or believed (see Searle 1992: 184–5) and so is presumably no longer part of the Background. It seems, then, that at least some aspects of the Background are accessible to consciousness. The concept of a 'manifest assumption' does as good a job as any of making sense of all of this.

33   In his early work on speech acts, Searle (1969) made a claim that follows from this principle: the study of the full range of speech acts people can perform with linguistic expressions in contexts can be confined to the study of explicitly performative sentences. Gazdar (1981) shows that this is false: even explicitly performative sentences do not always determine the speech acts they can be used to perform and it is not the case that for every speech act achieved pragmatically, there is a corresponding explicitly performative sentence.

Recanati (forthcoming a) provides a more sustained exploration of Searle's Principle of Expressibility, and its relation to his thesis of the Background, than I have given here; in particular, he argues against Searle's position that Background-dependence applies not only to the truth-conditional content of utterances but also to thoughts, beliefs and intentional states quite generally.

34   Andreas Kemmerling has pointed out to me that, although many people attribute this view to Frege, he did not hold it in quite this form. For him, Thoughts were ontologically prior to whatever may be considered their parts or constituents, so it is misleading to say that the *sense* of a sentence (i.e. a thought) is *determined* by the sense of its constituents. The level of unstructured thoughts is basic, and while, for their own epistemic purposes, humans impose a structure on thoughts (perhaps a function/argument structure), numerous different structurings are possible. According to Kemmerling (personal communication, 1999), Frege would have accepted the Compositionality Principle only in a version which contains relativizations to methods of decomposing thoughts (senses) and sentences: 'Let M be an acceptable method of decomposition of Thoughts-and-sentences-expressing-them, then the sense/reference of an M-decomposed expression is determined by the sense/reference of its M-constituents and the manner in which they are M-combined.' (Frege is most explicit on this in his (1892b); see especially p. 49 of the (1980) reprint. For useful discussion of Frege's view, see Janssen (1997a: 420).)

Like most linguists nowadays who refer to a Principle of Compositionality, my discussion in this section is concerned only with compositionality as a property of aspects of human psychology. The compositionality of linguistic meaning (logical form) is a function of the mental language faculty and the compositionality of propositional thought (or 'content', or a psychologized version of 'sense') is a property of mental representation. This makes for an important difference from Frege's Platonist conception: the only decomposition of sentences, or of thoughts, that is relevant is the one that human minds actually manifest.

35   The Compositionality Principle has a long history and a range of interpretations, varying in the strictness of the syntax–semantics relation required, and in the way in which component terms such as 'meaning' or 'semantic value' are defined. It can be viewed as an empirical claim about natural language, or as merely a methodological principle or evaluation criterion in the development of semantic theories. For discussion of these and other issues, see Welsh (1986), Janssen (1997a, 1997b) (the latter a short version of the former), Grandy (1990b), Partee (1995) and Woodfield (1999). For linguistic data which seem to weigh against the general truth of the principle, see Lahav (1989, 1993), Pelletier (1994) and, in what appears to be a conversion to the linguistic underdeterminacy view, Fodor (2001). For a position similar to the one I am proposing (that is, sentence-type meaning is compositional, but determination of the proposition expressed depends on non-compositional processes of pragmatic enrichment), see Powell (2000, forthcoming) and Blutner (1998, 2002); the latter also makes a strong case against the possibility of any principle of 'semantic/pragmatic' compositionality.

36   Some caution is necessary here, since we are able to think about our thoughts, or at least some of them, thanks to our metarepresentational capacity. For instance, I may think about a belief I once had, say, the belief that humans are basically good, that it is not true and reflect on how I have come to this conclusion. The form of this reflective thought is: 'It is not true that "humans are basically good",' that is, the mental representation of the original thought is itself represented; it is embedded in the representation which is my current thought. Furthermore, 'metarepresentational thoughts' may be incomplete in a way that is not possible for the simple thoughts I am confining myself to in this section. For instance, on the basis of overhearing someone's conversation I might form the thought/belief that there are no longer any serins in Britain, without having any idea what a serin is (is it an animal, a bird, an insect, an outdated occupation, a mode of dress, etc?). My thought is not the same as that expressed by the speaker, who knew what she was talking about; mine is incomplete, semi-propositional, and it too has a metarepresentational component, namely 'serin'. For my current concerns, I am ignoring the many interesting issues that arise in this realm of reflective (or representational) thought/belief. See Sperber (1982/85 and 1997a).

37   Levine (1988: 233) argues for the 'pointer to a percept' conception of mental demonstratives rather than the 'percept itself' conception: 'I have many percepts in play at any one time, yet I do not demonstratively pick out each object of which I have a percept. The act of focusing my attention on one object within my perceptual field and thinking of it "*this* is red", seems to involve a separate representation from the perceptual representation of the object itself. That is, there is the percept – present to mind, representing an object – and there is the act of pointing to it as a way of picking out the object it represents for selective attention.' I find this distinction persuasive and so adopt the 'pointer' symbol for the rest of the discussion.

38   What I'm adverting to here is sometimes called the dual-component view of thoughts: thoughts have a 'narrow', subjective, internal aspect and a 'wide', objective, external aspect, so may be individuated in two distinct ways. Just as two thoughts with the same narrow content may have distinct wide content (as with the tomato-directed thoughts described in the text), so two thoughts with different narrow contents (and so different causal roles in mental life) may have the same wide content (that is, the same truth con-

ditions). There are many contentious issues in this area, especially regarding the notion of narrow content; see, for instance, McGinn (1982), Fodor (1990), Recanati (1993, chapters 11 and 12) and Jacob (1997).

39   There are phenomena, which I have not explored here, that might undercut my conclusion to some extent. I mention three examples. Perry (1986: 145) says 'there is no reason that thoughts that employ representations in the language of thought should not have unarticulated constituents, just as statements that employ sentences of natural language do.' He makes a case for the existence of beliefs of the 'It is raining' sort, which exclusively concern the local weather conditions of the believer and so need not have any location constituent (even of an indexical sort). Sorenson (1991) argues that there is vagueness in Mentalese, that is, that some of its predicates and quantifiers have borderline cases (e.g. the conceptual equivalents of 'tall', 'lazy', 'messy', 'numerous', 'somewhat'), so that sentences, hence thoughts, in which they appear are not truth-evaluable. However, he claims that the sources of vagueness in the essentially private language of Mentalese are different from those in public natural languages used for communication. Giaquinto (1997) discusses cases of what he describes as 'informative but propositionless' thought; these are thoughts which apparently include a constituent whose content is indeterminate across a range of possibilities. One of his examples is the thought 'The Venus Fly Trap is not an animal', where there is a range of possible 'animal' concepts and the thinker doesn't seem to have any particular one in mind, so that the thought does not determine a unique proposition but rather a proposition schema. It is nonetheless an informative thought in the sense that from it can be inferred certain true propositions, e.g. a Venus Fly Trap is not a cat. This is an extremely interesting and plausible possibility, which may not, however, weaken the general point that, indexicality aside, Mentalese sentences do not underdetermine their truth-conditional content, are not context-sensitive. After all, the point about these schematic thoughts is that they simply do not have determinate truth-conditional content.

2

The Explicit/Implicit Distinction

'I just think that some people tell lies.'
'But I'm not a liar, Winnie,' protested Joan anxiously. 'I'm not, honestly.'
'Some people,' Winnie murmured, writing with her pine-needle.
'You're not fair, Winnie Todd,' quivered Joan, throwing down her Christmas trees. 'I know you mean me.'
'I didn't say so, did I? I just said – some people.'
'Well you looked at me.'
'Did I?'

(from 'Keel and Kool' by Janet Frame)

In the previous chapter I made the case for a strong essentialist linguistic underdeterminacy view. That is, 'what is said' (the proposition expressed) by an utterance is inevitably not fully determined by the meaning of the linguistic expression used to convey it. The other, more glaringly obvious, evidence of utterance meaning outstripping linguistic meaning is the widespread occurrence of implicatures, those propositional forms which are not constructed on the frame provided by linguistic meaning but are the result of inferential processes which take the pragmatically developed frame as a premise. In this chapter I shall consider ways in which the distinction between the proposition (explicitly) expressed by the speaker and the propositions she has implicated may be drawn. More broadly, I'll be looking at views on what can be called the explicit/implicit distinction in human verbal communication, most of which are currently held by someone in the field.

The work of Paul Grice is pivotal in any discussion of the explicit/implicit distinction, although he did not use this terminology; I will tend to see all the other theorists mentioned as endorsing, modifying or reacting against him. It is not, in fact, a binary distinction in everyone's view and it will become clear that, on the explicit side in particular, there are various other distinctions to be made. There will be some critical assessment in this chapter so that some positions can be removed from further consideration. The inconsistency of a view with the underdeterminacy thesis will be taken as grounds for finding it inadequate. In the following two chapters, I will discuss semantic/pragmatic analyses of several quite restricted areas of language data, including, at some length, 'and'-conjunctions and negation. In the light of those discussions and analyses, I will return, in the final chapter, to more theoretical issues concerning the semantics/pragmatics and explicit/implicit distinctions, including the nature of lexical meaning.

2.1 Semantics/Pragmatics Distinction

2.1.1 Truth-conditional semantics and formal pragmatics

The point of departure in a discussion of the explicit/implicit distinction in verbal communication is the semantics/pragmatics distinction. All the various ways of drawing the former will involve some relation to the latter. The relation has been held by some to be one of identity: linguistic meaning (semantics) gives you explicit content, and the residue of utterance meaning (pragmatically derived) is the implicit import (implicatures) of the utterance. Of course, this identity comes out in different ways depending on your characterization of the semantics/pragmatics distinction. As emphasized in the previous chapter (section 1.5), within the theoretical framework I am using, this is taken to be a distinction between decoded and inferred meaning. This seems like the right *type* of semantics/pragmatics distinction – a distinction between two sorts of cognitive process involved in the overall interpretation process – to interact with a distinction between ways in which assumptions are communicated through verbal utterances (that is, explicitly or implicitly). Looked at in this way, though, there is certainly not a neat correlation between the two. That possibility can be undermined from both directions: on the one hand, linguistic underdeterminacy, entailing extensive pragmatic input at the level of explicitly communicated assumptions, puts paid to a characterization of the explicit in purely semantic terms; on the other hand, some of the encoded content of an utterance makes itself felt in constraining the implicit import (implicatures) of the utterance rather than by contributing to the assumptions explicitly communicated. This latter point will be discussed more fully in section 2.3.7.

Work in pragmatics arising out of formal approaches to semantics has tended towards a view that can be summed up by Gazdar's (1979) formula: 'pragmatics = meaning minus truth conditions'.[1] The assumption behind this, of course, is that truth conditions are what a semantic theory must deal in. Although Larson and Segal (1995) do not present such a crude formula, it follows from their characterization of semantics that they too must hold a similar view of pragmatics. However, they locate their semantic work within a Chomskyan psychological competence view of language, which suggests that a complementary pragmatic theory will be similarly psychologically oriented. Gazdar's (and others', including Thomason and Montague) semantic theory is couched in terms of interpretation functions, whose values are sets, so it is an essentially mathematical rather than psychological theory. It follows that his pragmatic theory must be similarly formal and mathematical (as he himself explains – Gazdar 1979: 1–7). I will give just a brief indication of what this means in practice: sentences (rather than utterances) have a range of potential implicatures (and also presuppositions, but I leave them aside here); there is a set of rules for generating these 'im-plicatures', as they are labelled; (actual) implicatures are those im-plicatures that are left after a process of contextual cancellation has taken place; there is a set of cancellation rules, so, for instance, an im-plicature which is incompatible with either a proposition given in the context or an entailment is cancelled. Dinsmore (1982) discusses some of the pitfalls that this sort of account is prey to, one of which is the following: 'G's system is strikingly circular. It generates im-plicatures and pre-suppositions as features of sentences, then allows these to be cancelled in contexts. But the assignment of im-plicatures and pre-suppositions itself reflects generalisations about implicatures and presuppositions in actual use' (Dinsmore 1982: 47). Other considerations which make it clear that this approach cannot be carried over to a cognitive processing account are the formal pre-given notion of context it uses and the impossibility of extending the account to particularized implicatures (see discussion of the generalized/particularized distinction in section 2.2.3), which constitute the vast bulk of implicatures in communication.

For a formally oriented pragmatist such as Gazdar, it is not surprising that the explicit/implicit distinction, psychological and communicative as it is, is of no interest at all. The index of his book on pragmatics contains no entry for it, not even for the relatively simple and formalizable distinction drawn by Grice between saying and implicating. Whether one is in sympathy with the formal enterprise or not, it has to be appreciated as being all of a piece. Tensions begin to arise when aspects of the formal truth-conditional orientation and concerns of a communicative and cognitive processing sort are lumped together. I think that something of this sort is going on in Levinson (1988, 2000), where we find, on the one hand, the equation of sentence semantics with truth conditions and the idea that linguistic expressions carry potential implicatures along with them, coupled with, on the other hand, a concern for a workable saying/implicating distinction and recognition of the linguistic underdeterminacy thesis.

2.1.2 Semantic/pragmatic circles

Implicit in Levinson (1983) and explicit in Levinson (1988, 2000) is an equation of 'what is said' (the explicit) with sentence semantics and of 'what is implicated' (the implicit) with pragmatics. For instance, he writes: 'the "said" can be taken to be truth-conditional content, the proposition expressed, the output of the process of semantic interpretation; the proper domain of a theory of *linguistic meaning*. The "implicated" can be taken . . . to include all the processes of pragmatic inference; it is the proper domain of a theory of communication' (Levinson 2000: 186–7, my italics). This equation inevitably leads him to the view that some implicatures (the 'generalized' ones; see section 2.2.3 below) play a systematic role in the derivation of the truth-conditional content of the sentence/utterance (that is, its semantics). This is what Levinson calls the problem of pragmatic input to linguistic semantics. These implicatures are involved in the processes of disambiguation, indexical resolution, reference assignment, generality narrowing (enrichment) and completion of subsentential utterances, which are necessary in deriving the truth-conditional content of the sentence/utterance. Here are some of his examples and his explanations of them:

(1) a. He's an indiscriminate dog-lover; he likes some cats and dogs.
     b. He likes [[some cats] and dogs].
     c. He likes [some [cats and dogs]].

(2) a. He likes some-but-not-all cats.
     b. He likes some-but-not-all [cats and dogs].

The second sentence in (1a) is syntactically ambiguous, interpretable either as (1b) or (1c); in most contexts (1b) conversationally implicates (but does not entail) (2a), and (1c) implicates (but does not entail) (2b), but (2b) is incompatible with the content of the first sentence in (1a), which entails that he likes all dogs, so the correct structure is predicted to be the one in (1b). This is indeed the preferred interpretation of (1a). It seems, then, that these implicatures, arising as a result of an adaptation of Grice's first quantity maxim,[2] enjoining speakers to be as informative as required, are instrumental in the disambiguation process which is essential in arriving at 'what is said' by the utterance.

The next example involves indexical resolution:

(3) a. John came in and he sat down.
     b. John$_x$ came in and he$_x$ sat down.
     c. John$_x$ came in and he$_y$ sat down.
     d. John$_x$ came in and the man$_y$ sat down.

The preference for the coreferential interpretation in (3b) over the disjoint reference in (3c) is explained, apparently, by the generation of the implicature, ' "he" refers to "John" ', which is derived via a version of Grice's second maxim of quantity, enjoining speakers to say no more than they must. Here 'he' is the minimal (least informative) referring term possible (compare: 'the man', as in (3d), or a second occurrence of 'John') and its use licenses the hearer to infer the 'most obvious' referent; that is, John.[3]

He gives a further range of cases, based on examples from Cohen (1971) and Wilson (1975: 151), which he labels 'intrusive constructions' because pragmatic inference 'intrudes' into their semantics; that is, they have the property that 'the truth conditions of the whole depend in part on the implicatures of the parts' (Levinson 2000: 198). They include comparatives, conditionals and other logical connective constructions:

(4) a. Driving home and drinking several beers is better than drinking several beers and driving home.
     b. If each side in the soccer game got three goals, then the game was a draw.
     c. She either got married and had a child, or had a child and got married; I don't know which.

      d.   Because the police have recovered some of the gold, they will no doubt recover the lot.

(5)   a.   Driving home and *then* drinking several beers is better than drinking several beers and *then* driving home.

      b.   If each side in the soccer game got *exactly* three goals, then the game was a draw.

      c.   She either got married and *then* had a child, or had a child and *then* got married; I don't know which.

      d.   Because the police have recovered some *but not all* of the gold, they will no doubt recover the lot.

The idea is that the truth-conditional content of each of the examples in (4) involves a pragmatic contribution (a narrowing or enrichment), which is highlighted in the corresponding representations in (5). Each of these pragmatic contributions is an implicature, dependent on one or other of Levinson's inferential heuristics which he claims follow from Grice's quantity and manner maxims.[4] This type of example, in which a contentious case (e.g. an 'and'-conjunction, or a scalar term like 'some' or 'three') is embedded in the scope of an operator is of considerable interest and will be discussed again later in the chapter as providing a useful test for distinguishing pragmatic contributions to truth conditions from implicatures proper (see section 2.6.3).

What examples (1), (3) and (4) demonstrate is that disambiguation, indexical resolution and enrichment are pragmatic processes that contribute to the recovery of the proposition expressed by an utterance. Relevance theorists need no convincing on this score, since this involvement of pragmatics is a necessary consequence of linguistic underdeterminacy, and has been recognized and emphasized since the very beginnings of the theory (see Wilson and Sperber 1981). In fact, I will take the stronger position that the pragmatically derived components highlighted in (5) may contribute, not only to the proposition expressed by utterances of these complex constructions (conditionals, etc.), but also to the proposition expressed by utterances of the simpler component constructions, such as the following:

(6)   a.   He drank several beers and drove home.

      b.   Both sides in the soccer game got three goals.

What I want to take issue with is Levinson's insistence that (a) these are cases of implicature rather than simply pragmatic inferences which contribute to the proposition expressed, and that (b) because this demonstrates an interdependence between 'what is said' and pragmatic inferences (he would say 'implicatures'), so, correlatively, there is an issue of interdependence between linguistic semantics and pragmatics (jeopardizing semantic autonomy). I concentrate on the second of these in this section since the implicature issue needs the scene-setting given in later sections. Here is what he says on the interdependence issue:

> Grice's account makes implicature dependent on a prior determination of 'the said'. The said in turn depends on implicature: it depends on disambiguation, reference fixing, . . . [etc.]. But each of these processes, which are prerequisites to determining the propo-

sition expressed, themselves depend crucially on implicatures. Thus what is said seems
both to determine and to be determined by implicature. Let us call this 'Grice's circle'
... the theory of linguistic meaning is dependent on, not independent of, the theory of
communication.   (Levinson 1988: 17–18; 2000: 186–7)

Grice did not consider disambiguation or reference assignment to be governed by
the conversational maxims and he did not recognize the enrichment facts, so that,
on his account, 'what is said' is determined by conventional linguistic meaning and
a minor appeal to contextual best fit (to handle disambiguation and reference), and
'what is implicated' is determined by application of the maxims to the saying of
what is said. Levinson is certainly right that this is not workable: the gap between
encoded linguistic meaning and the proposition expressed by an utterance is far
greater than Grice envisaged and whatever pragmatic principles are responsible for
the derivation of implicatures are also involved in amplifying the encoded linguistic meaning into the proposition expressed. What does not follow, however, is that
this 'Gricean circle' entails an inevitable circularity or interdependency between an
account of linguistic meaning and an account of the pragmatic inferences involved
in utterance understanding.

The problem here, I think, stems from the ongoing assumption (which follows
from the Gazdarian formula) that sentence semantics is to be equated with truth-
conditional content (the proposition expressed by an utterance of the sentence).
Taken literally, it is difficult to see how anyone could accept it, since patently the
specificity of the truth-conditional content of an *utterance*, given the assignment of
particular contextual values to indexicals, takes it beyond anything one would want
as part of *sentence* semantics (encoded meaning). As Stalnaker (1980) points out,
this obvious fact need not get in the way of formulating a compositional semantic
theory which simply treats certain elements of content as unexplained givens (see
note 1 of this chapter). The implication of Stalnaker's view is that it is possible to
pursue a truth-conditional approach to natural language which is compatible with
both the underdeterminacy thesis and with semantic autonomy; this certainly seems
to be what is aimed at by the conditional T-sentence approach of Burge and
Higginbotham, discussed in the previous chapter. (For some doubts about its feasibility, see Recanati, forthcoming a, and Carston, 2000b.) The idea within relevance
theory is rather different in that two kinds of semantics are distinguished,
linguistic and truth-conditional. Linguistic semantics is concerned with the context-
invariant meaning encoded in the linguistic system and naturally takes its place
within a wider theory of utterance meaning. The domain of truth-conditional
semantics, on the other hand, is propositional forms, whether of utterances or
unspoken thoughts. This second conception of semantics is very much in line with
Stalnaker's (1970) position that formal truth-conditional semantics is the study of
propositions, and so is independent of linguistics: 'the subject has no essential connection with language at all, natural or artificial' Stalnaker (1970: 274). The first
kind of semantics (concerned with encoded linguistic meaning) is autonomous with
respect to pragmatics; it provides input to pragmatic processes and the two together
make up propositional forms, which constitute the domain of truth-conditional
semantics.

Levinson's view that this position is one of effectively giving up on semantics ('semantic retreat') was discussed (and, I hope, rebutted) in the previous chapter. In fact, when we look at the 'bite the bullet' approach that he finds most promising, it seems to bear remarkable similarity to this relevance-theoretic position. This is what he says with regard to the theories he favours, which are Discourse Representation Theory (see Kamp 1981; Kamp and Reyle 1993) and File Change Semantics (see Heim 1983):

> To adopt a metaphor, in these proposals there is a common slate, a level of proposi-
> tional representation, upon which both *semantics* and pragmatics can write – the con-
> tributions may be distinguished, let's suppose, by the colour of the ink: *semantics* in
> blue, pragmatics in red! *Semantics* and pragmatics remain modular 'pens' as it were:
> they are separate devices making distinctively different contributions to a common level
> of representation. The slate thus represents the *semantic* and pragmatic content of accu-
> mulated utterances, and it is this representation as a whole that is assigned a model-
> theoretic interpretation.   (Levinson 1988: 22; 2000: 193, my italics)

The blue ink 'semantics' here is not truth-conditional semantics but something much more like the relevance-theoretic notion of linguistic semantics as decoded meaning: it is subpropositional (hence the need for the red contributions to the common level of propositional representation) and, crucially, it is representational; that is, it involves translation from one symbolic system (phonological/syntactic) into another (logico-conceptual), and it is the latter which, having been appropriately filled in by the pragmatic pen, is given a 'real' semantics ('a model-theoretic interpretation'). So it's all here: the two kinds of semantics and the autonomy of the first kind (linguistic semantics) from pragmatics.

The lesson to take from the 'pragmatic intrusion' facts is clear enough: we should not identify the proposition expressed ('what is said') and linguistic semantics. Once these have been prised apart, it can be seen that Levinson's allegations of circularity separate into two distinct charges: semantic–pragmatic circularity and saying–implicating circularity. I hope the comments in the previous paragraphs have seen off the supposed problem of the interdependency of semantics and pragmatics. But what about the alleged saying/implicating circle? A circular relationship between these does seem to be inescapable once the extensive role of pragmatics in determining truth-conditional content is accepted (it was not recognized by Grice) and put together with the standard Gricean assumptions that (a) any material derived via conversational principles constitutes an implicature, and (b) implicatures arise from application of the maxims to 'the saying of what is said' and so require the prior determination of what is said. Indeed, it seems to be an unworkable circularity since what is said cannot be fully determined without implicatures and implicatures can only be determined on the basis of what is said. The point is that the Gricean assumptions are not compatible with there being pragmatic (maxim-driven) input to what is said, and as the truth of the latter seems indisputable (anyway, it is not disputed by Levinson or relevance theorists), it is the Gricean assumptions that must be revised.

Levinson's approach is to maintain assumption (a) and to effect a minimal modification to (b). This involves a system of default inference rules attached to particular lexical items and constructions (a picture with close affinity to Gazdar's account of 'im-plicatures'), which are implemented in the process of deriving 'what is said' and either maintained as part of what is said (truth-conditional content) or cancelled if incompatible with encoded material, entailments or contextual assumptions. This makes it possible to preserve the essence of assumption (b) since only a very circumscribed and distinct type of pragmatic inference contributes to what is said. However, it effects a huge change to the way in which pragmatics is conceived, involving a split into two totally distinct subtheories, the one accounting for default inferences and labelled GCI (generalized conversational implicature) theory (see note 4 of this chapter), the other accounting for the derivation of more context-dependent implicatures. The two systems run their own distinct modes of inference, in accordance with their proprietary pragmatic principles; the first is a component of an overall theory of grammar, while the second is simply part of general reasoning. The relevance-theoretic approach, on the other hand, drops the two Gricean assumptions and maintains a unitary account of pragmatic inference, constrained by the same communicative principles(s) whether the inference effects a contribution to the proposition expressed (the truth-conditional content of the utterance) or is a distinct implicated assumption. A range of 'local' pragmatic processes apply during the on-line derivation of the proposition expressed, but these do not involve a special set of default inference rules. These issues and the differences between the two approaches are taken up again briefly in section 2.3.4, by which time more of the background story will be in place.

I'll move on now to look at the views of the philosopher at the centre of all this, whose saying/implicating distinction was developed in the context of philosophical concerns rather different from those that motivate a cognitive theory of utterance interpretation.

2.2 Grice: Saying/Implicating

2.2.1 Odd statements but true

[T]he precept that one should be careful not to confuse meaning and use is perhaps on the way toward being as handy a philosophical vade-mecum as once was the precept that one should be careful to identify them.   (Grice 1967/89b: 4)

In the lecture from which this quote is taken, the first in the set of William James lectures collectively entitled 'Logic and Conversation', Grice's primary concern is to block certain applications of a pattern of linguistic argument employed by some ordinary-language philosophers against particular philosophical positions and questions. The analyses under attack from this group, whom Grice calls A-philosophers, tend to be of the constitutive philosophical kind, answering questions of the sort 'what is it to ____?'; for instance, 'what is it to perceive a physical object?' and 'what is it to know that P?' One of these was Grice's own bid to re-establish the causal theory of the perception of material objects, which required as an essential part what he called 'sense-datum' statements of the form: 'x looks (feels, sounds, etc.) G to me' (Grice 1961/89b). The objection, apparently raised by followers of Wittgenstein, was that the making of such statements in many of the most ordinary cases of object perception was incorrect. For instance, it is not legitimate to say 'it looks red to me' when referring to a patently red British pillar-box a few feet away. These statements can only be correctly made in circumstances in which either it is false that the x in question has the property G or there is some doubt about whether x is G. If this objection is warranted then the causal analysis of perception is threatened.

Here is one more example of this kind of linguistic objection. In advancing certain theses and proofs, G. E. Moore made a number of assertions involving the concepts 'know' and 'certain'; for instance, 'I know this is a hand' (indicating one of his hands), 'I am certain that I am awake at this moment'. Again, the idea was that the theses, in the establishing of which these statements were made, are undermined by misuses of the expressions 'I know' and 'I am certain'. Malcolm's (1949) objection is that it is incorrect to use these expressions unless there is some question at issue, some doubt about whether or not the state of affairs described in the complement clause obtains. Since there is absolutely no doubt in these cases, Moore's use of the expressions is illegitimate.

Much hangs on what is meant by an incorrect or illegitimate use here; is it the case that the statements made are false, or that they are merely inappropriate, or is it that no statement is made at all? It is not clear that the A-philosophical objectors made the sort of underlying distinctions between sources of meaning that are necessary for these questions to be answerable, since they were generally of the persuasion that once you had given an account of the ways in which an expression was properly used you had said all there was to say about its meaning. Grice believed otherwise, and insisted in this lecture on making a distinction between the truth or falsity of a statement, on the one hand, and its aptness or oddity, on the other. Moore's statements are true, however bizarre and pointless they may seem from the point of view of ordinary conversation, and so also are the sense-datum statements.[5]

As the opening quote indicates, Grice is keen to distinguish meaning from use, but there are two, minimally though importantly distinct, ways of interpreting this. The idea, of course, is to distinguish between the sense of the crucial word or phrase and the conditions under which it is appropriately used. Because the focus is on particular lexical items: 'know', 'try', 'looks', 'voluntary' and the natural-language counterparts of the logical connectives, it seems reasonable to assume that the distinction at issue is that between semantics and pragmatics. And so it is, but it is even more centrally concerned with the distinction between what is said and what is implicated by the speaker of the sentence containing the particular word or phrase. In the end the question that concerns Grice (I think) is: what statement(s) can the philosopher who has uttered that sentence, as part of his thesis or proof or exposition of a problem, be held to be making? What part of the meaning that we find ourselves taking from the philosophical utterance pertains to its truth or falsity? What is it that the philosopher has said as opposed to merely implicated? The distinction is between 'what is stated' and 'what is conversationally implicated' or, as it is given in the second lecture, 'the said' versus 'the implicated'.[6]

It is true that this way of thinking about the points in this lecture ('Prolegom-ena') requires a reading of it on which it is more closely tied to the second lecture ('Logic and conversation') than is usual, at least in discussions of Grice within linguistically based pragmatics, where usually little, if any, overt tie-up is made. This is probably because the second lecture has provided the basic precepts for a general theory of utterance understanding, so has been hugely influential in prag-matic work within the fields of linguistics and communication studies, while the first lecture is more apparently exclusively philosophical. However, Grice is clear, at the end of the first lecture, that he intends the system of conversational princi-ples, discussed in the second, to provide the tools for explaining the 'incorrectness' of use noted by the A-philosophers, thereby separating it off from the more funda-mental matter of the truth/falsity of the criticized utterances:

> inappropriateness connected with the nonfulfilment of such speaker-relative conditions is best explained by reference to certain general principles of discourse or rational behaviour. It is my view that most of the A-philosophical theses which I have been con-sidering are best countered by an appeal to such general principles; but it has not been so far my objective to establish this contention . . . it will be my hope that their utility for this . . . purpose might emerge as a byproduct of their philosophical utility in other directions.   (Grice 1967: 20–1)

Let's take an example from the first lecture and see how Grice's principles of con-versational use, given in the second, account for the inappropriateness of a state-ment while leaving untouched its truth (or falsity):

(7)   a.   It looks red to me.
      b.   It isn't in fact red.
      c.   It looks red to me and it is in fact red.

In many contexts an utterance of (7a) would communicate (7b). This is not because it is part of the statement made (what is said) by (7a), as the cancellation of it in (7c) shows; (7c) is not a contradiction as it would be if (7b) were part of what is said (that is, if it pertained to the truth of the utterance). The reason (7b) is often communicated by (7a) is that it is frequently only relevantly informative to utter (7a) when the speaker has reason to believe that the more informative 'it is red' is not true. The relevance and/or informativeness of statements is quite distinct from their truth, and in the case where the stronger statement is known to be true it follows that the weaker one must also be. In other words, the proposition in (7b), when conveyed by (7a), is conversationally implicated.

The Moore cases work in a similar way; Moore wanted some examples of obvious truisms as a preliminary stage of a bigger project (of establishing his 'proof of an external world'). What could be more obviously true than 'this is a hand' and 'this is another hand', said by a speaker holding up first one of his hands and then the other. Of course, in the vast bulk of ordinary conversational exchanges such utterances would be quite odd, precisely because they don't comply with standard expectations of relevance and informativeness. In relevance-theoretic terms, they do not interact fruitfully with contextual assumptions to give the hearer contextual effects. In Gricean terms, they would tend to carry the conversational implicature that there is some doubt around regarding their truth, an implicature which is clearly false. Using Searle's concept, we can say that the propositions they express generally belong in the Background, so when they are brought into the foreground, through an utterance, they carry implications that something unusual is going on.

In fact, the concept of 'what is said', developed in the second lecture, is only minimally distinct in what it picks out from the concept of the conventional (encoded) truth-conditional content; the only points of adjustment required are displayed transparently by linguistic constituents in the sentence employed: ambiguous forms and referential indeterminacies. And in the fifth lecture, where a more systematic (though clearly not intended to be definitive) account of 'saying' is given, this difference is glossed over entirely; 'what is said' is characterized as that aspect of the speaker's meaning (in Grice's special reflexively-intentional sense of 'meaning') which coincides with the meaning of the sentence employed.[7] Conventional implicature should be mentioned here, since it falls on opposite sides of the two divides (it is semantic and it is implicated). However, setting it aside for the moment (as Grice seems to have done when giving this analysis), the two distinctions – semantics/pragmatics and saying/implicating (conversationally) – seem to be essentially coextensive but operating at different levels. They are not so much different dividings up of the phenomena of utterance meaning as different ways of construing one and the same carve-up. The distinction between conventional truth-conditional content (semantics) and content which arises from conditions of communicative use (pragmatics) is a classification of types of meaning; the distinction between saying and implicating concerns two different sorts of things a speaker may *do* in producing an utterance (including a philosopher presenting a thesis), two different ways of communicating.[8]

Linguistic underdeterminacy is not recognized by Grice, and would not serve his purpose of countering the A-philosophical views. For this reason, some feel that Grice's strategy misfires, for instance Travis (1991). I will discuss this shortly (see section 2.4.1 below); for the moment, what I hope to have established is that one of the basic motivations (perhaps *the* fundamental one) for Grice's pragmatic system is this one of disposing of certain crucial applications of the 'illegitimate use' charge made by some ordinary-language philosophers.

A comment made by Grice in later years, when looking back over his work, makes it clear that he intended the meaning/use distinction in the first lecture to mesh more or less exactly with the saying/implicating distinction in the second one, or, at the very least, that the meaning arising from conditions of use is to be kept distinct from what is said: 'the idea of Conversational Implicature, which emphasized the radical importance of distinguishing (to speak loosely) what *our words* say or imply from what *we* in uttering them imply; a distinction seemingly denied by Wittgenstein, and all too frequently by Austin' (Grice 1986: 59). Conversational implicature was seen as an important and 'useful philosophical tool' by Grice and other philosophers in the 1970s (for instance, Walker 1975). Its use in linguistic pragmatics and, even more so, its treatment as a level of representation in an account of utterance processing were later developments. It is possible that its character has altered somewhat in these different hands, a point I'll try to bear in mind when making comparisons between Grice's philosophical pragmatics and the cognitive processing pragmatics developed within relevance theory.

2.2.2   Contextual contributions to 'what is said'

The small gap between the conventional linguistic meaning that contributes to truth-conditional content and the complete truth-conditional content or 'what is said', is, on Grice's conception (at least in the second lecture), bridged by reference assignment and by sense selection in the case of ambiguous words or structures. In a brief discussion of an utterance of 'He is in the grip of a vice', he says: 'for a full identification of what the speaker has said, one would need to know (a) the identity of x [some particular male person or animal], (b) the time of utterance, and (c) the meaning, on the particular occasion of utterance, of the [ambiguous] phrase *in the grip of a vice*' (Grice 1967/75/89b: 25). How, then, in his view, are these non-conventional but essential elements of what is said identified by the addressee of the utterance?

It seems that for Grice the correlation of 'conversational' maxims with 'conversational' implicatures was total. He did not envisage any role for conversational maxims in discerning 'what is said'; indeed, this was the whole point, since the statement made or the proposition expressed, the minimal truth-conditional content of the utterance, was to be distinguished from those aspects of utterance meaning that were a function of such considerations as its appropriateness, informativeness, relevance in a particular context (considerations that are irrelevant to its truth-evaluation). It follows then that the context-sensitive matters of reference assignment and choice of a sense in the case of ambiguity were not seen as guided by conversational maxims. Neale (1992: 530) casts some doubt on this, finding in a passage from an early paper by Grice an indication that the Cooperative Principle and conversational maxims (especially the maxim of relation) do play a role in the resolution of ambiguities and referential indeterminacies:

> [I]n cases where there is doubt, say, about which of two or more things an utterer intends to convey, we tend to refer to the context (linguistic or otherwise) of the utterance and ask which of the alternatives would be relevant to other things he is saying and doing, or which intention in a particular situation would fit in with some purpose he obviously has (e.g. a man who calls for a 'pump' at a fire would not want a bicycle pump). Nonlinguistic parallels are obvious: context is a criterion in settling the question of why a man who has just put a cigarette in his mouth has put his hand in his pocket; relevance to an obvious end is a criterion in settling why a man is running away from a bull.   (Grice 1957/89b: 222)

This is a nice piece of textual excavation, but it is far from obvious that what Grice intended here bears any close relation to whatever he intended by his later maxim of relation, 'Be relevant'. The criterion here, as in the discussion of disambiguation and reference resolution in the second of the William James lectures (Grice

1967/75/89b: 25), seems to be the rather vague one of best contextual fit. If this is
an early precursor of the conversational maxim of relevance, it is very odd that there
is no mention of the role of this maxim in these resolutions at the level of 'what is
said' in the crucial 1967 lecture. This is the lecture in which there is a discussion of
what is involved in grasping what is said by an utterance of 'He is in the grip of a
vice', and in which the conversational maxims are set out and an account is given
of the sort of work they do; they are presented as solely involved in the derivation
of conversational implicatures.

As I remarked in the previous chapter, there is an interesting tie-up here with
truth-conditional semanticists, who obviously see linguistic ambiguities and referential indeterminacies as lying within their purview (you can't say anything about
the truth conditions of a sentence/utterance without attending to these in some way
or other). Conversational implicature, on the other hand, can be completely ignored,
since it lies outside truth conditions and is entirely a matter of the pragmatics of
use. In the recent quite cognitively oriented truth-conditional approach of Segal
(1994) and Larson and Segal (1995), the following divisions among performance
systems are made: 'The cognitive systems will include at least (a) a parser (b) a
system that identifies the referents of indexicals and assigns them to the relevant
parts of the sentence (c) a pragmatics system' (Segal 1994: 112, footnote 3). Note
the distinction between (b) and (c), which parallels Grice's distinction between the
contextual identification of referents and intended senses of ambiguous words, on
the one hand, and the work of the conversational maxims on the other. It seems
that this is quite a widespread view on accounts which are not concerned with the
actual processes involved in utterance understanding.[9]

Some other philosophers, however, made the point early on that the maxims, or
at least the Cooperative Principle, must be involved in the recovery of these contextual elements of 'what is said'; for instance:

> Not everything that is M-intentionally conveyed with the help of the Co-operative Prin-
> ciple is to be accounted a conversational implicature. For one thing, in ordinary cases
> of ambiguity we rely on that principle to determine which sense is intended; if I say
> 'The bank is mossy' I can usually rely on the accepted purpose of the talk-exchange to
> disambiguate my remark. . . . The Co-operative Principle often helps to determine to
> what item a speaker is referring when he uses a proper name or a definite description,
> . . . It is the Co-operative Principle which enables the speaker to convey that the Tom
> he is talking about is the Tom we have both left, and that by 'the candle on the dresser'
> he means the one we can both see and not some other candle on a dresser in
> Timbuctoo.   (Walker 1975: 156–7)

Similarly, Katz (1972: 449) discusses a case of reference assignment involving the
first maxim of quantity and concludes 'Since identification of the referent . . . can
depend on maxims . . . and on the pattern of argument for implicatures, determining what is said depends on the principles for working out what is implicated.' While
Stalnaker's early work suggested, along with that of most formally oriented semanticists, that context disambiguates on its own, more recently he says 'the Gricean
principles and maxims clearly play a role in resolving ambiguity and fixing contextual parameters as well as in generating conversational implicatures' (Stalnaker
1989: 9).

From a more linguistically and psychologically oriented perspective, Wilson and Sperber (1981: 156–9) make the same point: 'hearers invariably ascribe sense and reference to utterances (within the limits allowed by the grammar) in such a way as to preserve their assumption that the conversational maxims have been observed'. And in this same paper they give their first statement of the wider role they see for pragmatic principles in determining the proposition expressed by the utterance.

As mentioned in the previous section, other linguistically based approaches to pragmatics, such as Levinson (1988, 2000), have seen this point too, but apparently take this to indicate that these context-sensitive features of utterance understanding must therefore be treated as involving implicatures. Walker (1975) took this as so obviously not the case that it did not need discussion: 'one would not say that the intended sense was conversationally implicated' and, in the case of referent determination, 'the speaker does not conversationally implicate what item it is' (1975: 157). It is all the more obvious within a cognitive account of communication and interpretation, among whose concerns is the articulation of the thought-level representations which are the end product of the understanding process, some of which are added to the interpreter's store of assumptions. If all pragmatically derived elements are treated as implicatures we are left with no candidate for what is said, or the explicit utterance content, other than the logical form of the linguistic expression used, which is standardly subpropositional. But we do not communicate logical forms (though we do communicate *via* logical forms), and we do not retain logical forms in memory; we communicate and remember assumptions or thoughts or opinions, which are fully propositional. So a distinction has to be made between pragmatic inference that contributes to the recovery of the explicitly communicated content and pragmatic inference that eventuates in implicated assumptions.

Sperber and Wilson (1986a/95b) rightly emphasize the importance of Grice's work in initiating an inferential approach (as opposed to the all-out code model) to utterance interpretation. But the difference between the Gricean view and the one discussed in the previous section, on which the explicit/implicit and semantic/pragmatic are equated, is negligible. For Grice, the maxim-driven inferential work which arose from the communicative use of expressions was confined to conversational (and other non-conventional) implicatures (the implicit). When it came to what is explicitly communicated, Grice was pretty much of a code theorist.

2.2.3   Implicature: conventional and conversational

While 'what is said' is largely determined by conventional (encoded) meaning, it is not the case that all encoded meaning goes into determining 'what is said'. I am alluding here to the well-known, though brief, discussions by Grice of what he termed conventional implicatures, cases of encoded meaning which do not contribute to the statement made by the utterance, its truth-conditional content. The cases he mentioned are the connectives 'moreover', 'but' and 'therefore' (at least on its parenthetical use) (Grice 1967/68/89b: 120–2), and in his last work, 'on the other hand' and 'so' (Grice 1989a: 361–2). While the 'what is said' of an utterance is the propositional component of the basic (or ground-level) speech acts of the utterance, such as asserting, telling, and asking, these implicature-generating elements of conventional meaning comment on, or relate one to another, the ground-level speech acts. That is, they indicate less central (higher-order) speech acts, such as contrasting, adding, or explaining, which are dependent on the more basic speech acts:

(8) a.   Ben is nice but he drives a Ford Capri.
     b.   Ben is nice.
     c.   Ben drives a Ford Capri.
     d.   There is a contrast between (b) and (c).

The idea is that an utterance of (8a) would make the two ground-level statements, given in (b) and (c), and also the higher-level comment on those statements given in (d). As Grice puts it (about another example): 'The truth or falsity of his words is determined by the relation of his ground-floor speech acts to the world; consequently, while a certain kind of misperformance of the higher-order speech act may constitute a semantic offence, it will not touch the truth-value . . . of the speaker's words' (Grice 1989a: 362).

In short, the conventional or semantic content of an utterance comes in two types, the descriptive content, which affects the truth-value, on the one hand, and the merely indicative (as in 'indicating'), which generates implicatures, on the other. The account of encoded semantic content within relevance theory also makes a distinction between two types of meaning: the conceptual and the procedural, as briefly mentioned in the previous chapter. The conventional implicature cases discussed here fall on the procedural side. However, this distinction is rather different in flavour, reflecting the representational and inferential (computational) picture of cognition within which the theory is developed; it is discussed in section 2.3.7.[10]

Moving to the pragmatic side of Grice's view of utterance meaning involves a move to conversational implicature. The crucial feature of these aspects of speaker meaning is that they are dependent on the assumption that the conversational maxims, or at least the Cooperative Principle (CP), are being observed. Grice was adamant that they be calculable/workable out: 'for even if it can be intuitively grasped, unless the intuition is replaceable by an argument, the implicature (if present at all) will not count as a conversational implicature; it will be a conventional implicature' (Grice 1967/75/89b: 31). He gave a rough working-out schema which was to serve as a model of the inferential process, taking as premises what is said, the maxims (including the CP) and contextually available information. Some (for instance, Grandy 1989: 519) have taken this to be a requirement not on the hearer, for whom intuitive grasp is sufficient, but merely on the theorist, who must be able to provide a 'rational reconstruction' of the derivational process. Others are of the view that Grice's requirement was the stronger one, that an account must be given of how the hearer arrived at (worked out) the implicature (Neale 1992: 527; Recanati 1993: 245). On the relevance-theoretic view, it is assumed that a central aim of the account of utterance interpretation is to explicate the non-demonstrative inference process carried out by the hearer's cognitive system in arriving at an interpretation, which, naturally, includes conversational implicatures.

Problems with Grice's working-out schema and with other features of his account of conversational implicature, in particular the concept of maxim flouting allegedly involved in the derivation of a range of cases, have been pointed out.[11] Of the many issues that could be pursued here I limit myself to two, which will bear on the analyses pursued in the next chapters: (a) the absolute nature of the distinction between 'what is said' and 'what is implicated', and (b) the lack of theoretical import in the distinction between generalized and particularized conversational implicatures.

It is clear that Grice intended the distinction between 'saying' and 'implicating' to be sharp. As we saw with the philosophical problem cases, 'This looks red to me' and 'I know this is a hand', the statement made by the utterance may be true while its conversational implicature is false. The opposite situation arises in another case discussed by Grice, that of the referential use of incorrect definite descriptions:

(9) Jones's butler mixed up the hats and coats.

Grice (1969a: 142), says: 'if the speaker has used [referentially] a descriptive phrase (i.e. "Jones's butler") which in fact has no application, then what the speaker has *said* will, strictly speaking, be false . . . but what he *meant* may be true (e.g. that a particular individual [who is in fact Jones's gardener] mixed up the hats and coats)'. On this account of the referential use of descriptions, the singular proposition, according to which the property of mixing up the hats and coats is predicated of the particular individual the speaker has in mind, is implicated, while the proposition expressed (what is said) is a general Russellian proposition. So in the case of a mistaken description, what is implicated may be true while what is said is false.

The examples in section 2.1.2 of so-called 'pragmatic intrusion' into the proposition expressed are not to be construed as cases of implicature. Although Grice did not recognize the facts about linguistic underdeterminacy which give rise to these pragmatic contributions to the explicit level, he did confront a similar problem in his attempt to give conditionals a semantic analysis which maintained their truth-functionality. The details of the account are not to the point here, but his reaction to the apparent involvement of implicature in the truth-conditional content of a conditional on this analysis is worth noting. He saw it as a definitive problem for his analysis: 'I am afraid I do not yet see what defense (if any) can be put up against this objection' (Grice 1967/89b: 83). (However, he does seem to have finally capitulated, in his Retrospective Epilogue, and allowed for implicatures to fall in the scope of certain operators; I discuss this in section 2.6.3.) I shall assume throughout that a clear distinction is to be maintained (though I will reassess its significance in later chapters): utterances communicate a bundle of propositions; some are explicitly communicated and some are implicatures. If it seems that a conversational implicature is contributing to the truth conditions of an utterance, I will take this as a reason to consider the pragmatically inferred material to be an aspect of the proposition expressed and not an implicature at all.

Conversational implicatures were described under two headings by Grice: generalized and particularized. Particularized implicatures are those 'in which an implicature is carried by saying that *p* on a particular occasion in virtue of special features of the context, cases in which there is no room for the idea that an implicature of this sort is normally carried by saying that *p*' (Grice 1967/75/89b: 37). One example should suffice:

(10)   Bill goes up to Scotland every weekend.

In different specific contexts this could implicate 'Bill's mother is ill', 'Bill has a girl-friend in Scotland', 'Bill gets as far away from London as he can when he can', 'Bill still hasn't got over his obsession with the Loch Ness monster', etc.

Generalized implicatures, on the other hand, are characterized as follows: 'the use of a certain form of words in an utterance would normally (in the absence of special circumstances) carry such-and-such an implicature or type of implicature' (Grice 1967/75/89b: 37). The only examples Grice gives at this point are the following, where an utterance of the sentence in (a) would normally (in the absence of any particular defeating features of context) implicate the proposition in (b); (11b) supposedly arises due to an apparent violation of the first maxim of quantity at the level of what is said; Grice doesn't say which maxim is involved in the case of (12) but others (Horn 1984b; Levinson 1987a) have taken it to be the second maxim of quantity or relevance.

(11)   a.   X is meeting a woman this evening.
       b.   The woman X is meeting is not his wife, mother, or sister.

(12)   a.   I broke a finger yesterday.
       b.   The finger was my own.

In a later paper, Grice returned to the particularized/generalized distinction and said of generalized implicatures: 'These are the ones that seem to me to be more controversial and at the same time more valuable for philosophical purposes' (1981: 185). He gives the example in (13a) as an illustration, where it follows from the manner maxim of orderliness (as it applies to narratives, at least) that the actions described took place in a certain sequential order, giving the implicature in (13b):

(13)   a.   He took off his trousers and he got into bed.
       b.   He took off his trousers before he got into bed.

The rest of that paper is devoted to using this philosophical tool to defend a Russellian analysis of definite descriptions, according to which (14a) is true (because there is no king of France), against a presuppositional analysis which finds this sentence truth-valueless (this is discussed a little more in chapter 4). Omitting details and motivation here, the idea is that an utterance of the sentence in (14a) gives rise to the generalized implicature in (14b); its cancellability, shown in (14c), is taken as evidence that it is an implicature and an account of its derivation is given, employing a manner maxim of 'conversational tailoring'.

(14)   a.   The king of France is not bald.
       b.   There is a king of France.
       c.   The king of France is not bald because there is no king of France.

Many of the examples that bothered the A-philosophers would also, I take it, be explained in terms of generalized implicature: 'It looks red to me' would quite generally implicate that there is some doubt about its redness, etc.

So it seems that Grice distinguished this class of conversational implicatures because they are the ones that served his purpose in defeating the A-philosophical views. As they hold very widely across different contextual conditions, it is easy to confuse them with aspects of the conventional (encoded) content of the linguistic expressions used. Some linguistically oriented pragmatists have taken the generalized/particularized distinction as absolute and as involving different sorts of pragmatic theory. As mentioned earlier, Levinson (1988, 1995, 2000) has developed a taxonomy of types of generalized implicatures and a system of default inference rules which are attached to particular lexical items, such as 'and', 'the', partitive 'some', 'looks', 'know', etc. On this outlook, the theory of generalized conversational implicatures is a theory of preferred interpretations. I have suggested elsewhere that this is a wrong turning in the development of pragmatic theory (Carston 1990/95).

Various people have denied that there is an absolute distinction among conversational implicatures: from a computational, AI-based perspective, Hirschberg (1985/91) in her study of scalar implicature, says that while the cases called generalized are more context-independent than particularized ones they are still context-dependent; within a relevance-theoretic framework, I have argued for a continuum of cases from those that are one-offs through various degrees of context dependence to those that arise in the vast majority of contexts and require quite particular contexts to prevent them going through; Geurts (1998b) expresses scepticism about the neo-Gricean notion of GCI and prefers to treat all conversational implicatures as context-dependent inferences; from within the philosophy of language, Neale (1992: 524, footnote 18) claims the distinction was 'theoretically inert (for Grice)'. On all these views, all conversational implicatures involve the same inferential mechanisms and are guided by the same principles of rational communicative behaviour, whether they arise across a range of contexts or are restricted to very specific contexts.[12]

Individual cases of what have been called generalized implicature do have some interesting properties, however. For instance, all of the cases discussed by Grice seem to implicate either that a stronger proposition than the one expressed by the speaker is the case, as in (15a)–(15c), or that a stronger proposition is not the case, as in (15d) and (15e):

(15) a. I broke my finger.
      b. He took off his trousers before he got into bed.
      c. There is a king of France and he isn't bald.
      d. It is not red.
      e. X is not meeting his wife/sister/daughter.

And it is worth noting that all of the reanalyses of cases of Gricean implicature as cases of pragmatic contributions to the proposition expressed, in accordance with the underdeterminacy thesis, involve cases of generalized implicature, as will be illustrated in chapters 3 and 4 on 'and'-conjunction and negation. This is not to say that everything that has been labelled a generalized implicature should be so reconstrued; we need to proceed on a case-by-case basis.

The Gricean picture can be summarized in the figure below, where S is a speaker and where the concept of 'meant' here is that which Grice analysed in terms of a complex of intentions on the speaker's part.[13] There is one proviso, which is that, if I am right about the lack of any real distinction between generalized and particularized implicatures, the bottom level should drop out of the picture.

Penultimately, a minor issue (which may, however, prove to have wider significance than it seems at first): whether or not entailments and conversational implicatures are mutually exclusive categories. Neale (1992: 528–9) says: 'Intuitively, it seems desirable that no proposition be both an entailment and a conversational implicature of the same utterance.' Two questions arise: why is this desirable and did Grice intend such an absolute distinction? The second question raises the usual problems of Gricean textual exegesis and I have seen and heard both 'yes' and 'no' responses to it. I tend to go with the 'yeses'. One reason for this lies in an answer to the first question, concerning the desirability of distinguishing entailment from implicature. As discussed in the previous section, one of Grice's aims in introducing the 'useful philosophical tool of implicature' was to stave off certain ordinary-language arguments against particular philosophical positions by distinguishing the matter of the truth or falsity of clauses of these theses from the issue of their appropriateness/oddity. Patently, the entailments of these theses affect their truth/falsity; if an entailment of a statement is false then that statement must be false, and that would certainly constitute a strong objection to it. The falsity of a conversational implicature, on the other hand, does not affect the truth value of what is stated, so that if a statement, made as part of a philosophical thesis, communicates a false implicature, that is not a threat to the validity of the thesis. So a clear distinction between entailments and conversational implicatures seems not

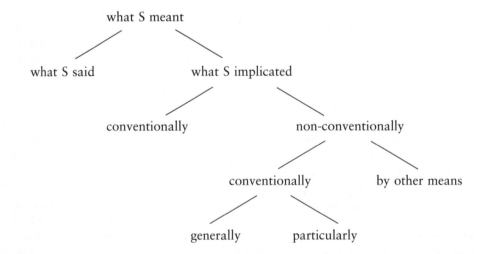

only desirable but essential to the primary impetus behind Grice's introduction of the notion of conversational implicature.

Furthermore, the diagnostics that Grice gives for conversational implicature at the end of the second lecture (Grice 1967/75/89b: 39) weigh heavily against the possibility of implicated entailments. They are cancellable without giving rise to contradiction, which is surely not a property of an entailment, and 'a conversational implicatum will be a condition that is not included in the original specification of the expression's conventional force' while entailments are, arguably, part of the intrinsic meaning (conventional force) of the expression. Less compelling, but suggestive, is the complete absence, from the many examples he gives of conversational implicatures, of any cases where the implicature is also an entailment. In this respect, Grice's (1981) account of the existential implication (presupposition) carried by definite descriptions is interesting:

(16)   a.   The king of France is bald.
       b.   The king of France is not bald.
       c.   There is a king of France.

In both the positive and the negative cases, he takes it that the existential implication in (c) is, in some sense, backgrounded and he introduces a new maxim (of 'conversational tailoring') to explain this: the speaker's choice of the abbreviated form 'The F', rather than the expanded Russellian conjunctive form, effects this backgrounding. Maintaining the Russellian semantics for the definite description and assuming wide scope of negation at the level of what is said, he explains the preferred narrow scope understanding of (16b) as the result of the existential implication arising as a generalized conversational implicature. Why is this not also seen as an implicature in the positive case in (16a), where the manner maxim also seems to account for the backgrounding effect? The answer seems to be: it can't be an implicature because it's an entailment.

So, although I stand with Sperber and Wilson (1983) and with Bach (personal communication) on not in fact wishing to exclude the possibility of an entailment, whether of encoded linguistic meaning or of the proposition expressed by an utterance, being implicated by a speaker, there seems to be reasonably strong evidence that Grice ruled this out. In a cognitive account of utterance interpretation, a rather different enterprise from Grice's, there is nothing inherently undesirable in a proposition which is a (semantic) entailment being also a (pragmatic/conversational) implicature, since the terms belong to different sorts of theories. Whether or not an entailment is an implicature depends on the cognitive mechanism involved in its derivation. In section 2.3, where I look at the relevance-theoretic use of the term implicature, possible examples of implicated entailments will be considered.

This section can be usefully rounded off by a quick look at Grice's last thoughts on this general area. In his Retrospective Epilogue (1989a, strand 5), he addresses the issue of whether there is any 'kind, type, mode, or region of signification which has special claims to centrality' and he finds two possibilities: the dictive and the formal, which, as far as I can see, are the 'what is said' (the truth-conditional content of an utterance) and the conventional or encoded linguistic meaning (what is given by the linguistic *forms* employed). Naturally, this gives rise to four categories of meaning: (a) the formal and dictive: for instance, the proposition expressed by 'Snow is white'; (b) the formal and non-dictive: for instance, the conventional implicatures indicated by 'but', 'moreover', etc.; (c) the non-formal and non-dictive: these are all cases of conversational implicatures, which are not semantically encoded and do not contribute to truth-conditional content; (d) the non-formal and dictive. What lies in this last category? For me it would be all those contributions to the proposition expressed by the utterance which have been pragmatically (that is, non-formally) derived; that is, manifestations of linguistic underdeterminacy. But what sort of thing does Grice have in mind? It might be thought that the only elements he could include here are the results of reference assignment and disambiguation, but I doubt that he would want this, given his conception of these and the fact that they are so clearly linguistically (that is, formally) indicated. The examples he in fact gives are very interesting and, perhaps, show a development in his thinking about the relation between conventional content and what is said. One of them is 'Heigh-ho' uttered in a suitable context, thereby saying something like 'Well, that's the way the world goes', though this is not part of the conventional meaning of the words used. The other example I save for later (chapter 5). What is clear from this late discussion of these two 'central types of signification' is that linguistic semantics (formal encoded meaning) is to be distinguished from the truth-conditional (dictive) content of an utterance.

2.2.4 Saying, meaning and 'making as if to say'

Grice seems to have wanted two things from his concept of 'what is said': (a) that it depart as little as possible from conventional linguistic meaning, and (b) that it constitute the truth-conditional content of an utterance, where the concept of truth-conditional content at issue seems to be the minimal proposition rather than the often richer one which the speaker intended. But no matter how minimal one goes with truth-conditional content, there is still a gap between these two construals, as the facts of 'semantic underdeterminacy' establish: linguistic meaning falls far short of full propositionality, let alone of the proposition expressed by the speaker.

A crucial further property of 'what is said', as the diagram on p. 112 shows, is that it falls under what the speaker meant; in fact, within Grice's analysis of the various species of non-natural meaning (all reducible to intentional states of the communicator) 'what is said' is characterized as involving a close coincidence of speaker meaning and linguistic expression meaning. This gives rise to a problem noted by several people: in those cases where it seems that the speaker does not mean what her words mean, nothing is said. This arises in cases of rhetorical use of expressions, as in metaphor, irony, hyperbole and, perhaps, meiosis/litotes. As Grice himself put it in the third William James lecture: 'Nothing may be said, though there is something which a speaker makes as if to say' (Grice 1967/78/89b: 41). A speaker using the sentences in (17) ((17b) intended ironically) does not 'say' the propositions expressed by uttering them; the first clause of the definition of 'what is said' (see note 7 of this chapter) is not met:

(17) a. Jane is a raging inferno today.
      b. It's a great day for a picnic.
      c. You are the best father in the world.

The requirement that 'saying' entail 'meaning' and the move from 'saying' to 'making as if to say' bring a bunch of problems with them; I'll briefly summarize these, but without seeking solutions within the Gricean framework, since some suggestions will arise later (see section 2.5) and, more important for me, these problems do not arise within the relevance-based framework:

(a) The account does not seem to accommodate what would be literally understood from slips of the tongue and other misuses, since one cannot unintentionally say something; in such cases, either nothing is said (and nor does the speaker make as if to say anything), or the close coincidence requirement has to be relaxed.

(b) In the case of many tropes, nothing is in fact said because the conventional content of the sentence uttered (plus disambiguation and reference fixing) does not coincide with any proposition meant by the speaker. It seems, then, that although what the speaker meant in these cases is supposed to come in at the level of implicature, there is no vehicle by which a conversational implicature is carried, since implicatures are characterized as following from the saying of what is said. The move to 'making as if to say', as well as being unclear in itself, raises new problems (see Bertolet 1983).

(c) The Gricean account of the tropes depends on the flouting of the first maxim of quality: do not *say* what you believe to be false. However, in these cases nothing has been said so, trivially, the maxim is not violated and the account on which an implicature is required in order to preserve the supermaxim of quality (try to make your contribution one that is true) cannot get off the ground (see Wilson 1995 for discussion).

The two problem areas are slips of the tongue and non-literalness, both of which fail the requirement of a coincidence of speaker meaning and sentence meaning. Bach (1994a, 1994b) provides one solution to this problem: drop the requirement that 'saying' entails 'meaning'; Sperber and Wilson (1986a/95b) have a more radical solution which involves dropping the concept of 'saying', as Grice conceived it, altogether. Their concepts of the proposition expressed by the utterance and of explicatures are discussed in the next section.

My account of the Gricean distinction between saying and implicating is far from complete. As Neale (1992: 512) says: 'It is at least arguable that the "Theory of Conversation" is a component of the "Theory of Meaning" and that, even if this is not the case, the two bear on each other in important ways and are most usefully discussed together rather than in isolation.' I'm sure he is right about this, although I have confined myself largely to discussing aspects of the theory of conversation alone; no doubt, placing it in the wider context of the (analytical, conceptual) theory of meaning would accentuate its philosophical temper and dissociate it all the more from a cognitive processing account. This point will arise again in section 2.5.2 where I look at the even stricter, more pared down concept of 'what is said', advocated by Kent Bach.

2.3 Sperber and Wilson: Relevance-theoretic Distinctions

The programme of formulating an adequate account of the cognitive processes and representations involved in utterance interpretation, an account set squarely within the computational view of the mind, brings with it a significant change of perspective. We can no longer leave as vague or mysterious the means for resolving ambiguity and referential indeterminacy. Nor will we be thinking of conversational implicature as a 'useful tool for philosophical analysis', but rather as a representational level, derived in a particular way and playing a particular role in the process of understanding. And we cannot accept a meagre boosting of linguistically given content to minimal propositionality if this does not figure as a representational level in the inferential process of recovering utterance meaning.

2.3.1 Explicature

The domain of relevance-theoretic pragmatics is ostensive stimuli (the paradigm case being linguistic utterances), what they ostensively communicate, and how this is achieved. The set of assumptions (propositions) ostensively communicated are those for which the communicator's stimulus (utterance) makes it mutually manifest (to communicator and audience) that she intends to make them manifest (or more manifest) to the audience. (See 'communicative intention' and 'ostensive-inferential communication' in appendix 1.) Of course, any stimulus (including an ostensive one) may convey other kinds of information, some covertly communicated, some inadvertently transmitted (see Wilson and Sperber 1993a), but from now on, when I talk of communicated assumptions (propositions) these are to be taken as *ostensively* communicated assumptions (propositions).[14]

The assumptions communicated by a speaker fall into two classes: 'explicature' and 'implicature'. Sperber and Wilson's (1986a/95b: 182) definitions are as follows:

(I)   An assumption communicated by an utterance U is *explicit* [hence an 'explicature'] if and only if it is a development of a logical form encoded by U.
      [*Note*: in cases of ambiguity, a surface form encodes more than one logical form, hence the use of the indefinite here, '*a* logical form encoded by U'.]

(II) An assumption communicated by U which is not explicit is implicit [hence an 'implicature'].

Let's concentrate on the concept of 'explicature' for the moment. There are two points worth emphasizing here. The first is that the explicature/implicature distinction applies only to those assumptions that fall within the speaker's *communicative intention*. This opens up the possibility of a difference between the proposition expressed by the speaker and her explicature(s): the proposition expressed may or may not be communicated; only when it is communicated is it an explicature of the utterance. This distinction is essential to the standard relevance-theoretic account of non-literalness, taken up in section 2.3.6; in cases of metaphorical or ironical use, it seems that the proposition expressed is not explicated. It is also essential to the account of non-declarative utterances, such as imperatives, interrogatives, hortatives and others, since, if we follow the standard speech-act line on these, all of the following have the same propositional content, but the only case where that proposition is communicated (hence explicated) is (18a), the declarative:

(18) a. Billy is going home.
　　　 b. Go home, Billy!
　　　 c. Is Billy going home?
　　　 d. Would that Billy would go home.

I'll consider the imperative in a little more detail later in this section.

Second, clearly the content of explicatures comes from two distinct sources, the linguistic expressions used and the context, and it is derived in two distinct ways depending on its source, by linguistic decoding or by pragmatic inference. As discussed at length in the previous chapter, the logical form, which is the output of the decoding phase, virtually never constitutes a fully propositional entity, but is rather a schema for the inferential construction of fully propositional assumptions. Several utterances with one and the same propositional content may differ with regard to the relative contributions of decoding and inference to that content. So, although the explicatures of such (declarative) utterances may be the same, they will vary in their degree of explicitness:

(19) a. Mary Jones put the book by Chomsky on the table in the down stairs sitting-room.
　　　 b. Mary put the book on the table.
　　　 c. She put it there.
　　　 d. On the table.

An utterance of any one of (19a)–(19d) could be used, in different contexts, to communicate explicitly one and the same proposition (or thought or assumption). Clearly (19c) and (19d) leave a great deal more to pragmatic inference than does (19b), which in turn is less explicit than (19a). Given the essential nature of the underdeterminacy thesis, as argued in the previous chapter, no linguistic expression will achieve full explicitness; that is, will fully encode the propositional form communicated. What we really have here are two different explicit/implicit distinctions: one which is the explicature/implicature distinction and another which is, in effect, identical to our semantics/pragmatics distinction. Within relevance theory, this second distinction, on which explicit = encoded and implicit = inferred, has been argued to be the basis of a theory of style; it concerns the choices a speaker makes about where a hearer/reader needs strong direction and where he can be left to make his own (inferential) choices (see Sperber and Wilson 1986a/95b: 202–24; Blakemore 1989a). As I understand it, the latter is a somewhat informal use of explicit/implicit (though widely used in other pragmatics frameworks), and it is redundant, as it merely restates the encoded/inferred distinction. I shall reserve the terms 'explicit' and 'implicit' for the explicature/implicature distinction from here on.

Levinson (1987b: 723) raises an apparent problem for the definition of explicature. He says that, in distinguishing explicature from implicature, the criterion offered by Sperber and Wilson is 'that explicatures must contain the encoded SR (semantic representation) or LF (logical form) as a proper subpart', and the problem with this is that some clear cases of implicatures meet that condition. He gives the following example:

(20)   A: If Thatcher has won the election, she'll have won three times.
       B: Thatcher has won.
       Implicature: Thatcher has won three times.

B has communicated that Thatcher has won three times, but the logical form of her utterance 'Thatcher has won' is a proper subpart of this representation, so, according to the criterion just given, this ought to be an explicature; however, it is, without doubt, an implicature, so the criterion is making wrong predictions. This piece of reasoning is correct, but one of its premises is wrong; Levinson has missed the crucial concept of 'development' in the definition of explicature and so misrepresented the relevance-theoretic criterion. This implicature is not derived by a process of pragmatically developing the decoded content of B's utterance; plainly, it is derived purely inferentially, by a straightforward deductive inference, one of whose premises is the assumption which *is* derived by development of the encoded content, 'Thatcher has won the election.' The 'criterion' provided by the definition of explicature is a *derivational* one, which is stronger than the one assumed by Levinson: explicatures do, inevitably, contain the SR as a proper subpart, but it is not the case that every communicated assumption that happens to contain a constituent which matches the SR is an explicature.

As discussed in some detail in the preceding chapter, there is a range of processes, which can be loosely called cases of pragmatic enrichment (or development), that are required in the recovery of the proposition the speaker intended to express (an explicature, if she communicated it). An early discussion of this phenomenon appears in Wilson and Sperber (1981), who look at the example in (21a). Let us suppose that the outcome of the two processes of disambiguation and reference assignment (in a particular context) is as given in (21b), which is fully propositional (so truth-evaluable):

(21)   a.   John plays very well.
       b.   John Murray plays some musical instrument very well.
       c.   John Murray plays the violin very well.
       d.   John Murray should be admitted to the National Youth Orchestra.

As they say, in most instances a hearer would interpret (21a) as expressing something more specific than (21b), say (21c), in circumstances of John Murray playing the violin in front of the speaker and hearer. They note a couple of important features of (21c): it entails (hence is more informative than) (21b), and it is on the basis of (21c) rather than (21b) that the implicatures of the utterance would be worked out, for instance (21d) in an appropriate context. An important question arises here that did not arise for the Gricean approach, according to which (21b) would be 'what is said'. The question is how far the process of pragmatically developing the logical form goes and what constraints there are on it, or, in other words, how it can be determined, for any given instance of a pragmatic inference, whether it is a contribution to the proposition expressed or an independent implicated assumption. Various criteria for distinguishing the proposition expressed (or basic explicature) from implicature have been proposed (see, for instance, Carston 1988/91 and Recanati 1989b/91, 1993), some of which are discussed in section 2.6, and the outline of some actual derivations of explicatures and implicatures in subsection 2.3.4 is intended to show that the ultimate arbiter is the relevance-based comprehension strategy itself.

So far I've considered only the explicature that an utterance has when the proposition the utterance expresses is communicated (overtly endorsed) by the speaker, but in fact Sperber and Wilson's idea is that utterances typically have several explicatures. A development of the logical form may be such that the propositional form (proposition expressed) is embedded in a range of different sorts of higher-level descriptions, including (weak) speech-act[15] and propositional-attitude descriptions (Wilson and Sperber 1993a: 5–6). For instance, Mary's reply to Bill's question in (22) might have the explicatures given in (23):

(22) a. Bill: Did your son visit you at the weekend?
      b. Mary (visibly happy):   He did.

(23) a. Mary's son visited her at the weekend.
      b. Mary says that her son visited her at the weekend.[16]
      c. Mary believes that her son visited her at the weekend.
      d. Mary is happy that her son visited her at the weekend.

The hearer may actually represent only some subset of these (though the speaker has made manifest her intention to make the others manifest as well). In a situation in which, for instance, Bill knows that Mary has been worrying about a growing rift between her son and herself, he may represent just (23a) (the base-level, we could say, explicature) and the higher-level explicature (23d). These are the explicitly communicated assumptions most likely to give rise to contextual effects (that is, to be relevant). In some other case, a higher-level explicature describing the speaker's belief[17] might be the major contributor to the relevance of the utterance; for instance, in a context in which this representation could overturn or modify the hearer's existing representation of the speaker's beliefs. The importance of higher-level explicatures (in which the proposition expressed is embedded) is most apparent when we look at cases of non-literalness, on the one hand, and at cases of non-declarative utterances, on the other.

On the relevance-theoretic account, an utterance of a sentence in the imperative mood communicates an explicature which describes a certain state of affairs as both achievable (or, 'potential') and desirable (to some degree x), to the speaker or the hearer or, perhaps, a salient third person; these indeterminacies have to be pragmatically resolved. For example, in an appropriate context, an utterance of (24a) could communicate the higher-level explicatures in (24b)–(24d) (S for the speaker, H for the hearer):

(24) a. Buy some milk.
      b. S is telling H to buy some milk.
      c. It is moderately desirable to S (and achievable) that H buy some milk.
      d. S is requesting H to buy some milk.

As on certain speech-act accounts, the idea here is that the proposition expressed is the same as that expressed by the corresponding declarative; here it would be 'the hearer buy(s) some milk'. This propositional form of an imperative is subject to the various enrichment processes already discussed with regard to declarative cases: disambiguation, reference assignment, propositional completion and propositional strengthening. The italicized forms beneath the following examples are rough indications of the sorts of enrichments that might have to be made:

(25) a. Stop him!
          [(*You*) *stop Bruce from getting into a fight with Sid!*]
      b. Have a bath!
          [(*You*) *bath your body very soon!*]
      c. Give this decision some thought!
          [(*You*) *give this decision an appreciable amount of thought!*]

These propositional forms are clearly not explicatures of the imperative utterance, however, since they are not communicated (they are not presented as actual but merely as potential and desirable). It is the higher-level representations which are explicitly communicated, so for an utterance of (24a) it is (24b)–(24d). (See Wilson and Sperber 1988a; Wilson 1991; Clark 1991, 1993a, for fuller accounts of this analysis of imperatives and of other non-declarative utterances.)

The distinction between higher-level explicatures and the explicated propositional form of the utterance is interesting from another point of view too. Several classes of sentential adverbial have been analysed by theorists as not being part of the propositional form of the utterance:

(26) a. Frankly, I'm unimpressed.
      b. Confidentially, she won't pass the exam.
      c. Happily, Mary's son visited her this weekend.
      d. Unfortunately, I missed the train.
      e. Obviously, I'm going to miss the deadline.
      f. Possibly, we're too late.

'Frankly' and 'seriously' are cases of illocutionary adverbials; 'happily' and 'unfortunately' are cases of evaluative (attitudinal) adverbials and 'obviously' and 'perhaps' are evidential adverbials. It seems that the propositional form (and hence the truth-conditional content) of these utterances does not include the contribution made by the adverbial.[18] Where, then, do these elements make their contribution? They each decode into a mentally represented concept,[19] which must feature in some representation derived by the hearer. There is a neat answer to this in the system Sperber and Wilson have developed: they contribute to a higher-level explicature. This is most easily seen in the case of the illocutionary adverbials, which slot straightforwardly into the role of modifier of a speech-act verb in the higher-level speech-act description:

(27)   a.   I tell you frankly that I'm unimpressed.
       b.   I inform you confidentially that she won't pass the exam.

Evidentials comment on what the speaker sees as the degree of evidential support for the proposition expressed, which may in turn affect the degree of conviction she represents herself as having in the truth of the proposition expressed (that is, the propositional attitude explicature):

(28)   a.   It is obvious (obviously true) that the speaker is going to miss the deadline.
       b.   The speaker strongly believes that she is going to miss the deadline.
       c.   It is possible that the speaker and X are too late [for . . .].
       d.   The speaker weakly believes that she and X are too late [for . . .].

And, in similar vein, for the evaluative adverbials:

(29)   a.   It is a happy eventuality that Mary's son visited her this weekend.
       b.   It is unfortunate that the speaker missed the train.

There is probably a further range of indeterminacies to be pragmatically resolved here: 'obvious to whom?', 'happy for whom?', 'unfortunate in whose opinion?', etc.
    So far so (relatively) good, but this brings us to a problem with the definition of explicature as given above. Let's look at some more complex cases involving sentence adverbials:

(30)   a.   Kim shouldn't pass the course, because she, frankly, hasn't done the work.
       b.   Kim might pass the course, although, confidentially, she hasn't done the work.
       c.   She has missed a lot of lectures and she, obviously, hates linguistics.

The argument has been that sentential adverbials contribute to higher-level explicatures, but in (30a) and (30b) they are modifying an embedded clause, which is certainly not a development of the logical form of the utterance, but is rather a constituent (a proper subpart) of the logical form of the utterance, and hence of the propositional form into which it is developed. It seems that either we are wrong about the role of these adverbials, or the propositional constituents into which the subordinate clauses are developed must be explicatures in their own right (or perhaps both).

In fact, the problem arises independently of the issue of the correct treatment of sentence adverbials. The simplest illustration is the case of an 'and'-conjunction:

(31) a. Sam went to a party and Jane watched a video.
      b. Sam went to a party.
      c. Jane watched a video.

Intuitions seem to be unequivocal that an utterance of (31a) communicates not only the conjunctive proposition but also the two constituent propositions, (31b) and (31c). So, again, these are explicatures which are embedded within the proposition expressed by the utterance. The point carries over to examples like those in (30) but without the sentence adverbials, so (32a) communicates explicitly both (32b) and (32c), as well as the more complex proposition of which they are constituents:

(32) a. Kim shouldn't pass the course because she hasn't done the work.
      b. Kim shouldn't pass the course.
      c. Kim hasn't done the work.

What all these examples show is that the definition of explicature given above is too restrictive. On the basis of the cases considered so far, (30)–(32), it looks as if it should be amended so as to include communicated entailments of the proposition expressed. However, there are other cases where the intuition of explicitness of communication applies to subpropositions which are not entailed by the proposition expressed. The following examples are based on one from Sperber and Wilson (1995a: 294, footnote a), who acknowledge the problem that this sort of case raises for the definition of explicature:

(33) a. I'm telling you that it's not possible.
      b. It's not possible.

(34) a. I'm totally certain that Emily will come.
      b. Emily will come.

A speaker of the utterances in (33a) and (34a) who explicates the proposition expressed in each case, also explicitly communicates (33b) and (34b) respectively, though these are not entailments of the proposition expressed (the truth of P does not follow from the truth of my telling you that P or from the truth of my being totally certain that P).

As well as not being a necessary feature of an explicature, the property of being entailed (and communicated) may not be sufficient either. Consider the following, in which an utterance of the sentence in (a) communicates the proposition in (b):

(35) a. (Confidentially) the judge is my father.
      b. The judge is a man.

(36) a. (Unfortunately) I bought some pork.
      b. I bought some meat.

Intuitions seem to vary across individuals as to whether the propositions in (b) in each case are explicatures or implicatures, so in these cases we need to look to more theoretical considerations. Notice that while examples (30)–(34) involve clauses within clauses and so propositions within propositions (once the proposition expressed has been pragmatically constructed), examples (35) and (36) are single clauses and the proposition they express contains no propositional subparts. It is the multi-clausal nature of (30)–(34) which has, so far, been the essential property in motivating the need for a broader definition of explicature, since in each case it is the possibility of explicating a subproposition contained within their propositional form that is not met by the current definition. This cannot arise for examples (35) and (36) because they are single-clause cases, so they should comply with the current definition; according to that definition, the communicated proposition shown in (b) in each case is not an explicature because it is not a development (an inferential enrichment) of any element of encoded meaning. On the assumption that the notion of a development of an encoded semantic representation is central to the account of explicature and should remain so, these cases fall outside its range. In the next section, I will suggest that they are indeed implicatures, since they are derived entirely inferentially (in fact, deductively) as are implicated conclusions quite generally.

So it seems that being a communicated entailment of the proposition expressed may be neither necessary nor sufficient for qualification as an explicature. At the least, it is not necessary, as the examples in (33) and (34) attest. It is worth noting that the intuition that the embedded propositional form is communicated, hence explicated, does not go through if the person of the main clause subject is changed or if the main verb semantics is altered in certain ways:

(37) a. John is telling us that it's not possible.
      b. The child is quite certain that Emily will come.
      c. I hope that it's not possible.
      d. I doubt that Jane will come.

The speaker of these utterances is not explicitly communicating the proposition expressed by the embedded clauses, 'it's not possible', 'Emily will come' (and is probably not communicating them at all). The relevant difference between the two cases is plain to see: in uttering (33) or (34), the speaker is expressing her commitment to the truth of the embedded proposition, while, in uttering any of (37a)–(37d), she is not. The point is that if the proposition expressed by an utterance itself expresses speaker commitment to a subproposition contained within it, then if the proposition expressed is communicated so must be the subproposition. A similar point can be made about the cases involving the factive-type entailments, such as

(30)–(32); in communicating (overtly endorsing) the proposition expressed by the utterance, the speaker cannot but communicate (endorse) the contained propositions that are entailed.

So what we are after in a modified definition of explicature is a characterization that encompasses the following *communicated* assumptions/propositions: (a) the proposition expressed, (b) embeddings of the proposition expressed in higher-level descriptions, and (c) propositional subparts of the proposition expressed. I suggest that the following quite minor amendment of the original definition does the job:

> (III)   An assumption (proposition) communicated by an utterance is an 'explicature' of the utterance if and only if it is a development of (a) a linguistically encoded logical form of the utterance, or of (b) a sentential subpart of a logical form.

Ideally, this would be made a little more precise (for instance, what exactly is meant by a 'sentential subpart' of the logical form?), and perhaps streamlined by a single characterization of 'development of a logical form' and 'development of a sentential subpart', so as to eliminate the disjunctive element of the definition, which might suggest we are not dealing with a unified phenomenon. However, as it stands, I think it is descriptively adequate and relatively clear. Note that, as with the original definition, the main work is done by the two central concepts: '(ostensively) communicated' and 'development (pragmatic enrichment)'.

Let's return to the example which first prompted the revision, (30a) (repeated here for convenience), and look at its explicatures:

> (30)   a.   Kim shouldn't pass the course, because she, frankly, hasn't done the work.

Assuming that the proposition expressed by this utterance is (38a) and that it is communicated, the utterance may have the following explicatures, in accordance with clause (a) of the definition:

> (38)   a.   Kim shouldn't pass the course because she hasn't done the work.
> b.   S is saying that Kim shouldn't pass the course because she hasn't done the work.
> c.   S believes that Kim shouldn't pass the course because she hasn't done the work.
> d.   S is sad that Kim shouldn't pass the course because she hasn't done the work.

In addition, it will have the explicatures in (39) and (40), in accordance with clause (b) of the definition:

> (39)   a.   Kim shouldn't pass the course.
> b.   S believes Kim shouldn't pass the course.
> c.   S is saying that Kim shouldn't pass the course.

(40)   a.   Kim hasn't done the work.
       b.   S believes that Kim hasn't done the work.
       c.   S is telling H frankly that Kim hasn't done the work.

While these may be communicated (that is, the speaker's intention to make them manifest to the hearer is itself made mutually manifest), this is not to say that the hearer will represent all of them; it is almost certain that he will not. He is likely to represent (40c) because the use of 'frankly' in this utterance makes it highly manifest and so, given the Principle of Relevance, likely to have cognitive effects.

Note that, according to this amended definition, as with the original one, the entailment cases in (35) and (36) do not qualify as explicatures, because, although they may be communicated, they are not developments of any sentential part of the decoded semantic representation of the utterance. It seems that only those entailments which are 'visible' in, and detachable from, the propositional form of the utterance are candidates for explicaturehood, and there may be an interesting complementarity with those entailments that can be implicated, a point touched on again in section 2.3.3 on implicature. This is backed up by differences in the functioning of the sentence adverbials in the clear cases of explicated entailments, on the one hand, and in these non-transparent cases, on the other. While the adverbials can play their standard role in higher-level descriptions involving the former (as in (40c)), this is just not possible with this second set of cases:

(41)   a.   Confidentially, the judge is my father.
       b.   ?S is telling H confidentially that the judge is a man.
       c.   Unfortunately, I bought some pork.
       d.   ?It is unfortunate that S bought some meat.

An utterance of (41a) does not explicitly communicate (41b) and an utterance of (41c) does not explicitly communicate (41d).

2.3.2   Multiple speech acts and multiple logical forms

As the last section made clear, an utterance may explicitly communicate a multiplicity of assumptions (propositions). Now I will consider two other related ideas that may have implications for the account of explicature given so far: (a) that an utterance may consist of two (or more) distinct speech acts, one in a subsidiary, 'commenting on', relation to the other; (b) that an utterance (or a speech act) may have a multiplicity of logical forms, hence of propositions expressed (with distinct sets of truth conditions).

Within relevance theory, as in a number of other approaches, it is assumed that talk of the truth conditions of an utterance is shorthand for talk of the truth conditions of the proposition expressed by the utterance, since it is propositions (or conceptual representations of them) that are the primary bearers of truth/falsity. Until fairly recently, most semanticists and pragmatists have assumed that every utterance expresses a single proposition and so has a single set of truth conditions.

However, Wilson and Sperber (1993a: 23–4) suggest that certain sorts of utterances might express more than a single proposition, hence have more than a single set of truth conditions, and that intuitions about *the* truth conditions of an utterance as a whole, and assessments of an utterance as being true or false, are really judgements about the truth conditions and truth value of that proposition that makes the major contribution to the overall relevance of the utterance. The specific cases they have in mind here are utterances with illocutionary adverbials or parenthetical phrases like 'I think'. From different perspectives, and for a different range of cases, Bach (1999b) and Neale (1999) have made similar suggestions. They both point out that an utterance can express several propositions, which may differ in truth value, and suggest that when intuitions that the utterance has a single value are fairly robust, this seems to reflect a prior judgement concerning which of the propositions expressed carries the most conversational weight.

Bearing these ideas in mind, recall Grice's characterization of conventional impli-cature devices such as 'on the other hand', 'moreover', 'therefore' and 'but' as sig-nalling the performance of a higher-order, subsidiary speech act, dependent on the central (ground-floor) speech act(s) (Grice 1989b: 121–2, 362). In his view, the utterance in (42) consists of *three* speech acts, two of them of a basic-level sort, (43a) and (43b), the third a higher-order one, (43c), which comments on (the per-formance of) the lower-level ones:

(42)   My brother-in-law lives on a peak in Darien; his great aunt, on the other hand, was a nurse in World War 1.

(43)   a.   My brother-in-law lives on a peak in Darien.
       b.   His great aunt was a nurse in World War 1.
       c.   (a) contrasts with (b)

The view that with a single utterance a speaker might perform, in addition to some basic speech act(s), some dependent or parasitic speech acts, has been taken up by a number of people, including Bach and Harnish (1979: 219–28), Recanati (1987a: 36–40), Ifantidou (1993, 1994), Bach (1994b: 147–9), who calls them split-level utterances, and Bach (1999b: 328), who talks of '*utterance* modifiers, as opposed to sentence modifiers, because they do not modify the content of the sentence but instead characterize the act of uttering it'. (Note that neither they nor relevance-theorists in general apply this sort of analysis to all the cases that concerned Grice; for instance, most of them would not wish to apply it to 'but'.)

The specific cases characterized in this way by Ifantidou (1993, 1994) are par-enthetical phrases involving speech-act or propositional-attitude verbs, such as those in (44) and (45):

(44)   a.   I suppose your house is very old.
       b.   Your house is, I suppose, very old.
       c.   Your house is very old, I suppose.

(45)   a.   I promise (you), I'll take Jane to Paris.
       b.   I'll take Jane, I promise (you), to Paris.
       c.   I'll take Jane to Paris, I promise (you).

Building on observations of Austin (1946) and Urmson (1956), but working within relevance theory, she develops the idea that these utterances involve two communicative acts (or illocutionary units), one dependent on the other. The parenthetical use of these verbs is thereby distinguished from their main clause use, which comprises a single speech act:[20]

(46) a. I suppose that your house is very old.
      b. I promise that I will take Jane to Paris.

As well as having a strong basis in intuition, this approach is backed up by syntactic evidence which emerges clearly when comparable cases involving imperatives and interrogatives are considered:

(47) a. I beg you to come with me to Cyprus.
      b. I beg you, come with me to Cyprus.
      c. Come with me, I beg you, to Cyprus.
      d. Come with me to Cyprus, I beg you.

(48) a. I wonder whether we'll ever be able to afford a house.
      b. I wonder, will we ever be able to afford a house?
      c. Will we ever, I wonder, be able to afford a house?
      d. Will we ever be able to afford a house, I wonder?

While the declarative form is the same in both main and subordinate clauses, imperative morphology only occurs in main clauses (the embedded counterpart taking an infinitive form), and interrogative subject–auxiliary inversion only occurs in main clauses. In the parenthetical use of 'I beg you' in (47b)–(47d), there is imperative morphology on the content clause indicating that it is a main clause, while in the main-clause use of 'I beg you' in (47a), the content clause is clearly a subordinate complement clause. The same general point applies to the examples in (48), where the subject–auxiliary inversion in (48b)–(48d), absent from (48a), indicates that the question is a main clause. So, in the parenthetical cases there is no subordination but rather something more like a juxtaposition of two main clauses (parataxis), for instance, 'I beg this of you. Come with me to Cyprus.'

   Assuming this is correct, what is the function of the parenthetical clause? The standard answer echoes Grice's discussion of 'on the other hand': parentheticals perform second-order speech acts, which comment on the first-order main one. They comment on the way in which the speaker is performing it or on the way in which the hearer is to take it. Urmson (1956: 205) says the role of parentheticals is 'to orient the hearer aright towards the statements with which they are associated'; Blakemore (1990/91) describes them as telling the hearer something about how he is to process and understand the basic-level speech act, and Hand (1993: 499) talks of them as 'fine-tuning' the interpretation of the basic one, their role being 'to intensify or attenuate the speaker's illocutionary commitment' to the main utterance. Let's look at one simple example of this, drawing the relevance-theoretic concept of explicature back into the picture. An utterance of (49a) consists of the two communicative acts (or two subutterances)[21] given in (49b) and (49c), where (49c) points to, and depends on, (49b), as indicated by the demonstrative 'this':

(49)   a.   Mary is in the garden, I think.
       b.   Mary is in the garden.
       c.   I think this.

The first of these communicative acts, (49b), taken in isolation, might have the following explicatures:

(50)   a.   S says that Mary is in the garden.
       b.   S believes that Mary is in the garden.
       c.   Mary is in the garden.

What the second-order speech act (the parenthetical) does is effect a modulation of the higher-level explicature in (50b), slightly weakening the degree of conviction that the speaker communicates herself as having in the proposition expressed.[22]

In some instances of third-person parentheticals, the commenting speech act may have its own independent relevance in addition to its role of affecting the interpretation of the basic speech act. An utterance of (51a) consists of the two communicative acts in (51b) and (51c), and (51c) will tweak the interpretation of (51b) by adjusting the degree of speaker endorsement that is communicated; deriving this will require an inference by the hearer based on his knowledge of the speaker's opinion of Chomsky's views. In addition, however, the proposition expressed by the parenthetical comment, (51d), may be worth processing in its own right, as a piece of information that interacts fruitfully with one's existing store of beliefs about Chomsky's views.

(51)   a.   The human language capacity, Chomsky believes/says, cannot be explained by natural selection.
       b.   The human language capacity cannot be explained by natural selection.
       c.   Chomsky believes/says this.
       d.   Chomsky believes/says that the human language capacity cannot be explained by natural selection.

Wilson and Sperber (1993a), Ifantidou-Trouki (1993) and Ifantidou (1994) have suggested extending the double speech-act account to (at least some of) the sentence adverbials discussed earlier, 'frankly', 'unfortunately', etc. These share various characteristics with parenthetical phrases like 'I think/suppose/hope': they are generally separated off intonationally from the clause they modify and they can appear clause-initially, medially or finally. A double speech-act approach also seems well suited to utterances such as those in (52a)–(52b); the adverbial here occurs together with a speech-act verb, which is in some non-canonical form (gerund, infinitive), so that it is much less obvious than assumed in the previous section that the adverbial simply slots into place, modifying the main verb form of a higher-level explicature of the main clause. On this view, then, an utterance of (52a) consists of two communicative acts, (53a) and (53b), the second parasitic on the first in much the same way as the previously discussed parenthetical phrases.

(52) a. Speaking confidentially, the company is about to go bust.
      b. To put it frankly, the company has no future.

(53) a. The company is about to go bust.
      b. (In telling you this) I am speaking confidentially.

The upshot is as described in the previous section, though achieved by a slightly different route. The secondary, dependent speech act, (53b), effects an adjustment to the interpretation of the basic one, in this instance by modifying its higher-level explicature concerning the speech act performed, so that the explicatures of (53a) are as follows (S for speaker, H for hearer):

(54) a. S is telling H confidentially (or: in confidence) that the company is about to go bust.
      b. S believes that the company is about to go bust.
      c. The company is about to go bust.

Strictly speaking, the secondary commenting type of speech act must have its set of explicatures too, roughly as follows:

(55) a. S is saying that she is speaking in confidence.
      b. S believes that she is telling H this in confidence.
      c. S is telling H this confidentially.

While these are communicated (that is, the utterance makes mutually manifest an intention to make them manifest), they are of such little relevance in these cases that a hearer is very unlikely to represent them.[23]
   The double illocutionary act (or split-level utterance) approach extends naturally to the class of what are sometimes called 'textual' adverbials, which pertain to aspects of organization of a text or discourse, for instance, 'first of all', 'finally', 'in conclusion', 'briefly', 'to sum up', 'in a nutshell', 'by the way', 'above all', etc. But whether the account should be extended to the full class of what have been called by syntacticians 'disjunct constituents' is not so clear. Espinal (1991) includes in this class non-restrictive (appositive) relative clauses, as in (56a), disjunct (appositive) noun phrases, as in (56b), disjunct adjectival phrases, as in (56c), and vocative phrases, as in (56d), as well as the parenthetical phrases and sentence adverbials just discussed.

(56) a. Pat's book, (which was) published by Blackwell, has sold two million copies.
      b. Len Kingston, a former greengrocer, has become mayor of London.
      c. There is a problem, difficult to pinpoint exactly, with my analysis.
      d. Mary, my love, everything is going to be all right.

Espinal provides an account of the syntax of disjunct constituents, according to which they are represented as occupying a structural plane independent from that of their host clause, the pair making up a three-dimensional syntactic object. This treatment applies equally to all the types of disjunct constituent, as do the various general conditions she proposes on the way in which the conceptual content of the host clause and disjunct constituent are related in the interpretation process. (See also Haegeman 1991 for related ideas.) While this unified approach to the grammar of these constructions looks very promising, there is, I think, an important semantic/pragmatic distinction to be made among them. The function of some of them is to perform a subsidiary speech act which comments on the more basic one; this is the case with the parenthetical phrases, and the illocutionary and textual adverbials, all of which share the property of being able to appear clause-initially, medially or finally. However, others, such as the appositives, quite clearly provide independent propositional content, or, at least, modify the *content* of the main clause rather than signal how the basic speech act is to be taken by the hearer. They are much more restricted in their location than the parentheticals; they have to appear immediately following the noun phrase they modify. While the parentheticals and sentence adverbials 'help the understanding and assessment of what is said rather than being a part of what is said' (Urmson 1956: 212), the disjunct constituents in (56a)–(56c), like their host clause, 'say something' of their own, albeit usually something of a less prominent sort than what is said by the main clause.[24]

According to the account so far, while an utterance may consist of several speech acts or subutterances, each of which communicates a variety of explicatures, still each speech act has been taken to express just one proposition and so to have a single set of truth conditions. This latter assumption has to be reconsidered now. In many instances, intuitions about the truth-conditional content of an utterance seem to be unequivocal, so in (52a), for instance, there is strong agreement that the proposition expressed is that the company is about to go bust and that the utterance is true if and only if this proposition is true. In these consensus cases, it is the basic explicature of the ground-level speech act that constitutes the truth-conditional content of the utterance. But there are cases where judgements tend to become a little more hedged. Consider the proposition expressed and the truth conditions of utterances involving non-restrictive relative clauses and other appositives, such as (56a)–(56c) above. Suppose Pat's book has indeed sold two million copies, but that it was in fact published by MIT Press, and suppose that while Len Kingston is the mayor of London, he has never been a greengrocer, then what truth value judgement do people who know these facts give to the utterances? It seems that if forced to make a binary choice, most people will say that the utterances are true, but, given a little more leeway for discussion, some people, at least, will say that while the main point is true there is also something false being said; others might be reluctant to deliver any judgement of truth or falsity for the *utterance*.

The point here is that there are two propositions expressed in each of these utterances, but one of them is secondary to the other, syntactically marked as such, and so generally has less communicative significance or weight. If this is right, then it may be that when an utterance expresses more than a single proposition, as these seem to do, people's intuitions about the truth-conditional content of the utterance are really intuitions about which one of these carries the main relevance (cognitive effects), which one matters most, which one it would be most reprehensible to get wrong.[25] This view of things would be supported if we could find structurally similar cases where the truth value judgement is apparently more influenced by the disjunct constituent, and where this correlates with an apparent increase in the conversational relevance of the dependent clause. The following seem to be such cases (and see also Bach 1999b: 346, note 25):

(57) a. Pat's book, which has sold two million copies, was published by Blackwell.

      b. Len Kingston, the newly elected mayor of London, was a greengrocer.

Here the appositive sentence/phrase does seem to enter into judgements of truth or falsity, so if it is known to be false, that may well be sufficient for the whole utterance to be found false. Presumably this is because selling two million copies of a book is at least as significant as who its publisher is, and whether or not Len Kingston is the newly elected mayor of London is likely to be more relevant than whether he has ever been a greengrocer.[26]

This is an appropriate point at which to pause and take stock, by looking at the ways in which the multiple speech acts view and the idea of multiple propositions expressed, considered together, partition the content of an utterance. The general picture is one in which a single utterance may consist of several speech acts (or subutterances), some ground-level and some higher-order ones, dependent on the ground-level ones, and then each of these units may express several propositions (each developed from a linguistically given logical form).[27] On the basis of the distinctions made so far, an utterance of (58) has the pragmatic structure laid out in (59):

(58) Mary's husband, who is, I believe, a New Zealander, works for British Telecom.

(59) *First-order speech act:*
      a. Mary's husband, who is a New Zealander, works for British Telecom.

      Logical forms (hence, after enrichment, propositions expressed):
      b. Mary's husband works for British Telecom.
      c. Mary's husband is a New Zealander.

      Second-order speech act (consisting of a single logical form):
      d. I believe this.
      (commenting on (c), the secondary proposition expressed by the basic speech act)

Each of (b)–(d) may make manifest a range of higher-level explicatures, the commentary speech act fine-tuning one of those arising for (c).

Recall now the further complication, discussed in the previous section, according to which sentential subparts of the logical form of an utterance may be explicated and their higher-level explicatures modified by sentence adverbials or parenthetical phrases. Here is such a case, with its pragmatic structure unpacked in (61):

(60)   Mary wants to have a baby and her husband, I think, intends to leave her.

(61)   *First-level speech act:*
       a.   Mary wants to have a baby and her husband intends to leave her.

       Logical form (hence, after enrichment, proposition expressed):
       b.   Mary wants to have a baby and her husband intends to leave her.

       Sentential subparts of logical form which may be explicated:
       c.   Mary wants to have a baby.
       d.   Her husband intends to leave her.

       Second-order speech act (consisting of a single logical form):
       e.   I think this.
       (commenting just on (d), the second conjunct of the conjunctive speech act)

Again, each of (b)–(e) may make manifest a range of higher-level explicatures; the commentary speech act in (e) fine-tunes one of the higher-level explicatures of (d). The following example is similar, but involves sentence adverbials, one of which modifies a sentential subpart of the logical form of the basic speech act:

(62)   Confidentially, Clive won't get the job because, apparently, he criticized the chairman.

An utterance of (62) consists of three speech acts (two of them dependent cases commenting on different parts of the logical form of the basic speech act), each of which has a logical form, and one of these logical forms has two sentential subparts ('Clive won't get the job' and 'he criticized the chairman'). Each of these five has its set of potential explicatures.

A variety of somewhat technical questions arise. Can dependent (second-order) speech acts have multiple logical forms? Are there third-order speech acts, that is, cases where a parenthetical comment is made on a parenthetical comment? The answer to the first of these seems to be affirmative:

(63)   a.   The president will, [I'm quite sure, [though I don't like him]], make a fair decision.
       b.   [In simple words, [understandable by any child]], leave my chocolates alone!

In these examples, a parenthetical commenting speech act, marked by the outermost brackets, contains an appositive or subordinate clause which has its own logical form and so, arguably, expresses a distinct, albeit backgrounded, proposition, for example, 'I don't like the president' in (63a). Regarding the second question, third-order speech acts may be possible, but more often it seems that when several secondary speech acts occur they are on a par with each other, all commenting on the ground-level speech act(s). For instance, in (64a), does 'confidentially' comment on the assertion that 'it is fortunate for us that he's been transferred to another branch' or on just the basic-level assertion 'he's been transferred to another branch', on which the parenthetical 'fortunately for us' also comments? I leave the following examples for the reader's consideration, without further discussion.

(64) a. Confidentially, he's being transferred to another branch, fortunately for us.
      b. Unfortunately, his wife, I believe, is a dipsomaniac.
      c. Apparently, I seem to recall, George worked for the BBC.

Obviously, a complete account of the pragmatic structure of utterances will need to attend to this and other matters.

Finally, I want to point out that despite extensive use of the notion of the 'proposition expressed' in this section (and indeed in the sections to come), we have no definition or characterization of it. Nor is there any obvious role for the concept to play in the relevance-theoretic account of verbal communication and utterance interpretation; notably, it doesn't figure in the definition of 'explicature', for which encoded logical forms (and their sentential subparts) are the basic input. The concept of the proposition expressed has long held, and still does hold, a central place in philosophical accounts of the semantics of natural-language sentences. However, as used in relevance theory, it has been transformed beyond recognition: sentences do not express propositions, speakers do, so that recovery of the proposition(s) expressed requires consideration of speaker's intentions and, therefore, a good deal of pragmatic inference. The only remnant of its standard use that remains is the idea of a representational level of explicit content that may not be communicated (speaker-meant), and it is on this basis that it has seemed important to maintain it as distinct from explicature. The two crucial phenomena are non-declaratives and cases of non-literal language use. The account of loose and metaphorical uses given in chapter 5 will cast doubt on there being a need, after all, for any concept other than the encoded logical form and explicatures in accounting for metaphor. As for non-declaratives, while I cannot undertake a proper investigation of those here, I do want to suggest that the idea that imperatives and interrogatives express propositions (hence have truth-conditional content) is quite anomalous, as borne out by the oddity of B's response to A in the following:

(65) A: Go home now.
      B: That's true.

And while we may want some means of referring to the content that a declarative and its corresponding imperative, interrogative and hortative have in common, and we may call this, as speech-act theorists have, 'the proposition expressed', it does not follow that this plays a particular role in the process of interpreting non-declaratives. In fact, this propositional form seems to be functionally inert; the cognitive effects of an imperative utterance come from the interaction of its (higher-level) explicatures with contextual assumptions. Again, the encoded logical form (what that exactly is in the case of imperatives, interrogatives, etc., is an interesting and, as yet, unanswered question) and the explicitly communicated assumptions (explicatures) may satisfy all our descriptive requirements. I will, in fact, use the term 'proposition expressed' in the following chapters, but this is a mere matter of convenience; what is really being discussed is one set of processes involved in arriving at the explicatures of the utterance, that is, those pragmatic enrichments of logical form that do not involve embedding in a higher-level description, such as 'S believes that . . .'. I return briefly in the final chapter to the issue of the status of the 'proposition(s) expressed'.

The main point of this section has been that a single utterance may communicate not only several explicatures, but several *sets* of explicatures, each set developed from a distinct logical form encoded by the utterance. As a result, talk of *the* truth conditions of an utterance is often misleading and confusing. In those cases where there do seem to be clear intuitions concerning *the* truth-conditional content of the utterance, this may be attributable to there being one particular explicature, among the many, that is understood as carrying the greatest relevance. I move now to the other sort of communicated assumption/proposition: implicatures. Discussion here will be briefer, since it is the explicitly communicated content of utterances that is the central focus of this book.

2.3.3   Implicature

First, it should be made clear that, whereas the earlier discussion of implicature, in the section on Grice, included two quite distinct notions, conversational implicature and conventional implicature, the latter will not figure at all here. There simply is no such thing as 'conventional' implicature in relevance theory (or, we would argue, in reality). Most of the linguistic phenomena categorized by Grice as devices of conventional implicature are given a quite different treatment – as procedural constraints on the inferential processes required in deriving conversational implicatures (this will be discussed briefly in section 2.3.7). So from now on, any talk of implicatures is to be understood as meaning 'conversational' implicatures.

While the conceptual schema delivered by the encoded logical form of an utterance provides the frame on which explicatures are developed and so is an intrinsic part of their content, the conceptual content of an implicature is supplied wholly by pragmatic inference. Naturally, the linguistic meaning of an utterance constrains the implicatures derived but none of that linguistic meaning features in the propositional forms implicated.

Some utterances may have no implicatures at all, for instance, cooperative responses to requests for information from a stranger, such as what time it is, where a certain building/street is located, etc. The respondent can be confident her utterance is relevant to the questioner (has cognitive effects for him) since his request has made that evident, but, in many instances, she won't have any specific expectations about the particular context in which it will be processed or the particular effects it will have. On the other hand, as will be seen with some of the examples that follow, for some utterances, it is an implicature rather than an explicature that carries the main relevance (is the main locus of cognitive effects).

For Sperber and Wilson, implicatures come in two sorts: implicated premises and implicated conclusions. Implicated premises are a subset of the contextual assumptions used in processing the utterance and implicated conclusions are a subset of its contextual implications. What characterizes these subsets is that they are communicated (speaker-meant), hence part of the intended interpretation of the utterance.[28] Consider B's response to A:

(66) A: Let's go to a movie. I've heard *Sense and Sensibility* is good. Are you interested in seeing it?
       B: Costume dramas are usually boring.

Understanding B's utterance requires deriving the following implicatures:

(67) a.   *Sense and Sensibility* is a costume drama.
       b.   *Sense and Sensibility* is likely to be boring.
       c.   B isn't very interested in seeing *Sense and Sensibility*.

Once we have an account of how (67a) is derived, the other two follow fairly straightforwardly: (67b) follows deductively from the proposition expressed by B's utterance and (67a); (67c) follows deductively from (67b) and from a further, easily accessible, assumption that people do not generally want to go to movies they expect to be boring. These are implicated conclusions. But what about (67a), an implicated premise, on which all this hinges? A assumes that B's response will meet his expectation of relevance, and the most obvious way it could do this is by supplying an answer to A's previous question. The presumption of optimal relevance licenses him to use the most accessible of the assumptions made available by the concepts encoded in B's response in interpreting the utterance. He may already know that *Sense and Sensibility* is a costume drama, but even if he doesn't, constructing this assumption will be relatively low-cost, since it follows a well-worn comprehension route which is the most direct one for finding an answer to his yes/no question. Note that none of the inferred assumptions in (67) follows deductively from the basic explicature of B's utterance, though (67b) and (67c) are derived deductively (by modus ponens) once other particular assumptions have been accessed. So the overall picture is one of a non-demonstrative inference process, driven by the search for an optimally relevant interpretation. (The processes involved in deriving implicatures (and explicatures) are considered in a little more detail in the next section.)

Following Grice, it is often maintained that implicatures are cancellable without giving rise to a contradiction. There are two ways in which cancellation can arise, explicitly and contextually: '. . . a putative conversational implicature that *p* is explicitly cancelable if to the form of words the utterance of which putatively implicates that *p*, it is admissible to add *but not p*, or *I do not mean to imply that p*, and it is contextually cancelable if one can find situations in which the utterance of the form of words would simply not carry the implicature' (Grice 1978/89b: 44).

The exact interpretation of the criterion is open to discussion,[29] but the following is a pretty standard application of the procedure for testing whether the propositional forms in (67) are cancellable:

(68)   a.   Costume dramas are usually boring but *Sense and Sensibility* is not a costume drama.
       b.   Costume dramas are usually boring but *Sense and Sensibility* is not likely to be boring.
       c.   Costume dramas are usually boring but B is interested in seeing *Sense and Sensibility*.

The 'form of words' of B's utterance is conjoined with a form of words which expresses the negation of the alleged implicature and the result is 'admissible', where this is taken to mean non-contradictory, as it standardly is (see Levinson 1983; Walker 1975; Neale 1992; Cappelen 2000). Hence, as expected, these elements of utterance meaning are cancellable.

However, it has been objected (by Burton-Roberts, personal communication) that while implicated premises are cancellable as required, the alleged implicated conclusions are not, because they follow *deductively* from the given set of premises. He takes the position that these communicated assumptions are not, therefore, really implicatures and claims, furthermore, that Grice would not have treated them as such. This is worth a moment's consideration, since many people get worried (needlessly, in my view) by the deductive element in the relevance-theoretic account, finding this somehow not properly pragmatic (see, for instance, Levinson 1989; 2000, epilogue). It is true that once the implicated premise has been accessed, the conclusion follows deductively and so is not cancellable. But this is irrelevant to the cancellation criterion at issue, which is not concerned with *how* a given proposition was derived (whether deductively or otherwise). The test was applied in (68) in a perfectly standard Gricean way and the result was positive in each case. As for Grice's own views on conversational implicature, a quick perusal of his standard examples reveals some cases of what, I think, are implicated conclusions, although it is difficult to be sure since the derivational process is never more than hinted at. Consider the following (from Grice 1975/89b: 32):

(69)   A: Smith doesn't seem to have a girlfriend these days.
       B: He has been paying a lot of visits to New York lately.
       [B implicates that Smith has, or may have, a girlfriend in New York.]

No doubt many subsidiary premises are required, but the basic structure of the inferential process here seems to be as follows, with the implicature concerned, (70d), derived as the deductive conclusion of the proposition expressed, given in (70a) and the implicated premises in (70b)–(70c):

(70)   a.   Smith has been paying a lot of visits to New York lately.
       b.   If Smith is visiting New York a lot these days there must be some attraction for him there.

    c.   A possible attraction for Smith to visit a place a lot is that he has a girlfriend in that place.

    d.   Smith may have a girlfriend in New York.

The main difference between Grice and Sperber and Wilson here is that the latter give a much more explicit account of how implicatures are actually derived and that happens to involve some deductive inference, but only as a subsidiary part of a bigger non-demonstrative inference process.

It's true that implicated premises often seem to have a special 'feel' to them and to be, in some sense, more pragmatically interesting than implicated conclusions. As noted by Curcó (1995, 1997), they often play a pivotal role in verbal wit and in other rhetorically effective uses of language, such as the following:

(71) A: Who was that gentleman I saw you with last night?
       B: That was no gentleman. That was a senator.

(72) A: Where are you going?
       B: To the departmental meeting.
       A: (There's no need.) It's only for research-active staff.

Both the humorous effect of (71) and the wounding effect of A's second utterance in (72) depend on implicated premises that the hearer has to access in order to reach an interpretation that satisfies his expectation of relevance: 'Senators are not gentlemen' and 'B is not (or is not considered) a research-active member of staff'. A detailed investigation of these sorts of cases lies beyond my scope here, but it may well be that the effectiveness of the implicated premise is, at least partly, due to its non-deductive derivation.

As regards the classification of communicated assumptions into explicatures and implicatures within relevance theory, the status of both the premise and the conclusions in (67) is clear. Since they are not developed out of the schema linguistically encoded by the utterance, they are all implicatures. Perhaps they will not qualify as such in some other framework that makes further distinctions among communicated propositions. However, most other pragmatists I know of also assume these are implicatures; see, for instance, Levinson's (1987b) discussion of example (73) (mentioned already in section 2.3.1), and Recanati's (1989b: 320) discussion of an example with essentially the structure of (74):

(73) A: If Thatcher has won the election, she'll have won three times.
       B: Thatcher has won.
       Implicature: Thatcher has won three times.

(74) A: Did Jim go to the party?
       B: I don't know, but if anyone was there, Jim was there.
       C: Bill was there, so certainly somebody was there.
       Implicature: Jim was there.

The proposition they label an implicature in each of these cases is an implicated conclusion derived deductively.

It is high time that an important point, which alters the terms of the discussion completely, was acknowledged: it is pragmatic inference quite generally that is cancellable/defeasible. So, given the underdeterminacy thesis, which entails that pragmatic inference plays a major role in the derivation of explicatures (and of uncommunicated proposition(s) expressed, if there are any), it follows that elements of the explicit conceptual content of an utterance are also cancellable. And, since I am going to put forward the possibility that certain entailments may be implicatures, it will follow that not all implicatures are cancellable. On these grounds, the cancellability diagnostic is undermined from both sides and should probably be disregarded; the most it might be expected to achieve is to distinguish encoded linguistic meaning from pragmatically inferred meaning, but even there it falls short, since, in cases of ambiguity, an encoded meaning can be cancelled without contradiction. (See Sadock 1978, for a discussion of this point; Grice 1978/89b: 44–5, pointed out some other failings of the test.)

Let's take the two sides of the argument in turn. On the relevance-theoretic view, a standard assertive utterance of each of the (a) members of the following examples, in an appropriate context, expresses and, in fact, explicates the proposition in each of the corresponding (b) members. However, as the expressions in (c) in each case show, the pragmatically inferred content of that explicature is clearly cancellable without creating a contradiction (albeit not without creating some sense of oddity in the given context, as is also usually the case with implicature cancellation):

(75) a. She's ready.
      b. Karen is ready to leave for the airport.
      c. She's ready but Karen isn't ready to leave for the airport.

(76) a. I've had breakfast.
      b. I've had breakfast today.
      c. I've had breakfast but I haven't had it today.

(77) a. He ran to the edge of the cliff and jumped.
      b. Lionel ran to the edge of the cliff and jumped over the edge of the cliff.
      c. He ran to the edge of the cliff and jumped (up and down) but he stayed on the top of the cliff.

Theorists with strong Gricean leanings (for example, Neale 1992; Bach 2001; and, in particular, Cappelen 2000) maintain that it is not possible to cancel elements of his much narrower conception of the proposition expressed by an utterance ('what is said'). This just seems to be wrong. Consider (78c), where the 'form of words' of the utterance, given in (78a), is conjoined with the negation of the proposition it expresses in a certain context, as given in (78b). There is no contradiction here, and nor would there be on application of the test to the alternative sense of 'in the grip of a vice', or to any other assignment of a referent to 'he':

(78) a. He is in the grip of a vice.
      b. Part of Peregrine's anatomy is held fast in a clamping device.
      c. He is in the grip of a vice but no part of Peregrine's anatomy is caught in a clamping device.

Cancellability without contradiction is, therefore, not a sufficient condition for some element of utterance meaning to be an implicature.

Turning now to the issue of whether it is a necessary condition, consider the following example, (minimally adapted) from Wilson and Sperber (1986a):

(79) X: Does John drink slivovitz?
       Y: He doesn't drink any alcohol.
           a.   Slivovitz is alcohol.
           b.   John doesn't drink slivovitz.
                c.   Whisky is alcohol.
                d.   John doesn't drink whisky.

They present all of (a)–(d) as implicatures of Y's utterance, with (a) and (c) as implicated premises and (b) and (d) as implicated conclusions. Working within relevance theory, Vicente (1998) has pointed out that both (b) and (d) are entailed by the proposition expressed, 'John doesn't drink alcohol'. She sees this as a reason for denying them the status of implicatures, while I find it extremely difficult to see how they could be anything else. For one thing, given that they are communicated by the utterance, they are either explicatures or implicatures, and they cannot be explicatures because there is no logical form (or sentential subpart of a logical form) from which they could be developed. Second, the example runs exactly parallel to the following, where there is no dispute about (a)–(d) being implicatures of Y's utterance:

(80) X: Have you read Susan's book?
       Y: I don't read autobiographies.
           a.   Susan's book is an autobiography.
           b.   Y hasn't read Susan's book.
                c.   All of Dirk Bogarde's books are autobiographical.
                d.   Y hasn't read any of Dirk Bogarde's books.

The only difference between the two cases is that there happens to be an entailment relation between the proposition expressed and the (alleged) implicatures in (79b) and (79d), but no such entailment relation in (80). The derivation process in both cases is the same: in order to establish the relevance of Y's utterance as an answer to his question, X has to access the premise in (a) in each case, from which the conclusion in (b), which answers his question, follows. There is not even, necessarily, any difference in the accessibility of the premises in the two cases, since X may or may not already have them stored in his encyclopaedic knowledge concerning alcohol, in the one case, and concerning Susan's book, in the other; if he does, he can retrieve them ready-made; if he doesn't, he has to construct the premise in accordance with a standard procedure (employed also in (66) above). In the (c)/(d) pairs in each case, there is only one possible processing route: the hearer looks into his encyclopaedic entry for alcohol, in the one case, and pulls out his assumption that whisky is alcohol, from which, given the proposition expressed, the conclusion in (d) follows; in the other case, he consults his knowledge of autobiographical books and retrieves the assumption about Dirk Bogarde's books, from which, given the proposition expressed, the conclusion in (d) follows.

The same point can be applied to cases of implicated premises. Consider the following examples in parallel:[30]

(81) Sue: Are you inviting Jessica to your party?
      Kim: No. I'm only inviting close friends.
      Implicated premise: Jessica is not a close friend of Kim's.
      Implicated conclusion: Kim is not inviting Jessica to her party because
                              Jessica is not a close friend of hers.

(82) Jim: Would you like to listen to my Rolling Stones record?
      Sam: No. I'd rather listen to some real music.
      Implicated premise: Jim's Rolling Stones record is not real music.
      Implicated conclusion: Sam doesn't want to listen to Jim's Rolling
                              Stones record because it is not real music.

In each case, the negative answer to the original question raises a further (implicit) question: 'why not?' This is indirectly answered in the follow-up clause in each case, which requires the accessing of the given premise in order to arrive at an answer (the implicated conclusion). There is a difference between the two cases, but it is not a processing difference: in (82), the proposition expressed (and explicated) by Sam, that he'd rather listen to some real music than to Jim's Rolling Stones record, entails the implicated premise, that Jim's Rolling Stones record is not real music; there is no such entailment relation between the proposition expressed by Kim's utterance in (81) and her implicated premise.

Each of the entailment cases fails the cancellability test, as we would expect; adding the negation of the implicature to the words originally uttered gives a contradiction:

(83) a. He doesn't drink any alcohol but he does drink slivovitz.
      b. I'd rather listen to some real music than listen to Jim's Rolling Stones
          record but I don't mean to imply that the Rolling Stones record
          is not real music.

So, as well as not being sufficient to qualify some aspect of utterance meaning as an implicature, non-contradictory cancellability is not a necessary property of implicatures either.

I would argue too that the entailment examples discussed earlier (in section 2.3.1), which do not conform to the definition of explicature, must, if they are communicated, be implicatures. Consider them as uttered by B in response to A's question in the following:

(84) A: Have you invited any men to the function?
      B: I've invited my father.
      Implicature: B has invited at least one man.

(85) A: I can't face lentil bake again tonight; I'm desperate for some meat.
      B: Good. I've just bought some pork.
      Implicature: B has just bought some meat.

These are, perhaps, more difficult cases to accept, since it seems that the alleged implicature in each case is not just entailed, but that the crucial shift is from a particular word to an intrinsic component of its meaning. However, following Jerry Fodor's powerful arguments against lexical decomposition (and any sort of internal structure to lexical concepts), the relevance-theoretic assumption is that lexical decoding is a straightforward one-to-one mapping from monomorphemic words to conceptual addresses and it is these simple, unstructured conceptual correlates of words that figure in the logical form.[31] The conceptual address for FATHER gives access to a logical entry which specifies the inference to MALE and the conceptual address for PORK may have a logical entry that specifies the inference to MEAT (see Sperber and Wilson 1986a/95b, chapter 2). In these cases, deriving the communicated assumptions that B has invited a man, in (84), and that B has bought some meat, in (85), is an entirely inferential process, in fact a straightforward deductive inference, so the mechanism involved is essentially the same as that for any implicated conclusion. These entailments are the complement class of those that are sentential subparts of the logical form of the utterance, which are detachable from it and able to be developed into explicatures.

Note that the possibility of implicated entailments marks another difference between Grice, for whom entailments and implicatures were mutually exclusive (recall the discussion in section 2.2.3), and relevance theorists (or some of them, at least). In my view, the concept of 'entailment' and the concept of 'implicature' belong to different explanatory levels or different sorts of theory, the one a static semantic theory, the other a cognitive processing pragmatic theory.

I move on now to other matters. An important point that Sperber and Wilson make about implicatures is that they may be communicated with variable degrees of strength. In many of the examples discussed so far, the implicatures are strongly communicated; that is, there can be little doubt that they fall within the speaker's informative intention. They are fully determinate. Consider again examples (79) and (80). The speaker expects the hearer to supply not merely something like the premise in (a) and conclusion in (b) but a premise and conclusion with just their logical content. However, this does not carry over to (c) and (d) in either example, where it is much more up to the hearer exactly what premises he accesses, and therefore what further conclusions he draws. Clearly, the speaker encourages him to explore a certain conceptual field (kinds of alcohol, autobiographical books) but can have no expectation that he will recover specific instances within the range. As Grice pointed out, there may be a degree of indeterminacy regarding speaker meaning when that meaning is implicated rather than said (Grice 1975/89b: 40). Consider again an example discussed in chapter 1:

(86)   I'm feeling better today.

It is reasonably clear what the speaker explicates here, but what does she implicate? She could be communicating any number of assumptions within quite a wide range concerning her ability to function today, her readiness to get on with work, her improved state of mind, the possibility of going without Nurofen, etc. There is no precise assumption or set of assumptions that can be pinned down as those she must have specifically intended to inform the hearer of. Nevertheless, she clearly intends the hearer to derive more than the explicit content of her utterance and the more that she intends is constrained to lie within a particular conceptual range. In short, she has weakly communicated a range of implicatures, some subset of which the hearer will in fact represent, thereby bearing some responsibility for the particular assumptions he chooses as part of his interpretation of the utterance. Sperber and Wilson (1987a) describe this property of indeterminacy of implicatures as follows:

> An utterance that forces the hearer to supply a very specific premise or conclusion to arrive at an interpretation consistent with the principle of relevance has a very strong implicature. An utterance that can be given an interpretation consistent with the principle of relevance on the basis of different – though of course related – sets of premises and conclusions has a wide range of weak implicatures. Clearly, the weaker the implicatures, the less confidence the hearer can have that the particular premises or conclusions he supplies closely reflect the speaker's thoughts, and this is where the indeterminacy lies.   (Sperber and Wilson 1987a: 706)

This idea of weak implicatures plays a central role in the relevance-theoretic account of metaphor and other tropes, and in the notion of 'poetic effect' more widely (see Sperber and Wilson 1986a/95b, sections 4.6 and 4.8; Pilkington 1992, 1994, 2000).

Finally, some matters of classification. The explicature/implicature distinction is essentially a distinction between two ways of deriving communicated assumptions: by developing a linguistically given logical form and by pragmatic inference. The distinction between implicated premises and implicated conclusions is, transparently, a distinction between two different inferential roles that implicatures may play in the derivation process. In some pragmatic frameworks, implicatures are classified in various other ways: for instance, according to how frequently they arise (whether generally or just in particular contexts), according to the different principles/maxims involved in their derivation (see Horn 1984b, 1989, on Q- and R-implicatures, and Levinson 1987a, 2000, on Q-, I- and M-implicatures), or according to the kind of linguistic element that triggers them, hence talk of 'scalar' and 'clausal' quantity implicatures (see Gazdar 1979; Levinson 1983). None of these three classifications carries any weight in relevance theory: there is no generalized/particularized distinction, but a continuum of cases from the very frequent to the one-off; the system runs on a single communicative principle, so all implicatures are necessarily 'relevance' implicatures; labels such as 'scalar' are, as in all frameworks, simply convenient ways of referring to implicatures with similar semantic bases.

In the chapters to follow, some of the aspects of utterance meaning that have been traditionally assumed, within Gricean frameworks, to be implicatures will be shown to be more appropriately construed as pragmatic contributions to explicatures.

2.3.4 Deriving explicatures and implicatures

In this section, I try to give an idea of how the comprehension process works on the relevance-theoretic conception. The pragmatic inferential system is triggered into operation by an utterance which is perceived by the addressee as directed at him. In processing this stimulus, the addressee's pragmatic system employs the following strategy, which is warranted by the presumption of optimal relevance carried by all utterances:

Relevance-theoretic comprehension strategy
(a) Consider interpretations (disambiguations, reference assignments, enrichments, contextual assumptions, etc.) in order of accessibility (i.e. follow a path of least effort in computing cognitive effects).
(b) Stop when the expected level of relevance is reached.[32]

When the communicative stimulus is a verbal utterance (as opposed to a non-verbal ostensive gesture or sound), the pragmatic system has a quite precise and well-articulated piece of evidence to work with: the decoded semantic representation, or logical form. On the relevance-theoretic account of the derivation of explicatures and implicatures, interpretive hypotheses concerning both types of communicated assumption are made rapidly, on-line, 'locally' and in parallel. According to Sperber and Wilson (1997/98a), the mechanism that mediates the inferences from logical form to communicated propositions is one of 'mutual parallel adjustment' of explicatures and implicatures, constrained by the comprehension strategy. The result should consist of (sets of) premises and conclusions making up a valid argument, as in the examples in the previous section, but the important point is that the reasoning need not progress step by step from premises to conclusions. For instance, a particular conclusion, or type of conclusion, might be expected on the basis of considerations of relevance and, via a backwards inference process, premises constructed (explicatures and implicatures) which will make for a sound inference to the conclusion. The process may involve several backwards and forwards adjustments of content before an equilibrium is achieved which meets the system's current 'expectation' of relevance.

Expectations about where the relevance of an utterance will lie are considerably constrained when it occurs as a response to a question, which is the case for several of the examples I will discuss. Standard questions indicate that a certain sort of information would be relevant (have cognitive effects) to someone (the questioner herself in all the examples I will consider). In the case of yes/no questions, the relevant information would be a confirmation or denial of the propositional form of the question; in the case of wh-questions, it would be a conceptual constituent that fills the wh-slot in the incomplete logical form encoded by the questioning utterance. (For a more precise relevance-theoretic account of questions, see Sperber and Wilson 1986a/95b; Wilson and Sperber 1988a; Clark 1991.) An account of what makes questions themselves relevant (that is, of the way in which they comply with the presumption of optimal relevance carried by all utterances) remains to be given and I do not attempt it here.

First, let's take a case that, intuitively, has no implicit import (no implicatures):

(87) Passer-by: I'm looking for Whitby Street. Can you tell me where it is?
      Speaker: It's the second one down on the left.

The following is a schematic outline of the, patently non-demonstrative, inference that the passer-by's pragmatic system performs in comprehending the speaker's utterance. It should be noted that here, and in the analyses that follow, interpretive hypotheses are given in rough English paraphrases which, while adequate for illustrative purposes, may be quite remote from the actual conceptual representations employed by the pragmatic system.

(88) a. S has uttered sentence with logical form: [it is the second one down on the left] (*Output of linguistic decoding*)
      b. S's utterance is optimally relevant to me. (*Presumption of relevance*)
      c. S's utterance will achieve relevance by providing an answer to my question. (*Standard expectation created by the asking of a question*)
      d. Whitby Street is the second street on my left as I proceed down Hinkley Road. (*First accessible reference assignments and enrichments which will yield an answer to question*)

Some of the pragmatically supplied elements in the hypothesized explicature in (d) have been made highly accessible by concepts in the passer-by's own utterance (e.g. the referents assigned to 'it' and 'one'), while the enrichment of 'down on the left' depends also on immediately perceptible features of the environment. No implicatures are derived, since the speaker has given a direct answer to the question, which has sufficient effects to satisfy (b), the expectation of relevance. It has sufficient cognitive effects because it supplies exactly the information that the question indicated would be relevant.

Very often, however, a response to a question does not provide a direct answer and the addressee has to infer an implicated answer. Other things being equal, indirectness requires more processing effort than directness, so the addressee is entitled to assume extra or, at least, different cognitive effects from those achieved by a direct answer. For instance, in the next example, Bob's response to Ann's question has the strongly implicated conclusion shown there, but on the basis of the indirectness of the response, it can be expected to have further intended implications (i.e. implicatures):

(89) Ann: Shall we play tennis?
      Bob: It's raining.

      Explicature: It's raining at location$_{A/B}$
      Implicated premise: If it's raining in location$_x$ then it's not possible to play tennis at location$_x$
      Implicated conclusion: Ann and Bob can't play tennis at location$_{A/B}$

In understanding Bob's utterance, the basic explicature constructed from the logical form has to be enriched with a location constituent in order that the implicated conclusion be properly warranted. In this case, the location is anchored to the place of utterance but, as Bob's utterance of the same sentence in the different context in (90) shows, this is not always the case. The location constituent isn't given, but has to be inferred.

(90)   Context: Bob and Ann live in London. Bob has just got off the phone
                   from talking to his mother who lives in New Zealand.
       Ann: How's the weather over there?
       Bob: It's raining.

The following step-by-step account of the pragmatic processes involved in under-standing Bob's utterance in (89) is closely modelled on those given in Sperber and Wilson (1997/98a) and, in greater detail, in Wilson and Sperber (2000):

(91)   a.   Bob has uttered sentence with logical form: [it is raining]   (*Output
            of linguistic decoding*)
       b.   Bob's utterance is optimally relevant to Ann.   (*Presumption of
            relevance*)
       c.   Bob's utterance will achieve relevance by providing an answer to
            Ann's question.   (*Standard expectation created by the asking of a
            question*)
       d.   If it is raining in a particular location then it is not likely that one
            can play tennis in that location.   (*Highly accessible assumption
            which might help to answer Ann's question*)
       e.   It is raining at Ann and Bob's location.   (*First accessible enrichment
            of Bob's utterance which could combine with (d) to yield an answer
            to Ann's question*)
       f.   Ann and Bob can't play tennis at their location.   (*Inferred from (d)
            and (e); satisfies (c); accepted as an implicature of Bob's utterance*)
       g.   They can't play tennis at their location because it is raining at their
            location.   (*Further highly accessible implicature inferred from (d)
            and (e), which, together with (f) and various other (weaker)
            implicatures, such as (h), satisfies (b), the general expectation of
            relevance*)
       h.   Ann and Bob will have to find some other entertainment. They could
            go to the cinema, etc.

The extra inferential effort required by Bob's indirect reply to Ann's question is offset by extra effects, specifically, the strongly communicated implicature in (91g) which supplies a reason for the negative answer to her question, and perhaps other weakly communicated implicatures, such as those in (91h).

Several caveats need to be registered with regard to the derivation in (91). First, I have obviously made no attempt to give an accurate representation of the logical form of the utterance, which might well not reflect the expletive 'it' subject required in English, but be better rendered as [raining]. Second, the indicative mood of the sentence Bob uttered would automatically communicate a higher-level explicature, involving the weak speech-act description in (92a) and, in the absence of indications to the contrary, the system will infer the propositional attitude description in (92b):

(92) a. Bob has said that it is raining at location$_{A/B}$.
      b. Bob believes that it is raining at location$_{A/B}$.

The second of these plays a crucial role in whether the pragmatic system accepts (91e)–(91h) as a satisfactory interpretation of the utterance. If (92b) is not conveyed, say Bob is communicating his dissociation from the proposition that it is raining at their location (if he's being ironical, for instance), then (91e) is not explicated and (91f)–(91h) are not implicated. The utterance will communicate a different set of explicatures and implicatures. However, I am confining my attention in this section to straightforward assertion cases, which do communicate a basic-level explicature. Third, following the comments given above about mutual adjustment of explicit content and implicit import, it should be clear that the steps in the derivation are not sequential; interpretive hypotheses are made in parallel and adjusted so as to achieve a final stable state of sound inference. So, it could be that both the implicated premise in (91d) and the implicated conclusion in (91f) were accessed before the enrichment of the logical form given in (91e). Alternatively, an enrichment hypothesis might have occurred first and then been confirmed by the resulting implicated conclusion which provides an answer to Ann's question.[33]

In the next example, the secretary answers the client's question directly, but continues with a further utterance that seems, in effect, to be a response to an implicit question that she takes to have been raised by her direct answer to the client's overt question. This process of anticipating questions, hence where relevance lies for an interlocutor, seems to be a very common practice among speakers.

(93) Client: Can I speak to Mr Prescott?
      Secretary: No, I'm sorry. He's busy.

Let us focus on the interpretation of the secretary's second utterance 'he's busy'. The derivation process might go as follows:

(94) a. S has uttered sentence with logical form: [he is busy]
      b. S's utterance is optimally relevant.
      c. S's utterance will achieve relevance by explaining why C is not permitted to speak to Mr Prescott. (*Expectation of relevance created by S's assertion that C cannot speak to Mr Prescott*)
      d. Mr Prescott is busy. (*First accessible reference assignment which could enter into an explanation of Mr Prescott's unavailability*)
      e. A sufficient reason for someone not being available to speak to is that they are busy. (*First accessible assumption which might help explain why C cannot speak to Mr Prescott now*)
      f. C cannot speak to Mr Prescott now because Mr Prescott is busy. (*Inferred from (d) and (e), satisfying (c), so accepted as an implicature of S's utterance*)

Notice that this is not, in fact, completely parallel to the previous case; there has been a process of reference assignment, but no enrichment involving the supply of an extra constituent to the explicature. That sort of process may seem unnecessary in this case, but consider the implicated premise in (94e). The plausibility of this is not obvious as it stands, and nor is the instantiation of it that is used here, that Mr Prescott's being busy is a sufficient reason for him being unable to speak to the client. Supposing Mr Prescott runs a law firm and is never unoccupied during his working day, that is, he is always busy to some extent or other; even so, he might be prepared to break off at times and talk to a client. There are degrees of, and kinds of, busyness (as there are of many other properties). In this example, the secretary is communicating a concept of fairly intense and focused busyness. It is difficult to see how to characterize what is communicated by the word 'busy' by adding further conceptual constituents (comparable to the location constituent in the previous example). Sperber and Wilson (1997/98a) suggest that what goes on here is that the speaker intends to communicate a concept that is not linguistically encodable by an utterance, call it BUSY*, and the addressee, following the standard comprehension procedure, is able to construct it pragmatically from the concept lexically encoded by 'busy'. It is this concept that features in the explicatures and implicatures of the utterance:

(95) a. Mr Prescott is busy*.
      b. A sufficient reason for someone not being available to speak to is
          that they are busy*.
      c. C cannot speak to Mr Prescott now because Mr Prescott is busy*.

So both examples (89) and (93) require an enrichment of the logical form of the utterance in deriving the intended explicature, but in (89) this is an additional conceptual constituent, while in (93) it is an adjustment (a narrowing) of an encoded conceptual constituent. As Sperber and Wilson (1997/98a: 196) put it: 'The explicit content (explicatures) of an utterance, and in particular the meaning of specific expressions, is adjusted so as to warrant the derivation of implicatures which themselves justify the expectations of relevance created by the utterance act.'

Finally, let's reconsider an earlier example, which does not involve an explicit question; the utterance is given in (96a) and a possible basic explicature in (96b):

(96) a. He plays well.
      b. John Murray plays the violin well.

As well as reference assignment, disambiguation of the verb 'play', and supplying of an object argument 'the violin', the concept encoded by 'well' may have to be modulated, in accordance with anticipated implicatures. Let's consider two different sorts of context. In the first, the speaker and the addressee are friends attending a concert together, who do not know and have no particular interest in the violinist, John Murray. Then, the import of the utterance in (96a) may be geared more toward the end of maintaining a companionable feeling between the friends than making an informative remark about John Murray; the implicatures in such a case are weakly communicated and may follow more from the fact of utterance than from the proposition expressed (see Žegarac 1998, and Žegarac and Clark 1999, for a relevance-theoretic account of these sorts of phatic interactions). In the second context, however, the speaker is the director of the National Youth Orchestra and the addressee is Mrs Murray, mother of John, who is manifestly anxious that her son might gain a place in the orchestra. The director, who is aware of what is at stake, utters (96a) to Mrs Murray. Arguably, the explicature developed from the logical form of his utterance is not identical to (96b), but involves a pragmatic enrichment of the concept encoded by the word 'well', call it WELL*, so that an implicated conclusion that John has a good chance of getting a place in the orchestra is warranted:

(97)   a.   John Murray plays the violin well*.
       b.   Someone who plays the violin well* has a good chance of getting a
            place in the orchestra.
       c.   John Murray has a good chance of getting a place in the orchestra.

If this is right, we have a case where both kinds of enrichment occur: the recovery of an unuttered constituent and the narrowing of an encoded concept. The idea of on-line *ad hoc* concept formation in utterance understanding is explored further in chapter 5.

   There are some interesting general features of the relevance-theoretic account of the recovery of explicatures and implicatures which are worth drawing out. They can perhaps be appreciated by considering some of the observations of Stephen Levinson, who is quite sceptical about the whole approach. He characterizes the notion of explicature as 'a special kind of implicature . . . that embellishes logical form in limited ways', commenting that 'for the existence of explicatures to be more than a terminological issue, they must have some specific identifying properties. The difficulty is to see how and why certain restricted kinds of pragmatic inference should alone have pre-semantic application, and, if so, why they should be derived by the identical apparatus that derives post-semantic implicatures (i.e. the Principle of Relevance)' (Levinson 2000: 238). First, we need to straighten out a skewing of terminology: it is not the case that an explicature embellishes a logical form, pragmatic inferences do that; rather, an explicature is a kind of representation that results from the pragmatic embellishment of a logical form. Explicatures are clearly distinguished from implicatures by the way in which they are derived. Second, if the derivational accounts given in this section can be sustained, Levinson's worry about one and the same pragmatic principle/strategy (the 'identical apparatus') being involved in the derivation of both explicatures and implicatures is undercut. The crucial mechanism is one of mutual adjustment of communicated propositions until they stabilize into sound patterns of inference that meet the expectation of relevance. This process is only possible if the full range of pragmatic tasks falls under one and the same interpretive strategy or principle.

   Recall now the discussion, in section 2.1.2, of what Levinson calls 'Grice's circle', that is, the dependence of 'what is said' on implicatures and the dependence of implicatures on (a prior determination of) 'what is said'. The shift from an abstract analysis of the issue to an on-line cognitive processing account alters the picture considerably and offers a solution to the apparent problem. The set of assumptions finally settled on as the 'correct' interpretation must meet the general expectation of relevance raised by the utterance and must comprise sound patterns of inference; in all instances, at least one of the premises (the explicated one) is constrained by the logical form of the utterance; in some instances, conclusions and perhaps other premises (implicatures) are constrained by specific assumptions about where the relevance of the utterance will lie. What seems to be a circle when considered purely analytically, becomes, in practice, a matter of satisfying a set of simultaneous constraints with no requirement on the order in which elements of the solution are recovered.

Levinson's own (partial) solution to the interdependence of what is explicitly and what is implicitly communicated involves the application of default rules attached to certain linguistic forms. For instance, a scalar term as in 'some of the x' carries a generalized implicature 'not all of the x',[34] which ensures that an utterance of (98a) communicates both (98b) ('what is said') and (98c), provided the default inference is not blocked by an inconsistent contextual assumption:

(98)   a.   I like some of Woody Allen's films.
       b.   I like at least some (maybe all) of Woody Allen's films.
       c.   I don't like all of Woody Allen's films.

I am not going to try to assess the idea of default rules and generalized implicatures here, but even supposing it works satisfactorily for scalar cases like this one and for some others that depend on particular lexical items, it cannot work for the full range of cases where the proposition(s) expressed by an utterance are affected by pragmatic inference. The example in (98) is a case of what Levinson calls 'generality narrowing' (i.e. strengthening or enrichment), and so are the following:

(99)   a.   Larry's book is about negation.
       b.   Since the surgeon came quickly, he cannot be blamed.
       c.   Recovering the lost data is going to take time.

In (99a), the narrowing involves a specification of the relation between Larry and the book (whether he wrote it, is reading it, borrowed it from the library, recommended it to his reading group, etc.). In (99b), what it is to 'come quickly' has to be specified since 'suppose we have an emergency in the hospital, and the surgeon started jogging from his home when he should have jumped in his car; no judge would judge [(99b)] true' (Levinson 2000: 185). And (99c) is trivially and irrelevantly true unless there is some specification of the amount of time involved. But there is no element of linguistic form in these examples which carries the required (default) inference, and, more fundamentally, these are not cases of context-general inference anyway: the relation between Larry and the book varies with context as do the specifications of 'come quickly' and 'take time'.

Another phenomenon Levinson mentions in making the case that there are 'implicatural contributions to "what is said"' is ellipsis. In this regard, he presents and discusses the first two of the following examples (Levinson 2000: 183):

(100)   A: Which side got three goals?
             (Q-implicates 'which side got three-and-no-more goals?')
        B: Tottenham Hotspurs.   [got three-and-no-more goals]

(101)   A: They won't visit Mary's parents.
        B: Old grudge.

(102)   A: *The Times* gave it only a tiny mention on the back page.
        B: Typical.

Example (100) is a straightforward case of linguistic ellipsis, where the propositional form of the question provides a schema for the answer to slot into. The pragmatic enrichment (a Q-implicature in this case, according to Levinson) that applies to the question is carried over into the interpretation of the elliptical utterance; here, it is a strengthening from the alleged encoded meaning of 'at least three' to 'exactly three'. But the examples in (101) and (102), taken from Barton (1990), are very different; although subsentential, they are not cases of linguistic ellipsis proper at all, and, as Levinson himself says of (101): 'complex reasoning and not rule-application is involved in proposition recovery' (2000: 184). In other words, the process involved in recovering the proposition expressed, say (103), is not a case of straightforward copying into an available propositional schema, and default inferences or generalized implicature play no discernible role. Rather, the pragmatic inferences involved depend on the presence of particular contextual assumptions.

(103)   There is an old grudge between the Simpsons and Mary's parents.

In general, subsentential utterances require a considerable measure of context-particular pragmatic inference in order for the proposition expressed to be recovered so that no general solution to Levinson's circle can be provided by an account in terms of generalized or default inferences. (For further discussion of the comprehension of subsentential utterances, see the next section).

Lastly, recall that Levinson follows Grice in equating pragmatic (maxim-driven) inference and implicature, even while recognizing, as Grice did not, that (a) the processes of disambiguation and reference assignment are maxim-dependent, and (b) there are considerable further processes of pragmatic enrichment involved in determining the explicit content of an utterance. According to him, it follows from this set of assumptions that generalized *implicatures* (and, in fact, some particularized *implicatures* as well) contribute to the proposition(s) expressed. But this is a very confusing way of characterizing the situation. It is completely out of step with one of the defining properties of conversational implicatures which is that they lie outside the proposition expressed (not affecting the truth conditions of the utterance), a property assumed by Grice and maintained by most pragmatists since him, even those who recognize the role of the maxims in deriving the proposition(s) expressed, such as Walker (1975), Recanati (1989b/91, 1993), and Bach (1994a). It also threatens to obscure another important distinction, that between communicated assumptions (i.e. those propositions that constitute the interpretation of the utterance) and the inferential steps involved in arriving at them. It is not obvious that every step of the non-demonstrative process should be construed as generating a communicated assumption; in particular, it is not obvious that the disambiguation, reference assignment and enrichment processes involved in deriving the proposition expressed should be so construed.

Consider again the coreference case discussed in section 2.1.2:

(104)   a.   John came in and he sat down.
        b.   John$_x$ came in and he$_x$ sat down.
        c.   John$_x$ came in and he$_y$ sat down.

On Levinson's view, the preference for the coreferential interpretation in (104b) over the disjoint reference in (104c) is due to a pragmatic principle which he calls the I-principle ('I' for informativeness), based on Grice's second quantity maxim ('Do not make your contribution more informative than is required'). The inferred coreference is, therefore, said to be a case of I-implicature. But just what proposition is implicated?

(105)   a.   John came in and he, John, sat down.
        b.   'He' refers to whoever 'John' refers to.

It surely cannot be (105a) since that is 'what is said', the level of explicit representation, to which the (alleged) implicature is supposed to have contributed. It seems, then, that it must be (105b), a propositional form with metalinguistic elements, representing a hypothesis about reference assignment. By parity of reasoning, each pragmatic resolution of an ambiguity and each enrichment of logical form must involve an implicature of this sort:

(106)   a.   'Ring' (in this utterance) means 'piece of jewellery'.
        b.   'Tired' (in this utterance) means 'tired to degree x'.
        c.   'Too heavy' (in this utterance) means 'too heavy to carry on a bike'.

But are these really among the assumptions that make up the interpretation of the utterance, those propositions which, once recovered as the object of the speaker's communicative intention, the addressee may then accept or reject, depending on whether or not they mesh with his existing representation of the world, assumptions that he may add to his mental store of knowledge and retrieve later to use as contextual assumptions in the processing of subsequent utterances? The answer is surely 'no'; rather, what are represented in (106) are inferential steps taken in the process of recovering the propositions that do fall within the speaker's communicative intention.

On the relevance-theoretic account, tentative interpretive hypotheses concerning intended referents and senses are made on-line and are subsequently confirmed or disconfirmed, depending on whether or not they contribute to an overall interpre-

tation that meets the expectation of relevance. So, in the case of inferred coreference, there is no *implicature* along the lines of (105b); rather, there is an interpretive hypothesis, like (105a), regarding the *explicature* of the utterance.[35] If this then
functions as a premise in a sound pattern of inference that accords with the relevance-based comprehension strategy, the hypothesis is confirmed and so is retained
as one of the assumptions communicated by the utterance. In conclusion, then,
equating pragmatic inference with implicature blurs important distinctions; among
the many pragmatic inferences involved in understanding an utterance, some result
in implicatures while others contribute to explicatures.

2.3.5   Subsentential utterances, saying and explicating

Subsentential utterances often prove an interesting sort of test case for the adequacy
of accounts of verbal communication. Here, by way of reminder, are some of the
types of example that have come up in passing in previous sections:

(107)   a.   Michael's father.
               Communicates: The man near the door is the father of Michael
                               Blair.
        b.   On the top shelf.
               Communicates: The marmalade is on the top shelf.
        c.   Ann: They won't visit Mary's parents.
             Bob: Typical.
               Communicates: It is typical of the behaviour of the Simpsons that
                               they won't visit Mary's parents.
        d.   Confidentially, Sam is seriously ill.
               Communicates: I am telling you confidentially that Sam is
                               seriously ill.

I include (107d) as a case in which, given the multiple speech-act (hence multiple
logical-form) account outlined in section 2.3.2, the adverbial 'confidentially' has its
own logical form distinct from that of its host clause. This looks like a candidate
for a subsentential logical form and there may be various other cases of embedded
fragments which have subsentential logical forms (appositional noun phrases, for
instance).

   However, my focus in this section is on examples, like (107a)–(107c), which occur
unembedded and alone. They seem to be genuine instances of subsentential utterances rather than cases of syntactic ellipsis, such as the following, in which an apparently subsentential utterance is really fully sentential:

(108)   a.   A: Where's Sue?
             B: At home.
        b.   A: Mary will come to the party.
             B: Bill won't.

B's utterance in (108a) is an ellipsed version of 'Sue is at home' and in (108b) of 'Bill won't come to the party'. So, in these cases, arguably, the logical form of the utterance is fully sentential, with a bunch of empty syntactic categories in the phonologically unrealized positions, and recovery of the missing material is a matter of grammatical reconstruction. Unlike these ellipsis cases, the examples in (107) can occur discourse-initially (precisely because they do not rely on a linguistic antecedent) and there is some indeterminacy regarding the conceptual material to be supplied in constructing the proposition communicated.[36]

There are two questions I would like to raise concerning these subsentential utterances: (a) what would Grice's position on them have been (that is, what is it that is 'said' by uttering them)? (b) does the concept of 'explicature' as so far developed apply satisfactorily to the propositions communicated by the utterances in (107)?

It is not clear what Grice would have said about fragmentary utterances of this sort. On the one hand, it is obvious that contextual material *has* to be supplied in order to achieve full propositionality (truth-evaluability). On the other hand, this is not a matter of either disambiguation or reference assignment, and there is quite a strong intuition that it is very odd, probably in fact false, to say that someone *said* that 'X Y Z' when the only constituent actually verbalized was 'Z'. As discussed earlier, one of the impetuses for Grice in developing the saying/implicating distinction was his concern to defend certain philosophical theses, and, naturally, they and their supporting principles and statements were framed in full sentences. I don't suppose Moore would have felt comfortable with an utterance of 'my hand', made with a look of certainty, as a datum for his theory of knowledge, nor Grice with 'a red pillar-box' or just 'red' as possible L-statements in his causal theory of perception. Perhaps these and other philosophical issues dominated Grice's concerns to the extent that he did not address some of the more ordinary and banal aspects of everyday non-philosophical communication. There is some irony, then, in his choice of terms for his account of language use: 'the logic of *conversation*', '*conversational* maxims', '*conversational* implicatures'. Most conversation is full of subsentential utterances, which do not seem to be accounted for in his scheme; it follows that there is no basis for the inference (calculation) of most of the conversational implicatures communicated in the rough and tumble of quick spontaneous exchange, since crucially in the Gricean system they follow, as it is put, from the saying of what is said.[37] Similar, and other, problems will be shown (in section 2.5.2) to arise for Bach's even narrower concept of 'what is said'. In developing his account and discussing the range of cases it covers, he too does not mention the ubiquitous phenomenon of subsentential utterances.

Now, what about the explicature(s) of a subsentential utterance? Explicatures by their very nature are full of elements which have been supplied pragmatically; the degree of 'development' of the encoded content is variable, but usually includes considerably more than the mere reference assignment and disambiguation of Grice's 'what is said'. It follows from the relevance-driven view of interpretation that the linguistically encoded element of an utterance is not generally geared towards achieving as high a degree of explicitness as possible, but that the speaker, taking account of the addressee's immediately accessible assumptions and the inferences he can readily draw, should try to encode just what is necessary to ensure that the inference process arrives as effortlessly as possible at the intended meaning. A speaker who fails to heed this, or gets it wrong, causes her hearer unnecessary processing effort (for instance, pointless decoding of concepts which are already activated or highly accessible to him), and runs the risk of not being understood or, at the least, of being found irritatingly pedantic and/or patronizing. The theory predicts that, in many contexts, a subsentential utterance will be more appropriate than a sentential one.

The term 'explicature' has the further fortunate property that it is not in lay usage; we do not go about reporting to each other that so-and-so explicated that P. It is a technical term, the introduction of which didn't just effect a minor amendment to the notion of 'saying'. It is getting at something rather different, in one sense something more abstract (it's not an assertion, an order, or any other speech-act type of thing), in another sense more concrete (a communicated thought/assumption that is developed out of the encoded content). So the move from 'what is said' to the concept of 'explicature' marks a change in the view of what a pragmatic theory is to account for, what the crucial components of 'what is communicated' are.

Stainton (1994) gives a relevance-theoretic account of the interpretation of an example like (107a), according to which a speaker who utters 'Michael's father', is employing a bare noun phrase, without any further linguistic structure (specifying slots to be contextually filled), and is thereby communicating the proposition 'The man near the door is the father of Michael Blair'. Given an easily imagined context (say, a party given by Michael Blair, who is a college friend of the interlocutors, etc.), in which the addressee can readily access this propositional form, the noun-phrase utterance may be more relevant than utterances of either of the following:

(109)   a.   The man near the door is Michael's father.
        b. $[_{IP} [_{NP} e] [_{I'} [_{I} e [_{VP} [_{V} e][_{NP}$ Michael's father$]]]]]$

In making the case for the relevance of the noun-phrase utterance as against the full sentence in (109a), Stainton points out that, since (109a) contains more words than 'Michael's father', understanding it requires certain inferential tasks not required by the noun-phrase utterance: 'words which need to be disambiguated, enriched and assigned reference. Is "man" to be taken as human being – as in "earth man" – or as male human being? In saying "the man", which man is the speaker referring to? Is "near" to be taken as near for two planets, near for two cities, near for a missed target, or near for two medium sized objects? And so on. . . . Discovering the propositional form of an utterance of the more explicit [(109a)] may, therefore, require more processing effort than discovering the completed logical form of an utterance of [(107a)] . . .' (Stainton 1994: 277). One possibility here is that, given the context, there is, highly accessible to the addressee, an assumption schema along the lines of '*The man near the door is x*', where, crucially, the italicized string is not to be taken as an expression of English but, rather, as an incomplete conceptual structure, a constituent of the language of thought (whose component concepts may well not be identical to any lexically encoded concepts). The conceptual material decoded from the noun phrase, and perhaps pragmatically enriched itself, slots directly into the accessible frame, resulting in the communicated proposition.

This line of argument does not look so promising in the case of (109b), where the only overtly articulated constituent is 'Michael's father', the other positions not being phonologically realized. One might think that the processing effort involved here is the same as that required by the superficially identical noun-phrase utterance. Stainton sidesteps this point, saying that since (109b) is an elliptical sentence, it cannot appear in the discourse-initial position that the noun-phrase utterance occurs in and, therefore, there is no issue concerning which of them would be more relevant in the given context. This may well be right, in which case nothing more need be said. However, just suppose, for the sake of argument, that this structure could be employed, not functioning as strict syntactic ellipsis here, but instead translating into a conceptual structure with open conceptual slots corresponding to each of the linguistically given empty categories. Wouldn't it then be as economical in its processing effort requirements as the bare noun-phrase utterance, if not even more so? I don't think so. First, there must be more effort involved in decoding this more elaborate linguistic representation than in decoding the noun phrase, and, given the putative highly activated schema 'The man near the door is x', the conceptual structure with open slots decoded from (109b) would be largely redundant. Second, a point not explored by Stainton, there is a degree of indeterminacy about the proposition expressed by an utterance of 'Michael's father' which is not accommodated by the structure in (109b). Rather than the propositional form 'The man near the door is the father of Michael Blair', the addressee might recover 'The father of Michael Blair is standing beside Michael Blair' (or any other of a wide range of possibilities). As discussed in chapter 1, the speaker may have no specific expectation about which precise proposition within an acceptable range the addressee should recover, and different addressees might recover different ones, any of which is satisfactory as regards the primary point of identifying a particular individual as Michael Blair's father. On this basis, the conceptual structure decoded from the fully sentential structure in (109b), say something like 'Someone/something [$_{pred}$ $V_{stative}/V_{dynamic}$ Michael's father]' will not necessarily mesh with the assumption schema most accessible to the addressee, for instance, 'x is standing beside Michael Blair' or 'x is the uneasy looking man gulping down the alcoholic punch'. The only way round this would be to allow for a range of fully sentential logical forms to be recovered from the utterance of 'Michael's father', presumably, in fact, the full set of possible elliptical sentences in which the only overtly articulated constituent is 'Michael's father'. The addressee's pragmatic system would then have the task of disambiguation, that is, of choosing among these logical forms on the basis of the most accessible conceptual schema for constructing a complete propositional form. So, it does look as if the minimal noun-phrase utterance, rather than either of the fully sentential structures in (109), provides the least costly route for the hearer to access the communicated proposition in the given context, and is, therefore, the one that a speaker who is trying to be optimally relevant should choose.

In his work on non-sentential communication, Stainton is primarily concerned to establish that the proposition communicated by a subsentential utterance, such as those in (107), is not a case of implicature but is communicated explicitly and is, in fact, asserted (see also Stainton 1997, 1998). As far as I can see, the possibility that the cases given could be treated as implicatures does not arise on either a

Gricean or a relevance-theoretic account. For Grice, the communicated proposition cannot be an implicature since that would leave the utterance without any 'what is said' and so no way of calculating the alleged implicature. From the relevance-theoretic point of view, since the given communicated proposition is clearly derived by pragmatically developing the encoded subsentential logical form it must be an explicature. No doubt, in particular contexts, these utterances also communicate other propositions which are, in fact, implicatures.

According to Stainton, the person who utters 'Michael's father' not only explicates but also asserts that the man near the door is the father of Michael Blair. What this amounts to on the relevance-theoretic account is that the speaker is taken to have also communicated a higher-level explicature expressing her belief in the proposition expressed. Of course, as Stainton acknowledges, subsentential utterances can be used to communicate a variety of other propositional attitudes and so to perform a range of other types of speech act:

(110)   a.   Out!   (Ordering the addressee to get out of the room)
        b.   Just one!   (Permitting the addressee to have just one cake)
        c.   Gently, gently!   (Advising the addressee to be gentle in his handling of a difficult situation)
        d.   The meter.   (Reminding the addressee to go and put more money in the parking meter)
        e.   A £40 fine.   (Warning the addressee that parking in a certain position could result in a £40 fine)
        f.   Sally?   (Enquiring whether it was Sally on the phone)
        g.   Where?   (Requesting the addressee to reveal where he has put the marmalade)

On a relevance-theoretic analysis, (110a) would have the higher-level explicatures in (111a) and (111b), and, given certain other paralinguistic information, such as tone of voice, and appropriate contextual assumptions concerning the power relations between the speaker and the addressee, it could be interpreted as an order (see discussion of speech acts in Sperber and Wilson 1986a/95b: 243–54).

(111)   a.   The speaker is telling the addressee to get out of the room.
        b.   It is desirable to the speaker (and potential) that the addressee get of the room.

The way in which explicit communication is characterized in relevance theory seems to accommodate subsentential utterances quite satisfactorily. Linguistic communication (and any other ostensive communication involving a code) makes possible the strongest form of communication, since it enables the communicator to make strongly manifest her informative intention to make some particular assumption strongly manifest. Still, as the linguistic underdeterminacy thesis underlines, there are many degrees of explicitness, and phrasal utterances like 'Michael's father', 'In there', and 'Typical' are simply cases where, occurring within broader situations of human social engagement, the most efficient linguistic stimulus for a

given communicative purpose is a very minimal one. While the notion of weak communication, of indeterminacy of communicated assumptions, is most often discussed
in connection with implicit communication (as in section 2.3.3), it is plainly a property of explicit communication too. Fragmentary utterances display this property of
indeterminacy in an especially clear way, since the hearer has considerable leeway
in how he represents the recovered content ('The man near the door is the father
of Michael Blair', 'The father of Michael Blair is the diffident looking guy in the
pink shirt', etc.). The extent of indeterminacy of explicature is considered in chapter
5, where the move to accommodating loose uses of linguistic expressions at the
explicit level entails that even the constituents of an utterance which are encoded
may not ensure the determinacy of those parts of the explicature they represent.
However, in the next section, I outline a different, more established line on non-
literal linguistic use.

2.3.6   Explicature and non-literalness

As emphasized in Sperber and Wilson (1986a/95b), a proposition expressed by an
utterance may or may not be actually (ostensively) communicated; that is, it may
or may not be an instance of P in the schema 'the speaker makes mutually manifest her intention to make manifest to the addressee that P'. The proposition
expressed by a metaphorical utterance or some other kind of loose use is not communicated in this sense, so is not an explicature, but rather serves as an effective
and efficient means of giving the hearer access to those assumptions which are communicated. Consider utterances of the sentences in (112a) and (113a)–(113c):

(112)   a.   Jane is my anchor in the storm.
        b.   The speaker says that Jane is her anchor in the storm.

(113)   a.   This steak is raw.
        b.   The room is silent.
        c.   Mike is bald.

The proposition expressed by the metaphorical utterance in (112a) involves predicating of Jane a property (of being an anchor) which the speaker patently does not
believe holds of her. The only explicature communicated by the utterance is the
higher-level one in (112b), where the proposition expressed is embedded in a (weak,
generic) speech-act description, which does not entail speaker endorsement. What
is communicated is a range of weak implicatures concerning the role Jane plays in
the speaker's life; the conceptual structure encoded by the phrase 'my anchor in the
storm' gives the hearer immediate access to a range of other properties associated
with anchors in storms and encourages him to select some subset of those that can
be predicated of a human being: say, reliable and stable when life gets difficult,
helpful in calming the speaker when she is disturbed, preventing her from being
'swept off course', etc. It is indeterminate exactly which of these the speaker implicated, but it is clear that she intended the addressee to recover some such assump-

tions within a constrained range of possibilities. The speaker may have had no specific individual assumptions in mind but rather a complex and probably ineffable
concept of Jane's significance in her life. The addressee has to take some responsibility for the specific propositions he recovers in interpreting the utterance.

In the more mundane cases of loose talk in (113), the speaker again does not
explicate the proposition literally expressed (since it is mutually manifest that the
steak is underdone rather than raw, that the room has a very low level of noise,
that Mike has quite a few wispy strands of hair). Rather, the property encoded in
the predicate gives access to a range of other properties that can be truthfully predicated of the subject; in the case of (113a), the implicatures might include that the
steak is underdone, it is inedible, the speaker is disgusted by it, she wants it to be
cooked more, etc. These are rather stronger than the sort of implications communicated by the metaphor in (112); it seems that when the property literally predicated belongs to a completely different category of entity (is a category mistake, in
other words), as in (112), the communication is far more evocative, it requires more
searching on the part of the hearer (more processing effort) and so gives rise to more
effects.

The crucial underpinning of this account is Sperber and Wilson's (1986a/95b)
concept of the interpretive use of a representation, which is contrasted with the more
familiar descriptive use, on which the representation is used to represent a state of
affairs and is true or false of that state of affairs. A representation with propositional content (such as a thought or an utterance) is interpretively used when it is
used to represent the propositional content of another representation; in such a case
the relation between the representation and what it represents is one of logical
resemblance. Two representations resemble one another interpretively in a context
if and only if they share analytic and contextual implications in that context. Like
all resemblances, interpretive resemblance is a matter of degree.

As well as the obvious kinds of interpretive use of utterances, such as reporting
speech or thought, there are cases of speculation or reflection in which an utterance
is used to represent a type of utterance or a kind of thought whose intrinsic properties are felt to be worth considering; for instance, a thought like 'if only human
beings could free themselves of desire they could be happy'. In any of these cases,
the proposition expressed may not be explicated by the speaker, that is, endorsed
by the speaker herself. However, there is, according to Sperber and Wilson
(1986a/95b, 1987a), an even more fundamental and general level of interpretive
use: every utterance is used interpretively to represent a thought of the speaker's;
that is, the propositional form of the utterance is an interpretation of the propositional form of the speaker's thought.

This is where metaphor, and loose use more generally, come in, on the standard
relevance-theoretic account. In cases of the literal interpretation of a thought, the
proposition expressed doesn't just resemble, but is identical to, the propositional
form of the speaker's thought, identity being the extreme case of resemblance and
literalness a special case of interpretive resemblance. When the speaker talks loosely
or metaphorically there is a relation of non-identical resemblance between the two
propositional forms. Then, again, the proposition expressed is not explicated (com-

municated) but is used as an efficient means of giving the hearer access to those assumptions the speaker does endorse and is communicating. In this account of loose talk, the full rendering of which I have not given here, we can see an interesting asymmetry in the way Sperber and Wilson view two apparently complementary pragmatic processes: enrichment or strengthening of encoded content and broadening or loosening of encoded content. As I've emphasized in this chapter and the last, linguistic underdeterminacy entails that there is much work of pragmatic completion and enrichment at the level of the proposition expressed. Loosening of encoded content, on the other hand, is assumed to have no effect on the proposition expressed; rather, the effects all come in at the level of implicature. In this respect the relevance-theoretic account has stayed in line with the Gricean approach, on which the proposition expressed by the utterance is not communicated (it is not meant, hence it is not said); the communicated propositional content of the utterance is entirely implicated. Grice moved to a concept of 'making as if to say'; Sperber and Wilson have an unexplicated proposition expressed. This has long been the standard relevance-theory position (Sperber and Wilson 1986a/95b, 1986b, 1987a, 1990; Wilson and Sperber 1988b; Wilson 1994); however, in some recent work, a more radical alternative has been advocated on which both conceptual loosening and enrichment are seen as pragmatic processes which affect the level of explicit content (see Wilson 1995; Carston 1996b/97a). I explore this possibility in chapter 5 and advocate a symmetrical account of the two processes. This, I believe, will mark the final severing of the cognitive theory of communication from its logical, philosophical forebears, for on this view the pragmatic contribution to explicature includes not only developments that build on encoded linguistic meaning, but also adjustments that broaden it, and so, effectively, drop or override elements of encoded content. The result is an explicitly communicated assumption which is very remote from any notion of 'the proposition expressed' in the existing philosophical or semantic literature.

Cases of irony, such as the standard example in (114a) below, involve representation by resemblance at yet another level, on the relevance-theoretic account, since the thought that an ironical utterance represents is itself being used to represent a thought or utterance, which is attributed to someone other than the speaker herself at that moment, and to which the speaker tacitly expresses an attitude of dissociation. Ironical utterances are analysed as cases of echoic interpretive use, where an 'echoic' utterance is one which tacitly attributes a thought/utterance to someone and, also tacitly, expresses an attitude to that thought/utterance. I will not motivate or explain this account further here, but in the context of the present section the point is that the proposition the speaker expresses is, again, not explicated. The explicatures the utterance does have are the higher-level ones given in (114b) and (114c):

(114) a. It's a lovely day.
       b. The speaker has said that it's a lovely day.
       c. The speaker thinks it is ridiculous to believe/assert that it's a lovely day.

Any implicatures that the utterance may communicate depend on the attitudinal explicature in (114c), for instance:

(115)   a.   It's a ghastly day.
        b.   We can't possibly go for a picnic today.
        c.   The addressee [who predicted a lovely day] has got it badly wrong.
        d.   The addressee is a foolish optimist.

Ironical use is a very different sort of phenomenon from the loose or metaphorical use of linguistically encoded concepts, since it involves a whole further level of metarepresentation. In this respect, it is like reported speech or thought and other cases of attributive use; the proposition expressed by utterances of this sort also represents a thought of the speaker's which is itself a representation of another thought or utterance, to which the speaker may express either a corroborative or a dissociative attitude. As will be seen in chapter 5, the divorce between the two tropes, metaphor and irony, is even more marked on the unitary treatment of enrichment and loose use of linguistic expressions explored there. On that account, adjustments to conceptual content at the level of the propositional form (narrowings, loosenings) eventuate in an explicated (communicated) proposition expressed, while an ironical utterance expresses a proposition that is not part of what is explicitly communicated. In fact, ironical utterances are one of the few phenomena that give some weight to the position that we need to maintain a concept of 'proposition expressed' (as distinct from explicature). After all, we seem to have quite strong intuitions that the proposition expressed (hence the truth conditions of) an utterance of (114a) are that it is a lovely day, whether it is uttered seriously or ironically. For detailed discussion of this account of irony, see Sperber and Wilson (1981, 1986a/95b: 237–43), Martin (1992), Wilson and Sperber (1992), Seto (1998), Sperber and Wilson (1998b).

2.3.7   Blakemore: the conceptual/procedural distinction

There is one last theoretical piece left to complete this account of relevance-theoretic concepts bearing on the explicit/implicit distinction. I have emphasized the role of pragmatic input in arriving at the explicatures communicated by an utterance, given the often meagre contribution from linguistically encoded content. To doubly dissociate the semantic/pragmatic distinction from the explicit/implicit, I need to point out that there are cases of encoded meaning which do not enter into the explicit level of communication, but which play their part at the level of what is implicitly communicated.

Blakemore (1987) took up the standard cases of Gricean conventional implicature ('but', 'moreover', 'therefore'), added some further cases of her own ('after all', 'you see', 'also') and investigated how these linguistic devices function within a cognitive pragmatic theory. As observed by Grice and others, they do not seem to contribute to the truth-conditional content, the proposition expressed by the utterance, but Blakemore found that rather than making conceptual contributions to some other level (implicatures), they appear to function more like filters on, or pointers to, the pragmatic inferences the hearer is to carry out. For example, simplifying her account somewhat, 'but' (on its 'denial of expectation' use) constrains the hearer to process the clause that follows it in such a way that it contradicts and eliminates a proposition potentially present in the context, most likely one derived from the preceding clause. Consider Bob's response to Ann's question in the following:

(116)   Ann: Are you interested in seeing *Sense and Sensibility*?
        Bob: Hmm. Costume dramas are usually boring, but it does have some great actors in it.

As discussed in section 2.3.3, the proposition expressed by the first clause of Bob's utterance, taken in isolation, seems to implicate that he is not very interested in seeing *Sense and Sensibility*. However, the implicated conclusion that Ann will ultimately derive as the answer to her question is that, on balance, Bob *is* moderately interested in seeing the film. This is explained by Blakemore's analysis, because 'but' indicates that the interpretation of the clause that follows it is to include a proposition that contradicts a highly accessible assumption and replaces it.

Suppose the exchange goes differently; Bob hasn't got beyond his 'hmm' and Ann, who is very keen to see the film, comes in with:

(117)   A: It should be good. After all, Emma Thompson is in it.

Here, 'after all' indicates that the addressee is to process the following clause in such a way that it provides evidence or backing for some highly accessible assumption(s), here the propositions communicated by the preceding utterance, some of which, an explicature and an implicature, are given in (118):

(118)   a.   *Sense and Sensibility* should be good.
        b.   We should go to see *Sense and Sensibility*.

The interpretation of the 'after all, Q' utterance is given in (119), with (119a) the basic explicature, (119b)–(119c) implicated premises and (119d)–(119e) implicated conclusions:

(119)   a.   Emma Thompson is in *Sense and Sensibility*.
        b.   If Emma Thompson is in a film, the film is likely to be good.
        c.   If the film is likely to be good, we should go to see it.
        d.   *Sense and Sensibility* is likely to be good.
        e.   We should go to see *Sense and Sensibility*.

The semantics of 'after all' has played a guiding role in the accessing of the implicated premises which together with the explicature provide an argument which backs up the assumptions in (118). Whether or not Bob agrees with the proposition in (119b), which expresses a positive view of Emma Thompson, Ann's use of 'after all' leaves him in no doubt that he is expected to access it as part of the interpretation of her utterance. For more detailed accounts of these and other 'non-truth-conditional' connectives, see Blakemore (1987, 1989b, 1990, 1992, 2002).

Blakemore's most important and very influential conclusion was that the elements of meaning encoded by these expressions are procedural rather than conceptual; rather than encoding constituents that enter into the representational content of an utterance, they indicate, guide, constrain, or direct the inferential phase of comprehension. The procedural idea is, at least in part, a consequence of the kind of explanation of utterance interpretation that relevance theory provides and of the broader approach to the mind within which it is developed (representational and computational): conceptual meaning enters into representations; procedural meaning indicates particular computational processes. Expressions that indicate an inferential procedure are just the sort of effort-saving devices you would expect to feature in a code which is subservient to a relevance-driven processing mechanism, a mechanism which is geared to deriving cognitive effects at least cost to the processing resources of the system. Given their function of reducing the inferential work that the addressee has to do in order to understand the utterance, procedural encodings seem to be intrinsically communicative and, therefore, unlikely to occur as elements of the language of thought.

On Blakemore's (1987) account, it looked as if all conceptual encodings contribute to the explicit side of communication, while procedural encoding constrains inferences affecting the implicit side (implicated premises and conclusions). However, as discussed in chapter 1, there are various other linguistic elements, such as pronouns and demonstratives, which, while they have a bearing on the truth conditions of the utterance they occur in, do not contribute their encoded content to the proposition(s) expressed. Recall the registering in the antecedent of conditional statements of truth conditions of the referential constraint(s) encoded by 'this', 'she', etc. It seems to follow that they are best construed as involving a different type of encoding from those whose encoded meaning does supply a constituent to explicit content. And once one sees that the essential function of procedural encodings is to constrain processes of pragmatic inference, it begins to seem likely that linguistic systems will include procedural elements that play a guiding role, not only in the derivation of implicatures, but in the full range of pragmatic tasks.

Wilson and Sperber (1993a) develop this idea: they suggest that pronouns and demonstratives encode procedural information that reduces the search space for the pragmatic process of reference assignment, and that various elements of linguistic form, including the indicative, imperative or subjunctive mood, rising or falling intonation, inverted word order, and some particles and markers like 'please' and 'let's' constrain the process of inferring the higher-level explicatures expressing the speaker's propositional attitude and speech act. So, for instance, an utterance of (120a) might communicate the explicatures in (120b)–(120c):

(120)   a.   Open the window, please.
        b.   S wants and considers it potential that H open the window.
        c.   S is requesting H to open the window.

It is important to note here that the imperative morphology does not encode the *concept* of requesting or of any other speech-act type, nor does it encode anything *conceptual* concerning the speaker's attitude to the propositional content [H open the window]. It provides a procedural constraint (concerning the desirability and potentiality of the state of affairs described) on the attitude and speech act that is to be inferred. As part of a different utterance this constraint might result in an interpretation on which the speaker is taken to be ordering or warning or advising or permitting the hearer. The procedural marker 'please' in (120a) provides a further indication that it is the speaker (rather than the addressee) to whom the potential state of affairs is desirable and that she does not assume she has the social power to compel the hearer's compliance (as in an order, for instance).

Although procedural encoding does not play a major role in this book (it does make an appearance in section 3.7.2), it is an important idea in relevance theory, one with the potential to bring some light to bear on the interaction of linguistic, paralinguistic and gestural ostensive acts, which, after all, often occur together in a single communicative act. For instance, a smile, a demonstration with a hand or head movement, a tentative or strident tone of voice, can all affect the inferential process of arriving at the intended interpretation of an utterance. If these can be said to encode anything it is surely not something conceptual but rather something procedural. Finally in this regard, consider how the conceptual/procedural distinction may help explain the little puzzle thrown up by the following examples:

(121)   a.   Did John pass the exam?
        b.   Yes.
        c.   He did.
        d.   He did, he did.
        e.   Yes, he did.

The responses in (121b) and (121c) seem to express the same proposition, that is, that John passed the exam, and so to be truth-conditionally equivalent. But while the response in (121d) is repetitive and redundant (though doubtless with certain cognitive effects thereby achieved), that in (121e) is not. If 'yes' is taken to encode something procedural, say, a constraint to the effect that an affirmatory interpretation is to be constructed, then we can begin to see an account of the difference emerging. While the utterance in (121d) consists of two instances of one and the same elliptical sentence that must be conceptually completed in the identical way, there is rather more leeway in what is to be recovered by a procedural constraint, so that 'yes' in (121e) may function merely to intensify the speaker's positive response.[38]

To sum up the whole of section 2.3, I'll give a stark taxonomy of the different combinations of semantic and pragmatic roles that specific linguistic devices may have: in terms of what they encode (conceptual or procedural information), the communicative level at which they function (explicit [= explicature] or implicit [= implicature]), and whether they contribute to the truth conditions of the utterance or not. An illustration of each of the possible combinations is taken from the utterance in (122).

(122)   She doesn't like cats but, happily, she has agreed to look after Fleabag.

(a)   'cats' – conceptual, explicit, truth-conditional (contributes its content to a proposition expressed);
(b)   'she' – procedural, explicit, truth-conditional (constrains the derivation of a proposition expressed);
(c)   'happily' – conceptual, explicit, non-truth-conditional (contributes its content to a higher-level explicature);
(d)   indicative mood indicator – procedural, explicit, non-truth-conditional (constrains the derivation of a higher-level explicature);
(e)   'but' – procedural, implicit, non-truth-conditional (constrains the derivation of implicatures).

Note that in each case there are two semantic classifications, reflecting the two semantic distinctions in play: truth-conditional vs. non-truth-conditional, and conceptual vs. procedural. These distinctions crosscut each other, which raises questions such as whether one is more fundamental than the other, whether they belong to different levels of theorizing, etc. It seems clear enough that for the kind of decoding (translational) semantics which provides the input to pragmatic inference, it is the conceptual/procedural distinction which matters. As suggested in earlier sections, it is unlikely that the truth-conditional/non-truth-conditional distinction plays any kind of central role in this communicative theory. Every fully propositional representation has a determinate truth condition, which includes explicatures (whether basic-level, lower-level or higher-level) and every implicature. However, the label 'non-truth-conditional', as applied to utterances, has been used for a variety of quite disparate phenomena, including sentence adverbials, parenthetical phrases, mood indicators, and discourse connectives and particles. Once we have the cognitive semantic distinction between conceptual and procedural encoding, and the pragmatic distinction between explicatures and implicatures, both independently motivated, the notion of 'non-truth-conditional' meaning can be dropped. For further discussion, see Carston (1999b), Blakemore (2000, 2002) and Iten (2000).

2.4 Travis and Recanati: Enriched 'What is Said'

2.4.1 Contextualist saying

The philosopher Charles Travis has for many years expounded (a version of) the linguistic underdeterminacy view[39] and pointed out its implications for the Gricean concept of 'what is said':

> words are sensitive to their speakings in the semantics they bear, varying semantics across speakings. So any semantics they might bear in saying something to be so is one they bear only occasion-sensitively. Their semantics as part of their language, e.g. English, is at most a proper part of their semantics on an occasion of expressing a thought, and underdetermines what thought they would thus express. . . . Their fixed,

language-contributed semantics must, in general, be supplemented if they are to be properly assessable as to truth, that is, if they are to count either as true or as false. (Travis 1991: 242)

Travis thinks that Grice's counteroffensive against the A-philosophers, specifically Austin and Wittgenstein, misfires, precisely because it depends on his concept of 'what is said', which fails to accommodate the basic fact about language described in the quote just given: that linguistic expressions are 'speaking-sensitive', as he puts it.[40]

I have argued that there is much pragmatic input to the level of the proposition(s) expressed (which when communicated are explicatures in relevance theory), and that many of Grice's most philosophically important cases of 'generalized' conversational implicature turn out to be pragmatic contributions to the proposition expressed (developments of the stark unexpressed logical form of the utterance). Does it follow from this that Grice's cause is lost? Is it the case that when he used 'it looks red to me' as a crucial L-statement within his causal theory of perception, and when Moore, looking for blatant truisms, stated 'I know this is my hand', they were saying something which somehow includes the condition of doubt being in the air. I am less sure about this than Travis is. If Travis is right, and Grice hasn't defeated the A-philosophical theses, then he has nonetheless made a sharp and hugely beneficial distinction between semantics (that is, 'language-contributed semantics', in Travis's terms) and pragmatics, which, adapted into cognitive scientific terms, is proving very useful in an account of utterance interpretation. However, there are contexts and contexts, and even the most generalized of pragmatic inferences doesn't always go through; given Moore's context (looking for indisputable truisms) I don't find it problematic that his statement is the odd but true one that he knows that what he is holding up is his hand. The philosophical context blocks the standard pragmatic inference that someone is doubtful about this.

Be all that as it may, both Travis (1981, 1985, 1991, 1997) and Recanati (1989b/91, 1993, 1994) develop an account of 'what is said' which they take to be in the tradition of Austin, Donnellan and Wittgenstein and which is much richer pragmatically than Grice's. This is a contextualist view of saying, which has much in common with the relevance theory view of the proposition(s) expressed (or explicated) by an utterance. What these philosophers loosely termed ambiguity, Recanati is able to recast in crisper terms, thanks to Grice's semantics/pragmatics distinction, which provides the basis for the drawing of a further very useful distinction: between linguistic semantic ambiguity, on the one hand, and propositional 'ambiguity' on the other. So, for instance, Recanati (1989a) takes up Donnellan's apparent 'ambiguity' account of the referential and attributive understandings of definite descriptions (e.g. 'Smith's murderer') and defends it against those who, following Grice, require that the referential understanding be treated as an implicature because it is pragmatically derived. Recanati shows that there is a third alternative, one which captures Donnellan's intuitions concerning the different truth conditions of the two uses, without assuming a linguistic ambiguity, and which derives the referential understanding by pragmatic inference from the attributive (Russellian) semantics. In other words, this is a contextualist account of what is said by a speaker when she uses a definite description in a particular way.[41] I have tried to do the same thing for the different truth-conditional possibilities for 'and'-conjunctions (see Carston 1988/91, 1993, and the next chapter of this book).

2.4.2 Availability to intuitions

Recanati (1989b/91; 1993: 245–50) makes a strong psychological claim about the level of 'what is said'. The claim is that we have conscious access to/awareness of this level, and that this distinguishes it from linguistic meaning (logical form), to which we do not have such access; we have only *tacit*, sub-doxastic (unconscious) knowledge of linguistic meaning, as we do of many other linguistic properties (syntactic, phonological). Furthermore, 'we have *distinct conscious representations* for "what is said" and for "what is implicated" by a given utterance: both are consciously accessible, and are consciously accessible *as distinct*' (Recanati 1993: 245). He argues that this requirement, in fact, follows from Grice's insistence that (conversational) implicatures be calculable (be workable out by both the speaker and the addressee), even though the Gricean concept of 'what is said' does not meet the requirement. To illustrate, recall an earlier example repeated here, focusing on Bob's response to Ann's question:

(123)   Ann: Shall we play tennis?
        Bob: It's raining.

According to the Gricean notion of 'what is said', Bob has expressed the proposition that it is raining in some place or other (this is indeterminate). Recanati's claim is that there is no intuitive basis for this, that neither the speaker nor the addressee is aware of this proposition as part of what is communicated. They are aware of the following two communicated propositions (assuming the relevant location is North London) and of the inferential connection between them:

(124)   a.   It's raining in North London.
        b.   We can't play tennis in North London.

Recanati's aim is to use this property of conscious access to provide a criterion for distinguishing 'what is said' from 'what is implicated'. The need for some means of making this distinction arises once the underdeterminacy thesis is adopted, because it follows from it that when some aspect of utterance meaning is derived pragmatically, that meaning could be either an implicature or part of what is said. The simple, clear dictum 'if it's pragmatic then it's an implicature' no longer holds. Here is the criterion that Recanati proposes:

Availability Principle: In deciding whether a pragmatically determined aspect of utterance meaning is part of what is said, that is, in making a decision concerning what is said, we should always try to preserve our pre-theoretic intuitions on the matter.

(Recanati 1989b: 310; Recanati 1993: 248)

Let's consider the result of applying the criterion to a couple of examples. Take an utterance of the sentence in (125a):

(125) a. Robert broke a finger last night.
       b. Robert broke a finger, either his own or someone else's, on the night immediately prior to the time of utterance.
       c. Robert broke his own finger on the night immediately prior to the time of utterance.
       d. Robert can't play in the game today.

According to a Gricean view, what is said is roughly as given in (125b), assuming reference assignment and disambiguation. But the Availability Principle denies that this is what is said, since it is not available to the conscious awareness of the speaker and addressee, neither of whom would accept it as what was said; the pragmatic inference that it was Robert's finger that was broken is, on this intuitive basis, part of what is said, and the implicature in (125d) intuitively follows from this rather than from (125b). There is a similar outcome for an utterance of the sentence in (126a):

(126) a. It will take us some time to get there.
       b. There will be a period of time between our departure and our arrival.
       c. It will take us a fairly long time to reach our destination.
       d. We won't have time to go to a theme park along the way.

What is said, according to a standard Gricean account, is given in (126b), but this is very unintuitive and addressees have no conscious awareness of it. However, they do have conscious access to (126c), (126d) and the inferential move from the one to the other; (pre-theoretic) intuition has it that the pragmatically determined element of meaning concerning the lengthiness of the time involved is part of what is said and, according to the criterion, this should be respected.[42]

Gibbs and Moise (1997) claim to have experimental results which support the utility of the Availability Principle. They presented their subjects with sentences similar to those in (125a) and (126a) above, and asked them to select 'the paraphrase which best reflects what speakers said in uttering these sentences'; the choice was either between a minimal paraphrase (a Gricean 'what is said'), as in the (b) cases, and an enriched what is said (explicature) as in (c), or between an enriched what is said and an implicature, as in (d). Across a range of experimental conditions, the vast majority of subjects favoured the enriched paraphrases ((c) in the two cases above). The different experimental arrangements included one which involved preliminary training in the Gricean saying/implicating distinction, another in which a piece of text preceding the utterance made the implicature highly manifest, and another in which the context provided was quite favourable to the minimal paraphrase. The results appear to confirm that speakers have reasonably clear intuitions about what is said, that they take it to be quite richly pragmatically augmented, and that they can distinguish it from assumptions that the speaker merely implicates.

However, in my view, we should be quite sceptical about results from this type of off-line, opinion-seeking 'experiment'. It is far from obvious that asking people to verbalize their views about what is said will elicit reliable responses about anything of theoretical import; for all we can tell, people might interpret the question 'what did the speaker *say*?' as 'what did the speaker mean?' or 'what was the main point the speaker made?' This may or may not coincide with the operative notion of what is said in an account of utterance understanding, and different people might have different interpretations, so that the results could reflect a medley of judgements about different facets of the utterance. Even if people do have conscious access to a representational level that matches Recanati's enriched notion of 'what is said', it does not follow that their folk or lay understanding of the everyday phrase 'what is said' matches the theoretical notion. These doubts are supported by the results from a replication of the experiments, by Nicolle and Clark (1999), who found that some subjects opted for what, according to any theoretical framework, is an implicature rather than either a minimal or an enriched 'what is said'. Clearly, then, there are pre-theoretic intuitions that should not be preserved in making the saying/implicating distinction.[43]

The Availability Principle gives considerable weight to intuitions. While I agree that they often play an important role in getting an analysis going, especially when there is a strong consensus, I doubt that they can be relied on to help much in disputed cases, the very ones for which we turn to a principle or criterion for help. The variety of views that have been expressed in the literature about the level at which, for example, the pragmatically derived relations between conjuncts, or the pragmatic differences between a referential and an attributive understanding of definite descriptions, should be captured, reflects the variability of intuitions. Here's another sort of case, discussed by Recanati (1996). The speaker is watching a poker game and utters 'Claire has a good hand,' but he is mistaken because Claire is not actually present in the situation, she is not one of the players in the game the speaker is watching. Then, '[the] utterance is not true – even if Claire is playing poker in some other part of the city and has a good hand there' (Recanati 1996: 446). I'm inclined to agree with this judgement, but others are not; intuitions about this are just not consistent. Many semanticists would take it that what the speaker has said is, in fact, true despite it being very different from what he intended to say. Misuses of definite descriptions, similar to this misuse of a name, have given rise to a great variety of intuitions among philosophers. Consider a referential use of a definite description such as 'Smith's murderer', in the utterance 'Smith's murderer is insane', used to refer to the man behaving oddly in the dock of the courtroom: suppose he (Perkins) is not in fact Smith's murderer and he is not in fact insane (just extremely nervous), but the actual murderer, who is still at large, is indeed insane. Some people (Russell, Grice, Neale, Larson and Segal) would say that this utterance does express a true proposition; it is not the one that the speaker meant/intended (that one is pragmatically derived and so is an implicature), but it is what is strictly and literally said. Others (including Recanati, Wettstein and, perhaps, Donnellan) would claim that the proposition expressed here is 'Perkins is insane', which is false.

Of course, you might say that each of these writers has his or her own theoretical axe to grind, and so does not reflect the sort of pre-theoretic intuitions Recanati is appealing to. Unfortunately, though, my experience of consulting students new to pragmatics is that their, truly pre-theoretic, intuitions are just as varied. So the problem with Recanati's Availability Principle is not so much that it is wrong, as that it seems to be inert in a great many cases. There are two possible reasons for this that occur to me. The first was discussed in section 2.3.2, where it was suggested that an utterance may express more than one proposition, that is, there may be more than a single 'what is said', perhaps each with a different relevance weighting. (See note 27 of this chapter for a brief discussion of this idea as applied to definite descriptions and names, an application developed by Neale, 1999). This seems a likely potential source for varying intuitions. The second is that one of the assumptions on which the principle depends, which is that we have no conscious access to sentence meaning, is not obviously correct. In his discussion of the output of the modular language processor, Fodor assumes 'that type-identity [of the linguistic expression employed in an utterance] and *at least some aspects of logical form* are phenomenologically salient [accessible to conscious awareness]' (Fodor 1983: 89, my emphasis). Similarly, I see no reason to think we are completely bereft of intuitions about what the words in our language mean, though these intuitions are easily mixed with intuitions about standard usage. We do seem to be able to consciously access the conceptual content of words with fairly concrete meanings, for example, 'cat', 'butter', 'house', 'jump', 'sing', 'read'. If this is right, we have two sorts of intuitions about 'what is said': intuitions about what proposition the speaker intended to express and intuitions about what the sentence she used means (or, at least, about the meaning of some of the lexical items in it). In certain sorts of problematic case, such as those just discussed in which an expression is used mistakenly in referring to someone, these two sets of intuitions pull in opposite directions.

This mix of intuitions is also very evident in cases of non-literalness; for instance, metaphors such as 'John is a lion'. Some would say that the one robust intuition we have about this is that it is false, a categorial falsehood in fact, and that it is recognition of this that leads us as hearers-processors to look for the intended implications, which are potentially true, or at least not ruled out as false on grounds of sortal incorrectness. That is essentially how metaphors work, according to Grice and others. However, Recanati's (1995) position on non-literalness entails that 'John is a lion' can be true and so does the move to an explicature treatment of metaphor within relevance theory (to be discussed in chapter 5). Informal enquiries into pre-theoretic intuitions about this case indicate that they vary too. Even in a clearly delineated context (say, John has just performed an act of great courage and nobility), there are some who judge that an utterance of 'John is a lion' is true (because he is brave, etc.), and there are others who judge that it is false (because he is a human being). Everyone might be prepared to agree that what the speaker *meant* is that John has a quality of majestic courage, and that we pragmatically infer this from her use of the word 'lion', and yet intuitions appear to be divided about whether this is what the speaker can be said to have said or not. The same goes for the cases of 'Claire' and 'Smith's murderer' above. So while intuitions about what a speaker has said are worth consideration, unless there is a strong consensus of opinion, they have to be regarded as unclear data, judgements which might have more than one possible source. They do not provide a criterion for distinguishing what is said from what is implicated in contentious cases. I return briefly to this interesting matter of intuitions and their sources in chapter 5. See also the discussion in Bach (2002), where he too argues that intuitions about what is said should be treated with great caution and not made the basis of any theoretical criterion.

To conclude this section, the Travis/Recanati concept of 'what is said', as inevitably involving extensive pragmatic input, is very close to the relevance-theoretic view, though there the terms are 'proposition expressed' and 'explicature'. Given that the term 'what is said' is essentially Grice's term and so is most salient in people's minds as a minimal unenriched propositional form, I think Travis and Recanati would do well to find some other term(s) – perhaps 'proposition expressed' and 'explicature'.[44]

2.5 Bach: What is Said/Impliciture/Implicature

2.5.1   Impliciture vs. explicature

Bach (1994a, 1994b) maintains a distinction between what is said and what is implicated, though he makes some fairly far-reaching changes to Grice's conception of the former, which we'll look at in the next section. In his view, the Gricean distinction is essentially right, but it is not exhaustive; it leaves out a crucial intermediate level. He is in absolute agreement with relevance theorists and Recanati about the role of pragmatics in arriving at the proposition(s) that the speaker intends to express. He distinguishes two sorts of pragmatic process involved in this: completion and expansion. Completion is required for those cases which, even given disambiguation and reference assignment, are not yet fully propositional, such as those in (127). Expansion may be required for those which, although fully propositional, are patently not yet the proposition that the speaker intended to express, as in (128), where a possible expansion is given in the square brackets:

(127) a. Mary is too short. [for what?]
       b. We've finished.   [what?]
       c. It's raining. [where?]
       d. Paracetamol is better.   [than what? in what regard?]

(128) a. No one [in my family] likes my spaghetti bolognese.
       b. She screamed at him and [as a result] he left the room.
       c. Mary and Sue climbed the mountain [together].
       d. He has [exactly] three cars.
       e. There are [approximately] 150 students in the class.
       f. I haven't [ever] eaten slugs.

These are representative of the sorts of examples that Bach gives. In passing, I note that not everyone working in this area (including myself) would agree that all the examples in (128) are fully propositional before expansion; for instance, (128a) is probably incomplete before a pragmatic process fixes the quantifier domain, and it may be that the cardinal number terms (as in (128d)) are sense-general and so always require pragmatic specification (see Carston 1990/95, 1998a; Atlas 1992). Notice also that some of these expansions involve a logical strengthening of the proposition: (b) and (c), and also (d) if you take the semantics of 'three' to be equivalent to 'at least three'; some involve a logical weakening: (a) and (e); others, Bach (1994a: 279) claims, are neither logical strengthenings nor weakenings: (f), and also (d) if you take the semantics of 'three' to be 'precisely three'. However, they are all cases of what he calls 'lexical strengthening'.

Bach calls this level 'impliciture' because it is what is implicit in what is said (on his narrow, semantically-oriented construal of 'what is said'), and he confines the adjective 'explicit' to what is given semantically. He takes issue with the Sperber and Wilson term 'explicature': 'I find this use of the term misleading, inasmuch as the conceptual strengthening involved in expansion or completion is not explicit at all' (Bach 1994b: 141). A couple of small points in favour of 'explicature' are that it has an accompanying verb 'explicate' (parallel with 'implicature'/'implicate') and that it is aurally and graphologically more clearly distinguishable from 'implicature' than is 'impliciture'. Sperber and Wilson are very clear that an explicature is an amalgam of the encoded and the pragmatically inferred, so that explicitness is a matter of degree and explicatures are more or less explicit, none being fully so, as discussed in section 2.3.1. As also mentioned, there does not seem to be much point in having an explicit/implicit distinction that coincides exactly with the already established decoding/inference (semantic/pragmatic) distinction. Finally, as the discussion of Bach's notion of 'what is said' will show, many utterances will simply not communicate anything explicitly on his account (those where the speaker does not mean what she (allegedly) says).

Bach's picture of verbal communication seems to[45] encompass the following four levels:

a. logical form or semantic representation of the linguistic expression used (a propositional schema);
b. what is said (minimal proposition or propositional radical);
c. pragmatically developed (completed and/or expanded) propositional form ('impliciture'/'explicature');
d. pragmatically inferred propositional forms (implicature(s)).

Note that in the relevance-theoretic account there is no level corresponding to the second of these. In the next two subsections, I'll take a closer look at this concept of 'what is said', trying to assess the role it plays in communication and whether or not there is a case for its psychological reality in the process of utterance interpretation.

2.5.2 What is said and linguistic meaning

Bach's reconstrual of the notion of 'what is said' has the following two features:

(a) saying that P does not entail meaning that P (communicating that P); and
(b) the elements of what is said must correspond to elements in the linguistic expression (sentence).

From the latter there follow two divergences from the way Grice (as far as we can tell) construed 'what is said':

(c)   P need not be fully propositional but may be just a fragment of a proposition, what Bach calls a 'propositional radical';
(d)   connectives such as 'but' and 'so' are taken to be elements of what is said rather than belonging in a separate category of non-truth-conditional linguistic meaning: conventional implicature.

Taking (a) first, 'what is said' does not fall under a speaker's communicative intention; Bach dismantles the entailment relation that Grice took to hold between what a speaker says and what a speaker means. An advantage of disconnecting these two is that 'saying' then applies, not only to literal assertions, but also to the literal content of metaphorical and other figurative utterances, doing away with the need for the theoretically awkward distinction between 'saying' and 'making as if to say' (discussed in section 2.2.4). It also applies to certain verbal mistakes, such as incorrectly applied referring descriptions and slips of the tongue, and to utterances where one produces a sentence with full understanding but does not communicate (mean) anything, such as cases of translating, and recitations or rehearsals of a verbal piece. In short, saying figures in a uniform way in all utterances. Its primary role in utterance interpretation, Bach says, is to provide the linguistic basis on which the hearer infers implicitures (explicatures) and implicatures, i.e. those representations that *do* fall under the speaker's communicative intention.

Moving to (b), this is what Bach (1994b: 142–4) calls the criterion of close syntactic correlation, and it has obvious similarities to the Isomorphism Principle mentioned in chapter 1. He claims that Grice wanted to give this principle greater weight than he found himself able to, and that he was hampered by a mistaken view of sentence connectives, which led him to his category of conventional implicature. Here is the crucial part of his discussion of Grice:

> what is said must correspond to 'the elements of [the sentence], their order, and their syntactic character' (1969b/89b: 87). Here he [i.e. Grice] mentions that how something is put may enter into what is said. His example concerns reference. He allows that someone who utters [1] and someone who (in 1967) utters [2] might not say the same thing
>
> [1]   Harold Wilson is a great man.
> [2]   The British prime minister is a great man.
>
> but he does not commit himself on this point.   (Bach 1994b: 142)

First, there is a subtle misrepresentation here, since if one goes back to this characterization of 'what is said' given by Grice (and reproduced in full in note 7 of this chapter), he does not say that 'what is said' *must correspond* with the elements of the sentence. There is no talk of a 'correlation' between the lexical items and syntax of the expression uttered and the elements of the 'what is said', though of course the compositional semantics of the sentence used by the speaker is a crucial component in determining 'what is said'. Bach produces this quote in other papers too (e.g. Bach 1994a: 274; 1999b: 336), and again the words 'must correspond to' lie outside the quotes; this is because they are Bach's words, not Grice's. Second, if Grice did believe that this was essential to the concept of 'what is said', why would he hesitate over [1] and [2]? It would follow automatically that something different is said in the two cases. So I am less sure than Bach is that he finds support for his position in Grice's own view.

As shown above in (c), one result of strict adherence to the criterion of close syntactic correlation is that what is said need not be even a minimal proposition; it may be a *propositional radical*, as in the examples in (127). The test for 'what is said' in any given case is provided by the following schema: '*S said that . . .*' or, adopting the perspective of the hearer at the time of the utterance, '*S is saying [to me] that . . .*'. The idea is that those elements of the original utterance that can embed in the schema without infelicity, that is, which can be indirectly quoted, are elements of what was said by the utterance. Bach calls this the IQ test. Compare the applications of the test in (130) to the utterances in (129):

(129) a. Mrs Jones, the local councillor, has won the lottery.
       b. Hey, Mary, Mrs Jones has won the lottery.

(130) a. S says that Mrs Jones, the local councillor, has won the lottery.
       b. ??S says that, hey Mary, Mrs Jones has won the lottery.

While the appositive phrase in (129a) can be indirectly quoted and so is an aspect of what is said by the original utterance, the vocative 'hey, Mary' cannot and so is not part of what is said by an utterance of (129b). The point here, though, is that each of the propositionally incomplete cases in (127) can be embedded acceptably in this schema, without the need for any further elaboration; the semantic underdetermination is simply carried over into the 'that' clause:

(131) a. S said that paracetamol is better.
       b. S said that it is/was raining.

However, there is another class of utterances which are like the semantically incomplete cases indirectly quoted in (131) in that they encode only a fragment of a proposition, but for which it would seem that the syntactic correlation criterion coupled with this indirect quotation test gives a different result. These are subsentential utterances (phrasal or lexical) such as those in (132):

(132) a. John's father.
       b. On the table.
       c. Can't see.
       d. Typical.
       e. Telephone.

These patently do not embed successfully in the indirect quotation schema: e.g. 'S said that John's father', etc. The reason for this is obvious: they don't meet the sub-

categorization requirement on 'say that'; the complementizer 'that' must take a sentential complement. They can of course be directly quoted ('S said "John's father" ')
as can all the fully sentential cases, but this is just the quoting of a linguistic string
and not the concept that Bach is after.

So it looks as if 'what is said' by an utterance may be subpropositional only if it
happens to have been expressed by a natural language *sentence*. In the case of these
subsentential utterances, apparently, *nothing is said*. But there does not seem to be
anything principled about this difference of outcome between the two cases. 'What
is said' is supposed to provide the linguistic basis on which, together with contextual information and constraining pragmatic principles, the hearer can infer
what the speaker is communicating, and, of course, that is exactly what the semantic representation of these subsentential utterances (the propositional fragments
they encode) does provide. The distinction between the two types of case which is
entailed by this concept of 'what is said' seems unwarranted.

Let's consider for a moment the impliciture (explicature) that could be communicated by these little utterances. I set aside cases where they are answers to an
immediately preceding question and so slot into a matching site left open by the
question form. Take again the case of (a) 'John's father', uttered at a party by me
to a friend when I, knowing that she has long wanted to meet John's father, spot
him across the room. As already discussed in chapter 1 and briefly in section 2.3.5
above, there is considerable indeterminacy as regards which proposition I have
expressed and which proposition the hearer will construct. Any of those in (133),
and a variety of others, might do:

(133)   a.   The man who just came in is the father of John Sims.
        b.   The man near the door is the father of John Sims.
        c.   The father of John Sims is that guy over there wearing a green suit.

What falls within the speaker's communicative intention is not any particular propositional form but a propositional range, and the addressee is free, within the
constraints imposed by pragmatic principles (consistency with optimal relevance
assumptions, for instance), to construct whichever proposition in the range is most
accessible to him.

The very minimal semantic information encoded in the utterance provides the
linguistic basis for the pragmatic system to work on, without any need for a level
of 'what is said'. I see no reason to think that things are different for fully sentential utterances which happen to fit the 'Speaker said that . . .' formula. In other
words, the processes involved in recovering what is communicated can proceed
directly from level (a), the propositional schema which is the representation decoded
from the linguistic expression employed. The concept of 'what is said' is not consistent in its application across types of utterances, nor does it seem to play any role
in the understanding process beyond that played by the decoded logical form of the
utterance. In short, it appears to be redundant, at least within the sort of cognitive
processing theory I am interested in here.

A brief word now on point (d), the idea that certain connectives, such as 'but',
'therefore' and 'so', should be treated as part of what is said rather than as indi-

cating distinct implicated propositions (non-central speech acts). Bach (1994b) believes that, while Grice adhered to the syntactic correlation criterion, he was driven to exclude 'but' and 'therefore' from 'what is said' because he could not see a way 'to explicate [their] import over and above p and q without using a third clause, an additional conjunct, e.g. to the effect that there is a relation of consequence or contrast between p and q. . . . [so that] what is said would contain one more clause than is contained in the sentence used to say it. This further conjunct would not correspond to a clause in that sentence and could not count as part of what is said' (1994b: 145). As already argued, the evidence that Grice held the correlation criterion is far from compelling. Moreover, evidence that reasoning along the lines just quoted entered into Grice's categorization of an element of utterance meaning as a conventional implicature is non-existent. His few discussions of these cases are entirely concerned with whether or not the item contributes to the truth-conditional content of the utterance or not (see Grice 1975/89b: 25; 1968/89b: 120–1; 1989a: 361); these cases are deemed conventional implicature because their falsity does not seem to falsify the utterance. I would hark back here to Grice's original motivation for the saying/implicating distinction: he wanted to isolate the core statements being made by certain philosophers in their attempt to establish particular theses. So, for instance, 'x looks red (to me) but y looks green (to me)' is to be taken as making a true statement iff the speaker has a sensory perception of redness on looking at x and a sensory perception of greenness on looking at y; the implication of some sort of contrast between the first conjunct and the second is just as irrelevant to this as any implications that there may be doubt about the redness of x and/or doubt about the greenness of y. The test case would, of course, be a connective that patently does affect truth conditions, but which is like 'but' or 'therefore' in that it could be argued, just as plausibly, that another whole clause is needed to explicate its import. The obvious example is 'because' on its basic content use:

(134)   a.   The chair was wet because it had rained overnight.
        b.   The chair was wet, it had rained overnight and the cause of the
             chair's wetness was the overnight rain.

It seems clear (as clear as anything can be in this area) that the truth conditions of an utterance of the sentence in (134a) are as given in (134b); if the chair had not been affected by the rain at all (having been indoors all night) but was wet from having been thrown into a full bath-tub, the utterance would surely be false. I believe that on these grounds Grice would have taken 'because' to contribute to what is said. He would not have used the implicature strategy to save, from a charge of falsity or impropriety, a philosopher who had uttered 'P because Q' in a situation in which there was no causal relation whatsoever between the states of affairs described by Q and P. Yet we have a two-conjunct sentence with a three-clause specification of truth conditions, which is an instance of the sort of general situation that Bach believes led Grice to conclude that 'but' did not contribute to what is said. Sadly, I've been unable to find any discussion by Grice of this crucial test case sort of example; however, I believe that the evidence of his concern for what is said as the minimal truth-conditional content of the utterance, and the lack of evidence of any worry about the technicalities of formally representing what is said, are sufficient to establish that, while 'because' is to be seen as part of what is said, 'but' is not.[46] On Bach's conception, though, all connectives are taken to be part of 'what is said' provided they signify relations between the propositions expressed.

He does recognize a distinct set of cases which do not contribute to 'what is said', but which instead provide a kind of higher-level comment on the utterance itself. This phenomenon was discussed in section 2.3.2 of this chapter in the context of utterances which consist of two or more subutterances or speech acts (see also Bach 1994a: 276–7; Bach 1999b: 356–60). He includes in this class illocutionary adverbials such as 'frankly', 'seriously', 'confidentially', additives like 'by the same token', 'moreover', 'in fact', concessives such as 'although', 'in any case', 'nevertheless' and a whole host of other cases. He claims that they do not pass the IQ test, but, as already mentioned in note 23 of this chapter, this is very debatable. In this regard, consider the following, where the commenting element is italicized:

(135) a. Bill said that he didn't have the money and that, *moreover*, he couldn't get time off work.
       b. Sam said that his mother was, *nevertheless*, in good spirits.
       c. Mary said that, *for the record*, she was happily married, but, *off the record*, she was about to get a divorce.
       d. Beth said that *frankly* she'd had enough of John's lies.

I find these perfectly acceptable and in clear and striking contrast with (136b/b'):

(136) a. Jim: My dear, I don't give a damn.
       b. ??Jim said that, my dear, he didn't give a damn.
       b'. ??Jim said that, his dear, he didn't give a damn.

If this is right, the IQ test does not correctly distinguish between saying and commenting. I suspect that is because the natural-language verb 'say', used in the schema, does not reflect the theoretical notion of 'saying' that Bach is trying to establish.

There may be other problems with the test. Cappelen and Lepore (1997) amass a great many examples in support of their contention that ordinary reporting of what someone has said may be considered correct, even true, despite the content of the embedded clause differing in a range of ways from the content of the linguistic expression used in the original utterance. This is perhaps too obvious to need great elaboration: the complement clause may omit material present in the original, as in summaries; it may include additional material, to make up for the absence of some other source of information which had been present in the original situation of utterance; it may substitute referring expressions in the original with other coreferential expressions, etc.[47] Reports of ironical utterances are particularly interesting in this respect; Larson and Segal (1995: 453) discuss the case of Jason who, after sitting through a particularly awful philosophy talk, expresses his view by uttering (137) with heavy sarcasm:

(137)   That was really brilliant.

(138)   a.   Jason said that the talk was really brilliant.
        b.   Jason said that the talk was pretty dire.

Cappelen and Lepore maintain that what Jason said cannot be reported correctly by (138a), but can be by (138b), and Larson and Segal suggest (138a) is only true if the irony in the original is somehow reflected in the report, perhaps by a mimicking of Jason's original sarcastic tone of voice; they add: 'This suggests that the verb *said* is sensitive to more than just the strict and literal content of people's utterances. Rather, what people are held to say encompasses their pragmatic, communicative intentions' (Larson and Segal 1995: 454).

The 'simple, intuitive test' which Bach relies on, that 'what is said is specifiable by a *that*-clause embedded in a matrix clause of the form *S said that* ...' (Bach 1994a: 278), seems to involve some sort of quite mechanical embedding of the surface syntactic structure used by the utterer (with just the essential deictic shifts, for instance, from 'I' to 'she'). This is not in line either with ordinary intuitions about reporting or with the (presumably more rigorous) judgements of semanticists concerned with when a reporting sentence can be said to be true. Add to this its unclear predictions in the commenting speech-act cases and the fact that it just doesn't work with subsentential utterances (despite it being the case that a speaker employing one of these is as much in the business of saying something as a speaker who employs a full sentence) and the conclusion has to be that it does not look like a test to rely on.

Bach insists that there is a distinction between 'what is said loosely speaking' and 'what is said strictly speaking' and that this is a distinction to which those of our inferential mechanisms responsible for recovering speakers' communicative intentions must be receptive because 'such inferences must be sensitive to the *semantic content of sentences* if sentences are to provide the linguistic basis for identifying speakers' communicative intentions' (Bach 1994b: 137, my emphasis). He is concerned with what is strictly and literally said, and this, it appears, is a semantic entity. It need not be fully propositional, so need not specify a determinate truth condition, yet it is not, apparently, just the logical form delivered by linguistic decoding. So what sort of a semantic entity is it? I address this question in the next section.

2.5.3   What is said and indexicality

Let's consider the role in Bach's account of the two pragmatic processes that Grice recognized as necessary additions to conventional linguistic expression meaning in determining 'what is said': reference assignment and disambiguation. Bach has much more to say about the former than the latter, so I'll concentrate on that. I find him holding two slightly, but crucially, different positions in his writings on the fixing of indexical reference and so on the nature of 'what is said'.

Bach (1987) takes the view that reference is essentially a pragmatic issue, a matter of speaker's intention and hearer's inference, with just a small class of exceptions.

According to Taschek's (1990) review of Bach (1987), this is the 'astonishing view ... that an expression's referring function, when it has one, never makes a semantic contribution to the sentences in which it occurs'. From the point of view of the cognitive pragmatic framework I am pursuing, this 'astonishing' view seems absolutely right: speakers, not linguistic forms, refer and part of the pragmatic inferential phase, as opposed to the decoding phase, of utterance understanding is working out what the speaker is referring to.

I'll focus on Bach's discussion of pronouns (used to refer). He, in fact, distinguishes pronouns which refer *semantically* from those which refer pragmatically, and only those referents determined in the first way, i.e. semantically, are constituents of 'what is said'. What makes certain cases of reference determination genuinely semantic, according to him, is that they do not involve consideration of the speaker's communicative intention. The distinction he has in mind is the by now familiar one between pure indexicals and the rest. Following Kaplan (1977/89a), a pure indexical ('I' being the paradigm case) specifies/encodes a rule (a 'character'), which is a function from the context of utterance to a referent; an utterance containing such an indexical has a semantically determined, though context-relative, truth condition. Bach distinguishes the notion of 'narrow context', which plays a role in semantics, from contextual information in the broad sense, which is anything the hearer takes into account, in accordance with pragmatic maxims/principles, in reaching the *intended* interpretation of the utterance. 'Narrow' context consists of a small, well-defined set of objective parameters, including, and perhaps exhausted by, the speaker, the addressee, the time, the day and the place of utterance.[48]

Bach (1987: 176–7) compares the following two utterances:

(139)   a.   I am ready to go now.
        b.   He was ready to go then.

Corresponding to the indexicals 'I' and 'now' in (139a) there are the contextual parameters of speaker and time of utterance, so what is said by an utterance of this sentence in a particular context is '*a* is ready to go at *t*', where *a* is the speaker and *t* is the time of utterance. However, the indexicals 'he' and 'then' in (139b) are different; their reference is not a simple function of narrow context; it is dependent on the speaker's referential intention, hence on broad context and the pragmatic principles or maxims that a hearer uses quite generally in arriving at a confirmed hypothesis about what a speaker meant. Bach's position on these is that their reference does not contribute to 'what is said' but rather to the impliciture of the utterance (the proposition the speaker intended to communicate). So what is said by an utterance of (139b)? He proposes the following:

(140)   A certain male person was ready to go at a certain time prior to the time of utterance.

He recognizes that this is not synonymous with (139b) and seems to intend it as a rough way of indicating the sort of 'open' proposition that is what is said in this case; the two instances of 'a certain . . .' are to be understood as constraints on the pragmatic reference-fixing process, the result of which will appear in that singular proposition which is the impliciture of the utterance. Understood in this way, (140) is very similar, if not identical, to the sort of logical form or assumption schema that is the output of the linguistic decoding process on a relevance-theoretic conception: an incomplete conceptual representation with variables whose value, to be fixed by pragmatic inference, is constrained by the encoded (procedural) meaning of the referring expressions.

Here are a few observations about this distinction between semantic reference and pragmatic reference. First, this is clearly another quite major departure from Grice's view of 'what is said'; recall his discussion of the example of 'He is in the grip of a vice' according to which the referent of 'he' is a crucial component of what the speaker has said. Bach's conception, then, is very much closer to encoded linguistic meaning than Grice's; overall, it differs from Grice's just as much as Recanati's enriched notion does, although their divergences take opposite directions. Second, it is unclear how, or indeed whether, the IQ test is able to reflect 'what is said' by an utterance which contains 'pure' indexicals. Recalling that '. . . the "that"-clause in an indirect quotation *specifies* what is said in the utterance being reported . . .' (Bach 1999b: 339, my emphasis), consider application of the test to Mary's utterance in (141a):

(141)   a.   Mary: I'm leaving tomorrow.
          b.   Mary is saying that she is leaving tomorrow.
          c.   Mary said that she was leaving the next day.
          d.   Mary said that Mary is leaving on Wednesday, 3 June 2000.
          e.   John said that Mary said that a certain female person was leaving the next day.

While trying to be as strict in using the indirect quoting schema as Bach requires, the most natural applications are those in (141b) and (141c). However, given the account of semantic reference just outlined, it would seem that neither of these succeed in specifying what is said, which should include the referents of 'I' and 'tomorrow'; these are most obviously reflected in (141d), but this is a very unnatural report of the utterance and it is not the one favoured by Bach himself (1994b: 136–7) in reporting a first-person utterance. There is a further possible problem with the strict but natural reports, which is that they contain the pronoun 'she' and what is said by such a non-pure indexical is something like 'a certain female'. So supposing it was John who uttered one of the indirect quotations in (141b) or (141c), then application of the IQ test to his utterance should give the report in (141e), which now seems to misrepresent both what he said and what Mary said.

Third, recall that one of the advantages claimed for the proposed notion of 'what is said' is that it applies uniformly to all utterances including cases where nothing is being communicated. In this regard, consider (142) as uttered by someone as part of the process of translating a French text or as part of a recitation or rehearsal:

(142)   We are here at last.

According to the account given, semantic context must supply values for the pure indexicals, 'we', 'here' and, perhaps, the present tense, but these cannot come from the context of the current utterer (i.e. the translator or reciter), since there may be no corresponding contextual parameter (for instance, no referent for 'we') and, even if there were, it would give the wrong result. The relevant referents come from somewhere else, perhaps the original author's context, or the context of a narrator or one of the characters within the text; figuring out what is the right context seems to be a properly pragmatic process, that is, one that requires consideration of the current speaker's intentions, and this *precedes* the assigning of supposedly intention-free semantic values. For discussion of a related problem, see Predelli (1998). Anyone who holds that there are cases of semantically determined, as distinct from pragmatically determined, reference has to address these points.

I have found no discussion of disambiguation to accompany the account of reference determination in what is said, but since it seems obvious that this is a process that also crucially depends on a speaker's communicative intention, hence on broad context and communicative principles, it cannot be involved in what is said as construed here, but must also make itself felt only at the level of impliciture. I conclude that, to the (minimal) extent that this semantic view of what is said departs from the concept of decoded linguistic meaning, it raises many problems and has no obvious advantages. Pure indexicals are the one possible point of difference, but the only strong case is 'I', and nothing at all will be lost by including its reference assignment with the rest, even if pragmatic principles are seldom required for the purpose.

While I think that the account just given is the one Bach generally endorses, he gives a curiously different picture in Bach (1994a). Consider the following exchange, focusing on the pronoun 'she' in B's response to A:

(143)   A: I wonder when Mildred gets back from Paris.
        B: She's back.

There are various ways of indirectly reporting what B has said:

(144)   a. B said that Mildred's back from Paris.
        b. B said that Mildred's back.
        c. B said that a certain female person is back.
        d. B said that she's back.

The first of these would be rejected by Bach, in all his writings on the matter, as involving a loose use of the concept of 'saying that', since there is nothing in B's utterance which corresponds with the constituent 'from Paris'. He is after a strict notion of 'speaker saying' and, according to the preceding discussion, would favour the 'definite indefinite description' in (144c). It is not clear why he doesn't go for (d), a direct copy of the original utterance, which gives a perfectly satisfactory report of B's utterance and complies very strictly with the Syntactic Correlation Principle.

However, the main point here is that Bach (1994a: 282) favours (b), with the referent 'Mildred' as a constituent of 'what is said', in what seems to be a move away from the strict semantic notion, back towards the Gricean notion, though he maintains the view that what is said may not be fully propositional (need not determine a truth condition). The reason given for this being the right conception of what is said is that the presence of a linguistic expression ('she') mandates recovery of a referent; 'an indexical is there in the sentence', whereas there is no linguistic element requiring recovery of the constituent 'from Paris'. Similarly, when the linguistic form used is ambiguous, a choice is obligatory (except in the case of a pun), so that just the operative meaning appears in 'what is said' (see Bach 1994a: 290, note 20). So it seems that in discerning 'what is said' one must consider the speaker's intention in two instances: assignment of referents to indexicals, and determining the 'operative meaning' in the case of ambiguous expressions. That is, these two, and just these two, pragmatic processes are involved in determining what is said; note that by 'pragmatic' I don't just mean that aspects of context somehow contribute, but rather that whatever pragmatic principle or maxim you employ in the derivation of the expanded proposition expressed (impliciture/explicature) and implicatures, it is also required to account for hearers' generally successful performance of these two tasks.

Summing up, the concept of 'what is said' in Bach (1987), which is supported by comments in Bach (1997/99a) and Bach (2001), is one on which only certain indexicals, the pure ones, have their reference fixed, the others having the constraint they encode spelled out by some sort of indefinite definite ('a certain . . .'). Disambiguation, like assigning of values to non-pure indexicals, cannot be achieved by narrow context alone, but has to involve speaker intentions. A consistent application of the narrow context idea would exclude any process of disambiguation at this purely semantic, speaker intention-free, level. So 'what is said' is a very messy entity: a set of propositions or propositional radicals with some referents fixed and some not.

The concept of 'what is said' in Bach (1994a) is even more of a mixed bag. Although its primary role is still that of providing the *linguistic* basis for the hearer's inference to what the speaker is communicating (implicitures and implicatures), its own recovery/derivation requires a partial involvement of the speaker's communicative intention. Some inferential pragmatic work is required, but other equally, if not more, immediate inferential developments of logical form, such as the recovery of the constituent 'from Paris' in example (143B), are excluded because there is no linguistic expression corresponding to them in the utterance. (There are those who would dispute this, claiming that in the case of (143B) there is, in fact, a phonologically null indexical element 'from x' indicating that a contextual value must be supplied; see discussion in section 2.7.)

I repeat the conclusion of some pages ago, reinforced now by these additional considerations: there appears to be no role for a level of 'what is said' to play in an account of the representations and processes required in the interpretation of utterances. All that Bach conceives of in this regard for 'what is said' is achieved by linguistic meaning (logical form).

2.5.4   What's to be said about 'what is said'?

It might be useful at this stage to set out the three general conceptions of 'what is said' that we've looked at in this chapter (allowing that there are variations among the supporters of each of these). Taking Grice's as the starting point, the other two are the outcome of moves in opposite directions from each other, the one to a narrower, more linguistic conception, the other to a broader, more pragmatic conception:

Semantic 'what is said'	Gricean 'what is said'	Pragmatic 'what is said'
• may be subpropositional	• fully propositional but minimally so	• fully propositional
• no involvement of communicative intentions	• involvement of communicative intentions?	• full involvement of communicative intentions
• narrow 'objective' contextual parameters	• limited role for context	• broad context
Supporters:	*Supporters:*	*Supporters:*
Bach	Berg	Relevance theorists
Kaplan?	Cappelen	Travis
	Other truth-conditional semanticists	Recanati

Given the independently motivated representational level of encoded linguistic meaning, logical form, it is tempting to conclude that the traditional, semantically oriented concepts of 'what is said', as construed by Grice or Bach, should be laid to rest. The process of utterance interpretation goes directly from linguistic meaning to explicature (or 'implicature'), without any intermediate level of 'what is said', at which some or all referents are assigned and perhaps candidate senses are selected. However, Bach insists that facts about the cognitive processes involved in under-standing an utterance simply have no bearing on the legitimacy of a purely seman-tic notion of what is said. He says: 'The concept of what is said does not concern the nature of the hearer's inference to the intended content of the utterance but merely the semantically determined portion of the information available to that inference' (Bach 1999b: 338). A distinction between information available to a hearer and what a hearer does with that information sounds quite similar to the well-known Chomskyan competence/performance distinction (knowledge vs. use of that knowledge) and is certainly valid. But there is another very clear distinction to be made between sources of information available to the hearer: information encoded in the linguistic expression used and extralinguistic contextual information. This distinction is both highly intuitive (involving no division among the class of indexicals – they all encode a referential constraint and they all have their value fixed contextually) and it corresponds with the representational levels involved in the interpretation process: logical form, on the one hand, and the communicated propositions, on the other. While kinds of information and their roles in processing need not correspond, there is certainly no bar to them doing so.

Finally, I note that, for many philosophers of language, a minimal notion of 'what is said' seems almost inevitably to enter into discussions of natural language semantics. This is so even among those who acknowledge the legitimacy of a pragmatically enriched proposition expressed. So Bach has 'what is said' and 'impliciture', Salmon (1991) has a 'technical and artificially strict sense' of saying and an ordinary everyday sense, and Recanati, in recent work, has c-content (what is said$_{min}$) and i-content (what is said$_{max}$) (see note 44 of this chapter). So although I see no place for a concept of 'what is said', in either Grice's or Bach's sense, within the sort of cognitive processing-oriented account that I am committed to, I have to allow that perhaps it has a role to play in some other sort of account of what is involved in utterance meaning.[49]

2.6 Pragmatic Meaning: Enrichment or Implicature?

The question in the title of this section used not to arise; an aspect of utterance meaning that could be shown to have been pragmatically inferred was automatically categorized as an implicature, a communicated assumption distinct from, external to, what had been explicitly said. For the most part, there went hand in hand with this assumption the view that the semantic aspect of an utterance is its truth-conditional content. I'll briefly mention some examples of this line of reasoning. Here's the first one:

(145)   a.   The door is closed.
        b.   The door of room 5, 20 Gordon Square, is closed.

On a Russellian account of definite descriptions, the example in (145a) presents a problem because it appears not to respect the uniqueness part of his semantics (there are many doors in the universe). One solution to this (among several others) is as follows: (i) the description is completed in such a way that it does denote a unique entity in the world (say, as in (145b)); this completion process is clearly a pragmatic matter, so (ii) the proposition expressed by an utterance of (145a) is the patently false one that there is an entity which is unique in having the property of being a door and it is closed, while what is meant is a pragmatically inferred proposition, say the one in (145b), which may well be true. Russell's semantics for 'the door' is maintained, what is said is false and absurd, and the strong intuition that something else, of a perfectly reasonable sort, has been communicated is explained as an implicature involving a uniquely denoting description. (For critical discussion of this sort of account, see Millican (1990) and Larson and Segal (1995: 329–30).

A second example, from Richard (1990: 120), concerns 'and'-conjunctions:

(146)   a.   Tonto jumped on to his horse and he rode into the sunset.
        b.   Tonto rode into the sunset and he jumped on to his horse.
        c.   Tonto jumped on to his horse and rode into the sunset. Not necessarily, however, in that order.

Richard says the strong intuition that (146a) and (146b) communicate a certain order of occurrence is to be explained pragmatically, as is evident from the cancellability, without contradiction, of this element of meaning, shown in (146c). So it follows that strictly and literally these say the same thing – that a jumping occurred and a riding occurred – and the one is true iff the other is true. The implication of an order of events is an implicature, different in each case, and as such does not enter into the semantic level, the level of what is said. (I discuss the analysis of 'and'-conjunctions in much more detail in the next chapter.)

Third, consider the notorious issue of belief contexts:

(147) a. Mary believes that Twain is alive.
       b. Mary believes that Clemens is alive.

The problem here, given a particular view of proper names (that of direct reference theorists), is that, although the proper names are coreferential (hence make the same contribution to semantic content), it is widely felt that these two utterances could differ in truth value and so must be truth-conditionally distinct. The strategy, again, is to show that the felt difference is pragmatic rather than semantic, and so, contrary to intuitions, does not enter into what is strictly and literally said; (147a) and (147b) express the same proposition: 'Mary believes of a that he is alive', where a is the individual referred to by 'Twain' (and by 'Clemens') and the difference between the two utterances is explained as a difference of implicature, hence not a truth-conditional difference. (See critical discussion in Recanati 1993, chapter 17).

Many more examples of this Gricean gambit could be given. It is notable that, in all three cases, the implicature analysis rides roughshod across strong intuitions that the implication in question does contribute to truth conditions hence, for most people (though not Bach), to what is said. Presumably, examples like this motivated Recanati's Availability Principle (see section 2.4.2). Although I have argued that this principle leaves us stranded when intuitions conflict, it does seem to be good policy to heed intuitions when they are coming through loud, clear and consistent, as in these cases.

Furthermore, according to the linguistic (semantic) underdeterminacy view, established in chapter 1, the logical form of a linguistic expression seldom, if ever, determines a truth condition, so that pragmatics is inevitably required in the recovery of a fully propositional representation. Even such essential elements of what is said as referents of referring expressions require principle-guided pragmatic inference and these cannot be relegated to implicature except on pain of never recovering a proposition expressed (hence no truth-conditional content for the utterance). There is no direct inference from 'x is pragmatic' to 'x is an implicature (so not truth-conditional)'.

In this context it's worth mentioning a (methodological) principle frequently employed by philosophers of language following Grice: 'Modified Occam's Razor' (MOR), according to which 'Senses (linguistic meanings) are not to be multiplied beyond necessity' (Grice 1967/78/89b: 47). This is essentially a principle of theoretical economy; it entails that, instead of positing a linguistic ambiguity to account for multiple interpretations of a linguistic expression, pragmatic principles and inferences, which are independently motivated, should be employed, wherever possible. Advocates of the implicature accounts of 'and'-conjunctions and belief contexts just discussed above would employ this principle to counter suggestions that 'and' is ambiguous between a truth-functional meaning and a temporal sequence meaning, and 'believe' is ambiguous between an opaque and a transparent reading.

However, once underdeterminacy and its implications are recognized, it becomes clear that employment of this principle can, at best,[50] take us only part of the way to a full account; having established that some aspect of utterance meaning is to be accounted for pragmatically rather than semantically, the issue remains whether it contributes to explicature (Recanati's enriched 'what is said') or is an independent, implicitly communicated, proposition. Obviously, MOR cannot choose between two pragmatic options. The same goes for Grice's standard diagnostics for conversational implicature, the two most generally employed being calculability (on the basis of conversational maxims) and cancellability without contradiction. These hold for all pragmatic (maxim-dependent) meaning, whether an implicature or a contribution to truth-conditional content. It is for this reason that some of us have played with other criteria in an attempt to find a principled basis for deciding between the two pragmatic possibilities in any given case.

Recanati (1989b/91, 1993) has proposed the Availability Principle. I have argued, in section 2.4.2, that since intuitions are so often variable and manipulable, they cannot provide the basis for a general reliable criterion and that the principle is based on the erroneous claim that while we have conscious access to the level of 'what is said' (explicature) we do not have conscious awareness of (any aspects of) linguistic meaning.

2.6.1 Minimalist principles

In Carston (1988/91), I discussed two 'minimalist' principles which, though seldom made explicit, seem to guide philosophers in distinguishing pragmatic contributions to the proposition expressed (what is said) from implicated meaning; they are minimalist in that they reflect a concern to keep pragmatic contributions to the explicit level, the level of 'what is said', to a minimum. These are the **Linguistic Direction Principle** and the **Minimal Truth-Evaluability Principle**. I argued that neither of these is satisfactory, at least not for a cognitive account of utterance interpretation. I shall discuss them only briefly here.

The logical form or semantic representation which is the result of linguistic decoding contains variables and/or slots which require filling by pragmatic inference. Recanati calls this sort of pragmatic process 'saturation'. According to the Linguistic Direction Principle, a pragmatically derived element of utterance meaning may contribute to the level of what is said if and only if it is required to give a value to a slot or variable in the decoded semantic representation, that is, iff it is a case of saturation. The obvious examples are indexical elements, such as pronouns and demonstratives, which can be viewed as marking a slot to be contextually filled and as imposing a constraint on how it should be filled (singular/plural; male/female; inclusive/exclusive, etc.). Are there any others? Cases of grammatical ellipsis, as in

(148), seem to involve a variable or slot, but the unexpressed material here is to be entirely recovered by grammatical means:

(148) a. Jane wants apple pie and Bill [. . .] chocolate mousse.
   b. Although [. . .] unwell, Sam gave a brilliant lecture.
   c. Vlad likes football and so does Nick.

Pragmatic inference is not only not required to saturate these slots, it is prohibited from overriding the grammatically dictated value; for instance, (148a) cannot be understood as Jane wants apple pie and Bill loathes chocolate mousse, even if it is blindingly contextually salient that Bill does indeed loathe chocolate mousse.

There are some other examples which have been suggested in the literature as involving pragmatic saturation of linguistically given slots, but there is no general consensus on these:

(149) a. Kate's picture is hanging in the Tate.
   b. Everyone went home early.
   c. I haven't eaten.

For the genitive form in (149a), the grammar might supply a relation variable whose value has to be pragmatically fixed: picture painted by Kate, picture of Kate, picture owned by Kate, Kate's favourite picture, etc. There may be a domain variable for the bare quantifier in (149b) whose value, again, has to be supplied by pragmatic inference: everyone in the linguistics department at UCL, everyone at Bill's party, etc. And for (149c) it may be that a temporal span slot accompanies the past perfect tense, so pragmatic determination is required, a likely value in this example being 'today' or 'in the last several hours'.

According to Bach's (1994a) notion of 'what is said', his second and more liberal conception, pragmatic contributions at this level are restricted to those that are required for saturation, that is, he follows the Linguistic Direction Principle. He distinguishes between syntactically generated slots or variables, which must be filled in order to arrive at what is said, and those which, while conceptually necessary, are not linguistically mandated, so do not have to be filled in order to arrive at what is said. The examples he has in mind include 'finish' as opposed to 'complete', 'eat' as opposed to 'devour', 'try' as opposed to 'attempt'. For instance:

(150) a. He completed the essay.
   b. * He completed at midnight.
   c. He finished at midnight.

Supposing the referent of 'he' is 'Nick', then what is said in (150a) is 'Nick completed the essay', while what is said in (150c) is 'Nick finished at midnight'. Even if it is perfectly clear that what he finished is the essay, it is not a constituent of what is said, as there is no syntactically specified slot for an object. So what is said is not fully propositional (does not have a determinate truth condition). The result for subsentential utterances such as 'Michael's father' would be similar: on the assumption that it doesn't come embedded in a logical form full of variables, what it says, on Bach's view, must fall well short of a full proposition. This is enough to make this notion of 'what is said' very questionable for many. It falls between two stools: it is more than the decoded linguistic meaning and it is less than a level to which a truth-conditional semantics can be applied. Others who support the idea that pragmatic contributions to 'what is said' conform strictly to the Linguistic Direction Principle ensure that it is fully propositional by being much more liberal than Bach in postulating hidden variables or covert indexicals in the logical form of sentences, including those in (149) and (150c); their view is discussed further in section 2.7.

In Bach's case, there is the further issue that he distinguishes two other representational levels: impliciture and implicature, where impliciture is very close to the relevance-theoretic level of basic explicature and to Recanati's enriched 'what is said': it is a fully propositional development of the logical form and is communicatively intended; it involves a considerable contribution from pragmatic inference, not just to complete it (make it truth-evaluable), but also to ensure that it is the propositional form that the speaker intended. So, the issue of distinguishing among the contributions of pragmatic inference arises again: which result in constituents of an impliciture and which are implicatures? Bach does not address this.

The second minimalist principle overlaps in its predictions to a large extent with the first, except where what the first determines is subpropositional. The Minimal Truth-Evaluability Principle says that a pragmatically derived element of utterance meaning may contribute to the level of what is said if and only if it is required to arrive at a complete proposition, that is, a truth-evaluable entity. Anything beyond that is to be considered an implicature. I think that Grice observed this second minimalist principle; his discussions concerned with distinguishing what is said from what is implicated (whether conventionally or conversationally) focused on distinguishing those aspects of overall utterance meaning which were necessary in determining a truth value for an utterance from those that were not. The implicature analyses, mentioned at the beginning of section 2.6, of definite descriptions that do not denote a unique entity, of 'and'-conjunction relations, and of the opacity of belief contexts, are also 'minimalist' in this way about what is said. And the principle seems to guide accounts that equate the domain of truth-conditional semantics with what is said; Cappelen and Lepore (1997) and Reimer (1998) cite many proponents of this view, including Davidson, Kaplan and Soames (see note 8 of this chapter).

So why don't we accept this principle? To answer this it is useful to look at utterances whose logical form seems to require just reference assignment and/or disambiguation in order to be minimally propositional (hence truth-evaluable), but which are either trivially true or blatantly false, and so do not fall within the set of assumptions which comprise the intended interpretation of the utterance:

(151) a. It'll take time to understand Relevance Theory.
       b. Delays are possible.
       c. Something's happened.
       d. I haven't eaten.
       e. There's nothing on telly tonight.

The minimal propositional forms assignable to (151a)–(151c) are virtually always trivially true: every undertaking takes a span of time, delays are always within the realm of what is possible, at any point in (human) time, there has been some occurrence or other. The minimal propositional forms assignable to (151d)–(151e) are obviously false, since the speaker has eaten in her life, and there is something or other on the telly. The general point for the two types of case is the same: across the vast majority of contexts, this propositional form does not interact productively with the hearer's existing assumptions about the world. It is either already so well known that it cannot be made more highly manifest to the hearer, or it is so plainly untrue that it will not be treated by the hearer as a manifest assumption at all; in both cases a local process of pragmatic strengthening is required in order to recover a propositional form which could be informative and relevant. For instance, (151c) might be strengthened to (152a) and (151e) to (152b):

(152)   a.   Something of an untoward sort has happened [on the motorway].
        b.   There's nothing worth watching on the telly tonight.

Recanati (1993) calls these cases of 'free enrichment', distinguishing them from saturation, as the impetus for the pragmatically derived material is entirely cognitive, not indicated by any linguistic element. It might be noted that, in the positive case, the pragmatic process results in a propositional form which is logically stronger than the minimal one, while in the negative examples, the process results in a logically weaker one ('There's nothing on telly', arguably, entails 'There's nothing worth watching on telly'). The process is local in each case, that is, it strengthens or makes more precise a constituent of the proposition. Relative *logical* strength of propositions is just not to the point; in both cases the proposition derived by the pragmatic process is *cognitively stronger* in the sense that it is more informative/relevant than the minimal one; it has more cognitive effects.

Minimalists would probably agree that the minimal propositions derivable from (151a)–(151e) are not what the speaker meant, while the representations in (152a)–(152b) are; they would insist, however, that the minimal proposition is what was said and that what was *meant* in each case is an implicature. This is, in fact, at odds with Grice's position that what is said is meant, though he doesn't seem to have been wholly consistent on this matter. More to the point, in the current context of a cognitive account of ostensive communication and inferential interpretation, is the fact that minimal propositions of this not-meant (not-communicated) sort are not among the constructs of the theory, as they are neither communicated assumptions nor the vehicle by means of which these assumptions are recovered.

Delivering the propositional forms intended by the speaker (or forms sufficiently similar to them) is what pragmatic maxims/principles are all about; they are not employed so as to enable recovery of a minimally truth-evaluable proposition, which, more often than not, neither falls within the speaker's communicative intention nor has any role to play in the interpretation process. Neither of the two principles will do for the theory of the cognitive representations and processes involved in ostensive-inferential communication.[51] The linguistic underdeterminacy thesis entails that there is considerable pragmatic work involved in arriving at the proposition the speaker intends to express; the users of one or other of these minimalist principles have either ignored the import of this thesis for an account of verbal communication, or are involved in some other endeavour altogether, perhaps an attempt to carve out a level that might serve as the appropriate domain of a semantic theory of some sort. For further discussion, see Carston (1988/91) and Recanati (1989b/91, 1993), and for a defence of Gricean minimalism, see Cappelen (2000).

2.6.2 Functional independence

In Carston (1988/91), I suggested a different sort of principle for deciding on whether or not a pragmatic inference resulted in an implicature or contributed to an explicature. This was called the Functional Independence Principle; the idea behind it was that the proposition expressed (the explicature) and implicatures should play independent roles in the mental life of the hearer; if an alleged implicature was such that its role in subsequent inferences such as the derivation of contextual effects subsumed the role of the alleged proposition expressed, then the alleged implicature was most likely really a pragmatic aspect of the proposition expressed.

The idea is perhaps best conveyed through examples. The truisms and blatant falsehoods in (151a)–(151e), have few, if any, cognitive effects, so that the richer propositions, such as (152a)–(152b), which are pragmatically inferred, subsume their inferential role and go well beyond it. By the Independence Principle, it follows that these richer propositions are not implicatures but the proposition explicitly expressed by the utterance. A more striking case, perhaps, is the following 'and'-conjunction, where it is apparent that a cause–consequence connection between the two conjuncts is communicated:

(153) a. He applied bleach to the sink and the dirt dissolved.
       b. His application of bleach to the sink caused the dirt to dissolve.

Assuming that the causal connection is not part of the decoded meaning but is derived pragmatically, it could be an implicature or it could contribute to the proposition explicitly expressed. According to the Functional Independence Principle, the latter construal is the correct one, since whatever cognitive effects the truth-functional conjunction may have, they are but a proper subset of those that the pragmatically derived, causally connected proposition has. That is, there is no independent role for the truth-functional conjunction to play.

Recanati (1989b/91) finds the principle inadequate, at least in one of its manifestations, and provides a clear counterexample. He characterizes it as follows:

Independence Principle: conversational implicatures are functionally independent of what is said; this means in particular that they do not entail, *and are not entailed by*, what is said. When an alleged implicature does not meet this condition, it must be considered as part of what is said.

(Recanati 1989b: 316; my italics)

First, this is not quite right; nowhere in the paper did I endorse that part of the statement that I have italicized. As discussed in section 2.3.3 above, it seems quite possible to me that a speaker could implicate an entailment of the proposition her utterance expresses, for instance:

> (154)   A: Did you buy any fruit?
>   B: I bought some apricots and a couple of apples.

Here, it is at least arguable that B implicates that she bought some fruit, which is the answer to A's question. Unlike Grice, relevance theorists do not claim that entailments and implicatures are necessarily mutually exclusive; indeed, they are concepts that function at different explanatory levels. However, Recanati's main point concerns the non-italicized part of his statement of the principle, and this I did say at various points throughout the article. Here is his counterexample:

> (155)   A: Was there anybody rich at the party, who might be asked to pay for the damages?
>   B: Jim is rich.
>   A: Yes, but did he go the party?
>   B: I don't know, but I can tell you that if *anybody* was there, Jim was there.
>   A: *Somebody* was there – this I know for sure (I saw John going there). So it looks as if the damages will be paid for, after all.
>   (Recanati 1989b: 320)

It is clear that the beginning of A's last reply, 'Somebody was there', implicates that 'Jim was there', given the premise supplied by B's previous utterance, 'If anybody was there, Jim was there'. This implicature, that Jim was there, entails the proposition explicitly expressed, that somebody was there. So, according to the Independence Principle, it should be considered a part of what is said rather than a genuine implicature. This prediction is simply wrong. There are a couple of points to make here. First, in the paper I vacillate between a functional characterization of the notion of independence that I'm looking for and a logical characterization. The logical characterization is simpler and clearer: an implicature should not entail the proposition expressed; it is this that Recanati takes up and he shows, correctly, that it cannot be right. The argument that I have levelled against the minimalists applies here too: it is a mistake to assume that logically based principles necessarily have a cognitive correlate.

The rather vaguer notion of 'functional' independence concerns the requirement that the proposition expressed by the utterance should have a role to play, distinct from and independent of its implicatures, in the hearer's inferential processing, specifically that it should function independently as a premise in arguments (see Carston 1988/91: 35). Interestingly, this condition seems to be met by the example in (155): 'Jim was there' is the conclusion of a deductive inference, one of whose premises is the proposition expressed by the utterance, namely 'Someone was there'; so the functional characterization seems to predict correctly the status of 'Jim was there' as an implicature rather than a pragmatic contribution to the level of what is said. A more compelling counterexample to the principle would involve a communicated assumption which, like the example here, is clearly an implicature, but which is an *implicated premise* (rather than an implicated conclusion) and entails what is said; I have not come across such a case.[52]

However, it is not clear to me that 'functional independence' is worth any kind of vigorous defence; it was in fact intended as only a useful heuristic and should probably never have been elevated by the label 'principle' at all. I was (and am still) of the view that the communicative principle of relevance itself or, more particularly, the comprehension strategy that follows from it, effects a sorting of pragmatic inferences into contributions to the proposition expressed (explicature) and implicatures, and so subsumes whatever correct predictions 'functional independence' might make. Strongly constrained by his bid for an interpretation which meets his expectations of relevance, the addressee's pragmatic inferential work is apportioned between proposition expressed (explicature) and implicatures by a mutual adjustment process resulting in logically sound arguments, as described in section 2.3.4.

Unlike the relevance-theoretic principle, the various minimalist principles, the Scope Principle (which is yet to be discussed) and the Availability Principle are not to be thought of as principles that govern hearers in their utterance-understanding processes, but as useful tools that pragmatic theorists can turn to in order to reach, or justify, particular analyses of utterance meaning. Bearing this in mind, I move to what has turned out, in practice, to be the most useful criterion or test for distinguishing between these two roles that pragmatic contributions may play.

2.6.3 Embedding tests

Along with the Availability Principle, Recanati (1989b/91) proposed a further principle, called the Scope Principle, which is intended to provide the pragmatist (as opposed to the addressee engaged in utterance interpretation) with a criterion for delineating the distinction between explicating/saying and implicating:

> **Scope Principle:** A pragmatically determined aspect of meaning is part of what is said (and, therefore, not a conversational implicature) if – and, perhaps, only if – it falls within the scope of logical operators such as negation and conditionals.

The insight embodied in this principle had already been employed for some time as a kind of test for toning up intuitions about truth-conditional content. It seems to have begun with Cohen's (1971) use of an embedding procedure in order to demonstrate that Grice couldn't simultaneously maintain the truth-functionality of 'and' and of 'if'. On a Gricean account, the meaning of 'and' is identical to its truth-functional logical counterpart '&', so that the two conjunctive utterances in (156) have the same truth-conditional content (they 'say' the same thing). The difference in what they communicate, concerning the order in which the events described took place, arises at the level of conversational implicature (based on the manner maxim of 'orderliness'):

> (156) a. The old king has died of a heart attack and a republic has been declared.
>   b. A republic has been declared and the old king has died of a heart attack.

The problem with this analysis that Cohen pinpointed is apparent when the conjunctions are embedded in the antecedent of a conditional as in (157):

> (157) a. If the old king has died of a heart attack and a republic has been declared, then Tom will be quite content.
>   b. If a republic has been declared and the old king has died of a heart attack, then Tom will be quite content.

Given the alleged truth-functionality of 'and', the antecedents of the two conditionals must be truth-conditionally equivalent, and given the alleged truth-functionality of 'if', to which Grice was equally committed, it follows that the two conditionals in (157) must be truth-conditionally equivalent. However, this does not seem to be so: the temporal relation understood to hold between the conjuncts seems to be an integral part of the antecedents, so that the two conditionals are truth-conditionally distinct and could well differ in truth-value, Tom being happy with one sequence of events but unhappy with the other. The same result can be achieved by embedding the sentences under scrutiny in the scope of other operators, including negation, disjunction, and comparatives. If the only options in accounting for the temporal connection were a Gricean implicature or a richer semantics, there would be good reason to favour the latter, as Cohen did. Relevance theorists, however, have used the results of this embedding test, together with a pragmatic account of how the temporal ordering arises, to support an account on which this is a pragmatic contribution to the proposition expressed (explicature, enriched 'what is said' or i-content). This is the subject of the next chapter.

A number of theorists have concluded that in certain cases of a sentence/utterance that carries a conversational implicature, embedding that sentence in the syntactic scope of a logical operator results in the implicature becoming a part of the propositional content that falls within the scope of the operator. This is essentially Levinson's (1988, 2000) position (discussed in section 2.1.2). Another is Green (1998), who puts forward the 'Embedded Implicature Hypothesis: If assertion of a sentence S conveys the implicatum [implicature] that p with nearly universal regularity, then when S is embedded the content that is usually understood to be embedded for semantic purposes is the proposition (S & p)' (1998: 77). An instance of the sort of case he has in mind is given in (158a), which is standardly taken to implicate that the contact lens belonged to the speaker (or, more generally, to the agent of the losing). When this same sentence is embedded in the scope of negation as in (158b) or a disjunction as in (158c), this 'implicature' is judged to fall within the scope of those operators:

(158) a. I lost a contact lens in the accident.
        b. I didn't lose a contact lens in the accident, but Mary did.
        c. Either Mary lost a contact lens in the accident or Bob did.

Even Grice, in his last writings, seems to have been prepared to concede something along these lines: 'It certainly does not seem reasonable to subscribe to an absolute ban on the possibility that an embedding locution may govern the standard non-conventional implicatum rather than the conventional import of the embedded sentence . . .' (Grice 1989a: 375). He reached this position as a result of having been unable to find a solution to the problem that the negation of a conditional (where 'if' is assumed to be equivalent in its meaning to the material conditional of standard logic) denies not the material conditional but the 'implicature' that standardly arises when the conditional sentence occurs unembedded. (I omit details of the case as they are somewhat complex and not strictly to the point here.)

    These observations are at one with the view that pragmatic inference plays a fundamental role in determining the proposition expressed; however, they do not have to be taken as entailing that what is an implicature (a propositional form distinct from the proposition expressed) of a simple sentence/utterance changes its status when that simple sentence is embedded, becoming then part of the proposition expressed (the truth-conditional content). Rather, we have a pragmatic contribution to the proposition expressed in both cases (unembedded and embedded) and an implicature in neither. The interesting fact is that some pragmatically derived meaning does fall in the scope of logical operators and some does not, so that we have a test for distinguishing pragmatic contributions to the proposition expressed from conversational implicatures. The pragmatic inference of a temporal sequence relation between the states of affairs described in the conjuncts does fall in the scope of the conditionals in (157) and the subject ownership inference in (158) falls in the scope of the negation and disjunction. Similarly, the pragmatic inference which narrows the temporal span in (159a) to 'today' falls in the scope of the negation in (159b), and the inference of a particular quantifier domain, say 'the people who came to Jane's party' in (160a) also falls in the scope of the disjunction in (160b):

(159) a. I've showered.
        b. I haven't showered.

(160) a. Everyone left early.
        b. Either everyone left early or the ones who stayed on are in the garden.

Compare these with an application of the test to Bob's utterance in (161a):

(161) a. Ann: Does Bill have a girlfriend these days?
               Bob: He flies to New York every weekend.
        b. He doesn't fly to New York every weekend.
        c. If he flies to New York every weekend he must spend a lot on travel.

From Bob's answer to her question, Ann can infer that Bill probably does have a girlfriend (who lives in new York). But this pragmatic inference does not affect the propositional content in the scope of the corresponding negation in (161b), nor does it fall in the scope of the conditional in (161c); the consequent (that Bill must spend a lot on travel) depends just on the proposition that Bill flies to New York every weekend and not on him having a girlfriend there.

Similarly, a typical utterance of (162a) communicates that the speaker doesn't know where in the south of France Mary resides, but, as Green (1998: 73) points out, that is not understood as contributing to the proposition expressed by the more complex (162b) in which the original sentence is embedded. If it did, (162b) should be found tautologous (or, as he puts it, *prima facie* plausible), which is not the case:

(162)   a.   Mary lives somewhere in the south of France.
        b.   If Mary lives somewhere in the south of France, then I do not know where.

In accordance with the Scope Principle, what these embedding tests indicate is that the pragmatically determined elements of meaning in (156)–(160) are parts of the proposition expressed by those utterances, while the pragmatically determined elements in (161a) and (162a) are not; rather, they are truly cases of conversational implicature.

So the Scope Principle seems to provide a promising test. However, Recanati (1993) demotes it, in favour of the Availability Principle, because of the problem created by so-called metalinguistic uses of logical operators:

(163)   a.   I am not his daughter; he is my father.
        b.   If you use elevators and sidewalks you must be from America; in England we have lifts and pavements.

The significant feature of these examples is that some property other than truth-conditional content seems to be falling within the scope of the logical operator: in (163a) it is some connotation carried by a readiness to declare oneself someone's daughter which is the focus of the negation; in (163b) it is the use of the dialect-specific lexical items 'elevator' and 'sidewalk' that falls within the scope of the antecedent of the conditional. This sort of metalinguistic use can be applied to virtually any utterance property: phonetics, intonation, grammar, style, attitude, etc. I take it that the problem Recanati thinks this presents for the Scope Principle is that the principle can only fulfil its purpose of distinguishing the two types of pragmatic contribution if, as it is often misleadingly put, the operator is not being used metalinguistically. For instance, if the conditionals in the Cohen examples in (157) are being used in this way, then nothing follows about the truth-conditional content of the conjunctive antecedents; it could be that the metalinguistic focus is on the different order of presentation of the two conjuncts in the two examples and that the consequent in each case is in an implication relation with this feature of the antecedent rather than with its truth-conditional content.

In my view, more fully explicated in chapter 4, section 4.4 on metalinguistic negation, the operators in such cases are not being used in any special way; what the difference between descriptive and metalinguistic uses comes to is whether or not some feature, linguistic or conceptual, of the embedded material is being used meta-representationally. Provided one can discern this, one can tell whether or not the embedding test can be applied to provide evidence in distinguishing implicatures from pragmatic contributions to truth conditions. In many instances, this is perfectly clear, as in the examples in (163), which are usually pronounced with a very particular 'contradiction' kind of intonation pattern. But there are others where it is not so clear and then other considerations have to be brought to bear in deciding whether the use is descriptive or metarepresentational, and so whether the test can be properly applied or not. Used with care, the scope embedding test is a helpful tool, though it should probably not be given the status of a principle.

A further interesting complication comes from the possibility of an utterance having two or more propositions expressed (basic-level explicatures), as discussed in section 2.3.2 of this chapter. Consider an example involving a non-restrictive relative clause, which is pragmatically enriched as in (164b):

(164) a. Pat's book, which everyone scorned, has won the Nobel prize for literature.
 b. The book Pat wrote, which everyone in London literary circles scorned, has won the Nobel prize for literature.

In the following application of the embedding test, I try to use a consequent whose content is not obviously biased toward the main clause:

(165) a. If Pat's book, which everyone scorned, has won the Nobel prize for literature, she won't write any more.
 b. The book Pat wrote has won the Nobel prize for literature.
 c. Everyone in London literary circles scorned Pat's book.

The question is what, according to the sentence/utterance in (165a), is the basis for the claim that Pat won't write any more? Is it both of (165b) and (165c) or just the main clause (165b)? I think it is fairly clear that the answer is that the claim depends on (165b) alone and that (165c), the proposition expressed by the non-restrictive relative clause, in fact falls outside the scope of the conditional. On this mechanical application of the test, we would have to conclude that the pragmatic inference restricting the domain of 'everyone' to 'London literary circles' does not contribute to the truth conditions of the utterance. But recall that talk of the truth conditions of an utterance is really a shorthand for talk of the truth conditions of a proposition expressed by an utterance, and the utterance in (164a) expresses two propositions, one of which is syntactically marked as a secondary background element. Since it is antecedently clear that there are two propositions expressed here, the embedding test should be applied to each clause individually; then, if a pragmatically determined aspect of the meaning of the syntactically disjunct clause falls within the scope of logical operators, that element of meaning is a constituent of the proposition expressed by that subsidiary clause.

The test has also been used within relevance theory on cases which were described in section 2.3.2 as involving two speech acts, a central one and a higher-level commenting speech act, as in:

(166) a. Sadly, Mary hasn't got into Cambridge.
      b. Bill, frankly, has no linguistic ability.

When (166a) is embedded in the scope of a conditional as in (167a), there are two scope possibilities for 'sadly'; it may take the whole conditional in its scope or just the clause in the antecedent. We are concerned only with the latter here:

(167) a. If, sadly, Mary hasn't got into Cambridge she'll have to go to Hull.
      b. Mary hasn't got into Cambridge.
      c. It is sad that Mary hasn't got into Cambridge.

Even given the narrow scope interpretation of the adverbial, it seems clear that it falls outside the scope of the logical operator, as we might expect from the double speech-act analysis. However, there are other adverbials, which seem to have the same syntactic properties as the evaluative and illocutionary adverbials, but for which the test gives a different result:

(168) a. The play is, obviously, going to lose money.
      b. If the play is, obviously, going to lose money, it will close early.
      c. Bill has, allegedly, stolen the funds.
      d. If Bill has, allegedly, stolen the funds, we should question him carefully.

In the case of the evidential adverbial 'obviously' and the hearsay adverbial 'allegedly', the intuitions tapped by the embedding test are that the basis for the play closing early is that it is obvious that it's going to lose money, and the basis for questioning Bill carefully is that it is alleged that he has stolen the funds. According to the test, then, these adverbials do affect the proposition expressed by the host clause and so contribute to the truth conditions of the main speech act. Although I cannot pursue the implications of these differences here, it should be evident that, with judicious use, this embedding test can provide useful indications, not only concerning the role of pragmatic inference in utterance meaning, but also the contributions of encoded elements external to the main clause of the utterance. For extensive use of this test in developing analyses of different sentence adverbials and other parenthetical clauses, see Ifantidou (1993, 1994, 2001) and Ifantidou-Trouki (1993); for critical discussion of some applications of the test, see Asher (2000).

Finally, it will be interesting to see what the scope criterion indicates for cases of non-literal use, such as metaphor and other loosenings:

(169) a. If this argument is *rock solid*, the problem is solved.
      b. Paul isn't a *lion*; he's a *pussycat*.
      c. She summoned the chef because her steak was *raw*.

The issue here is whether the pragmatically inferred, non-literal meaning (communicated by the use of 'rock solid', 'lion', 'pussycat' and 'raw') contributes to the proposition expressed or is only implicated. For instance, is the negated clause in

(169b) inevitably true, since Paul (a human being) does not belong to a certain class of feline mammals, or could it be judged false by someone who believes Paul to have awesome qualities of courage and nobility? This is considered in chapter 5, where I explore the idea that pragmatic loosenings, like pragmatic strengthenings, can contribute to an explicitly communicated proposition.

2.7 Postscript: Hidden Indexicals or 'Free' Enrichment?

To complete this chapter's coverage of positions on the 'what is said' of an utterance (generally, equated with its truth-conditional content, or the proposition it expresses), I should consider a currently popular view among philosophers that the logical forms of many sentences contain various hidden indexicals (or 'suppressed parameters') and that, given disambiguation, the only pragmatic contributions to 'what is said' are those that involve fixing the values of indexicals (whether overt or hidden).

Recall the requirement on the Gricean notion of 'what is said' that it should be very close, if not identical, to what truth-conditional semanticists set out to assign as the semantic content of a sentence (discussed in section 2.2.1). This is most apparent in the following formulation of an assumption held by a large number of different approaches to semantics within the philosophy of language: 'An adequate semantic theory T for a language L should assign p as the semantic content of a sentence S in L iff in uttering S a speaker says that p.' Let us assume, with Reimer (1998), that the 'says' here is the Gricean notion (see note 8 of this chapter). Given the obvious facts concerning indexicals and unarticulated (or, at least, unuttered) constituents of 'what is said', it is difficult to see how this could be taken absolutely literally. While the Gricean 'what is said', on any given occasion of utterance, is fully propositional, with particular values given to indexicals, the semantics of an *indexical sentence S in a language L* clearly does not include any particular contextual values and is standardly non-propositional.

However, the approach to be discussed here manages to preserve the essence of this concern for a match between sentence semantics and 'what is said' without requiring their full content-identity. This is the view that all elements of 'what is said' by the utterance of a sentence are marked out in the logical form of the sentence, or, as Stanley (2000: 391) puts it, 'all truth-conditional effects of extra-linguistic context can be traced to logical form'. The idea is that whenever a constituent of truth-conditional content ('what is said') has been contextually supplied, the requirement that it be so supplied is indicated linguistically by an indexical (in the broad sense of 'indexical'); it might be a so-called 'pure' indexical (e.g. 'I', 'now', 'today'), a pronoun, a demonstrative or a covert variable (that is, a phonologically unrealized indexical occupying a particular structural position in logical form[53]). In other words, there are no truly unarticulated constituents, because, although some constituents do not appear in the surface syntax of the linguistic expression used, so are not perceptible, they are nonetheless articulated in the logical form of the expression. On this view, the Linguistic Direction Principle, one of the minimalist principles discussed in the previous section, correctly distinguishes pragmatic contributions to the proposition expressed from conversational implicatures. Given disambiguation, the only further pragmatic process which contributes to the proposition expressed is 'saturation' (slot-filling); there is no 'free' enrichment, where 'free' means not linguistically mandated. The domain of semantics is the interpretation of logical forms relative to contexts and semantic composition is fully reflected in the logical form. Obviously, this position entails the presence, in the logical forms of natural-language sentences, of quite a number of imperceptible elements.

In making his case, Stanley develops a particular line of argument against the existence of unarticulated constituents, hence against any process of free enrichment. It goes as follows: (a) he takes a simple case which has been argued to involve the addition of a constituent by a process of free pragmatic enrichment; (b) he embeds it in a larger structure which contains an explicit quantifier and in which the constituent in question can be understood as being bound by that quantifier; (c) he then shows that an account on which that constituent is wholly absent from the logical form is unable to predict this bound-variable interpretation, while an account on which a variable occurs in the appropriate position in logical form predicts both that interpretation (on which it is bound by the quantifier) as well as the unbound, deictic interpretation (on which the variable is free).

Here's the line of argument applied to perhaps the most famous case of an (alleged) unarticulated element, the location constituent standardly understood in interpreting an utterance of (170a). The simple sentence is embedded in a universally quantified sentence, as in (170b):

(170) a. It's raining.
       b. Every time John lights a cigarette, it rains.

There are (at least) two interpretations of (170b):

(171) a. For every time t at which John lights a cigarette, it rains at t at the location l in which John lights a cigarette at t.
       b. For every time t at which John lights a cigarette, it rains at t at some location which is salient in the context of utterance.

While the enrichment analysis can account for (171b), in which a single constant location constituent is recovered from context, it cannot account for the interpretation in (171a) (which, incidentally, is the preferred interpretation here), because the truth conditions it gives for the sentence in (170b) are as follows (assuming a temporal variable):

(172) An utterance of 'it is raining (t)' is true in a context c iff it is raining at t and at l, where l is the contextually salient location in c.

An account which posits a location variable (in addition to an assumed temporal variable) in the logical form can account for both readings; on reading (171a), the variable l is bound by the quantifier; on reading (171b), the variable is free and takes as its value the most contextually salient location. Therefore, the free enrichment analysis is inadequate and there is, after all, a location variable in the logical forms of both (170a) and (170b). The analogy is with overt indexicals such as 'she' in the following, which can be given both a bound and a free interpretation:

(173)   Every woman in the company was glad that she had an interesting job.

Stanley repeats the line of argument for sentences containing degree adjectives like 'short', 'fast' and 'old', whose truth conditions involve an implicit comparison class, as in (174a), for sentences containing quantifiers whose truth conditions depend on an implicit domain restriction, as in (174b), for sentences containing relational expressions, such as 'home', 'enemy', 'local', whose truth conditions depend on what they are related to ('home of x', 'local to y', etc.), as in (174c), and for a range of others that require propositional completion, such as (174d):

(174)   a.   Josie is short.   [short for a basketball player]
        b.   Every medicine bottle is kept on the top shelf.   [every medicine bottle in Gran's house]
        c.   Sam went to a local bar.   [a bar local to Sam's office]
        d.   There is enough beer in the fridge.   [enough beer to satisfy the needs of the guests at our barbecue]

When embedded in a quantified structure, each of these can be given a free or a bound variable interpretation, for instance:

(175)   a.   Most delegates visited a local bar.
        b.   Most delegates x visited a bar local to x.   [bound variable reading]
        c.   Most delegates visited a bar local to some contextually salient entity.   [free variable reading]

For each case, the crucial step in Stanley's argument is to point out that the free enrichment treatment, on which the constituent in question is not present in any covert form in any linguistic representation, can account only for the free variable reading, that is, the interpretation on which the logical form is supplemented by a representation of a contextually salient entity.

Let's consider how convincing this step is. Focusing again on the example in (170), although a variable is required in the operator-bound interpretation, (171a), there is no need for a variable of any sort on the other reading, (171b), nor for the interpretation of the simple, unquantified sentence (170a), so we could say that it is there in the one sort of case and not there in the others. This might seem to amount to an ambiguity account, whereby the linguistic form 'rains' encodes both 'RAINS' *tout court* and 'RAINS AT L', which would certainly be an unattractive prospect. But it is not the only way of understanding the proposal: the variable could come into being by a pragmatic process in the case where the intended interpretation is the bound variable one. Stanley, however, claims that this is not possible:

It is easy to see how an object or a property could be provided by pragmatic mechanisms; it need only be made salient in the context either by the speaker's intentions, or contextual clues, depending upon one's account of salience. However, denotations of bound variables are odd, theoretically complex entities. It is difficult, if not impossible, to see how, on any account of salience, such an entity could be salient in a context. Certainly, neither it, nor instances of it, could be perceptually present in the context. It is equally difficult to see how speaker intention could determine reference to such an entity.

An entity such as a denotation of a bound variable is a theoretical posit, part of the machinery of a particularly complex semantic theory. It is not something about which we have beliefs or intentions. They are therefore not supplied by pragmatic mechanisms.   (Stanley 2000: 414)

The truth of this claim is essential to the case against the free enrichment possibility, but it rests on certain assumptions about the nature of contexts and pragmatic processes, with which one could take issue. Stanley seems inclined to a very extensionalist view of context, consisting of perceptible objects and properties, while the operative notion of context on the cognitive relevance-theoretic view is of a set of mentally represented assumptions, some of which are representations of immediate perceptible environmental features, but most of which are either retrieved from memory or constructed on the basis of stored assumption schemas. It is an entirely open question at present just what these conceptual (language of thought) representations consist of, but it should not be ruled out *a priori* that there are assumptions whose mental representation involves variables bound by quantifiers, and that these can be accessed by addressees in the process of interpreting utterances, in particular utterances containing explicit quantifiers. A plausible case would be a general knowledge assumption about the way in which times and places pair up when a certain type of event (such as 'raining') recurs, so that from an appropriate temporal binding can be inferred a locational binding, and vice versa, as in the interpretation of 'Everywhere John lights a cigarette, it rains'.

These very programmatic remarks are primarily directed at example (170), the place constituent case. As regards the others that Stanley considers, it may indeed be that some of them have a covert indexical or variable in logical form. Perhaps the best candidates are the relational terms (e.g. 'local', 'friend', 'enemy', 'home'), which seem to behave syntactically very much like examples with overt indexicals. For instance, they give rise to 'weak crossover effects':

(176)   a.   [Every reporter]$_i$ was sponsored by her$_i$ local bar.
        b.   * Her$_i$ local bar sponsored [every reporter]$_i$.
        c.   Every reporter was sponsored by a local bar.
        d.   * A local bar sponsored every reporter. [where the bar is the reporter's local bar]

Just as the explicit pronoun 'her' in (176b) can't be bound by the quantified phrase 'every reporter', nor can '*a* local bar' in (176d), which does seem to indicate that there is an implicit element in this expression with the same properties as the explicit pronoun, as Stanley claims. However, there are still many cases for which a free enrichment account is at least a serious possibility and some for which a hidden variable account doesn't seem possible.

Bach (2000a) launches a battery of arguments against the case made by Stanley and Szabo (2000a) for a covert domain variable, f(i), occurring with quantifier phrases, such as 'every bottle'. I mention only a few of his considerations here. He points out that, unlike the relational examples, there is no particular lexical item imposing the domain-variable requirement and that many occurrences of quantified phrases, such as those italicized in (177), do not seem to require any domain restriction although, according to the covert variable view, they must be contextually assigned one:

(177) a. *All men* are mortal.
       b. *Hardly any food* is blue.
       c. That is *a lesser spotted woodpecker*.

Furthermore, even in cases of extreme specificity and explicitness, such as (178), the variable is present, apparently requiring yet further contextual specification:

(178) Most of the [retired people in Arkansas who voted for Dole in 1996, f(i)] were Republicans.

This distinguishes the quantifier domain variable from the other hidden variable cases Stanley discusses, whose position in logical form can be taken over by a phonologically realized linguistic constituent, which blocks a bound variable interpretation when the quantificational embedding procedure is pursued. This is seen in (179), where there is an overt location constituent, and in (180), where there is an overt relational constituent; the quantified (b) cases can only be understand as having (rather odd) unbound readings:

(179) a. It's raining in Weston-super-Mare.
       b. Every time John lights a cigarette it rains in Weston-super-Mare.

(180) a. Tom went to a bar local to Ely cathedral.
       b. Most journalists go to a bar local to Ely cathedral.

Then, contrary to Stanley and Szabo, Bach argues that the natural interpretation of examples such as (181)–(183) does not require a domain variable to be present in logical form and bound to the higher quantifier 'every room':

(181) In every room in John's house, he keeps every bottle on the top shelf.

(182) In every room in John's house, the personality of the designer is evident.

(183) In every house that John rents out, every passing car may be heard.

The natural interpretations in each case are, respectively:

(181′)   In every room in John's house, he keeps every bottle [*in that room*] on the top shelf.

(182′)   In every room in John's house, the personality of the designer [*of that room*] is evident.

(183′)   In every house that John rents out, every car passing [*that house*] may be heard.

In Bach's view, these communicated propositions are cases of impliciture arrived at by a process of pragmatic expansion of 'what is said'. He points out that the small but important differences in the understood domain in each case (italicized in each example) are an entirely pragmatic matter, governed by general knowledge about the relations between bottles and rooms, designers and rooms, houses and passing cars. All in all, Bach seems to me to have effectively undermined the case for a domain variable in the logical form of quantified sentences (but see the reply in Stanley and Szabo 2000b).

It begins to look as if decisions about this hidden variable issue can only be reached on a case-by-case basis. In this respect, consider the following set of examples, some of which have been discussed in previous sections as cases where the italicized constituents are recovered entirely pragmatically:

(184)   a.   Jack and Jill went up the hill [*together*].
        b.   Mary left Paul and [*as a consequence*] he became clinically depressed.
        c.   She took out the gun, she went into the garden and she killed her father [*with the gun*] [*in the garden*].
        d.   I'll give you £10 if [*and only if*] you mow the lawn.
        e.   John has [*exactly*] four children.
        f.   Louise has always been a great lecturer [*since she's been a lecturer*].

For most of these it is extremely difficult to see how one might argue for a hidden variable (or implicit argument), or why one would want to. In (184a), unlike the relational cases (e.g. 'local', 'distant', 'lover', 'protégé', etc.), there does not seem to be any lexical item carrying a variable for which 'together' could be the contextual value; rather, it arises from relevance-driven inference based on general knowledge about people on hill-climbing ventures, and is, no doubt, much encouraged by the NP-coordination (as opposed to S-coordination). Nor does this constituent appear to be able to enter into a binding relation with a quantifier. Similar points apply to the causal, instrumental and locative constituents in (184b) and (184c), which are entirely optional (being told that someone has killed her father *tout court* is quite relevant enough in some contexts), and to the pragmatic strengthenings in (184d)–(184f) which, again, appear to have no linguistic motivation but are warranted by considerations of contextual relevance. I am, of course, assuming that the supporter of hidden indexicals would not advocate an account of these examples as involving implicatures (rather than contributions to the proposition expressed). He could only do this at the cost of denying the effect of the bracketed elements on the truth-conditional content of the utterance which, in most instances at least, seems indefensible.

Leaving aside now the specifics of Stanley's arguments, I will finish this section with some general points against the idea of hidden constituents, based on an argument in Wilson and Sperber (2000). They start by considering the following exchange between Alan and his neighbour Jill who has just called by:

(185) Alan: Do you want to join us for supper?
       Jill: No thanks. I've eaten.

The sentence 'I've eaten' uttered by Jill is understood by Alan as expressing a proposition which includes an object of eating and a temporal specification, both of which are pragmatically inferred. The result is represented roughly in (186):

(186) Jill has eaten supper this evening.

On a hidden indexical view, the logical form of the sentence she uttered would contain two variables, one for the object and one for the temporal span:

(187) I have eaten x at t

Note that quite general and routine processes of reasoning will also supply these constituents: if someone has eaten she has eaten something; if someone has eaten (something) she has eaten at some time. Be that as it may, Wilson and Sperber go on to point out that in other situations the proposition expressed by a speaker who utters 'I've eaten', or its negation, might involve a specification of the place of eating, the manner of eating, and perhaps others. Their examples are:

(188) I've often been to their parties, but I've never eaten anything [*there*].

(189) I must wash my hands: I've eaten [*using my hands (rather than, sa, being spoon-fed)*].

They comment on this:

> more and more hidden constituents could be postulated, so that every sentence would come with a host of hidden constituents, ready for all kinds of ordinary or extraordinary pragmatic circumstances. . . . We see this as a *reductio* argument that goes all the way to challenging what we accepted earlier for the sake of argument: that the use of the perfect carries with it a hidden constituent referring to a given time span. There is no need to postulate such a hidden constituent: the same [entirely pragmatic] process that explains how 'eating' is narrowed down to 'eating supper' also explains how the time span indicated by the perfect is narrowed down to the evening of utterance. (Wilson and Sperber 2000: 238)

They go on to describe the postulation of hidden constituents as an *ad hoc* process, designed to limit as much as possible the gap between sentence meaning and proposition explicitly expressed, and argue that, although it is at odds with certain theoretical positions on semantics, there is strong evidence that there is a considerable gap and that given the relevance-theoretic view of pragmatic processing this is entirely to be expected.

I think this *reductio* argument can be carried a step further. On the assumption that logical forms are replete with hidden indexicals, it seems that many of them do not receive any contextual value on given occasions of use. For instance, the logical form of the sentence 'I've eaten' might contain four hidden constituents or variables:

> (190)   I've eaten [x] [in manner y] [at location l] [within time span t]

But in the exchange between Alan and Jill above, neither the manner nor the location are of any relevance at all, and would not receive any specific contextual value despite the fact that they are (allegedly) there in the logical form calling for contextual specification. Of course, the hidden indexical theorist might opt for an unspecified default value for these indexicals:

> (191)   I've eaten supper in some manner at some location this evening.

But, first, this doesn't seem to be the propositional content Alan recovers from Jill's utterance; there are strong intuitions that if a sentence, which actually encoded these 'some' elements, and so corresponded more directly with the alleged default-valued proposition, were in fact uttered, it would not have the same meaning as Jill's utterance of 'I've eaten'. Second, the hidden elements are envisaged as the covert counterparts of pronouns, which may be either free (and so given a contextual value) or bound by some operator in the sentence uttered. However, when a pronoun is free it *must* be given a contextual value if the utterance is to be understood and a fully propositional content recovered. Someone who can, for whatever reason, only find a contextual value for 'she' when interpreting an utterance of (192a), and so fills the other indexicals with nonspecific default values, won't have grasped the proposition expressed:

> (192)   a.   She put it there.
>   b.   Lisa$_i$ put something somewhere.

Another way out might be to propose that the sentence 'I have eaten' (and innumerable others) has a variety of logical forms, each with an array of variables, differing in number and type (including one with none), marking possible contextual completions. In the case of a sentence with four variables for different constituents, that means sixteen linguistically provided logical forms to cover the range of cases.

Whichever way you look at it, the covert indexical approach seems to require an unwelcome proliferation of entities, whether of logical forms or default values for variables. One of the nice features of the free enrichment account is that it is not straitjacketed in this way; by definition, only the relevant constituents are recovered. So, while recognizing that this issue is far from finally resolved, as things currently stand, I contend that there are at least three different sorts of pragmatic task involved in the derivation of the proposition(s) expressed by an utterance: disambiguation, saturation and free enrichment.[54,55]

2.8 Conclusion: From Generative Semantics to Pro-active Pragmatics

Grice's idea that there are prevailing standards of rational communicative behaviour, embodied in his Cooperative Principle and conversational maxims (see appendix 2), has effected a revolution in the way linguistically communicated meaning is thought about and analysed. What his idea entails is that communication is possible without the use of a code, that a communicator conveys her thoughts by, so to speak, opening her mind in a certain way to her addressee, so that he is able to infer (non-demonstratively, of course) her intention.

Work in the framework known as 'generative semantics' had aimed to pack into the deep semantic structures of the language the myriad elements of meaning that a single surface form might be understood as having (see Newmeyer, 1986, for discussion of this approach). For instance, the fact that a verb in the imperative mood (e.g. 'Leave now') might communicate an order, a request, permission or advice, was explicitly encoded at this level in distinct semantic representations; various deletion rules were postulated as operating on these structures, so as to account for the absence of the performative verb in the surface structure. Indefinite NPs (e.g. 'a symphony') provide another example: these might communicate a universal, an existential, a generic, or a specific understanding, each of which would, again, be encoded by a distinct operator at deep structure, all the different possibilities mapping on to a single surface structure via grammatical transformations of some sort. This sort of approach raised many worries, due to the baroque, arbitrary, and unconstrained derivational processes involved, and the apparent non-recoverability of the deleted content by any mechanical grammatical process.

With the advent of inferential pragmatics there came a complete methodological turn around. The questions that linguistic semantics should be trying to answer changed significantly. What is it about the imperative mood that makes it possible to communicate this range of speech acts? What is it about the indefinite that enables the range of interpretations that can be inferred from its use? From the recognition that language users bring a rich body of contextual assumptions to communication, and that they have specifically communicative inferential capacities, enabling them to augment considerably and easily the clues provided by linguistically encoded content, there follows a strategy which is the diametric opposite of that pursued in generative semantics: go for as lean a linguistic semantics as is possible. (See Nunberg and Pan, 1975, for an interesting early exposition of this altered perspective.)

Grice's basic insight has been hugely extended by two subsequent theoretical developments: (a) the acknowledgement of the radical linguistic underdeterminacy thesis, which takes pragmatic inference right into the proposition expressed ('what is said') by uttering a linguistic expression; and (b) the transplantation of inferential pragmatics from its original restrained social-philosophical milieu to the teeming underworld of human cognitive processing, a relocation brought about by relevance theory, which highlights its pervasive and prolific nature. The balance has tipped, from encoded meaning with a few inferential additions when necessary, to pro-active pragmatic inferencing constrained by bits of encoding.[56] (See Wilson, 1998b, for further discussion of the shift from the code model of communication to the inferential view and its implications.)

One important consequence of the underdeterminacy thesis and the thorough cognitivization of pragmatics is that the concept of what is explicitly communicated cannot be equated with linguistically encoded meaning, or with some minimal boosting of it so as to fill linguistically indicated slots or to meet some logical requirement of minimal propositionality. The notion has to answer to the cognitive imperative of playing an active role in the achievement of an overall interpretation which meets addressees' expectations of relevance. For further comparison of the explicit/implicit distinction construed, as it is here, as a distinction among communicated assumptions, and the standard saying/implicating distinction, according to which 'saying' is essentially a semantic notion, see Carston (forthcoming a).

The next three chapters trace some of the implications of the ideas in chapters 1 and 2 for several key domains of pragmatic theorizing: 'and'-conjunctions, negation, and loose (including metaphorical) uses of linguistically encoded meaning. Another domain of central importance in the context of the semantic/pragmatic and explicit/implicit distinctions is the range of phenomena standardly assumed to fall in the category of scalar implicature. I have addressed this in some detail elsewhere (see Carston 1990/95, 1998a).

NOTES

1 At the end of the book, Gazdar raises the question of whether the semantic autonomy thesis can be maintained. As he states it, this is the position that a complete theory of the truth conditions of natural-language sentences/utterances need make no reference to pragmatic properties. He leaves the question unresolved, after having found some apparent problems for the thesis, some of which were mentioned in the previous chapter (section 1.5). In his review of Gazdar's book, Stalnaker (1980) dismisses as clearly false the autonomy view as it is stated by Gazdar, due to indexicality and other obvious contextual dependencies of aspects of truth-conditional content. However, he points out that 'this rejection does not prevent us from holding that truth-conditional semantics is a self-contained subject matter that can profitably be studied in abstraction from pragmatics. A compositional semantic theory may take certain semantic determinants as unexplained givens: a domain of discourse, reference classes, assignments of referents to deictic pronouns. Its job is to explain how the contents of complex expressions are a function of the meanings of their parts, together with the semantic determinants. Pragmatics has the complementary job of explaining how the semantic determinants are determined by identifiable features of context' (Stalnaker 1980: 905). This more reasonable semantic autonomy view presumably lies behind the work of truth-conditionalists such as Higginbotham (1988), Larson and Segal (1995) and Stanley (2000). For some relevant discussion, see section 2.7 of this chapter.

2   I will not discuss Grice's system of maxims here or elsewhere; they are listed in appendix 2. They have been widely used and abused. With regard to a cognitive processing approach to utterance interpretation, they cannot compete with the relevance-based criterion (see Wilson and Sperber 1981; Sperber and Wilson 1986a/95b, 1987a, 1987b). The implicatures here are of the classic 'scalar' variety, where choice of a weaker element in a scale is taken to standardly implicate the inapplicability of stronger elements in the scale (see Horn 1972, 1984b, 1989).

As regards the analysis of example (1), it is not clear that the pragmatic inference is required for the disambiguation. The assumed encoded meaning of 'some' is equivalent to 'some and maybe all' or 'at least some'; this seems sufficient in itself to ensure that disambiguation goes in the right direction. The rejected reading would amount to: 'he likes all dogs; he likes some and maybe all [cats and dogs]', which, if not downright contradictory, is pragmatically odd, since one statement about liking dogs is immediately followed by an appreciably weaker statement (which is entailed by the previous one) about liking them.

3   I find this analysis inadequate, on several counts: (a) the maxim involved does not account for the referential inference, (b) there is an obvious, more minimal way of communicating the same proposition expressed (by a phonologically unrealized constituent), and (c) the alleged implicature, with its mention (as opposed to use) of particular linguistic items (e.g. 'he') does not look like anything one would want to attribute to a speaker's informative intention. I address this third point later in the chapter, but close assessment of Levinson's analyses lies beyond the scope of this book; for some discussion of his (and Horn's) two informativeness maxims (adaptations of Grice's quantity maxims) and the distinct classes of implicatures they generate, see Carston (1990/95, 1998a).

4   Levinson is in the process of developing a theory of default or preferred interpretations, a specialized submodule within pragmatics. These inferences are taken to be generalized conversational implicatures, in Grice's sense (see section 2.2.3). The theory involves a system of non-monotonic default rules which, while based on the two quantity maxims and the manner maxims, are attached to particular linguistic elements; for instance, in the absence of defeating contextual assumptions, a partitive use of 'some x' implies 'not all x', an 'and'-conjunction implies a temporal sequence and a marked expression such as 'not impossible' (as opposed to the unmarked 'possible') implies a marked (non-stereotypical) interpretation. Preliminary accounts appear in Levinson (1988, 1995) and a much more detailed exposition is given in Levinson (2000), to be reviewed in Carston (forthcoming b).

5   Some 'A-philosophers' employing the suspect linguistic manoeuvre are Austin (1956/57), Benjamin (1956), Malcolm (1949), Ryle (1949), and Wittgenstein (1953). (Is the 'a' in 'A-philosopher' as in 'asymmetry', 'amoral', etc.?) For useful discussion of Grice's response to these approaches, see Travis (1991) and Neale (1992).

6   The original version of the distinction, given in Grice (1961/89b), was 'stating' versus 'implying'. As Harnish (1976: 332, 337) points out, the shift to 'implicating' removed the unwanted 'logical' sense of 'imply', and, more important here, the shift from 'stating' to 'saying' enabled a broadening of scope to include 'telling' and 'asking' as well as 'stating'. See also discussion by Bach (1994b: 143).

7   The analysis of 'U (the utterer) said that p' is as follows:

U did something x (1)   by which U meant that p
(2)   which is an occurrence of an utterance type S (sentence) such that

(3) S means 'p'
(4) S consists of a sequence of elements (such as words) ordered in a way licensed by a system of rules (syntactical rules)
(5) S means 'p' in virtue of the particular meanings of the elements of S, their order, and their syntactical character.
                                        (Grice 1967/69/89b: 87)

8   Reimer (1998) lends support to the view that the Gricean 'what is said' and sentence semantics (construed truth-conditionally) are commonly assumed to be coextensive. She discusses the proper interpretation of the following assumption:

(X)   An adequate semantic theory T for a language L should assign p as the semantic content of a sentence S in L iff in uttering S a speaker says that p.

Reimer is responding to Cappelen and Lepore (1997), who attribute this assumption to a range of different approaches to semantics (from Davidson's to Kaplan's) and who find it an inadequate basis for a semantic theory, since many reports of what someone has said plainly overlap only partially with the semantic content of the original sentence uttered. Reimer retorts that they are wrong to take 'says' here in a pre-theoretic, ordinary usage sense; rather, as used by semanticists, 'says' should be (and standardly is) understood as the strict Gricean notion of 'saying'. For further discussion of this and of a more sophisticated rendering of the same general idea (employing the notion of hidden indexicals), see section 2.7.

9   As well as being the standard view among semanticists, some *pragmatists* in the Gricean tradition also make a strict distinction between the processes involved in disambiguation and reference assignment and those responsible for implicatures. For instance, Asa Kasher, in a series of articles about types of pragmatics, distinguishes an 'interface pragmatic system' from central pragmatics. Central pragmatics involves the operation of rational communicative principles of a Gricean sort and accounts for implicature, indirect speech acts, and stylistic effects, while the interface system seems to be concerned with the pragmatic aspects of 'what is said' and does not involve communicative principles (see Kasher 1991b: 390–1). Elsewhere, he makes a further distinction (of a Russellian sort), between 'acquaintance indexicals' and 'description indexicals', and says:

> As a first approximation to an analysis of the psychologically possible acquaintance indexicals, we make a peri-pragmatic suggestion: the pairing of such an indexical with the appropriate element of a context of utterance must be made by a perceptual input system, without recourse to the background beliefs accessible only to the central cognitive systems. On the plausible assumption that not too many aspects of any context of utterance are grasped by such informationally encapsulated systems, our suggestion imposes a psychological restriction on the class of possible acquaintance indexicals.   (Kasher 1991c: 571–2)

I take it that this is akin to a distinction between 'pure' indexicals ('I', 'you', 'here', 'now') and the rest of the indexicals, in which case it concerns only a small subset of the reference fixings involved in arriving at what is said. This issue arises again in section 2.5.3 in a discussion of Bach's distinction between narrow context and broad context, which rather closely parallels the (more psychologically oriented) distinction Kasher is making between perceptual system pragmatics and central system pragmatics.

10   The notion of 'conventional implicature' is generally felt to be one of the least satisfactory aspects of Grice's framework. For recent far-reaching critiques of the concept and well worked-out suggestions for different treatments of the crucial phenomena, see Rieber (1997), Bach (1999b), Blakemore (2000) and Iten (2000).

11   Interesting criticisms of the working-out schema are given in Wilson and Sperber (1986a) and Neale (1992: 528–9). Problems with the maxim-flouting account of metaphor, irony and other tropes are shown in Harnish (1976), Hugly and Sayward (1979), Wilson and Sperber (1981), Sperber and Wilson (1981), Sperber and Wilson (1986a/95b), Sperber and Wilson (1986b).

12   Green (1998: 86) divides conversational implicatures into three categories: particularized, generalized and nearly universal, and finds that the 'nearly universal' have certain characteristics that the merely 'generalized' do not have. I see this as a further indication that what we are dealing with here is a continuum with regard to degree of generality rather than a theoretically important split between the particular and the general.

13   Grice's early analysis of what it is for an individual to mean something by an utterance x (where 'utterance' refers not only to linguistic productions but to any communicative (i.e. ostensive) behaviour) was as follows:

> '[S] meant something by x' is (roughly) equivalent to '[S] intended the utterance of x to produce some effect in an audience by means of the recognition of this intention.'   (Grice 1957/89b: 220)

This analysis underwent many revisions, both by Grice himself and by others, but the crucial reflexivity of intention was retained.

14   Sperber and Wilson use the term 'assumption' throughout their work for those units of content communicated by utterances. It has been objected (by Kent Bach for one) that this is a somewhat inappropriate term since, on the whole, these are not something which is 'assumed' or given, but rather are new additions to the conversation. In fact, although they are clearly not assumed by the hearer, they are assumed by, or at least are presented as assumed by, the speaker (which is not the case for the 'proposition' expressed). Then, if they are taken up by the hearer, they are added to his assumptions about the world, that is, they are numbered among those mental states that can play a causal role in his behaviour. For my part, however, I will use 'assumption', 'thought', and 'proposition' pretty much interchangeably. They are all loaded terms and I hope that, by being used in this indiscriminate way to pick out one and the same entity, they will neutralize each other's unwanted connotations and that readers will feel free to think in terms of whichever one they prefer.

15   By a 'weak' speech-act description, I mean one that does not carry the sort of speaker commitments of specific speech acts like 'asserting that', 'requesting that', etc. (which express speaker commitment to the actuality or desirability, respectively, of the states of affairs described in the proposition expressed). The idea is that propositional forms (enriched logical forms) may be integrated into assumption schemas such as 'X says that P' (or 'X tells H that P') and 'X tells Y to P', where these are merely speech-act reflections of different ways in which a representation can be entertained by someone (as a description of an actual state of affairs or of a potential and desirable state of affairs). See also note 16 below, and for further discussion, see Sperber and Wilson (1986a/95b: 247–54), Wilson and Sperber (1988a) and Clark (1991, 1993a).

16   Declarative indicators, such as the indicative mood in this example, encode the information that their clause represents an actual or possible state of affairs, or, equivalently,

that their clause comes with a belief attitude attached; this applies to all clauses, main or embedded. When actually *uttered*, declarative indicators in the main clause ensure that the *utterance* counts as a case of 'saying that', or 'telling H that', but since there is an array of uses of declarative sentences on which the speaker is not endorsing the propositional content (non-literal cases such as ironical uses, jokes and various (tacitly) attributive uses), this notion does not entail speaker commitment (that is, the belief attitude may not be held by her).

The dearth of distinct terms here is regrettable, but I must emphasize that 'says that' here is quite different from Gricean 'saying' (as discussed above). Gricean 'saying' is a generic term for the three central speech acts of *stating* that *p*, *asking* whether *p*, and *enjoining* someone to make it the case that *p*, and it does entail speaker commitment ('speaker meaning', in his terms), and it involves no pragmatic input beyond sense and referent selection. The relevance-theoretic notion of 'saying' has none of these properties. Besides, as far as I am aware, Grice did not propose a level at which the fact of the speaker's saying what she said is represented. This relevance-theoretic notion of 'saying that' is also distinct from its ordinary usage in reported speech, where the embedded clause in an utterance of, for example, 'Tony Blair says that life will improve for all of us' may be a very satisfactory report, while not coinciding with the propositional form of any of Tony Blair's utterances (it may be an implicature of one of his utterances or simply a summary with a range of implications in common with propositions he has expressed).

17   As Ifantidou (1994: 69–70) points out, there is an omission here in the Gricean account. Grice (1978/89b: 42) makes it clear that he does not wish the communication of the propositional attitude of speaker belief in what she says to be treated as a conversational implicature: 'it will not be true that when I say that *p*, I conversationally implicate that I believe that *p*; for to suppose that I believe that *p* . . . is just to suppose that I am observing the first maxim of quality on this occasion.' Since it is obviously not part of what is said, nor a conventional implicature (because it depends on the maxims of quality), there doesn't seem to be any place within the Gricean framework for the representation of the speaker's believing that *p*.

18   It turns out that the facts are rather more subtle than this: illocutionary (e.g. 'frankly') and attitudinal (e.g. 'sadly') adverbials do not contribute to the truth conditions of the utterance, while evidentials (e.g. 'clearly', 'possibly') and, much more obviously, hearsay adverbials (e.g. 'allegedly', 'reportedly') do contribute to truth conditions. See Ifantidou-Trouki (1993), Ifantidou (1994, 2001) for detailed discussion of these differences and how they might be accounted for. Bach (1999b) also looks at a range of these adverbials but divides them up differently from Ifantidou. He makes a distinction between 'utterance modifiers', which include illocutionary adverbials, and 'content modifiers', which include attitudinal and evidential adverbials, and he suggests rather different analyses for the two types of case.

19   Arguments for this are given in Wilson and Sperber (1993a) and Ifantidou (1994, 2001). At this point it may seem that no arguments are needed. However, recall the distinction between conceptual and procedural encodings considered briefly in the previous chapter, and to be discussed again shortly (in section 2.3.7). The point of the arguments is to show that these adverbials are not cases of procedural meaning. Truth-conditional semanticists of natural language sentences (see, for instance, Lycan 1984; Asher 2000) are quite clear that these can be given a truth-conditional semantic analysis. Asher disputes the relevance-theoretic classification of these as 'non-truth-conditional', but there is, in fact, no real conflict between the two positions, as far as I can see. The semanticists are concerned with the truth-conditional content of a *sentence* and the relevance-

theorists (like the speech-act theorists) with the truth conditions of an *utterance*, by which is meant the truth conditions of the proposition expressed by the utterance. See Carston (1999b: 119–21), where I try to disentangle some of the complications caused by this duality of usage. Problems with the notion of *the* truth-conditional content of an utterance are discussed in the next section of this chapter.

20 Recall that, as argued in section 2.3.1, although these are single speech acts, the content of the complement clause can, on occasion, be communicated and so qualify as an explicature of the utterance. So an utterance of (i) may explicate (ii):

(i) I firmly believe that we will win.
(ii) We will win.

Note also that this view of the main clause cases is directly at odds with Davidson's (1968) paratactic analysis of indirect speech, extended by Lepore and Loewer (1989) to propositional attitude reports. According to that sort of account, the complementizer 'that' in (iii) and (iv) is to be analysed as a demonstrative indicating the juxtaposed representation (of a thought or utterance), as in (v) and (vi):

(iii) Mary said that Tony will be waiting for us.
(iv) I believe that Tony will be waiting for us.
(v) Mary said that. Tony will be waiting for us.
(vi) I believe that. Tony will be waiting for us.

For discussion and criticism of this account, see Segal and Speas (1986), and Hand (1993).

21 I remain agnostic here regarding the precisely correct characterization of these examples, whether as cases of a single utterance consisting of two (or more) speech acts, or as cases of two distinct utterances, or subutterances, or discourse units. For my purpose in this section, these different modes of description can be used pretty much interchangeably, though, no doubt, they entail differences of detail that will be important in the final analysis.

22 Urmson (1956: 196) points out that even a parenthetical phrase like 'I hear' or 'I am told' does not seem to diminish the speaker's commitment to the truth of the proposition expressed to such an extent that she is taken to be dissociating herself from it and so not communicating it. The effect is one of 'fine-tuning' it, not wiping it out. In this respect, it is interesting to note the anomalous nature of (i) and (ii) (variations on Moore's paradox), as opposed to (iii):

(i) ?Your house is, I don't suppose, very old.
(ii) ?Your house is very old, I don't suppose.
(iii) Your house isn't very old, $\begin{cases} \text{I don't suppose.} \\ \text{I suppose.} \end{cases}$

The only exception to this seems to be the rather heavy-handed irony-indicating formula, 'I don't think' positioned clause-finally:

(iv) She's a good and loyal friend, I don't think.

23 Jim Higginbotham has pointed out to me an interesting fact about these sentence adverbials (in English, at least) that remains to be explained, which is that they seem to be acceptable as elements in reported speech.

(i)   He said that, frankly, he didn't give a damn.
(ii) She said that, fortunately, he wasn't dead.
(iii) He said that she was, obviously, right.
(iv) She said that, allegedly, he was a crook.

This is certainly not true of all disjunct constituents, for instance, vocative phrases, and there are differences of opinion even in the adverbial cases. Bach (1999b) claims that illocutionary adverbials cannot be reported in this way, so for him (i) is unacceptable, and that this is quite generally not possible for utterance (as opposed to sentence) modifiers. My intuitions go with Higginbotham, rather than Bach, on this matter, and I also find acceptable indirect reports across a broad range of the parenthetical cases, such as 'I think', 'I fear', etc., provided, of course, the necessary deictic shifts (of pronouns, tense, etc.) are made in the report:

(v)   She said that her sister would, *she thought*, pull through.
(vi) He said that although his mother was completely devoted, his father, *he feared*, was having an affair.

This is of some interest for the double speech-act view since it seems to indicate that these still constitute a single unit in some sense (a single utterance).

24 There is a third semantic/pragmatic type of disjunct constituent, known as 'domain' or 'point of view' adverbials. Examples are 'morally', 'logically', 'linguistically' and 'from a lay point of view'. They have similar syntactic properties to the other sentence adverbials, being intonationally separated from the clause they modify and being able to occur in various positions (initially, medially, finally). However, what distinguishes them from illocutionary and evaluative adverbials, on the one hand, and appositives, on the other, is that they seem to make a direct contribution to the truth conditions of the proposition expressed by their host sentence, so, for instance, (i) and (ii) are clearly truth-conditionally distinct (one could be true while the other is false) and (iii) is quite consistent:

(i)   Legally, Gertrude has done nothing wrong.
(ii) Morally, Gertrude has done nothing wrong.
(iii) Linguistically, this example is interesting, but logically it is not.

For discussion of these adverbials, see Bellert (1977) and Bertuccelli Papi (1992).

25 Both Neale (1999) and, in particular, Bach (1999b) use this idea of an utterance expressing several distinct propositions, one or other of which may carry less communicative weight (relevance) than the other(s), to motivate an account of elements like 'but'. Bach's aim is to debunk the problematic notion of 'conventional implicature', by showing that the phenomena so labelled are properly analysed in terms of the independently required notion of a secondary proposition expressed by an utterance. The fact that, when forced to make a categorical true/false assessment of an utterance containing 'but', people are generally prepared to judge it true provided the conjuncts are true, even if they do not believe there is any contrast between them, is explained in the same way as the appositional cases: the proposition expressed by the 'but' element is of less import. Relevance theorists also do away with the notion of 'conventional implicature' but take a quite different stance on both the semantics and pragmatics of elements like 'but'. See, in particular, Blakemore (1987, 1989b) and the brief discussion in section 2.3.7 of this chapter.

26 Note that the claim is that these utterances express two separate propositions (perhaps a *sequence* of propositions as Neale (1999: 48–9) puts it), not a single conjunctive propo-

sition. This is supported by the shifting judgements about the truth value of the *utterance* depending on the import of the different propositions, since while a conjunction is falsified by the falsity of a single conjunct, several distinct propositions do not constitute an entity that is simply true or false. In her analysis of the subordinating conjunction 'although', Iten (1998) reaches a similar conclusion: an utterance of 'S1, although S2' expresses, not a single conjunctive proposition 'P & Q', but two distinct propositions 'P' and 'Q', and utterances of this sort evoke a pattern of truth-conditional intuitions similar to those for the appositive cases, with the clause prefaced by 'although' generally having less weight in judgements of the truth/falsity of the utterance. How far this point carries over to other cases of syntactic subordination remains to be seen.

27   The notorious phenomenon of referentially used definite descriptions provides another case for which it has been argued that two propositions are expressed. Within the relevance-theoretic framework, Rouchota (1994b) proposes that an utterance of (i), on which 'Smith's murderer' is used by a speaker to refer to the convicted murderer standing in front of her in the courtroom, call him Perkins, expresses both of the propositions in (ii)–(iii). Indeed, arguably there is a third, effectively hidden in here, that Perkins is Smith's murderer.

> (i)   Smith's murderer is insane.
> (ii) Whoever is Smith's murderer, x, is insane.
> (iii) Perkins$_x$ is insane.

Neale (1999) makes a similar proposal, to the effect that there is a primary general proposition expressed, of the standard Russellian sort, and a secondary singular proposition involving the referent Perkins. Both authors are keen to present an alternative to the standard Gricean view according to which the general proposition is the one expressed by the utterance with the singular proposition arising only as an implicature. One advantage of their alternative is that it provides an explanation of the widely recognized conflicting intuitions about the truth value of an utterance like (i) in the case where the description is faulty, that is, Perkins is not Smith's murderer.

Neale extends the multiple proposition approach to an account of utterances involving demonstrative descriptions like 'that man in a woolly hat' and proper names. These three cases of (alleged) multiple propositions look quite different from the ones I've been considering, as their source is certain properties of noun phrases rather than manifestly distinct structures in the linguistic form, such as a host clause and a comma-ed-off disjunct constituent. Neale suggests that the source of the two (or more) propositions is certain (ordered) lexical instructions carried by proper names and by the determiners 'the' and 'that'.

28   Note that implicatures are both parts of the (intended) interpretation and may be among the cognitive effects (strengthenings of contextual assumptions, contextual implications, etc.) which go to establishing the relevance of the utterance. This dual role is not problematic; specifically, it does not entail that every implicature must have further cognitive effects. While many implicatures do give rise to further cognitive effects, this is not a necessary property of implicatures. For an interesting discussion, see Gutt (1991: 194, note 8).

29   Cappelen (2000) interprets the passage from Grice differently. First, he points out that there is some imprecision in Grice's discussion, saying that while it makes sense to add together forms of words or to add together propositions, it is not clear what's involved in adding a proposition to a form of words (which is what, on a very literal reading, Grice could seem to be saying). Cappelen opts for an interpretation according

to which the cancellation test involves adding a proposition to a proposition, specifically the Gricean 'what is said' to the negation of the alleged implicated proposition. On the other interpretation, which I have made, the words uttered have added to them a form of words which expresses the negation of the alleged implicature. This is the way the cancellability test has always been applied in my experience and it is strongly supported by Grice's talk of adding 'but not p' or 'I do not mean to imply that p' to the form of words used in the utterance. Cappelen's construal is geared toward his primary aim of establishing that the Gricean minimal notion of 'what is said', which is immune to cancellation, on his stipulatory interpretation, is the right concept of the proposition explicitly expressed by an utterance. His argument against the enriched relevance-theoretic concept is that it involves cancellable elements, which are, therefore, really implicatures.

30 Both of these examples appear in unpublished work of Deirdre Wilson, who, I think, first suggested the possibility of implicated entailments.

31 See Fodor (1981b, 1998), for extensive and compelling arguments against lexically encoded concepts having any kind of internal structure (definitional or otherwise), arguments that, in fact, extend to most concepts (construed as mental representations), whether lexicalized or not. According to Fodor, even in the very few cases where an adequate definition can actually be formulated (consider in this regard the hopelessness of trying to define 'pork', 'monkey', 'red'), the simple concept, say BACHELOR, and the complex one that defines it, say UNMARRIED MAN, are distinct concepts, though they have the same external content (that is, they express the same property). Concept identity and content identity are two distinct matters. Fodor (1998, chapter 3) argues that while you cannot entertain the mental representation BROWN COW without entertaining the mental representation BROWN, you can entertain the mental representation BACHELOR without entertaining the mental representation UNMARRIED. Similarly, the idea here is that, in deriving the intended interpretation of an utterance, one can recover the mental representation FATHER without necessarily recovering the mental representation MAN.

On the relevance-theoretic view, the one-to-one mapping from words to conceptual addresses is, however, a partial one, as only a fraction of the conceptual repertoire is lexicalized. It follows from the strong essentialist view of linguistic underdeterminacy (see chapter 1), that we can think many thoughts/concepts that our language cannot encode, and, due to our pragmatic capacity, we can communicate many thoughts/concepts that our utterances do not encode. The on-line pragmatic construction of *ad hoc* concepts is discussed in chapter 5. On this general point, Fodor and relevance theorists seem to part company, since Fodor appears to accept a code model view of communication, according to which the concepts communicated are identical with the concepts en/decoded. See discussion in Sperber and Wilson (1997/98a).

32 There are more and less sophisticated versions of the strategy depending on the different sorts of expectations of relevance the addressee has, from a naive expectation of *actual* optimal relevance to an expectation that allows for variations in both the ability and the willingness of the speaker to be optimally relevant. The naive expectation is employed by young children and develops progressively into the more knowing expectations, though adults may vary their expectations across speakers and situations, perhaps taking actual optimal relevance as the default. See Sperber (1994a) and Wilson (1999b/2000) for detailed discussion.

33 As discussed briefly in chapter 1, the representations manipulated by the pragmatic system are metarepresentational. So the inferential processes outlined in this section really involve premises and conclusions embedded in schemas like 'S intends me to believe that . . .'. At its most sophisticated, the expectation of relevance (on which neither

the competence nor the complete good will of the speaker is assumed) requires inferences which involve metarepresentations of several further orders (or levels). As Sperber (1994a: 197) puts it: 'Fully-fledged communicative competence involves, for the speaker, being capable of having at least third-order meta-representational communicative intentions, and, for the hearer, being capable of making at least fourth-order metarepresentational attributions of such communicative intentions.'

Note an important distinction: between comprehension of an utterance, on the one hand, and acceptance of the communicated assumptions, on the other hand. An addressee may recover the intended interpretation of an utterance, in which case the speaker's communicative intention will have succeeded, but not accept (some or any of) the assumptions communicated; that is, the addressee may not be prepared to adopt them as beliefs of his own, in which case the speaker's informative intention will have failed (see 'communicative intention' and 'informative intention' in appendix 1). An addressee who accepts the intended interpretation as true adds to his existing representation of the world the propositional forms which have been disquoted from the metarepresentational schemas; an addressee who rejects any of the communicated assumptions may nonetheless store them embedded at varying levels of depth in metarepresentational schemas (for instance, as representations of what the speaker intended him to believe). For relevant discussion of the role of metarepresentation in human mental life and communication, see Sperber (1994a, 1997a, 2000).

34   For those who endorse a generalized/particularized distinction between implicatures, all the implicatures in the relevance-theoretic analyses in this section fall on the particularized side. Levinson (1989: 466) has claimed that RT is intrinsically incapable of accounting for the generalized sort because it is 'a theory of "nonce-inference"' and 'there can be no way to get the universal regularities of GCI predictions out of a theory of "nonce-inference"; relevance theory was simply not concocted to deal with GCIs and should relinquish ambitions in that direction'. I think Levinson is wrong about this. Much of my work has focused on cases of what he calls generalized implicatures, including the strengthening of 'and'-conjunctions, negation narrowing and the interpretation of cardinal number terms (see, for instance, Carston 1998a). In all of these cases, however, I believe the pragmatic inference is not a GCI but contributes to the explicature. Sperber and Wilson (1995a) have given a relevance-theoretic account of the classic scalar implicature case, the inference to 'not all of the x' from 'some of the x', leaving it open whether this might, in fact, also be better construed as a case of pragmatic enrichment, something which Geurts (1998b) argues for.

35   There are some cases of implicatures which, arguably, supply material which contributes to the explicature; perhaps the best known of these are what are called 'bridging' implicatures:

   (i)   Kay went skiing in Italy. The snow was thick and soft.
   (ii) The dinner was a disaster. The cassoulet was dry and the wine was sour.
      (iii) There was snow on Kay's skiing trip.
      (iv) There was a cassoulet served at the dinner.
      (v)   There was wine at the dinner.

The idea is that the process of assigning a referent to the definite descriptions 'the snow', 'the cassoulet', and 'the wine' involves the accessing of an implicated premise such as those given in (iii)–(v). These are quite different from the cases I am rejecting as implicatures; they are not metalinguistic and they are plausible candidates for storage in memory and subsequent use in processing. (The classic paper on bridging assumptions is Clark (1977); see Matsui (1995, 1998, 2000) for a relevance-theoretic account and a survey of the literature on bridging.)

36   Stanley (2000) claims that there simply are no non-sentential assertions; he argues that many of the alleged cases, such as those in (107a) and (107b), are really elliptical and so, underlyingly, have a full sentential structure. Others do not qualify as genuine linguistic speech acts at all, but fall in with taps on the shoulder, winks and other bodily gestures of a communicative sort, all of which, according to him, are to be studied within a non-linguistic theory of general human reasoning. Elugardo and Stainton (forthcoming b) take issue with Stanley and defend the existence of non-sentential assertion. Clapp (forthcoming) also supports the existence of genuine non-sentential assertions and shows that these present a pressing problem for what he calls the 'standard model of truth-conditional interpretation'.

37   Clark (1996: 143–6) also points out this problem, within a broader discussion of the false assumption that 'what is said' is well defined for every type of utterance.

38   The notion of procedural meaning seems to me to be potentially very significant, but it does need a lot more development and elucidation. See Wharton (2000) for an interesting extension of the notion to interjections like 'ouch' and 'oops', which are, arguably, not linguistic elements at all. Bach (1999b) considers the conceptual/procedural distinction to be vacuous; Blakemore (2000) provides both a defence and a detailed analysis of it.

39   According to Travis's 'pragmatic view', as he calls it, the *semantics* of words is occasion-specific; that is, he seems to construe semantics as concerned with tokenings of words rather than with word types. On the view I am pursuing, the domain of linguistic semantics is linguistic expression types (this is recognized by Travis as 'at most a proper part of' the occasion-sensitive semantics of words), and there is a distinct truth-conditional semantic endeavour, whose domain is propositions or conceptual representations. I think that this too must be, for the most part at least, a semantics of types rather than tokens.

40   It seems that recently Putnam has joined with Travis in this view. He is quoted as saying in a 1997 lecture: 'a sentence, simply as a sentence, doesn't *have* a determinate content apart from particular speakings'. This quote appears in Berg (2002) who says that acceptance of this view entails that, if a semantic theory is supposed to determine for each sentence what its (truth-conditional) content is in general, semantics is not possible. Berg, however, does not accept the view and argues that every sentence expresses a determinate, albeit often quite vague and general, proposition. For instance, while the sentence 'there is milk in the refrigerator' can be used to express 'there is a puddle of milk in the bottom of the refrigerator' in one context, and 'there is milk suitable for coffee in the refrigerator' in another, the semantic content of the sentence is something weaker than this (roughly, 'the refrigerator contains some milk (no matter how little or in what form)') and is true whenever any one of the more specific propositions expressed is true. It follows, then, that a (truth-conditional) semantics for sentences is possible. This appears to be a defence of the standard position that sentence semantics is equivalent to 'what is said', in the Gricean sense, and it is, therefore, subject to the various points, made in this chapter and the last one, about the semantic underdeterminacy of sentences and the role of pragmatics in recovering the proposition expressed, including the supplying of values to indexicals and to expressions used to refer, such as 'the refrigerator' in the examples given.

41   Recanati (1993: 15.6) gives a slightly different treatment of both the semantics of definite descriptions and the pragmatic derivation of the referential use, though one that is still very much a contextualist account of the proposition expressed. Relevance-theoretic

accounts of the different interpretations of definite descriptions have been given by Rouchota (1992, 1994b), Bezuidenhout (1997b) and Powell (1999). All three share with Recanati the view that the referential interpretation is to be explained in terms of a pragmatic contribution to the proposition expressed, but differ in certain other respects. Rouchota and Powell argue for an abstract linguistic semantics for the definite article which entails that both the referential *and* the attributive (and any other) understandings are pragmatically derived; furthermore, this semantics is procedural, in the sense of section 2.3.7, rather than conceptual. Bezuidenhout discusses attributive uses of indexicals and gives a unified pragmatic enrichment account of the referential and attributive readings of both definite descriptions and indexicals.

42 Cappelen (2000), who is an advocate of the Gricean notion of 'what is said', claims that it does have a psychological role to play in utterance interpretation and that Recanati is wrong in believing that it is unavailable to consciousness. His argument for the latter point is as follows: it is possible, in any context, to cancel the element that Recanati wants to include in what is said (e.g. 'the time involved is fairly long' in the case of example (126)); the fact that the cancellation strikes the speaker as non-contradictory is, he claims, evidence that the Gricean 'what is said' is quite easily accessible to consciousness. See also note 52 below for a brief account of the cognitive role which is played, according to Cappelen, by the minimal 'what is said'.

43 See also Bach (2000b) for discussion of the problems in the design of these off-line questionnaire experiments. Anne Bezuidenhout and her colleagues have embarked on a potentially more revealing line of investigation using measures of a more on-line sort; the aim is to tap the actual processes of utterance interpretation to see whether there is evidence for recovery of a Gricean 'what is said' and/or the more pragmatically enriched representational level that Recanati and relevance theorists favour (see Bezuidenhout and Cutting 2002).

44 In his most recent work, Recanati has moved to some different terminology. In Recanati (2001), he talks of *what is said$_{max}$*, contrasting it with *what is said$_{min}$*, and, in Recanati (2000), of *i-content* (= intuitive truth-conditional content of the utterance), contrasting it with *c-content* (= compositionally articulated content of the utterance). The two sets of terms seem to be interchangeable, *i-content* and *what is said$_{max}$* labelling the pragmatically enriched level of explicit content, the other two terms labelling the minimal Gricean notion.

45 I say 'seems to' since sometimes it looks as if the first two levels do not pick out different elements or levels of meaning at all, but are simply different ways of construing one and the same aspect of utterance meaning. The terms 'logical form' or semantic representation locate this content in the linguistic system, while the concept of 'what is said' relativizes it to an utterance, to an *act* of communication, to language users. If so, 'what is said' just is the logical form of the linguistic expression uttered on a particular occasion. In his most recent statement on the matter, Bach (2001) characterizes 'what is said' as 'information encoded in what is uttered', but in the light of the wider discussion in the paper, it becomes clear that he intends this as a shorthand for 'encoded information plus contextually supplied values of (pure) indexicals', in which case there is a distinction between the logical form (level (a)), which is determined by the linguistic code alone, and 'what is said' (level (b)), which includes a certain element of contextual input as well.

46 It is worth noting that Frege (1892a: 73–7) made a clear distinction between what he called tonal elements, such as 'but', 'although', 'yet' and 'fortunately', on the one hand, which cannot affect the truth value of the sentence/utterance, and subordinating conjunctions such as 'because', 'since', 'after' and 'before', which have what he calls 'sense' and so do

have a truth-conditional effect. He gives a three-clause specification of the 'thoughts' expressed by the sentence 'Because ice is less dense than water, it floats on water':

    (i)   Ice is less dense than water;
    (ii) If anything is less dense than water, it floats on water;
    (iii) Ice floats on water.

47   In Sperber and Wilson's terms, the propositional form constructed from the embedded sentence is in a relation of interpretive resemblance (that is, resemblance in content as opposed to resemblance in form) to the propositional form of the original utterance, and the appropriate (optimally relevant) degree of resemblance will differ across contexts (see Sperber and Wilson 1986a/95b; Wilson and Sperber 1988b, 1992).

48   For further discussion of the narrow/broad context distinction, see Bach (1997/99a, 2000a, 2000b). Compare Kasher's (1991b) distinction between reference assignment by perceptual input system (presumably intention-free) and reference assignment by central systems (guided by rational communicative principles), mentioned above in note 9 of this chapter. Regarding membership of the class of pure indexicals, the only case mentioned with any certainty is 'I'; the next most favoured candidates are 'now', 'here', 'former', and 'latter'; then there is a range of other temporal cases such as 'today', 'yesterday', 'tomorrow', 'last week', 'next month', etc. However, problems with the sort of fixed, code-like reference determination that is entailed by the concept of pure indexicality have been pointed out for virtually all of these. Take 'here' for instance; it is obvious that on any occasion of use there are innumerable possible referents of a more or less space-inclusive sort (e.g. the spot where the speaker is standing, the room she is in, the building, the street, the city, the country, . . .) and that determining the right one is a matter of pragmatic inference. The point obviously applies equally to 'now'.

49   Bach (personal communication) says that the notion of what is said is also needed to label the content of the locutionary act [in fact, the rhetic, as opposed to the phonetic and phatic aspects of the locutionary act], as opposed to the il- or per-locutionary acts (in Austin's 1955/62 terms). And it is necessary to distinguish the locutionary act from these others in order to allow for cases where the speaker is communicating nothing or is communicating something utterly distinct from anything traceable to the words he is using. Bach and Harnish (1979: 288–9) defend the need for a concept of locutionary act (hence what is said) against attacks by Searle and by Katz. But, again, the sorts of cases mentioned here seem to be explainable in terms of encoded linguistic meaning; for instance, one might say of the first case: he isn't communicating anything but the sentence he uttered has the meaning such and such. Without embarking on an exploration of Austin's concepts, it is not obvious to me that Bach's concept of 'what is said' is quite the same beast as a locutionary act, which has 'a more or less definite "sense" and a more or less definite reference' (Austin 1955/62: 93). As already discussed, Bach (1987, 1997/99a, 2000b) argues quite forcefully that, with the possible exception of a few 'pure' indexicals, it is not possible to determine indexical reference without recourse to speaker intention (hence to whatever pragmatic maxim/principle mediates ostensive behaviour and recognition of the intention behind it). Since Bach's semantic notion of 'what is said' is intended to be intention-free, I don't see how it can be the same as the locutionary act, even supposing we care to preserve this latter notion, which I doubt.

50   Modified Occam's Razor is much used by philosophers of language, including those who give pragmatics an extensive role to play in establishing truth-conditional content (see, for instance, Recanati 1993, 1994). I am doubtful about its validity in a cognitive

account of utterance semantics and pragmatics such as relevance theory. Within a theory of utterance interpretation conceived as a matter of on-line cognitive processes, it might well be more economical to retrieve a clutch of stored senses and choose among them, than to construct an interpretation out of a single sense and contextual information, guided by principles of rational discourse. The more so if all senses of an ambiguous word are automatically activated by its phonological form (so they come very cheap), as much work in psycholinguistics seems to indicate. I am uneasy with the assumption that a monosemous analysis is always to be preferred to a polysemous one, though the 'if at all possible, go pragmatic' strategy that it entails is one that I generally follow myself, as it makes for much more elegant analyses and because, for the time being, we lack any other strong guiding principle.

51 Recanati (1993: 240–4) endorses my dismissal of these principles and extends it to a third which combines these two, the **Mixed Minimalist Principle**. The motivation for this is to exclude instances of conventional implicature cases like 'but' from being taken to result in a pragmatic contribution to what is said. Some theorists see 'but' as being like an indexical in setting up a slot to be contextually filled, so that according to the Linguistic Direction Principle the pragmatic work prompted by 'but' would contribute to the proposition expressed. Virtually everyone (except Bach; see especially Bach 1999b) is agreed that 'but' does not contribute at this level, so what the Mixed Minimalist Principle does is place a further constraint on those pragmatically filled slots that enter into what is said: their contribution must be required for the utterance to be truth-evaluable, i.e. to be fully propositional. This principle has the desired excluding effect, but is, of course, prey to the same objections as the other two minimalist principles.

52 Cappelen (2000) takes issue with my view that the minimal, Gricean 'what is said' is cognitively redundant, that is, that it does not play an independent functional role in utterance processing or in the subsequent mental life of communicators. His claim is that, in fact, it does have a unique cognitive role to play: it is the *default proposition* expressed by an utterance, that proposition no part of which can be subsequently cancelled by the speaker without creating a contradiction. Here's one of his examples:

(i)   He's had breakfast.
(ii) Karl has had breakfast today.
(iii) I don't mean to imply that he's had breakfast today, just that the rumour that he never has breakfast is false.

Suppose an utterance of (i) communicates the proposition in (ii), but suppose the speaker subsequently cancels part of this by uttering (iii). She doesn't contradict herself as she would, according to Cappelen, if she tried to cancel an aspect of the Gricean 'what is said'. He says: 'Since it is always possible that some later part of the conversation will make us revise an earlier interpretation, it is cognitively useful to have something to fall back on, a basic proposition that cannot be cancelled. The minimal Gricean proposition is the one interpreters cancel down toward.'

I don't find this a very strong argument for the cognitive utility of this minimal proposition, because I believe that any aspect of utterance meaning which is pragmatically derived can be cancelled without contradiction, including the assignment of Karl as the referent of 'he' in (i). (See discussion of cancellability in section 2.3.3 of this chapter.) Furthermore, the construal of cancellation as a conversational phenomenon rather than as a theorist's tool diminishes its import; a speaker may simply retract aspects of what she communicated earlier, even if they were, in fact, linguistically encoded rather than pragmatically inferred, and an addressee has to adjust his interpretation accordingly.

53 The use of the phrase 'hidden indexical' here must be distinguished from its use in the 'hidden indexical theory' account of the apparent difference in the truth conditions of belief attribution sentences such as the following:

> (i)   Jo believes that Cicero was a fine orator.
> (ii) Jo believes that Tully was a fine orator.

According to this theory, the strong intuition of a semantic difference between these sentences (which are formally identical but for their coreferring proper names) is to be accounted for by appeal to a contextually specified 'mode of presentation' m, different in each case. Speakers tacitly refer to m on an assertive utterance of (i) or (ii), m varies across contexts and it enters into the proposition expressed. However, calling this a 'hidden indexical' account is somewhat misleading, since there is no suggestion in this theory that there is some element present in the structure of the sentence whose referent is m; reference to m is achieved by the speaker without the guidance of any 'hidden' expression (see Reimer 1997 for further discussion). As I am using it, though, 'hidden indexical' is to be taken rather literally: there is a marker, though not one that is visible or audible, occupying a structural position in the logical form of the sentence.

54 In chapter 5, I will suggest that there is a fourth pragmatic task involved in deriving the proposition expressed, that of *ad hoc* concept construction, which raises a host of new issues. Among these is the interesting possibility, suggested to me by Richard Breheny, that saturation and *ad hoc* concept construction might provide all the pragmatic input needed in developing the logical form into the proposition expressed. If so, there would be no free enrichment of the sort that involves addition of a conceptual constituent to logical form and so the desired structural match between logical form and 'what is said' would be achieved. This possibility is briefly considered in Carston (2000b), from which much of the material in this section has been taken.

55 Taylor (2001) advocates a position similar to Stanley's, which he calls 'parametric minimalism'; according to this view, there is no free enrichment involved in determining the proposition expressed and many sentences carry suppressed parameters which must be pragmatically saturated, that is, whose semantic value must be contextually determined. In the case of 'it's raining', he suggests there is an unexpressed parameter hidden in the 'subsyntactic verbal argument structure' of the verb 'rain'; this is a theta-marked argument position, which takes locations as its value. Recanati (forthcoming b) presents sustained and sophisticated counterarguments to the cases made by both Taylor and Stanley for the presence of a free variable or suppressed parameter in the logical form of the sentence 'it's raining'. He also investigates some of the wider issues raised by this dispute and develops criteria for distinguishing truly unarticulated constituents (such as the location constituent frequently recovered in understanding utterances of 'it's raining') from those constituents which, while not perceptible in surface syntax, are in fact articulated in the logical form of the sentence concerned (for instance, the object constituent which is mandatorily recovered in understanding utterances of 'I've finished'). See also Breheny (2002), who claims that Stanley's argument for covert indexicals based on their apparent bindability by quantifiers rests on an overly strong notion of binding in natural language.

56 Of course, not everyone has embraced Grice's inferential perspective on communication, much less the relevance-theoretic account of utterance interpretation. For instance, the work of Seuren (1985, 1994) is a sustained attempt to develop a thoroughgoing code model account of the meaning that natural language can convey: it has numerous very rich deep semantic structures for sentences and, necessarily, a lot of complex machinery mapping these structures on to the much less elaborated and multiply ambiguous surface

structures. One consequence of this is that an encoded semantic structure in this system may look very much like a relevance-theoretic representation of the proposition expressed by an utterance, recovered by a combination of decoding and pragmatic inferencing. An example of this, which will come up in chapter 4, is the proposition expressed by an utterance of the negative sentence in 'I'm not his daughter; he's my father', which involves metalinguistic negation, a matter of pragmatics for me, a matter of linguistic semantics for Seuren (see section 4.4.4).

3

The Pragmatics of 'And'-Conjunction

and he saw this big red balloon tied to a lamp post, so and then he climbed up the lamp post and he untied the red balloon, and then he climbed down the lamp post and started walking down the stairs again and so he was walking and walking and walking . . . and then . . . I can't remember how the whole thing goes.

(Narrative told by child, aged 5: 9, from D. Hicks (1990), CHILDES database)

and men do not think they know a thing till they have grasped the 'why' of it.

(Aristotle, *Physics II*, 3)

3.1 Preserving the Truth-functionality of 'And'

The focus of this chapter is the meaning of the word 'and' and the range of relations between states of affairs that can be communicated by conjoining two sentences with 'and'. Our starting point is Grice's (1981) brief but influential remarks about the following two examples of 'and'-conjunction:

(1) a. He took off his boots and got into bed.
     b. He got into bed and took off his boots.
     c. P & Q = Q & P

Grice wanted to provide an alternative to the view that, in order to account for the different ways in which the two utterances in (1a) and (1b) would normally be meant and understood, the word 'and' needs to be assigned a sense additional to its logical truth-functional sense. His suggestion was that the understanding of (1a) and (1b) as communicating different sequential orderings of the actions described is to be attributed to his manner maxim of orderliness; in other words, the understanding is arrived at entirely pragmatically and the semantics of the word 'and' does not diverge from that of the logical conjunction operator. At the level of what is said, the two utterances are equivalent, truth-conditionally identical like their logical counterparts shown in (1c). He took the communicated temporal ordering to constitute a conversational implicature (a *generalized* implicature), and most neo-Gricean pragmatists concur with this view.[1]

Given the linguistic underdeterminacy thesis, this is, of course, not the only option available: the pragmatically inferred relation could be a case of an enrichment at the level of the proposition expressed (the truth-conditional content). Consider the following pertinent remarks by Mark Richard, who favours a Gricean implicature account: 'We do not come equipped with a meter that reliably distinguishes between semantic and pragmatic implications. Examples like that concerning "and" and temporal order help make the point that what seems for all the world like a truth-conditional implication may turn out not to be one' (Richard 1990: 123). I shall argue, to the contrary, that this *is* an instance of a truth-conditional implication, albeit one that is pragmatically derived. Richard's first statement, though, is surely right, whether on his own construal of semantics as truth-conditional content, or on the linguistically encoded meaning construal. As language users, we do not have reliable intuitions about which aspects of utterance meaning are linguistically encoded, which are pragmatic contributions to the truth-conditional content of our utterances and which are independent implicated propositions. The lack of any meter to distinguish between truth-conditional implications (whether linguistically encoded or pragmatically derived) and implicatures is what has led to the formulation of various criteria and tests to help make this distinction, as discussed in the previous chapter (section 2.6).

The importance of the Gricean suggestion is that it opens up the way to a pragmatic account. Grice saw himself as countering a suggestion of Strawson (1952) that there is a divergence between the ordinary meaning of the word 'and' and the conjunction operator, '&', of the propositional calculus, and that the word 'and' is in fact ambiguous. It is not clear to me that it is correct to attribute to Strawson a semantic ambiguity position, at least not if what is meant by this is that the lexical form 'and' encodes more than a single meaning/sense. As suggested in the previous chapter, it is equally possible that Strawson, along with some of the other ordinary-language philosophers, was putting forward a context-sensitive view of saying. If this is right, then the pragmatic position that I advocate is a working out of that idea, using theoretical tools not available to Strawson. This is how Recanati (1994) has interpreted the pragmatic enrichment account.

The pragmatic story, whether in terms of implicature or pragmatic enrichment of the proposition expressed, needs to encompass a much wider range of conjunctive relations than just that of temporal sequence (see discussions in Carston 1993, 1994a). Here is a representative set of examples:

(2) a. It's summer in England and it's winter in New Zealand.
     b. He handed her the scalpel and she made the incision.
     c. We spent the day in town and I went to Harrods.
     d. She shot him in the head and he died instantly.

    e. He left her and she took to the bottle.
    f. He was shortsighted and mistook her for a hatstand.
    g. She went to the yoga class and found it very calming.
    h. I forgot to hide the cake and the children consumed it.

Apart from (2a), these are all cases of so-called asymmetric or directional conjunction (see Schmerling 1975);[2] that is, their meaning is crucially affected by the order of the conjuncts. For instance, reversing the order of the conjuncts in (2d) would convey the idea that she shot him in the head after he had died, despite the fact that this runs counter to normal assumptions about how events of shooting and dying connect up. The pragmatic account takes the linguistic semantics of 'and' to be identical to that of the truth-functional logical conjunction operator (though this is questioned later in section 3.7.2), so that, as far as their logical forms are concerned, all the examples above are symmetric.

One of the strongest arguments in favour of this very minimal semantics for 'and', with the temporal and consequential relations accounted for pragmatically, is that any semantic account would have to allow for the encoding of a huge range of such relations. Let's look a bit more closely at the examples in (2). Utterance (2b) is the standard sort of case of a sequential relation between the two events described in the conjuncts, paraphrasable by 'and then', but the temporal relation most readily understood to hold for (2c) is one of containment, the going to Harrods having taken place during the time spent in town. As regards consequence relations, (2d), (2e) and (2h) can all be understood as involving some such connection, though each case is different: the event in the second conjunct of (2d) is directly caused by the one in the first conjunct (her shooting him is sufficient for his dying); in (2e) the event mentioned in the second conjunct is certainly understood as a reaction to the one mentioned first, though the cause–effect relation here is fairly indirect and requires a mesh of further conditions; in (2h) there is no temptation to talk of a causal relation: the leaving out of the cake is a factor enabling the children to get hold of it and devour it, but it is far from a sufficient condition for their doing so. Furthermore, while a relation of consequence between the conjuncts standardly involves a relation of temporal sequence between them, as in (2b) and (2d), it need not always do so: in (2f) his mistaking her for a hatstand is a causal consequence of his shortsightedness but the example cannot be paraphrased by 'and then'; similarly, in (2g) the release of tension is a result of the yoga class but is achieved as the class progresses not after it. And so on and on; the more examples one considers, the more fine-grained variations among the connections one finds. This suggests that the appropriate explanation is a pragmatic one, according to which communicators are calling on their general knowledge of how states and events in the world connect with each other.

Another argument frequently proffered against a rich semantics for 'and' and in favour of the pragmatic account is that the very same temporal and consequence relations arise when the 'and' is removed. That is, the non-conjunctive[3] (or asyndetic, in traditional terms) counterparts of these examples are understood as essentially identical to them with regard to the information they convey about the relations between the facts described by the individual sentences. (See Posner 1980; Schiffrin 1986; Carston 1988/91, 1990/95; Wilson and Sperber 1993b/98.)

(3) a. It's summer in England. It's winter in New Zealand.
     b. He handed her the scalpel. She made the incision.
     c. We spent the day in town. I went to Harrods.
         etc.

So, (3b) communicates that he handed her the scalpel before she made the incision, just as (2b) does. Similar observations can be made regarding all the other asyndetic counterparts of the explicitly conjoined examples, indicating that these relations are not a matter of the meaning of 'and' itself.[4]

While these parallels appear to be incontestable, there are other examples, which show that, though it may be the case that all the conjunct relations are equally well captured by non-conjunctive counterparts, the converse is not the case. That is, there are relations that can be communicated by the use of juxtaposed sentences but which do not seem to be communicated when these same sentences are conjoined by 'and'. As far as I know, the first person to point this out was Herb Clark (as noted by Gazdar 1979: 44), using the following example:

(4) a. John broke his leg. He tripped and fell.
     b. John broke his leg and he tripped and fell.

The point is that in (4a) the information communicated by the second sentence can be (and most often is) understood as providing an explanation of the event described by the first sentence. So the tripping and falling, though presented second, is understood as having preceded and caused the leg-breaking, presented first. This 'backward' relation between the events does not seem to be an accessible interpretation when the two sentences are conjoined as in (4b) (though this assessment will receive qualification in later sections).

In fact, this is just one of the relations or connections between two juxtaposed sentences which are precluded when they are conjoined with 'and'. Bar-Lev and Palacas (1980) have pointed out the extent of this phenomenon and the variety of its manifestations. They propose a semantic explanation for why 'and' appears not to allow certain sorts of connections between its conjuncts, thereby rejecting the bare truth-functional semantics for 'and'. The data they consider are of central importance in the semantic-pragmatic analysis of conjunction and their analysis, though not right in my view, captures an insight, which, when recast, leads to a satisfying account of the differences between the conjoined and non-conjoined cases given above. I will look at their account in section 3.3.

This issue has already been addressed to some extent within the relevance-theoretic framework, by Diane Blakemore, in the course of her work on discourse connectives (Blakemore 1987, 1992, 1997a). Her analysis explains the non-equivalence entirely in pragmatic terms and, crucially, involves the concept of a pragmatic processing unit, that is, an utterance, or subutterance, which is interpreted as a whole in accordance with the relevance-based comprehension strategy. In attempting to develop an account which embraces a wider array of cases than hers, I am very much building on her work. Essentially, the account involves coupling some simple observations about the linguistic properties of 'and'-conjunction together with the cognitive and pragmatic insights of relevance theory.

3.2 A Relevance-based Pragmatics of Conjunction

3.2.1 Cognitive scripts and accessibility

One of the most important factors contributing to the effort side of the optimal relevance definition is the accessing of contextual assumptions. They are either retrieved ready-made from memory or constructed from partially articulated assumption schemas in memory together with new information provided by the utterance. Though not a great deal is known about the organization of memory, it is widely assumed in cognitive studies that frequently experienced actions, events or processes and sequences of these are stored in chunks, as frames or scripts. Some of these may be relatively specific, such as the sequence of walking out of one's front door and locking it, of going to a restaurant for a meal, or of two people having an argument; these are representations of stereotypical scenarios which are clearly acquired through experience.[5] Others may be of a more skeletal or abstract nature, such as that humans generally perform actions with a purpose in mind, or that events in the world are usually causally connected to other events; these may have a more fundamental cognitive status, perhaps originating as part of innately given domain-specific capacities (for instance, 'theory of mind', 'naive physics', etc.).

So when we hear (2b), for instance, we are given immediate access to a bundle of stereotypical material of this sort, a surgical operation script, involving scalpels and the making of incisions, and, perhaps, a more general abstract schema about one person handing something to the other for that other to do something with it, etc. On the basis of this readily accessible information, it is instantly assumed that the making of the incision followed the handing over of the scalpel and the scalpel was used for making the incision; that is, the proposition expressed is enriched along the lines of (5a). This is by no means a logical necessity: the enrichment in (5b) is perfectly conceivable and internally consistent. In fact, it would probably lead to a greater array of cognitive effects than (5a), precisely because of its more unusual nature.

(5) a. He handed her the scalpel and a second or two later she made the incision with that scalpel.
    b. He handed her the scalpel and simultaneously she made the incision with her pocketknife.

The relevance-theoretic comprehension strategy (see section 2.3.4) provides an explanation for why the stereotypical interpretation in (5a) is the one chosen. The hearer constructs the most accessible interpretation (that is, the stereotypical one) and, provided that it satisfies his expectation of relevance, he stops there.[6] Abstracted from any narrative or conversational setting as the example is here, the default assumption is that this highly accessible interpretation does give rise to the expected range of effects, so the hearer doesn't go on to consider other less accessible interpretive hypotheses. Furthermore, the other logically possible interpretations, such as (5b), are not just less accessible, but massively much less accessible, and no particular one of them is more obviously available than dozens of others, so that even a hearer dissatisfied with (5a) could have no idea which hypothesis to try next. It follows that a speaker who wanted to communicate something other than (5a) would not be able to do so by uttering (2b) and, if functioning rationally, would not attempt to do so.[7]

The relevance-based account of the cause–consequence relations in (2d) and (2e) is essentially the same: we have all fairly frequently encountered and used scripts of shootings and dyings, and of human relationships in which one person leaves the other with a range of unhappy repercussions. In addition, we have more general assumption schemas concerning cause–effect relations in the physical world, cause–effect relations between human mental states, between mental states/events and behaviour, and between events in the world and mental events. The consideration of such connections appears to be a major feature of our cognitive life as we attempt to understand the world, in particular each other, and function adequately within it. So the assumption of a causal relation between the events described by the conjuncts comes readily to mind and, standardly, gives an adequate flow of effects.

3.2.2   Enrichment or implicature?

As Richard (1990) says (quoted in the previous section), there are strong pre-theoretic intuitions that these conjunct relations are truth-conditional implications, that is, that they contribute to the proposition expressed by utterances of 'and'-conjunctions. According to Recanati's Availability Principle, such intuitions should be respected in deciding whether a pragmatic inference contributes to 'what is said' (the proposition expressed) or is an implicature. The functional independence criterion and the operator-scope embedding tests, discussed in section 2.6, converge on the same conclusion. The embedding tests have been put to extensive use in the existing relevance-theoretic literature to support a pragmatic enrichment account of these relations (see Carston 1988/91, 1993; Wilson and Sperber 1993b/98). A few examples should suffice to make the point here; 'and'-conjunctions differing only in the order of their conjuncts are embedded in the scope of logical operators in the examples in (6): a disjunction, a comparative and a negation, respectively:

(6)   a.   Either he left her and she took to the bottle or she took to the bottle
            and he left her.
      b.   It's better to do your PhD and get a job than to get a job and do your
            PhD.
      c.   He didn't go to a bank and steal some money; he stole some money
            and went to a bank.

It can be seen that the Gricean treatment of the temporal and consequential connections as implicatures makes the false predictions that the proposition expressed by (6a) is redundantly repetitive, of the form 'Either P or P', and that (6b) is a non-sensical comparative, of the form 'It is better to P than to P', and that (6c) is self-contradictory, of the form 'Not P; P'. In fact, the two conjunctions in each example differ from one another in respect of the temporal and causal orderings understood to hold between the events described; that is, these relations make a crucial contribution to the proposition expressed by (hence to the truth conditions of) utterances of these sentences.

The same prediction follows from a relevance-theoretic derivation, only a part of which I give here (see fuller derivations in section 2.3.4). In the following exchange, understanding Bob's response requires a cause–consequence enrichment of the logical form of his utterance (along with various other pragmatic contributions), in order for the implicated conclusion to be inferentially warranted:

> (7) Context: Bob has broken his leg.
>   Ann: Are you entitled to accident compensation?
>   Bob: Well, a manhole was left uncovered and I fell in.
>
>   a. *Highly accessible contextual assumption:*
>   If you fall in a hole because of a manhole cover being left off, you are entitled to accident compensation.
>   b. *Proposition expressed (basic explicature):*
>   A manhole was left uncovered and as a result Bob fell in the hole.
>   c. *Implicated conclusion:*
>   Bob is entitled to accident compensation.

The explicit content of Bob's utterance is pragmatically adjusted in the process of recovering an indirect (implicated) answer to Ann's yes–no question. Treating (7b) as an implicature would simply leave the alleged minimal proposition expressed, of the form 'P & Q', with no role to play: it would not function as a premise in the derivation of the implicature in (7c), which together with other implicated conclusions, meets the expectation of relevance, and it would not enter into any of Ann's subsequent inferential activity, since the logically stronger (7b) subsumes any inferential role it could play. The conclusion is, then, that the relational inferences are pragmatic aspects of explicit content rather than implicatures. The process involved is one of free enrichment rather than saturation; I assume there is no case for a hidden indexical in 'and'-conjunctions linguistically mandating the pragmatic contribution.

In the next section, I'll consider (and reject) several attempts to account for the various interpretations semantically, that is, in terms of the encoded meaning of 'and'. One of these leads into a fairly extensive discussion of why certain 'backwards' relations (temporal, causal and other) cannot arise when the sentences are conjoined with 'and', although they do arise in the interpretation of merely juxtaposed sentences.

3.3 The Semantic Alternatives

Strong semantic accounts include the ambiguity view and the single rich lexical entry idea of Cohen (1971). According to the latter view, the sense of 'and' consists of a

set of features, including temporal sequence and cause–consequence. To accommodate the fact that not all these features are understood on every use of a conjunction, he says that features may be selectively pragmatically cancelled in particular
contexts. For instance, understanding the statement in (2a) about the seasons in two
parts of the world would involve cancellation of both the temporal and causal features. He claims that, unlike the semantic ambiguity position, his is as much in line
with Modified Occam's Razor (MOR) as Grice's logical 'and', since it involves a
single sense for 'and'.

I have given a range of arguments against both the ambiguity and the complex
sense analyses of 'and' in the references cited above, and will mention only a few
briefly here. First, Cohen's use of MOR is rather sophistical; if such a principle is
worth observing at all, then it can surely be further modified along the following
line: 'Semantic features are not to be multiplied beyond necessity', in which case his
rich multi-featured lexical entry falls foul of it as much as a semantic ambiguity
analysis does. Second, as with the ambiguity analysis, features proliferate as one
looks at more and more cases, like those in (2), which show that quite a number
of different temporal and consequence relations can arise. This creates a serious
problem for Cohen's idea, which the ambiguity account does not face: some of these
features are at odds with each other, for instance, 'temporal sequence', 'temporal
overlap' and 'simultaneity'. It follows that his set of features must be internally
inconsistent, which surely precludes them from constituting a single lexical sense.
Finally, the process of contextual feature cancellation is not explained. Can any
feature be cancelled or are some inevitably preserved (the truth-functional ones, for
instance)? Is cancellation effected by a communicative maxim or principle of some
sort or is it a simple consistency mechanism? If the latter, what prevents cancellation of one of the conjuncts itself when it is at odds with a contextual assumption
('not P' may be contextually salient to the hearer while he is processing an utterance of 'P and Q')? I take it that this idea of a single rich sense for 'and' cannot be
maintained, and move on now to another semantic account.

Bar-Lev and Palacas (1980: 139–40) (henceforth B-L and P) consider first a set
of data which are essentially variants of the Clark case, given in (4) above:

(8)   a.   Max didn't go to school; he got sick.
        b.   ≠ Max didn't go to school and he got sick.

(9)   a.   Max fell asleep; he was tired.
        b.   ≠ Max fell asleep and he was tired.

(10)   a.   Max fell; he slipped on a banana skin.
        b.   ≠ Max fell and he slipped on a banana skin.

In all these cases, a very natural interpretation of the (a) member of each pair, the
non-conjunctive variant, is that the second clause gives a reason for the first, which
is, therefore, in some relation of consequence to the second clause. So the clause
presented second is understood as temporally prior to the one presented first.[8] Later
in the paper they give a further range of examples, which show that there are other
restrictions on the set of possible relations between states of affairs presented con-

junctively, restrictions that don't affect those presented non-conjunctively. One of their examples is given in (11):

> (11) a. Wars are breaking out all over; Champaign and Urbana have begun having border skirmishes.
> b. Wars are breaking out all over and Champaign and Urbana have begun having border skirmishes.

This extension to the data will be considered later; it raises some quite new issues, I think. For the moment, I'll concentrate on the temporal/consequential examples in (2)–(4) and (8)–(10), which motivate B-L and P's analysis. They briefly point out that pragmatic maxims concerning the order in which we communicate material, such as Grice's manner maxim of orderliness, and Schmerling's principle of pragmatic priority, according to which we lay the groundwork for what we are going to say next (see Schmerling 1975: 229), make the false prediction that the pairs of examples above are equivalent. This is a point that is worth emphasizing, as the setting up of maxims or principles of discourse which stipulate that the order of utterance must match the chronology of the events described is widespread. Here are two more manifestations of the tendency:

> A. **Submaxim of Time:**   In so far as possible, make the order of saying reflect the order of events.
> (This is seen as just one dimension of a more general conversational maxim which enjoins a speaker to 'make her sayings "mirror" the world'.)
> (Harnish 1976: 359)

> B. **Temporal Discourse Interpretation Principle:**   Given a sequence of sentences $S_1, \ldots S_n$ to be interpreted as a narrative discourse, the reference time of each sentence S_i is interpreted to be: (a) a time consistent with the definite time adverbials in S_i, if any, (b) otherwise, a time which immediately follows the reference time of the previous sentence S_{i-1}.
> (Dowty 1986: 45)

These too predict that the temporal interpretation of the pairs of examples in (4) and (8)–(10) should be the same, contrary to fact. It looks pretty clear that attempts in this direction should be abandoned. (See Carston 1990/95, and, especially, Wilson and Sperber 1993b/98, who mount a strong case against such 'special-purpose sequencing rules', as they call them.)

B-L and P go on to say that, whatever the source of the meaning differences is, it cannot be to do with the order of the constituent clauses since this ordering is the same for the two members of each pair: 'on the contrary, the change of meaning is uniquely associated with the presence of "and". At this point it seems most natural to conclude that the cause of the change lies in the meaning of "and", rather than in a discourse principle of any sort' (1980: 140). While this is not an unreasonable conclusion to come to, it is by no means a necessary one. Note that the various discourse principles of information ordering actually get it right for the conjunctions (at least those so far considered). Where they fall down is in accounting for the relations that arise in the non-conjoined cases. So, what these observations most clearly entail is that these maxims should be dropped (assuming we don't want discourse principles whose domain is restricted to a subset of cases of linguistically encoded conjunction), and some other pragmatic principle brought into play, one which allows for the broader range of relations possible for the juxtaposed sentences, since these patently cannot be explained semantically. The communicative principle of relevance is such a principle. Then, in addition, it is necessary to account for the difference between the conjunctive cases and their non-conjunctive counterparts, which may be explainable in terms of the semantics of the lexical item 'and', as B-L and P claim. In fact, nothing in their observations up to this point excludes the possibility of a wholly pragmatic explanation, but it may be instructive to look at their semantic account.

On the basis of the examples (8)–(10), they propose that the semantics of 'and' is not the simple truth-functional semantics of the logical conjunction operator, but that it has a crucial feature specifying a relation of 'semantic command' between the two conjuncts:

(12)   The first conjunct, S′, semantically commands the second conjunct, S″;
        that is, S″ is not prior to S′ (chronologically or causally).

They claim that there is an analogy here with a syntactic concept of command, familiar from generative grammar, according to which A commands B as long as B is not higher (in a syntactic tree) than A. They don't develop this analogy, which remains impressionistic at best. In fact, syntactic theory over the past couple of decades has employed various notions of structural command, of which the most durable and useful has proved to be c-command, which bears little, if any, relation to the concept of 'semantic command' as given in (12). So I doubt that it's worth pursuing the possibility of an analogy between these different notions of 'command'.

Turning to the main point now, which is the proposed semantics for 'and', that S″ is not chronologically or causally prior to S′. This is an immediately appealing characterization in that it seems to encompass the whole spectrum of temporal and consequential relationships which the conjunctions in examples (2a)–(2h) and (8b)–(10b) can have and to exclude those that they cannot have. It covers the full range of temporal relations – simultaneity, overlap, containment, forward sequencing – and excludes backward sequencing; similarly, it allows for the full range of relations of consequence which the second clause may be in with the first, and excludes the first from being a consequence of the second. Furthermore, it is clear that this analysis leaves a considerable amount of appropriate work for pragmatics, in determining, for any particular case of a conjunctive utterance, precisely which, if any, temporal and consequential connection is to be taken to pertain. The relevance-based pragmatic analysis given in section 3.2 would go through, without any obvious changes being required, taking as its input the 'semantic command' characterization of conjunction. Finally, this semantics for 'and' avoids a range of problems which other attempts to give a semantic account have fallen prey to. As mentioned above, the semantic ambiguity account and Cohen's univocal multi-featured semantic account wind up having to proliferate a potentially infinite number of senses or features in their bid to account for the full set of subtly different temporal and consequential relations that different examples communicate. Worse still, some of these senses or features contradict others, for instance, simultaneity and sequentiality. So B-L and P's account seems to me to be the most promising of the semantic options on offer.

However, it turns out not to be satisfactory. For one thing, the difference between examples like (11a) and (11b) does not seem to be accounted for; I'll look at this case, together with a further range of data, in section 3.5.2. The account raises some other worries. First, it is not clear what the intended semantics of 'and' is, whether it has, say, three features, one specifying the truth of the first conjunct, another specifying the truth of the second conjunct, and the third stipulating the semantic command relation between the two, or whether it just has the semantic command feature with the truth features somehow derived from or implicit in it. Second, although it allows for the full range of temporal and consequential relations that can occur, what it seems to come down to is a clever way of finding a single descriptive statement which covers the set of examples. That is, there is nothing explanatory about it. Why should the 'backward' relations be excluded by the presence of 'and' but not by the mere juxtaposition of sentences? This might seem to be an unreasonable sort of question to pose. An explanatoriness requirement is a tall order in this realm, akin to asking for an explanation of why the word 'bread' means bread; lexical semantic facts simply aren't explainable, 'l'arbitraire du signe', as Saussure put it. However, in this particular case, I believe, a more explanatory account is possible, though, certainly, the focus won't be semantic. A deeper account will emerge from consideration of the syntactic differences between conjunctions and juxtapositions, and some basic facts about human cognitive processes.

A more substantial worry is that this semantic analysis is riven by counter-examples, cases which should make it apparent that the attempt to account for the restrictions on conjunctive interpretation in semantic terms is doomed to perpetual inadequacy, no matter how artfully done. The sort of counterexample which springs to mind, if one takes B-L and P at face value, is the following:

(13) a. She lives now in Crouch End and she lived in Muswell Hill three years ago.
      b. The boy is dead and he was shot by the soldiers.

The state of affairs recounted in the second-conjunct of (13a) is clearly chronologically prior to that expressed in the first one. The event described by the second conjunct of (13b) is causally implicated in the state of affairs described by the first one. In a charitable spirit, one might allow that semantic indications in the conjuncts themselves overrule the semantic command requirement on 'and', so 'used to live' explicitly places the second-mentioned state of affairs before the 'lives now' state of affairs; similarly, for the sequence encoded by 'was shot' and 'is dead'. All the same, if this semantic command requirement really is an intrinsic feature of the *semantics* of 'and' we would expect some sort of oddness or tension in these examples, if not a downright contradiction, between the dictates of semantic command, which preclude the temporal priority of the second conjunct, on the one hand, and the temporal order imposed by the explicitly given linguistic content in the conjuncts, on the other. I assume that intuitions are agreed that there is nothing contradictory or even mildly uneasy about these examples.

B-L and P (1980: 142–3) discuss an example of Gazdar's (1979: 69–71) which raises the same problem in a different form:

(14)   If the old king has died of a heart attack and a republic has been formed, and the latter event has caused the former, then Tom will be content.

Leaving aside the argument between Cohen (1971) and Gazdar (1979) which prompted the example, my point, again, is that on the semantic command analysis, the three-conjunct antecedent of this conditional should have a contradictory feel, since we are being told both that a cause–consequence relation between the second conjunct and the first is precluded and, then, that just such a relation holds. In discussing this example, B-L and P say: 'The two original conjuncts "float" with respect to each other, no semantic relationship implied, or not implied . . . in [14] ["and"] implies logical conjunction alone, with the third conjunct spelling out an otherwise unavailable meaning' (1980: 143). This seems right, but I don't see how it is compatible with the semantic command feature which, contrary to what this quotation says, does indeed imply (in fact encode) that a particular relationship is excluded. There is a marked inconsistency here which may indicate that B-L and P are working with a notion of semantic command which differs from the one they actually formulate. I am unable to work out what it could be. In trying to find a reformulation that would bring the notion into line with their discussion of the Gazdar example, I was driven back to an ambiguity analysis which involves listing all the possible relations between the conjuncts and which, of course, includes, as one sense, the truth-functional definition, which is the one needed to explain this example. I take it as established that the ambiguity analysis is out of the running and conclude that examples (13) and (14) provide strong support for the pragmatic account.

In fact, the information that imposes the 'backward' temporal and causal relations does not have to be encoded in the conjuncts, as the following examples indicate:

(15)   a.   She did her BA in London and she did her A-levels at home in Leeds.
       b.   The plant died and it was Mary who forgot to water it.

It is not the semantic content of the conjuncts that dictates the chronology, since the tenses in the conjuncts in each case are the same, but general knowledge about the order in which people usually do A-levels and BAs in our society and about the life and death of houseplants. So what's going on here is that pragmatically derived information is overriding the alleged semantics. This runs counter to everyone's conception of the nature of semantically decoded versus pragmatically inferred content. The fundamental characteristic of pragmatically derived meaning is its cancellability or suspendability (see Grice 1967/89b; Horn 1972, among many others), while semantic content is invariant, context-independent and uncancellable.[9]

Even more interesting in this regard, and with much broader implications than these cases, is the following example, due to Larry Horn:

(16) A: Did John break the vase?
      B: Well, the vase broke and he dropped it.

Here the event of dropping the vase is readily understood as having preceded and caused the breaking of the vase, although this belies the order of the conjuncts. Now, there is certainly something more going on here than in the cases previously considered. The speaker is avoiding explicitly expressing the proposition that John broke the vase, the utterance of which would be briefer and more direct than the one she has produced. What she communicates explicitly is two of the crucial premises the hearer needs in order to arrive at the conclusion that John did break the vase. She is making the hearer do some extra inferential work in deriving an answer to his question and so, in relevance-theoretic terms, the utterance should convey effects that the more direct utterance would not, which indeed seems to be the case. There is more to be said about how this example works and I'll take it up again later in the chapter. The important point here is that whatever the effects this response has, in the context of the preceding question, they are not effects derived via contradiction, contrary to what the 'semantic command' analysis entails.

As ever, there are two levels at which the inferentially derived relation between the conjuncts of this example could be established: at the level of the proposition explicitly expressed or at the level of implicature. That is, either (1) the pragmatically enriched proposition expressed (the basic-level explicature) is something along the lines of 'The vase broke as a result of John's dropping it', or (2) the proposition expressed does not include any specification of a cause–consequence relation and, perhaps, not even any temporal ordering; the two events are simply represented as having occurred in the recent past. Then the inferred cause–consequence relation is derived as an implicature, that is, an implicated conclusion, derived deductively from the conjunctive proposition expressed together with the highly accessible general knowledge proposition that dropping a vase is very likely to cause it to break. I would opt for the second of these possibilities, but a commitment need not be made at this stage, because the point here is that, either way, there is a problem for the semantic command analysis of 'and'. Taking the first option, the proposition expressed would directly contradict the semantic content from which it is developed, since this specifies that the second conjunct cannot be causally prior to the first. There is no such contradiction and again B-L and P would have to say that a pragmatic enrichment was somehow cancelling some semantically encoded material.

Taking the second option, we have an implicature which contradicts the proposition explicitly expressed. This sort of situation *can* arise; for instance, in the case of ironical utterances, where a speaker dissociates herself from the proposition expressed and implicates an assumption or set of assumptions which contradict, or are at odds with, the semantic content of the proposition expressed. In such instances, the proposition expressed is not an explicature, in relevance-theoretic terms; that is, it is not part of what is communicated (endorsed by the speaker) but is rather a vehicle for the communication of some other assumptions (and attitudes). In Grice's terms, the speaker 'makes as if to say' something in order to implicate something else. This, however, is surely not the case with B's utterance in (16); B is no less committed to the truth of the proposition expressed than to the implicated cause–consequence relation; indeed, the derivation of the latter depends on the assumed truth of the former. So the contradiction predicted by the semantic command analysis must hold between the base-level explicature of the utterance (which precludes the causal priority of the second conjunct) and the implicated conclusion that the dropping event (described in the second conjunct) caused the breaking event (described in the first conjunct). Again, there is no such contradiction and, in fact, there could not be, since this situation would involve a speaker simultaneously communicating (that is, giving her backing to), not merely expressing, two contradictory assumptions. I take this to be a *reductio ad absurdum* of the 'semantic command' analysis of 'and'.

There is nothing unique about Horn's example; with a little thought, one can come up with contextualizations which alter the supposedly fixed (semantically encoded) forward-directed temporal and causal relations of the Clark case in (4):

(17)   A: Bob wants me to get rid of these mats. He says he trips over them all the time. Still, I don't suppose he'll break his neck.
       B: Well, I don't know. John broke his leg and HE tripped on a Persian rug.

The same exercise can be performed for examples (8b)–(10b) (with the help of some marked intonation, probably a fall–rise, on the second conjunct). The upshot of all this is that the 'semantic command' analysis of 'and' has to be abandoned.

In the next section, I'll change tack temporarily and consider the non-conjunctive (or juxtaposed) sentence pairs, which, in their turn, have highly preferred interpretations. I'll come back in section 3.5 to the 'and'-conjunctions and give an account of why some interpretations favoured for the juxtaposed sentences are precluded from their 'and'-conjoined counterparts. This will be a wholly pragmatic account, grounded in claims about cognitive processing. Finally, the somewhat marked examples in (16) and (17), in which it seems an 'and'-conjunction does allow a backward temporal and cause–consequence relation, have to be accommodated by this pragmatic account; I return to them briefly in section 3.6.

3.4 Cognitive Fundamentals: Causality and Explanation

Let's consider the interpretive possibilities for juxtaposed sentences. The second sentence in each of (4a), (8a), (9a) and (10a) is understood as providing an explanation of some sort for the state of affairs described in the first, as if answering an implicit 'why?' or 'how come?' Recall that it's this explanatory role that the second conjunct of an 'and'-conjunction seems unable to play:

(8)   a.   Max didn't go to school; he got sick.
       b.   Max didn't go to school and he got sick.

(10)   a.   Max fell; he slipped on a banana skin.
       b.   Max fell and he slipped on a banana skin.

What is an explanation? What distinguishes an explanation from other types of information, such as (mere) descriptions? The standard answer to this, at least since Aristotle, is that an explanation starts with what is taken to be a correct description of a state of affairs and gives an account of what necessitated, or at least constrained, that state of affairs to be as it is. Scientific explanation aims at causal sufficiency, but more mundane conversational explanation may be satisfied with much less, with citation of possible reasons, or enabling conditions, for instance. Given a relatively broad construal of what might pass as explanatory, it does seems that the second sentence in each of (8a)–(10a) gives an explanation (cites a cause or a reason) for the state of affairs described in the first.

The prevalence of this sort of explanatory interpretation for the juxtaposed cases is made evident by an example that B-L and P mention in passing at the end of their paper:

(18)   a.   Max can't read and he's a linguist.
       b.   Max can't read; he's a linguist.

The natural and immediate interpretation of the conjunction in (18a) is that there is some sort of contrast (or adversative relation) between these two facts about Max. Such an interpretation is entirely in line with our existing assumptions about linguists and the ability to read. The interesting case is (18b), where it seems that we take the information that Max is a linguist as an explanation for his inability to read. On the face of it, this is pretty surprising. It runs directly counter to the standard assumption, which would lead us to take these as contrasting properties, highly unlikely to co-occur, and there is no linguistically encoded content which could override the stereotypic assumption and force this interpretation upon us, as in 'this is *because* he is a linguist', for instance.

In section 3.1 above, I noted that the temporal and consequential relations observed for 'and'-conjunctions also arise for their non-conjoined counterparts; this is one of the points standardly proffered as evidence that the relations need not be seen as part of the semantics of 'and' itself. However, the examples in (2) and (3), used to illustrate this point, did have to be chosen rather carefully; consider the following:

(19)   a.   He hit her and she screamed.
       b.   She screamed and he hit her.
       c.   He hit her. She screamed.
       d.   She screamed. He hit her.

While the forward-directed cause–consequence relation is strongly favoured in the two conjunction cases, (19a) and (19b), this is not inevitably so for the juxtaposed cases in (19c) and (19d). In both cases, the second sentence might well be taken as giving the cause or reason for the behaviour described in the first. Both the cause–consequence and the fact–explanation interpretations are compatible with commonsense assumptions about human interactions, and, without further contextualization, neither is obviously preferable to the other. What's interesting about (18b), though, is the dominance of the fact–explanation interpretation. After all, a cause–consequence interpretation is no more implausible than the fact–explanation one; also, it would better reflect a forward temporal relation and the idea that background information is given first: 'here's a general property of Max which has had the consequence that . . .'. Such a relationship can be made to seem more plausible than the fact–explanation one, by changing the example to bring it into line with prevailing assumptions about the inability to read and job prospects:

(20) a. Max can't read and he's a street-cleaner.
      b. Max can't read. He's a street-cleaner.
      c. Max is a street-cleaner. He can't read.

However, this doesn't seem to make much difference to the interpretation process; while a forward cause–consequence relation is highly accessible in the conjunction case in (20a), in both (20b) (which mirrors the ordering of the conjuncts in (20a)) and (20c), the second sentence is readily taken as an explanation for the fact observed in the first.

So the (temporary) shift of focus in this section is, from a consideration of why certain relations are precluded from the interpretation of 'and'-conjunctions, to similar considerations regarding the juxtaposed sentences and, in particular, to the dominance of the explanatory interpretation of the second one. The account of the latter will not amount to very much more than an earnest assertion that we are explanation-seeking creatures, so that, in general, when we register a new fact/assumption about the world, we look for an explanation for it. When the source of that new fact is an utterance, the speaker can assume that a further utterance on her part which supplies an explanation for it will be relevant to the addressee.

Either the world is a vast causal nexus and our mental representation system has evolved in such a way as to accurately reflect this, or, the world is not like this, being perhaps just 'the totality of facts', but we have, nevertheless, developed this highly effective (that is, survival-promoting), even if inaccurate, way of representing it and acting on it. However 'it' may really be, there is overwhelming evidence that in our striving to achieve a satisfactory understanding of events in the world we very much go in for organizing our interpretations in terms of cause–consequence relations; we will cleave to implausible, unevidenced causal accounts rather than have none at all (hence God, the First Cause and *causa sui*).

Work in many areas of cognition demonstrates this. For instance, in their study of the sort of reasoning that humans employ when required to make 'judgements under uncertainty', Tversky and Kahneman (1982) have demonstrated the great ease with which people construct causal accounts for outcomes which they could not predict. In the field of social psychology a dominant paradigm is 'attribution theory' which sees humans as lay scientists attempting to infer causes (find explanations) for the effects they observe, including, crucially, the causes of particular instances of human behaviour (see Kelley 1972). Many people investigating the inferential processes involved in text comprehension, whether in AI, psychology or pragmatics, have remarked on the fundamental role of causal assumptions in understanding a text as a coherent whole rather than as a series of unrelated statements (for instance, Schank 1975; Keenan, Baillet and Brown 1984; Myers, Shinjo and Duffy 1987; Singer 1994; Noordman and Vonk 1998). There is considerable evidence that we are much better at remembering both real and fictional sequences of events that are causally connected than those that are just temporally connected (Abbott and Black 1986: 129–30).

In these various disciplines, there is extensive use of the notion of causal schemas; that is, of knowledge structures consisting of a package of propositional representations, concerning two or more states of affairs, which are explicitly represented as causally related. As discussed in section 3.2.1, we seem to have a great many stable schemas of this sort; for instance, the death from shooting scenario, the dropping and breaking of vases, etc. However, given the ease with which causal connections are imposed on novel sequences there would seem to be other less fully scripted, more flexible, causal schemas, varying in their degree of articulation and in the number and type of open slots they employ, thus allowing for the construction of new causal sequences. In the absence of established or adaptable causal schemas, the default procedure might be as general as 'Given two states of affairs P, Q, the one hotly followed by the other, consider P as having caused Q'.

The automatic reflex-like nature of the causal-link-making mechanism in our mental life is demonstrated by work on perceptual processes. Michotte (1963) showed the irresistible tendency in humans to perceive sequences of events in terms of causal relations, even when the perceiver is fully aware that the relation between the events is coincidental and the apparent causality is illusory. For example, although it is reasonable, given our knowledge of the world, for us to believe that the collision of one billiard ball with another has caused the movement of that other, we do not actually believe that a patch of green light projected on a screen and moved along to make contact with a patch of red light causes the subsequent movement of the red light, but we nevertheless inevitably perceive it as doing so. Building on this, Rock (1983) talks of the 'coincidence–explanation' principle in accounting for the favoured perception of ambiguous sensory stimuli. He claims that the perceptual system prefers, wherever possible, to account for all co-occurring changes, correlated events or apparent regularities in the percept in terms of a common cause; there is an implicit aversion to unexplained or coincidental variation or regularity. He continues: 'Temporal contiguity alone is a powerful determinant of perceived causation . . . So, for example, if a loud noise occurs just as a light goes out, there is a feeling that the one has caused the other or that they are co-caused. This is a clear example of rejecting coincidence even though we "know" better' (Rock 1983: 137–8).[10]

In our understanding of human behaviour and social relations, causes and consequences are no less central and considerably more diverse. Much of our cognitive life is given over to explaining and predicting people's actions/behaviour. Describing this activity calls for a wider array of terms than 'cause' and 'effect'. On the causing side of the relation, we talk of people as having 'reasons', or 'motives' for behaving in certain ways, of their being driven, forced, induced, seduced, tempted, enabled, allowed, etc., by others or by circumstances, to act in certain ways; on the effect side we talk of consequences, results, outcomes, achievements, side-effects, etc. At the centre of all this lies our attribution to each other of such mental states as beliefs, desires and intentions (discussed in chapter 1, section 1.4). This folk-psychological theory, or theory of mind, appears to emerge in the normal child between the ages of three and four years (Leslie 1987a, 1987b). In conjunction with the cause–consequence concept, already a fundamental feature of the child's representational system, it gives rise to the ability to explain episodes of human behaviour in terms of mental causes. The answer to the question 'why did Mary look in the box?' moves from 'because there were chocolates in there' to 'because she *thought/knew* there were chocolates in there and she *wanted* some'. Quite generally, establishing the agency of a state of affairs is only a small part of what matters to us; we want to know the agent's motives, his intentions, the extent to which he knew what he was doing, etc. This sort of 'intentional' explanation has manifold social and moral implications; on this basis, responsibility is assigned, blame and credit are allotted, excuses or mitigating factors may be found, punishments and rewards are meted out, social relations are strengthened or weakened.

While nature may or may not be a system of causes and effects, what is clear is that it is not a system of explanations. We have to construct explanations for ourselves and we may communicate them to one another. Explanations are the products of minds, possibly only human minds. Explanations are 'meta-' with regard to causes and reasons. They are answers to questions of a certain sort, usually of a 'why?', and sometimes of a 'how?', sort. Aristotle's doctrine of 'the four causes', the formal, the material, the final and the efficient, is now generally construed as a taxonomy of types of explanation and provides a useful way of thinking about the sorts of relations between facts which we take to be explanatory. A *formal explanation* of a state of affairs, x, will be concerned with what constitutes an x; a *material explanation* of the same state of affairs will be concerned with the means by which x came to be; a *final* (or *teleological*) *explanation* concerns the ultimate purpose of x; an *efficient explanation* concerns the immediate 'trigger' for the occurrence of x. To illustrate, consider each type as a response to a 'why/how' question raised by the description in (21):

(21) The chicken crossed the road.
     Formal: She was on the east side at 2.00 and by 2.10 she was on the
                  west side.
     Material: She hopped like crazy for ten minutes.
     Final: She wanted to join Elmo on the other side.
     Efficient: Elmo told her to get on over, or else.

While both the final and efficient types are natural responses to the English 'why?', the formal may seem better prompted by 'How do you know (that she crossed the road)?' (a point that will be taken up again later) and the material by 'How did the chicken . . . ?' But they are all explanatory: they all involve the citing of a cause, reason or enabler of the state of affairs described by (21), or of the belief that the state of affairs pertains. This distinguishes them from the answers to the 'who?', 'what?', 'when?' and 'where?' type of questions, that do not function as explanations (at least not primarily). As the discussion so far would lead us to expect, explicit conjoining of (21) with any of these destroys the explanatory relation:

> (22)   a.   The chicken crossed the road and she hopped like crazy for ten minutes.
>   b.   The chicken crossed the road and she wanted to join Elmo on the other side.
>   etc.

This point will be taken up again in section 3.5.1, where I consider why this interpretation is impossible and whether these four types of explanation exhaust the relations precluded by 'and'-conjunctions.

There are good and bad explanations (but not good and bad causes), there are real reasons and bogus reasons (rationalizations) that may be offered as explanations for behaviour, and there are great individual differences in what people will accept as satisfactory explanations. But when it comes to the explanation interpretation of utterances such as those just given and the earlier (8a)–(10a), (18b), (19c), (19d), (20b) and (20c), such evaluative considerations are essentially post-interpretive. Taking the second utterance as explanatory of the first is simply the first strategy tried; when the effects it yields are puzzling, as in the case of (18b), where Max's being a linguist is hardly a compelling explanation of his inability to read, the next interpretation accessed and checked for adequate relevance, I think, is one on which the speaker is taken as giving a facetious explanation, rather than as doing something else entirely, such as just listing two facts about Max or predicating a property of Max and then giving a plausible consequence of that property.

Why is it the first strategy tried and why is it maintained even when far from satisfactory? It follows from a fundamental organizing principle of our cognitive make-up, which requires that our representations of individual states of affairs reflect them as being embedded in a mesh of (broadly speaking) causal relations with other states of affairs. A representation that cannot be so integrated will generally not be found relevant (it won't have cognitive effects). Relevant information is information that connects up with one's existing representation of the world so as to effect certain improvements on it; such 'improvements', or positive cognitive effects, include (a) the provision of confirmatory evidence, or stronger grounding, for some existing assumptions, (b) the disconfirmation and elimination of others, (c) the derivation of further implications which follow from the new and the existing representations jointly, and (d) the reorganizing of information, perhaps into schemas, so as to make subsequent information processing less effortful.

Another way of thinking about relevant information is as information that answers questions one has or, equivalently, that fills in incomplete representations (assumption schemas). An explicit question tells the hearer what sort of information the questioner regards as desirable or relevant (that is, rich enough in effects

to be worthy of attention). As Wilson and Sperber (1988b) put it, questions interpretively represent[11] relevant thoughts or propositions; while yes–no questions
express complete propositions which call for confirmation or disconfirmation, wh-
questions express incomplete (that is, not fully propositional) logical forms which
represent the sort of complete proposition the questioner considers relevant. The
kind of completion required is explicitly indicated by the wh-word: what, when,
how, why, etc. For instance, a 'why P?' question can be understood as interpretively
representing an assumption schema of the sort 'P because ____', indicating that the
provision of an explanatory proposition would be relevant.

In the juxtaposed utterances we are considering, for instance (10a) repeated here,
there is no explicit question:

(10)   a.   Max fell. He slipped on a banana skin.

But, as the preceding discussion of causal representation and its fundamental role
in our mental lives is intended to suggest, when we register a new piece of information P, for instance, that Max fell, we standardly construct a 'P because ____'
assumption schema, the completion of which will be relevant to us. So a speaker is
usually safe in assuming that a hearer presented with a description will automatically formulate a 'why?' question (or, equivalently, access a 'P because ____'
schema); she can anticipate this, and perhaps pre-empt an explicit question, by
supplying an explanation, which is bound to achieve the expected standard of relevance. Conversely, hearers, looking for interpretations which meet their expectation of optimal relevance, will take the second utterance as explanatory of the first
unless there are overwhelming reasons not to. The relation is so readily accessible
that it is usually not encoded; that is, the speaker does not preface the second utterance with 'That is because . . .' or 'The reason is that . . .'. The decoding of these
would put the hearer to extra work, which would be justified only if it gave rise to
some effects which were additional to those yielded by the standard low-effort
employment of the explanatory strategy.

Finally, recall that the cause–consequence relation understood to hold in many
conjunctive cases, such as (2d), repeated here, is a pragmatic enrichment of the
encoded logical form; that is, it contributes to the proposition expressed (the basic-
level explicature), and so to the truth-conditions of the utterance.

(2)   d.   She shot him in the head and he died instantly.

What about the cause–consequence relation understood to hold in the case of (10a)
above, to the effect that Max's slipping on a banana skin caused him to fall. I think
this is an implicature rather than an explicature, though it is a very strongly communicated one. The derivation process is very similar to that given for example (93)
in section 2.3.4; I reproduce the crucial part of the derivation:

(23)   a.   S's utterance will achieve relevance by explaining why or how Max
            fell. (*Expectation of relevance created by S's assertion that Max
            fell*)

    b.   Max slipped on a banana skin. (*First accessible reference assign-ment which could enter into an explanation of Max's falling*)

    c.   A standard reason for someone falling is that they slipped on a banana skin. (*First accessible assumption that might help explain how Max fell*)

    d.   Max fell because he slipped on a banana skin. (*Inferred from (b) and (c), satisfying (a), so accepted as an implicature of S's utterance*)

The following seems to be a likely generalization: an inferred cause–consequence relationship between states of affairs functions as a pragmatic enrichment when the utterance expresses a single conjunctive proposition and as an implicature when it holds between a sequence of propositions expressed.[12]

3.5   Relevance Relations and Units of Processing

I return now to the issue of the relations that can be understood to hold between the states of affairs described in the conjuncts of an explicit 'and'-conjunction, and, in particular, to why certain relations possible in the juxtaposed cases are not possible in the 'and'-conjunctions. There are two questions here:

(a)   Since the bid for explanations of observed and communicated facts is so fundamental, apparently the first strategy pursued in the interpretation of the second sentence uttered in the juxtaposed cases, why is it precluded from the interpretation of 'and'-conjunctions?

(b)   Supposing an adequate answer to this question can be given, does it provide the whole story of the differences between conjunctions and juxtapositions? That is, can all the precluded relations be understood as cases of explanation? Pre-empting a little, it is not obvious that the sort of exemplification relation understood in (11a) ('Wars are breaking out all over; Champaign and Urbana have begun having border skirmishes') can be included here, and there is a variety of other 'elaboration relations', as they are often called, which can arise between juxtaposed cases but not between conjuncts. The second question, then, is how are these other differences to be explained?

I address these questions in order in the next two subsections.

3.5.1   The conjunction unit

The claim is that the second conjunct can never function in an explanatory role *vis-à-vis* the first conjunct. It's important to distinguish this from the claim being made by the 'semantic command' analysis, that the state of affairs described in the second conjunct can never be understood as the cause of the first. We have already seen that this latter view is false, as shown by the Horn example in (16), repeated here (and by appropriate contextualizations of (8b)–(10b)):

(16) A: Did John break the vase?
      B: Well, the vase broke and he dropped it.

Although the interpretation of B's response will, doubtless, involve deriving the assumption that John is responsible for the breaking of the vase, I don't think there is any temptation here to describe B as explaining to A that John caused the breaking of the vase. Rather, B gives A two facts and leaves it to him to do as he likes with them. The 'semantic command' analysis of 'and' misses the point: it makes the false prediction that 'and' excludes the possibility of the second conjunct being understood as temporally or causally prior to the first and it bypasses what really needs to be accounted for, which is the preclusion of an explanatory role for the second conjunct.

In her study of such discourse connectives as 'so', 'moreover', 'furthermore', 'after all', and 'you see', Blakemore (1987: 119–20) notes a contrast in the acceptability of conjunctions in which they are made to occur, whether explicitly or implicitly (that is, encoded or left to inference):

(24) a. The road was icy and [so] she slipped.
      b. She's good-looking and [furthermore/moreover] her father's rich.
      c. ? She slipped and [you see] the road was icy.
      d. ? She passed the French exam and [after all] she is a native speaker.

Taking out the 'and' to render them non-conjunctive makes all four equally acceptable. As discussed in the previous chapter, Blakemore's analysis of the semantics of these connectives is in terms of directives to the hearer to put the proposition they introduce into a particular inferential relation with other available propositions; in this way, she achieves a uniform characterization and these connectives seem to form a natural class, distinct from truth-conditional connectives such as 'after', 'before', 'while', 'because', 'unless', etc. So the question is why they should split into two groups when used in an 'and'-conjunction. Part of the answer is given by the following observation: 'the proposition introduced by "you see" must be relevant as an explanation. That is, it is relevant as an answer [to a question] raised by the presentation of the first proposition. . . . The same point applies to the connection expressed by "after all"' (Blakemore 1987: 123). The rest of the answer, of course, has to address the preclusion of the explanatory function from a conjunction.[13]

Blakemore's claim is that, when a speaker produces an explicit conjunction, it is that complex conjoined proposition that carries the presumption of optimal relevance and not the constituent propositions (the conjuncts) individually. That is, it is the conjunction as a whole, which is the unit that should satisfy the presumption of optimal relevance. It follows from the communicative principle of relevance that a hearer is entitled to assume that he won't be required to expend processing effort gratuitously; that is, that the effort demanded will be adequately rewarded by cognitive effects. A hearer presented with a conjoined sentence is being required to undertake the processing that follows from the lexical and syntactic structure involved in conjoining and can therefore expect effects that would not follow from the conjuncts taken individually. The individual conjuncts may be relevant in their own right, but there is no automatic presumption that they will have adequate effects individually.[14]

This single processing unit idea receives some support from the fact that a conjoined subject, phrasal or sentential, may function as a syntactic unit with a single determiner or complementizer, and take a singular verb:

(25) a. Friends, whose [kindness and encouragement] has . . .
      b. My [hope and wish] is to . . .
      c. That [John had an affair and Mary left him] is a sad fact.

Further support comes from work in discourse analysis. Schiffrin (1986, 1987) looked at a wide range of attested conversations, comparing uses of 'and' with 'zero' (no connective), and concluded that a primary use of 'and' by speakers was to signal to hearers that the new utterance was to be understood as a continuation of either the immediately preceding utterance or an earlier one which had been interrupted or sidelined in some way. As she puts it, ' "and" often displays an upcoming utterance as part of a not yet completed interactional unit' (Schiffrin 1986: 57).

Let's consider some of the earlier examples as processing units meeting the expectation of relevance as a whole. As the examples in (2) (a few of which are repeated here) illustrate, conjunctions are frequently taken to communicate a chronological sequence of events and, where relevant, the state of affairs described by the second conjunct is taken as a consequence of the first.

(2) b. He handed her the scalpel and she made the incision.
     e. He left her and she took to the bottle.
     g. She went to the yoga class and found it very calming.

In cases such as (2b)–(2g), the cognitive effects of the conjunction unit crucially hinge on these assumed relations; for instance, the effects of (2b) may include implications concerning the working relationship between the 'he' and 'she', and the nature of the activity they are engaged in, which will depend on the assumption that the second action described followed closely on the first and the first was a necessary precursor of the second (that is, she needed the scalpel in order to perform her incision). The particular scenario understood here will be taken as an instance of a more general stereotypical schema, about people working together to perform an operation, and it might prompt some adjusting of standing assumptions in this schema about male and female roles. Assuming that schemas (sets of related propositions, stored together) really are cognitive units, and there is much evidence to support this (see Anderson 1980; Lloyd 1989), I suggest that, in at least a great number of cases, conjunctions will map directly on to such units rather than on to individual propositions. Their relevance will lie, at least partially, in the reinforcing effect they have on the schema as a whole and the modifications they might introduce to subparts of the schema.

Example (2a) was included as a case that did not give rise to a directional interpretation, and (18a) might be another such case where reversal of the conjuncts
makes little difference to the interpretation.

(2)   a.   It's summer in England and it's winter in New Zealand.

(18)   a.   Max can't read and he's a linguist.

Symmetric these may be, but, given what I've said about the principle of relevance
applied to conjunctions, they ought to have some effects that follow from their
having been conjoined. The obvious sort of effect here is, broadly speaking, one of
contrast.[15] In (2a) the effects would involve various comparative judgements about
England and New Zealand, the activities one could pursue there at this time of year,
the way the two landscapes might look, which place one might prefer to be in, etc.
In (18a) where it is two properties, predicated of a single individual, which seem to
be understood contrastively, the effects might principally consist of implications
(and questions) about the sort of abilities and character that Max might have, given
this unusual co-occurrence of attributes.

If it is correct that a conjunction is processed as a single unit for relevance, then
the last step in the account of the exclusion of explanatory interpretations from
conjunctions follows directly: one conjunct cannot function as an explanation for
the state of affairs described in the other, since an explanation is an answer to a
'why?' or 'how come?' question and 'questions and answers are by their very nature
planned as separate utterances, each one satisfying the principle of relevance individually' (Blakemore 1987: 123).

This account applies in a pleasing way to some examples which exhibit rather
different properties from those of the cases considered so far:

(26)   a.   Jim has a new girlfriend. He goes to New York every weekend.
       b.   Jim has a new girlfriend and he goes to New York every weekend.

There are various possible interpretations of (26a), including a cause–consequence
one, on which (26a) and (26b) are essentially the same, schematically 'P (and) so
Q'. But what I'm concerned with here is an interpretation of the juxtaposition in
(26a) which is not possible for the conjunction in (26b). The solution just proposed,
for the restrictions on conjunction interpretation, predicts that the second conjunct
of (26b) will not be able to function as an explanation of the fact given in the first
conjunct, which indeed seems to be the case. As we have seen, this is the sort of
relation that juxtaposed utterances, on the other hand, frequently enter into.

However, the backwards causal relation which hearers are likely to understand
for the juxtaposition in (26a) is different from that discussed so far. It is obviously
not the case that Jim's going to New York every weekend is a cause or a reason for
his having a new girlfriend. Rather, it is the fact of his going to New York every
weekend that gives the speaker grounds for her *belief* that Jim has a new girlfriend;
that is, it plays a causal role (as a premise) in her deriving this conclusion. It is not

too surprising that this is an accessible interpretation for the juxtaposed utterances, since, as is widely acknowledged, it is often the intended interpretation of a 'because'-clause, as in (27a):

(27) a. Jim must have a new girlfriend, because he goes to New York every weekend.
      b. Jane has left, because her son isn't here.

The two scope possibilities for 'because'-clauses are clearly evident in (27b): it can be interpreted either as giving the reason for Jane's having left, or as providing evidence for the speaker's belief that she has left. This is the often discussed distinction between a content relation and an epistemic relation (see, for instance, Sweetser 1990; Oversteegen 1997). Further context is required to choose between the two possibilities in this case.

This 'reason for believing' interpretation of the juxtaposed utterances in (26a) is easily handled within relevance theory, which, as outlined in chapter 2, section 2.3.1, claims that an utterance may communicate several propositions explicitly So, for instance, the first utterance in (26a), used literally, would have at least the following explicatures:

(28) a. The speaker is saying that Jim has a new girlfriend.
      b. The speaker believes that Jim has a new girlfriend.
      c. Jim has a new girlfriend.

So a 'why?' question can be raised in reaction to any of these and the second utterance taken as explanatory of any of them. In the case of (26a), the second utterance, 'he goes to New York every weekend', is most likely to be taken as an explanatory follow-up to (28b), the higher-level explicature representing the speaker's propositional attitude, rather than to (28c), the proposition expressed, which has been the target of the explanation in all the previously discussed juxtaposed cases.

In the next section, a new group of examples is considered, showing that there are relations other than explanation, that can be communicated by using juxtaposed sentences, but which cannot be communicated if the two sentences are conjoined in a single unit. I shall try to extend the account already given to cover these.

3.5.2 Elaboration relations

The story given above for the prohibition on an explanation relation between conjoined sentences turned on the fact that an explanation is an answer to a 'why?' question (whether explicit or implicit) and, as quoted above from Blakemore, 'questions and answers are by their very nature planned as separate utterances'. This would indicate that the account should extend beyond 'why?' questions to other types of question. The following examples, suggested by Deirdre Wilson, show that this is so:

(29)   a.   I ate somewhere nice last week; I ate at McDonald's.
       b.   I ate somewhere nice last week and I ate at McDonald's.

(30)   a.   I met a great actress at the party; I met Vanessa Redgrave.
       b.   I met a great actress at the party and I met Vanessa Redgrave.

The juxtaposed variants here do not communicate an explanation; the second utterance in each of (29a) and (30a) does not give a cause or a reason for the event described in the first utterance, or for the speaker's belief in the proposition it expresses, nor do they provide an analysis (a formal explanation) of any of the concepts in the first utterance. They do have an amplificatory function, though, and are readily understood as responses to questions, prompted by the first utterance. In fact, the first utterance in each of (29a) and (30a) seems specifically designed to raise the questions 'where?' and 'who?', respectively, which the second utterances answer. Again, conjoining these with 'and', as in (29b) and (30b), knocks out that interpretation and causes a strikingly different one to come to mind (involving some sort of contrastive relation).

Notice that these differences between the (a) and (b) versions could not be accounted for at all by the semantic analysis in terms of 'semantic command', nor by any other semantic analysis for that matter. They follow, however, from the observation that 'and'-conjunctions are single processing units, meeting the pragmatic criterion of optimal relevance as a whole. It may be that questions of the 'who?', 'what?', 'where?', 'when?' sort have to be more deliberately provoked, as they are in these cases, than does the 'why?' or 'how come?', explanation-requiring, sort of question, whose insistent appearance has already been noted, in discussing the juxtaposition examples in (18)–(20).

It is also interesting to note which sorts of sentence-level linguistic entities can be conjoined and which cannot. For convenience I'll refer to the declarative, the imperative and the interrogative as sentence types, and represent the types as follows: P, P!, and P? Clearly, an acceptable conjunction can be formed by conjoining two sentences of the same type, but there seem to be certain restrictions on the mixing of types:

(31)   a.   [P! and Q]
            Mow the lawn and I'll lend you my stilettos.
       b.   [P and Q!]
            He'll be here soon and make sure dinner is ready.
       c.   [P and Q?]
            You'll get back together and will it make you happy?
       d.   [P? and Q]
            ? Will you be happy with him and you'll have to give up your job.
       e.   [P? and Q] where Q is answer to P?
            ?? Why did he leave her and she did nag at him all the time.

There are varying degrees of acceptability here, but (31e) seems to be the least happy of these attempted conjunctions, with (31d) also somewhat uneasy. It looks as if question–answer conjunctions are not possible, which is what the account of the exclusion of the fact–explanation interpretation of conjunctions predicts. It may be that the only [P? and Q] type that we can get away with is, in fact, interpreted as [P?] [R and Q] where R is the inferred answer to P?, so (31d) is understood as:

(32)   Will you be happy with him? You won't be and you'll have to give up your job.

It is noticeable that the acceptability of this sort of conjunction drops markedly when the intended answer to the question isn't immediately apparent:

(33)   Why did the chicken cross the road and she is such a featherbrain.

If these observations are right, there is a quite general restriction on the conjoining of an interrogative and declarative, and (31d) is more accurately represented as a case of sentence-initial 'and':

(34)   Will you be happy with him? And you'll have to give up your job.

So the single processing-unit nature of conjunction, coupled with the observation that, in various of the juxtaposed cases, the second utterance appears to be answering an implicit question raised by the first, provide the ingredients for an account of why so many of these relations cannot be communicated by a conjoined utterance.

Other relations possible for juxtaposed cases but excluded from conjunction are exemplification and restatement or reformulation. Bar-Lev and Palacas (1980) mention some of these, including (11) above, repeated here, and (35):

(11)   a.   Wars are breaking out all over; Champaign and Urbana have begun having border skirmishes.
       b.   Wars are breaking out all over and Champaign and Urbana have begun having border skirmishes.

(35)   a.   Language is rule-governed: it follows regular patterns.
       b.   Language is rule-governed and it follows regular patterns.

With regard to these and others,[16] they say: ' "and" is mutually exclusive with other conjoining relationships, including exemplification, conclusivity, and explanation. . . . In nontemporal, noncausal cases, "and" is inadmissible in relationships heading in either direction, forward or backward' (B-L and P 1980: 143–4). These observations seem to be essentially correct, but I do not think that B-L and P's analysis can account for them. The conjunctions in (11b) and (35b) do meet their 'semantic command' requirement, since the second conjunct is not interpretable as temporally or causally prior to the first, but the following question then arises: why is it that they cannot be understood in the same way as the juxtaposed cases? This question is not addressed by B-L and P.

Elaboration relations, which include exemplification and restatement, have received a lot of attention recently, in the coherence theory literature.[17] The relation of elaboration is one type of coherence relation, which is usually kept distinct from a variety of other backward-directed relations such as evidence, justification, and explanation. Classifications of these relations vary, but frequently cited subtypes of elaboration are exemplification, restatement and several varieties of specification. Here are a couple of examples of the 'specification' relation, taken from Mann and Thompson (1986):

(36) Your behaviour bothers me. You come in drunk and you insult the waiter.

(37) Karen is so photogenic. She has a really brilliant smile.

They categorize (36) as a case of 'generalization–instance', that is, the second utterance provides an instance of the abstract generalization in the first, and (37) as a case of 'whole–part' specification. These, again, are cases where conjoining the clauses with 'and' blocks the relation.[18] The account given so far can be extended to these various examples falling under the general elaboration label, in that the second utterance in each case can be understood as answering an anticipated question: for (11a) 'where are wars breaking out?', for (35a) 'what does it mean to say language is rule-governed?' or 'why?', for (36) 'what's the problem with the behaviour?' or 'why?', for (37) 'in what respect is she photogenic?' or 'how?'

However, there is more to be said about at least some of these examples. In cases such as (35a), where the second utterance can be construed as another way of putting the first, it is, in relevance-theoretic terms, an *interpretation* of the first utterance (rather than a description of a state of affairs). This way of thinking about reformulations, or restatements, has been discussed within relevance theory by Blakemore (1993, 1996, 1997a). In the course of this work, she has analysed a variety of conceptual (as opposed to procedural) discourse markers, whose function seems to be to tell the hearer that the utterance they preface (or some part of it) is a representation of a preceding utterance (or some part of it), rather than a description of a state of affairs. This group of markers includes 'that is', 'in other words', and 'in short'. Here is one of her examples:

(38) a. At the beginning of this piece there is an example of an anacrusis.
     b. *That is*, it begins with an unaccented note which is not part of the first full bar.

(from Blakemore 1997a: 8)

The relation of (38b) to (38a) is more or less identical to that of the second utterance to the first in (35a) above, although there is no explicit indicator of the relation in (35a). It would be natural to suppose that the second utterance in (35a) is interpreted as a reformulation of the first utterance, one which gives the hearer easier access to the contextual assumptions against which processing the proposition expressed by the first utterance will achieve an array of effects. Put differently, these are cases of 'formal' explanation (see discussion of explanation types in section 3.4 above); they involve *explaining* the meaning of 'anacrusis' and of 'rule-governed' (as applied to language), thereby enabling the hearer to derive further contextual effects from the first utterance (assuming he did not already have a full grasp of the meaning of these expressions). This explanatory, question-answering role of the second utterance accounts for the non-occurrence of the relation in (35b), the conjoined counterpart of (35a). Formal explanations (that is, explications of the meaning of expressions) will, necessarily, involve the interpretive use of a representation.

Finally, consider the exemplification relation, exemplified in (11a) above (perhaps also in (37) despite its 'specification' labelling), and here in (39a), a relation which disappears when the two sentences are conjoined:

(39) a. I always pick the wrong queue;[19] yesterday I ended up waiting a quarter of an hour to get to the checkout.
      b. I always pick the wrong queue and yesterday I ended up waiting a quarter of an hour to get to the checkout.

The second utterance in (39a) could be comfortably prefaced by 'for example' or 'for instance'. In Carston (1992: 164), I suggested that exemplification is a way of providing evidence (inductive support) for a claim. Blakemore (1997a, 2001) gives some substance to this idea, pointing out that the recognition of a particular state of affairs as an example brings with it an assumption that it is *typical* in some respect, and that, therefore, there is a set of other cases which have the same property. She says 'it is the suggestion that there are other cases which could have been cited which makes exemplification such a good means of providing evidence for the claim exemplified' (Blakemore 1997: 13). To make a claim and then to present evidence for it is to produce two utterances, each of which carries the presumption of relevance individually; this explains why exemplification is not a possible relation between the conjuncts of an 'and'-conjunction, since they comprise a single unit processed for relevance.

The relations discussed in these sections, which can arise for juxtaposed cases but not for conjunctions, are explanation, evidence, reformulation and certain sorts of elaboration; logical consequence is another (see note 16 of this chapter). They all have in common the property that they are not relations 'out there' in the world; they are relations that hold only in minds, perhaps only in human minds. They are relations between representations. On the other hand, the temporal and cause–consequence relations, which may hold between conjuncts, are very much out there, or, at least, are assumed by us to be out there; we register them perceptually and we represent them in our factual beliefs.

In the next section, I leave the two-unit cases and concentrate on completing the account of the pragmatics of 'and'-conjunctions, focusing on the forward-directed temporal sequence relation so typical of these examples.

3.6 Processing Effort and Iconicity

A temporal sequence relation is very often inferred to hold between the state of affairs described by the first conjunct and that described by the second. The pragmatic account of this, given in section 3.2.1, relied heavily on the idea of highly accessible narrative scripts, in which these sequential relations are represented. But this cannot be the whole story, since there is a range of other cases in which sequential (and cause–consequence) enrichment cannot be a result of scripted knowledge. Consider the following:

(40) a.   Sally cooked some vegetables and she began to feel more optimistic.
      b.   Mary put on her tutu and did a highland fling.
      c.   Bill saw his therapist and fell down a manhole.

(41) a.   Tonto rode into the sunset and he jumped on to his horse.
      b.   Bill went to bed and he took off his shoes.

Each of the examples in (40) is taken to communicate a temporal sequence, though none of them involves a stereotypical scenario in which they are represented as sequential.[20] The examples in (41), on the other hand, give ready access to a script: the 'jumping on to a horse and riding into the sunset' script and the 'taking off shoes, etc. and getting into bed' script, so the question they raise is why the stereotypical script does not lead to a backwards temporal relation being inferred as holding in the two examples. Why isn't (41b) understood as 'Bill went to bed after he took off his shoes'?

I've dismissed accounts that rely on a pragmatic maxim or principle which enjoins speakers to present their descriptions of states of affairs in the order in which these took place in the world. These are kinds of iconicity principles, as is made explicit in Harnish's (1976: 359) supermaxim: 'Be representational; in so far as possible, make your sayings "mirror" the world', from which his more specific mirroring sub-maxims of time and space follow.[21] For the reasons already given, in section 3.3, it would not be a good move to reinstate maxims of this sort, although they do seem to account for the persistent interpretation of 'and'-conjunctions as involving temporal sequence, even in cases like (41a)–(41b), where this runs counter to stereotypical assumptions and leaves us with a weird interpretation.

The explanation is, I think, a general cognitive one rather than a specifically pragmatic one; it concerns the relative ease/difficulty of certain processing paths. The processing of proximal stimuli of an unintended sort cannot but take place in a certain order. When a certain (visible or auditory) event, e_1, occurs in the world, and is followed by a second event, e_2, and both of these are picked up by the appropriate sensory transducer and processed perceptually and conceptually, the processing of a representation of the first event begins before the processing of a representation of the second event. So, to a significant extent, the processing of the second event takes place in the context of the prior processing of the first event, rather than vice versa. We have no choice but to process an awful lot of information in this way; it impinges on our receptors in the order in which it occurs. Given this utterly banal fact (true doubtless of other sentient beings too), the human cognitive system presumably finds it natural (easy) to process other stimuli (those designed by humans, including ostension) in a similar way.

This cognitive explanation enters into utterance interpretation, hence pragmatics, by virtue of the rather obvious fact that utterance processing involves effort. In the absence of explicit (encoded) signposts telling a hearer what temporal relations hold between states of affairs described in a single processing unit, as is often the case with 'and'-conjunction, an order of presentation that matches the temporal order of the events is the least costly in processing effort demands. There is no need for principles or maxims enjoining iconic representation; it follows from the precepts of relevance theory that, other things being equal, a speaker will cause her hearer as little processing effort as possible in achieving the intended cognitive effects of her utterance.[22]

Mental scripts of stereotypical sequences of events represent their real-world temporal relations, so, in many instances, the temporal sequence inference is supported by both general ease of processing considerations and a script which represents events as occurring sequentially. When there is no script, as in the examples in (40), the natural processing track is taken, and when there is a clash between a script and this most accessible route, as in the examples in (41), it is the latter that seems to prevail.

However, we have seen earlier a couple of cases which might appear to be exceptions to these generalizations; I repeat them here:

(42)   A: Did John break the vase?
       B: Well, the vase broke and he dropped it.

(43)   A: Bob wants me to get rid of these mats. He says he trips over them
            all the time. Still, I don't suppose he'll break his neck.
       B: Well, I don't know. John broke his leg and HE tripped on a Persian
            rug.

It seems that, despite the order in which the conjuncts are presented here, the temporal order the hearer will recover accords with that of the standard script (first the dropping then the breakage, first the tripping then the leg-breaking).

In fact, it is not too difficult to envisage a context in which (41b) is understood in such a way that it is not at odds with the standard scripted temporal sequence: suppose a parent is trying to persuade a child that she should take off her shoes before she gets into bed, by citing her older brother, Bill, whom the child takes as a role model, as having done so. In this context, the utterance will have a particular, fairly marked pattern of accentuation and intonation (as is also the case for (42B) and (43B)):

(44)   BILL went to bed and | HE took off HIS shoes.
       [upper case indicates accented syllables; | marks intonation phrases
       (IPs); there is a fall–rise contour in each IP]

In all three examples, what is presented is not a narrative, but an argument or example intended to encourage the hearer to reach a certain conclusion: that John did break the vase, that one can hurt oneself badly from tripping on a mat or rug, and that the child should take off her shoes before she goes to bed. The relevant conclusion follows from the information expressed in the two conjuncts and a further premise concerning temporal and/or cause–consequence relations, which is highly accessible to the hearer, either via a script (vase dropping and breaking) or via the context (the child knows that her mother wants her to take off her shoes before she goes to bed). While a full explanation of these interesting examples remains to be given, they clearly have certain special features which distinguish them from the narrative cases, which have been the focus of this section, and for which the most accessible assumption is that the temporal ordering of the events described matches the order of their utterance (even when this conflicts with a stereotypical script). The marked intonation contour in examples (42)–(44) demands extra attention, thereby indicating that the standard least-effort processing route is not to be followed here. Although the issue of the temporal ordering of the states of affairs described does enter into the interpretation of these examples, it is not part of the proposition explicitly expressed by the speaker but is left for the hearer to access as a distinct proposition; at most it is weakly implicated by the speaker. For further discussion of these 'non-narrative' cases, see Blakemore and Carston (1999).

3.7 Residual Issues

3.7.1 Pragmatic enrichment or unrepresented Background?

I have argued against a number of different semantic accounts of the relations that can hold between the conjuncts of an 'and'-conjunction and, in the case of 'semantic command', those that cannot. The pragmatic account of the various temporal, consequential and other conjunct relations that I have favoured has a very cognitive flavour to it: knowledge structures in the form of stereotypical scripts have played a large part, as has the idea that the human mind is constantly looking for and assuming causal relations among the states of affairs it perceives and conceives, and an iconic processing route was claimed to be the least effortful, other things being equal.

I have presented these conjunct relations as cases where pragmatically inferred meaning contributes to the proposition explicitly expressed (that is, to the truth-conditional content of the utterance). This view recalls an interesting issue that arose towards the end of chapter 1, in the context of the discussion of Searle's concept of the Background. The question there was: which, if any, elements of the great mass of contextual/background material go into the proposition expressed? Alternatively, which unencoded elements of total utterance meaning enter into the proposition expressed (that is, enrich the encoded logical form) and which do not? Which unencoded elements does the hearer actually infer? Consider the following familiar utterances:

(45) a. I've had breakfast.
      b. She ran to the edge of the cliff and jumped.
      c. She gave him the key and he opened the door.

Temporal sequence is inferred in (45b) and (45c); in addition, it has been claimed that, in each of these cases, a hearer recovers an unarticulated constituent, in the process of deriving the proposition the speaker intended to express: 'today', for (45a), 'over the cliff' for (45b), 'with the key she gave him' in (45c). But Searle points out that there are a number of other elements of meaning which, though not literally expressed, are assumed by both speaker and hearer; for instance, that the 'having' of breakfast was an instance of ingesting in the normal way through the mouth, that the jumping over the cliff took place in a situation in which the laws of gravity held, and that the door opening was performed in the normal way by putting the key in the keyhole in the door rather than, say, by gouging a hole in it. Are these elements of the Background also recovered and represented by the hearer as part of the proposition expressed by the speaker? If so, what limits are there on this process of building in material? If not, why not, what distinguishes them from the constituents that are recovered and represented?

I don't think that any of these Background elements of meaning would be represented by the hearer of these utterances, except in the unusual case of a context in which there was some doubt about their holding. In general, elements are inferred only if they are likely to make a positive contribution to the relevance of the utterance, that is, only if they contribute to the derivation of cognitive effects. The point about the Background is that it is a body of taken-for-granted, *unrepresented* dispositions and manifest assumptions, which make it possible for the *representations* that are our actual thoughts and utterances to be meaningful. There is a question about what exactly is in the Background and what is not, and there are possible disruptions of the Background, which cause aspects of it to lose their background status and become represented, but these matters do not bear on the concept itself.

With regard to the examples in (45), it does seem that the relevance of (45a) depends on the breakfast having taken place 'today', and that of (45b) depends on the jumping being 'over the cliff'. Cognitive effects follow from these. Nothing more follows from the breakfasting having been in the normal ingesting way or from the jumping having been subject to gravity, though much may have followed from these *not* being in force. As for the instrumental inference of 'with a key' in (45c), I suspect that that is one that comes for free, along with the other material, in the door-opening script, whether relevant in the particular case or not. Scripts may be viewed as some sort of intermediate structure, between unrepresented Background and particular propositional representations of non-stereotypical knowledge.

3.7.2   The semantics of 'and' and the logic of 'and'

This chapter began by rehearsing Grice's pragmatic account of the temporal sequence relation which is understood in many 'and'-conjunctions: it is a (generalized) conversational implicature derived via the manner maxim of ordering. For Grice, this was but one instance of his general project to preserve the view that the semantics of certain natural-language expressions does not depart from that of their logical operator counterparts (negation, conjunction, disjunction, the conditional, the universal quantifier, the existential quantifier and the iota operator). It is probably fair to say that the debate over whether the equivalence holds has not been finally settled in any of the particular cases, though some, such as the conditional, have been much more contentious than others.

In arguing for a pragmatic account of the various rich conjunct relations, I have, so far, been content to go along with the apparent conclusion that the semantics of natural-language 'and' is captured by the standard truth table for '&'. However, although the arguments in the preceding sections all point to a minimal meaning for 'and', there is no reason to suppose that in a cognitively-realistic decoding semantics the characterization of the meaning of 'and' (or of any other natural-language connective) should match the definition of the corresponding element in a logical calculus, whose semantics is resolutely truth- and reference-based. This sort of translational semantics, which provides the linguistic input to pragmatic processing, is not directly concerned with the relation between linguistic forms and the external world, but with the relation between linguistic forms and the cognitive information they encode.

As outlined in section 2.3.7, within the relevance-theoretic approach to utterance understanding, there is an important strand of semantic investigation, based on the distinction between conceptual and procedural encoding, initiated by Blakemore (1987). So within this framework, a natural question to ask is whether 'and' encodes a concept (as assumed so far) or a procedure. Of course, whatever the answer, it must preserve the fundamental logical property of 'and', which is standardly captured by the deductive rule of 'and'-elimination:

(46)   *And-elimination*
    a.   *Input*:   (P and Q)
         Output: P
    b.   *Input*:   (P and Q)
         Output: Q

Among the English connectives which have been argued to encode procedures are 'but', 'moreover', 'after all', 'so', 'although' and 'whereas'. One of the preliminary observations often made in discussions of these examples is that they do not contribute to the truth-conditional content of utterances in which they appear. For any one of these cases, call it c, an utterance of '$P, c\ Q$' is true if and only if P is true and Q is true. In other words, a truth-statement for these cases would be identical to the truth-statement for an 'and'-conjunction. Similarly, if they were given a truth table, it would be identical to the truth table for 'and', though we would hasten to say that, of course, this did not exhaust, or even begin to capture, their meaning (which has a crucial 'non-truth-conditional' component). They appear, therefore, to be truth-*functional* unlike such truth-*conditional* connectives as 'because', 'after', 'before' and 'when', for which it is not possible to give a complete truth-table, as no truth value can be computed on the basis of just the information that each of their constituent propositions is true.

In practice, the connectives in class c are not generally given a truth table, nor submitted to truth-conditional analysis. The reason for this seems clear for those cases like 'moreover', 'after all', 'so' and denial-of-expectation 'but': they are not conjunctive in that they do not form complex sentences or well-formed formulas. Rather, they are discourse connectives, whose meaning specifies the sort of inferential relation which the utterance they prefix enters into with existing contextual assumptions. Like the juxtaposed cases discussed in this chapter, '$P, c\ Q$' consists of two separate sentences (and so two processing units): 'P' and '$c\ Q$', each of which would constitute a distinct input to a truth-conditional semantics. Note that from '$c\ Q$' there follows deductively 'Q', so that the deductive output of the two units making up '$P, c\ Q$' is identical to that of 'P and Q', shown in (46). Others in this class of procedural connectives, such as 'although', 'whereas' and, perhaps, 'since', are syntactically conjunctive; as subordinating conjunctions, the clause they prefix can only occur as a subpart of a single sentence (or well-formed formula). Sentences of the form 'P although Q' are, therefore, just as much input to a would-be complete truth-conditional semantics for natural-language sentences as those of the form 'P and Q'.[23]

Let's entertain the possibility that the information encoded by 'and' is procedural. Before considering what that procedure might be, recall what a procedural encoding is supposed to do. It doesn't contribute a constituent to a representation, as a conceptual encoding does; rather, it constrains or facilitates some aspect of the pragmatic inferential phase of utterance interpretation. For instance, indexicals reduce the search space for referents, and discourse connectives indicate the type of contextual assumptions or implications to be accessed. In this chapter, we have seen that the sorts of relations between two segments that can be communicated when they are 'and'-conjoined are quite a lot more limited than the range that is possible when the segments are merely juxtaposed, which suggests that the presence of 'and' exerts a constraining effect on interpretation. However, given the arguments of the preceding sections, it cannot be that an 'and'-constraint encodes anything about temporal or causal relations; what is responsible for the restrictions on conjunct relations is, rather, the fact that an 'and'-conjunction comprises a single processing unit. So, if 'and' encodes a procedure, it must amount to something like 'treat the propositions I connect as a single unit for pragmatic processing'. Such a procedure would, like those encoded by pronouns, function as a constraint on the derivation of the proposition expressed by the utterance, limiting the process of pragmatic enrichment.

However, there are strong reasons to doubt that a procedural account is right. The proposal given is the only plausible possibility, but it looks very much as if it is redundant, since the formation of a single unit of coordinated parts is already achieved through the syntax. An alternative suggestion is that 'and' has no linguistic meaning at all, whether conceptual or procedural, and that the restrictions on the relations that can be pragmatically inferred, compared with those for the juxtaposed cases, are purely a function of syntactic coordination. The truth-functional properties of 'and' would fall out readily from such an assumption. Rather than having elimination rules as part of a logical entry attached to an 'and' concept, the truth of the propositions conjoined by a semantically empty 'and' would simply follow as it does in the case of bare juxtapositions: P logically implies P; Q logically implies Q.[24]

Naturally, the Gricean advocacy of the equivalence of other natural-language connectives and determiners to their truth-conditional counterparts can be similarly questioned. Westerstahl (1985) and Breheny (1999: 28) claim that determiners ('a', 'the', 'every', etc.) are context-dependent and distinct from their logical counterparts. Both Atlas (1989) and Seuren (2000) have argued that natural-language negation is not to be equated with the truth-functional logical notion. Both pursue a unitary semantic analysis of 'not', neutral between the various different interpretations it can be given; Atlas opts for a very general abstract sense and Seuren for a speech-act notion of rejection.

The following general conclusion about natural-language semantics and logic seems to me to be well worth pursuing: 'The logical properties of the sentences of natural languages are best seen as epiphenomenal on the semantic and cognitive processing of the sentences in question. They emerge when semantic processes and properties are looked at from the point of view of preservation of truth through sequences of sentences, which is the defining question of logic, not of semantics' (Seuren 2000: 289). That there might well be divergences between cognitive semantics and logical semantics does not follow directly from the linguistic underdeterminacy thesis, but the two certainly harmonize. What underdeterminacy clearly entails is that few, if any, natural-language sentences have fixed, determinate truth conditions. The truth relation holds between thoughts and states of affairs, so between propositions expressed by utterances (semantic/pragmatic hybrids) and states of affairs. Then, it is systems of thought, rather than linguistic systems, for which a truth calculus, that is, a logic, should be devised. If this is right, there is no obvious reason to suppose, or to consider it desirable, that what natural-language connectives and determiners encode is identical to the context-free, truth-based properties of logical operators; rather, there is some reason to expect differences in at least some cases.

3.8 Conclusion: From Generalized Conversational Implicature to Propositional Enrichment

Let me briefly sum up how the analyses in this chapter illustrate the theoretical positions, taken in the previous chapters, on the semantics/pragmatics distinction and the explicit/implicit (= explicature/implicature) distinction. I have rejected semantic analyses which endeavour to attribute the various possible temporal and cause–consequence relations between the conjuncts to the meaning of 'and' itself. These relations are a product of pragmatic inference. In this, I am at one with Grice and neo-Griceans, like Gazdar, Levinson and Horn. The standard assumptions of this general position, however, are that 'and' is semantically equivalent to '&' and that the pragmatically inferred relations are generalized implicatures. These assumptions have not been supported here. I have considered other minimalist possibilities for the meaning of 'and', including that it has no linguistic semantics at all, and I have argued that the pragmatically inferred relations are cases of enrichment, contributing to the proposition expressed by the utterance, hence to its basic-level explicature. This analysis is a clear demonstration of the strong linguistic underdeterminacy view: encoded linguistic meaning may do little more than provide a skeletal framework which is both augmented (into explicatures) and complemented (with implicatures), by fast, effective mechanisms of pragmatic inference.

The source of the interpretive differences between 'and'-conjunctions and corresponding 'and'-less sentence juxtapositions is that, while the latter comprise two distinct utterance units, the 'and'-conjunctions are single pragmatic processing units which meet relevance expectations as a whole rather than individually. This is the crucial ingredient in explaining the inaccessibility of a wide variety of possible relationships between states of affairs described by the conjuncts, including a range of explanatory relations and other question–answer-type relations.

I hope that the account in this chapter goes some way towards puncturing Levinson's (1989) allegation that relevance theory is incapable of accounting for the phenomena that he classifies as generalized implicature (see note 34 of chapter 2). On his account, the 'conjunction-buttressing' inferences, as he calls them, are generalized I-implicatures, that is, pragmatic inferences governed by a maxim that enjoins stereotypical informational enrichment. (Horn 1984b, 1989, takes essentially the same position.) However, once we drop the untenable assumption that a pragmatic inference inevitably results in an implicature, it becomes pretty clear that these 'and'-enriching inferences have to be taken as contributions to the explicit content of the utterance.

This opens the way to a reconsideration of other cases of alleged generalized implicature, including the well-known scalar implicature cases, exemplified in (47):

(47) a. I like some of Woody Allen's movies.
          Implicature: I don't like all of Woody Allen's movies.
      b. Jim has four children.
          Implicature: Jim has no more than four children.
      c. Sarah is a poet or a philosopher.
          Implicature: Sarah isn't both a poet and a philosopher.

The case for the inference to be accounted a pragmatic contribution to the explicit content of the utterance seems to have been won for cardinal number expressions (see Carston 1990/95, 1998a; Horn 1992b); it remains unsettled in the case of the non-cardinal scalar terms (but see Geurts 1998b).

NOTES

1   Neo-Griceans who support this 'generalized implicature' view include Gazdar (1979), Horn (1972, 1984b, 1989, 1996), Atlas (1989), and Levinson (1987a, 1988, 1995, 2000). In Stephen Levinson's view, this is just one instance of what he takes to be an important and prevalent phenomenon, for which he has developed a specific theory: generalized conversational implicature (GCI) theory. As mentioned in the previous chapter (see especially note 4), he treats GCI as a distinct phenomenon from particularized impli-

cature (PCI): generalized implicatures arise quite generally across contexts unless they are blocked by specific salient assumptions, while particularized implicatures are 'nonce' inferences, dependent on specific contextual assumptions for their derivation. GCI theory is conceived of as a module within pragmatics, having its own distinct pragmatic principles and formalized in a system of default inference rules. The temporal sequence relation arising for 'and'-conjunctions is one of the examples that is taken to fall within this theory.

Although the term 'generalized conversational implicature' comes from Grice, Levinson's work is a significant departure from his. There is no evidence that Grice gave any theoretical weight to a distinction between generalized and particularized conversational implicature, and the postulation of a system of default logical rules, attached to particular lexical items, runs counter to the aim of accounting for pragmatic inference in terms of quite general conversational maxims rooted in considerations of human rationality. With regard to the case of 'and', the GCI approach runs into a number of problems: it does not account for the wide range of subtly different temporal, cause–consequence and other relations, which 'and'-conjunctions can communicate (see the examples in (2)); it postulates a default inference rule for temporal sequence attached to 'and', but the same inference goes through for juxtaposed cases (see the examples in (3)); it cannot account for the fact that temporal sequence may be assumed, on the basis of conjunct ordering, even when it is inconsistent with highly accessible general knowledge (and so should be defeated according to GCI theory). For some discussion of Levinson's position, see Carston (1990/95, 1998a) and section 3.8 of this chapter. However, his latest and fullest rendering of GCI theory (Levinson 2000) remains to be considered in detail.

2 Like most others discussing the general properties of sentential 'and'-conjunctions, I am not considering an apparently exceptional class of examples, of which the following are three:

   (i)   She's gone and ruined her dress now.
   (ii) I've got to try and find that document.
   (iii) Do me a favour and shut it.

As Schmerling (1975) points out these do not behave syntactically or semantically like cases of logical conjunction.

3 I may be using the term conjunction in a rather nonstandard way. Many authors write of (asyndetic) conjunction relations when discussing what I am calling juxtaposed or 'non-conjunctive' cases; some would say the conjunction relation is implicit (inferred) in these cases, to distinguish them from the explicit (encoded) cases when a linguistic connective is present. Furthermore, they would make a distinction between coordinating conjunction (whether encoded or inferred) and subordinating conjunction (whether encoded or inferred). However, I don't think that my simple distinction in this chapter between what I call conjunctions (examples where the linguistic element 'and' is present) and juxtapositions (where there is no linguistically given connective), should cause any conceptual difficulties.

4 This line of argument has to be employed with care. Consider the following (mis)use of it:

   (i)   John is tall but Bill is short.
   (ii) John is tall. Bill is short.

Since the juxtaposed sentences in (ii) communicate a contrast comparable to that of (i), a blind application of the argument would suggest that the connective 'but' does not encode anything about a contrast, and that this is pragmatically inferred in both cases. For independent reasons, it's clear that this is not right, and appropriate choice of examples makes it evident:

(iii)   John is rich but he is tall.
(iv)   John is rich. He is tall.

While no relation of contrast is communicated by (iv), the use of 'but' in (iii) ensures its presence, however odd it may seem, indicating that this is what is encoded by 'but'.

5   Anderson (1980) discusses the notion of schema in general and considers a range of evidence for its status as a real cognitive unit. Brewer (1999) gives a brief history of the role of schemas, frames and scripts in psychology and artificial intelligence, and supplies a useful reference list.

6   Other pragmatic accounts give a lot of weight to stereotypical interpretation too. For instance, Levinson's (1987a, 1988, 2000) I-principle (Principle of Informational Enrichment) entitles hearers to derive implicatures which are stereotypical enrichments of the information encoded by the utterance. However, this principle makes some false predictions, and offers nothing by way of explanation for why hearers should enrich stereotypically (when they do) instead of in more unusual (and interesting) ways. For critical discussion of Levinson's account, see Carston (1990/95, 1994a); Wilson and Sperber (1993b/98).

7   The account of the pragmatic derivation of the temporal relation between the conjuncts which I gave in Carston (1988/91) was a little different; there I saw it as a byproduct of the necessary assignment of temporal reference to the past tense of the verbs in each of the conjuncts, so for (2b) 'handed' and 'made'. The result of this process looked like the following:

X handed Y the scalpel at t & Y made the incision at $t + n$
(where t is some more or less specific time prior to the time of utterance and $t + n$ is some more or less specific time, later than t)

This made it more like a saturation account; Grice and others accepted reference assignment as one of the few processes required to bring the linguistic content up to a complete proposition. There are various problems with this (see Recanati 1989b; 301, footnote 3; Wilson and Sperber 1993b/98), the most obvious being that it won't account for cases involving temporal spans rather than specific times. I see no reason now to attach it so closely to a reference fixing process; along with the various cause–consequence relations, it can be accounted for by a free enrichment process, which involves highly accessible assumption schemas and the relevance-theoretic constraint.

8   Another example which they present with this set is of the variety known as 'pseudo-imperative':

(i)   Stand up, and I'm going to break your arm.
(ii)   Stand up; I'm going to break your arm.

As with the other pairs, these are not equivalent in the meaning they communicate. They are, however, very different from the others and raise several further issues, so I leave them aside here. See Clark (1991, 1993a) for a survey of ideas about these cases and for a relevance-theoretic account.

9   This statement will seem a little strong in the light of the observations in chapter 5, where I make a case for the loose use of linguistic expressions bringing about alterations

to the proposition expressed which involve the loss of some encoded linguistic content. However, I think it will be evident that these cases, where a pragmatic loosening is warranted, are very different from what would be required here, which is that general world knowledge completely reverses some alleged lexical content.

10   These observations stand in opposition to the Humean view that the causal idea is the result of a lengthy period of experiencing, sensorily, repeated occurrences of spatio-temporal contiguity between objects or events. To the contrary, Michotte's experiments indicate that some causal connections are directly perceived (as opposed to all being a function of higher-level cognitive processes). Furthermore, Michotte claimed, causally connected events do not necessarily have to be experienced repeatedly for the causal link to be forged (it's enough to be bitten by the dog once). Given this, he thought it probable that even very young infants perceive events as cause–effect episodes rather than as mere sequences. The results of recent experimental work support this prediction. Leslie and Keeble (1987) have suggestive evidence that 6-month-old infants already perceive cause–effect relations, providing a strong case for the innateness of the assumption and for the early stage at which it is operational (along with other concepts concerning the properties of physical objects, of course). For recent discussion of these matters and of the nature of causal cognition more broadly, see Sperber, Premack and Premack (1995).

11   This is an instance of the important distinction made in relevance theory between descriptive and interpretive representation, touched on briefly in chapter 2, section 2.3.6. Descriptively used representations represent states of affairs directly. Interpretively used representations (thoughts or utterances) represent other representations; utterances are always first-order interpretive in that they represent thoughts, but they may be interpretive to further orders, for instance, if they report speech or thought. The interesting thing about questions is that they are intrinsically (semantically) interpretive: they represent certain relevant (or desirable) assumptions. See Sperber and Wilson (1986a/95b, chapter 4, sections 7 and 10), Wilson and Sperber (1988a), Clark (1991).

12   There is an interesting comparison to be made between this implicature account of the cause–consequence relation in (10a) and the following examples: (i) is from Frege and is discussed by Neale (1999: 48); (ii) is similar in the information it conveys but the clauses are differently ordered:

   (i)   Napoleon, who recognized the danger to his right flank, personally led his guards against the enemy position.
   (ii) Napoleon personally led his guard against the enemy position, having recognized the danger to his right flank.

Frege says there are two thoughts expressed in (i) and Neale agrees but suggests that, instead of the conjunction of two propositions that Frege seems to assume, the utterance expresses a sequence of propositions:

   (iii) Napoleon personally led his guards against the enemy position.
   (iv)   Napoleon recognized the danger to his right flank.

There is also the third thought, that his knowledge of the danger to his right flank was the *reason* for Napoleon leading the guards against the enemy position, that is, a cause–consequence relation is conveyed. Frege thinks this third thought is 'just lightly suggested' rather than expressed, and Neale agrees with him on this, saying that this third thought is not a proposition expressed but rather an implicature. Like these examples, and more obviously so, an utterance of (10a) expresses a sequence of propositions, rather than a single complex conjunctive proposition, and the analysis is also that the cause–consequence relation constitutes an implicature rather than a development of a logical form into a proposition expressed (explicature).

13   Interestingly, 'after all' and 'you see' can apparently occur comfortably in a 'but'-conjunction:

> (i)   She failed the exam but, after all, she's been unwell all year.
> (ii) He has the qualifications but, you see, he doesn't get on with the boss.

Blakemore (1987: 125–41) suggests that, on its denial of expectation use, 'but' is not a coordinating conjunction at all, but a (non-truth-conditional) discourse connective; if this is right, each of (i) and (ii) consists of two processing units and it is not surprising that explanation-indicating devices can be acceptably employed.

14   I do not mean to imply that, in contrast with the conjunction examples, the juxtaposed cases are inevitably treated as two processing units, each independently satisfying the optimal relevance criterion. All the examples considered in the text do seem to function as effectively two utterances, but one can conceive of cases where they might function conjunctively, so be treated as a single unit, and of other cases where the first one might have a scene-setting, background-giving role, such that its purpose is essentially as a bit of context against which the second is to be processed.

15   It is certainly not the case that all of the adversative relations that can be expressed by the use of 'but' can also be achieved by 'and'-enrichment. Kitis (1995) discusses examples involving two apparently contrasting clauses which are nevertheless interpreted differently depending on the presence of 'and' or 'but':

> (i)   Her husband is in hospital and she is seeing other men.
> (ii) Her husband is in hospital but she is seeing other men.

The difference here is explainable in terms of the conjunctive nature of (i), a single processing unit, and the non-conjunctive nature of the denial-of-expectation 'but' in (ii). While the speaker of (i) communicates an attitude of surprise/outrage that the two conjuncts in (i) are true together, the speaker of (ii) suggests that the inference that one might have drawn from the first segment, that she is having a miserable time, is illegitimate. See Blakemore and Carston (1999) for more discussion of these cases.

In the course of a discussion of epistemic modality, Papafragou (1997) mentions two examples where replacing 'but' by 'and' results in unacceptability:

> (iii) He may be a university professor, but he sure is dumb.
> (iv) ? He may be a university professor and he sure is dumb.

An explanation of this difference remains to be given but, again, it seems highly likely that the conjunctive nature of 'and' as opposed to the non-conjunctive nature of the 'but' here will enter into the account.

16   Bar-Lev and Palacas (1980) also give the following pair of examples:

> (i)   There are his footsteps: he's been here recently.
> (ii) There are his footsteps and he's been here recently.

The conclusion, or logical consequence, relation which can be understood to hold for (i), but not for (ii), is yet another distinct case from the, broadly speaking, 'elaborative', or amplificatory, relations I am discussing in this section. I considered this case at length in Carston (1993). Again, the observation that 'and'-conjunctions comprise a single processing unit plays a crucial role; the other component of the explanation concerns the fact that the logical consequence relation is an inferential one and inferential relations, quite generally, hold between distinct processing units. It follows that a conjunction unit may function, as a whole, as a premise in an argument, or, as a whole, as a conclusion in an argument, but that it cannot communicate a premise–conclusion relation as holding between its constituent propositions.

17   Coherence theorists generally assume that there is a fixed set of discourse relations (for instance, cause, reason, enabler, evidence, justification, specification, exemplification, restatement, etc.) which play a central role in the coherence of discourses and texts, and, therefore, in judgements of the acceptability or well-formedness of texts. There are various attempts to provide a (usually hierarchical) taxonomy of these, with results varying from four basic relations to several hundred of a more fine-grained sort (see, for instance, Sanders, Spooren and Noordman 1992, 1993; Hovy and Maier 1994). Lascarides and Asher (1993) provide a more formal treatment of some of the these relations, integrating defeasible rules of discourse relation assignment (specifically, narration, background, result, explanation, elaboration) with the discourse structure building mechanisms of the DRT framework.

Some theorists assume that the identification of discourse relations in a text is a crucial aspect of understanding it (for instance, Hobbs 1979, 1983; Mann and Thompson 1986, 1988). Blakemore (1997a, 2001) is critical of these approaches, disputing both the possibility of finding any definitive set of coherence relations and the need for recovery of propositions expressing these relations in understanding a discourse. She shows that the understanding of an utterance or discourse depends, not on the classification of the coherence relations it exhibits, but on how it achieves relevance. For an interesting discussion of the different goals and predictions of coherence theory and relevance theory, see Giora (1997) and Wilson (1998a).

18   While the elaboration relations discussed in this section are precluded by 'and'-conjunction, this is not the case for all those subtypes of the relation given in the literature. As well as 'generalization–instance' and 'whole–part', Mann and Thompson (1986) mention 'set–member', 'process–step' and 'object–attribute', respectively exemplified by the following:

(i)   I love to collect classic automobiles. My favourite car is my 1988 Duryea.
(ii)   It's time to make the cake. I start by taking out the milk and eggs.
(iii) I'm Officer Jordan. I was born in 1952 and I joined the police force in 1970.

Arguably, each of these conjoins quite happily with 'and' into a single unit and seems to preserve the relation in question. I draw two lessons from this. First, there is still some way to go in giving the full account of 'and'-conjunctions. Second, this may well be just another indication of the arbitrary nature of the sets of relations drawn up by the coherence theorists and of the labels the different relations are given; motivating the relations is an ongong concern (see Knott and Dale 1994).

19   The use of a variety of different punctuation marks across the juxtaposed cases (whether full stops, colons, semicolons, etc.) is a rough indication of some of the different relations that hold between the two units. See Nunberg (1990) for some ideas about the sort of information communicated by these marks.

20   Lloyd (1989, chapter 8) makes the case for what he calls a *narrative psychodynamics*, that is, for narrative with its characteristic temporal sequentiality as a basic structure of cognition, whose basic connective is 'and then'. He develops this idea in the context of

a discussion of the properties of human thought which distinguish it from logical ideals of rational thought, and writes of us posing to ourselves an urgent 'what next?' question, seeking plot, rather than proof. This idea is worth exploring further, but I can't do that here.

21 Iconic representation involves a pictorial element, which makes it not wholly conceptual or descriptive; there is a degree of isomorphism between the representation and what it represents, usually a second-order relation between (a) the relations between the external entities, and (b) the relations between their corresponding internal representations (see Recanati 1993: 113). Iconicity (naturalness) of linguistic form is supported in functionalist literature on syntax; see especially Haiman (1983, 1985, 1994), and for useful discussion of the role of iconicity in the formalist/functionalist debate, Newmeyer (1998, chapter 3). More directly relevant to pragmatics, Sweetser (1990: 87–93) discusses iconicity at the cognitive level, which inevitably enters into language use.

22 Just as the submaxim of manner concerning orderliness in the narration of events is subsumed by the processing effort considerations that are fundamental to relevance-theoretic pragmatics, so too are the other manner submaxims, of brevity and clarity, at least to the extent that these make correct predictions. As discussed in section 3.3, the orderliness maxim gets it wrong in a number of cases of juxtaposed utterances, and brevity may be sacrificed, if the more succinct of two possibilities requires more processing effort than the longer option, for instance, 'condiments' versus 'salt and pepper'.

23 Although syntactically conjunctive, it may well be that what utterances of this sort express is two distinct propositions rather than a single conjunctive proposition. This position is argued for by Iten (1998, 2000, forthcoming); see also relevant discussion of multiple-proposition analyses in section 2.3.2 of chapter 2.

24 It is worth noting that Schiffrin (1986), who investigates the use of 'and' in a wide range of kinds of discourse, using mostly naturally occurring data, comes to a conclusion that supports the idea that 'and' has no linguistic semantics distinct from its syntactic conjoining function: 'I show that *and* is used in everyday discourse to build idea structure and to continue speakers' actions. Although both findings support a minimalist semantics for *and*, they also suggest that the truth-functional meaning of *and* bears less on its use in discourse than does its grammatical role' (Schiffrin 1986: 41).

4

The Pragmatics of Negation

Thus for every thought there is a contradictory thought; we acknowledge the falsity of a thought by admitting the truth of its contradictory. The sentence that expresses the contradictory thought is formed from the expression of the original thought by means of a negative word.

The negative word or syllable often seems to be more closely united to part of that sentence, e.g. the predicate. This may lead us to think that what is negated is the content, not of the whole sentence, but just of this part.

(Frege 1918b/77: 48)

In the previous chapter, a number of possible semantic-pragmatic analyses were considered: according to two of these, the semantics of the linguistic system supplies the full understood content of the element in question, while according to two others, much of the work of constructing the intended meaning is left to pragmatics. These four general options can be summarized as follows:

1   semantic ambiguity with pragmatic disambiguation;
2   rich semantic univocality with selective pragmatic cancellation (Cohen's approach);
3   minimal univocal semantics with conversational implicature (the Gricean approach);
4   minimal univocal semantics with pragmatic enrichment at the level of explicit content (the relevance-theoretic approach).

In this chapter, I look again at these approaches and at some further possibilities. I will focus on the multiple understandings of negated sentences in natural language. Trying to find an adequate account of how negation works has taxed many minds over the centuries. Though the problem remains unsolved, the analyses that it has spawned, and the arguments mounted to support them, are illuminating. My main aim here is to explore more fully the sorts of analytic options that arise as a result of recognizing the existence of two interacting sources of meaning: the semantic properties of the linguistic code and the rich inferential resources of the human mind. This latter, I shall continue to insist, is standardly much underestimated in accounts of verbal communication, including accounts of negation. Again, I will favour an approach on which a weak univocal semantics is pragmatically enriched in interpretation. Many utterances of negative sentences will be shown to require pragmatic narrowing, akin to that already seen for 'and'-conjunctions, and some negative utterances involve a tacitly (that is, not linguistically indicated) metarepresentational use, whose pragmatic recovery brings with it a further element of pragmatic enrichment of the proposition expressed.

4.1 Some Data and Some Distinctions

In accordance with the literature on the topic, I take it that there are (at least) the following two distinctions involved in the understanding of utterances of negative sentences: (a) the scope distinction, and (b) the representational distinction.

4.1.1 The scope distinction

It is well known that the sentence in (1a) may be understood in the two distinct ways given in (1b) and (1c):

(1)   a. All the children haven't passed the exam.
      b. Not all the children have passed the exam.
      c. None of the children have passed the exam.

While (1b) leaves open the possibility that some have passed the exam, this is excluded from the stronger (1c). Standard logical notations for these two interpretations are given in (2) and (3), respectively:

(2) $-(\forall x[Cx \rightarrow Px])$
    or: $-$[every x: x child] (x passed the exam)

(3) $\forall x[Cx \rightarrow -Px]$
    or: [every x: x child] $-$ (x passed the exam)

The difference lies in whether the 'not' is understood as having wide scope over the sentence (specifically, in this case, over the universal quantifier 'all'), as in (2), or as having narrower scope (specifically just over the VP 'pass the exam'), as in (3).

Discussions of this duality have often been enmeshed with that other deeply explored phenomenon of 'presupposition', in particular, the presupposition of existence carried by the following sort of example:

(4)   The present king of France is not bald.

This may be understood in two different ways, apparently depending, again, on the breadth of the scope of the 'not':

(5) a. The present king of France is non-bald (he has an excellent crop of curls).
     b. It's not the case that the king of France is bald (since there is no king of France).

In (5a) the 'presupposition' that there is a present king of France is preserved, while in (5b) it is cancelled. In logical notation these are, respectively:

(6) a. $(\imath x\ Kx) - Bx$
         or: [the x: x king of France] $- (x$ is bald)

     b. $-[(\imath x\ Kx)\ Bx]$
         or: $-$[the x: x king of France] $(x$ is bald)[1]

As widely remarked, interpretation (a) is by far the more natural (the more accessible) of the two. The (b) understanding, though certainly possible, is highly marked; it requires quite a special context or some sort of follow-up explanation, such as that given in brackets in (5b).

4.1.2 The representational distinction

This is perhaps more familiarly known as the object language/metalanguage, or use/mention, distinction. The following two sentences can be understood in two distinct ways as indicated by the follow-up material in (a) and (b):

(7) a. We didn't see the hippopotamuses. But we did see the rhinoceroses.
     b. We didn't see the hippopotamuses. We saw the hippopotami.

(8) a. She's not pleased with the outcome. She's angry that it didn't go her way.
     b. She's not pleased with the outcome. She's thrilled to bits.

In the (a) cases, the predicate falling within the scope of the negation is being used literally, it is taken to be descriptive of some aspect of the world, and the follow-up statement, also taken descriptively, is consistent with the prior negation. The logical structure of the utterances (ignoring scope distinctions) is, schematically: Not P; Q. In the (b) cases, on the other hand, such a descriptive understanding, would lead to a contradiction. In (7b) it's being claimed, first, that we didn't see a certain set of animals and, then, that we did see them. In (8b) it's being claimed that she doesn't have some property F ('being pleased') and then that she does have some property G ('being thrilled') that entails her having property F. The logical structure of these utterances (again ignoring matters of scope) is, roughly: Not P; P.

But, of course, the (b) cases are not understood in this way; they are taken not to be incomprehensible self-contradictions, but to be communicating an objection to some non-descriptive aspect of the material falling within the scope of the negation. In (7b), the plural suffix for 'hippopotamus' is being objected to as wrong; in (8b), the adjective 'pleased' is being objected to as too weak or understated a way of describing the subject's state of mind. In other words, the material over which the negation has its effect is taken to be mentioned rather than used by the utterer; it is a case of metarepresentational use, of representation by resemblance, rather than of descriptive use (see appendix 1 for these terms). The contradiction is blocked because the representation is, as it were, in quotation marks, sealed off from inter-action with the propositional content of the follow-up comment. This may be pictured, schematically and roughly, as: Not 'R'; S, where R and S are sentences, and S entails R.

While the first distinction, the scope distinction, concerns *how much* or *which part* of the sentence falls under the mantle of the negation, the second concerns the nature of the material that so falls, whether it is being used descriptively or metarep-resentationally. Since we have here two two-way distinctions, there are, in principle at least, four ways in which a given negated sentence may be understood:

(a)   narrow-scope descriptive
(b)   narrow-scope metarepresentational (mention)
(c)   wide-scope descriptive
(d)   wide-scope metarepresentational (mention)

The following examples, all involving the sentence 'All of the kids didn't pass the exam' (though sometimes with quite marked accentuation), with different sorts of follow-up clause, are intended to instantiate the four possible interpretations, (a)–(d), respectively:

(9)   a. All of the kids didn't pass the exam. They will all have to resit it.
          (The property that the entire set of children is said to lack is the prop-
          erty of having passed the exam.)

      b. All of the kids didn't PASS the exam. They all got A GRADES.
          [Upper case roughly indicating accented syllables.]
          (It is not sufficiently informative/appropriate/relevant to say just that
          they passed the exam; they in fact got A grades, which entails that they
          passed it.)

      c. All of the kids didn't pass the exam. Some of them failed quite badly.
          (What is denied is that the entire set of children have the property of
          having passed the exam; some, at least, failed it.)

      d. All of the KIDS didn't pass the exam. All the CHILDREN passed the
          exam.
          (An objection is made to the use of the colloquial word 'kids' which
          occurs in the subject of the negative sentence.)

So it does seem that all four possibilities arise and the two distinctions are real and distinct from each other.

Consider, however, a further case:

> e. All of the KIDS didn't pass the exam; there weren't any KIDS taking it; it was just for the mature students.

The ground for the use of the negation here is someone's mistaken assumption (pre-supposition) that there was a group of children who sat the exam in question. Which of the four cases does this represent? The negation has wide scope but is the material within its scope being used descriptively or metarepresentationally? Opinion in the literature is divided: for some it is just a case of ordinary wide-scope negation providing evidence that the semantics of negation is fundamentally wide in scope. For others, it has the same special, marked, 'meta-' feel to it that cases (b) and (d) have, and is to be treated as similarly involving metarepresentation. Much depends here on the relation assumed to hold between the proposition expressed by the negative sentence and the (existential) proposition that some children sat the exam. This issue comes to the fore with sentences of the form: 'The F is not G', which have received such enormous philosophical attention. Let's try out the four possibilities raised by the two distinctions on one of these:

> (10) a. The president of New Zealand is not foolish. He is an intelligent man.
> (Narrow-scope descriptive: what's being denied is his having the property of being foolish.)
>
> b. The president of New Zealand is not FOOLISH. He's a complete IDIOT.
> (Narrow-scope metarepresentational: the weakness of the adjective 'foolish' in describing the president is being objected to, and the follow-up provides a stronger predicate which entails it.)
>
> c. The president of New Zealand is not foolish. There is no president of New Zealand.
> (Wide-scope descriptive: one of the logical implications of the subject of the unnegated sentence is denied: that there is a president of New Zealand.)
>
> d. The PRESIDENT of New Zealand is not foolish. There IS no PRESIDENT of New Zealand. (or: The PRIME MINISTER of New Zealand may be.)
> (Wide-scope metarepresentational: an objection to an utterance of the unnegated sentence is being made on the grounds that it 'presupposes' something false: that New Zealand has a president.)

In this example, the two wide-scope possibilities seem to be falling together. Some, in fact, would say that the third logical possibility (c), that of wide-scope descriptive negation, does not arise for this sort of case, that the unnaturalness of this 'pre-supposition'-cancelling case must be captured by the so-called 'metalinguistic use' of the negation operator (in my terms, the mentioned or metarepresented nature of the material falling under the scope of the negation). Now, it is clear from the quan-tified cases that there is a wide/narrow scope distinction to be made. I hope it is also clear that presupposition cancellation (still relying on a fairly intuitive notion of 'presupposition') is not confined to existential or factive entailments that emanate from *subject* position. Consider the examples in (11):

(11) a. Mary hasn't gone to meet the king of France.
         (There is no current king of France.)
     b. My neighbour doesn't regret selling her Saab.
         (She didn't sell it in the end.)
     c. I haven't stopped being an academic.
         (I never was one.)

The definite description in the *predicate* of (11a) is responsible for the existential 'presupposition'; (11b) is standardly taken (by those who favour presuppositions) to presuppose 'My neighbour sold her Saab' and (11c) to presuppose 'I have been an academic', both arising from the predicates of their respective sentences. Assuming that the 'not' in each of these cases negates the predicate (so it is inter-nal, narrow in scope), the question raised by (9e) and (10c) arises here too: are these cases of ordinary descriptive negation or instances of metarepresentational negation? The real issue is whether or not descriptive negation (whether wide or narrow in scope) is inevitably presupposition-preserving. If so, either these presup-positional elements can only be cancelled via metarepresentational use or there are different senses or uses of 'not', such that one is presupposition-preserving and the other is presupposition-cancelling. So there are, potentially, three ambiguities here: wide vs. narrow scope, presupposition-cancelling vs. presupposition-preserving, descriptive vs. metarepresentational. That makes for eight logical possibilities in interpreting a negative sentence, although, as we have seen, some of these seem to fall together.

Finally, another sort of example to bear in mind, as we look at treatments of negation in the next sections, is the case of adverbially modified predicates:

(12) a. Fred didn't scrub the potatoes.
     b. Fred didn't scrub the potatoes with sand-paper.
     c. Fred didn't scrub the potatoes with sand-paper in the bath-tub.
     d. Fred didn't scrub the potatoes with sand-paper in the bath-tub at
         midnight.

Depending on the particular pattern of stress in each case and on follow-up clauses, different constituents in these may be understood as being the focus of the nega-tion. If, as has been claimed, the unmarked pattern of stress is at the end of a sen-tence, there is a preferred understanding in these cases; for instance, in (12c) the unmarked understanding would be that while Fred did scrub the potatoes with sand-paper he didn't do this in the bath-tub. However, virtually any other constituent can be the negated constituent, given an appropriate heavy stress, so that all of these sentences can receive a range of interpretations; the more constituents they have, the more the possibilities. Does this make them *n*-ways ambiguous, *n* equal to the number of constituents?

In what immediately follows, I will set aside the clear metalinguistic cases, such as (7b) and (8b); whatever the best way to characterize them may be, it is standardly seen as not a matter of the semantics of the language. Any bit of linguistic form (from a single speech sound through to whole texts) can be used in this metalinguistic way; I will look at this use of negation with metarepresented material in its scope in section 4.4. For the moment, the focus is on the scope distinction and the 'presupposition'-preserving/cancelling distinction. The question to kick off with is whether these distinctions are encoded into the linguistic system as lexical or structural ambiguities, or they arise from the way in which humans use a linguistically univocal 'not' in communication. My aim is to dispose of the ambiguity option, so as to concentrate on the range of ways in which an account in terms of a univocal semantics with a heavy contribution from pragmatics has been envisaged.

4.2 Semantic Ambiguity Analyses

4.2.1 Lexical ambiguity and/or scope ambiguity?

There are two ambiguity possibilities:

(a) 'Not' is *lexically* ambiguous, as between a sentence operator, NOT_1, and a predicate operator, NOT_2, and/or 'not' is *lexically* ambiguous as between a presupposition-preserving and a presupposition-cancelling operator.

(b) Sentences with the surface form [$_{IP}$ NP [$_{VP}$ not . . .]] are structurally ambiguous, i.e. 'not' is an element that can take up one of two positions in some underlying level of logico-syntactic structure.

The Russellian position (supported by Grice 1981/89b, and Neale 1990) is one of scope ambiguity, as in examples (5) and (6) above. This is a *logical* ambiguity and it is not clear that it amounts to what we nowadays mean by *linguistic* ambiguity; Russell did not entertain a semantics/pragmatics distinction, so correlatively made no distinction between (conventional, encoded) semantic content and the proposition expressed by an utterance.[2] Van der Sandt (1988), however, does see the approach as entailing a linguistic ambiguity; in a discussion of Russell's theory of positive and negative sentences containing definite descriptions he says:

> That theory was the first proposal to use the syntactic notion of scope to solve a problem that was regarded as presuppositional by Frege before him, and by many

others after him. . . . Russell's analysis has the merit of solving the logical problem posed by non-denoting terms [e.g. 'The current king of France'] without affecting classical logic. *The price is that two logical forms are postulated for sentences that, according to many, are not ambiguous but merely admit of different uses.* Furthermore Russell's analysis does not explain why the reading with narrow scope for the negation is strongly preferred and the other reading strongly marked. (Van der Sandt 1988: 168–9, my emphasis)

The objections raised against ambiguity accounts in the next section apply only to a construal of the scope ambiguity as a property of the language system itself; merely being capable of being used to express two distinct propositions does not make a sentential form a case of linguistic ambiguity (given the possibility of pragmatic involvement). Recall, in this regard, the pragmatic account of the many possible propositions expressed by 'and'-conjunctions in the previous chapter.

Karttunen and Peters (1979) clearly take an ambiguity position, distinguishing what they call 'ordinary negation' and 'contradiction negation'; the first takes as its domain just the proposition expressed by the corresponding positive sentence, the second pertains to the total meaning of the target sentence. For instance, both (11b) and (11c) above are cases of contradiction negation, which, according to Karttunen and Peters, is responsible for denying a conventional implicature (a presupposition, according to other frameworks) in each case, carried by the verb 'regret' in (11b), and by the verb 'stop' in (11c). On their account, using the formal system of Montague, the grammar of the language has distinct rules for the formation and the semantics of each of the two types of negative sentence. Like Russell, Karttunen and Peters assume a bivalent logic and their distinction is essentially a matter of scope.

Many of those who assume that natural-language semantics is presuppositional employ a three-valued logic, the third value usually being 'neither true nor false', to capture the intuition that you can't assign a truth value to a sentence whose presupposition is not fulfilled; following Strawson (1950, 1952), 'the current king of France is wise' is neither true nor false because its existential presupposition is not met. These sorts of accounts generally posit two negation operators, with distinct (three-valued) truth tables, one for presupposition-preserving negation, the other for presupposition-cancelling negation. (For discussion and references, see Gazdar (1979: 64–6.) A slightly different three-valued approach is taken by the presuppositionalist, Pieter Seuren (1985, 1988). He distinguishes two kinds of falsity, minimal falsity and radical falsity (which arises when a presupposition is not fulfilled) and, correlatively, a 'minimal' negation operator, which preserves presupposition, and a 'radical' negation operator, which does not. Finally, Horn (1985, 1989), who is anti-presuppositionalist and advocates a bivalent logic, can also be understood as holding an ambiguity position. Though he talks of a duality of *use* of negation, he characterizes metalinguistic negation as if it is semantically distinct from descriptive negation (see discussion in section 4.4.2).

I don't believe the word 'not' is lexically ambiguous, nor that negative sentences inevitably have two syntactic logical forms in which 'not' takes different scopes. Without looking at the detail of particular ambiguity proposals, I shall try, in the next section, to amass considerations that weigh against ambiguity, but, as will be seen, it is difficult to find anything in the way of definitive counterevidence.[3]

4.2.2   Arguments against ambiguity

The first and most popular argument against a *lexical* ambiguity is the argument from one-to-one translatability. This has become, by now, a fairly standard argument to trot out against putative ambiguities, one that I have used myself in arguing against the semantic ambiguity of 'and' (Carston 1994a). As Gazdar (1979: 65–6) points out, lexical ambiguity is a language-specific phenomenon, that is, a lexical ambiguity in one language is typically not retained by a translation into another language; consider, for instance, English 'ring', 'pen', 'board', 'bank', 'fan', each of which are translated by two distinct forms in other languages. This gives us a test to apply in trying to determine whether a linguistic expression that has two distinct interpretations should be considered linguistically ambiguous or not. For instance, while the two understandings of 'ring' are translated by two different forms in other languages, the various different interpretations of a 'P and Q' sentence are not, suggesting that the source of the diversity in this case is pragmatic.

Care is needed in applying the test, however, since it is not the case that if a single form in one language is translated by more than one form in another language, the form in the first language is necessarily ambiguous. For instance, the term 'brother-in-law' in English may be translated into Russian by one of several forms, depending on whether the property in question is one of being a sister's husband, a wife's brother, or a husband's brother, and there are languages which have a single form for the relations expressed in English by the two words 'sibling' and 'cousin'. So the line of reasoning is not that if a single form in L1 has two understandings and these are translated into L2 by two forms, then the form in L1 is necessarily ambiguous; no decision can be made between ambiguity and univocality (sense-generality) on that sort of basis. Rather, the reasoning is that if a single form in L1 has two understandings and this form is translated into all/most other languages by a single form which also evinces the same understandings, then the form is not linguistically ambiguous, but is sense-general as regards the two understandings. The wide-scope/narrow-scope distinction and the presupposition-preserving/presupposition-cancelling distinction, in the interpretation of negative sentences, are found across a wide range of languages, quite possibly all, and in each language, there is a single form used to express these different meanings (see discussion in Horn 1989: 366). So it looks very much as if there are not distinct lexical items which just happen (by accident as it were) to have the same phonological (and graphological) form, that is, homonyms, but rather that the interpretive distinctions arise quite systematically due to perfectly general cognitive/pragmatic factors acting on a single lexical item.

Just about everyone who mentions this translation argument finds it a compelling one, for instance, Burton-Roberts (1989b: 39), Van der Sandt (1988: 91), and Horn (1989: 366). Even Seuren (1988: 222), who favours an ambiguity account, takes the translation point very seriously and, on that basis, concedes that the sort of ambiguity that characterizes 'not' is very different from other cases of lexical ambiguity. But just how strong is this translation argument? I think it is a pretty good argument against the idea that there are really two unrelated homonymous lexical items, 'not₁' and 'not₂', but I find it difficult to believe that this is what is being claimed by ambiguists. Homonymy entails unrelatedness of senses (or, at least, that no synchronic sense connection is made by native speakers). But would anyone really want to claim of the different interpretations of 'not' that they are unrelated, that native speakers do not see any connection among them (that the meanings of 'not' are discrete in a comparable way to the two senses of 'ring', the sound and the circle). I assume that the only lexical ambiguity position which could be up for consideration is one of polysemy, that is, that there is a single lexical item 'not' which has two or more (related) senses. But polysemies may show up fairly systematically across languages, since universal properties of conceptualization may lead to certain basic senses or uses of words being extended in reasonably predictable ways.[4] So the translation argument is unable to distinguish between a case of polysemy and a case of monosemy (that is, a single general sense with different pragmatic manifestations in use). This, then, removes an obstacle to the ambiguity case, provided the ambiguist is prepared to accept a polysemy analysis rather than a homonymy.

So we must look for further arguments against viewing 'not' as an ambiguous lexical item. In fact, though, virtually all the literature against the ambiguity of negation employs tests geared to distinguishing homonymy and monosemy, so this is not going to be a straightforward process. Van der Sandt (1988, chapter 4) and Atlas (1989, chapter 2) discuss the famous tests from Zwicky and Sadock (1975) for separating cases of ambiguity from cases of sense-generality, with a view to applying them to negative sentences which have two different interpretive possibilities. One of these is the VP-anaphor test and the reasoning behind it is as follows: if a sentence is ambiguous, then in a conjunction in which this sentence is the first conjunct, VP-pronominalization in the second conjunct can take place only if the interpretation assigned to the anaphoric expression is the same as that assigned to the antecedent. So crossed interpretations, that is interpretations on which the antecedent receives one interpretation and the anaphoric expression another, are excluded. If it turns out that apparently crossed interpretations are all right, it must be that the sentence in question is vague or unspecified, rather than ambiguous, with respect to the two interpretations.

Let's see how the test works for a fairly clear case of each of homonymy, polysemy and sense-generality. First, as a clear case of homonymy, we'll take 'bank': 'bank₁' = financial institution; 'bank₂' = side of a river.

(13) a. John went to a bank.
      b. John went to a bank and {so did Bill.
                                    {Bill did so too.

Of the four conceivable interpretations in (14), only (14a) and (14d), arise naturally ((b) and (c) might be possible in contrived cases of jokes and verbal games):

(14) a. John went to a bank$_1$ and Bill went to a bank$_1$.
  b. John went to a bank$_1$ and Bill went to a bank$_2$.
  c. John went to a bank$_2$ and Bill went to a bank$_1$.
  d. John went to a bank$_2$ and Bill went to a bank$_2$.

The 'crossed' understandings are ruled out, which is what we would expect given the ambiguity of 'bank' and the fact that the VP anaphor gets its *sense* from its antecedent: 'went to a bank'.

Now, take a case of a sense which is clearly general as regards some feature of meaning, for instance, 'neighbour', which is unspecified for gender:

(15) I've come to depend on my neighbour and so has Jane on hers.

Here it seems that all four understandings are possible; that is, the crossed understandings, on which my neighbour and Jane's are known to be of different gender, are fine. Gender is not a feature of meaning that the VP anaphor picks up from its antecedent, which reflects the fact that 'neighbour' is a single lexical item unspecified for gender.

Third, consider the test applied to two (of the few) cases which are generally agreed to be polysemous: 'model', which has the two related senses 'example to imitate' and 'person who poses for artists', and 'glass', which has a container and a content sense:

(16) a. My sister Rachel has always been a model for me, and so she was for the sculpture class.
  b. When we went out, Richard bought me three glasses and so did Sally.

Intuitions may not be so sharp here, but I don't think that crossed readings are possible for either of these; in (16a), Rachel is understood as being either a fine example in both conjuncts or as posing for artistic reasons, and in (16b) Richard and Sally both bought three drinks or three glass containers for drinks. If this is right, polysemy falls in with homonymy in precluding mixed readings and, on these grounds at least, the test is available for adjudicating between a polysemous and a monosemous (sense-general) analysis of 'not'.

This test and others, such as one involving conjunction reduction, have been used successfully to settle some contentious cases; for instance, whether a feature of 'purposiveness' is part of the semantics of verbs like 'cut', 'hit' and 'knock over':

(17) a. John cut the chicken and, in the process, also his thumb.
  b. Enraged, Brian knocked down his wife and also an innocent bystander.
  c. Pat hit the wall and so did Mary.

In each of these cases, crossed understandings seem all right; for instance, in (17c) Pat can be understood as having purposely hit the wall and Mary as having done so accidentally, and vice versa. So the test tells us that the verb is not semantically specified for purposiveness (though this can be built in pragmatically).

Unfortunately, negation is not a straightforward case for these tests. As is often pointed out, there is a relation of privative opposition between the two scope interpretations:

(18)   a.   [Every x: x a child] – (x pass the exam)   entails:
            –[Every x: x a child] (x pass the exam)
       b.   [The x: x king of France] – (x bald)   entails:
            –[The x: x king of France] (x bald)

This gives rise to particular problems in trying to assess the status of the different readings. Zwicky and Sadock (1975) themselves believe that their tests cannot distinguish ambiguity from sense-generality in cases of privative opposition, such as the case of the two senses of 'dog', where the one sense 'species *canis*' is entailed by the other 'male *canis*', but not vice versa. Kempson (1975) follows them in this and claims that it is therefore impossible to establish empirically whether or not there is a genuine semantic ambiguity in a case like this. If that is true, it must also be impossible to establish by these means that negation is or is not ambiguous. Atlas (1977, 1989: 48–52), on the other hand, argues against the alleged privative opposition problem and for the applicability of the tests to the negation case. He considers the following example:

(19)   The King of France is not wise (since France is not a monarchy) and the same thing goes for the Queen of England (who is a typical Windsor).

The bracketed material shows the interpretation intended in each case: the first conjunct is to be taken as wide in scope, cancelling the existential implication (presupposition), and the second as narrow in scope, preserving the existential implication (presupposition). Atlas (1989: 74–5) claims to find the crossed non-factive/factive readings quite acceptable, thereby gaining support for his view that negation is sense-general rather than ambiguous. Like van der Sandt (1988: 91), my intuitions fail me with this example; too many factors seem to intervene. Without the bracketed material there is clearly one interpretation that comes to mind first and that is the one on which the two conjuncts are understood as preserving the existential presupposition, but this is because this is the much preferred reading for pragmatic reasons. The most I feel able to say is that, assuming the possibility at all of the presupposition-cancelling understanding of the first conjunct, the crossed reading is not obviously ruled out here, but it is certainly mighty weird.

The test isn't any more decisive if we try to run it on a case where different scopes of negation are at issue, without affecting anything presuppositional:

(20)   a.   All the girls didn't pass the exam and the same goes for all the boys.
       b.   Not all the girls passed the exam and none of the boys passed it.
       c.   None of the girls passed the exam and not all of the boys passed it.
       d.   All the girls didn't pass the exam and all the boys didn't pass the exam.

The logically possible crossed readings of (20a) are given in (20b) and (20c); I find it difficult, if not impossible, to get these readings of (20a). But note that it is also quite difficult to get crossed readings from the unreduced conjunction in (20d), which does not require sameness of sense. What this shows is that there is a general problem here in separating out bare semantic intuitions from those having to do with strongly preferred understandings: uncrossed parallel readings of conjuncts are generally preferred and this tendency increases when the differences involve logical scope relations such as those between negation and quantifiers, which are notoriously hard on people's processing capacities. So, again, the test as applied to negated sentences is inconclusive. This may simply reflect a more general problem underlying Zwicky and Sadock's tests: they conflate sentential meaning with truth conditions, and their concept of an acceptable reading or understanding seems to be more a matter of appropriateness/naturalness than of semantic possibility. In short, there is plenty of room in there for pragmatic interference, so that a crossed reading could be rejected on grounds of pragmatic inaccessibility rather than semantic impossibility.[5]

At this point, it is tempting to turn to Grice's Modified Occam's Razor (MOR) and suggest that if we can give a pragmatic account of what is going on, that is, if we can derive the understandings of negative sentences by pragmatic inference from a single semantics, then that is preferable to positing two or more senses. As mentioned in chapter 2 (section 2.6), however, it is not at all obvious that MOR is a valid principle in a cognitively based pragmatics, in which processing effort plays an important part. So for want of strong argument but no lack of strong conviction, I appeal to pre-theoretic intuitions about the meaning of 'not', which, I think, come down pretty unanimously for a single sense. Only once enmeshed in theory (and logical theory at that) does the idea of an ambiguity in 'not' take hold. I note also that, in his most recent work, Seuren, a staunch defender of the reality of semantic presupposition (as distinct from mere entailment), has abandoned the view that natural-language 'not' is ambiguous and has argued instead for a univocal semantics of 'not' as a rejection operator (see Seuren 2000). This follows in part from a general distinction he makes between a *logic* for natural language (in which there are two (or more) negation operators) and a cognitively oriented *semantics*.

In the next section, I look at some analyses that assume a univocal semantics for 'not' (usually of the standard bivalent truth-functional sort) and derive other interpretations pragmatically. As soon as one starts to look to a pragmatic account, the question arises as to which of the readings, if any, is to be taken as the semantics and which derived pragmatically. Given two understandings or readings, R+ and R−, of a linguistic form, L, there would appear to be three possibilities:

1   R+ is semantically encoded in L and R− is derived pragmatically from R+.
2   R− is semantically encoded in L and R+ is derived pragmatically from R−.
3   Neither R+ nor R− is semantically encoded in L; rather, both are derived pragmatically from the encoded content of L, whatever that is.

Examples of all three of these proposals will be shown in what follows; I will try to assess the arguments presented for each, before settling on the only position that,

I believe, is fully coherent and accommodates both the range of data given above and the intuitions regarding preferred and marked (echoic) understandings.

4.3 Strong Pragmatic Analyses

4.3.1 Analyses in the Gricean spirit

The rather odd title for this section is motivated by a disparity between standard assumptions about a Gricean account and the actual account Grice gives of sentences of the form 'The F is not G' in Grice (1981/89b). I will consider the latter in the next section. Here, I look at what, before reading Grice (1981/89b), I took to be the Gricean account of negation and what many others too have assumed to be a standard Gricean approach. Following the methodological dictates of MOR, the account favours a univocal weak semantics and a pragmatic derivation of the stronger understanding in terms of conversational implicature.

Atlas (1989) characterizes what he takes to be a Gricean account of the wide/narrow scope difference as follows:

> The Gricean view . . . permits a negative utterance semantically interpreted as a sentence negation to [conversationally] implicate a predicate negation that entails the existential presupposition. (A negative utterance semantically interpreted as a predicate negation would straightforwardly entail it.) And of course there are contexts in which no implicature of the sentential negation is intended. Letting R− stand for the sentential negation, R+ for the predicate negation, the function PRAG for the Gricean inference, and K for kinds of context, we may abbreviate the Gricean claims by the formulae:
> PRAG (K*, R−) = R+
> PRAG (K**, R−) = R−
>
> (Atlas 1989: 143–4, notation modified)

He is principally concerned with example (4), repeated here:

(21)   The present king of France is not bald.

The Gricean analysis of the internal negation understanding that he assumes is as follows:

(22)   what is said: $-([\iota x: x \text{ king of France}] (x \text{ bald}))$
       what is conversationally implicated: $[\iota x: x \text{ king of France}] - (x \text{ bald})$

The implicature entails the existence of a unique king of France and so preserves (or reinstates) the 'existential presupposition', although the semantics (logical form) is 'presupposition'-cancelling. Atlas (1989: 143) gives a sketchy account of how the inferential account based on Gricean maxims of informativeness and relevance might go; I won't look at this here.

Let's briefly consider how this general approach applies to a case of the interaction of negation and quantification, which does not involve a definite description:

(23)   Everyone isn't hungry.

Here the preferred reading appears to be the wide-scope one, giving the 'Not everyone' interpretation. This may be because of the ready availability of the unambiguous lexical item 'no one', hence of a compact way of expressing the alternative: 'No one is hungry'. Assuming, in line with a Gricean analysis, that wide scope is semantically ordained for negation, there is no pragmatic adjustment to this; what is said is what is communicated:

(24)   what is said: $-([$every $x: x$ person$]$ $(x$ hungry$))$

The narrow-scope interpretation is possible and, presumably, would be pragmatically derived when the context was such that predicate negation would be the more relevant/informative, etc., interpretation.[6] In such a (special, particular) context the communication would come out as follows:

(25)   what is said: $-([$every $x: x$ person$]$ $(x$ hungry$))$
        what is implicated: $[$every $x: x$ person$]$ $-$ $(x$ hungry$)$

However, from a natural-language utterance point of view, there seems to me to be something missing from the representation of example (23), which is, one might say, a 'presupposition' that there are (exist) some entities about which one is talking. This is as much presupposed here, and in many ordinary uses of the universal, as it is in uses of a definite description. It is assumed that there is a non-empty set or domain of entities over which the quantifier ranges (as it is put). Let's assume a particular context in which the relevant domain is a group of friends at a picnic, then clearly what is communicated is that not all of *the picnickers* are hungry, or, less likely but possible, that no one in the group is hungry. Either way, there is some sort of existential 'presupposition' lurking here, to the effect that a certain group of people exist. The point is that it lies outside the scope of the negation on both of these interpretations (see relevant discussion in note 5 of this chapter).

These observations naturally carry over to 'king of France' examples. On the standard wide-scope negation interpretation of a universally quantified case the existence of some (more than one) kings of France is presupposed.

(26)   Not all of the present kings of France are bald.

The same holds, of course, for a narrow scope of negation interpretation:

(27)   None of the present kings of France is bald.
        or: All of the present kings of France are non-bald.

This is not to say that a wide-scope negation which cancelled this presupposition is impossible. If we create an even more off-the-wall variant of the famous example, we might have such a case:

> (28)   All of the present kings of France aren't bald; there aren't any present kings of France.

This underlines the observation made earlier, that narrow- versus wide-scope negation should not be equated with presupposition-preserving versus presupposition-cancelling negation (a point made forcibly by Burton-Roberts (1991, 1993/97)). It would seem, then, that there are two distinguishable pragmatic functions here: one for scope-narrowing, the other for presupposition-preservation.

The general Gricean mode of analysis of the different interpretations of negation assumes a weak, wide (widest) scope for negation and derives the stronger (narrower) understandings (including, in particular, the presupposition-preservation meaning) pragmatically. Its adherents over the years include Horn (1972, 1984a, 1988, 1989, 1992a), Kempson (1975), Boer and Lycan (1976), Gazdar (1979), Atlas (1977, 1989) and Levinson (1983, 1987a, 1988). Horn points out that there is a fairly systematic pattern of implicature where

> logically contradictory negation is pragmatically strengthened to contrary negation. This arises, for example, in the default interpretation of the following negative sentences, where neither is standardly understood as the straightforward denial of its positive counterpart:
>
> (A)   I don't like you.   (implicates that I dislike you)
> (B)   I don't think I can come.   (implicates that [I think] I can't come)
>
> (B) is an instance of so-called 'neg-raising'. The motivation for expressing each of the negative sentences in a weaker form, with the stronger understanding conveyed pragmatically, is essentially one of hedging or politeness. In such cases, as Harnish (1976: 360) says, 'the speaker wants to communicate a certain belief . . . without saying it, as if he might want to leave the "I didn't say that" bridge unburned.'   (Horn 1992a: 262)

This 'standard Gricean' account would, I assume, generalize quite naturally to the cases such as (12) above, for instance (12d) repeated here, where the scope possibilities are more numerous:

> (12d)   Fred didn't scrub the potatoes with sand-paper in the bath-tub at midnight.

This too would be taken as a case of external negation at the level of what is said and, for any case of an understanding on which the 'not' is taken to focus on some greater or smaller internal constituent, this would be captured at the level of conversational implicature: for instance, 'not (in the bath-tub)'.

It is notable that, in all of the cases discussed in this subsection, there is an entailment relation between the alleged conversational implicature and the 'what is said'; this situation always raises a question about whether the pragmatic inference really does deliver an implicature. Recall some of the criteria and tests, discussed in chapter 2, for distinguishing between implicature and pragmatic contributions to what is said: availability (to conscious awareness), functional independence, embedding in the scope of a logical operator. The application of any of these to the analyses discussed would indicate that this pragmatic inference is, in fact, constitutive of 'what is said' and so not an implicature: for instance, speakers and addressees have no conscious awareness of a weak wide-scope, presupposition-cancelling proposition, and, even with a follow-up clause explicitly denying a presupposition, they find the negative sentence highly marked; the pragmatically narrowed proposition subsumes any inferential role that could be played by the weak semantic 'what is said'; when embedded in a conditional, comparative, disjunction, etc., the presupposition-preserving understanding is just as salient as when it occurs unembedded. There will be a similar result on a relevance-theoretic derivation, involving the mutual pragmatic adjustment of explicit content and implicature (as discussed in section 2.3.4); the weak logical form of the negative sentence is pragmatically augmented so as to warrant implicatures expected in particular contexts.

The various analyses mentioned in this section have the following features in common:

1 a semantically univocal negation operator;
2 a weak, wide-scope semantics for negation;
3 a 'presupposition'-cancelling semantics, i.e. all of the logical implications of the positive sentence are suspended; the negative sentence itself has no entailments;
4 a derivation of the preferred narrower scope (and presupposition-preserving) understandings through a Gricean inferential procedure, employing one or other of the maxims, and giving rise to conversational implicatures which capture those aspects of the utterance which are understood as falling outside the scope of the negation.

These are just the analytical components one would expect of a follower of Grice, given his general position in the 1967 William James lectures on Logic and Conversation that, semantically, the natural language expressions 'not', 'and', 'or', 'if', 'all', 'some', and 'the' do not diverge from their logical operator counterparts, any other interpretations following from facts about language use and constituting conversational implicatures. However, as I shall go on to discuss now, Grice's own story has a further twist to it.

4.3.2   Grice: structural ambiguity and implicature

In his discussion of sentences of the form 'The F is G', Grice (1981/89b) follows Russell very closely. He wishes to preserve the Russellian quantificational unpacking of definite descriptions and (most significant in the present context) the *scope ambiguity* of the negation operator. First, he establishes that the most satisfactory formal counterpart of (the surface form of) the sentence 'The king of France is bald' is one employing a term-forming iota-operator: $G (\iota x.Fx)$, rather than one for which the iota-operator functions like a quantifier. His reason for preferring this notation is that there is no clear distinction in sense between the following English sentences:

(29) a. The king of France is not bald.
      b. It is not the case that the king of France is bald.

That is, despite the different surface positions of 'not', they are equally (un)suscep-tible to being interpreted as presupposition-cancelling (neither is readily understood in this way) or as presupposition-preserving (the much preferred understanding in both cases). So both are formally equivalent to $-G$ ($\iota x.Fx$), that is, a representation which, like the English sentences, masks the two scope possibilities. He continues:

> We are then committed to *the structural ambiguity* of the sentence 'The king of France is not bald'. The proposed task may now be defined as follows: On one reading 'The king of France is not bald' entails the existence of a unique king of France, on the other it does not; but in fact, without waiting for *disambiguation*, people under-stand an utterance of 'The king of France is not bald' as implying (in some fashion) the unique existence of a king of France. This is intelligible if *on one reading (the strong one), the unique existence of a king of France is entailed, on the other (the weak one), though not entailed, it is conversationally implicated.* (Grice 1981/89b: 272, my emphasis)

Much of the rest of his paper is taken up with developing a pragmatic account of how this implicature arises, employing a manner maxim of 'conversational tai-loring', which is the somewhat vague (as it should be, according to Grice) 'Facili-tate in your form of expression the appropriate reply'. Here is a brief outline of how the account goes: given the Russellian truth conditions for definite description sentences (a set of three conjuncts: there is an F, there is at most one F, whoever is F is G), there is a variety of natural-language sentences that could be used to express them, including a three-clause conjunction, such as 'There is a king of France, there is only one and he is bald'. On the basis of the manner maxim, the speaker's choice of the abbreviatory linguistic form in 'The king of France is bald', rather than a longer form involving conjunction, licenses the hearer to infer that only that one of the truth conditions which is not part of the abbreviated form is up for considera-tion (or reply). Correlatively, the speaker of the corresponding negative utterance has tailored her utterance in such a way as to indicate which of the three truth con-ditions of the positive sentence is the focus of her negation, that is, just the third one, contributed by the predicate. On that basis, the hearer can infer that she is implicating the existence of a unique F.

My main concern is to highlight a particular difference between the 'Gricean' analyses above and what Grice is advocating here. The salient and (to me) surpris-ing part of Grice's analysis of 'The F is not G' is his assumption of a structural ambiguity *and* an implicature account of the preferred narrow (presupposition-preserving) understanding, when the implicature account alone would seem to do the trick (i.e. account for the natural, preferred understanding on which the exis-tential implication is taken to hold). Neale (1990: 163–4) notices this difference between the Russell–Grice account and that of Kempson (1975) (given in section 4.3.1) and says: 'Kempson (1975) appears to disagree with Russell by suggesting that (i) [= 'The king of France is not bald'] is unambiguously represented as (i_2) [= wide-scope reading], presumably in deference to the fact that (i_1) [= narrow-scope reading] entails (i_2). It is not clear to me that this approach has any advantages over the Russellian–Gricean account.'

It seems reasonable to wonder whether, on the other hand, the Russell–Grice account has any advantages over the Kempson account. They are not identical positions and there should be some way of choosing between them. On economy grounds, it seems clear that the position of Kempson (and others) is preferable. What point is there in having both a (strong) reading R+, and a (weak) reading R– which is standardly interpreted, via pragmatics, as R+? There is an odd and unmotivated duplication in the account. The equivalent set-up for another connective, say 'or', would be for 'p or q' to have one reading R+ on which it is exclusive and another reading R– on which it is inclusive, but this reading R– is standardly interpreted, via pragmatics, as R+. As far as I know, neither Grice nor any Gricean has advocated such an analysis, and it would clearly run counter to Modified Occam's Razor, which is grounded in general economy considerations in theory building.

However, in the negative sentence we are considering, the alleged ambiguity is *structural* rather than *lexical*. The two readings are not characterized by a difference in particular symbols at any point, say two different negation operators, – and ~. The difference is captured in the syntax of the logical representations, the arrangement of the symbols:

(30)   a. $-\exists x\ [KFx\ \&\ \forall y\ (KFy \rightarrow x = y)\ \&\ Bx]$
       b. $\exists x\ [KFx\ \&\ \forall y\ (KFy \rightarrow x = y)\ \&\ -Bx]$

So talk of 'multiplying senses' doesn't carry over directly here. Further, it might be argued that postulating a syntactic (as opposed to a lexical) ambiguity does not lead to any proliferation of the elements needed in giving an account of the semantics of the language (English) since the syntactic rules involved (of the logical language employed for the task) are required anyway. Perhaps this is the reason for Grice finding an ambiguity acceptable here, but not in the case of 'and' or 'or'. Still, this account involves postulating two types of logical form (or sentence senses) in the language, when a full explanation postulating only one can be given. It combines ambiguity and implicature in an account of the two understandings of a particular linguistic form; these are usually taken to be mutually exclusive alternatives in explaining an interpretation. Furthermore, if these different scope possibilities are syntactically generated, there seems to be something missing from the account, which is an explanation of why it is that the negation doesn't turn up just as freely in front of the conjunct headed by the universal quantifier; that is, why there isn't a narrow-scope reading on which non-uniqueness is taken to be what falsifies the positive sentence.

It might be that what underlies the maintenance of an ambiguity is the uneasy conjunction of ideas about the notion of 'what is said': it is the truth-conditional content of the utterance and (yet) it is closely related to the conventional meaning of the sentence uttered. Perhaps, the (implicit) line of reasoning runs as follows: on some uses, the truth-conditional content of 'The F is not G' includes the condition that there exists an F and, on others, it does not, so both meanings must be con-

ventional meanings of the sentence. This may be why Grice does not consider
the conversational implicature account of how the existential implication arises to
be sufficient; implicatures are not supposed to contribute to the truth-conditional
content of an utterance. If this is what motivates the analysis, it will clearly lose its
force once the radical underdeterminacy of truth-conditional content by linguistic
meaning is taken on board. Then, when we speak of the semantics/pragmatics distinction, the relevant notion of semantics concerns the meaning encoded in the forms
of the linguistic system, and these seldom provide more than a schematic structure
on which to build a fully truth-conditional representation; given this, there is no
reason, in principle, why presupposition-preservation shouldn't be both pragmatically derived and an element of the truth-conditional content of the utterance.[7]

I move on now to an approach which gives full weight to the underdeterminacy
thesis and favours a quite abstract univocal semantics of sentence-types of the form
'The F is not G', a semantics which does not constitute the truth-conditional content
of *any* utterance of the sentence.

4.3.3   Sense-generality and implicature

In a series of papers, culminating in his 1989 book, Jay Atlas has developed and
defended his 'semantic generality' thesis, which is a particular manifestation of the
underdeterminacy thesis: '*The sense-generality of a sentence radically underdetermines (independently of indexicality) the truth-conditional content of its utterances*'
(Atlas 1989: 31). With respect to the negation issue, what this comes to is the view
that 'not' is semantically unspecified as regards its scope: it has neither wide nor
narrow scope as a matter of its semantics (it is neither presupposition-cancelling nor
presupposition-preserving). Whether the understanding of a negative sentence on a
particular use is one of narrow or of wide scope, that understanding will involve
pragmatic 'construction'; neither is a direct reflection of the semantics of the negation operator.[8]

He describes his approach as 'radically radical pragmatics', to distinguish it from
the so-called 'radical pragmatics' position which developed as a result of the work
of Grice and is exemplified by the analyses given in section 4.3.1. The following
features distinguish his view from the standard Gricean position:

(a)   The semantics is neutral between the two (or more) readings (understandings)
      in question.[9]
(b)   Pragmatic specification is essential in arriving at the proposition expressed (the
      truth-conditional content of the utterance); it is a 'completion' process, though
      not, I assume, a saturation process, that is, one that is indicated by a hidden
      indexical or slot in linguistic form.
(c)   So some of those aspects of utterance meaning which are treated as implica-
      tures by the neo-Griceans are, for Atlas, pragmatically inferred aspects of truth-
      conditional content.
(d)   Hence the work of pragmatic (conversational) maxims is not confined to the
      derivation of conversational implicatures but is crucially involved in arriving
      at the proposition expressed.

(e)   So, according to him, there is no longer any clear distinction between 'what is said' and 'what is implicated'.

What the two approaches (the Gricean and Atlas's) have in common is an anti-ambiguist stance. Atlas (1989), entitled *Philosophy without Ambiguity*, gives considerable space to discussion of the difference between linguistic ambiguity (lexical and structural) and generality of sense, and to the various tests that have been proposed in the literature to decide which is in play in any given instance of two (or more) understandings of a linguistic expression. He uses a number of these, as reviewed above in section 4.2.2, to provide evidence against the ambiguity of 'not', so, by implication, for his sense-generality approach. However, even if the tests do succeed in removing the ambiguity (polysemy) option, they do not choose between his scope-neutral semantics and the weak, wide-scope, semantics of the Griceans. Atlas is bound then to advance some independent argument which supports his more abstract semantics and so he does in Atlas (1977, 1979, 1989). Let's consider this issue now.

First, he highlights the salient differences by the use of the stark formulae in (I) and (II), where the notation is to be understood as follows:

R− stands for the externally negated understanding
R+ stands for the internally negated understanding
Nrep stands for the semantic representation with negation unspecified for scope
$K_{i,j,k,etc.}$ are kinds of contexts
PRAG is a function, representing the Gricean inference, which takes as input the semantics and the context and delivers an 'understanding' as output

I.   The Gricean position: II.   Atlas's position:

$$\text{PRAG } (K_i, R-) = R+ \qquad\qquad \text{PRAG } (K_i, \text{Nrep}) = R+$$

$$\text{PRAG } (K_j, R-) = R- \qquad\qquad \text{PRAG } (K_j, \text{Nrep}) = R-$$

As he says (Atlas 1977; 1989: 140–9), the crucial difference is that, on his treatment, both understandings require some pragmatic work, while on the Gricean account only the internally negated (presupposition-preserving) understanding does, the externally negated being a direct reflection of the encoded sense. Atlas believes that his 'symmetrical' treatment is to be preferred to Grice's 'asymmetrical' treatment. His main argument[10] can be summarized as follows:

(a)   The two understandings (external ('presupposition'-cancelling) and internal ('presupposition'-preserving)) of a negative sentence, abstracted from particular contexts, are *phenomenologically of equal status*.
(b)   On the standard Gricean account they are treated as asymmetric, in that only for the narrow-scope understanding does the function PRAG do any work. In the wide-scope case, PRAG is 'degenerate', in that the interpretation is a direct reflection of the semantics.

(c)   On Atlas's scope-neutral semantics, the two understandings are treated as sym-
      metric; neither is a direct reflection of the semantics, so the function PRAG
      has work to do in both cases.
(d)   So, while the Gricean account fails to represent the phenomenological equal-
      ity of the two understandings, the Atlas account succeeds in capturing it.
(e)   Therefore, Atlas's semantics is to be preferred.

In assessing this argument, we first need to be clear what he means by the property of 'phenomenological equality' of the two understandings of negated sentences.
He says that, when confronted with a negative sentence of the form 'The F is
not G', abstracted from specific contexts, competent speakers know that it has (at
least) these two uses or understandings and do not judge one as 'less a function of
the meaning of the sentence than the other' (Atlas 1989: 142). That is, the claim
seems to be that a native speaker will find either one of the understandings (presupposition-cancelling or presupposition-preserving) as likely to come to mind as
the other.

I cannot claim to have clear-cut intuitions across the full range of negation
cases, including the various possibilities of negation interacting with quantifiers. However, like most people, I do have immediate intuitions about the sentence-
types Atlas is concerned with, of the form 'The F is not G', and they do not mesh
at all with his. His appeal to the phenomenological equality of the wide- and
narrow-scope understandings of this sort of sentence seems especially wayward,
given that hardly a person writes about these without pointing out that the
narrow ('presupposition-preserving') understanding is highly 'preferred' (Wilson
1975; Kempson 1975; Grice 1981/89b; van der Sandt 1988; Burton-Roberts
1989b, etc.). Even though most of these writers favour a wide-scope semantics, they
recognize that, as an *understanding* of a negative sentence, it is frequently marked
as compared with the narrow ('presupposition'-preserving) understanding; Kempson (1975: 87), for example, writes of these cases as 'unnatural interpretations of negative sentences'. Isn't it precisely because we (native speakers
and theorists alike) do not find the two understandings to be phenomenologically
equal that the case for the special category of logical implication known as
'presupposition', has been made, has enjoyed a lengthy life and is still far
from extinct (see Seuren 1988; Burton-Roberts 1989a, 1989b)? It is the very
phenomenological *in*equality of the understandings that underlies the anti-
presuppositionalists' assumption that they had better find a way of accounting
for why one reading (the presupposition-preserving negation) is so clearly preferred
to the other.

The upshot then, as far as I can see, is that we have not been given a reason for
preferring the sense-general account to the wide-scope semantics. In fact, the widespread intuitions of unequal phenomenological status might be taken to point to a
preference for the Gricean semantics. According to Atlas, the phenomenological
salience of two readings or understandings of a sentence, in the absence of a specified context, indicates that both are the outcome of general pragmatic processes.
Since Grice and the Griceans look to pragmatics to account for 'preferred' understandings, they seem to assume this too. Given this much common ground between
the contenders, the overwhelming consensus of intuitions that the one understand-

ing is marked (highly salient) and the other unmarked (low in salience) favours the Gricean over the Atlas account.

However, not everyone shares the basic assumption here: Burton-Roberts (1989b) takes the unnatural, marked nature of the presupposition-cancelling interpretation to be evidence *against* such a wide-scope semantics for 'not' and in favour of a univocal presupposition-preserving negation. I shall look at his views in some detail in section 4.4 and will argue that his conclusion is based on a rather impoverished, insufficiently cognitive, conception of the role of pragmatics in interpretation. I doubt that we should draw any general conclusion about the role of semantics or pragmatics from a perceived asymmetry in the salience of possible understandings of any given linguistic form. All such an asymmetry indicates is that one understanding is more accessible than the others, so more likely to be relevant, in the absence of particular contextual assumptions. This might arise because one is the result of standard cognitive processes while the other (less salient one) reflects the bare semantics; alternatively, though, there could be several pragmatically derived possibilities, one of which is more accessible than the others.

A consideration in favour of the Gricean semantics is that it does, at least, give us a semantics to work with. We have a reasonably clear idea of what it means for the negation operator to be semantically wide, including presuppositions in its domain. Apart from a few remarks to the effect that semantic representations should be given the form of computer programmes (Atlas 1977: 335; 1979), remarks which were not repeated in his 1989 book, Atlas does not address the issue of what a scope-neutral semantics for 'not' would look like. He can only tell us that it is not wide-scope nor narrow-scope and it is not, therefore, equivalent to the truth-functional negation operator. As a result of this blank as far as the semantics is concerned, we can have little idea what the input to the Gricean inferential procedure (PRAG) is to be. Burton-Roberts (1991: 171–2) notes this, and goes on to point out a further problem, which comes from Atlas's apparent recourse to Gricean pragmatics. He observes that Atlas considers a major implication of his work to be that '[t]here is no straightforward distinction between "what is implicated" and "what is said"' (Atlas 1989: 146). As Burton-Roberts says, it follows from this that PRAG cannot, then, be Gricean inference, since Gricean pragmatics consists of inferential mappings from propositions ('what is said') into propositions ('what is implicated'), requiring the very distinction that Atlas is undermining. There are echoes here of Levinson's discussion of 'Grice's circle', which arises once linguistic underdeterminacy of the proposition expressed is taken on board, making it appear that 'what is said' is dependent on 'implicatures'. As discussed in chapter 2 (sections 2.1.2 and 2.3.4), the standard Gricean account cannot handle this, so has to be modified or replaced.

Clearly, Atlas's basic position of the 'radical underdeterminacy' of what is said (or the proposition expressed) by linguistic meaning is completely at one with the basic thesis of this book. His treatment of negation as semantically scope-neutral, giving to pragmatics a more essential and pervasive role than any earlier account, is a nice application of the general position. While I don't find his own argument for the sense-neutral (as opposed to the wide-scope) semantics very compelling, there may well be other reasons for adopting it and working out its details, such as the strong independent case for a scope-free semantic representation of sentences with multiple quantifiers.[11] Finally, as we've seen in previous chapters, a radical under-determinacy stance entails a major departure from the Gricean account of saying and implicating. Atlas hasn't really followed up the consequences of his radicalism, one of which is that a distinction has to be made between pragmatic inferences that contribute to the proposition expressed and those that deliver implicatures, and, as a result, a different account of the way pragmatic inference works in utterance comprehension has to be constructed.

4.3.4 Pragmatic narrowing of negation

Whenever the relationship between two understandings of a linguistic expression is one of entailment, that is, when one of the readings is stronger (more informative) than the other, there is a second pragmatic approach (additional to conversational implicature) to be considered: enrichment at the level of the proposition expressed. Internal (or narrow-scope, or predicate, or presupposition-preserving) negation entails external (or wide-scope, or sentential, or presupposition-cancelling) negation; therefore, the stronger interpretations of negative sentences are candidates for this second kind of pragmatic account. For the purposes of demonstrating this, I will assume, for the time being, that the linguistic semantics of 'not' is the same as that of the bivalent truth-functional negation operator and that it has maximally wide scope in the logical form of the sentence (while conceding that Atlas's scope-neutral account may well prove the better way to go ultimately).

As far as I am aware, the earliest published proposal to treat the stronger interpretations of negative sentences as cases of pragmatic narrowing of the proposition expressed (hence as affecting truth conditions) appears in Wilson and Sperber (1981), where they discuss the example in (31), which is standardly interpreted as an internal (predicate) negation, entailing ('presupposing') (32):

(31) Lydia's sister didn't play a piano sonata.

(32) Lydia has a sister.

They say:

> Suppose that [31] is semantically interpreted as expressing the external negation [33]:
>
> [33] It is not the case that Lydia has a sister who played a piano sonata.
>
> [33] is entailed by the more specific internal negation (34):
>
> [34] Lydia has a sister who didn't play a piano sonata.
>
> A properly defined maxim of informativeness could lead the hearer to interpret [31] as expressing [34] rather than [33] . . . [32] is neither entailed nor conversationally (nor conventionally) implicated by [31]: it is part of the proposition the speaker is taken to have expressed, but a part not determined by semantic rules alone.   (Wilson and Sperber 1981: 176, note 5)

Like the pragmatic enrichments of 'and'-conjunctions, discussed in the previous chapter, this pragmatic strengthening of the truth-conditional content of negative utterances is one of those cases treated by many Griceans as 'generalized' conversational implicatures, or default pragmatic inferences (see Levinson 1988, 2000). The reanalysis here captures the strong intuition that the different scope and presuppositional possibilities affect the truth-conditional content of the utterance, an intuition which motivated Atlas's account and may well have lain behind Grice's (and Russell's) structural ambiguity.

It has been objected to the position represented in the quote above that the 'maxim of informativeness' referred to could be interpreted in such a way that it obliges the speaker to utter (34), if that is what she means, rather than the weaker (31) (see Burton-Roberts 1999: 357–8). Since the more explicit sentence form in (34) is available, why shouldn't the addressee, on hearing (31) instead of (34), infer that the speaker has no commitment to Lydia having a sister? I think this is a legitimate charge against certain neo-Gricean accounts, but, as I'll try to establish, it does not have any force against the relevance-theoretic approach (which can be seen as, or as replacing, the 'properly defined maxim of informativeness', referred to in the quote).

Neo-Gricean accounts, such as Horn's (1989) and Levinson's (1988, 2000), generally have two informativeness maxims (based on Grice's two quantity maxims), one enjoining speakers to be fully informative (the Q-principle), the other to not be unnecessarily informative (the I-principle), and different sorts of implicatures follow depending on which of these is taken to be in force. Given a weak wide-scope semantics for negation, the pragmatic inference to a stronger (presupposition-preserving) interpretation, such as that in (34), clearly requires that it is the I-principle ('be informationally minimal', 'leave it to hearers to enrich along stereotypical lines'), rather than the Q-principle, that is operative. Horn and Levinson, therefore, have to impose certain constraints on their principles to ensure that the right one comes into play at the right time, and so to meet Burton-Roberts's objection.

However, this sort of issue simply does not arise on a relevance-theoretic account, because there is a single principle in operation ('every utterance conveys a presumption of its own optimal relevance') and it follows from the processing effort side of the definition of the presumption of optimal relevance (see appendix 1), that speakers should not be, and are expected not to be, as explicit as possible. They should encode only what they cannot rely on their addressees to infer easily. On this basis, a speaker should choose the longer and more explicit sentence in (34), rather than that in (31), only when she has reason to think that the hearer will not easily and immediately perform the pragmatic inference of negation narrowing on (31), perhaps, for instance, because the hearer has already expressed doubt about the existence of Lydia's sister (see discussion in Carston 1999a: 370–2).

In the contexts that come most readily to mind, the pragmatic narrowing in question will be an essential and immediate part of the process of satisfying the addressee's expectation of relevance. Consider, for instance, a natural setting for an utterance of (31); it is almost bound to involve an issue concerning whether Lydia's sister (whose existence is assumed) did or did not play a piano sonata, each of the two possibilities carrying certain implications for the addressee. In order to derive any of these implications, the explicit content has to be pragmatically adjusted so that the existential 'presupposition' is outside the domain affected by negation.[12] The problem of a non-denoting definite description, like 'the current king of France', which has occupied so much philosophical thought, seldom arises in communication and when it does, it is usually manifest as an assumption of one of the conversationalists which is deemed mistaken by another who corrects it. For instance:

(35)   [Bob has just come back from a soirée at Lydia's.]
        Ann: I suppose Lydia did her dance routine and her sister played a
               piano sonata.
        Bob: Lydia's sister didn't play a piano sonata; Lydia hasn't got a sister.
               We did get a piano sonata from her girlfriend, though.

Bob's negative utterance appears to be an instance of the wide-scope, presupposition-cancelling negation, which is provided directly by the semantics, on a Gricean account, or is one of the possible pragmatic fixings, given Atlas's sense-general semantics. However, an account along those lines misses the salient feature, recognized by everyone in the field, that, in practice, this wide-scope negation has a special marked (echoic, some would say) feel to it. This, then, may involve a different use of the negation operator, a 'metalinguistic' use, as Horn and Burton-Roberts claim, or a wide-scope use of an ordinary descriptive negation operator but with metarepresented material in its scope, as I claim. These possibilities, so far ignored in this survey of 'strong pragmatic' approaches, are pursued in the next sections.

Here is a summary of the different positions considered so far on the semantics and pragmatics of 'not':

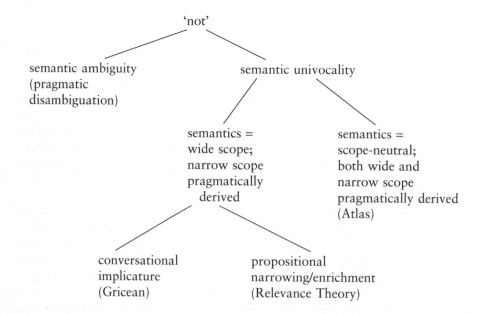

This is very schematic, of course; it does not differentiate among a range of quite different ambiguity positions (for instance, Russell/Grice, Seuren), nor among the various neo-Gricean implicature accounts. Granted these finer distinctions, it might seem that the field of possibilities is covered, but this is not so. There is the further logical possibility, which is that of a univocal internal 'presupposition'-preserving semantics with the wide-scope 'presupposition'-cancelling understanding derived pragmatically. A position of this sort is, essentially, what has been proposed by Burton-Roberts (1989a, 1989b), whose ideas I consider in the next section. This brings the representational distinction back into the picture and, accompanying it, there are some further interesting issues concerning the role of pragmatics in determining the explicit content of an utterance.

4.4 'Presupposition'-cancelling Negation and Metalinguistic Negation

4.4.1 Semantic presupposition and negation

In his book *The Limits to Debate* (1989b), and in a series of papers (1989a, 1989c, 1991, 1993/97), Noel Burton-Roberts has forcefully expounded and defended the view that natural languages are presuppositional and the logic that they reflect is a two-valued one with gaps. He has concentrated his attention on sentences of the shape 'The F is G', which he claims *semantically* (that is, as sentences of the language) presuppose, rather than merely entail, the existence of an F. In defending this thesis, he has, of course, had to discuss negation in some detail. The main tenets of his position are as follows:

1 English is a presuppositional language, some of whose sentences (those with false presuppositions) may be truth-valueless (neither true or false).
2 'Not' is an *un*ambiguous operator, whose semantics is that of the classical truth-functional negation operator: '*Not*-A is true (false) iff A is false (true)'.
3 'Not' is maximally wide in its scope, but is neither presupposition-cancelling nor, strictly speaking, presupposition-preserving, though its default meaning is p-preserving.
4 Where p-cancellation is made to take place, it gives rise to an unnatural, marked understanding, which involves a contradiction at the literal level and consequent pragmatic reanalysis of the negated sentence as containing some mentioned (metarepresented) material.

Let's consider the, somewhat paradoxical-seeming, third point more closely. The negation operator is neither p-cancelling nor p-preserving, or, as Burton-Roberts (1993/97: 83) puts it: 'the denial-of-A *neither logically affirms nor logically denies* the contingent presuppositions of A'. Yet the denial of A inevitably winds up being understood as presupposition-preserving (as affirming the contingent presuppositions of A). So in the case of an utterance of a sentence of the form 'The F is not G', the 'not' cancels all the entailments of 'The F is G' except for the presupposititional one 'There is an F'. The overwhelming intuition that this presupposition is in fact preserved is not, on this account, taken to be a direct function of the negation itself, a feature which distinguishes it from virtually all other presuppositional theories. (Burton-Roberts, 1993/97, shows that Strawson's 1950, 1952, presupposition-preserving negation operator does not yield an internally coherent semantic account of presupposition and negation.) So how is p-preservation explained on this account?

First, recall that, in the previous section, the explanations of this phenomenon, which all came from analysts opposed to a semantic notion of presupposition, were in terms of pragmatic mechanisms – Gricean maxims or optimal relevance considerations. This is not so for Burton-Roberts (henceforth B-R), whose account is essentially semantic. B-R (1989b: 148–50) describes the existential presupposition of 'The F is not G' as a default *semantic* implication, and B-R (1993/97: 36–8) explains it as the result of an interaction of the semantics of the negative sentence (which, to repeat, neither cancels nor preserves presuppositions) with a fundamental 'Cognitive Principle of Bivalence' (CPB), according to which human cognition operates in terms of truth vs. falsity, affirmation vs. denial. Given this principle, the status of the proposition 'There is an F' has to be resolved one way or the other. As B-R (1993/97: 83–4) puts it, 'speakers will irresistibly cognise that a proposition that is (a) *in a domain of denial* but (b) *not denied* is (c) in some sense *affirmed*'. So the proposition 'There is an F' is tacitly affirmed by default (that is, in default of being denied). This is the bare bones of B-R's account of the interaction of semantic presupposition and negation; to spell out and motivate the (very interesting) details would require considerable space and take us some way off course (see the discussion in Burton-Roberts 1993/97, 1999, and Carston 1999a).

The key features of the account which matter to the rest of the discussion in this chapter are that the negation operator does not (cannot) cancel presuppositions and the presupposition-preserving understanding, which is the natural unmarked one, is not explained pragmatically. This is the common core of Strawson's and B-R's views and from here on I shall take it to be the semantic presuppositionalist position (although, in fact, many of Strawson's presuppositionalist descendants have assumed two negation operators, one p-preserving, the other p-cancelling). In considering B-R's account of negation, I will try not to become embroiled in the arguments for and against the existence of semantic presuppositions. Like the Griceans, I see no call for a semantic concept of presupposition, but B-R presents a tightly argued case for the affirmative and his revised logical definition of semantic presupposition does seem to be immune to many of the criticisms levelled at the standard definition.[13] Since I wish to raise some objections to his analysis of negation, to the extent that that analysis bolsters the case for his presuppositional view, my observations will be anti-presuppositional, albeit at one remove.

In his review of Atlas (1989), B-R (1991: 170–1) employs Atlas's notation to contrast three positions on negation. Positions (A) and (B) are already familiar to us: the Gricean wide-scope analysis and Atlas's scope-neutral analysis respectively. B-R adds (C) as the third logical possibility and as a rudimentary representation of his own stance:

A. Wide Scope   B.   No Scope   C.

PRAG $(K_i, R-) = R+$ PRAG $(K_i, Nrep) = R+$ PRAG $(K_i, R+) = R+$
PRAG $(K_j, R-) = R-$ PRAG $(K_j, Nrep) = R-$ PRAG $(K_j, R+) = R-$

where:
R− stands for the externally negated understanding
R+ stands for the internally negated understanding
Nrep stands for the semantic representation with negation unspecified for scope
$K_{i,j}$ are kinds of contexts.

    This is a usefully clear way of presenting both the similarities and the broad differences between the positions. They are similar in that they are all committed to the semantic univocality of negation; B-R (1989b) has effectively countered the prevailing assumption that a presuppositional semantics commits one to an ambiguity of negation (see note 5 of this chapter). The particular semantics in each case is different. It might look as though what we have here is (A) wide-scope, (B) neutral scope, and (C) narrow scope. However, this is not quite right, and in this respect the R+ and R− notation used across the three analyses is misleading; (C) has been left unlabelled for a reason. It is not to be taken as narrow-scope, in the general sense, but as presupposition-preserving. While these come to the same thing in the simplest instances of 'The F is not G' sentences, they are to be distinguished, as we saw above, in more complex examples involving quantifiers and/or factive predicates. Another difference, not evident from these schematic pictures, lies with the function PRAG in (C), which is not some simple mirror-image of its function in (A) but, at least as envisaged by B-R, a very different kind of process of 'pragmatic reanalysis', as we shall see.

    Like everyone else (except perhaps Atlas), B-R takes the preferred reading of the following negated sentences, (36a)–(38a), to be one on which their presuppositions, (36b)–(38b) respectively, are preserved:

  (36) a. The king of France isn't bald.
        b. There is a king of France.

  (37) a. I don't regret inviting him to my party.
        b. I invited him to my party.

  (38) a. I haven't stopped smoking.
        b. I have smoked (in my life).

On his account, these are straightforward reflections of natural-language semantics and the inherently bivalent nature of thought; no pragmatic explanation is called for. As he puts it, the expressive capacity of the language is such that these understandings are the only ones it sanctions. He then has the task of explaining how it is that utterances in which a presupposition is cancelled can be acceptable, especially when followed by an explicit denial of the presupposition.

Examples (39a)–(41a), though marked, are quite acceptable utterances. On B-R's account, they are predicted to be contradictions, as shown in (39b)–(41b), respectively, where the semantically based presuppositional analysis is indicated:

(39) a. The king of France isn't bald: there is no king of France.
      b. There is a king of France and he is non-bald; there is no king of France.
(40) a. I don't regret inviting him to my party – he's a gate-crasher.
      b. I invited him to my party and I don't regret doing so; he is a gate-crasher.
(41) a. I haven't stopped smoking – I've never smoked in my life.
      b. I have smoked in my life and I have not stopped smoking; I have never smoked in my life.

B-R (1989a, 1989b) follows the lead of Horn (1985, 1989) and treats (39a)–(41a) as involving what they call metalinguistic negation (MN), which they take to be a pragmatic phenomenon quite distinct from standard truth-functional descriptive negation. It has the approximate meaning 'I object to U' or 'U is inappropriate/unassertable', where U is an utterance of the positive counterpart of the negative sentence. For the examples under discussion, the idea is that an utterance of the positive form, say 'The king of France is bald', is being rejected as inappropriate because one of its presuppositions, here the existential one, is not fulfilled, as the follow-up clause makes explicit. The metalinguistic understanding of the negative sentence is derived by a hearer when the descriptive, truth-based, understanding, which is accessed first, is rejected for some reason.

   On B-R's account, it is the contradictory, and so unacceptable, interpretation, arising from the semantics of 'not' and the cognitive bivalence principle, which triggers the search for some other way of construing these utterances and results in the metalinguistic interpretation. B-R's primary commitment is to establishing the presuppositional nature of natural language and his interest in a metalinguistic analysis of (39a)–(41a) is geared to this end. Horn, on the other hand, stands with the anti-presuppositionalists, in that he believes that there is no such semantically based relation, additional to the semantic relation of entailment, and that 'presuppositional' effects are to be understood entirely pragmatically.[14] Before examining the analysis of the problem examples more closely, we need to look at the phenomenon of metalinguistic negation; in the next subsection, I briefly consider Horn's account, and, in the following one, I suggest a different approach worked out within the relevance-theoretic framework. In section 4.5, I return to the 'presupposition-denial' issue, present some problems for Burton-Roberts's account and offer an alternative.

4.4.2 Metalinguistic negation

At the beginning of this chapter, we saw some cases where some of the material in the scope of the negation operator was clearly used, not to represent some aspect of the external world, but to represent a representation. This phenomenon is usually known as 'metalinguistic' negation and the following are typical examples:

(42)   a.   Jane doesn't eat tom[eɪDouz]; she eats tom[aːtouz].
        b.   The points aren't at different locuses; they're at different loci.
        c.   She hasn't read some of Chomsky's books; she's read everything he ever wrote.
        d.   I won't deprive you of my lecture on negation; I'll spare you it.
        e.   We're not halfway there; we've got halfway to go.
        f.   Poor old Mr Dean's not a bachelor; he's an unmarried man.

The properties standardly cited as characterizing metalinguistic negations are: (a) they consist of a negative sentence followed by a 'rectification' clause; (b) they are rejoinders to previous utterances, aspects of which they reject; (c) when spoken, they tend to receive the so-called contradiction intonation contour (involving a final rise within the negative clause), with contrastive stress on the offending item and on its correction in the second clause; (d) taken descriptively, they are (truth-conditional) contradictions; (e) addressees are often garden-pathed by them, in that their first interpretation of the negative sentence is descriptive, and, when they process the second clause, they find they must 'go back' and reanalyse the negative sentence as metalinguistic; (f) they involve an element of quotation, or mention, or representational use.

The examples in (42), which do appear to have these properties, are entirely representative of the sort of example given by B-R (1989a, 1989b) and reasonably representative of the type of example given by Horn (1985, 1989, chapter 6). The negation operator itself is said by Horn and B-R to be interpreted as 'I object to U', where U is an utterance of the corresponding positive sentence. The aspect of the utterance that is objected to is something other than its truth-conditional content: phonetic in (42a), morphological in (42b), a generalized conversational implicature (allegedly) in (42c), a conventional implicature in (42d), an attitudinal element in (42e), stereotypical connotations (of the eligible bachelor) in (42f). This is summed up by Horn (1989: 363): '[metalinguistic negation is] a device for objecting to a previous utterance on any grounds whatever, including the conventional or conversational implicata it potentially induces, its morphology, its style or register, or its phonetic realization'. This statement is quite typical: while 'any grounds whatever' would seem to include truth-conditional content (believing someone's utterance to be false is a good ground for objecting to it), it is always followed up by a list which does not include it and the very term 'meta*linguistic*' might seem to suggest that it is elements of form and not propositional content that are targeted. Most people seem to assume that since descriptive negation deals with truth-conditional content, this other kind of negation, used to register an objection, need not and does not. I shall return to this matter in the next section.

So we have two uses of the negation operator; the question is whether the distinction between them is to be captured pragmatically, or is a semantic matter. Horn wrestles with the issue of how to characterize the relationship between these two ways of interpreting a negation; he insists that it does not amount to a semantic ambiguity, an ambiguity within the linguistic system itself, and calls it a pragmatic ambiguity, a 'built-in duality of use', which extends to other linguistic operators such as 'if', 'or' and 'and' (see Horn 1989: 379–82). However, in the absence of any further delineation, the concept of 'pragmatic ambiguity' is vague, and does not seem to have any specific application; given the linguistic underdeterminacy thesis, virtually every linguistic expression is pragmatically ambiguous. A number of writers have puzzled over what it might be taken to mean (Burton-Roberts 1989b; Foolen 1991; van der Sandt 1991; Carston 1994b/96a), without reaching any consensus.

Horn himself is somewhat inconsistent in his discussion, writing of 'an extended metalinguistic use of a basically truth-functional operator' (Horn 1985: 122), followed soon after by reference to 'this special or marked use of negation, irreducible to the ordinary internal truth-functional operator' (Horn 1985: 132); he gives no account of how the metalinguistic understanding of 'not' is derived from the logical one. Despite his avowals to the contrary, it seems to me (and to van der Sandt 1991, 333) that Horn's is essentially a semantic ambiguity position. In fact, it involves a twofold ambiguity. There is an ambiguity in the negation operator itself: the one is the logical, truth-value-reversing, negation, the other is a non-truth-functional operator expressing objection or rejection. And the further ambiguity lies with the nature of the material falling in the scope of the negation, whether it is a proposition or an utterance. This double ambiguity is inevitable for Horn since, in his view, utterances and, in particular, such non-truth-conditional and formal properties of utterances as those at issue in the examples in (42), are just not the sort of thing that can fall in the scope of a *propositional* operator, such as logical 'not'. I will maintain, to the contrary, that 'not' is univocal; whatever its correct semantics is on a descriptive use (generally assumed to be the standard truth-functional operator), that carries over to its so-called metalinguistic use. The crucial factor (once again) in this account is a process of pragmatic enrichment which eventuates in a fully propositional representation for the 'not' to operate on, albeit one which contains an element of metarepresentation. It is only with the recognition that pragmatic inference is not confined to the derivation of implicature, but also plays a key role in determining the explicit content of an utterance, that this sort of account becomes possible, an account on which the overwhelming intuition that 'not' has the same meaning on all its uses is preserved.

4.4.3 Negation and echoic use

I have argued, in Carston (1994b/96a) and Carston and Noh (1995), that, of the standardly cited properties of metalinguistic negation (MN from here on) given in the previous section, only the last one, concerning metarepresentational use, is essential. I won't repeat the various arguments here, except for one that bears on the positive account I want to give.

Horn (and many others, for instance, Burton-Roberts 1989b, van der Sandt 1991, 1994, and Foolen 1991) characterizes MN as a rejoinder to another utterance, which is metarepresented in the scope of the negation and one of whose properties is objected to. It's pretty clear that there need be no *actual* previous utterance; (43a) is one of Horn's own utterances (from his acknowledgement note in Horn 1985: 121), (43b) is taken from a billboard advertising a car-sales yard, and (43c) was uttered by Clive James as a voice-over accompanying a television programme (called *Postcard from Cairo*, I think) at the point at which we were shown him riding on a camel:

(43)   a.   I would like to single out for special thanks [...] Their contribu-
             tions were not important – they were invaluable.
       b.   We don't sell cheap cars; we sell cars cheap.
       c.   It wasn't as painful as it looked; it was more painful.

In none of these cases was there any previous utterance or text to which these were a response. Of course, they can be accommodated, by simply broadening the requirement to 'actual or *potential* utterance', but then the question is whether another utterance need be involved at all. In Horn's acknowledgement in (43a), he could be attributing (to the reader or to himself at another time) the *thought* or opinion that these people made important contributions, and in (43b), what the advertisers are attributing to us, the viewer, is the thought that they sell cheap cars.

Noh (1998b, 2000, section 3.2.1.1) reinforces this point with the following example:

(44)   A: Their contributions were important.
       B: Right, but YOUR contributions were not important, they were
             invaluable.

As she says, (44B) works very similarly to (43a): the negation has to be understood as involving a metarepresentational element (and it has the various other properties typical of MN). However, it is not understood as an objection to A's previous utterance, but rather as rejecting a thought or view that someone (perhaps A) could be holding.

This sort of metarepresentational negation is a more general phenomenon than is usually acknowledged. While there may be a substantial subset of cases pertaining to linguistic form and so properly called meta*linguistic* negation, a generalization is missed if the possibility of representing an attributed propositional content (whether of an utterance of a thought) is not recognized as involving the same general process; such cases might be called meta*conceptual* negation.

The two main features of my account of these cases of metarepresentational negation (extended to include the sort of examples just considered) are the following: (a) the essential property is that (some, at least) of the material falling within the scope of the negation operator is to be understood as 'echoically used', in the sense of Sperber and Wilson (1986a/95b), Wilson and Sperber (1988b, 1992); and (b) the negation operator itself acquires no special meaning/interpretation ('I object to U') in these cases, but is standard descriptive truth-functional negation. I leave the second of these for the next subsection.

A representation is used echoically when it attributes some aspect of its form or content to someone other than the speaker herself at that moment and expresses an attitude to that aspect. The attribution may be overt (encoded) or tacit (to be inferred), and, similarly, the expression of attitude may be overt or tacit. Hence, all of the following can involve echoic use:

(45) a. A good time to buy, he said.
      b. A good time to buy, I don't think.
      c. A good time to buy, indeed.
      d. She eats tom[eɪDouz].
      e. I don't eat tom[eɪDouz]; (I eat tom[ɑːtouz].)

In (45a), the attributive nature of the utterance is made explicit; the speaker may be merely reporting someone's utterance or she may be echoing the proposition that it is/was a good time to buy in order to express (tacitly) her own attitude to it, an attitude of either an endorsing or a dissociating nature. In (45b), a dissociative attitude is made explicit. In (45c), both the attribution of the propositional content and the attitude to it are tacit; when that attitude is dissociative (which would have to be pragmatically inferred), the utterance is a case of irony (see Wilson and Sperber 1992). In the last two examples, what is attributed is a formal aspect of the utterance, here phonetic form. In (45d), the attribution (probably to the person referred to by 'she') and the speaker's attitude are tacit; in (45e), a standard case of metalinguistic negation, the attribution is tacit while the attitude of dissociation is made perfectly explicit by the use of the negation. This, I have argued, is the only essential property of the cases discussed under the label of 'metalinguistic negation', and it extends equally to cases where it is a thought, or the truth-conditional content of an utterance, that is echoed, cases of 'metaconceptual negation'.[15,16]

4.4.4 Truth-functional negation and metarepresentational enrichment

Probably, the more contentious part of my view is that the negation operator here is no different from the negation in any descriptive (non-metalinguistic) case. This is inimical to both Horn and B-R, who are adamant that the word 'not' in cases of metalinguistic negation is interpreted non-truth-functionally. B-R has to take this line, as the only truth-functional negation operator he can countenance in his presuppositional semantics is one that does not cancel presuppositions (and the echoic negation can do just that). Horn's conviction, on the other hand, comes from the fact that a truth-functional negation, by definition, takes as its argument a (truth-evaluable) proposition, while the target of negation in the metalinguistic cases can be any one of a ragbag of formal and other non-truth-conditional properties of an utterance.[17] He says of an early attempt on my part to establish the truth-functionality of the negation operator in MN:

> We are now back to the ultimately incoherent view that negation is invariably a truth function – even when it takes as an argument the 'echoic use of language'. If there is

no category mistake here, there is at the very least a good deal of explaining to do, since Carston is forced by her neomonoguism to propositionalize every target of metalinguistic negation, from grammatical usage to phonology, from register to musical technique. Occam's razor cuts more ways than one; when we bear in mind what a truth function must be a function of, we recognize the implausibility in the view that negation is invariably truth-functional.   (Horn 1989: 434)

I will try to meet this 'incoherence' charge now by (a) presenting a range of examples of metarepresentational use in the scope of operators, which clearly do not call for any special 'meta-' understanding of the operators themselves, and (b) showing how a simple process of pragmatic enrichment results in the recovery of a propositional form over which the descriptive negation operator has scope. (For earlier attempts, see Carston 1994b/96a; Carston and Noh 1995/96; and for a recent more detailed one, see Noh 1998b, 2000, chapter 3.)

Quotations, echoes and other representations employed for purposes other than referring to, or describing, aspects of situations in the world are very common elements of verbal communication generally. As shown in the examples in (45), this non-descriptive use of a representation may or may not be overtly signalled. When overtly signalled, by, for example, a verb of saying or quotation marks, there seems to be no problem in grasping the proposition(s) falling in the scope of truth-functional operators:

(46) a.   Americans say 'tom[eɪDouz]' and Brits say 'tom[aːtouz]'.
      b.   The army slaughtered everyone in the village or, according to them, 'ethnically cleansed' it.
      c.   If you say 'sidewalk', you must be American.
      d.   The correct plural of 'mongoose' is not 'mongeese' but 'mongooses'.

We have here a conjunction, a disjunction, a conditional and a negation; some part of the representation within the scope of each of these operators is used non-descriptively. However, there seems to be no temptation to say that, as a result, these operators must be understood as having some interpretation other than their standard truth-functional meaning. The truth conditions are clear enough in each case; for instance, (46a) is true if and only if it is the case that Americans pronounce the word in question as 'tom[eɪDouz]' and the British pronounce it as 'tom[aːtouz]'.

In the next set of examples, which involve exactly the same operators, there is no encoded indication that there is an element of non-descriptive or echoic use; this has to be pragmatically inferred:

(47) a.   Americans eat tom[eɪDouz] and Brits eat tom[aːtouz].
      b.   The army annihilated, or ethnically cleansed, the village.
      c.   If you use a sidewalk, you must be American.
      d.   They're not mongeese but mongooses.

Is it reasonable to suppose that these operators, which are, let us assume, semantically truth-functional, lose their truth-functionality as a result of the absence of an explicit signal that material in their scope is being used non-descriptively? Surely not. What sort of causal connection could there be between the move from overt to tacit echoic use and a fundamental change in the meaning of a logical operator? I contend that there is none and that the interpretation of the operators in (47) is the same as that in (46): ordinary descriptive conjunction, disjunction, conditional and negation.

A further consideration weighing against Horn's 'I object to U' interpretation of negation in the metalinguistic/echoic cases is that it is very difficult to see how it will accommodate the variety of encodings of negation that we can find in such cases, including 'not at all', 'not any more', 'not ever', 'not anywhere', 'neither . . . nor', 'it is unlikely that', 'I doubt that':

(48) A: I want some tom[a:touz].
      B: We're not eating tom[a:touz] any more; from now on it's tom[eɪDouz].

(49) A: Johnny's eaten some of the cakes.
      B: It's highly unlikely (I very much doubt that) Johnny's eaten SOME of the cakes; he will have eaten ALL of them.

(50) a. I haven't seen monGEESE anywhere; I have seen monGOOSES
      b. Neither Mary nor Bill LIKES rock music; they both have consuming PASSion for it.

Many of these involve negative polarity items, e.g. 'any', 'anywhere', 'at all', which is a clear sign that they are not part of the echoed representation (within which the polarity will reflect that of the (positive) echoed representation) but rather contribute to the expression of the negation. On Horn's view, these presumably acquire a metalinguistic interpretation, which distinguishes them from their meaning in fully descriptive utterances. Let's take just one of the examples above, though the problem arises for all of them. The Hornian interpretation of B's utterance in (48) would be 'I object to the (potential) utterance "we are eating tom[a:touz]" . . .'. How does the 'any more' mesh with this? As far as I can see, it doesn't. However, if we assume that the negation here is no different from a negation in an entirely descriptive utterance, there is no problem, since the meaning of 'not . . . any more' remains constant whether or not there is echoed material in its scope.

Noh (1998b, 2000, section 3.2.1.3) makes the further point that the functions ascribed to metalinguistic negation can be achieved without the use of 'not'. Consider, for instance:

(51) A: Would you like some tom[eɪDouz]?
      B1: I'd rather have some tom[a:touz].
      B2: Sorry. I only eat tom[a:touz].

On a descriptive understanding, the proposition expressed by B1 is contradictory: 'I'd rather have some tomatoes than have some tomatoes.' But there is an understanding, easily recoverable here, on which it is not contradictory: 'I'd rather have something described as tom[a:touz] than have something described as tom[eɪDouz].' There is no negation operator here, nor in B2, and yet the metarepresentational analyses are in every other respect just like the MN cases; I assume we would not want to claim that 'rather' and 'only' are being used in any special 'meta-' way in these examples.

These various observations strongly indicate that what distinguishes metalinguistic (or echoic) from descriptive negation is not the way in which the operator itself functions or is understood, but is rather the presence of metarepresented forms or contents in its scope. If this is right, that is, if the negation involved in these metarepresentational cases is truth-functional, then there must be a propositional form on which it operates.[18,19] This means that the metarepresented element contributes somehow to truth-conditional content. But how? After all, what we seem to have so far is a mix of descriptive and metarepresentational elements, which cannot be directly composed into a single-level representation:

(52)   a.   not (Johnny's eaten 'some' of the cakes); he's eaten 'all' of them
       b.   not (I eat 'tom[eɪDouz]'); I eat 'tom[a:touz]'

In order for the bracketed material to constitute a determinate truth-conditional content, it needs an element of pragmatic enrichment. The sort of material that has to be supplied pragmatically, fairly obviously, has to capture the shift from the descriptive to the metarepresentational and, in addition, express the concern with the 'right' way of putting something:

(53)   a.   not (Johnny's eaten quantity x of the cakes where x is properly described as 'some'); Johnny's eaten quantity x of the cakes where x is properly described as 'all'
       b.   not (I eat what is properly called 'tom[eɪDouz]'); I eat what is properly called 'tom[a:touz]'

These are very rough natural-language renderings of the propositional forms derived, but do at least give a quite clear idea of the sort of enrichment involved.[20] By embedding the lexical forms, in (53a), and the phonetic representations, in (53b), in descriptive expressions along the lines of 'is properly called/described/expressed', the incomplete and non-composable representations in (52) become complete propositional forms, with the metarepresented elements introduced descriptively like any legitimate case of quotation or mention. Note that this applies just as much to the follow-up clauses as to the negations and that they could be uttered, with these interpretations, quite independently of the preceding negations.

This process is certainly not limited to cases of so-called metalinguistic negation:

(54)   a.   The intelligent bloke sure is dumb.
       b.   The pretty girl is (indeed) pretty.
            (adapted from Noh 1998b, section 3.4.3)

On an entirely descriptive interpretation, neither of these will meet a hearer's expectation of relevance: (54a) is internally contradictory and (54b) is a tautology.

However, in an appropriate context, these are not treated as pointless, irrelevant utterances; rather, an element of echoic use is recovered, so that (54a) can be interpreted as expressing disagreement with someone else's judgement of the bloke's intellectual powers, and (54b) as agreeing with someone else's assessment of the girl as pretty:

> (55) a. The bloke described as 'intelligent' sure is dumb.
>   b. The girl described as 'pretty' is (indeed) pretty.

In fact, tacitly echoic elements do not just occur in examples like (47)–(55), where recognition of the echoic element is essential if the utterance is to achieve any cognitive effects at all. They also occur in utterances which are perfectly interpretable and relevant at a wholly descriptive level, so as to achieve some extra (humorous or mocking) effects. For instance, the following could be uttered by an English commentator presenting a programme on the landmarks of Paris:

> (56) The striking modernity of the glass [paɪraːmɪːd] is a perfect foil for the classically ornate façades of the Louvre.

The speaker makes a descriptive statement about the pyramid structures in the courtyard of the Louvre and tosses in a playful echo of the English pronunciation of a young French woman he has just interviewed.

In the next section, I return to the issue of 'presupposition'-denial cases. They are exemplified in (39a)–(41a), repeated here as a reminder; their crucial property is the explicit denial, in the follow-up clause, of a presuppositional element:

> (39) a. The king of France isn't bald; there is no king of France.

> (41) a. I haven't stopped smoking – I've never smoked in my life.

They are most readily contextualized and understood as involving echoic negation.

4.5 The Pragmatics of 'Presupposition'-denial

Recall the two main types of semantic/pragmatic analysis of utterances of negative sentences that are still in play: on the one hand, the Gricean and relevance-theoretic accounts, on which presupposition is a pragmatic phenomenon, and, on the other, Burton-Roberts's account, on which presupposition is a semantic matter. They agree in just one respect: semantically (that is, in terms of the meaning encoded in the language system), there is a single negation operator, or a single meaning for 'not'. However, they differ in every other respect: this single negation operator is quite different in its functioning, on the two views, and the respective roles of semantics and pragmatics in accounting for the p-preserving and p-cancelling cases are virtually the opposite of each other. This is perhaps made more vivid by the following contrasting (and very schematic) representations of the way the two approaches treat negative sentences of the form 'The F is not G':

I.   Burton-Roberts (presuppositionalist):
     Semantically: The F is not-G   (p-preserving)
     Pragmatically: not [The F is G]   (p-cancelling)

II.   'Griceans' and relevance-theorists (anti-presuppositionalists):
     Semantically: not [the F is G]   (p-cancelling)[21]
     Pragmatically: The F is not-G   (p-preserving)

The apparent symmetry should not mislead us, though, into assuming that the p-cancelling representations here (pragmatically derived in the one case, semantic in the other) are in fact identical. While this is descriptive truth-functional negation on the Gricean view, it is a special (pragmatically derived) metalinguistic negation on Burton-Roberts's view. In the next section, I will argue against B-R's position that p-denial examples are descriptive contradictions and that they are (therefore) *necessarily* metalinguistic (echoic). If these arguments hold, then his account cannot stand and the way is open for an alternative account in terms of a presupposition-cancelling negation operator and relevance-theoretic pragmatic inference, which is developed in section 4.5.2.

4.5.1   'Presupposition'-denial and contradiction

B-R characterizes p-denial cases as descriptive contradictions (B-R 1989b: 234–5); he takes it that this follows from his presuppositional story, according to which the negation operator is semantically incapable of cancelling presuppositions. It follows that p-denials, which are interpretable in a non-contradictory way, have to be metalinguistic (and so, as he puts it, fall outside the descriptive power of the language system). It is the literal contradiction that triggers the metarepresentational reanalysis. In this subsection, I simply gather together evidence, some of it already presented in different places by various writers (pro- and anti-presuppositionalist), which collectively makes a strong case for the non-contradictory nature of the p-denial cases. My strategy (pursued in even more dogged detail in Carston 1998c), is to take 'standard' cases of metalinguistic negation (such as the examples in (42)), show that they have some property, and then check the p-denials for the same property, revealing that they do not have it.

   First, consider the following point from Kempson (1986a: 85) concerning the possibility of an evidential interpretation of the second clause:

(57)   a.   He didn't see the sign: he was looking the wrong way.
       b.   We didn't see some mongeese; we saw some mongooses.
       c.   She didn't eat some of the cakes; she ate all of them.
       d.   I'm not his daughter; he's my father.
       e.   The king of France isn't bald: France doesn't have a king.
       f.   She hasn't stopped drinking: she has never been a drinker.

Descriptively used negations, like descriptively used positives, are often followed by a clause which provides evidence for the belief expressed in uttering the first clause (recall the discussion of juxtaposed cases in the previous chapter). The example in (57a) is a clear case of this: that he was looking the wrong way provides evidence for my belief/assertion that he didn't see the sign. However, when we move to (57b)–(57d), some of the cases standardly cited as readily giving rise to a metalinguistic interpretation, we find the second clause does not have this function. The fact that we saw some mongooses is not evidence that we didn't see some mongeese; even more clearly, the fact that she ate all of the cakes is not evidence for the belief expressed by the preceding negation but is in fact strong evidence for its opposite, that she *has* eaten some of the cakes, and the same goes for (57d). The evidential relation is one that is rooted in the way events and states of affairs connect up in the world, in temporal, causal and other relations to each other. It is not surprising that this is not how the metalinguistic negations and their follow-up clauses are understood because they are, precisely, not making statements about the way things are in the extra-linguistic world.

What about the p-denials in (57e) and (57f)? Like (57a), an evidential relation is readily taken to hold between the second clause and the first. The fact that France doesn't have a king can be taken as evidence in support of the contention that the king of France isn't bald. In line with this, these two cases, like (57a) and unlike the unequivocally metalinguistic cases, can be conjoined by a causal connective such as 'because' or 'since' (descriptively used). Compare the following:

(58) a. He didn't see the sign because he was looking the wrong way.
      b. ! I'm not his daughter because he's my father.
      c. The king of France isn't bald because France doesn't have a king.

The next sets of data are intended to demonstrate that the very property that led to the standard metalinguistic cases being called 'paradoxical negations' does not seem to extend to the 'presupposition'-denial cases. The basic fact that I will be appealing to in making the point is that for any two descriptive statements, P and Q, which are contradictory, whether they themselves involve negation or not, each entails the negation of the other:

(59) a. She murdered him; he's still alive.   (P; Q)
      b. If she murdered him he is not still alive.   (If P then not Q)
      b'. If he is still alive she didn't murder him.   (If Q then not P)
      c. She loves him; she does not love him.   (P; Q)
      d. If she loves him she does not love him.   (If P then not Q)
      d'. If she does not love him she does not love him.   (If Q then not P)

Now, as Horn (1989: 431–2), following Cormack (1980), points out, standard metalinguistic negations seem to be paradoxical because their positive counterparts are entailed by their correction clause. That is, given the schematic representation of these examples as 'Not R; Q', the following seems to be the case 'Since/if Q, then not (not R)', which, by double negation, gives us 'Since/if Q, then R':

(60) a.   I'm not happy; I'm ecstatic.
      a′. Since/if I'm ecstatic, I'm (certainly) happy.
      b.   I'm not his child; he's my father.
      b′. If he is my father then I am his child.
      c.   The king of France isn't bald; there isn't a king of France.
      c′. ! Since there isn't a king of France, the king of France is bald.
      d.   Kim doesn't regret inviting Bob to her party; Bob gate-crashed/she
           didn't invite him.
      d′. ! If Kim didn't invite Bob to her party then she regrets inviting him.

The examples in (60a) and (60b) exhibit the same property as those in (59), a consequence of being descriptive contradictions. The examples in (60c) and (60d), on
the other hand, do not; in fact, they seem to have the contrary property in that this
very manipulation gives rise to a contradiction, as is the case for any other instance
of denying an entailment:

(61) a.   ! If Mary likes cats then she doesn't like any animals.
      b.   The king of France isn't bald; he has long black hair.
      b′. ! If the king of France has long black hair then the king of France
           is bald.
      c.   Kim doesn't regret inviting Bob to her party; she is glad he came.
      c′. ! If Kim is glad that Bob came to her party she regrets inviting him.

The evidence, then, indicates that the juxtaposition of a negative 'presuppositional' sentence and a sentence which negates its (or one of its) presupposition(s)
does not constitute a literal contradiction. This looks like trouble for B-R's semantically based 'presupposition' position. He claims that all cases of MN are literal
contradictions and it is the need to resolve this contradictoriness that triggers the
move to the MN interpretation.[22] Given a presuppositional semantics, which precludes a descriptively p-cancelling negation, p-denials, which require a p-cancelling
negation, have to be interpreted as cases of MN, so they too must be literal contradictions. According to him, this is the crucial generalization uniting all cases of
MN, and it is missed by those who, like Horn, take the semantics of 'not' to be
wide-scope and p-cancelling. 'On a presuppositional semantics, and only on a presuppositional semantics, this generalization holds good . . . a properly general and
explanatory account of metalinguistic negation itself implies a presuppositional
semantics' (B-R 1989b: 235). But the generalization simply does not hold, and the
presuppositional semantics makes a wrong prediction.
    Since the p-denial cases are not intrinsically contradictory, the claim that their
only (non-contradictory) interpretation is a metalinguistic/echoic one is also undermined. However, the intuition that these cases are, in fact, frequently understood
as metalinguistic/echoic is widely shared. A reasonable conclusion is that while they
are standardly metalinguistic in use, they are not metalinguistic as a matter of logical
necessity. Their metarepresentational nature is pragmatically (i.e. communicatively)
motivated, rather than being forced by a presuppositional semantics. The account
given in the next subsection reflects this outlook.

4.5.2   Negation and two kinds of pragmatic enrichment

I shall give an analysis of the p-denial cases by putting together (a) the relevance-theoretic analysis, given in section 4.3.4, of the p-preserving interpretation, as a case of pragmatic narrowing, and (b) the different sort of pragmatic enrichment, discussed in section 4.4.4, required in understanding cases of tacit echoic use, which is frequently involved in the use of p-denials.

B-R makes several criticisms of the anti-presuppositionalist (Gricean) pragmatic approach. First, he points out that the semantically given, wide-scope, p-cancelling negation fails to account for the marked, non-preferred status of the 'presupposition'-cancelling interpretation. This is a valid criticism, but there is a simple solution to it, which I shall come to very soon. B-R continues his critique in the following vein: 'What, on a non-presuppositionalist semantics, would trigger, and provide the rationale for, a pragmatic reanalysis of the negation as metalinguistic? Nothing whatsoever. . . . Such non-presuppositional theories thereby entirely fail to predict that, let alone explain why, the examples in Set I [presupposition denials] do, as a matter of empirical fact, fall together with those in Set II [the standard cases of MN, as in (42)], evincing all the special features characteristic of metalinguistic uses of negation' (B-R 1989a: 120).

Quite generally, the 'rationale for a pragmatic reanalysis' is provided by the failure of the previous analysis to meet a pragmatic criterion. Within relevance theory, this means a failure to deliver a satisfactory range of cognitive effects. Deriving a contradiction, which gives rise to no cognitive effects and so cannot establish the relevance of the utterance, is just one clear way in which such a failure may arise. This may, in fact, be what goes on in at least some occurrences of the denials in (39a)–(41a), repeated here, those occurrences which involve garden-pathing and reanalysis, though the contradiction involved will be a pragmatically derived one.

(39)   a.   The king of France isn't bald: there is no king of France.
(40)   a.   I don't regret inviting him to my party – he's a gate-crasher.
(41)   a.   I haven't stopped smoking – I've never smoked in my life.

There is nothing, as far as I can see, to rule out an explanation along these lines, despite assuming the wide-scope, p-cancelling, semantics of negation. It will simply involve adding a further step of pragmatic processing to the pragmatic enrichment account of the p-preserving interpretation already given. Schematically, the picture I propose of the phases involved in understanding such instances of p-denials is as follows:

(62)   semantically: not [The F is G]; there is no F
        via pragmatic enrichment (a):   [The F is not-G]; there is no F
        via pragmatic enrichment (b):   not ['The F is G' is properly said]; there
                                              is no F

Let's consider a concrete example of a p-denial, thinking of it now in communicative rather than semantic terms, as an utterance produced and processed over time. I repeat example (35), introduced at the end of the relevance-theoretic account in section 4.3.4, which occurs in a moderately realistic context:

(35)   [Bob has just come back from a soirée at Lydia's.]
       Ann: I suppose Lydia did her dance routine and her sister played a piano sonata.
       Bob: Lydia's sister didn't play a piano sonata; Lydia hasn't got a sister. We did get a piano sonata from her girlfriend, though.

Ann clearly assumes that Lydia has a sister, and what is relevant to her is whether or not this person played a piano sonata. So, although the negation is semantically wide-scope, hence has no entailments (that is, it cancels so-called 'presuppositions'), it is pragmatically narrowed so as to focus on the sonata-playing, thereby yielding certain cognitive effects (e.g. Lydia's sister wasn't seeking the limelight for once, etc.). This is the standardly preferred narrow-scope, 'presupposition'-preserving, interpretation, and is just one of many instances of the process of pragmatic strengthening at the level of the proposition expressed. Ann would be bound to leave it at that, were it not that, some milliseconds later, when she has processed the next utterance unit, she finds herself with a contradiction: Lydia has a sister and Lydia doesn't have a sister. The overall interpretation of the two clauses is not consistent with the expectation of optimal relevance and a reanalysis is sought. Here, as in most instances, this will be a move to an echoic (metalinguistic) analysis.

I don't want to give the impression that the three levels shown in (62) are always inevitably involved or that they are of equal status. The semantic level differs from the two pragmatic levels in that no final interpretation will ever involve it alone. It is the input to the pragmatic inferential processes, an input which comes from the linguistic system, not as a whole logical form, but bit by bit (perhaps word by word). There are only two levels of actual interpretation and they are identical with B-R's levels, but they are both levels which are the outcome of pragmatic processes, governed by a single communicative principle (the principle of relevance).

In fact, the picture given in (62) is not the only one possible for these utterances. I think there are four possible processing routes for p-denials, for all of which the semantic input is the same wide-scope, uncommitted negation:

1.   *first pass:*   pragmatic narrowing (p-preserving)
     second pass: echoic reanalysis (p-cancelling)

This is the processing track just discussed, and the one that captures exactly the same intuitions as B-R's analysis, including the intuition of p-preservation under negation, but without assuming a presuppositional semantics or a semantic contradiction. However, in many actual contexts, comparable to the one just given, there is another possibility:

2.   *first and only pass:*   echoic interpretation recognized straight off (p-cancelling)

This is the case of an utterance for which the echoic interpretation is the most accessible one to the hearer (the least effort-requiring). Of course, the first accessible interpretation to Ann in (35) might well be one on which she takes Bob to be echoing and denying an element of her previous utterance, most likely her predicate 'play a piano sonata'. However, what I have in mind is an interpretation on which the whole utterance is taken to have been echoed so that the presupposition is cancelled. Suppose that, in the same context, Bob had uttered the following in response to Ann:

> (63) Bob: You've got it wrong. Lydia doesn't HAVE a sister, that's her GIRLfriend; so, NO, Lydia's SISTER didn't play a piano sonata.

The difference here is that the presupposition-denial ('Lydia doesn't have a sister') precedes the negative sentence at issue (and I've also added some plausible accenting which gives further interpretive clues). This ordering of the clauses blocks the standard presupposition-preserving understanding of 'The F did not G' utterance: since the so-called correction clause (the explicit presupposition-denial) is processed first, it is part of the context for the processing of the following negative sentence whose negative scope is not narrowed so as to preserve the presupposition. There is no contradiction derived, no reanalysis required, but rather the utterance is recognized on the first processing pass as an echoic negation. There are, no doubt, other sorts of contexts where this occurs, contexts where it is just obvious that the speaker is in the business of echoing someone else's utterance or where this is a habitual mode of interaction between the interlocutors.

The other two possibilities are less likely, but possible in principle:

3. *first pass:*   pragmatic narrowing   (p-preserving)
    second pass: pragmatic widening   (p-cancelling)

What this amounts to is undoing or repairing a pragmatic strengthening or enrichment. This seems to be going on in the following (non-presuppositional) cases:

> (64) a. I have had breakfast. I used to have it regularly as a boy when I worked on my uncle's farm, but nowadays I prefer to hang out for a good lunch.
>
>   b. *Edina:* Have you eaten?
>   *Patsy:* No – not since 1973.
>   (from *Absolutely Fabulous*, BBC2, 9 February 1994)

The on-line temporal enrichment of the first sentence in (a), and of the proposition apparently expressed by Patsy's 'no' in (b), is a narrowing from the semantically encoded, unspecified temporal span of time preceding the time of utterance, to a much shorter span contained within the day of utterance. A pragmatic reanalysis takes place as a result of the second clause in each case which is at odds with that temporal enrichment; the original pragmatic narrowing is subsequently pragmatically broadened. Here is a p-denial case where the same sequence of pragmatic processes might take place:

(65)   A: You always hedge everything. Isn't there anything you feel straight-
            forward simple certainty about?
       B: Well, yes, there are a few things I feel sure about. For instance, the
            king of France isn't bald and he isn't hairy and he isn't tall and he
            isn't short; there isn't any king of France.

Finally, what is probably the least likely option:

4.   *first and only pass:*   descriptive interpretation   (p-cancelling)

This shouldn't be seen as purely the output of semantics, though it is identical to
it; pragmatic inference would be involved in deciding that this is the intended interpretation. Say we are wig-makers to royalty, well aware of which European countries have monarchs and which don't, and we are making a list of the hirsute
monarchs and the bald monarchs, and one of us remarks: 'well, the king of France
is neither bald nor hairy', implicating that that's one less to have to worry about.
   I return now to the first scenario, which is the central one here, and which is the
direct rival to B-R's account of p-denials. I think my picture, given in (62), has quite
a lot going for it:

(a)   It captures the marked feel that most people comment on for the 'presupposition'-
      cancelling use; this markedness (the extra effects) arises from the double
      processing here just as it does on B-R's approach.
(b)   It is consistent with the p-denials, (39a)–(41a), not being intrinsically (that is,
      semantically) contradictory, which the evidence in the previous section strongly
      indicates is the case. In this respect the analysis has a definite edge on B-R's
      (1989a/1989b) account which requires, against the facts, that they are seman-
      tically contradictory, and on his (1993/97) account, according to which they
      are contradictory as a function of semantic encoding and the dictates of cog-
      nitive bivalence.
(c)   The naive unexamined intuition that there is something contradictory here is
      accounted for by the standard non-presuppositionalist account of the preferred
      'presupposition'-preserving understanding. The beauty of this is that it is a
      pragmatic account and so it is consistent with the non-contradictory seman-
      tics of the two clauses, while meeting B-R's demand for a 'rationale for the
      pragmatic reanalysis'.

   There is a final piece of evidence which makes starkly apparent how much more
satisfactory the two-level pragmatic approach is than the semantic presuppositional
account. This hinges on what happens when we reverse the order of the negative
presuppositional sentence and the correction clause as in example (63). This makes
no difference to the metarepresentational (echoic) nature of the utterance, but it
does make an important difference to the interpretive process and so to whether or
not a hearer is likely to be garden-pathed into deriving a contradiction. Let's see
how the two accounts (B-R's and the pragmatic enrichment account advocated here)
handle a clause reversal of the p-denial cases:

(66) a. There is no king of France: so, the king of France is not bald.
      b. The king of France is not bald: there is no king of France.

(67) When did you give up smoking?
      a. I've never smoked in my life (so) I haven't given up smoking.
      b. I haven't given up smoking; I've never smoked in my life.

B-R's account seems to predict that both the (a) and the (b) cases have to be understood as metalinguistic (echoic), and, crucially, that the interpretive stages involved
in arriving at that understanding are the same in the two cases: on a first pass, the
negated presuppositional sentences are taken to be presupposition-preserving; then,
understood in conjunction with the other clause, a contradiction is reached and,
finally, the negative clauses are reanalysed as involving echoic use. Spelling out the
interpretive levels for (67a) looks something like this:

(68) I've never smoked in my life. I haven't given up smoking.

level 1:   (semantics plus bivalence)
             not-P.   P and not-Q

             (where P = I have smoked in my life, and Q = I am an ex-smoker now)
             Result: logical contradiction: not-P.   P

level 2:   pragmatic reanalysis (giving metalinguistic P-cancelling negation):
             I've never smoked in my life. not ['I have given up smoking'].
             not-P. not ['P and Q']

    But this cannot be right. Placing the 'correction'/explanation clause first effec-
tively prepares the way for the wide-scope interpretation of the negative presuppositional sentence. As with example (63), intuitively, there is no garden-pathing here,
no logical contradiction and so no pragmatic *re*analysis. The (a) versions of (66)
and (67) do not have the marked feel that is typical of the (b) versions, in which
the 'correction' or explanation clause follows the negated clause. In short, the level-
1 analysis shown here does not take place; an interpretation of the sort given as
level 2 is accessed on a first processing pass.
    The relevance-theoretic account on which an all-inclusive semantics for negation
is coupled with a psychologically realistic on-line processing view of pragmatics can
capture the intuitive interpretive differences between the (a) and (b) examples, as it
is sensitive to the ordering of the clauses. Given the context created by the first
explanatory clause in each of (66a) and (67a), in which the presupposition is explicitly denied, the subsequent negative utterance may well achieve relevance on its
semantically given p-cancelling (non-echoic) understanding and will not need to be
narrowed to exclude the 'presupposition' from its scope. Or if, as is very likely, these
are intended as echoic of a previous utterance (say, the question in (67)), and this
interpretation is sufficiently accessible to the hearer, they will be so interpreted on
a first pass. Either way, and this is the important point, there is no intermediate
stage of p-preservation, something which seems unavoidable on B-R's account.

The general analysis of p-denials that I am proposing involves three levels of meaning, the semantic and the two pragmatically adjusted understandings, as shown in (62). This could be viewed with Occamite suspicion, since both of the original competitors (the Gricean account and B-R's) had only two. My claim, however, is that it takes three levels to do justice to the interpretive facts; economy principles can be brought into play only when the analyses being assessed all cover the same set of data, which, as I've shown, is not the case here. This talk of counting levels should really be dropped and replaced by counting interpretations, or pragmatic analyses, in which case there are two here, as in both the previous accounts; it's just that neither of them coincides with what is semantically encoded.[23] In fact, the richer account I'm proposing calls for no increase in semantic apparatus (in this regard it comes cheaper than B-R's presuppositional semantics) or in cognitive or pragmatic principles. What it does postulate is more interpretive work being done with these pragmatic principles than either of the original accounts allows for. What lies behind both of those approaches, especially B-R's, is a conception of pragmatics as a fairly thin icing on a substantial semantic cake. This is evident from his assumption that natural, unmarked interpretations should be reflected in the semantics, while less preferred, more marked, ones arise pragmatically (Burton-Roberts 1989b: 40). It follows from the view of pragmatics emerging from the cognitively based, relevance-theoretic framework, that exactly the reverse is the case: pragmatic inference is natural and substantial, and encoded meaning may be not only minimal, but also unnatural from the point of view of what utterances communicate. (These points are argued more fully in Carston 1998c, 1999a.)

4.6 Conclusion: From Multiple Semantic Ambiguity to Univocal Semantics and Pragmatic Enrichment

I finish this chapter by highlighting the central point, which I hope stands out against the detail, and which bears directly on the main theme of this book, that is, the extensive role of pragmatics in determining the explicit content of utterances:

> The negation operator in natural language can be given a univocal, truth-functional semantics, which is maximally wide in scope, and all the other interpretations – a narrow-scope understanding, constituent negation, the presupposition-preserving meaning, an objection to some echoed (or metalinguistic) material – can be accounted for pragmatically in terms of enrichments of one sort or another at the level of the proposition expressed by the utterance.

Jay Atlas reports having reached a similar conclusion: 'not' is not ambiguous but is 'general in sense among exclusion and choice-negation interpretations [presupposition-cancelling vs. presupposition-preserving], among contradictions and contraries, among wide-scope and narrow-scope interpretations, and even, I suspected, among object-language and metalanguage uses' (Atlas 1989, preface, ix).

This is very much in keeping with the methodological turnaround I mentioned in the conclusion of chapter 2: given that we have a communicative inferential system capable of constructing detailed interpretive hypotheses on the basis of quite minimal linguistic clues, the need for several distinct encodings to capture the different possible interpretations of a linguistic form, or for a single but highly elaborated sense, evaporates. A quite lean, schematic and abstract encoding is often sufficient. Unfortunately, Atlas gives us little idea of what the abstract general sense of 'not' could be. He claims that it cannot be the same as the classical truth-functional negation operator (1989: 131), while I have found no reason so far to assume it is anything else. Even if it is semantically scope-neutral, as he maintains (that is, it does not take any particular scope in the logical form of *sentences* in which it appears), it can still be characterized in the standard way as a *propositional* operator: 'not P is true/false if and only if P is false/true'. Of course, the *sentence* itself generally won't supply a fully propositional form over which the 'not' can operate, and, even if it did, it is likely that it would not be the proposition the speaker intends it to operate on in her utterance; determining that is a matter for pragmatic inference.

However, as noted in the discussion of the semantics of 'and' (section 3.7.2), it no longer seems inevitable, nor even particularly desirable, as it did on the Gricean approach, for the semantics of the apparent counterparts in natural language of logical operators to be identical to the semantics of those operators. If it is right that natural-language sentences do not encode propositions and so are not directly truth-conditional, it might well be that natural-language connectives do not encode truth-functional properties either, though these may be pragmatically recovered and enter into the propositions expressed by utterances of sentences containing them. But while I am at one with the general outlook (the semantics of natural language is a distinct matter from logic), I have so far seen no compelling reason to drop the (univocal) truth-functional semantics for 'not'.[24,25]

NOTES

1   Here the iota operator is treated as forming a quantifier. Grice (1981/89b: 271–2) suggests a different interpretation of this symbol, as a term-forming operator (see section 4.3.2). The pros and cons of various different notations in reflecting the Russellian truth conditions for definite description sentences are discussed by Neale (1990, chapter 2).

2   Neale (1990: 67) says that what Russell was concerned with was the propositions expressed by utterances rather than abstract sentence types, though this distinction was not made explicit at that time. The assumption is that a sentence expresses a proposition, whose truth conditions are the truth conditions of the sentence, sentence semantics being construed in wholly truth-conditional terms, without any concern for the gap between encoded sentence meaning and truth conditions. This proposition is determined in accordance with the minimal truth-evaluability principle, as discussed in chapter 2, section 2.6.1. Grice's 'what is said' is a direct descendant of this view.

3   In the context of looking at strong semantic positions, we might wonder what an account along the lines proposed by Cohen (1971) for 'and' might look like. Recall that this was a univocal multi-featural semantic entry, which required selective contextual cancella-

tion of features. It should be fairly clear that this has to be instantly dismissed as a possibility for negation (and Cohen certainly does not suggest it); it would be transparently internally contradictory, with an entry like [+presup, −presup] or [+wide scope, +narrow scope].

4   For instance, in her work on polysemy, Sweetser (1986, 1990) suggests that certain metaphorical extensions of senses are universal: extensions from the physical domain to the epistemic and speech act domains. From this point of view, she develops a polysemy account of the meanings of modal verbs and various connectives. Papafragou (2000), on the other hand, advocates a monosemous view of modals, with the other related 'senses' derived pragmatically. More generally (in chapter 5), she takes a critical look at the notion of polysemy and argues that 'much of the workload of so-called polysemy can be re-allocated to either ambiguity or semantic indeterminacy [monosemy]'.

5   It has been claimed by many that a semantic theory of presuppositions requires a semantic ambiguity of negation (a p-preserving operator and a p-cancelling operator), and it is certainly true that most theories of the one incorporate the other. This fact can be used in two ways: (a) on the one hand, if a strong case can be made for semantic presupposition, then this gives support to an ambiguity of negation; (b) on the other hand, it can be, and has widely been, used to undermine the ambiguity account: since the semantics of natural language is greatly complicated by a logical relation of presupposition, which requires either a trivalent logic or a bivalent logic with gaps, other things being equal, the usual considerations of theoretical parsimony weigh against both a presuppositional semantics and so an ambiguity of negation (see, for instance, Thomason 1973; Kempson 1975; Wilson 1975; Atlas 1989; Gazdar 1979; Martin 1982; Horn 1985).

     However, Burton-Roberts (1989a, 1989b, 1993/97) has argued convincingly that a presuppositional semantics, far from carrying with it a commitment to a semantically ambiguous negation operator, is *incompatible* with it; a semantic account of presupposition entails that negative sentences cannot be p-cancelling, so introducing a p-cancelling operator (in addition to an assumed p-preserving negation operator) is tantamount to acknowledging the existence of counterexamples to the basic thesis. He argues further (Burton-Roberts 1991) that while there may be a scope ambiguity of negation, this leaves presuppositions intact (that is, presuppositions slip through the net of even wide-scope negation). In short, the issue of the ambiguity or univocality of negation is, in fact, independent of the presuppositional issue.

6   The situation seems to be different in the existential quantifier case:

     (i)   Someone isn't hungry.

The natural and immediate interpretation here is that there is someone such that that person is not hungry, i.e. predicate negation. If we wish to maintain the external negation as the semantics, we get the following Gricean analysis:

     (ii)   what is said: $-([Ex: x \text{ person}] (x \text{ hungry}))$
             what is implicated: $[Ex: x \text{ person}] - (x \text{ hungry})$

This, again, preserves the 'existential presupposition' that there is an existing person about whom one is talking. The question arises whether the semantically given wide-scope negation ever surfaces as the understanding (as what is communicated). It's not clear that it does, except in the echoic sort of case where the negation is a corrective rejoinder to someone else's affirmative statement 'Someone is hungry' (see discussion of echoic (or metalinguistic) negation in section 4.4). Horn (1989, sections 4.3 and 7.3) offers an explanation for the missing wide-scope negation understanding in terms of his principle of 'the division of pragmatic labor'.

7   Burton-Roberts (1999: 357–8) considers (Gricean) accounts that treat the existential entailment/presupposition as a conversational implicature to be misguided: 'it is typical of conversational implicatures to be generally closer to the communicative *point* of an utterance than what is actually "said". But exactly the opposite is true of presuppositions. That there is a French king could hardly be further removed from the communicative point of (the usual p-preserving understanding of) an utterance of *The king of France is not bald*.' I think this is right; Grice's recourse to conversational implicature for this sort of case is a very clear instance of his conception of it as 'a useful philosophical tool', rather than as a level with communicative import. As we will see in section 4.3.4, this criticism does not carry over to the relevance-theoretic account on which, via a pragmatic process of negation narrowing, the 'presupposition' is preserved at the level of explicit content ('what is said'). Burton-Roberts (1999) considers the Gricean and the relevance-theoretic accounts to be essentially the same; however, there are important differences, differences that make all the difference, in my view. One of these is this shift from an implicature account to a propositional enrichment account and there are others (see discussion in Carston 1999a, and in section 4.3.4 of this chapter).

8   Atlas (1989: 69) refers to the scope-neutral semantics for negation as the Atlas–Kempson thesis, acknowledging the parallel work of Ruth Kempson (1975, 1979). However, as far as I can see, her position, which has evolved over the years, has never been identical to his. In her 1975 book she was clearly a Gricean, as described in section 4.3.1; with the development of relevance theory, she moved to the view that the internal negation was the result of pragmatic enrichment at the level of the proposition expressed (see Kempson 1986a, 1988). With this move, she does come close to the Atlas view in that both of them, together with relevance-theorists in general, assume that pragmatic inference may contribute to the proposition expressed. I think she has remained constant, however, in assuming a wide-scope semantics for negation, which distinguishes her position from Atlas's and aligns her with the general Gricean approach.

9   Atlas (1989: 62, 132) stresses that sense-generality is to be kept distinct from vagueness of predicates. Vague terms, like 'few', 'heap', perhaps 'bald', and colour words, do not have sharply demarcated senses, while sense-general linguistic elements, such as negation, may do.

10 Atlas (1989: 140–1) gives another, less direct, argument, in which he makes an interesting analogy with a theory of navigation which is successful in getting sailors from one place, say, Dover, England, to a distant point on the globe, say, Wellington, New Zealand, but which is based on the false premise that the earth is flat. His point seems to be that while the general Gricean theory of conversational inference (language use) is successful in accounting for how hearers arrive at the full signification of an utterance (that is, at speaker's meaning), it is less clear that such a theory can tell us anything about 'the *actual* meanings of English expressions'. The import of this is hard to assess. It is true that, on the Gricean analysis, the starting point (i.e. the semantics) for the pragmatic constructive process could be wrong despite the theory leading to the right result, but this, of course, is equally true of Atlas's alternative analysis. He is assuming the standard Gricean inferential apparatus in his own account, so the property of having a useful theory, which nonetheless involves a false premise, might apply also to his sense-general semantics, to the extent that it is given any actual content.

11 In order to avoid a proliferation of ambiguity and some counterintuitive implications for utterance processing, a case has been made for multiply quantified sentences, as in

(i), having a logical form in which the relative scopes of quantifiers are not specified, this being left to a subsequent process:

(i) Few examiners marked many papers.

See, for instance, Kempson and Cormack (1981, 1982) and, in particular, Bach (1982), who discusses Kempson and Cormack's two-level semantic approach, arguing instead for a single level of scope-neutral (hence subpropositional) semantic representation, with particular (fully propositional) understandings derived pragmatically. Hobbs (1996) takes a similar position, pointing out that the following sentence has 120 possible scopings, and yet people seem to be able to assign it a specific interpretation without first having to compute the set of possibilities and then choose among them:

(ii) In most democratic countries most politicians can fool most of the people on almost every issue most of the time.

Since negation interacts scopally with quantifiers, so increasing the range of logically possible interpretations, this analysis of quantifiers makes Atlas's idea that negation has a similarly scope-unspecified presence in logical form all the more plausible.

12 The relevance-theoretic line of reasoning was anticipated in Wilson's (1975: 99–104) Gricean account of the preferred interpretations of presuppositional sentences. She employed the manner maxims (specifically, those enjoining brevity and clarity) in arguing for a pragmatic account of presupposition-preserving interpretations of semantically univocal (wide-scope) negated sentences. The idea is that, other things being equal, an utterance of (i) is an unnecessarily prolix and very obscure way of attempting to communicate (ii), so a speaker observing the maxims will not do this, and a hearer interpreting (i) will assume that the negation applies to the relation between the subject and predicate, there being no briefer or clearer way of expressing that.

(i) Lydia's sister didn't play a piano sonata.
(ii) Lydia doesn't have a sister.

In subsequent relevance-theoretic terms, a speaker observing the optimal relevance constraint would not use (i) to communicate (ii), since to do so would be to put her hearer to some quite pointless processing effort: he would be made to decode concepts (concerning the playing of a piano sonata) from which nothing would follow; all the intended cognitive effects would follow from an utterance of the briefer and non-redundant (ii).

13 Burton-Roberts's treatment does not necessitate any of the massive complications brought about by a three-valued logic of presupposition but rather preserves the classical definitions of the logical connectives. Negative existential sentences, such as 'The F does not exist', which are paradoxical on standard presuppositional accounts, cause no problem on his revised account. However, for criticisms see Atlas (1991), Seuren (1990) and Turner (1992).

14 B-R (1989a, 1989b) claims that Horn's commitments lead him into a double bind whereby he is explicitly supporting the view which disavows the existence of semantic presupposition and, simultaneously, due to his treatment of these examples as metalinguistic negations, implicitly supporting the semantic presuppositionalists. Horn (1990) continues to protest his freedom from this error, maintaining his overt support for a

presupposition-free semantics. I think that one consequence of the account of the p-denial cases that I develop in section 4.5 is a vindication of Horn's general stance with regard to these examples and the evaporation of any appearance of dilemma. This is discussed in more detail in Carston (1998c), Burton-Roberts (1999) and Carston (1999a).

15   There is a small point of disagreement between Noh (1998b, 2000, chapter 3) and me regarding exactly what kind of metarepresentational use is involved in the MN examples. Noh thinks that 'echoic use' is too restrictive and that the right notion is one of simply attributive representation, dropping the attitudinal component (see her section 3.3.2). I prefer to maintain the 'echoic' characterization, since these cases are not simply attributive in the way that quoting or reporting someone's utterances/thoughts are, and the main cognitive effects seem, on the whole, to hinge on the expression of attitude. (See also Iwata 1998, who supports the 'echoic' analysis and develops it further by exploring the notion of the 'focus of echo'.)

Van der Sandt's (1991, 1994) reanalysis of a range of MN cases appears, on the surface, to be similar to mine, as he maintains that the negation in these cases is truth-functional descriptive negation, and in its scope is an echo-operator, which has within its scope the full informative content of a previous utterance (including presuppositions, conventional and generalized conversational implicatures, as well as the truth-conditional content). His notion of 'echo', however, is not the same as the relevance-theoretic one, being more akin to the notion of 'attributive' use, without an attitudinal component, so to that extent he aligns with Noh rather than me. But, as she points out (Noh 2000, section 3.2.2), his analysis is overly restrictive: it applies only to the metarepresentation of (previous) *utterances* and then only to their informational content, leaving echoes of elements of linguistic form unexplained.

16   The different types of metarepresentational use in linguistic communication are discussed in Noh (1998b, 2000, chapter 2) and Wilson (1999b/2000). The unifying feature of the many varieties of metarepresentation (quotations, mentions of words and concepts, echoic attributions and allusions, etc.) is that they involve *representation by resemblance* (as opposed to descriptive truth-based representation). The degree of resemblance between the original representation and its metarepresentation varies with context and is governed by relevance considerations (effort and effect); strict identity is a special case of resemblance and is seldom attempted by a speaker or expected by a hearer.

An interesting suggestion made by both these authors is that even standard 'descriptive' negation may actually involve metarepresentation, though not of an echoic, attributive sort. Quite generally, it is possible to metarepresent, as well as utterances and thoughts, more abstract representational entities like propositions and hypotheses. The suggestion is, then, that descriptive negation may involve the metarepresentation (and denial) of just such an abstract entity. An advantage of this idea is that it captures the widespread intuition that negative sentences/utterances are marked, relative to their corresponding positives, and that the processing of a negative in some sense assumes the availability of the corresponding positive (see Horn 1989, chapter 3).

17   Both Foolen (1991) and Moeschler (1992b, 1997) also find highly problematic the idea that the negation involved in MN is the standard propositional operator, though both apparently favour a univocal semantics for 'not'. Following Atlas (1989), Foolen advocates a sense-general semantics, something like 'signifying inadequacy', which is neutral between descriptive inadequacy and metalinguistic inadequacy, one or other of which has to be pragmatically derived on any given use. However, cases involving metalinguistic inadequacy are not, according to him, amenable to truth-conditional interpretation, since it does not make sense to ask about them whether they are true or false (Foolen 1991: 234). Moeschler advocates a procedural, non-truth-conditional semantics

for 'not'; he represents this as a set of mutually exclusive conditions in a branching tree, such that when set A is met the result is descriptive negation, when set B is met the result is metalinguistic negation, and so on, for other types (polemic negation, illocutionary negation, etc.). This, in fact, looks more like a polysemy account than a univocal semantics.

18   From their own theoretical perspectives, both van der Sandt (1991, 1994) and Geurts (1998a) also argue for a truth-functional negation in these sorts of cases. Geurts includes 'form denials', along with 'information denials' (which he subdivides into proposition, presupposition and implicature denials), in the class of logical negations. He presents additional arguments to those I have given against Horn's claim that MN means 'I object to U', including the point that while Horn's characterization leads one to expect that MN cannot occur in embedded positions, this is simply not so:

   (i)   In America, people don't eat tom[a:touz] but tom[eɪDouz].
   (ii)   Barney claims that Mary didn't eat two but three bananas.
   (iii) Mary is convinced that the king of France isn't bald because there is no king of France.

The embedded negations here seem to involve metalinguistic (echoic) elements just as much as unembedded cases, indicating that 'metalinguistic negation is just as much part of the language as ordinary descriptive negation' (Geurts 1998a: 283).

19   Although Horn and others talked of MN as registering an objection to *any aspect what-soever* of a previous utterance, this is simply not true of the particularized conversational implicatures of a previous utterance (as pointed out and discussed by Chapman 1993, 1996). This is explained on the truth-functional analysis, because it follows from it that the negation affects the truth-conditional content of the proposition which it has scope over rather than properties of a (previous) utterance (see discussion in Noh 1998b, 2000, chapter 3). This raises an interesting question about so-called generalized conversational implicatures, the status and treatment of which has been a background theme of the last few chapters (conducted largely in notes). These have featured as absolutely central cases in Horn's (1985, 1989, 1992a) discussions of MN; for instance:

   (i)   Some men aren't chauvinist; all men are.
   (ii)   She didn't finish her PhD and get a job; she got a job and finished her PhD.

The idea is that what's being objected to and corrected is a generalized conversational implicature ('Not all men are chauvinist', 'She finished her PhD before she got a job') carried by an utterance of the corresponding positive sentence. This differ-ence between the generalized and particularized cases might seem to lend weight to the neo-Gricean GCI/PCI distinction. In fact, however, as I've argued in chapter 3 and elsewhere, these should not be construed as implicatures at all (that is, as consti-tuting a representational level distinct from the proposition expressed), but rather as cases of on-line local pragmatic enrichments which contribute to the propositional content and so, whether echoically used or not, fall in the scope of the truth-functional negation.

20   In Carston (1994b/96a) I considered the example in (i) (originally from Noel Burton-Roberts) and suggested a pragmatically enriched propositional form along the lines of (ii) (fine-tuning probably required), with standard truth-functional 'not' and quoted material within its scope:

(i)   Her dissertation is not eSOTeric; it's esoTERic.
(ii) Not [her dissertation is correctly described by pronouncing 'eSOTeric']; her
      dissertation is correctly described by pronouncing 'esoTERic']

I noted that Seuren (1990: 444) has proposed a very similar sort of representation, but as an underlying *semantic* representation, an element of the language
system itself, which undergoes complex movement and deletion rules to give the
surface form in (i). As Burton-Roberts (1990: 467–8) points out, this seems to
entail that a sentence like 'Her dissertation is esoteric' is indefinitely many ways ambiguous (It would have another semantic representation for 'proper spelling', another
for 'proper morphology', etc.) On the account I am advocating, the representation
in (ii), rather than being construed as a level of underlying linguistic representation,
is the outcome of pragmatic inferential processes, which interpret the (surface) linguistic clues given by the utterance itself. (See short discussion in the conclusion of chapter
2.)

   The really big issue here concerns the nature of metarepresentation, in particular, the
metarepresentational use of natural language. Questions include: Is it essentially a
semantic or a pragmatic phenomenon, or something else altogether, a reflex in public
language of a fundamental cognitive capacity perhaps? Is it a feature of the language
faculty and, if so, does that entail that every sentence has various logical forms with, as
it were, quotation marks around certain constituents? If it is not a part of the grammar,
then how does it arise in interpretation?

21 The semi-formal representation here with the 'not' placed outside the positive sentence
    reflects the one-place propositional connective of the Fregean logical system. Horn
    (1989) prefers the Aristotelian predicate denial formulation and has rather good argu-
    ments for it, so an alternative representation of this level might be [The F is-not G] as
    a way of capturing the idea that 'not' is a mode of predication. Nothing hangs here on
    the difference in the formulations since both encompass so-called presupposition-
    cancellation.

22 In fact, many cases of MN, besides those concerned with mistaken presuppositions,
    are not contradictions. Horn himself has never seen this as a necessary property of the
    phenomenon; for instance, in Horn (1989: 494), he gives the following, clearly non-
    contradictory, attested example as a case of MN:

    (i)   A sociopath wouldn't get through the first ten minutes of my films. They are
          too slow. Someone isn't killed in the credits.
                              (from a newspaper interview with Brian de Palma)

He also claims that 'any negation which takes scope over a [sentential] conjunction, disjunction, or conditional must be metalinguistic' (Horn 1989: 476), so that the following, also clearly non-contradictory, examples have to be interpreted metalinguistically,
according to him:

    (ii) It's not the case that Chris won and Sandy lost.
    (iii) It is not the case that if X is given penicillin he will get better; it might very
          well have no effect on him.

Koenig (1991: 150), who takes it that MN can be used to reject the truth-conditional
content of a previous utterance, claims the following non-contradictory cases are just as

much metalinguistic (echoic) as would be those in which the highlighted terms are swapped with each other:

(iv) The weather is not HOT, it is WARM.
(v)   He didn't IMPOSE some ridiculous rules, he SUGGESTED some.

A number of other descriptively non-contradictory cases, which are, nevertheless, most naturally interpreted as involving metarepresentational negation, are discussed in Carston (1994b/96a), Carston (1998c) and Noh (1998b, 2000, chapter 3).

23 As Burton-Roberts (1999) points out, his own account similarly involves three levels, only two of which, (ii) and (iii), are actual interpretive possibilities:

(i)   encoded semantics: Not [the F is G]
(ii)   by Cognitive Tendency to Bivalence: [the F is not-G]
(iii) reanalysis into MN: Not ['the F is G']

The main differences between our positions concern: (a) the semantics of 'not' and so of the sentence form 'The F is not G'; (b) the mechanism responsible for the first interpretation, on which the presupposition is preserved; and (c) the principle responsible for the rejection of that interpretation in a p-denial case, leading to the reanalysis in terms of MN. (See Carston 1999a, for discussion of each of these.) The main difficulty with B-R's account, in my view, is its rigidity: the processing sequence given in (i)–(iii) applies in every instance of a p-denial, whatever the context, or the ordering of the clauses, so that it is impossible for the metarepresentational interpretation to be accessed without the p-preserving interpretation having been constructed first and rejected.

24 Seuren (2000) advocates a redefinition of the so-called truth-functional operators in natural language ('and', 'or', 'not', 'if . . . then') as 'commitment-specifying' operators; he focuses on negation specifically, developing an account of it as a univocal rejection operator, which can take as its argument any of the following: propositional content, a formal linguistic feature or a presupposition. This marks a major shift from his long-held semantic ambiguity position, which involved a minimal negation and a radical (= presupposition-cancelling) negation, both of them truth-functional operators, though these continue to play their part in a specification of the (trivalent) *logical* properties of language. I find both his general stance on the connectives and the particular account of negation extremely interesting, but cannot pursue them here since that would require extensive consideration of his well-developed 'discourse semantic' framework, within which they are embedded, and the accompanying strong antipathy to any pragmatic approach (whether Gricean or relevance-theoretic). Despite the major theoretical differences between Seuren's approach and that of relevance theory, many of the underlying premises and intuitions are very similar (see, in particular, the discussion of the relation between logic and natural language semantics in Seuren 1995, 2000).

25 The further question that inevitably arises in the context of a relevance-theoretic approach to natural-language semantics is whether an element of linguistic form encodes conceptual or procedural information. I have opted for a conceptual approach since it seems to me that 'not' has the standard properties of conceptual meaning (for instance, it is compositional and truth-evaluable). However, a case has been made for a procedural treatment of metalinguistic negation by Yoshimura (1995, 1998), and a quite general procedural account of 'not' on all its uses is advocated by Moeschler (1992a, 1992b, 1997).

5

The Pragmatics of On-line Concept Construction

By a kind of necessity of language, my expressions, taken literally, sometimes miss my thought; I mention an object, when what I intend is a concept. I fully realise that in such cases I was relying upon a reader who would be ready to meet me half-way – who does not begrudge a pinch of salt.

(Frege 1892b/1980: 54)

Or again if someone were to say 'He's just an evangelist,' he might mean, perhaps, 'He's a sanctimonious, hypocritical, racist, reactionary, money-grubber.'

(Grice 1989a: 361)

In previous chapters, the focus has been on pragmatic inference whose contribution to the explicit content of an utterance (the proposition expressed, or explicature) is to complete or strengthen the meaning of a constituent of the logical form of the utterance. In this chapter, I will consider the putatively opposite, or complementary, process of loosening or broadening aspects of encoded conceptual content. As mentioned briefly in chapter 2, according to the standard relevance-theoretic treatment, this works quite differently from content narrowing or enrichment, in that its effects are registered at the level of implicature alone. On this view, loose use, which is taken to include certain kinds of figurative use, such as metaphor and hyperbole, does not contribute to the proposition expressed, which, consequently, is not among the thoughts communicated by the speaker. I suggest a different account in this chapter, an account on which the complementarity of the processes of narrowing and broadening is reflected in the proposition expressed, which is, therefore, explicated in both sorts of case.

5.1 Encoded Concepts and Communicated Concepts

There are atomic concepts and there are complex concepts; atomic concepts are simple unstructured entities and complex concepts are structured strings of atomic concepts. I follow Jerry Fodor in assuming that concepts encoded by (monomorphemic) lexical items are atomic and so not decompositional; they don't have definitions (sets of necessary and sufficient component features) and they are not structured around prototypes or bundles of stereotypical features (for the arguments, see Fodor et al. 1980; Fodor 1998; Laurence and Margolis 1999). If a complex concept (i.e. a structured conceptual string) is linguistically encoded, the linguistic form involved is standardly a phrase and the concept is determined (at least in part) compositionally. The discussion of concepts in this section is concerned just with *lexically* encoded concepts and the pragmatically derived concepts that they are taken to communicate in particular contexts, hence just with atomic concepts.

According to the relevance-theoretic view, an atomic concept consists of an address or node in memory which may make available three kinds of information: logical content, encyclopaedic or general knowledge, and lexical properties. Each of these kinds of information has its own format. The logical entry consists of a set of inference rules, or 'meaning postulates', which capture certain analytic implications of the concept, generally falling far short of anything definitional. The encyclopaedic entry comprises a wide array of different kinds of knowledge, including commonplace assumptions, scientific information, culture-specific beliefs and personal, idiosyncratic observations and experiences. Some of this information may be stored as discrete propositional representations, some of it may be in the form of integrated scripts or scenarios (as discussed in chapter 3), and some may be represented in an analogue (as opposed to digital) format, perhaps as mental images of some sort. This entry is internally structured in terms of the degree of accessibility of its constituent elements to various processing systems, such as the utterance comprehension system. Accessibility is an organizing principle that entails more or less constant rearrangement of the internal structure of the entry; differences in both the frequency and recency of use in processing of specific items of information affect their accessibility and, at any moment, newly impinging information may effect changes in the accessibility hierarchy of the entry, or of specific subsections within it. The third sort of entry, the lexical one, specifies such properties as the phonetic form and the phonological and syntactic properties of the linguistic form that encodes the concept.

Consider the concept CAT: its logical entry contains an inference rule whose output is ANIMAL OF A CERTAIN KIND; its encyclopaedic entry contains general knowledge about the appearance and behaviour of cats, including, perhaps, visual images of cats, and, for some people, scientific knowledge about cats, such as their anatomy, their genetic make-up, or their relation to other feline species, etc., and, for most people, personal experiences of, and attitudes towards, particular cats; its lexical entry, for an English-speaker, includes the phonetic structure and grammatical properties of the word 'cat'. While concepts such as CAT, SING and CLEVER probably have all three entries, some concepts lack one of the three (or, conceivably, even two of them). For instance, if the word 'or' encodes a concept, it may well have a logical entry but no encyclopaedic entry; proper names are generally assumed to have no logical properties; if we have an atomic concept which can be expressed by the English phrase 'best childhood friend', that concept probably has a logical and an encyclopaedic entry, but it has no lexical entry (in English, at least); for further discussion, see Sperber and Wilson (1986a/95b: 83–93). Now, there are many questions raised by this general picture. For instance, is there really a clear logical/encyclopaedic distinction, and, if so, how is it determined in particular cases? What is involved in 'having' (knowing or possessing) a concept? Clearly, one must know its logical properties, but, in most cases, these fail to distinguish a particular concept from a whole bunch of other, related but distinct, concepts (e.g. CAT, DOG, COW, HORSE, all have the single meaning postulate ANIMAL OF A CERTAIN KIND). Equally clearly, one need not have much, if any, of the potentially vast range of encyclopaedic information about its denotation. Third, propositional thought is said to be conducted in a conceptual format, but which, if any, of these three kinds of information are integral to, or carried along with, a concept when it features in a thought? These are hard questions and way beyond my scope here. For the purposes of this chapter, I shall simply adopt the incomplete story as just outlined, though towards the end I will briefly consider the possibility that word meanings are often not full-fledged atomic concepts, but rather schemas for the construction of such concepts.

In the next two subsections, the expression 'ad hoc concept' features quite prominently. This term is used to refer to concepts that are constructed pragmatically by a hearer in the process of utterance comprehension. The idea is that speakers can use a lexically encoded concept to communicate a distinct non-lexicalized (atomic) concept, which resembles the encoded one in that it shares elements of its logical and encyclopaedic entries, and that hearers can pragmatically infer the intended concept on the basis of the encoded one. The description of such concepts as 'ad hoc' reflects the fact that they are not linguistically given, but are constructed on-line (on the fly) in response to specific expectations of relevance raised in specific contexts. There is considerable evidence that the human conceptual capacity is flexible and creative in this way; for instance, Barsalou (1987, 1992) has shown how, in different contexts and for different purposes, people can incorporate different information from long-term memory (encyclopaedic entries) to form distinct concepts for a single category. For example, under some conditions, the category of cats is conceptualized as having the property 'chase birds', in others it is not; for certain purposes, a concept of the category of sports takes the property of 'winners and losers' as central, while, for others, this property is absent or demoted in importance.[1]

It is hardly surprising that this capacity is exercised in communication and interpretation, where it is given the extra impetus and direction of the presumption of relevance, so that any required construction of concepts is guaranteed to be relatively easy to achieve (low in processing cost) and to have a satisfactory array of cognitive effects. It's worth noting that an ad hoc concept recovered in the process of understanding an utterance need not be an entirely novel or one-off occurrence, though it may be. The basic characteristic of an ad hoc concept is that it is accessed in a particular context by a spontaneous process of pragmatic inference, as distinct from a concept which is accessed by the process of lexical decoding and so is context-invariant (that is, one that comprises the standing meaning of the word in the linguistic system). So, for instance, a speaker may use the word 'happy' in a particular context to communicate a concept which, although not encoded by the lexical form, is an established component of the hearer's conceptual repertoire, one that features as a constituent of certain of his thoughts. It might be a concept of a particular emotional state of deep relaxed contentment that he associates with long, lazy, summer days they have spent together on a Greek island. Such a concept could have a logical entry (for instance, it would entail the more general lexical concept HAPPY) and an encyclopaedic entry, though no lexical entry. Alternatively, the communicated concept might be a quite new construction for the hearer and, having accessed it in the process of understanding a particular utterance, he might never employ it again. To distinguish pragmatically derived (that is, *ad hoc*) concepts from lexicalized ones, I will represent them with an asterisk, for instance, HAPPY*.

5.1.1   *Ad hoc* concepts via narrowing

The following kind of example in which a logical form is pragmatically enriched in the process of deriving the basic explicature of the utterance has been discussed in earlier chapters:

(1)   a. On the top shelf.   [THE MARMALADE IS . . .]
      b. It's snowing.   [IN KATHMANDU]
      c. I've got nothing to wear to the party.   [NOTHING APPROPRIATE]
      d. You can enter the club if you're 18.   [AT LEAST 18]
      e. He handed her the scalpel and she made the incision.   [AND THEN]
      f. The police hit the suspect and she had to go to hospital.   [AND AS A RESULT]
      g. He begged her not to jump.   [OVER THE EDGE]

Understanding either of the first two examples in a specific context requires the recovery of whole constituents, a subject term in (1a) and a location in (1b), by a process of 'free' pragmatic enrichment. Arguably, the same holds for the other examples in (1), for which a particular outcome of the enrichment process is suggested in brackets, although cases such as the quantifier domain specification in (1c) are controversial (see chapter 2, section 2.7). In the two conjunction examples, the linguistically encoded meaning specifies no particular connection between the events; the temporal relation in (1e) and the cause–consequence relation in (1f) are pragmatically inferred, perhaps via highly accessible general knowledge schemas concerning relevant ways in which events connect up. Note that in (1e) the second conjunct is further narrowed by the obvious assumption that the incision was made with the scalpel mentioned in the first conjunct. Similarly in (1g), a further constituent may be recovered so that, in an appropriate context, the utterance could be taken to communicate that he begged her not to jump off the ledge of a high building.

I mention the examples in (1) so as to set them aside for the rest of the chapter. The focus now is on a rather different type of enrichment, where, rather than adding a conceptual constituent, the pragmatic process targets a particular lexical item and strengthens the concept it encodes. Consider the concept encoded by the italicized word in each of the following:

(2)   a.   Ann is *happy*.
       b.   I want to meet some *bachelors*.
       c.   The *birds* wheeled above the waves.
       d.   The path is *uneven*.
       e.   Tom has a *brain*.
       f.   *Something*'s happened.

The example in (2a) was discussed briefly above, the idea being that the encoded concept HAPPY is quite general, covering a wide range of states of positive feeling, while the concept communicated and understood in a particular context is considerably narrower and denotes a much more specific state. This is plainly the case for the full range of 'emotion' words: 'sad', 'angry', 'pleased', 'afraid', 'upset', 'depressed', etc., each of which applies to a great gamut of quite distinct states of mind. In this regard, consider the following attested example:

(3)   Kato (of O. J. Simpson): He was upset but he wasn't upset.

This utterance looks contradictory on the surface, but, in the context of a witness being questioned about Simpson's state of mind on the day when his wife was murdered, it was understood as communicating that he was in a certain kind of upset state of mind, but that he was not in another (more intense, perhaps murderous) mental state. The word 'upset' was understood as expressing two different concepts of upsetness, at least one, but most likely both, involving a pragmatic strengthening of the more general lexical concept UPSET.

In the case of (2b), suppose the context is one in which the speaker has made it clear that she wants to settle down and have children, then the relevant concept, BACHELOR*, is narrower than the encoded concept whose extension is the set of unmarried adult males; 'eligibility for marriage' is a crucial component of the derived concept. In the case of (2c), the BIRD* concept inferred would be confined to sea birds, and so would exclude sparrows, robins, owls, woodpeckers, etc. The remaining examples have in common that the proposition resulting from linguistic decoding, reference assignment and disambiguation is a trivial truism: all paths are uneven to some extent or other, human beings standardly have a brain, and at any moment in time it is true to say that something has happened (in virtually any location). Some pragmatic narrowing down is required, of the degree of unevenness in (2d), of the sort of brain Tom has in (2e), and of the nature of the event in (2f).

In similar vein, recall the set of examples discussed in chapter 1, where perfectly literal uses of the verb 'open' may communicate quite distinct concepts of the action of opening:

(4) a. Jane opened the window.
     b. Bill opened his mouth.
     c. Sally opened her book to page 56.
     d. Mike opened his briefcase.
     e. Pat opened the curtains.
     f. The child opened the package.
     g. The carpenter opened the wall.
     h. The surgeon opened the wound.

Arguably, the word 'open' encodes a single general concept, while each of the more specific concepts expressed in these examples involves a different manner of opening. Sometimes different ways of performing some action are lexicalized; for instance, each of the verbs 'saunter', 'amble', 'shuffle', 'march', 'stride', 'totter', 'hobble', encodes different ways of walking. In the case of acts of opening, cutting, hitting, and many others, while some differences of manner are incorporated into lexicalized concepts (e.g. 'mow' and 'slice' for kinds of cutting, 'punch' and 'slap' for hitting), many are not, but can be readily pragmatically inferred from the general lexical concepts OPEN, CUT and HIT. Note that other cases involving the manner in which an action is performed, such as (1g) above ('jump *over the edge*'), might also be better thought of as cases of concept enrichment (so JUMP*).

In the different sort of case of a natural kind concept, such as that encoded by 'fish' in the next examples, the enrichment process results in a concept of a particular subcategory of the kind, here a particular sort of fish:

(5) a. One by one, she prised the fish out of their shells.
     b. The fish leapt above the waves alongside the boat.
     c. He smashed the glass bowl and the fish wriggled on the floor.
     d. The fish savagely attacked the young swimmer.
     e. We had some delicious fish in a mornay sauce.

In short, in all of these cases, the extension of the concept pragmatically constructed is a subset of the extension of the lexical concept from which it has been derived. This is shown schematically in (6), where L is the extension of the lexical concept and C^* is the extension of the narrowed *ad hoc* concept, which is the relevant concept in each case.

(6)   L

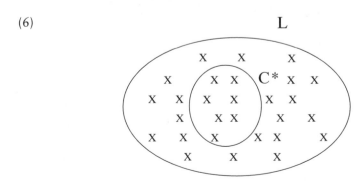

Focusing on example (2b), 'I want to meet some bachelors', let's consider how the pragmatic process of narrowing works. Suppose, as above, that the context is one in which the addressee knows that the speaker, who is a woman, wants to get married and have children. Having accessed the lexical concept BACHELOR, which makes available its associated logical and encyclopaedic information, he uses a subset of this information to construct a more specific concept BACHELOR*, which is relevant (that is, gives rise to cognitive effects) in the context. The encyclopaedic entry might well contain information about certain sorts of bachelor, the irresponsible, fun-loving, forever-young-and-free sort, the elderly, solitary, misogynous sort, and those who are youngish, heterosexual, and capable of long-term commitment, i.e. eligible for marriage. Given the hearer's alertness to the speaker's marital interest, it is probable that information about this third sort of bachelor will be more highly activated than that about either of the others, so it will be accessed first, together with the logical entry, and used to construct the *ad hoc* concept. Provided this gives rise to a satisfactory range of cognitive effects, it is retained as the intended interpretation. In different contexts, other narrowings might be effected, yielding concepts which denote different subsets of the category of unmarried adult males.

One of the features of relevance theory which distinguishes it quite sharply from standard Gricean theory is the view that these strengthenings, of both types exemplified in (1) and (2)–(5), may contribute to the explicit level of communication. On the Gricean approach, they have the status of implicatures, that is, communicated assumptions which are independent from, external to, the core proposition communicated by the utterance ('what is said'). Relevance theorists favour the former view because, in many instances at least, these appear to contribute to the truth-conditional content of the utterance, to what makes it true or false. In chapter 2, I presented various arguments and tests which support this view; assuming it is correct, the proposition expressed by (2b) is as in (7), where BACHELOR* represents the concept that results from narrowing the encoded concept BACHELOR.

(7) S_x WANTS AT T_i TO MEET SOME BACHELORS*

It is the interaction of this propositional form (which is the basic explicature of the utterance) with contextual assumptions that will give rise to cognitive effects; for example, it might strengthen the addressee's assumption that the speaker is keen to get married, it might imply that she would like to meet the addressee's neighbour who has the BACHELOR* property, etc.

As discussed in chapter 2 (section 2.3.4), the derivation of explicatures and implicatures standardly involves a process of mutual parallel adjustment of the two kinds of communicated assumption, which continues until the interpretation meets the addressee's expectation of relevance. So, in some instances, the pragmatic process of narrowing a lexical concept down to a more specific one involves a kind of backwards inference, the particular concept being constructed so as to warrant some antecedently expected implicature. Consider the following exchange, focusing on Ann's response:

(8) Bob: The New Age Psychic Synergy movement promises to reveal the
            secret of lasting peace and happiness. Will you come with me to
            their meeting?
     Ann: No, thanks. I'm already happy.

As is standard with rejections of offers and requests, Ann's direct 'no' answer to
Bob's question raises a 'why?' question; that is, it creates a specific expectation of
relevance regarding her next utterance, which is that it will provide an explanation
for her refusal. Knowing this, Ann utters 'I'm already happy'. But that utterance
does not yield an adequate explanation without a measure of pragmatic narrowing,
because the encoded concept HAPPY applies to a wide range of positive states of
mind of varying quality and durability, not all of which would render a visit to the
Psychic Synergy Society redundant or undesirable. In accordance with the presumption of optimal relevance, Bob infers the more specific concept HAPPY*, which
denotes a mental state of calm contentment of a long-lasting sort (rather than, say,
a transient state of joyous intensity). This provides the premise needed to validate
the expectation that Ann is communicating an explanation for her refusal. In a
somewhat truncated form, the interpretation of Ann's utterance, which is warranted
by Bob's expectation of relevance, is as follows:

(9)   Explicature: ANN IS HAPPY*
      Implicated premise: IF A PERSON IS ALREADY HAPPY* SHE/HE DOESN'T
                            NEED ADVICE FROM THE PSYCHIC SYNERGY
                            MOVEMENT
      Implicated conclusion: ANN IS NOT INTERESTED IN GOING TO A PSYCHIC
                               SYNERGY MEETING BECAUSE SHE IS ALREADY
                               HAPPY*

For more detailed examples, showing how the parallel adjustment process eventuates in explicatures with *ad hoc* concepts as constituents, see Sperber and Wilson
(1997/98a) and, especially, Wilson and Sperber (2000).
    Finally, with regard to the examples just discussed, notice that there is nothing
inherently context-dependent about the linguistic encodings that are pragmatically
adjusted, that is, there is nothing in the linguistic forms at issue that indicates that
a process of conceptual strengthening has to take place. From the linguistic point
of view, it is an optional rather than a mandatory process, and so occurs only in
particular contexts. Compare this with another set of cases often discussed as involving pragmatic enrichment or specification:

(10)   a.   I've been *here* since Saturday.
       b.   Things are better *now*.
       c.   Tracy has a *fast* car.
       d.   The Pritchards are *rich*.

For each of the italicized words, there is a range of possible instantiations. For
instance, in (10a), the relevant location might be the country the speaker is in

(say, she normally lives in Italy, but is currently visiting England), the city, the street, the building, the room, or the very spot where she is standing as she speaks, each one narrower than the last and entailing it (if she's in the University College library, then she is in London, hence in England, etc.). In (10a) and (10b), the indexical elements are overt indicators that a pragmatic process of contextual specification is obligatory, though it is left to pragmatic constraints to determine how narrow it should be. It is unlikely that these cases encode a concept (an address in memory with a logical and/or an encyclopaedic entry); they may encode a procedure (see chapter 2, section 2.3.7), or a concept schema, a pro-concept. In (10c) and (10d), although there is no *overt* indexical element indicating that pragmatic enrichment is required, these scalar adjectives seem to be inherently context-dependent, so that pragmatic specification is in fact mandatory. In one context, 'fast' in (10c) might be taken to express 'fast enough to get to Birmingham by lunchtime', in another 'fast enough to catch up with a speeding criminal', in another 'fast enough to compete in a car rally', and so on, each of these being different ways of completing the concept schema encoded by 'fast'. Given the mandatoriness of the enrichment process for scalar adjectives, it seems likely that there is a *covert* indexical element in their encoded meaning marking this as required. (For further discussion of this sort of case, see Breheny 1997, section 4.)

With regard to the examples of conceptual narrowing in (2)–(5), where it is assumed that the lexical item concerned encodes a full-fledged concept, the process of inferring a stronger concept (which denotes a subset of the entities denoted by the lexical concept) seems to be a kind of 'free' enrichment. It is free from linguistic dictate and is entirely motivated by pragmatic considerations, that is, considerations of relevance.

5.1.2   The problem of concept broadening

The other, apparently opposite, process of loosening or broadening, is exemplified by the following, where the loosely used concept is the one encoded by the italicized lexical item:

(11)   a.   There is a *rectangle* of lawn at the back.
       b.   This steak is *raw*.
       c.   On Classic FM, we play *continuous* classics.
       d.   Ken's a (real) *bachelor*.   [where Ken is technically married]
       e.   Here's my new *flatmate*.   [referring to a newly acquired cat]
       f.   Jim's bedroom is a *rubbish dump*.
       g.   Mary is a *bulldozer*.

The area of lawn referred to in (11a) is very unlikely to be truly a rectangle (with four right angles, opposite sides equal in length); rather it is approximately rectangular, and this holds for many other uses of geometrical terms: a 'round' lake, a 'square' cake, a 'triangular' face, etc. In (11b), the steak, perhaps served in a restaurant, is not really raw but is much less cooked than the speaker wishes; in (11c), the classical music played on the radio station is interspersed with advertisements and other announcements, so not strictly 'continuous'; in (11d), Ken is a married man who behaves like a bachelor (of a certain sort), and so on. In each case, a logical or defining feature of the lexically encoded concept is dropped in the process of arriving at the intended interpretation. These *pragmatically* motivated cases of loose use should be distinguished from cases of *semantic vagueness*, where there is no clear cut-off point between what a predicate is strictly true of and what it is not. For example, at what stage is it no longer true to say of a person that he or she is 'young' or is a 'child'? There seems to be a range of borderline cases where a person is neither clearly a member of the category nor clearly not a member. Other concepts with this property are encoded by colour terms (for instance, 'blue'/'green'), scalar adjectives like 'warm', 'tall', 'rich', and the famous case of 'heap' (how many grains of sand are required to make a heap of sand?). The concepts encoded by the examples in (11), on the other hand, are generally agreed to have clear category borders as a matter of their semantics, and what is going on is that speakers are using them loosely for a particular communicative purpose.[2]

The idea that linguistically encoded meaning can be relaxed has not been given much attention in pragmatics outside the relevance-theoretic framework, though there has been quite widespread expression of doubt about the possibility of a systematic pragmatic account of any such process.[3] In the context of a discussion of words which seem to have two related meanings, one stronger than the other, Grice (1978/89b: 48) says:

> If one makes the further assumption that it is more generally feasible to *strengthen* one's meaning by achieving a superimposed implicature, than to *make a relaxed use* of an expression (and I don't know how this assumption would be justified), then Modified Occam's Razor would bring in its train the principle that one should suppose a word to have a less restrictive rather than a more restrictive meaning, where choice is possible.   (my emphasis [RC])

Atlas (1992), who works within a Gricean view of pragmatics, refers to this passage and responds as follows to the uncertainty expressed in the parenthesis:

> The 'strengthening' assumption can be justified by discovering that there is an intelligible inference that brings about the strengthening of a speaker's meaning – intelligible in the sense that such inferences can be formulated and rationalized – but no intelligible inference that brings about the relaxation of a speaker's meaning. Loose uses of words don't seem particularly rule-governed.

Similarly, Seuren (1993: 226), who eschews pragmatic explanations quite generally, says:

> the maxims seem unable to explain why a sentence like *All the girls in her class admired Joanna* is not taken to imply that Joanna admired herself, although Joanna is herself a girl in her class. The logical analysis of this sentence does, of course, entail that Joanna admired herself. But the normal natural language interpretation of the sentence takes that entailment away. And though the maxims may perhaps lead to the addition of invited inferences, or implicatures, over and above the logical entailments, they will have a difficult job removing logical entailments.

If this outlook is right, the examples in (11) seem to pose quite a problem for semantic/pragmatic analysis. It seems pretty clear that we cannot 'go semantic': the concept encoded by the lexical item 'flatmate' does not include non-humans in its extension, 'continuous' surely doesn't mean the same as 'frequent', and the category of bachelors should not include some married men, etc. Loose use is a pervasive phenomenon and, given our highly developed 'mind-reading' communicative capacity, with the role of the linguistic system being merely to provide clues or pointers, it is not a particularly surprising phenomenon. Despite the pessimism expressed in the quotes above, I believe that an adequate pragmatic theory has to address these cases where the linguistic underdeterminacy thesis manifests itself as what we could, somewhat paradoxically, characterize as a kind of linguistic *over*determinacy, in the sense that the encoded content is overly restrictive. A cognitive account, which emphasizes the role of the differential accessibility of information in understanding utterances, may be better able to meet the challenge of loose use than a more logically oriented, rule-bound account.

With a few notable exceptions, neo-Griceans have tended to steer clear of loose use.[4] However, before moving to a relevance-theoretic account, it is worth noting some features of Grice's own comments on relevant examples. First, immediately following the remarks quoted above (Grice 1978/89a: 48), he considers what he takes to be non-literal uses of the adjectives 'loose' and 'unfettered' when they are applied to the noun 'life': 'John led an unfettered life' versus 'John led a loose life'. Both cases involve what he calls 'transferred' senses, rather than simply specificatory or stronger senses, the idea being that in addition to their basic sense which applies in a physical domain, they have a further sense arising from their projection into a social or psychological domain. He regards the meaning of 'loose' here, with its overtones of dissipation, to have become a distinct encoded sense of the word, while that of 'unfettered' is quite general and is predictable from its basic sense, so it does not comprise an additional derivative sense of the word. Although he does not pursue the point any further, the implication is that the meaning of 'unfettered' in 'unfettered life' is pragmatically derived from the single encoded sense of 'physically free from chains or bonds'. It is clear that the understood meaning – that John led a life which was free from responsibilities and cares – cannot be accounted for by any sort of strengthening process such as would be achieved by the 'superimposing' of an implicature; rather, there is some sort of relaxing of the encoded meaning, which involves the dropping of the feature concerning *physical* restraints.[5] In another inconclusive but suggestive passage, in much later work, Grice discusses the meaning of a particular utterance of 'He's just an evangelist', quoted in the epigraph to this chapter. Again, the intended interpretation has the characteristics of the sort of loose use of lexical concepts that I'm interested in here. It seems to involve a dropping of the encoded (conventional) PREACHER concept and the picking out of a set of relevant encyclopaedic properties: HYPOCRITICAL, REACTIONARY, etc. The example appears in his 'Retrospective Epilogue' (Grice 1989a: 361), where he discusses the two central categories of meaning, the formal (linguistically encoded) and the dictive (what is said). What is most significant is that it is cited as an example which is non-formal and *dictive*, that is, a case in which the meaning is part of what is said but is not given by the conventional meaning of the lexical form in the language system. Since this seems to be directly at odds with the characterization of 'what is said' elsewhere in Grice's work (see discussion in chapter 2 of this book), it is unclear to me whether, and if so how, he regarded this sort of case as being explainable by his account of conversational logic. Nevertheless, it bears an interestingly close relation to the *ad hoc* concept treatment I will shortly suggest for cases of loose use.

In outline, the standard relevance theory account of loose talk, including metaphorical talk, goes as follows (for more detail, see Sperber and Wilson 1986a/95b: 231–7). In some (perhaps many) instances, a speaker chooses to produce an utterance which is a less-than-literal (that is, a loose) interpretation of the thought she intends to communicate. This will arise when she judges that the communication of her thought is facilitated by such a non-literal utterance, in that it makes the thought more accessible to the hearer than a literal one would, or when there isn't an utterance available to provide a literal means of expression of the thought. For instance, although it might be possible to spell out one's thoughts about the unacceptable steak by use of a literal utterance such as: 'This steak is hopelessly undercooked and the idea of eating it is disgusting to me', an utterance of (11b) 'This steak is raw' may communicate all the same implications, but in a far more economical way. More often (and perhaps even in the previous case), it is just not possible to find a literal utterance to express the thought one has and a loose/metaphorical use is not just the best, but the only, way to communicate it. Even a fairly conventional metaphor such as 'Mary is a bulldozer' seems to be such a case; it carries implications (and communicates a 'picture' of Mary) for which there just is no literal equivalent.

Quite generally, the proposition expressed by an utterance is, in the first instance, not a representation of a state of affairs in the world (so is not used descriptively), but a representation of the thought(s) that the speaker seeks to communicate (so is used interpretively). This is reflected in the upper part of the diagram in (12), adapted from Sperber and Wilson (1987a: 708):[6]

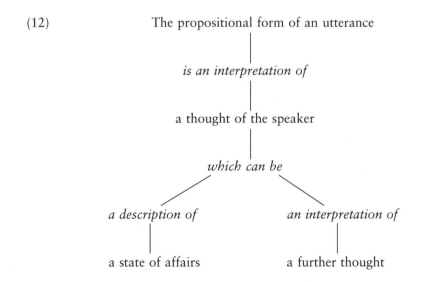

(12)   The propositional form of an utterance

                              is an interpretation of

                          a thought of the speaker

                                which can be

        a description of   *an interpretation of*

        a state of affairs   a further thought

When a propositional representation represents another propositional representation, the relation between them is one of *interpretive resemblance*, that is, one of a greater or lesser degree of shared content; the more logical and contextual implications they share the more they resemble each other. The limiting case of resemblance between representations is strict identity, in which case all such implications are shared and the interpretation is a literal one. But this is not to be generally expected of an utterance, where very often the relation between its propositional form (that is, the proposition it expresses) and the propositional form of the thought the speaker wants to communicate by the utterance is one of non-identical resemblance, that is, the interpretation is not a literal one (see Wilson and Sperber 1988b: 139). It is important for what is to come to be very clear about where the relation of non-literalness is located in this picture; it is the relation between *propositional forms* of utterance and thought, not between encoded linguistic meaning and thought communicated (though, of course, literal encoded linguistic meaning provides a conceptual skeleton for the propositional form of the utterance). According to the relevance-theoretic view, utterances do not come with a presumption that the proposition they express is true (endorsed by the speaker), or is a literal interpretation of the thought being communicated. Rather, utterances come with a presumption of optimal relevance, and it is often more relevant to express a proposition which is plainly false and in a relation of non-identical resemblance with the thought(s) being communicated. Of course, this depends on the addressee being able to distinguish quite easily the communicatively intended implications of the proposition expressed from the unintended ones.

According to this account, the proposition expressed by (11b) above, 'this steak is raw', would be as given in (13a), which is in a relation of non-identical resemblance with the thought the speaker wants to communicate. The hearer, employing the standard comprehension procedure, derives contextual implications in their order of accessibility, such as those in (13b), and retains them as aspects of the intended interpretation (so implicatures) provided they have sufficient cognitive effects:

(13) a. STEAK$_X$ IS RAW
      b. STEAK$_X$ IS VERY UNDERCOOKED
          STEAK$_X$ IS INEDIBLE
          STEAK$_X$ IS DISGUSTING

The upshot of this is a kind of sorting of the logical and encyclopaedic properties of the encoded concept RAW into those that are taken to have been communicated as applying to the steak and those that have not. In this case, the definitional property NOT COOKED, among others, will have been rejected; either it is inhibited (hence low in accessibility) due to activated contextual assumptions about steaks served in restaurants being cooked, or, if accessed, it is abandoned as its inconsistency with these strong contextual assumptions prevents it from having cognitive effects. This is a case which reflects the left-hand branch of the diagram in (12): the proposition expressed by the utterance is a non-literal interpretation of the speaker's thought concerning the gross undercookedness and inedibility of the steak, which is a description of a state of affairs in the world. The account of the metaphorical statements in (11f) and (11g) goes in essentially the same way: only certain properties of rubbish dumps are taken to apply to John's bedroom (presumably, professional garbage collectors don't deliver truck-loads of rubbish to John's room, for instance), and only certain properties of bulldozing machines are understood as pertaining to Mary. On this account, metaphors are treated as cases of loose use; while their departure from strict literalness is generally more striking than that of such mundane cases as those in (11a)–(11c), the difference is not one of kind, but only of degree.

Although Grice did not attempt an account of ordinary loose use, he did sketch a treatment of metaphor, using the example of an utterance of the sentence in (14a):

(14) a. You are the cream in my coffee.
      b. YOU ARE MY PRIDE AND JOY

As with all his accounts of tropes (irony, hyperbole, meiosis), a maxim of quality (truthfulness) plays an essential role (Grice 1975/89b: 34). According to him, a hearer of (14a) derives the proposition strictly and literally expressed, recognizes it as a blatant falsehood (a category mistake), and takes the speaker to be overtly violating (flouting) the first maxim of truthfulness ('Do not say what you believe to be false') in order to get across an implicature, such as (14b), which does preserve truthfulness. The problems with this sort of account have been well aired (see, for instance, Hugly and Sayward 1979; Levinson 1983, section 3.2.5; Sperber and Wilson 1986b; Wilson 1995; Wilson and Sperber 2000), and I won't go into them here. What interests me is that although the relevance-theoretic account of metaphor, as outlined above, is very different from the Gricean story and considerably more explanatory, there is one central aspect of his account which has been carried over into the more cognitive approach. That is the assumption that the proposition expressed by a metaphorical utterance is not communicated. Grice wanted to maintain that 'what is said' has, as part of its definition, that it must be meant by the speaker (in his technical sense of speaker meaning, which involves speaker endorsement), so he moved to a different term in discussing metaphorical utterances: 'what a speaker makes as if to say'. The speaker of (14a) does not say anything, she merely makes as if to say something (namely, that the addressee is the cream in her coffee); only the implicatures of the utterance are meant (or communicated) by the speaker. This holds also for the standard relevance-theoretic account of metaphorical utterances and of loose use quite generally. For instance, in the case of 'This steak is raw', the proposition expressed is as given in (13a), and this is not an explicature of the utterance, but just a vehicle for the communication of a range of implicatures, such as those given in (13b).

This, then, marks a clear asymmetry in the relevance-theoretic treatment of concept narrowing/strengthening and concept broadening/loosening. Cases of concept narrowing contribute to the propositional form of the utterance; that is, enrichment is taken to be one of those pragmatic processes, along with reference assignment and disambiguation, that are involved in arriving at an explicitly communicated assumption, an explicature. Loosening, on the other hand, has no such role; the lexical concept, which provides the point of departure for the loose use, stays in place in the propositional form of the utterance, which simply resembles the one the speaker has in mind to communicate. The question of why there should be this asymmetry arises, since, on the face of it at least, these look like two opposite and symmetrical processes of pragmatically constructing a new concept from a lexically encoded one: narrowing vs. broadening. In fact, as will emerge in the next section, this way of talking is quite misleading as there are not really two distinct processes at work. Rather, there are two possible outcomes (a narrower concept or a broader one) of what is essentially a single process: a process of picking and choosing from among the elements of logical and encyclopaedic information that are made available by the encoded concept. The only difference between them is that, in the case of narrowing, all the logical properties are retained, while in the case of loosening, some of them are dropped. Both outcomes involve a move away from strict literalness, albeit in opposite directions (above and below literalness), so we might well expect that either both sorts of result figure in the proposition expressed by the utterance, or that neither does.

In fact, in the last few years, recognition of the human facility for constructing *ad hoc* concepts in on-line understanding has led to an approach on which such concepts, whether cases of strengthening, or broadening, or a combination of the two, have been taken to enter into the proposition explicitly communicated. In the next section, based on Carston (1996b/97a), I start to look at some of the implications of moving to this more uniform analysis, which obviously entails some departures from the original relevance-theoretic account just outlined.

5.2 A Symmetrical Account of Narrowing and Broadening

There are at least the following two ways of symmetrifying the account: bring narrowing into line with the standard treatment of loose use which does not affect the proposition expressed, or bring loosening into line with the propositional content-boosting account of enrichment. I'll look at these in order, fairly swiftly dismissing the first possibility and arguing for the view that both kinds of concept adjustment work together in determining the proposition(s) explicitly communicated.

To unify narrowing with the established relevance-theoretic account of loose use would entail not building a more specific concept in the enrichment case, but simply using the lexical concept as a jumping-off point to cognitive effects, as it is for loose, including metaphorical, uses. That is, at the level of the proposition expressed, the lexical concept would remain and the effects of pragmatic enrichment would emerge as implicatures. This would, of course, involve a move back in the direction of the Gricean concept of 'what is said'. It would extend the import of the upper part of the diagram given in (12), since many more, in fact virtually all, utterances would have a propositional form which was in a relation of non-identical interpretive resemblance with the thought being communicated. Cases of strengthened meaning could be seen as involving a particular type of interpretive resemblance where the logical implications of the proposition expressed by the utterance would be a proper subset of those of the thought of the speaker.

This may be workable for lexical concepts with rich encyclopaedic entries, such as BACHELOR, with its various sets of stereotypical bachelor properties, which comprise chunks or units within the overall encyclopaedic entry. For example, in (2b), the most accessible chunk of encyclopaedic information might consist of the following set of properties: YOUNGISH, HETEROSEXUAL, FREE TO MARRY, WILLING TO MAKE A COMMITMENT, etc. (along with the logical property UNMARRIED MAN), from which implications such as the following could be inferred:

(15)   a.   S wants to meet some men who are free to marry.
       b.   S wants to meet some men who are willing to commit to a relationship.

A relevance-driven sorting process, similar to that assumed in the loose-use cases, would ensure that other possible bachelor stereotypes, e.g. that of the fussy, old, misogynous type of bachelor, would be bypassed, as would the pope, and various others, who are technically bachelors but do not have the relevant properties.

However, there are a number of cases of enrichment for which this just won't work. While a range of implications can be easily derived from a lexical concept used loosely, this is not so for at least some instances of enrichment. What concept broadening entails is that, in effect, the original (lexical) concept makes available more information than you need, so you can simply disregard whatever does not contribute to relevance (cognitive effects), on the particular occasion. But, of course, the opposite is the case in many instances of narrowing/enrichment; here what the lexical concept makes available is often rather less than one needs to derive the intended effects. Examples (2e) and (2f) are such cases: nothing follows from these literal and trivial truths, and the concepts of 'having a brain' and, especially, of 'something' in 'something's happened' do not obviously give access to a rich set of encyclopaedic assumptions from which the more specific intended concept is built. These enrichments are effected in some other way, relying on inferences that follow more directly from the presumption of relevance itself: that Tom has a brain worth drawing attention to, and that something out of the ordinary has happened.

Furthermore, treating cases of pragmatic enrichment as not affecting the proposition expressed, but simply resulting in implicatures, would quite generally give a very odd result within relevance theory. The relevance of the utterance, its effects, would seem to derive from an interaction of contextual assumptions alone, with the proposition expressed playing no role. This is exemplified in (16) and (17), where it can be seen that the cognitive effects follow from an implicature (an implicated premise) in each case, which represents a particular strengthening, of 'happy' and 'have a brain', respectively, together with other accessible assumptions.

(16)   Proposition expressed: ANN IS HAPPY
       Implicature: ANN IS HAPPY*
       Contextual assumption: IF ANN IS HAPPY* SHE DOESN'T NEED HELP FROM THE PSYCHIC SYNERGY SOCIETY
       Contextual implication: ANN DOESN'T NEED HELP FROM THE PSYCHIC SYNERGY SOCIETY

(17) Proposition expressed: TOM HAS A BRAIN
      Implicature: TOM HAS A VERY ABLE BRAIN
      Contextual assumptions: SOMEONE WITH A VERY ABLE BRAIN COULD
                                    DO THE JOB
                                    TOM IS POSSIBLY THE RIGHT PERSON FOR
                                    THE JOB
      Contextual implication: TOM COULD DO THE JOB
      Contextual strengthening: TOM IS VERY LIKELY THE RIGHT PERSON
                                    FOR THE JOB

This is the sort of case that my functional independence heuristic (discussed in section 2.6.2) was designed to adjudicate: as given in (16) and (17), the proposition expressed has no inferential function independent from that of the alleged implicature, so this picture cannot be right. The pragmatic inference should, therefore, be understood as contributing to the proposition expressed, rather than as resulting in an implicature. This heuristic was conceived as a mere preliminary to the relevance-theoretic account, which subsumes it, and precludes the situation laid out in (16) and (17) from arising: it is part of the definition of cognitive effects, hence of relevance itself, that they must follow from an inferential interaction of the proposition expressed and contextual assumptions (see Sperber and Wilson 1986a/95b: 107–23). I conclude, then, that this tack, a partial retreat back to Grice, as it might be seen, is not the right way to attempt to provide a symmetrical relevance-theoretic treatment of the pragmatics of the narrowing and broadening of encoded meaning.

So let us consider the opposite possibility: bringing loosening into line with the existing account of narrowing. This would involve building into the proposition expressed an *ad hoc* concept, which is a weakening of the encoded lexical concept. In parallel with the representation in (7) of the propositional form of a strengthening case, we would have the following propositional form for (11b), where RAW* represents the concept that results from a particular relaxing of the encoded concept RAW:

(18) STEAK$_Y$ IS RAW*

As on the original account, there follows an array of contextual implications, communicated with varying degrees of strength: the steak is insufficiently cooked, the steak is inedible, the speaker is very unhappy with the state of the steak, the speaker wants this steak replaced by another which has received more cooking, etc.

This is the position that I am going to adopt but it needs to be approached with care. It involves a fairly radical shift of perspective in that there is a dropping of (part of) the logical entry of the lexically encoded concept, usually considered integral to the meaning of the lexical item and, therefore, to the proposition expressed by the utterance. So, before looking at the actual processes involved in constructing this sort of concept, I'll consider some of the consequences of making the move, several of which appear, initially at least, to be problematic.

5.2.1   Consequences of the unified account

This section is divided into six points; the first two consider consequences which could be viewed as quite general objections to an *ad hoc* concept account of loose use and the remaining four are concerned with some of the knock-on effects within relevance theory of adopting the account.

[1]   Someone might object that one upshot of this account is that some words are virtually never used literally, that is, to communicate their encoded meanings; for instance, 'silent' meaning NOISELESS (which would strictly speaking apply only to a soundproof chamber), 'empty' meaning CONTAINING NOTHING, 'continuous' meaning WITHOUT INTERRUPTION, 'rectangle', 'square', 'hexagon', etc. (abstract geometric forms not actually found in nature), etc.[7] The validity of this objection would depend on the assumption that it is very implausible that words are not used literally at least some of the time. But this assumption is not very compelling; it seems quite clear that we simply do have (probably innate) concepts of geometrical perfection and that we use these as a point of departure in entertaining other concepts, which are approximations to them. That this might extend to quite a range of the concepts encoded in natural language should not be seen as troublesome but as a downright useful feature of language. Suppose one were in the business of designing a public representation system for a species identical to humans except for their not yet having such a system in place. This species would have all the other cognitive capacities of the human species, including a sophisticated theory of mind, that is, the ability to attribute complex mental states (such as higher-order beliefs and intentions) to conspecifics, the ability to draw elaborative inferences from newly impinging stimuli by placing them in a context of existing assumptions, and the ability to recognize conceptual and other resemblances from a range of points of view. I think a designer might well opt for a public representation system with quite minimal and even generally uninstantiated encodings (in the sense that little, if anything, in the actual world falls under the encoded concept), since these more fundamental abilities could be relied on to make the appropriate adjustments, with relative ease, in a number of directions. Perhaps then, more often than not, our communication is non-literal in just this way.

[2]   Second, one might wonder what has become of the notion of the truth-conditional content of the utterance. In fact, it is not clear that we really want such a notion in our pragmatics at all, especially if, as relevance theorists argue, the proper domain of a truth-conditional semantic theory is thoughts/assumptions (or, at least, their propositional forms), rather than sentences or utterances. However, suppose we did think there was good reason to maintain that notion, then the new account has a consequence that seems highly problematic for it. An utterance of 'Mary is a bulldozer' can be true, provided Mary has certain properties that appear in the encyclopaedic entry of the lexical concept BULLDOZER and which are central to the new non-lexical concept BULLDOZER*. But, so the argument would go, we have robust intuitions that 'Mary is a bulldozer' is false and 'Mary is not a bulldozer' is true (trivially and patently). And these intuitions are explained by the

presence of the literal encoded concept in the proposition expressed by the utterance. The revised account violates these clear intuitions.

Well, just how robust are these intuitions and what is their source? We can, after all, agree or disagree with someone who utters 'Mary is a bulldozer', as in (19), or even say 'that's *true*' or 'that's *not true*':

(19)   A: Mary's a bulldozer (or: a bit of a bulldozer).
       B: Yes, she is; I'd prefer not to have her on the committee.
       C: She's not really a bulldozer; in fact, she's quite insecure.

Surely what is being denied by C quite explicitly is not that the lexical concept BULLDOZER applies to Mary (which would be a patent truism and completely irrelevant to the conversation A, B and C are having), but that the *ad hoc* concept BULLDOZER* applies to Mary. Similarly, having understood what A is saying about Mary, B expresses her agreement directly; she is not expressing a blatantly false proposition in order to indirectly (via implicature) agree with A about the sort of personality Mary has. These intuitions seem to be at least as strong as, and completely at odds with, the intuition that (the sentence) 'Mary is a bulldozer' is false. Examples in which a loose or metaphorical use of a concept occurs in the antecedent of a conditional, or in a factive subordinate clause, point in the same direction:

(20)   a.   If Mary is a bulldozer, she'll be ideal on the committee.
       b.   Since Mick is a loose cannon at the best of times, I think we should keep him out of any delicate negotiations.

It seems pretty clear that what is being communicated by (20a) is that if Mary is of a certain aggressive disposition, unmoved by the views of others, etc., she'll be ideal on a particular committee. If the arguments based on these various examples are right, it looks as if the source of the original intuition, that 'Mary is a bulldozer' is false, is not the proposition expressed by the utterance (so not its truth-conditional content), but rather the conceptual content of the *logical form* of the utterance, specifically our knowledge of the encoded meaning of the word 'bulldozer'.

[3]   Consider now a more theory-internal consequence. If both strengthenings and broadenings are taken to contribute to the proposition expressed by the utterance, then won't the propositional form of the utterance always be virtually identical to the propositional form of the thought the speaker wants to communicate, so that the distinction between them, discussed in the previous section and reflected in the top half of the diagram in (12), falls away? On the old account, this distinction involved a relationship of non-identical interpretive resemblance between the proposition expressed by a loose or metaphoric utterance and the thought the speaker wants to communicate. According to the new account, the speaker has the thought 'STEAK$_y$ IS RAW*' and the propositional form of her utterance of the sentence 'This steak is raw' is also 'STEAK$_y$ IS RAW*'.

Before directly addressing this point, I should emphasize that the concept of 'interpretive resemblance', arguably one of the most constructive innovations of relevance theory, is not threatened. It plays a fundamental role in the account of irony, indirect quotation and other cases involving the reporting, or echoing, of someone else's thought, or the content of their utterance, where the relation between the original representation and the one used to represent it is typically one of non-identical resemblance (mere overlap of logical and contextual implications). What these cases have in common is that they involve a metarepresentational use which a hearer must recognize if he is to properly comprehend the utterance: there is a fundamental difference between an utterance in which a speaker expresses her own view and one in which she reports or echoes that of someone else. See Wilson (1999b/2000) for extensive discussion of these, and other, kinds of metarepresentational use of language.

However, the cases of loose/metaphorical use we are discussing here are not of this sort (though, of course, they may be put to such use). The speaker of 'This steak is raw' or 'Mary is a bulldozer', is representing her own current thought and it looks as if, on the new account, the proposition expressed by her utterance, and recovered by the hearer, is more or less identical with her thought; both contain the concept RAW* or BULLDOZER*. I say 'more or less' since, in fact, it is quite likely that the concepts they contain are not absolutely identical; there is always leeway for individual differences where pragmatic inference is concerned. But this is just as true of cases of concept strengthening which are generally judged as perfectly literal, such as the example of 'I want to meet some bachelors' discussed in section 5.1.1; the speaker and the hearer may entertain slightly different concepts, BACHELOR* and BACHELOR**, or RAW* and RAW**, without successful communication being impeded. This general fact is beside the point here, the point being that the speaker of the utterance and the hearer, who has understood the utterance, both employ concepts which are distinct from the linguistically encoded one in the crucial respect that they exclude one or more of its logical or defining properties; for example, NOT COOKED AT ALL, PIECE OF MACHINERY.

This symmetrical treatment of pragmatic strengthening and broadening entails that the relation of interpretive resemblance at issue in loose use essentially holds between a lexical concept and the concept it is used to communicate. So there is a further relation of interpretive resemblance not shown in the scheme in (12), a layer which comes in above those which are shown. Adopting this perspective involves a double shift in the locus of the crucial relationship: from one that holds between proposition expressed and thought communicated to one that holds between encoded linguistic meaning and proposition expressed (= thought communicated), and from a global relation between whole propositional forms to a local relation between constituent concepts. While two propositional forms resemble each other to the extent that they share logical and contextual implications, two concepts can be said to resemble each other to the extent that they share logical and encyclopaedic properties. An *ad hoc* concept formed by strengthening a lexical concept seems to involve elevating an encyclopaedic property of the latter to a logical (or content-constitutive) status, as in the case of ELIGIBILITY FOR MARRIAGE in the concept BACHELOR*; an *ad hoc* concept formed by the loosening of a lexical concept seems to involve dropping one or more of the logical or defining properties of the latter. In both cases the resultant concept is in a relation of interpretive resemblance with the lexical concept.

[4]   The next worry is closely related to the previous issue and equally theory-internal. Starkly put, it is the following: the new account seems to have the result that metaphorical (and other loose) uses are no less *literal* interpretations of speakers' thoughts than standard literal uses are. Let's see how this apparent paradox arises. Recall that, according to Sperber and Wilson, an utterance is a literal interpretation of the thought the speaker wants to communicate when the proposition it expresses has the same set of logical and contextual implications as the thought. A slightly different formulation of the same view is: 'The comprehension of every utterance involves [. . .] a process of identifying relevant implications. When the proposition expressed is itself among the implications on which optimal relevance depends, the result is a literal interpretation' (Sperber and Wilson 1987a: 708). Now, according to the proposed symmetrical account, the proposition expressed incorporates *ad hoc* concepts formed by loosening lexical concepts (for example, STEAK$_y$ IS RAW*, MARY IS A BULLDOZER*). These propositional forms look very much like literal interpreta-tions of the thoughts the speaker wants to communicate; at the least, the primary source of non-literalness, the difference between RAW and RAW*, etc., is no longer a feature of the relation between the propositional form of the utterance and the propo-sitional form of the thought. The propositional form of an utterance of the sentence 'Mary is a bulldozer' resembles the speaker's thought about Mary no less than the propositional form of an utterance of the sentence 'I need a bulldozer to clear the field' resembles the speaker's thought that she needs a bulldozer to clear a particular field.

So, on the symmetrical account, the distinction between utterances that are literal and those that are non-literal (or 'less-than-literal', as it is standardly put) interpre-tations of the speaker's thought seems to have collapsed. Yet, surely, we want to pre-serve the essence, if not the precise formulation, of such statements as: 'the hearer is not invariably entitled to expect a literal interpretation of the speaker's thought, nor is such an interpretation always necessary for successful communication to take place. A less-than-literal interpretation of the speaker's thought may be good enough: may indeed be better on some occasions than a strictly literal one' (Sperber and Wilson 1986b: 158). The essential point is that we frequently use elements of en-coded linguistic meaning non-literally, either because this is the most efficient way of communicating our thoughts, or because our language does not provide us with any literal means. It follows from the underdeterminacy thesis that many of the con-cepts that feature in thought are not encoded in public linguistic systems. The con-clusion to be drawn here parallels that made for the immediately preceding point on interpretive resemblance: the proper location of any distinction between the literal and non-literal interpretation of a thought is in the relation between the encoded lin-guistic meaning and the proposition expressed, rather than between the proposition expressed and the thought (which no longer differ in the crucial respect). Further-more, the relation is typically a local one, between lexical or phrasal concepts (lin-guistically encoded), and the atomic or complex concepts (elements of thought) that they are used to communicate. The use is a literal one if the logical/definitional prop-erties of the linguistic encoding are preserved; it is non-literal if they are not.

[5]   A bold claim of relevance theory since its inception has been that verbal com-munication is not governed by any maxim of truthfulness or presumption of liter-

alness. It has been argued that such maxims are either redundant or, in the case of Grice's first maxim of quality: 'Do not say what you believe to be false' (Grice 1975/89b: 27), simply wrong.[8] One of the arguments against truthfulness maxims has turned on the pervasive phenomenon of loose use. According to the old account, the proposition expressed on a loose use is standardly strictly false and not endorsed by the speaker (e.g. BILL HAS A SQUARE FACE, LISA HOPPED ON HER BIKE AND FLEW DOWN THE STREET), yet hearers seem to be generally unaware that any norm has been violated. According to the new account, however, the proposition expressed in a case of loose use *is* endorsed by the speaker; it sufficiently closely resembles the thought which she intends to communicate (e.g. BILL HAS A SQUARE* FACE). So, does the shift in treatment bring with it the consequence that we are, after all, following a maxim of truthfulness?

The response here builds directly on the responses to the previous two points. What Grice's first maxim of truthfulness applies to is his minimal notion of 'what is said', which is essentially the conventional linguistic meaning of an utterance (disambiguated and with the reference of indexicals determined). Now, while it does follow from the proposed symmetrical treatment of loose-use cases that the speaker endorses the proposition her utterance expresses, the point is that this proposition, which may contain various kinds of *ad hoc* concepts, departs even more radically than it did before from the *literal linguistic meaning* of the utterance, so that Grice's first maxim of truthfulness will virtually never be met. This maxim is inoperative for two reasons: (a) people frequently use elements of linguistic meaning non-literally (that is, without endorsing the encoded meaning) as simply the best available means by which to lead a hearer to the proposition(s) they do endorse, (b) as argued in earlier chapters, especially chapter 2, given a level of linguistically encoded meaning (logical form), which is not communicated, and a set of (pragmatically derived) explicatures and implicatures, which are communicated, there seems to be no role for the Gricean conception of 'what is said', so nothing for this maxim to apply to. This is not to deny that hearers standardly derive from utterances propositions which they take to be true (or probably true), but that follows from the process of deriving cognitive effects in accordance with their expectation of relevance, rather than from any presumption concerning the speaker's belief in the literal content of the sentence uttered or the minimal proposition expressed. For discussion of how truthfulness in communication follows from the pursuit of relevance, see Ifantidou (1994, 2001, section 4.2.2) and Wilson (1995).

[6]   Finally, a direct consequence of replacing the encoded concept by a pragmatically inferred concept in cases of loose use is that the proposition expressed is no longer just a vehicle for deriving communicated assumptions (implicatures) but is communicated itself, hence is an explicature. So, in such cases, the only level of meaning in the whole process of utterance interpretation that is not communicated is the logical form. This seems like a thoroughly positive outcome to me; there has always been a kind of redundancy in the standard account of loose use and metaphor in that there were two representational levels (logical form and propositional form) that were tools or vehicles for getting at what was in fact communicated. As suggested in chapter 2, section 2.3.2, it looks as if we may be able to dispense with a

concept of 'proposition expressed' as distinct from base-level explicature (though there is some thinking to be done here about irony and other utterances involving metarepresentational uses). The characterization of an 'explicature' as a communicated assumption which is a *development* of a logical form of the utterance (see chapter 2, section 2.3.1, for a slightly more detailed definition) can be maintained, provided that the notion of a 'development' of a logical form is understood to include pragmatic adjustments to linguistically encoded concepts which may involve dropping logical or definitional elements of the encoded concepts.

If this idea can be sustained, the diagram in (12) will need more radical revision than simply the addition of another layer of interpretive representation, as suggested in consequence [3] above. I tentatively offer the following as part of the new picture:

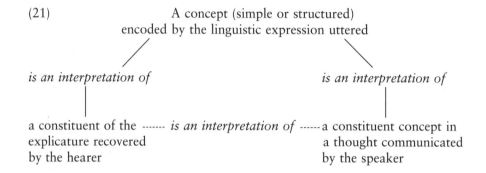

(21)   A concept (simple or structured)
                      encoded by the linguistic expression uttered

is an interpretation of   *is an interpretation of*

a constituent of the ------- *is an interpretation of* ------a constituent concept in
explicature recovered   a thought communicated
by the hearer   by the speaker

The vertical interpretive relation between encoded concept, on the one hand, and concept communicatively intended and concept understood, on the other, is the locus of the distinction between literal and loose (metaphorical) use; that distinction is essentially a function of linguistic underdeterminacy (encoded meaning typically does not determine explicitly communicated meaning). The horizontal interpretive relation, between the concept the hearer infers as an element of the basic explicature of the utterance and the thought component the speaker intends to communicate by her utterance, is rather different; it is not a direct reflection of linguistic underdeterminacy since the hearer's pragmatic inference has made up for that. The point here is that we have two mental representations and the relation between representations is always one of interpretive resemblance (measured in terms of shared implications), even if they are, in fact, identical (the limiting case). Furthermore, given that pragmatic inference is not algorithmic, but a kind of (strongly) constrained guesswork, strict identity between the speaker's thought and that derived by the hearer is not very likely and is not required for successful communication.

No doubt, there are other consequences of bringing the account of loose uses of concepts into line with concept enrichment cases, consequences which will emerge in due course. Confining ourselves to the six considerations just discussed, there seems to be nothing to deter us from unifying the picture by building both sorts of *ad hoc* concepts into the proposition expressed (explicature), although, unsurprisingly, the move makes necessary some modifications to the relevance-theoretic framework, specifically to the characterization of literal and less-than-literal interpretation. In the next subsection, I will look at some empirical data which provide the material for positive arguments in support of the new account.

5.2.2 Arguments for the unified account

We saw in the previous section, under consequence [2], that when a loosely used lexical concept occurs in the syntactic scope of a conditional or a negation operator, it seems that the *ad hoc* concept formed by broadening the lexical concept is understood as contributing to the antecedent of the conditional or as falling in the scope of the negation, and so is a constituent of the truth-conditional content of the utterance. This is an application of the embedding test for distinguishing implicatures from pragmatic contributions to the proposition expressed, which was discussed in chapter 2. For instance, in example (20b), it is because Mick has the attribute represented by LOOSE CANNON* (which entails the property CAUSES RANDOM DAMAGE), rather than the encoded property LOOSE CANNON, that it seems advisable to keep him out of any delicate negotiations. This supports the unified account of concept narrowing and broadening according to which both kinds of conceptual adjustment contribute to the proposition expressed by the utterance.

A second point in favour of the symmetrical account arises when we take a closer look at the outcome of loose use. The diagram given above in (6), to illustrate the relation between a lexical concept and an *ad hoc* concept formed from it by enrichment, shows that the set of entities falling in the denotation of the lexical concept L contains as a proper subset the set of entities in the denotation of the strengthened *ad hoc* concept C*. One might think that if we are dealing in symmetrical processes, then the corresponding diagram for concept loosening will look as in (22). In fact, it more often comes out looking like (23), where the picture is one of a kind of concept shift rather than of a simple broadening, where the denotations of the lexical concept and the concept which results from the 'loosening' process merely intersect:

(22)

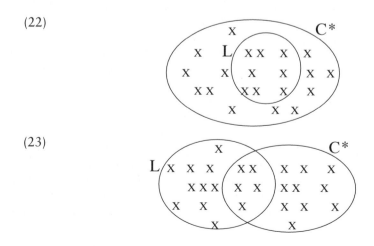

(23)

Consider in this regard the following examples, some of which are repeated from (11):

(24)   a.   There is a *rectangle* of lawn at the back.
       b.   This steak is *raw*.
       c.   The house was still and *silent*.
       d.   Ken's a (real) *bachelor*. [where Ken is technically married]

The encoded concept RECTANGLE is loosely used in (24a), since the lawn in question might have all sorts of little irregularities that render it not strictly rectangular (i.e. not having four right angles). If the denotation of RECTANGLE* includes all strict rectangles along with other shapes that deviate to some limited degree from strict rectangularity, then the relation between RECTANGLE and RECTANGLE* is captured by the diagram in (22). However, the denotation of the *ad hoc* concept might include some cases of strict rectangles while excluding others; it might, for instance, exclude those with two sides a mile long and the other two only a few inches long, the relevant concept here being one that can apply to lawns. If so, then the relation between RECTANGLE and RECTANGLE* is reflected in the diagram in (23); the denotations of the concepts merely overlap. The same two possibilities arise for all the other examples in (24) and, no doubt, for cases of loose use quite generally. For instance, the BACHELOR* concept formed from BACHELOR in (24d) applies to Ken who is technically married but behaves in the free and easy way of a certain sort of unmarried man. The extension of this concept might include all truly unmarried men as well as married men who behave like Ken; if so, then the relation between the denotations of BACHELOR and BACHELOR* is that shown by the diagram in (22). However, it is perhaps even more likely that the *ad hoc* concept excludes some unmarried men, those who live sober, responsible, perhaps celibate lives (such as the pope); then the relation between the denotations of the lexical concept and the new concept is as shown in the diagram in (23). Fairly clearly, the relation of conceptual overlap is not one of broadening alone but also involves some narrowing. A logical property is dropped (for instance, UNMARRIED), but, in addition, another property is given a defining role (for instance, EMOTIONALLY UNCOMMITTED or PROMISCUOUS).

The fact that both processes might be required in forming a communicated *ad hoc* concept makes it look all the more likely that they both contribute to the proposition expressed. It would be very hard to find a principled reason for supposing that, for the cases just discussed, the result of narrowing the concept RECTANGLE or BACHELOR figures at this level, while its simultaneous widening is registered only at the level of implicature. Once such combination cases are taken on board, it follows that those cases of broadening which are the true counterpart to narrowing, that is, those that are pictured by (22), must also contribute a new concept to the proposition expressed.

A third kind of supporting evidence for the proposed unified approach emerges from a consideration of categorial falsehoods and their trivial truth counterparts. This is going to take a little building up, however, before we reach the most compelling data. First, it is often pointed out that positive metaphorical utterances such as (25) are literal category mistakes (sortally incorrect), clearly flouting Grice's first maxim of truthfulness. Their negative counterparts, as in (26), are, therefore, trivial obvious truths, which do not flout the truthfulness maxim. They seem, however, to be no less metaphorical than the positive cases.

(25) a. Robert is a bulldozer.
      b. Sally is a block of ice.

(26) a. Robert isn't a bulldozer.
      b. Sally isn't a block of ice.

In fact, year after year, undergraduate students acquainted with the Gricean story, blithely write of both kinds of example that they are obviously false and so flout the truthfulness maxim. What is really at issue here, in my view, is not the literal truth or falsity of the global sentence/utterance, but the (in)applicability of the linguistically encoded predicates BULLDOZER and BLOCK OF ICE to human beings. It is this, I surmise, that the students are responding to, since it arises equally for the positive and the negative sentences. (Notice that we have here another shift of focus to the constituent word or phrase level, similar in certain respects to those discussed in points [3] and [4] in the previous section; it seems that, quite generally, this is where the distinction between literal and loose use is to be located.) Pursuit of an optimally relevant interpretation ensures that the logical properties of the encoded concepts are dropped in both kinds of case. This is so whether loose use is treated as contributing an *ad hoc* concept to the proposition expressed or not. For instance, on either account, the implicatures of (26b) include (27a) but not (27b):

(27) a. SALLY ISN'T AN EMOTIONALLY COLD PERSON
      b. SALLY ISN'T MADE UP OF SOLIDIFIED H_2O

Consider now another set of examples of obvious falsehoods, which have been discussed by Flieger (1996), who takes them to be also metaphorical; he calls them metaphorical negations, the idea being that a phrase consisting of a negated predicate (e.g. 'not a lion') is used metaphorically as a whole:

(28) a. Ari isn't a lion; he's a pussycat.
          [where Ari is, in fact, a member of the lion species]
      b. Dr Lucas isn't a surgeon; he's a butcher.
          [where Dr Lucas is a surgeon by profession]
      c. Sean isn't a human being; he's a wild beast.
      d. Frank isn't a human being; he's a buddha.
          [where both Sean and Frank are men]

In each case, the subject referent does in fact have the property (taken literally) that the speaker is denying he has and does not have the property (taken literally) that the speaker predicates of him in the next clause, and this is mutually manifest to speaker and hearer. These are interesting examples in the context of a discussion of pragmatic processes of enrichment and loosening, because while Flieger sees them as cases of metaphor (hence of concept loosening, in relevance-theoretic terms), they can just as well be described as cases where an enriched concept is negated. In (28a) for instance, while Ari is plainly a member of the species *Panthera leo*, what the speaker is really denying is that he belongs to a narrower category, which consists of fierce, proud and unapproachable lions; in (28b), where the speaker and the hearer know full well that Lucas is a surgeon by profession, what is being denied is that he belongs in the class of skilful careful surgeons. The same goes, *mutatis mutandis*, for (28c) and (28d). It is unsurprising that such examples can be seen as either cases of metaphorical (loosely used) negations or cases of negated strengthenings; it simply falls out from the concept of negation, the complementarity of concept narrowing and loosening, and the local nature of the processes involved.

It might seem that we have here the basis for an argument in favour of the proposed unified treatment of loosening and strengthening: given that there is both an enrichment and a loosening route to the single intended interpretation, and assuming, as I am, that enrichment contributes to the proposition expressed, so surely must the loosening. However, from an economy of processing point of view, an account in terms of loose use (of the negated predicate) looks very unlikely. It would clearly require less effort to strengthen the concept HUMAN BEING by, as it were, dipping into the accompanying encyclopaedic entry, pulling out a positive stereotype and negating it, than it would take to form the concept NON-HUMAN-BEING compositionally and then loosen that so as to include some actual human beings, such as Frank, in its denotation. In fact, the latter would not give quite the right result, since the vast category NON-HUMAN-BEING* would also have to be drastically narrowed so as to exclude a wide range of non-human-beings (tables, trees, trumpets, theories, etc.) which are unlikely to share the property being predicated of Frank (a property concerning uncivilized, inhumane behavioural tendencies perhaps). The local enrichment account meshes well with the widespread recognition that negations are more complex to process than their corresponding positives (negation being the marked member of the positive/negative opposition) and that the processing of a negation presupposes, in some sense, the availability of the corresponding positive (see Horn 1989, chapter 3). Of course, the narrowing of a lexical concept (LION, SURGEON or HUMAN BEING) makes for the widening of the containing phrasal concept (NOT [LION*], NOT [SURGEON*], etc.), but that is a function of a semantic composition of negation with a strengthened atomic concept and not of a pragmatic process operating on a phrasal concept.

So far, then, we have seen three distinct sorts of case of what seem to be metaphorical utterances: (a) those where an encoded property is patently inapplicable to its subject (the examples in (25)); (b) those involving the negation of such a patently inapplicable property (the examples in (26)); (c) those where a property that patently applies to the subject is negated (the examples in (28)). The first two of these appear to involve a pragmatic process of concept adjustment which results in the loosening of a lexically encoded concept (e.g. BULLDOZER and ICE) while the third results in the strengthening of a lexically encoded concept (e.g. SURGEON). There is, clearly, a fourth sort of case, which is the positive counterpart of (c): those where an encoded property obviously applies to the subject. It is this sort of case which, I think, provides clear support for the unified treatment of concept loosening and strengthening. Consider the following examples:

(29) a. Caroline is our princess.
      b. Uncle Bob is a sergeant-major.
      c. Tom is a human being (he's not a machine).

The idea with (29a) is that, while the Caroline in question is in fact a princess (for instance, Princess Caroline of Monaco), what the speaker intends to communicate about her is not that she has a certain status in a royal family, but rather that she is, perhaps, an adored and somewhat spoiled girl. The same holds, *mutatis mutandis*, for (29b), where, let us assume, Uncle Bob is known by all the conversational participants to have the rank of sergeant-major in the army, and for (29c). Are these cases of concept loosening or of concept enrichment? Flieger (1996) considers them to be cases of metaphor, along with the three previous sorts of cases; as he puts it, all have a 'figurative feel'. Martinich (1984/91), from whom the example in (29a) originates, also characterizes them as metaphors (albeit 'non-standard' ones, in his view, because they are literally true). A bid for consistency with the treatment of the other three kinds of case would suggest that these examples should be enrichments, so that one possibility for the proposition expressed in each case is, respectively, that Caroline is a certain sort of spoilt, wayward princess, that Uncle Bob is a particular type of sergeant-major (perhaps the authoritarian, humourless, etc., stereotype), and that Tom is a human being who clearly demonstrates certain frailties of the species.

My claim here, though, is that the pragmatic adjustment of the encoded concept could result in either a narrowing or a loosening in these cases, depending on the context and so on the accessibility ranking of the logical and encyclopaedic properties associated with the lexical concept. It is not too difficult to envisage a context in which the *ad hoc* PRINCESS* concept might not include the logical (definitional) property of the lexical concept (i.e. female member of royal house); for instance, in a context in which the hearer, who is about to meet Caroline, knows full well that she is the daughter of a king but doesn't know anything more about her, the utterance may be taken as a warning that she is wilful, pampered and high-handed. In such a case, the pragmatically inferred concept will be looser than the lexical concept PRINCESS, including in its denotation some people who are not members of any royal family. This loosening possibility holds similarly for the *ad hoc* SERGEANT-MAJOR* and HUMAN BEING* concepts. Whether these are, technically, simply enrichments or combinations of loosening and enrichment hinges on whether or not logical (definitional) properties are dropped, something which could vary from context to context.

The case for the symmetrical account of enrichment and loosening cases is supported by these considerations. What matters here, at least from a communicative point of view, is that the relevant concept is constructed out of the logical and encyclopaedic information which is made accessible by the encoded lexical concept. Whether the construction process is strictly speaking a loosening or an enrichment, or a combination of the two, does not seem consequential and certainly should not lead to two utterly different ways of treating the resultant concept.

Note, by the way, that the examples above which involve the pragmatic construction of a concept from the lexical concept HUMAN BEING, (28c), (28d) and (29c), seem to eventuate in three different *ad hoc* concepts, contrasting respectively with properties of wild beasts, buddhas and machines. The proposition expressed by these utterances can be represented as follows, where the different numbers of asterisks reflect the fact that the concepts differ:

(30) a. SEAN IS NOT A HUMAN BEING*; SEAN IS A WILD BEAST*
      b. FRANK IS NOT A HUMAN BEING**; FRANK IS A BUDDHA*
      c. TOM IS A HUMAN BEING***; TOM IS NOT A MACHINE*

Quite distinct concepts may be pragmatically constructed in different contexts from one and the same linguistically encoded concept.

The final argument turns on the observation that, in some instances, concept broadening has to take place before some other process, which is obligatory in the derivation of the proposition expressed, can occur. Consider the following cases:

(31) a. *That bulldozer in the back row* should be told to leave.
      b. I was stuck all evening beside *that robot from IBM*.
      c. Thank goodness, *the wilting violet* has finally left.

The italicized phrases in these examples are referential; in order to fully understand what is being explicitly communicated, the addressee has to identify the individual the speaker has in mind in using these expressions. Everyone seems agreed that assignment of reference is an essential process in grasping the proposition expressed by an utterance. However, in these cases, each of the phrases includes some loosely used (metaphorical) conceptual material, so that identifying the referent requires a prior pragmatic process of determining the intended *ad hoc* concept. In (31b) for instance, correct reference assignment proceeds via the concept ROBOT*, which is formed from the lexical concept ROBOT, by dropping the logical property MACHINE and, perhaps, by giving a defining status to an encyclopaedic property such as LACKING IN HUMOUR AND FEELING. There is much controversy around the correct treatment of both descriptive demonstratives, as in (31a) and (31b), and of referential uses of definite descriptions, as in (31c), which I have to sidestep here. However, in the demonstrative cases at least, which are intrinsically referential, it is widely agreed that the referent (or, on a cognitive account, a *de re* concept of the referent) must occur in the proposition(s) expressed. So the characterization given in (32) of the proposition(s) expressed by an utterance of (31a), where x is a *de re* concept of the referent, may not, I hope, run into too many objections:[9]

(32) X [BULLDOZER* IN BACK ROW] SHOULD BE TOLD TO LEAVE

In short, for an utterance containing a referring expression, the derivation of the proposition expressed requires that a referent be identified and, in certain cases, correct referent identification requires that an *ad hoc* concept be pragmatically inferred from an encoded concept, a process that may involve a broadening of that encoded concept.[10]

On the basis of the considerations in this section and of those in the previous section on the consequences of adopting a symmetrical account of enrichment and loosening, I conclude that there is a strong case for the position that both concept narrowing and concept broadening contribute to the proposition expressed. In particular, since the two possibilities are the results of a single process of relevance-driven pragmatic adjustment of encoded concepts, it makes no sense to maintain that only one of them (strengthening) makes a propositional contribution.[11] In the next section, I focus more specifically on metaphorical cases and the extent to which they are accommodated by this general account of pragmatic concept construction.

5.3 Metaphor: Loose Use and *Ad Hoc* Concepts

According to the relevance-theoretic approach, the metaphorical use of language is a kind of loose use and involves no special interpretive mechanisms or processes; it is understood in accordance with the standard procedure of evaluating interpretive hypotheses in their order of accessibility. It follows, then, that the relevance-driven process of interpreting a metaphor has the result that the logical and encyclopaedic information attached to the loosely used encoded concept is effectively sorted into two disjoint sets of properties: those which are taken to be part of the intended interpretation and those which are not, and in the set of excluded properties is some logical or defining feature of the encoded concept. Given the symmetrical account of narrowing and loosening, it also follows that an *ad hoc* concept, formed from the encoded one, contributes to the explicit content of the utterance, and that the denotation of the new concept includes, or at least overlaps with, the denotation of the encoded concept.[12]

5.3.1 Where does metaphorical meaning come from?

The account of metaphor in terms of loose use and relevance-driven processing has been, and continues to be, something of a breakthrough in the understanding of metaphor. However, my concern in this section is to suggest that, as so far expounded, it may be incomplete, perhaps needing to be supplemented by a further cognitive component in order to be fully explanatory.

I will largely confine myself here to cases of positive attributions of a property which, if taken literally, is inapplicable to its subject ('Mary is a steamroller/robot/icicle/gazelle, etc.'), and avoid the complications of the patently false negation cases ('Tom isn't a human being/man/surgeon, etc.'). So let's consider in a bit more detail how the loose-talk story works for the fairly standard, but still mildly evocative, metaphor in (33):

(33)   Robert is a bulldozer.

Sperber and Wilson (1986a/95b: 236) say the following about this example: '[it is] a fairly conventional metaphor whose interpretation involves bringing together the encyclopaedic entries for *Robert* and *bulldozer*, which do not normally come together in a subject–predicate relationship. The result will be a wide array of contextual implications, many of which, being contradictory, can be automatically discarded. The relevance of [(33)] will be established by finding a range of contextual effects which can be retained as weak or strong implicatures. Here there is no single strong implicature that automatically comes to mind, but rather a slightly weaker, less determinate range having to do with Robert's persistence, obstinacy, insensitivity and refusal to be deflected.' On the updated account, on which an *ad hoc* concept BULLDOZER* is constructed, the idea is that certain elements of the encyclopaedic entry of BULLDOZER which are highly accessible in the particular context are carried over into the construction of the new concept which, as a constituent of the explicature, warrants the particular implicatures derived.

This seems fine as far as it goes. But consider the sort of properties that are taken to have been communicated as pertaining to Robert: obstinacy, insensitivity, refusal to be deflected, not listening to other people's views, ruthlessness in pursuing his own interests, etc. The questions that need consideration concern where these properties have come from, and how they have been accessed. As indicated above, according to the general account of loose use, they are recovered via the encyclopaedic entry of the concept BULLDOZER. But how? These properties do not actually feature in that entry, since bulldozers (i.e. those large tractor-like machines used for moving earth, rocks, etc.) are not persistent and obstinate, nor do they ignore other people's views, refuse to be deflected, or ruthlessly pursue their own goals. Only human beings seem to have psychological properties such as these (taking them literally, as we must). It is difficult to see how any encyclopaedic sorting process can, by itself at least, effect the transition from the property BULLDOZER, which is literally inapplicable to Robert, to a set of attributes that may well be true of him, because none of those attributes are found in the encyclopaedic entry of BULLDOZER. Note that, in the quote above, Sperber and Wilson say the interpretation process involves bringing together the encyclopaedic entries for ROBERT and BULLDOZER. The idea here, I think, is that the first of these plays an important role in constraining the information selected from the second one because it exerts a considerable influence on the accessibility ranking of the information in the BULLDOZER entry. But this does not help with the problem at hand, which is that the required information is just not in there, so is not available to be promoted in accessibility. Nor, presumably, is it (yet) in the encyclopaedic entry for ROBERT since, if it were, the predication would be pointless and the utterance uninformative. Intuitively, what goes on is that properties of Robert interact somehow with properties of bulldozers thereby making highly accessible some different properties which can be plausibly predicated of Robert; it is the 'somehow' in this description that remains to be cashed out.

Searle (1979/91) and Martinich (1984/91) have made similar observations about the example in (34). None of the properties that we take to be attributed to Sally by this utterance (for instance, extreme emotional reserve, lack of generosity towards other people, etc.) are properties of blocks of ice.

(34)   Sally is a block of ice.

As Martinich (1984/91: 511) observes, an inferential process from the coldness of blocks of ice to the coldness of Sally trades on an equivocation in the meaning of 'cold' and so is not in fact a valid inference. Another way of putting it is to say that the relevant concepts in the encyclopaedic entries of 'bulldozer' and 'block of ice' have themselves to be taken as used metaphorically, so that what we have are metaphors within metaphors (loose uses within loose uses). However, that doesn't get us any closer to an explicit account of how the process works, since extending the context further by exploring the encyclopaedic entries of these metaphorically used concepts, at the next level as it were, does not break through the metaphorical web, into the realm of those properties that are being literally attributed to the human subjects in (33) and (34). For instance, it is not the case that the encyclopaedic information associated with the property of efficient land-clearing provides us with the sort of properties that we can understand as being literally attributed to Robert in (33), nor that the information associated with the concepts of coldness and hardness to the physical touch includes the sort of psychological traits that we understand as attributed to Sally by a speaker of (34). Pugmire (1998: 99) puts the point well when he says: 'a predicate does not project unmodified from a non-metaphorical into a metaphorical context. Iron cannot, *except metaphorically*, be stubborn, persistent, or headstrong.'

The predicated properties in (33) and (34) are not only false of their subjects, they are necessarily false; that is, according to our (naive) metaphysical understanding of the universe, the entity denoted by the subject just isn't eligible, in any situation, for the property denoted by the predicate. By contrast, there are cases, such as those in (35), where the encoded concept being metaphorically used *could* be literally true of the subject, whether it actually is or not. If it is in fact false, then this is merely a contingent matter, there is no category mistake (no violation of our naive metaphysics).

(35)   a.   My son is a baby.
       b.   Suzannah is a princess.
       c.   Bob is a soldier/surgeon/butcher/artist/magician.

A person's son might well be a baby; a female human called Suzannah could be a princess; a male person could be a soldier or a surgeon, etc. Let us suppose, though, that these sentences are uttered in a situation where it is mutually manifest to the speaker and hearer that the property denoted by the concept encoded in the predicate is not true of the person referred to at the time of utterance. In these cases, the general account of interpreting loose uses, in terms of a relevance-driven process of encyclopaedic sorting, is perfectly adequate; for instance, in (35a), properties represented in the encyclopaedic entry for BABY, such as their total dependence on their carers, their demands for immediate attention, their inability to consider other people's needs, etc., can be understood as literally true of a particular kind of adult person; similarly, certain (stereotypical) properties of actual princesses, such as that they are rich and privileged, and get treated with great care and deference, can be understood as attributed literally to Suzannah, and so on, *mutatis mutandis*, for the range of predicates in (35c).

So, while it is a general feature of metaphors that the literal meaning of a predicate is not what the speaker intends to communicate, there are two distinct cases: those where the property could (in some circumstance or other) hold of the entity it is predicated of and those where it simply could not because there is a crossing of fundamental type or category boundaries (machines and humans, inorganic matter and humans, material artefacts and emotions). The latter kind seems to raise a problem for an account which turns solely on the recovery of relevant properties from the encyclopaedic information attached to the encoded concept(s). In so far as this is a genuine problem for a loose-use account of the metaphors in (33) and (34), it must be all the more so for truly creative cases such as the following:

(36)   a.   The fog comes on little cat feet.

(from Carl Sandberg's poem *Fog*)

b.   Love is the lighthouse and the rescued mariners.

(from Oskar Davičo's poem *Hannah*)

c.   Life's but a walking shadow, a poor player, that struts and frets his hour upon the stage, and then is heard no more.

(Shakespeare: *Macbeth* V. v. 24–6)

These are highly evocative metaphors which fulfil the presumption of relevance, not through the communication of a few strong implicatures, but, rather, through a very wide range of weakly communicated implicatures. It is this that gives them their poetic quality (see Sperber and Wilson 1986a/95b: 199–200, 224, 235–7). Different hearers/readers may entertain different specific implications in accordance with the particularities of their own encyclopaedic knowledge systems (and their imaginative capacities). The question, again, is how we go from information plausibly stored in memory about cat feet to thoughts about fog, or from our knowledge about lighthouses to thoughts about the nature of love.

It might be supposed that these literary metaphors are of a very different nature from the conventional cases in (33) and (34), that they call for a special sort of measured effortful processing (with commensurately greater effects). A distinction is often made between time-limited comprehension and leisurely comprehension (see Gerrig 1989; Gibbs 1994, chapter 3; Pilkington 2000, chapter 4). While this seems a valid distinction (though perhaps better viewed as a continuum), I see no reason to suppose that different interpretive mechanisms are involved; rather, the expectation of relevance can be set at a higher level when temporal constraints are relaxed, so that more effort may be invested in exploring connections and going beyond the first few accessible levels of information, and the result should be an ever wider array of cognitive effects. The process is not different in kind from that involved in understanding the quite ordinary cases of the bulldozer and the block of ice, in (33) and (34). A complete explanation of how it is that we access the intended properties in these cases, and form the intended but unencoded concepts BULLDOZER* and BLOCK OF ICE*, should provide us with all the ingredients needed for a complete explanation of the creative cases.[13]

Recall that, in the previous section, we saw two subcases of the loose use of concepts, the 'pure' broadening case resulting in a proper subset relation between the denotations of the lexical concept and the *ad hoc* concept, shown again here in (37a), and the combination broadening/narrowing case resulting in a denotational overlap of the lexical concept and the *ad hoc* concept, shown again in (37b). A third possibility, which arises when we look at certain cases of metaphor, is that the denotations of the two concepts do not intersect at all, as shown in (37c).

(37) a.

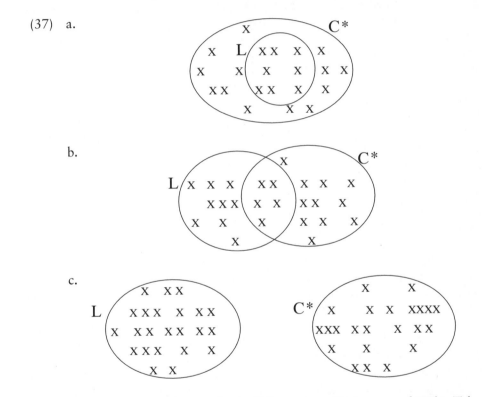

b.

c.

The contingent falsehood examples in (35) are most likely cases of (37b). Take, for instance, an utterance of 'Bob is a magician', in a context in which Bob, who is a surveyor by profession, has just rapidly produced a very nice meal for his flatmates out of a few unpromising old cans of food. What is communicated about Bob is that he has done something surprising, that he has made something highly improbable happen, he is quick and dexterous in his actions, his performance belies the onlookers' perception, etc. These are all properties that a professional magician is expected to have, so the *ad hoc* concept MAGICIAN* which is constructed in understanding this utterance includes in its denotation quite a few professional magicians, though probably not all, as well as non-magicians like Bob who have the properties in question.

However, when we turn back to the category-crossing cases, such as (33), (34) and (36), the appropriate picture seems to be that given by (37c). Support for this comes from the earlier observations that, in these cases, the properties that make up the *ad hoc* concept cannot be recovered from the encyclopaedic (or, indeed, logical) entry of the encoded concept. Consider again BULLDOZER and BULLDOZER*. The logical entry for the lexicalized concept BULLDOZER may contain an inference rule with the output HEAVY MACHINERY OF A CERTAIN SORT, or something along those lines, and its encyclopaedic entry includes information about its land-clearing function, its effectiveness in mechanically pushing away large volumes of earth, rocks and other debris, and about its physical appearance, perhaps represented by a visual image of some sort. The components of the *ad hoc* concept BULLDOZER* include representations of the properties mentioned earlier: obstinacy and persistence, insensitivity to other people's feelings and views, single-mindedness in pursuing personal interests, etc. It's not clear to me whether a one-off *ad hoc* concept is usefully thought of as having a logical entry, but for those people for whom BULLDOZER* has become a stable element of their conceptual systems, the likely logical entry is HUMAN TEMPERAMENT OF A CERTAIN SORT (this is certainly reflected in the many dictionaries that give a second sense to the word 'bulldozer'). The entities in the world that fall under these two concepts comprise disjoint sets. Another possible source of support for this third picture comes from linguistic semantic change. Among the processes which bring about such change the following three are often distinguished: lexical narrowing, lexical broadening and metaphorical transfer or shift (see Campbell 1998, chapter 10). For instance, the word 'insult' in English originally meant 'to jump on', but, through its repeated metaphorical application to a certain kind of uncomfortable psychological effect, the physical action meaning has been lost. This would seem to indicate that, at a particular time in the history of the language, the two concepts, INSULT (jump on), encoded by the lexical form 'insult', and INSULT* (offend), an *ad hoc* concept pragmatically inferred from it, referred to distinct non-overlapping categories of behaviour.

The question remains: how is the move from the lexically encoded concept to the *ad hoc* concept effected in these fundamental category-crossing cases? I have said that the crucial properties of the new concept in such cases are not to be found in the encyclopaedic entries of the lexically encoded concepts, BULLDOZER, ICE, LIGHTHOUSE, etc., but, of course, this information plays an important role in their recovery. Exactly what that role is and what else is required has not yet been made explicit in the relevance-theoretic account of metaphor (or in any other account of on-line metaphor interpretation that I am aware of). I have nothing new to offer here, my primary aim being the modest, albeit rather negative, one of placing the issue on the table as one that must ultimately be addressed. I'll simply mention briefly two lines of thought in the wider literature on metaphor which might be worth considering in this regard.

The first comes from psychological investigations of the general human capacity for making analogies between what may be quite disparate subject domains, a capacity that manifests itself most strikingly in creative thinking, both artistic and scientific, but which is also prevalent in everyday cognitive activity (see, for instance,

Holyoak and Thagard 1995; Gentner, Holyoak, and Kokinov 2001). This capacity is not well understood, but one point of agreement seems to be that a crucial element is the (partial) mapping or alignment of the *structures* of the different domains, that is, a matching of dimensions and relations (as opposed to a search for attributes shared by entities in the domains). For example, the scientific analogies between the atom and the solar system, or between sound transmission and waves of water, are based on similarities in the structures of the two systems rather than similarities in the entities themselves (electrons and planets, etc.). At the more mundane level, young children can readily perceive relational correspondences between, say, the domain of bird life and that of human life, aligning bird with person, nest with house, tree with backyard, singing with talking, etc. Once a structural alignment of two domains is assumed, correspondences can be read off from a position in the structure of one domain (the 'source' domain) to the corresponding position in the other (the 'target' domain). Perhaps the capacity to perform this sort of relational mapping is a component of understanding certain verbal metaphors. So, for example, the metaphorical utterance 'Ariel Sharon is a hawk' might involve a structural mapping from the domain of birds to the domain of politicians, with Sharon occupying the same position in the politician domain as the hawk does in the bird domain, so that characteristics such as political aggressiveness, readiness to make pre-emptive strikes, etc., might be read off from correspondences with the hawk's ferocity (among birds) and quickness in finding a prey and going for the kill. Exactly how such a story might go for our bulldozer case, I am less sure about. I take it that we want a mapping from, in the source domain, the movement of a bulldozer and its effects on the environment it moves through, to, in the target domain, the behaviour of a particular kind of human individual and its effects on the people who encounter it. Conceivably, then, particular correspondences can be read off, for instance, between a bulldozer's indiscriminate clearing of material in its path to a person's insensitive overriding of other people's views and feelings. (For more discussion of the possible role of structure mapping across domains in metaphor understanding, see Gentner and Markman 1997; Gentner et al. 2001; Holyoak and Thagard 1995, chapter 9.)

The second line of thought, sometimes occurring in combination with the first one, is the currently very popular view that there is a large number of pre-existing metaphorical schemes, which play a fundamental role in structuring some of our more abstract concepts (such as LIFE, LOVE, MIND, TIME) and which are readily available to the processes of utterance interpretation. Commonly discussed examples are LIFE IS A JOURNEY, THE MIND IS A CONTAINER, TIME IS A MOVING ENTITY, ARGUMENT IS WAR (see Lakoff 1993; Gibbs 1994). One very general scheme proposed by these authors is PSYCHOLOGICAL FORCE IS PHYSICAL FORCE, which enables us to understand psychological phenomena (traits of character, mental processes) in terms of physical (perceptible) phenomena. It may be this that underpins the 'bulldozer' example, or a much more specific scheme such as PEOPLE ARE MACHINES may be involved. Similarly, there might be a metaphorical scheme mapping emotions aroused by other humans, such as love, anger or grief, on to visceral experiences of the physical world (so perhaps underpinning the 'lighthouse and rescued mariners' case). If we really do have such schemes as part of our conceptual make-up, then part of the role of the relevant encyclopaedic information accompanying a metaphorically used lexical concept is to provide a connection with the appropriate metaphorical scheme. For instance, information about the physical movements of bulldozers and their effects instantiates one side of the mapping between physical forces and psychological characteristics, so that (perhaps) the bulldozer property of indiscriminately clearing away anything in its path maps to the human psychological trait of ignoring other people in the pursuit of one's own goals. Whether such schemes are really employed in this way in understanding metaphorical utterances remains to be seen; the idea has its critics (see, for instance, Glucksberg and McGlone 1999; Keysar et al. 2000), and its wider framework, according to which thought is fundamentally metaphorical, raises many questions (see, for instance, Murphy 1996).

A further issue, which should be acknowledged, though it lies well beyond my scope here, is whether an approach in terms of propositional *conceptual representations* (explicatures and implicatures) can ever do full justice to the processes and results of comprehending a metaphor. From a phenomenological perspective, what is striking about so many metaphors is their imagistic quality; for instance, the cat feet of the fog, the lighthouse and the rescue of the shipwrecked sailors. Even in the utterly banal bulldozer case, people report having a mental image of a bulldozer, perhaps two images that merge in a certain way, the one of Robert, the other of a bulldozer, aspects of the two being combined so that we *see* Robert *as* a bulldozer, or, in the case of 'that surgeon was a butcher', we may have a mental image of a figure dressed in surgeon's garb and in an operating theatre, but who is raising a cleaver to hack at the flesh on the table. What relationship there is, if any, between these apparently imagistic mental representations and the sort of representations I have been concentrating on – conceptual, propositional, syntactic – is something that needs to be explicated. For instance, could it be that we derive conceptual representations ('that surgeon was rough/brutal/behaved without appropriate care and skill', etc.) through scrutinizing the internal image, rather as we might form thoughts through looking at an external picture? If so, this would provide a ready explanation for the open-endedness and variability of metaphor interpretations. (See Davies 1983, and Moran 1989, 1997, for discussion of 'proposition' theories and 'image' theories of metaphor and possible relations between them.)

In many good poetic metaphors, there are other apparently non-propositional effects that are achieved: qualitative states of mind, such as sensations and feelings, are evoked and these, rather than anything conceptual, may be precisely what the poet is striving for through his creative use of words. Sperber and Wilson (1986a/95b: 224) suggest that (at least some of) the *affective* effects of poetic metaphors may turn out to be explainable in cognitive conceptual terms, through their account of weak communication which involves a slight increase in the manifestness of a very wide array of weakly manifest assumptions. See Pugmire (1998, chapter 7) for a discussion of whether or not metaphors might 'come down to nascent, inchoate thoughts or to devices for suggesting these' (1998: 98), and Pilkington (2000, chapters 6–8) for a searching discussion of the extent to which poetic effects can be adequately captured in entirely cognitive terms.

5.3.2 *Ad hoc* concepts, explicature and indeterminacy

In the previous subsection, I dwelt on the question of how we arrive at an interpretation of a metaphorical utterance. This question arises both for the original
relevance-theoretic account and for the slightly revised one involving *ad hoc* concepts. I'll focus now on this relatively recent idea that an *ad hoc* concept is constructed and functions as a constituent of what is explicitly communicated.[14] Recall
that this position simply follows from the idea that metaphor is a kind of loose use,
together with the symmetrical view of the effects of enrichment and loose use,
argued for in section 5.2. An interesting consequence is that it provides a nice way
of reflecting the often-discussed difference between a metaphor and its corresponding simile:

(38) a. Mary is a bulldozer.
      b. Mary is like a bulldozer.

(39) a. Love is the lighthouse and the rescued mariners.
      b. Love is like the lighthouse and the rescued mariners.

There are clearly great similarities in how the members of each of these pairs are
understood and in the result of the interpretation process; in fact, the implicatures
are probably the same, so, for both (38a) and (38b), Mary is understood to be obstinate, single-minded, insensitive to other people's feelings, etc. However, their overall
impact is not identical, the metaphor usually being experienced as somehow more
direct and forceful than the simile. Various observations can be made about what
might account for this felt difference. For instance, while the metaphor is literally
false, similes are standardly said to be trivially true (since everything is like everything else in some respect or other). But, as we've already seen, this is not the central
issue, since the corresponding negatives are just as much metaphors and similes,
although their truth/falsity status is reversed. It is sometimes said that while a
simile invites the addressee to make a comparison between two unlike things, a
metaphor requires the addressee to conceive of one thing as actually *being* another
(unlike) kind of thing. Whether or not this is right, an account of metaphor understanding which involves the construction of an *ad hoc* concept from an encoded
concept may reflect the felt difference, since similes do not seem to undergo such a
process. Compare (40a) and (40b) as possible propositions expressed by the simile
in (38b):

(40) a. MARY IS LIKE A BULLDOZER*
      b. MARY IS LIKE A BULLDOZER
      c. Mary is like a human being.
      d. A pear is like a fruit.

While it makes sense to say that Mary belongs to a particular category of BULL-
DOZERS*, there is no more sense in claiming that she is *like* a BULLDOZER* than

that she is like a human being (given that she *is* one). That is, (40a) is odd in much the same way as it would be odd to say that a pear is like a fruit, that a nuthatch is like a bird, or that a dog is like a mammal. The oddity lies in saying of an entity which is a member of some category that it is (merely) *like* that category. So while a metaphor and its corresponding simile may communicate the same set of implicatures, the difference between them may be captured by the fact that an *ad hoc* concept is constructed as part of the explicit content of the metaphor, while the lexically encoded concept is preserved in the simile, as in (40b).

Incorporation of an *ad hoc* concept in the proposition explicitly communicated by a metaphorical utterance has another interesting consequence. Recall that, according to the relevance-theoretic account, many metaphors involve weak communication; that is, the intention made mutually manifest by the speaker is not (or not only) to make strongly manifest some small number of specific assumptions but rather to make weakly manifest a wide range of assumptions (a conceptual space). In such a case, the implicatures of the utterance are indeterminate: the speaker has not singled out and endorsed any particular assumptions, but has rather encouraged the hearer to explore within the range of activated assumptions. Precisely which ones the hearer does in fact derive as implicatures of the utterance is, in large measure, a matter of his own choice and responsibility. The more creative or unusual a metaphor, the wider the range of possibilities and the weaker the speaker's endorsement of any specific implicated propositional form. This much has been part of the account since its beginnings in the 1980s. The point here is that, given the view that the hearer constructs an *ad hoc* concept that replaces the encoded concept in the explicitly communicated propositional form, the characteristic of indeterminacy must carry over from the implicatures of many metaphorical utterances to their explicatures.

All the implicatures derived by the hearer have to be inferentially warranted and the *ad hoc* concept plays a crucial role in this, since most of the implicated properties are features of its encyclopaedic entry. What we have here is the process of mutual parallel adjustment writ large. It may be that the time course of interpretation is such that, before he has a complete explicature, the hearer accesses a variety of particular assumptions from the, possibly vast, range activated by the utterance and treats them as potential implicatures of the utterance; if so, there is then a good deal of backwards inference involved in shaping the new concept which will figure in the explicature and ultimately warrant the set of implicated conclusions. The indeterminacy that pertains to implicatures, therefore, pertains equally to the *ad hoc* concept; that is, the relation between the concept constructed by the hearer and that in the speaker's own thought is one of sufficiently close resemblance rather than identity. There may be quite a range of subtly different concepts licensed by an utterance of, for instance, 'Robert is a bulldozer': BULLDOZER*, BULLDOZER**, BULLDOZER***, etc. No specific one is strongly communicated and the hearer's construction of any one of them is good enough for the communication to have succeeded. (For further discussion, see Wilson and Sperber 2000, especially pp. 243–5.)

A final question, which I merely raise without attempting to answer, concerns the extent of the process of *ad hoc* concept formation in metaphor understanding. Most of the examples above have involved single constituents, either a predicate or a referring expression, but, clearly, whole sentences can be used metaphorically, as in the following examples, where (41a) might describe a bad-tempered boss and his intimidated employees, (41b) might be a report on the state of a failing institution or company, and (41c) a characterization of the course of a destructive marriage or friendship:

(41) a. When the old lion wakes up and starts roaring again we had all better run for cover.
   b. Despite lavish nursing, the patient has yet to leave his sick-bed and take a few tottering steps in the sunshine.
   c. The buds of hope and love called out by a day or two of sunshine are frozen again and again till the tree is killed.

The proposition expressed by (41a) might involve several *ad hoc* concepts which compose together with some encoded concepts along the lines in (42):

(42) WHEN THE OLD [LION]* [WAKES UP]* AND STARTS [ROARING]* AGAIN WE HAD ALL BETTER [RUN FOR COVER]*

Another possibility is that longer stretches of the encoded conceptual structure, phrases or the whole logical form, are to be taken as used loosely (metaphorically) and a complex (structured) *ad hoc* concept pragmatically constructed on that basis:

(43) [[THE PATIENT] [HAS YET TO [[LEAVE HIS SICK-BED] AND [TAKE A FEW TOTTERING STEPS IN THE SUNSHINE]]]]*

Neither of these possibilities seems sustainable in the case of certain wholly metaphorical poems and stories (allegories or parables); rather, they would seem to be given an initial full interpretation (pragmatically disambiguated, enriched, etc.) within a frame or (fictional) domain, from which, subsequently or in parallel, their metaphorical interpretation is projected. This is, clearly, an issue that needs a lot more thought.

5.4 Word Meaning and Concepts

The discussion in this chapter has proceeded on the assumption that lexical items like 'cat', 'sing', 'open', 'raw' and 'happy' encode (atomic) concepts, where, on a mental representational construal, concepts are 'words of Mentalese', that is, constituents of sentences in the language of thought (Fodor 1975, 1998). The claim has been that, in *some* utterances containing these lexical items, the concepts they encode provide the starting point for a pragmatic process which results in a different concept, one which is narrower and/or broader than, or, perhaps in the case of some metaphors, different in some other way from, the lexical concept. What I want to consider now is the possibility that this view of word meaning is not right, that such 'conceptual encodings' are (in many instances, at least) not really full-fledged concepts, but rather concept schemas, or pointers to a conceptual space, on the basis of which, on *every* occasion of their use, an actual concept (an ingredient of a thought) is pragmatically inferred. The discussion is, I'm afraid, highly speculative, appealing to intuition rather than providing hard argument.

The idea that natural-language *sentences* do not encode (do not translate into) sentences in the language of thought but rather provide a template or schema for constructing such language of thought sentences has been fundamental to relevance theory since its beginnings: 'Linguistically encoded semantic representations are abstract mental structures which must be inferentially enriched before they can be taken to represent anything of interest' (Sperber and Wilson 1986a/95b: 174). At the same time, however, it has been assumed that, with the exception of indexicals and a few other expressions that encode procedures, most words encode (atomic) concepts, that is, constituents of thought. The suggestion here is that the abstract schematic nature of a decoded 'semantic' representation (or logical form) is manifest not only at the global sentence level (by variables, gaps and missing sections of propositional structure) but also at the local level of the basic elements of the representation. While sentences encode thought/proposition templates, words encode concept templates; it's linguistic underdeterminacy all the way down.

In chapter 1 (section 1.5.2), I discussed Fodor's (1998: 9) position that 'English inherits its semantics from the contents of the beliefs, desires, intentions, and so forth that it's used to express'. I suggested that, although this does not work for natural-language *sentence* types, which cannot be assigned a 'real' truth-conditional semantics, even by inheritance, it may work at the *lexical* level: words that encode concepts may inherit a referential semantics from the concepts (CAT, SING, OPEN, RAW, HAPPY, etc.) which they encode (and so activate in an addressee's mind when uttered). One upshot of questioning the view that lexical items encode anything recognizable as a fully fledged concept will be to cast doubt on even this rather meagre claim that word types in natural language can be thought of as having a truth-based semantics by inheritance.

Focusing on the word 'happy', let's consider the concept that it is supposed to encode, a concept which is to provide communicative access to a wide range of other more specific concepts, including one for a steady state of low-key well-being, another for a momentary experience of intense joy, another for the sense of satisfaction that accompanies a successful negotiation, and so on. (Note that these descriptions are necessarily circumlocutionary ways of indicating in natural language the nature of the *atomic* concept at issue.) The idea is that the lexically encoded concept HAPPY is distinct from all of these; it is more general and abstract than any of them, but provides the basis, in appropriate contexts, for processes of pragmatic enrichment so that addressees can come to grasp one of the more specific concepts and incorporate it into their representation of the speaker's thought. But what is not at all clear is whether we ever actually have (hence sometimes try to communicate) thoughts in which this very general lexicalized concept features as a constituent, or indeed what the property of being HAPPY is, as opposed to being HAPPY* or HAPPY**, etc. Could it be that the word 'happy' does not encode a concept, but rather 'points' to a conceptual region, or maps to an address (or node, or gateway, or whatever) in memory? This pointing or mapping provides access to certain bundles of information from which the relevance-constrained processes of pragmatic inference extract or construct the conceptual unit which features in the speaker's thought.

Sometimes it seems that Sperber and Wilson are envisaging something along these lines: 'Quite generally, the occurrence of a word in an utterance provides a piece of evidence, a pointer to a concept involved in the speaker's meaning. . . . A verb like "open" acts as a pointer to indefinitely many notions or concepts . . .' (1997/98a: 196–7). However, this is selective quoting; in between these two sentences they say: 'It may happen that *the intended concept is the very one encoded by the word*, which is therefore used in its strictly literal sense' (my italics). But when we try to think about the general concept OPEN and to have a thought in which such a general concept features, as opposed to any of the more specific concepts that we grasp in under-standing 'open one's mouth', 'open the window', 'open a can', 'open a discussion', etc., the experience is an odd one, as we seem to have no definite thought at all.

Recall Searle's point discussed in chapter 1, that we are unable to fully under-stand (assign a determinate truth-conditional content to) the following:

(44) a. Bob opened the grass.
      b. Chris opened the fork.
      c. Jane opened a hair.

According to him, although we understand each word in these sentences and their syntax is unproblematic, our Background does not supply us with any know-how concerning opening grass or forks or hairs. One way of construing this in the current context is that the verb 'open' points us to a particular region in encyclopaedic memory at which all manner of information about kinds of opening is stored, or at least made accessible, but it does not include what would be needed for us to construct the kind of full-fledged concept that could feature in a thought involving a relation between Bob and the grass, Chris and the fork, etc., a thought which could then be evaluated against some situation or event in the world involving Bob and the grass, Chris and the fork, etc., and judged true or false. Assuming we have referents for 'Bob' and 'the grass' but no other knowledge about a specific context, then all we get from an utterance of (44a) is that Bob performed some act involv-ing the grass and that that act can be described as one of 'opening'. Whatever mental representation we form from this contains not a descriptive concept, that is, one with a determinate denotation, but an interpretive, metarepresentational one. But surely, if the word 'open' encodes a concept, we should be able to have thoughts which include that concept, and there should be no particular difficulty in grasping the proposition expressed by 'Bob opened the grass'.

At the least, it seems that the 'concepts' encoded by bits of lexical phonological material are a rather different kind of thing from the concepts that feature as ingre-dients in our thoughts and in interpretations of our utterances. That there is a dis-tinction of this sort to be made is further supported by the general account of how *ad hoc* concepts are constructed: the lexical form maps to a 'conceptual' address in memory to which is attached a package (or packages) of information; we dip into this package and take out just a part of it. The process is always selective, there is always some subset of the activated information which is left behind or discarded, whether the ultimate upshot is one of a narrowing or a broadening, in the sense discussed earlier. The result is a concept, a constituent of the thought the speaker is communicating; however, the building materials for this process made available by the lexical item (perhaps including several conflicting properties or stereotypes, as in the case of 'bachelor') do not constitute a concept. If this is right, there is a sense in which all concepts are *ad hoc*, that is, temporary constructs arising for specific purposes at particular times, as Barsalou (1987, 1993) has claimed (see note 1 of this chapter).

Given the rich range and finely varied nature of the concepts that can be communicated by a single lexical form, it seems we have (at least) the following two options in giving an account of the encoded meaning of a word: multiple ambiguity, with each of the (related) meanings a full-fledged concept, or the very abstract, attenuated, schematic meanings, which come from taking the 'univocality' or 'monosemy' line (see Grice 1978/89b; Atlas 1989; Ruhl 1989) and which, I am suggesting, are not concepts. Even setting aside possible economy considerations, reflected in the well-known methodological principle of Modified Occam's Razor (see section 2.6), the ambiguity approach is ruled out as any sort of general solution since it's not a matter of some fixed set of (related) senses but of an apparently indefinite range of possibilities (see Sperber and Wilson 1997/98a: 186). So even if we decided that 'open' encodes, say, four distinct (but related) literal senses, the pragmatic account of *ad hoc* concept construction would be required for the myriad other meanings that arise in particular contexts. But once we have an effective account of these cases, the supposedly encoded meanings might as well be derived in the same general way, given an initial pointer to the right area of information in memory. Of course, individual concepts within the (indefinitely large) set of those communicable by 'open' differ greatly in their frequency of occurrence in thought and communication (compare a concept of the usual mode of opening one's mouth with one of an action of prising lips and teeth apart with one's fingers, etc.) so that some are retrievable more or less ready-made while others require a more constructive process. This conception of word meaning and concept communication goes at least some way towards accounting for the phenomenon of polysemy (the multiple related senses of a word).[15]

However, while this view of word meaning as very abstract and schematic is perhaps plausible for a range of cases, such as the verbal and adjectival encodings just discussed, it might be thought to be much less so when we turn to natural-kind terms, like 'cat', 'lion', 'water', 'tree'. There is a strong intuition that 'cat' encodes a concept CAT, which features in thoughts, and not just some abstract schema for constructing CAT* concepts or some pointer to knowledge about cats. Utterances such as those in (45) do not seem to be susceptible to the indeterminacy of those in (44), that is, we have no difficulty grasping a propositional content, even though we may judge it false and/or bizarre in other ways:

(45) a.   The cat next door reads Shakespeare.
      b.   Mr Jones was transformed into a cat for a few hours.

It is noticeable that natural-kind terms do not figure much in discussions on polysemy, perhaps a further indication of their stable conceptual content (which is not to deny their high susceptibility to figurative use). So perhaps there are different kinds of lexical meanings, with some words encoding full-fledged concepts, others encoding a schema or a pro-concept (see Sperber and Wilson 1997/98a on the latter) and others a procedure or inferential constraint.

Suppose it is right that there is a sizeable class of words that do not encode particular concepts (senses), but rather concept schemas, or pointers, or addresses in memory (which of these is the best metaphor remains unclear), what effect does this have on our depiction of the output of the linguistic processing system, the decoded logical form or 'semantic' representation? I think it doesn't make much difference; we just alter our construal of such representations as HAPPY, OPEN, etc. from being concepts, constituents of thought, to being labels for pointers or schemas. This is not a change that brings with it any new problems for a principle of semantic compositionality, which, as argued in chapter 1 (section 1.6.3), holds for encoded linguistic meaning (expression-type meaning) but not at the level of utterance content (proposition expressed). Not too surprisingly though, this way of thinking about word meaning raises tricky questions and has various knock-on effects within the overall conception of the relation between language and thought. It will require some reworking of the account of atomic mental concepts given at the beginning of this chapter, according to which they can have three associated entries: logical, encyclopaedic and *lexical*. Also, the introduction of a whole additional population of mental entities, which are distinct from concepts and don't seem to have any function in mental life except to mediate the word/concept relation, is not to be taken on lightly; on the other hand, this is simply a counterpart, at the lexical semantic level, to what we've already taken on at the sentence semantic level: proposition schemas, which mediate the sentence/thought relation. One challenging question that arises concerns acquisition: if word meanings are these abstract schematic entities that do not feature in our thinking about the world, how do we ever manage to acquire (learn) them?

Consider how the word meaning acquisition story goes on a Fodorian sort of account, according to which learning a natural language is 'learning how to associate its sentences with the corresponding thoughts. To know English is to know, for example, that the form of words "there are cats" is standardly used to express the thought that there are cats; . . .' (Fodor 1998: 9). So learning a word, say 'cat' or 'open', is learning to associate it with the corresponding concept, CAT or OPEN, on the basis of which the word inherits the semantics of the concept, namely that it refers to the property *cat* or the property *open*, respectively. There are two acquisitional processes here; the acquiring of the concept and the acquiring of the form–concept link, and giving a satisfactory explanation of these is no simple matter (see, for instance, Fodor 1981b, 1998, on concept acquisition, and Bloom 2000 on forging the word–concept link). However, on an account of word meaning according to which it is not a concept but something more like a general schema for building concepts, or a pointer to a range of concepts, the task of explaining acquisition appears to become much more difficult. How does a child acquire such an abstract entity as a schema or a pointer, something that doesn't play any role in her thoughts? For instance, suppose she already has several concepts of the OPEN* variety, which figure in her thoughts about the world, say one for the action of opening her mouth, another for opening a door, another for opening a carton of milk. On the current hypothesis, none of these concepts is the meaning of the word 'open', so she can't just map the phonological form /open/ on to one of those and thereby acquire the (adult) meaning of 'open'. Of course, in another sense, these are all (context-dependent) meanings of the word 'open', meanings that particular *tokenings* of the word 'open' have. So, at different points along the route to establishing a more or less stable meaning for the lexical form, various different form–concept correspondences may be made. The question, which won't receive any answer here, is how the more general schema or indicator arises and how it comes to be the meaning of the lexical expression *type*. There must be some process of abstraction, or extraction, from the particular concepts associated with the phonological form /open/ to the more general 'meaning', which then functions as a gateway both to the existing concepts of opening and to the materials needed to make new OPEN* concepts which may arise in the understanding of subsequent utterances.[16]

5.5 Conclusion: The Long Road from Linguistically Encoded Meaning to the Thought(s) Explicitly Communicated

On the picture of linguistic communication endorsed and developed in this book, the input to the system for utterance comprehension is a set of logical forms (and a set of procedural constraints), which have been decoded by the language processing system. The logical forms are often highly schematic conceptual structures, functioning as mere templates for the construction of fully propositional forms. The output of the pragmatic comprehension system is a set of assumptions or propositional forms, explicatures and implicatures, which constitute 'what is communicated' or speaker meaning. There seems to be no role in this account for any other, intermediate, level of 'what is said' or minimal proposition, which departs as little as possible from encoded meaning but has a determinate truth condition.

We started from the recognition that processes of disambiguation and reference assignment, essential in understanding any linguistic utterance, are fully pragmatic processes, in that they require considerations of speaker intentions which, all going well, are recognized through the workings of the relevance-based comprehension procedure. From there, we considered a range of cases that can broadly be called 'enrichment' processes, processes that hypothesize a development of the logical form on the basis of highly accessible conceptual material and retain that development if it functions fruitfully in the derivation of cognitive effects (that is, if it contributes to an interpretation which meets the presumption of optimal relevance). Some of these enrichments are like assigning a referent to a pronoun in that they involve giving a specific value to a variable or indexical present in the logical form; they are often called cases of 'saturation'. But there are others which don't appear to be linguistically mandated, so that their recovery is entirely motivated by pragmatic considerations; they are often called cases of 'free' enrichment. The most striking instances of this are non-elliptical subsentential utterances, such as 'On the top shelf' when there is no preceding utterance to supply 'the missing words'. Comprehension here is a pragmatic mind-reading exercise, *par excellence*: the speaker guesses that the addressee is looking for x and the addressee recognizes her intention to inform him that x is on the top shelf. However, there are also cases of fully sentential utterances which involve this sort of pragmatic supplementation. One of the most convincing is that of 'and'-conjunction, many instances of which are enriched by one or another of myriad temporal and cause–consequence relations (discussed at length in chapter 3). Another is the fixing of the scope of certain operators, such as negation, which, as argued in chapter 4, is maximally wide in scope as a matter of its linguistic semantics, but is frequently pragmatically narrowed in accordance with considerations of relevance. Finally, and much less generally noted, there are those cases where an encoded lexical meaning is pragmatically enriched.

These various different kinds of enrichment take us well beyond the linguistic meaning encoded in the expression used and, if the arguments in chapter 1 are correct, they take us beyond any meaning that *could* be expressed by relying just on the existing resources of the linguistic code, without recourse to pragmatic inference. This latter point is perhaps most evident in the case of lexical conceptual enrichment, since there seems to be a virtually indefinite range of finely distinct concepts that can be communicated by such apparently unambiguous adjectives as 'happy', 'upset' or 'tired', or verbs such as 'open', 'cut' or 'take'. Clearly, pragmatic enrichment processes also take us well beyond any minimal propositional development of the encoded template and so beyond anything that could be deemed the *semantic content* of the linguistic expression used (even the context-relative semantic content). However, if the main argument of this chapter is right, the cutting away of the notion of the explicitly communicated content of an utterance from its linguistic meaning is far more radical than the enrichment facts suggest. The view that concept broadening or loosening is simply another possible result of a single process of concept adjustment which contributes to the proposition explicitly communicated entails that elements of meaning which are generally taken to be intrinsic to linguistic meaning, meaning encoded in the language system, may be dropped from the proposition which that linguistic meaning has been used to explicitly communicate (as in the case of loose uses of 'raw', 'flat', 'fly', 'bulldozer', etc.). This is a logical outcome of a position according to which communication is first and foremost a kind of constrained mind-reading with linguistic (and perhaps other) codes just providing evidence (often rich and detailed evidence, but never a complete encoding, never a proof) of the thoughts being communicated.

From its inception, relevance theory has recognized a (very pragmatically elaborated) proposition expressed, as distinct from encoded linguistic meaning, on the one hand, and from explicature, on the other. If the arguments of the current chapter hold up, while the first distinction is fundamental and reinforced, much of the motivation for the second distinction (between an uncommunicated but pragmatically enriched propositional form and the communicated propositional forms) is lost. Even metaphorical utterances communicate the proposition they express, which is therefore an explicature of the utterance (the base-level explicature). Delivering the propositional forms intended by the speaker (or forms sufficiently similar to them) is what a system of pragmatic interpretation is all about. The claim here is that the pursuit of this goal does not involve any sort of way-station at which a propositional form is constructed which exhibits just those pragmatic adjustments that constitute (local) enrichments, so maintaining all encoded (literal) content, irrespective of whether this propositional form is communicated or not. If this is right, it marks a cleaning up within the theory itself. Not only is there no role for the sort of minimal proposition favoured by semanticists, there is no role for a much more pragmatically imbued proposition which does not, however, fall within the speaker's communicative intention.

The distinction between explicatures and implicatures, the two kinds of communicated assumptions, is primarily a derivational distinction and may have no greater import than that. Explicatures are derived by pragmatically filling in and adjusting the semantic scaffolding provided by the linguistic expression used, while implicatures are derived wholly pragmatically, though that inferential process may be constrained by encoded procedural meaning. Both may be communicated more or less strongly, and either may constitute the primary point of the utterance, that is, the main locus of cognitive effects. I suspect that it is these properties of communicated assumptions, that is, the strength with which they have been communicated and how much they yield in cognitive effects, that really count for the hearer, rather than whether they were explicated or implicated.

To finish, let's review our application of those three bits of heavyweight terminology: 'underdeterminacy', 'indeterminacy' and '(in)effability'. Quite generally, the encoded meaning of the linguistic expression employed in an utterance underdetermines the proposition that is explicitly communicated; this holds both at the structural level, in that there may be constituents in the communicated proposition that are not articulated in the decoded logical form, and at the level of lexically encoded conceptual meaning. It's worth noting that, as a result of the way in which the account of explicit communication has developed over these chapters, the 'linguistic underdeterminacy thesis' we have ended up with is rather different from that discussed in chapter 1 ('linguistic meaning underdetermines what is said') and is virtually uncontroversial: 'linguistic meaning underdetermines explicature'. The property of *in*determinacy, that is, of there being no fact of the matter, arises for certain instances of both explicatures and implicatures. In cases of weakly communicated assumptions, a *kind* of propositional form or a conceptual region or space may be made manifest, without the speaker giving her backing to any specific propositional forms of that kind or within that space, so that which of them is actually entertained by the hearer is largely a function of his own cognitive dispositions. Finally, the property of effability or expressibility of thoughts, discussed in detail in chapter 1, can be understood in two ways: as encodability in a natural-language form, or as communicability by a natural-language form. On the first understanding, the vast majority, if not all, of our thoughts are ineffable. On the second understanding, the vast majority, if not all, of our thoughts are effable, since this construal allows for the primary role of pragmatic inference in the process of coming to grasp the thought(s) that a speaker is attempting to communicate. In the case of novel creative metaphors we see all three properties, underdeterminacy, indeterminacy and ineffability (= unencodability), at their most extreme. Here too the limits of effability (= communicability) seem to be reached in the attempt to convey or evoke phenomenal states of mind, such as sensations, feelings and moods, by means of language.

NOTES

1   There are some important differences between Barsalou's view of concepts and the one assumed in this chapter. First, he, in fact, uses the term 'ad hoc' of categories rather than concepts; ad hoc categories are those that people construct in particular contexts to achieve particular goals (e.g. the category of 'things that can fall on your head', 'ways to keep stress to a minimum when writing a conference presentation'); the distinction is with common established categories, such as 'birds', 'furniture', 'games' (see Barsalou 1983, 1987, 1993). His robust finding is that subjects presented with ad hoc categories instantly conceive of them as having a structure similar to that of established categories; for instance, they judge certain members of the category to be its prototype and assign degrees of typicality to other members. As regards concepts, Barsalou's hypothesis is that they are quite generally not stored in long-term memory but are temporary, highly context-sensitive entities, constructed in working memory: 'people have the ability to construct a wide range of concepts in working memory for the same category. Depending on the context, people incorporate different information from long-term memory into the current concept that they construct for a category' (Barsalou 1987: 118). On this account, then, *every concept seems to be ad hoc*. If that is right, it follows that the meanings of words cannot be concepts, a position which is argued for in Barsalou et al. (1993). For the moment I will continue to assume that some concepts are stable, enduring mental structures and that some lexical items encode such stable concepts; however, in section 5.4, I'll suggest a different position on word meaning.

2   For some of the classical cases of vagueness, such as 'bald', there is the possibility of the different analysis according to which the semantics is absolute, e.g. HAIRLESS, but it is standardly used loosely, as is assumed in the text for 'raw', encoding UNCOOKED, and 'silent', encoding NOISELESS. Sperber and Wilson (1986b: 165) point out that this account provides a solution to (or dissolution of) the well-known 'baldness' paradox, that is, the conclusion that a man with a full head of hair is bald, which one can be led into by an inductive argument starting from the premises (a) that a man with no hair is bald and (b) that if a man with no hair is bald then a man with one hair is bald. The paradox does not arise if the second of these premises is simply denied, as follows from the categorical semantics (HAIRLESS): on that account, to describe a man who has one hair as bald is strictly speaking false, though it is, certainly, perfectly appropriate (relevant) as a loose use across many everyday circumstances. Of course, there is no suggestion here that this is the way out for the many other such 'sorites' paradoxes (from the Greek *soros* meaning 'a heap') that arise as a result of semantic vagueness. (For discussion of the paradoxes, see Sainsbury and Williamson 1997.)

3   An exception to this generalization is Jonathan Cohen, who, in a series of papers (1971, 1979/93, 1986) has developed the idea that words have very rich semantic encodings consisting of multiple features, which are selectively cancelled in context. The contextual elimination of features of meaning seems to be governed by some sort of principle of consistency. Recall his treatment of 'and' discussed briefly in chapter 3, section 3.3,

according to which the temporal and cause–consequence connections often communicated by an 'and' conjunction are elements of the semantics of 'and', elements which are cancelled in certain contexts. His approach could hardly be more different from Grice's in that a kind of loosening or relaxing of word meaning in context is taken to be commonplace while meaning enrichment is unnecessary. An upshot of Cohen's general approach is an account of metaphor (1979/93) which seems to be interestingly similar to the relevance-theoretic account developed later in this chapter; for instance, the semantic feature MACHINERY is dropped when 'bulldozer' is predicated of a human being. For further discussion of this, see note 12 below.

4   The exceptions are Bach (1994a, 1994b) and Recanati (1995), who both discuss a range of cases of non-literalness. Although Recanati is a Gricean in his treatment of implicature, his account of enrichment and non-literal uses (he concentrates on metonymy) is a huge departure from Grice and much closer to the relevance-theoretic outlook. He sees both processes as what he calls 'primary' pragmatic processes (as opposed to the secondary processes involved in implicature derivation), that is, as contributing to 'what is said', in his intuitive sense (see discussion in chapter 2, section 2.4). Moreover, these primary pragmatic processes are not governed by the Gricean maxims but rather occur in accordance with a criterion of accessibility: at any point in the on-line processing of an utterance, where there are competing candidates for the conceptual value of an element of linguistic form, the most highly activated one is chosen and, according to him, no other communicative principle or criterion is needed. This is a very cognitively oriented account and one of the first to allow for the effects of figurative uses of language to feature at the level of what is explicitly communicated. A comparison and evaluation of the predictions of this accessibility-based account and the relevance-based approach remains to be done.

5   Grice did not specify the sort of pragmatic account he envisaged for the comprehension of 'an unfettered life'. Perhaps he would have said that it works like any case of a metaphor in his system. However, it does not flout the maxim of truthfulness, since it is generally true that the lives in question are not fettered in the physical sense, so it does not follow the derivational pattern of the one case of metaphor he discussed: 'You are the cream in my coffee', which clearly is literally false (see Grice 1975/89b: 34). Perhaps, then, instead of a categorial falsehood, it is a trivial truth when taken literally (as in 'You are not the cream in my coffee') and so it flouts the first maxim of quantity ('Make your contribution as informative as is required'). However, it does not have the sort of blatant quality that is supposed to typify floutings, as in 'the cream in my coffee' examples, both positive and negative, a point which also applies to a great many other loose-use cases, such as those in (11). If the social-psychological meaning of 'unfettered' is not simply an extra sense of the word, then it has to be accounted for pragmatically, but it remains an open question how it could be derived on a Gricean account. According to relevance theory, it should follow from the general account of loose use about to be given.

6   This diagram is incomplete in a number of ways, which do not matter too much in the present context. For instance, the bottom level (of description and interpretation) can be divided into various distinct sorts of sub-case, and the right-hand path, which ends in the interpretation of a further thought, could be continued to another level (or levels), since that interpreted thought may itself be either a description of a state of affairs or an interpretation of yet another thought, and so on, through as many cycles of interpretive representation as the mind can handle. Note also that the scheme given here is slightly different from the one given in the central text on relevance theory (Sperber and Wilson 1986a/95b: 232). This is not the place to try to tease out the differences, which

may or may not be significant. I have chosen the (1987a) picture, coupled with the discussion in Wilson and Sperber (1988b) ('*every* utterance is interpretively used to represent a thought: the very thought the speaker wants to communicate', p. 139), for no better reason than that I find it more comprehensible than the original.

7 A number of people have pointed out to me that some of the words for which I am assuming a semantics with clear category boundaries can in fact co-occur with linguistic modifiers which entail differences of degree, thereby casting doubt on the assumed absolute semantics; e.g. 'this steak is *too* raw', 'these vegetables aren't *quite as* raw *as* those ones'. The primary target of this criticism is the word 'bald' when its meaning is given as TOTALLY HAIRLESS (see note 2 above); as this is such a controversial case, I have not included it in the discussion in this chapter of cases of loosely used absolute concepts. Itzak Schlesinger (personal communication) has noted that the issue is especially acute with 'bald' because the tendency is to provide modification (hedges) in the case of a person who is totally, or almost totally, hairless, rather than when they are only somewhat hairless; e.g. 'Paul is bald, but Jim is *completely* bald' rather than 'Paul is *somewhat* bald, but Jim is bald'. He points out that the prototype of a bald man is of one who in fact has some hair left and that being completely without hair calls for the modification of 'bald' because of its non-prototypicality.

These observations seem undeniable, but their implications for a semantic analysis are not clear. First, a lexical semantics based on prototypes does not seem to be feasible (see Fodor 1998). Second, facts about how a word is most frequently employed need not reflect its semantics, as the words for geometric figures indicate. Furthermore, modification by 'completely', 'totally', 'perfectly', etc., is found across the board, even for cases which are patently absolute, e.g. 'totally hairless', 'perfectly round', 'completely uncooked'. Finally, although I cannot explore it in detail, it may be that the strong underdeterminacy view advocated here, coupled with the idea of pragmatically derived *ad hoc* concepts, accommodates the modification facts. One possibility is that adverbial modifiers, such as 'not quite as *x* as', 'somewhat', 'very', etc., function as indicators to the hearer of the nature of the *ad hoc* concept he is to build. Then, since loose use is the norm in the case of 'bald' and the geometric terms, the adverbials 'completely' or 'perfectly' are perhaps used to ensure the hearer does not follow this usual track, but takes the following lexical concepts quite literally. For an interesting discussion of these issues (which was written before the advent of the *ad hoc* concept approach), see Reboul (1989), who supports Sperber and Wilson (1986b) in their advocacy of a non-fuzzy lexical concept BALD, which entails HAIRLESS, and suggests a solution to the apparent paradox that arises as a result for phrases like 'very bald' and '. . . balder than . . .'. See also Franken (1997) for a recent discussion of Reboul's work and of relevance-theoretic ideas on loose use more generally.

Lewis (1979/83) has presented an account on which, in effect, cases of loose use are treated as a pragmatic analogue to cases of semantic vagueness. According to him, words like 'flat', 'raw', 'hexagonal' and 'bald' are to be understood in relation to a particular standard of precision which may vary from context to context. He says: 'Austin's "France is hexagonal" is a good example of a sentence that is true enough for many contexts, but not true enough for many others. Under low standards of precision it is acceptable. Raise the standards and it loses its acceptability' (Lewis 1979/83: 245). Wilson and Sperber (2000) argue against this approach, and give a range of examples which cannot be construed as involving a continuum of cases with a range of possible cut-off points according to different standards of precision; for instance, the use of 'run' for 'go quickly on foot' in 'I must run to the bank before it closes', or 'glasses' for anything made for drinking from, such as polystyrene beakers, or 'Kleenex' for any brand

of disposable tissue. As they say, these are cases of words with sharp conceptual boundaries, whose loose use cannot be explained in terms of an 'ordered series of successively
broader extensions that might be picked out by raising or lowering some standard of
precision' (Wilson and Sperber 2000: 227). They argue that an account in terms of expectations of relevance explains how these absolute cases work and that it generalizes to
the other (possibly graded) cases, such as 'flat', 'hexagonal', etc., so that there is no need
to invoke degrees of truth or contextually variable standards of precision.

8   A convention or presumption of literalness says that it is generally assumed by hearers
that speakers are using language literally, unless this is clearly impossible (see, for
instance, Bach and Harnish 1979: 12, 61, 224; Lewis 1975; Searle 1969). This seems to
amount to a hearer's counterpart to Grice's speaker's maxim. It entails that a speaker
should be taken as endorsing the literal content of her utterance (equivalent to the
minimal notion of 'what is said'). So arguments against Grice's first maxim of quality
will generally mediate equally against the presumption of literalness.

   However, while loose uses are troublesome for the two maxims of truthfulness which
focus on 'what is said', they are quite consistent with Grice's supermaxim of quality:
'Try to make *your contribution* one that is true' (my emphasis), provided 'contribution'
here is taken to mean all communicated (speaker-meant) propositions. It doesn't follow
from this, though, that we need any such maxim in the relevance-theoretic account. That
the propositions communicated by an utterance are endorsed by the speaker (that is, put
forward as true or probably true) follows from the presumption of optimal relevance
and no separate maxim or principle is needed. (For further discussion, see Ifantidou
1994, 2001, section 4.2.2; Wilson 1995.)

9   There are, broadly speaking, two general analyses of complex demonstratives (as
opposed to bare 'this' or 'that') differing with regard to whether the descriptive
material is taken to contribute to the proposition expressed (hence the truth conditions)
or not. See the useful discussions on this in Braun (1994), Larson and Segal (1995, section
6.4) and Borg (2000). I have assumed that the descriptive material does make such a
contribution and that, therefore, in these metaphorical cases, an *ad hoc* concept formed
from the encoded description is a component of the proposition explicitly communicated. However, even if this is wrong and it is only a *de re* concept of the referent that
occurs in this propositional representation, the *ad hoc* concept has nevertheless played
a crucial preliminary role in the addressee's identification of that referent and so in the
derivation of the proposition expressed. Neale (1999, section 8) argues for an analysis
on which two propositions are expressed, a general one in which the descriptive material appears, and a singular one in which the object referred to appears; the latter is
dependent on the former, in that the object has to satisfy the description, so, again, for
the sort of examples I am considering, the pragmatic construction of an *ad hoc* concept
from the encoded concept is necessary for the determination of the referent.

   All three of these possible analyses have been proposed also for referentially used definite descriptions, but there is a fourth possibility according to which the referent does
not appear in the proposition expressed, in which case this particular line of argument
for the *ad hoc* concept contributing to the proposition expressed does not go through
(see Grice 1969a: 141–2; Kripke 1977; Neale 1990, chapter 3). However, this seems to
be something of a minority view nowadays; it is widely held that the referent does enter
into the proposition expressed, while the descriptive content may or may not (see
Recanati 1989a, 1993; Larson and Segal 1995, chapter 9; Rouchota 1992, 1994b;
Powell 1999; Neale 1999), in which case the points given above for the contribution of
an *ad hoc* concept to the proposition expressed in the case of demonstrative descriptions
carry over to definite descriptions (referentially used).

10 Similar points have been made by Papafragou (1995, 1996) and Recanati (1995) with regard to cases of metonymically used definite descriptions. Papafragou's idea is that in order to determine the intended referent in utterances like (i)–(ii), an addressee has to pragmatically infer a related concept on the basis of the concept encoded by 'burgundy hat' or 'saxophone':

(i) The burgundy hat left in a hurry.
(ii) The saxophone has the flu.

(Note that the relationship between the two concepts in metonymy is not one of interpretive resemblance as in the loose-use cases, but rather one of salient association. That is, the metonymically used concept, e.g. SAXOPHONE, makes the intended one, e.g. SAXOPHONE PLAYER IN BAND X, highly accessible, and on that basis the individual referred to, say Tom Spinx, is identified.)

Recanati (1995) gives a detailed account of those local (subpropositional) pragmatic processes that contribute to the proposition expressed by an utterance (such as disambiguation, instantiation of indexicals, enrichment of senses). He includes in this category of 'primary' pragmatic processes certain kinds of non-literal interpretation and discusses, in particular, metonymy. He shows that a pragmatic process which is mandatory in determining the proposition expressed may depend on an antecedent process of metonymic interpretation. The obligatory process he considers is that of the contextual provision of a specific relation between x and y in the genitive construction 'y's x' and the point is that this may require an antecedent process of non-literal interpretation in order to determine the identity of either 'x' or 'y'. His example is an utterance of 'Bring me the lion's sword', where 'the lion' is used metonymically to refer to a warrior whose shield is engraved with an image of a lion. As he puts it: 'This is a case in which it is not possible (even in principle) to determine the proposition literally expressed before one has determined what the speaker nonliterally means' (Recanati 1995: 229).

11 In Carston (1996b/97a, section 6), I played with a third unified (or symmetrical) position, according to which *ad hoc* concepts, whether a product of narrowing, broadening or a combination of both, are constructed only when 'necessary'. Such a process is necessary if the propositions the speaker intends to communicate cannot be derived without the formation of such concepts, as in the cases of reference assignment just considered (e.g. 'That bulldozer in the back row') and the fixing of the genitive variable mentioned in note 10. However, it is not necessary in most cases where a loosely used concept occurs in the predicate, as in (i) and (ii). Here the encoded concept licenses all the intended implications without having to be adjusted, so that the original relevance-theoretic account goes through quite satisfactorily:

(i) This steak is raw.
(ii) Maria is a nightingale.

(Of course, it also licenses various unintended implications (e.g. Maria has wings) but these are either too low in accessibility to be derived or, if they are, they are abandoned for lack of cognitive effects.) Although it is much less clear that this can work for enrichment cases, there may be a (non-deductive) way, in predication cases, of simply taking highly accessible properties from the encyclopaedic entry of the lexically encoded concept and directly attributing them to the subject referent without going via an *ad hoc* concept. For instance, in (iii), implicatures concerning John's relative youth, heterosexuality, and interest in marriage might be derivable without the setting up of a narrowed *ad hoc* concept BACHELOR*:

(iii) John is a bachelor.

This general position is very much in keeping with the relevance-theoretic procedure for comprehending utterances which involves following a path of least (processing) effort in forming interpretive hypotheses and stopping once one's expectation of relevance is realized. In effect, then, it's left to the procedure to 'decide' whether an *ad hoc* concept is constructed as part of the proposition expressed (explicature) or not. I think this idea is worth pursuing in order to see how workable it is and what its consequences are, but that is a project for the future.

It's interesting to note that, although the dominant claim from psycholinguistic find-ings is that metaphorical interpretation is as fast a process as literal interpretation (see note 13), this is not so in the case of metaphorical descriptions used *referentially* (e.g. 'My princess' used to refer to a cat). Successful reference assignment in such cases has been found to take significantly longer than it does for corresponding literal descriptions (e.g. 'My (spoiled) cat'); see Gibbs (1990); Onishi and Murphy (1993); Noveck et al. (2001). Exactly what lies behind this difference between metaphorical predicates and metaphorical referring expressions needs careful consideration, but it is a result which the third symmetry account would predict since the construction of an *ad hoc* concept would be necessary in the reference case but not in the predicate case. (Of course, there are other important relevance-based considerations here too: a speaker who chooses a metaphorical referring expression is bound to achieve effects additional to merely pro-viding the hearer with an efficient means for securing the intended referent and, as ever, more effect generally requires more effort.)

12 Cohen (1979/93, 1986) takes a position on metaphor and conceptual innovation, which might appear to be rather similar to this one, since it too involves the cancellation of features of lexical meaning. So, for example, the meaning of 'Jane has the face of a wild rose' is arrived at through the cancellation of certain of the features that, in his view, comprise the meaning of 'rose', such as 'has a spiky stem', which is inconsistent with what we know of women's faces. Detailed consideration of his position is beyond my scope here, but I think the differences between the two positions outweigh this superfi-cial similarity. The process is entirely a matter of pragmatics for relevance theorists, the crucial elements of interacting information being encyclopaedic and the process of deriv-ing the metaphorical meaning governed by the relevance-based comprehension proce-dure. For Cohen it is first and foremost a matter of the linguistic system itself, with all the meaning possibilities packed into rich multi-featural lexical semantic entries, which interact in particular *sentential* contexts so that only some of the features are maintained. This sort of decompositional lexical semantics has now been largely discredited (see, for instance, Fodor 1998), and, despite Cohen's (1979/93) lengthy attempt to find a prin-ciple to explain which of the many features of a word may be cancelled in metaphor and which may not be (empirical ones rather than inferential ones, categorical versus non-categorical, most important versus less important, and so on), the matter remains unresolved. I believe that it is, in fact, unresolvable if treated as a linguistic issue rather than a cognitive pragmatic one.

13 It is now a commonplace in the psychological literature that understanding metaphori-cally used predicates takes no longer, and so is no more effort-demanding, than under-standing those used literally. See, for instance, Gerrig (1989) and Gibbs (1994, chapter

3), where many of the experimental findings to this effect are cited. In a brief discussion of the relevance-theoretic view of 'metaphor-as-loose-talk', using the example of an utterance of 'My neighbour is a dragon', Gibbs makes the following critical point:

> [According to the relevance theory view] The indirect nature of metaphor calls for extra processing effort on the listener's part, but this is offset, according to the principle of optimal relevance, by extra effects not achievable by saying directly 'My neighbour is fierce and unfriendly'. . . . Although there may be instances when listeners or readers spend considerable mental effort teasing out the weak contextual implications of a metaphor, the psychological research once again clearly shows that listeners do not ordinarily devote extra processing resources to understanding metaphors compared with more literal utterances. The metaphor-as-loose-talk view, therefore, may not see metaphors as violations of communication norms but still incorrectly assumes that metaphors, and other tropes such as irony, obligatorily demand additional cognitive effort to be understood. (Gibbs 1994: 231–2)

There are several lines of response here: one is to deny that the relevance-theoretic account entails that metaphors are cases of indirectness, hence that they necessarily require more effort to understand than literal utterances; another is to point to the very standardized nature of the metaphors used in the experiments (of the 'dragon', 'bulldozer', 'block of ice' variety) and to suggest that 'full' understanding of truly creative cases really does take more time and effort. Regarding the first point, according to the relevance-theoretic account, the interpretation of literal and of loose (including metaphorical) utterances proceeds in the same way (implications are considered in their order of accessibility and the process stops once the expectation of relevance is fulfilled), so the account does not predict that loose (including metaphorical) uses will generally require more processing effort than literal uses. Indeed, it is to be expected on this account that, in appropriate contexts, a metaphorical interpretation of an utterance may be more easily derived than a literal one (see, for instance, the examples used in Gerrig's experiments). For further discussion of Gibbs's criticism and, more generally, of the processing effort issue for metaphor, see Pilkington (2000, chapter 4).

14 Over the past twenty odd years, Sam Glucksberg and his colleagues have been developing an account of predicate metaphors such as (i)–(iii) which, like the account given here, involves the creation of an *ad hoc* category or concept:

(i)   My job is a jail.
(ii) Lawyers are sharks.
(iii) That surgeon was a butcher.

Their claim is that each of these is, as it appears on the surface, a class inclusion statement (rather than, say, an implicit comparison): what is asserted is that the entity designated by the subject term is a member of a superordinate category referred to by the predicate expression. Understanding any of these is just like understanding 'A robin is a bird' except that 'bird' is a conventional name for a taxonomic category, whereas 'jail', 'shark', 'butcher' are borrowed names for *ad hoc* attributive categories that have to be created on the fly. So an utterance of (i) is understood as asserting that the speaker's job is a member of a category which can be roughly paraphrased as that of 'things/situations which are confining, unpleasant, externally imposed, difficult to get out of, etc.'.

Since this category, which we might represent as JAIL*, has no established lexical form, the word for a prototypical instance of such an externally imposed, confining thing, namely a jail, is used as a name for the more general category.

Given their common appeal to *ad hoc* concepts, it would be interesting to do a close comparison of this account (call it the G account) and the relevance-theoretic (RT) one. While the RT account is explicitly pragmatic and treats *ad hoc* concept construction as a relevance-driven process of uncovering a speaker's informative intention, it is quite unclear what drives the process of metaphor understanding in the G account; it doesn't seem to be conceived of in pragmatic mind-reading terms. Second, the RT account appears to be more general in that essentially the same processes are involved in understanding literal and loose use of language as well as metaphor (which is a kind of loose use). Third, the examples discussed in the G account are all cases of topic-vehicle metaphors (metaphorical predications); it may be that it is extendable to referential metaphors and whole sentence metaphors, but this remains to be made clear. Finally, the unlexicalized category which the metaphorically used term ('jail', 'shark', 'butcher') refers to is always described as 'superordinate' and this appears to mean superordinate to both the subject entity and the literal lexical category in the predicate. That is, the category JAIL* includes both the speaker's job and actual jails. It seems that the relation between the denotation of the *ad hoc* concept JAIL* and the denotation of the lexical concept JAIL could be either one of inclusion (diagram (37a)) or, if certain atypical jails (those with a more open rehabilitative regime, etc.) do not fall under the new concept, one of overlap (diagram (37b)). But what is the superordinate category a speaker refers to when predicating 'block of ice' of Sally, a category that contains humans of a certain reserved and unexpressive disposition and cubes of solidified H_2O? I have suggested that this, along with many other metaphors, is not a case of broadening (with or without some narrowing) but of concept 'transfer' (diagram (37c)); if this is right, then it is quite unclear that an account based on projecting properties from a prototype to form a superordinate category is sufficient, unsupplemented, to cover the full range of (even quite conventional) metaphors.

See the following for much fuller discussion of this approach to metaphor: Glucksberg and Keysar (1990, 1993), Glucksberg, Manfredi, and McGlone (1997) and Glucksberg (2001), and, for a computational realization, see Kintsch (2000). For another approach to metaphor which employs *ad hoc* categories/concepts and takes them to contribute to the proposition expressed by the utterance (hence to its truth-conditional content), see Nogales (1999).

15　The proper treatment of polysemy is currently the subject of considerable debate. In addition to the pragmatic approach advocated here and the ambiguity or 'sense enumeration' approach, there is the very interesting 'generative lexicon' account of Pustejovsky (1995). He points out that quite a wide range of cases of polysemy are systematic in that they occur across different languages; for instance, the various interpretations of 'enjoy' in (i) and of the adjectives 'sad' and 'fast' in (ii):

(i)　Mary enjoyed the novel.　　　　[enjoyed reading/writing]
　　 Mary enjoyed the beer.　　　　 [enjoyed drinking]
　　 Mary enjoyed the conversation.　[enjoyed listening to/taking part in]
(ii)　a sad person / sad face / sad day / sad music
　　 a fast car / fast track / fast race

He develops an account in terms of general mechanisms, including what he calls *type coercion* and *co-compositionality*, such that each polysemous word has a univocal semantics and what varies is how that semantics interacts with the semantics of the term it is in construction with. The approach is criticized by Fodor and Lepore (1998), and by Blutner (2002), who advocates a pragmatic approach. Bach (2001: 38–9) is in broad sympathy with the aims of Pustejovsky, if not the actual mechanisms proposed, since, in his view 'polysemy of this sort [i.e. the sort in (ii) above] seems too systematic to be relegated to pragmatics'. Just where such systematic relatedness in the different meanings that a word may communicate is to be located, that is, whether within the semantics of languages or in the conceptual knowledge available to pragmatic inferential processes, is an interesting question. It may be that there is no general answer and that it varies from case to case.

16   This acquisition question arises for any framework that takes seriously the underdeterminacy thesis at the lexical level. So, for instance, Blutner (2002) says: 'Given a polysemous lexeme, its meaning representation may either refer to a primary conceptual variant (representing its base sense), or it may be a more abstract unit referring to some form of underspecified structure'; he seems to favour the latter option. Similarly, those who advocate lexical meaning representations which contain various kinds of variables or covert indexicals are faced with this issue; see, for example, Szabo (2001) on scalar and/or evaluative adjectives such as 'high', 'old', 'intelligent', 'good', 'simple', and Taylor (2001) on 'suppressed parameters' in the subsyntactic structure of lexical items, such as a location parameter in the meaning of the verb 'rain'.

Recanati (1998) refers to work by Hintzman (1986) on a multiple-trace memory model of word-meaning acquisition, according to which each experience of a token (an utterance) of a word leaves an 'episodic' memory trace. On a new encounter with the word, all those accumulated traces are activated, but with different weightings (accessibility rankings) depending on the particular context, so that some subset consisting of the most strongly activated traces gives the meaning of the word on that specific occasion. This leads to the radical claim that there is no lexical meaning in the sense of a stable encoding: 'Words, as expression-types, do not have "meanings", over and above the collection of token-experiences they are associated with. The only meaning which words have is that which emerges in context' (Recanati 1998: 630). Whether one takes this extreme line or the more conservative one I am taking (on which words do encode something, albeit something very schematic, which simply sends the system off to a particular region in long-term memory), the multiple-trace model offers a suggestive approach to the question of how we acquire word meanings. On the more conservative view, it would need to be supplemented by an account of how the encoded schema or pointer emerges, or is abstracted, over time from the accumulation of traces of particular cognitive experiences of tokens of the word.

Appendix 1:
Relevance Theory Glossary

accessibility (of an assumption): the ease or difficulty with which an assumption can be retrieved (from memory) or constructed (on the basis of clues in the stimulus currently being processed); accessibility is a matter of degree and is in a constant state of flux depending on, among other things, what is occupying attention at any given moment.

cognitive effects: contextual effects in a cognitive system (e.g. an individual). (See also 'contextual effects' and 'positive cognitive effects'.)

cognitive environment (of an individual): the set of assumptions that are manifest to an individual at a given time. (See also 'mutual cognitive environment'.)

communicative intention: a higher-order intention to make it mutually manifest to audience and communicator that the communicator has a particular informative intention. (See also 'manifestness' and 'informative intention'.)

computation: a transformation of a set of symbols into another set of symbols in accordance with some mapping, rule or procedure, which is defined over syntactic (formal) properties of the input symbolic representation.

conceptual address: a mental label or node connecting and providing access to information of various sorts pertaining to a single concept (for example, CAT, LOVE, or AND): logical or computational rules and procedures, encyclopaedic information about the denotation of the concept and linguistic information about the natural-language counterpart of the concept. Some concepts may have only one or two of these types of information.

conceptual semantics: the category of linguistic semantics whose domain is those linguistic forms whose encoded meaning contributes concepts (or conceptual addresses or concept schemas) to the logical form (propositional schema) of an utterance, for example, 'cat', 'sing', 'silent'. (See also 'procedural semantics'.)

context: that subset of mentally represented assumptions which interacts with newly impinging information (whether received via perception or communication) to give rise to 'contextual effects'. In ostensive communication, this set is not pre-given but is selected by the hearer on the basis of the utterance and his bid for an interpretation consistent with the second principle of relevance.

contextual effects: the result of a fruitful (i.e. relevant) interaction between a newly impinging stimulus and a subset of the assumptions already in the cognitive system; there are three main kinds of contextual (cognitive) effects: supporting and so strengthening existing assumptions, contradicting and eliminating assumptions, combining inferentially with them to produce new conclusions. (See also 'contextual implication'.)

contextual implication: a conclusion inferred on the basis of a set of premises consisting of both contextual assumptions and new assumptions derived from the incoming stimulus (for instance, the 'proposition expressed' by an utterance) and not derivable from either of these alone.

descriptively used representation: a representation (whether mental or public) which represents a state of affairs (that is, something non-representational). It is truth-based representation; that is, the representation describes a state of affairs that makes it true. (Compare with 'representation by resemblance' and 'interpretively used representation'.)

echoic use (of a representation): the use of a representation (mental or public) to attribute another representation (mental or public) to someone else (or to oneself at some other time) and, crucially, to express an attitude to it. The representation represented may be linguistic/formal (e.g. phonological, syntactic) or semantic/conceptual and the relation between the two representations is one of resemblance.

explicature: an ostensively communicated assumption which is inferentially developed from one of the incomplete conceptual representations (logical forms) encoded by the utterance. (Compare with 'implicature'.)

higher-level explicature: a particular kind of explicature (see above) which involves embedding the propositional form of the utterance or one of its constituent propositional forms under a higher-level description such as a speech-act description, a propositional attitude description or some other comment on the embedded proposition.

implicature (conversational): an ostensively communicated assumption which is not an explicature; that is, a communicated assumption which is derived solely via processes of pragmatic inference. An alternative characterization: a contextual assumption or contextual implication intended (communicated) by the speaker; hence an implicature is either an implicated premise or an implicated conclusion. (Compare with 'explicature'.)

indeterminacy (of implicature or explicature): a property of those communicated assumptions whose propositional content as recovered by the hearer does not specifically fall within the speaker's informative intention, though her utterance encouraged the hearer to derive some assumptions, of which these are possible cases, among a restricted conceptual range.

informative intention: an intention to make manifest or more manifest to an audience a set of assumptions. (See also 'manifestness' and 'communicative intention'.)

interpretively used representation: a representation (whether mental or public) which represents another representation (whether mental or public) and resembles it in content (logical, semantic, conceptual). (See also 'representation by resemblance' and 'loose use', and compare 'descriptively used representation'.)

irony: a use of language by which a speaker tacitly communicates a mocking or, at least, dissociative attitude to a thought or view which she tacitly attributes to someone other than herself at the time of utterance. (See also 'echoic use'.)

loose use: a use of a representation (whether mental or linguistic) to represent another representation (whether mental or linguistic) with which it is in a relation of non-literal resemblance (i.e. it does not have some of its logical or defining properties, but does have a range of its salient encyclopaedic properties); for instance, 'France is hexagonal'. (See also 'interpretively used representation' and 'metaphor'.)

manifestness (of an assumption to an individual): the degree to which an individual is capable of mentally representing an assumption and holding it as true or probably true at a given moment.

metaphor: a kind of 'loose use' in which, typically, the logical properties of the representation (mental or public) are inapplicable but which gives rise to a range of weak implicatures and other cognitive effects. (See also 'representation by resemblance' and 'strong (vs. weak) communication'.)

metarepresentation: the use of a representation to represent (through a relation of resemblance) another representation (including, possibly, itself).

mutual cognitive environment: a cognitive environment which is shared by a group of individuals and in which it is manifest to those individuals that they share it with each other; every manifest assumption in a mutual cognitive environment is 'mutually manifest'. (See also 'manifestness' and 'cognitive environment').

non-demonstrative inference: an inference to the best explanation, which is not strictly valid (as opposed to a deductive inference which is valid); also known as hypothesis formation and confirmation. An interpretive hypothesis is made (it might be delivered by decoding or by a least-effort strategy for accessing assumptions) and subsequently confirmed or disconfirmed (for instance, by whether or not it leads to a satisfactory range of cognitive effects).

ostensive-inferential communication: communication which involves a stimulus which makes it mutually manifest to communicator and audience that the communicator intends, by means of this stimulus, to make manifest or more manifest to the audience a set of assumptions. It should be distinguished from 'accidental information transmission' and various 'covert' means of communication, where what is missing is the element of overtness characteristic of ostensive communication. (See also 'manifestness' and 'communicative intention'.)

ostensive phenomenon: a stimulus or behaviour that makes manifest an intention to make an assumption or assumptions manifest; that is, a behaviour backed by a 'communicative intention' (see also 'communicative intention').

positive cognitive effects: cognitive effects that contribute positively to the fulfilment of cognitive functions or goals.

presumption of optimal relevance:
1. *1986 definition:*
   (a) The set of assumptions *I* which the communicator intends to make manifest to the addressee is relevant enough to make it worth the addressee's while to process the ostensive stimulus.

    (b)   The ostensive stimulus is the most relevant one the communicator could have used to communicate *I*.

2.   *1995 definition:*
    (a)   The ostensive stimulus is relevant enough for it to be worth the addressee's effort to process it.
    (b)   The ostensive stimulus is the most relevant one compatible with the communicator's abilities and preferences.

(See also 'relevance-theoretic comprehension strategy'.)

principles of relevance:

1.   *First (cognitive) principle of relevance:*
Human cognition is geared towards the maximization of relevance (that is, to the achievement of as many contextual (cognitive) effects as possible for as little processing effort as possible).

2.   *Second (communicative) principle of relevance:*
Every act of ostensive communication (e.g. an utterance) communicates a presumption of its own optimal relevance.

procedural semantics: the category of linguistic semantics whose domain is those linguistic forms whose encoded meaning does not contribute a concept but rather provides a constraint on, or indication of, the way some aspect of pragmatic inference should proceed. Subtypes are (a) constraints on pragmatic inferences involved in deriving the explicit content of the utterance, for example, pronouns and tense; (b) constraints on the derivation of implicatures (intended contextual assumptions and contextual implications), for example, discourse connectives such as 'moreover', 'after all', 'but', 'so'. (See also 'conceptual semantics'.)

processing effort: this is the effort which a cognitive system must expend in order to arrive at a satisfactory interpretation of incoming information (involving factors such as the accessing of an appropriate set of contextual assumptions and the inferential work involved in integrating the new information with existing assumptions).

proposition expressed (by an utterance or speaker): that propositional form which is developed by pragmatic inferences building on the incomplete logical form decoded from the linguistic form employed in the utterance (hence it is an amalgam of decoded conceptual content and of pragmatically inferred concepts). The pragmatic inferences achieve disambiguation, the recovery of intended referents, and conceptual completion and enrichment, in accordance with the second principle of relevance. The proposition expressed may either be ostensively communicated itself (hence an 'explicature') or be merely a vehicle to enable the recovery of assumptions which are ostensively communicated (as in cases of 'loose use' according to the standard relevance-theoretic treatment, pre-1996).

relevance in a context:

classificatory definition:
An assumption is relevant in a context if and only if it has some contextual effect (cognitive effect) in that context.

comparative definition:
extent condition 1: an assumption is relevant in a context to the extent that its contextual (cognitive) effects in this context are large.

extent condition 2: an assumption is relevant in a context to the extent that the effort required to process it in this context is small.

relevance to an individual:

classificatory definition:
An assumption is relevant to an individual at a given time if and only if it has some positive cognitive effects in one or more of the contexts accessible to him at that time. (See also 'positive cognitive effects'.)

comparative definition:
extent condition 1: an assumption is relevant to an individual to the extent that the positive cognitive effects achieved when it is optimally processed are large.
extent condition 2: an assumption is relevant to an individual to the extent that the effort required to achieve these positive cognitive effects is small.

relevance of a phenomenon:

classificatory definition:
A phenomenon is relevant to an individual at a given time if and only if one or more of the assumptions it makes manifest is relevant to him.

comparative definition:
extent condition 1: a phenomenon is relevant to an individual to the extent that the positive cognitive effects achieved when it is optimally processed are large.
extent condition 2: a phenomenon is relevant to an individual to the extent that the effort required to achieve these positive cognitive effects is small.

relevance-theoretic comprehension strategy:
(a)   construct interpretations in order of accessibility (i.e. follow a path of least effort);
(b)   stop when your expectation of relevance is satisfied.
(Note: expectations of relevance may vary across different situations of utterance and with the relative developmental level of the hearer, from an expectation of actual optimal relevance, to more sophisticated and realistic expectations that allow for speakers' fallibility and/or deceptiveness; for detailed discussion, see Sperber 1994a.)

representation: anything used in such a way that it can be construed as being *about* something (as having *meaning*) as opposed to just being itself; aboutness may be truth-based or resemblance-based (see also 'descriptively used representation' and 'interpretively used representation'.)

representation by resemblance: the representation of one thing by another, based not on a relation of truth between the representation and the represented, but on a relation of similarity or resemblance between them; for instance, maps, pictures, gestural mimicry and utterances when they are used to represent other linguistic or propositional representations which they resemble either in formal features or in propositional content.

strong (vs. weak) communication: a communicated assumption ('explicature' or 'implicature') is strongly communicated when the 'informative intention' to make manifest that particular assumption is made highly mutually manifest; the degree of strength with which an assumption is communicated varies on a continuum through to cases of very weak communication, where there is some 'indeterminacy' regarding which specific assumptions within some conceptual range fall under the speaker's informative intention.

weak implicatures: implicated assumptions which are weakly communicated; in cases of evocative metaphor, for instance, rather than a few assumptions being made highly manifest, a wide range of assumptions is made weakly manifest and the interpreter must take a great measure of responsibility for the specific assumptions he represents as part of his interpretation. (See 'strong (vs. weak) communication'.)

Appendix 2:
Gricean Conversational Principles

The Cooperative Principle: Make your conversational contribution such as is required, at the stage at which it occurs, by the accepted purpose or direction of the talk exchange in which you are engaged.

Note: Grice presented this as a 'first approximation to a general principle' (Grice 1975/89b: 26).

Conversational Maxims and Submaxims

These will, in general, yield results in accordance with the Cooperative Principle. They are grouped according to four Kantian categories:

Category of quantity

1 Make your contribution as informative as is required (for the current purposes of the exchange).
2 Do not make your contribution more informative than is required.

Category of quality

Supermaxim: Try to make your contribution one that is true.

Submaxims:
1 Do not say what you believe to be false.
2 Do not say that for which you lack adequate evidence.

Category of relation

Be relevant.

Category of manner

Supermaxim: Be perspicuous.

Submaxims:
1   Avoid obscurity of expression.
2   Avoid ambiguity.
3   Be brief (avoid unnecessary prolixity).
4   Be orderly.
5   Facilitate in your form of expression the appropriate reply.

(this last one is from Grice 1981/89b: 273)

Note: The phrasing of the maxims seems to indicate that some of them concern only 'what is said': see the wording of the submaxims of quality/truthfulness; the manner maxims can only apply to how what is said is to be said. Others seem to apply to the whole of what is meant: the quantity maxims refer to the speaker's 'contribution'; the relation maxim seems entirely general. Opinions vary regarding both how strictly Grice's wording should be taken and what its implications are: see Neale (1992: 526), Wilson (1995), Ifantidou (2001, chapter 3).

References

Note: Dates given in the form '1962/89' refer first to the date of original publication and second to a subsequent reprinting which is the one actually cited.

Abbott, V. and Black, J. 1986. Goal-related inferences in comprehension. In Galambos, J., Abelson, R. and Black, J. (eds) *Knowledge Structures*, 123–42. Hillsdale, NJ: Lawrence Erlbaum.

Anderson, J. 1980. Concepts, propositions, and schemata: what are the cognitive units? *Nebraska Symposium on Motivation* 28: 121–62.

Asher, N. 2000. Truth conditional discourse semantics for parentheticals. *Journal of Semantics* 17: 31–50.

Astington, J., Harris, P. and Olson, D. (eds) 1988. *Developing Theories of Mind*. Cambridge: Cambridge University Press.

Atlas, J. 1977. Negation, ambiguity, and presupposition. *Linguistics and Philosophy* 1: 321–36.

Atlas, J. 1979. How linguistics matters to philosophy: presupposition, truth and meaning. In Oh, C. and Dineen, D. (eds) *Syntax and Semantics 11: Presupposition*, 265–81. New York: Academic Press.

Atlas, J. 1984. Comparative adjectives and adverbials of degree: an introduction to radically radical pragmatics. *Linguistics and Philosophy* 7: 347–77.

Atlas, J. 1989. *Philosophy without Ambiguity*. Oxford: Clarendon Press.

Atlas, J. 1990. Implicature and logical form: the semantics–pragmatics interface. Lectures at Second European Summer School in Language, Logic and Information, Leuven.

Atlas, J. 1991. Review of N. Burton-Roberts, *The Limits to Debate, Mind and Language* 6: 177–92.

Atlas, J. 1992. Why 'three' doesn't mean 3: scalar implicatures, truth-conditions and meaning. Unpublished ms. Pomona College, California.

Austin, J. L. 1946. Other minds. *Proceedings of the Aristotelian Society*, Supplementary volume 20: 148–87; reprinted in Austin, J. L. 1970. *Philosophical Papers*, 2nd edn, ed. J. Urmson and G. Warnock, 76–116. Oxford: Oxford University Press.

Austin, J. L. 1955/62. *How to do Things with Words*, 1955 William James Lectures, Harvard; published 1962. Oxford: Clarendon Press.

Austin, J. L. 1956/57. A plea for excuses. *Proceedings of the Aristotelian Society* 57: 1–30; reprinted in Austin, J. L. 1961. *Philosophical Papers*, ed. J. Urmson and G. Warnock, 123–52. Oxford: Oxford University Press.

Austin, J. L. 1962. *Sense and Sensibilia*. Oxford: Clarendon Press.

Bach, K. 1981/91. Referential/attributive. *Synthese* 49: 219–44; reprinted in Davis, S. (ed.) 1991, 17–32.

Bach, K. 1982. Semantic nonspecificity and mixed quantifiers. *Linguistics and Philosophy* 4: 593–605.

Bach, K. 1986. Thought and object: *de re* representations and relations. In Brand, M. and Harnish, R. (eds) 1986, 187–218.

Bach, K. 1987. *Thought and Reference*. Oxford: Clarendon Press.

Bach, K. 1993. Postscript, to the paperback edn of *Thought and Reference*, 302–19. Oxford: Clarendon Press.

Bach, K. 1994a. Semantic slack: what is said and more. In Tsohatzidis, S. (ed.) *Foundations of Speech Act Theory: Philosophical and Linguistic Perspectives*, 267–91. London and New York: Routledge.

Bach, K. 1994b. Conversational impliciture. *Mind and Language* 9: 124–62.

Bach, K. 1997/99a. The semantics–pragmatics distinction: what it is and why it matters. *Linguistische Berichte* 8, Special Issue on Pragmatics: 33–50; reprinted in Turner, K. (ed.) *The Semantics/Pragmatics Interface from Different Points of View*, 65–84. Oxford: Elsevier Science.

Bach, K. 1999b. The myth of conventional implicature. *Linguistics and Philosophy* 22: 327–66.

Bach, K. 2000a. Quantification, qualification, and context: a reply to Stanley and Szabo. *Mind and Language* 15: 262–83.

Bach, K. 2001. You don't say. *Synthese* 128: 15–44.

Bach, K. 2002. Seemingly semantic intuitions. In Campbell, J. K., O'Rourke, M. and Shier, D. (eds) *Meaning and Truth: Investigations in Philosophical Semantics*, 21–33. New York: Seven Bridges Press.

Bach, K. and Harnish, R. 1979. *Linguistic Communication and Speech Acts*. Cambridge, MA: MIT Press.

Bar-Lev, Z. and Palacas, A. 1980. Semantic command over pragmatic priority. *Lingua* 51: 137–46.

Baron-Cohen, S. 1995. *Mindblindness: An Essay on Autism and Theory of Mind*. Cambridge, MA: MIT Press.

Barsalou, L. 1983. *Ad hoc* categories. *Memory and Cognition* 11: 211–27.

Barsalou, L. 1987. The instability of graded structure in concepts. In Neisser, U. (ed.) *Concepts and Conceptual Development: Ecological and Intellectual Factors in Categorization*, 101–40. New York: Cambridge University Press.

Barsalou, L. 1992. Frames, concepts, and conceptual fields. In Lehrer, A. and Kittay, E. (eds) *Frames, Fields, and Contrasts*, 21–74. Hillsdale, NJ: Lawrence Erlbaum.

Barsalou, L. 1993. Flexibility, structure, and linguistic vagary in concepts: manifestations of a compositional system of perceptual symbols. In Collins, A. C., Gathercole, S. E. and Conway, M. A. (eds) *Theories of Memory*, 29–101. London: Lawrence Erlbaum.

Barsalou, L. et al. 1993. Concepts and meaning. *Chicago Linguistics Society* 29, *Papers from the Parasession on Conceptual Representation*, 23–61. Chicago: University of Chicago Press.

Barton, E. 1990. *Nonsentential Constituents: A Theory of Grammatical Structure and Pragmatic Interpretation*. Amsterdam: John Benjamins.

Barwise, J. 1988. On the circumstantial relation between meaning and content. In Eco, U.,

Santambrogio, M. and Violi, P. (eds) *Meaning and Mental Representations*, 23–39. Bloomington: Indiana University Press.

Barwise, J. and Perry, J. 1983. *Situations and Attitudes*. Cambridge, MA: MIT Press.

Bellert, I. 1977. On semantic and distributional properties of sentential adverbs. *Linguistic Inquiry* 8: 337–51.

Benjamin, B. 1956. Remembering. *Mind* 65: 312–31.

Berg, J. 2002. Is semantics still possible? *Journal of Pragmatics* 34: 349–59.

Bertolet, R. 1983. Where do implicatures come from? *Canadian Journal of Philosophy* 13: 181–91.

Bertuccelli-Papi, M. 1992. Determining the proposition expressed by an utterance: the role of 'domain adverbs'. *Textus* 5: 123–40.

Bezuidenhout, A. 1997a. The communication of *de re* thoughts. *Noûs* 31: 197–225.

Bezuidenhout, A. 1997b. Pragmatics, semantic underdetermination and the referential/ attributive distinction. *Mind* 106: 375–409.

Bezuidenhout, A. 1998. Is verbal communication a purely preservative process? *Philosophical Review* 107: 261–88.

Bezuidenhout, A. 2002. Generalized conversational implicatures and default pragmatic inferences. In Campbell, J. K., O'Rourke, M. and Shier, D. (eds) *Meaning and Truth: Investigations in Philosophical Semantics*, 257–83. New York: Seven Bridges Press.

Bezuidenhout, A. and Cutting, J. C. 2002. Literal meaning, minimal propositions, and pragmatic processing. *Journal of Pragmatics* 34: 433–56.

Blakemore, D. 1987. *Semantic Constraints on Relevance*. Oxford: Blackwell.

Blakemore, D. 1988. 'So' as a constraint on relevance. In Kempson, R. (ed.) 1988, 183–95.

Blakemore, D. 1989a. Linguistic form and pragmatic interpretation: the explicit and the implicit. In Hickey, L. (ed.) *The Pragmatics of Style*, 28–51. London: Routledge.

Blakemore, D. 1989b. Denial and contrast: a relevance theoretic analysis of *but*. *Linguistics and Philosophy* 12: 15–37.

Blakemore, D. 1990. Constraints on interpretations. *Proceedings of the 16th Annual Meeting of the Berkeley Linguistic Society. Parasession on the Legacy of Grice*, 363–70. Berkeley, CA: Berkeley Linguistics Society.

Blakemore, D. 1990/91. Performatives and parentheticals. *Proceedings of the Aristotelian Society* 91: 197–213.

Blakemore, D. 1992. *Understanding Utterances: An Introduction to Pragmatics*. Oxford: Blackwell.

Blakemore, D. 1993. The relevance of reformulations. *Language and Literature* 2: 101–20.

Blakemore, D. 1994. Echo questions: a pragmatic account. *Lingua* 94: 197–211.

Blakemore, D. 1995. Relevance theory. In Verschueren, J., Ostman, J.-O. and Blommaert, J. (eds) *Handbook of Pragmatics: Manual*, 443–52. Amsterdam: John Benjamins.

Blakemore, D. 1996. Are apposition markers discourse markers? *Journal of Linguistics* 32: 325–47.

Blakemore, D. 1997a. Restatement and exemplification: a relevance theoretic re-assessment of elaboration. *Pragmatics and Cognition* 5: 1–19.

Blakemore, D. 1997b. On non-truth-conditional meaning. *Linguistische Berichte* 8, Special Issue on Pragmatics: 92–102.

Blakemore, D. 2000. Indicators and procedures: *nevertheless* and *but*. *Journal of Linguistics* 36: 463–86.

Blakemore, D. 2001. Discourse and relevance theory. In Schiffrin, D., Tannen, D. and Hamilton, H. (eds) *Handbook of Discourse Analysis*, 100–18. Oxford: Blackwell.

Blakemore, D. 2002. *Linguistic Meaning and Relevance: The Semantics and Pragmatics of Discourse Markers*. Cambridge: Cambridge University Press.

Blakemore, D. and Carston, R. 1999. The pragmatics of *and*-conjunctions: the non-narrative cases. *UCL Working Papers in Linguistics* 11: 1–20.

Blass, R. 1990. *Relevance Relations in Discourse: A Study with Special Reference to Sissala.* Cambridge: Cambridge University Press.

Bloom, P. 2000. *How Children Learn the Meanings of Words.* Cambridge, MA: MIT Press.

Blutner, R. 1998. Lexical pragmatics. *Journal of Semantics* 15: 115–62.

Blutner, R. 2000. Some aspects of optimality in natural language interpretation. *Journal of Semantics* 17: 189–216.

Blutner, R. 2002. Lexical semantics and pragmatics. *Linguistische Berichte* 10: 27–58.

Boer, S. and Lycan, W. 1976. *The Myth of Semantic Presupposition.* Bloomington: Indiana University Linguistics Club.

Borg, E. 2000. Complex demonstratives. *Philosophical Studies* 97: 229–49.

Brand, M. and Harnish, R. (eds) 1986. *The Representation of Knowledge and Belief.* Tucson: University of Arizona Press.

Braun, D. 1994. Structured characters and complex demonstratives. *Philosophical Studies* 74: 193–219.

Breheny, R. 1997. A unitary approach to the interpretation of definites. *UCL Working Papers in Linguistics* 9: 1–27.

Breheny, R. 1999. *Context-dependence and Procedural Meaning: The Semantics of Definites.* PhD dissertation, University of London.

Breheny, R. 2000. Dynamic semantics and pragmatics. Unpublished ms. RCEAL, University of Cambridge.

Breheny, R. 2002. The current state of (radical) pragmatics in the cognitive sciences. *Mind and Language* 17: 169–87.

Brewer, W. 1999. Schemata. *The MIT Encyclopaedia of Cognitive Sciences.* Cambridge, MA: MIT Press.

Burge, T. 1974. Demonstrative constructions, reference, and truth. *Journal of Philosophy* 71: 205–23.

Burge, T. 1977. Belief *de re. Journal of Philosophy* 74: 338–62.

Burton-Roberts, N. 1989a. On Horn's dilemma: presupposition and negation. *Journal of Linguistics* 25: 95–125.

Burton-Roberts, N. 1989b. *The Limits to Debate.* Cambridge: Cambridge University Press.

Burton-Roberts, N. 1989c. Theories of presupposition: review article of R. van der Sandt, *Context and Presupposition. Journal of Linguistics* 25: 437–54.

Burton-Roberts, N. 1990. Trivalence, gapped bivalence and ambiguity of negation: a reply to Seuren. *Journal of Linguistics* 26: 455–70.

Burton-Roberts, N. 1991. Review of J. Atlas, *Philosophy without Ambiguity. Mind and Language* 6: 161–76.

Burton-Roberts, N. 1993/97. On preservation under negation. *Newcastle and Durham Working Papers in Linguistics* 1: 18–41; reprinted in 1997, *Lingua* 101: 65–88.

Burton-Roberts, N. 1994a. Apposition. *Encyclopedia of Language and Linguistics.* Oxford: Pergamon Press and Aberdeen University Press.

Burton-Roberts, N. 1994b. Ambiguity, sentence, and utterance: a representational approach. *Transactions of the Philological Society* 92: 179–212.

Burton-Roberts, N. 1999. Presupposition-cancellation and metalinguistic negation: a reply to Carston. *Journal of Linguistics* 35: 347–64.

Butler, K. 1995a. Compositionality in cognitive models: the real issue. *Philosophical Studies* 78: 125–51.

Butler, K. 1995b. Content, context, and compositionality. *Mind and Language* 10: 3–24.

Campbell, L. 1998. *Historical Linguistics.* Edinburgh: Edinburgh University Press.

Cappelen, H. 2000. Saying, implicating, and canceling: in defense of Grice on the semantics–pragmatics distinction. Unpublished Manuscript, Vassar College, New York.

Cappelen, H. and Lepore, E. 1997. On an alleged connection between indirect speech and the theory of meaning. *Mind and Language* 12: 278–96.

Carruthers, P. 1996. *Language, Thought and Consciousness: An Essay in Philosophical Psychology*. Cambridge: Cambridge University Press.

Carston, R. 1988/91. Implicature, explicature and truth-theoretic semantics. In Kempson, R. (ed.) 1988, 155–81; reprinted in Davis, S. (ed.) 1991, 33–51; reprinted in Kasher, A. (ed.) 1998, Pragmatics: *Critical Concepts*, vol. 4, 436–64. London and New York: Routledge.

Carston, R. 1990/95. Quantity maxims and generalised implicature. *UCL Working Papers in Linguistics* 2: 1–31; reprinted in 1995 in *Lingua* 96: 213–44.

Carston, R. 1992. Conjunction, explanation and relevance. *UCL Working Papers in Linguistics* 4: 151–65.

Carston, R. 1993. Conjunction, explanation and relevance. (Revised and extended version of Carston 1992.) *Lingua* 90: 27–48.

Carston, R. 1994a. Conjunction and pragmatic effects. *Encyclopedia of Language and Linguistics*, Oxford: Pergamon Press and Aberdeen University Press.

Carston, R. 1994b/96a. Metalinguistic negation and echoic use. *UCL Working Papers in Linguistics* 6: 321–39; revised version in *Journal of Pragmatics* 25: 309–30.

Carston, R. 1996b/97a. Enrichment and loosening: complementary processes in deriving the proposition expressed? *UCL Working Papers in Linguistics* 8: 205–32; reprinted 1997 in *Linguistische Berichte* 8, Special Issue on Pragmatics: 103–27.

Carston, R. 1997b. Relevance-theoretic pragmatics and modularity. *UCL Working Papers in Linguistics* 9: 29–53.

Carston, R. 1998a. Informativeness, relevance and scalar implicature. In Carston, R. and Uchida, S. (eds) 1998, 179–236.

Carston, R. 1998b. Postscript (1995) to 'Implicature, explicature and truth-conditional semantics'. In Kasher, A. (ed.) 1998. *Pragmatics: Critical Concepts*, vol. 4, 464–79. London and New York: Routledge.

Carston, R. 1998c. Negation, 'presupposition' and the semantics–pragmatics distinction. *Journal of Linguistics* 34: 309–50.

Carston, R. 1999a. Negation, 'presupposition' and metarepresentation: a response to Noel Burton-Roberts. *Journal of Linguistics* 35: 365–89.

Carston, R. 1999b. The semantics/pragmatics distinction: a view from relevance theory. In Turner, K. (ed.) *The Semantics/Pragmatics Interface from Different Points of View* (CRiSPI 1), 85–125. Oxford: Elsevier Science.

Carston, R. 2000a. The relationship between generative grammar and (relevance-theoretic) pragmatics. *Language and Communication* 20: 87–103.

Carston, R. 2000b. Explicature and semantics. *UCL Working Papers in Linguistics* 12: 1–44. Revised version to appear in Davis, S. and Gillon, B. (eds) *Semantics: A Reader*. Oxford: Oxford University Press.

Carston, R. forthcoming a. Relevance theory and the saying/implicating distinction. In Horn, L. and Ward, G. (eds) *Handbook of Pragmatics*. Oxford: Blackwell Publishing.

Carston, R. forthcoming b. A review of Stephen Levinson, *Presumptive Meanings: The Theory of Generalized Conversational Implicature. Journal of Linguistics*.

Carston, R. and Noh, E.-J. 1995/96. Metalinguistic negation is truth-functional negation, with evidence from Korean. *UCL Working Papers in Linguistics* 7: 1–26; reprinted 1996 in *Language Sciences* 18: 485–504.

Carston, R. and Uchida, S. (eds) 1998. *Relevance Theory: Applications and Implications*. Amsterdam: John Benjamins.

Castañeda, H.-N. 1966. 'He': a study in the logic of self-consciousness. *Ratio* 8: 130–57.

Castañeda, H.-N. 1967. Indicators and quasi-indicators. *American Philosophical Quarterly* 4: 85–100.

Castañeda, H.-N. 1990. Indexicality: the transparent subjective mechanism for encountering a world. *Noûs* 24: 735–49.

Chapman, S. 1993. Metalinguistic negation, sentences and utterances. *Newcastle and Durham Working Papers in Linguistics* 1: 74–94.

Chapman, S. 1996. Some observations on metalinguistic negation. *Journal of Linguistics* 32: 387–402.

Chng, S. 1999. *Language, Thought and Literal Meaning*. PhD thesis, University of Newcastle.

Chomsky, N. 1965. *Aspects of the Theory of Syntax*. Cambridge, MA: MIT Press.

Chomsky, N. 1966. *Cartesian Linguistics*. New York: Harper and Row.

Chomsky, N. 1979. *Language and Responsibility*. Sussex: Harvester Press.

Chomsky, N. 1980. *Rules and Representations*. Oxford: Blackwell.

Chomsky, N. 1986. *Knowledge of Language*. New York: Praeger.

Chomsky, N. 1987. *Language in a Psychological Setting*. Special issue of *Sophia Linguistica* 22, Sophia University, Tokyo.

Chomsky, N. 1988. *Language and Problems of Knowledge*. Cambridge, MA: MIT Press.

Chomsky, N. 1991. Linguistics and cognitive science: problems and mysteries. In Kasher, A. (ed.) *The Chomskyan Turn*, 26–53. Oxford: Blackwell.

Chomsky, N. 1992a/2000. Language and interpretation: philosophical reflections and empirical inquiry. In Earman, J. (ed.) *Inference, Explanation and other Philosophical Frustrations*, 99–128. Berkeley: University of California Press; reprinted in Chomsky, N. 2000, 46–74.

Chomsky, N. 1992b/2000. Explaining language use. *Philosophical Topics* 20(1): 205–31; reprinted in Chomsky, N. 2000, 19–45.

Chomsky, N. 1993. *Language and Thought*. Wakefield, RI: Moyer Bell.

Chomsky, N. 1994/2000. Naturalism and dualism in the study of language and mind. *International Journal of Philosophical Studies* 2: 181–209; reprinted in Chomsky, N. 2000, 75–105.

Chomsky, N. 1995. Language and nature. *Mind* 104: 1–61. Slightly modified version printed in Chomsky, N. 2000, 106–63.

Chomsky, N. 2000. *New Horizons in the Study of Language and Mind*. Cambridge: Cambridge University Press.

Clapp, L. forthcoming. On the interpretation and performance of non-sentential assertions. To appear in Elugardo, R. and Stainton, R. (eds) *Ellipsis and Non-Sentential Speech*. Dordrecht: Kluwer.

Clark, H. 1977. Bridging. In Johnson-Laird, P. and Wason, P. (eds) *Thinking: Readings in Cognitive Science*, 411–20. Cambridge: Cambridge University Press.

Clark, H. 1996. *Using Language*. Cambridge: Cambridge University Press.

Clark, W. 1991. *Relevance Theory and the Semantics of Non-declaratives*. PhD thesis, University of London.

Clark, W. 1993a. Relevance and 'pseudo-imperatives'. *Linguistics and Philosophy* 16: 79–121.

Clark, W. 1993b. *Let* and *let's*: procedural encoding and explicature. *Lingua* 90: 173–200.

Cohen, L. J. 1971. Some remarks on Grice's views about the logical particles of natural language. In Bar-Hillel, Y. (ed.) *Pragmatics of Natural Language*, 50–68. Dordrecht: Reidel.

Cohen, L. J. 1977. Can the conversationalist hypothesis be defended? *Philosophical Studies* 31: 81–90.

Cohen, L. J. 1979/93. The semantics of metaphor. In Ortony, A. (ed.) *Metaphor and Thought*, 64–77. Cambridge: Cambridge University Press; reprinted in Ortony, A. (ed.) 1993, 58–71.

Cohen, L. J. 1985. A problem about ambiguity in truth-theoretical semantics. *Analysis* 45: 129–34.

Cohen, L. J. 1986. How is conceptual innovation possible? *Erkenntnis* 25: 221–38.

Cole, P. (ed.) 1978. *Syntax and Semantics 9: Pragmatics*. New York: Academic Press.

Cole, P. (ed.) 1981. *Radical Pragmatics*. New York: Academic Press.

Cormack, A. 1980. Negation, ambiguity and logical form. Unpublished ms, University of London.

Cormack, A. 1998. *Definitions: Implications for Syntax, Semantics and the Language of Thought*. New York and London: Garland.

Crimmins, M. 1995. Contextuality, reflexivity, iteration, logic. *Philosophical Perspectives* 9: 381–99.

Curcó, C. 1995. Some observations on the pragmatics of humorous interpretations: a relevance theoretic approach. *UCL Working Papers in Linguistics* 7: 27–47.

Curcó, C. 1997. *The Pragmatics of Humorous Interpretations: A Relevance-Theoretic Approach*. PhD dissertation, University of London.

Dascal, M. 1981. Contextualism. In Parret, H., Sbisa, M. and Verschueren, J. (eds) *Possibilities and Limitations of Pragmatics: Proceedings of the Conference on Pragmatics, Urbino, July 8–14, 1979*, 153–77. Amsterdam: John Benjamins.

Davidson, D. 1967/84. Truth and meaning. *Synthese* 17: 304–23; reprinted in Davidson, D. 1984. *Inquiries into Truth and Interpretation*, 17–36. Oxford: Clarendon Press.

Davidson, D. 1968/84. On saying that. *Synthese* 19: 130–46; reprinted in Davidson, D. 1984. *Inquiries into Truth and Interpretation*, 93–108. Oxford: Clarendon Press.

Davidson, D. 1970. Semantics for natural language. In Visentini, B. et al. (eds) *Linguaggi nella società e nella tecnica*. Milan: Edizioni di Comunità.

Davidson, D. 1986. A nice derangement of epitaphs. In Lepore, E. (ed.) *Truth and Interpretation: Perspectives on the Philosophy of Donald Davidson*, 433–46. Oxford: Blackwell.

Davies, M. 1983. Idiom and metaphor. *Proceedings of the Aristotelian Society* 83: 67–85.

Davies, M. 1986. Tacit knowledge, and the structure of thought and language. In Travis, C. (ed.) *Meaning and Interpretation*, 127–58. Oxford: Blackwell.

Davies, M. 2000a. Persons and their underpinnings. *Philosophical Explorations* 3: 43–62.

Davies, M. 2000b. Interaction without reduction: the relationship between personal and sub-personal levels of description. *Mind and Society* 1: 87–105.

Davis, S. (ed.) 1991. *Pragmatics: A Reader*. Oxford: Oxford University Press.

Davis, W. 1998. *Implicature: Intention, Convention, and Principle in the Failure of Gricean Theory*. Cambridge: Cambridge University Press.

Dennett, D. 1969. *Content and Consciousness*. London: Routledge and Kegan Paul.

Dinsmore, J. 1982. Review of G. Gazdar, *Pragmatics: Implicature, Presupposition and Logical Form*. *Journal of Pragmatics* 6: 39–80.

Donnellan, K. 1966/91. Reference and definite descriptions. *Philosophical Review* 75: 281–304; reprinted in Davis, S. (ed.) 1991, 52–64.

Dowty, D. 1986. The effects of aspectual class on the temporal structure of discourse: semantics or pragmatics? *Linguistics and Philosophy* 9: 37–61.

Elton, M. 2000. The personal/sub-personal distinction: an introduction. *Philosophical Explorations* 3: 2–5.

Elugardo, R. and Stainton, R. forthcoming a. Grasping objects and contents. To appear in

Barber, A. (ed.) *The Epistemology of Language*. Oxford: Oxford University Press. (Paper read at the Epistemology of Language Conference, University of Sheffield, 10 July 2000.)

Elugardo, R. and Stainton, R. forthcoming b. Non-sentential assertions: a reply to Stanley. Manuscript, Carleton University, Ottawa.

Espinal, T. 1991. The representation of disjunct constituents. *Language* 67: 726–62.

Fauconnier, G. 1975. Pragmatic scales and logical structure. *Linguistic Inquiry* 6: 353–75.

Fauconnier, G. 1978. Is there a linguistic level of logical representation? *Theoretical Linguistics* 5: 31–49.

Fauconnier, G. 1985. *Mental Spaces*. Cambridge, MA: MIT Press.

Flieger, J. 1996. Metaphor and categorization. Seminar paper, School of Oriental and Asian Studies, University of London.

Fodor, J. 1975. *The Language of Thought*. New York: Thomas Crowell.

Fodor, J. 1978. Propositional attitudes. *The Monist* 61: 501–23; reprinted in Fodor, J. 1981c, 177–203.

Fodor, J. 1980. Methodological solipsism considered as a research strategy in cognitive psychology. *Behavioral and Brain Sciences* 3: 63–109; reprinted in Fodor, J. 1981c, 225–53.

Fodor, J. 1981a. Introduction: some notes on what linguistics is about. In Block, N. (ed.) *Readings in the Philosophy of Language*, vol. 2, 197–207. Cambridge, MA: Harvard University Press.

Fodor, J. 1981b. The present status of the innateness controversy. In Fodor, J. 1981c, 257–316.

Fodor, J. 1981c. *Representations: Philosophical Essays on the Foundations of Cognitive Science*. Brighton, Sussex: Harvester Press.

Fodor, J. 1983. *The Modularity of Mind*. Cambridge, MA: MIT Press.

Fodor, J. 1986. The modularity of mind. In Pylyshyn, Z. and Demopoulos, W. (eds) *Meaning and Cognitive Structure*, 3–18. Norwood, NJ: Ablex.

Fodor, J. 1987a. Why there still has to be a language of thought. In Fodor, J. *Psychosemantics: The Problem of Meaning in the Philosophy of Mind*, 135–54. Cambridge, MA: MIT Press.

Fodor, J. 1987b. Modules, frames, fridgeons, sleeping dogs, and the music of the spheres. In Pylyshyn, Z. (ed.) 1987, 139–50.

Fodor, J. 1989/90. Stephen Schiffer's dark night of the soul: a review of *Remnants of Meaning*. *Philosophy and Phenomenological Research* 50: 409–23; reprinted in Fodor, J. 1990, 177–91.

Fodor, J. 1990. *A Theory of Content and Other Essays*. Cambridge, MA: MIT Press.

Fodor, J. 1998. *Concepts: Where Cognitive Science Went Wrong*. Oxford: Clarendon Press.

Fodor, J. 2000a. *The Mind Doesn't Work That Way*. Cambridge, MA: MIT Press.

Fodor, J. 2000b. It's all in the mind: Noam Chomsky and the arguments for Internalism. *Times Literary Supplement* 23 June, 3–4.

Fodor, J. 2001. Language, thought and compositionality. *Mind and Language* 16: 1–15.

Fodor, J., Garrett, M., Walker, E. and Parkes, C. 1980. Against definitions. *Cognition* 8: 263–367; reprinted in shortened form in Margolis, E. and Laurence, S. (eds) 1999, 491–512.

Fodor, J. and Lepore, E. 1991. Why meaning (probably) isn't conceptual role. *Mind and Language* 6: 328–43.

Fodor, J. and Lepore, E. 1998. The emptiness of the lexicon: reflections on James Pustejovsky's *The Generative Lexicon*. *Linguistic Inquiry* 29: 269–88.

Fodor, J. and Lepore, E. 1999. Why compositionality won't go away: reflections on Horwich's 'deflationary' theory. RUCCS technical paper.

Fodor, J. and Pylyshyn, Z. 1988. Connectionism and cognitive architecture: a critical analysis. *Cognition* 28: 3–71.

Foolen, A. 1991. Metalinguistic negation and pragmatic ambiguity: some comments on a proposal by Laurence Horn. *Pragmatics* 1: 217–37.

Frame, Janet. 1951/91. Keel and Kool. In Janet Frame *'The Lagoon' and Other Stories*. London: Bloomsbury Press.

Franken, N. 1997. Vagueness and approximation in relevance theory. *Journal of Pragmatics* 28: 135–51.

Frege, G. 1892a/1980. On sense and reference. *Zeitschrift für Philosophie und Philosophische Kritik* 100: 25–50; reprinted in Geach, P. and Black, M. (eds) 1980. *Translations from the Philosophical Writings of Gottlob Frege*, 56–78; 3rd edn. Oxford: Blackwell.

Frege, G. 1892b/1980. On concept and object. *Vierteljahrsschrift für Wissenschaftliche Philosophie* 16: 192–205; reprinted in Geach, P. and Black, M. (eds) 1980. *Translations from the Philosophical Writings of Gottlob Frege*, 42–55, 3rd edn. Oxford: Blackwell.

Frege, G. 1918a/77. Der Gedanke. *Beitrage zur Philosophie des Deutschen Idealismus*; reprinted in English translation under the title 'Thoughts' in Frege, G. 1977, 1–30.

Frege, G. 1918b/77. Die Verneinung. *Beitrage zur Philosophie des deutschen Idealismus*; reprinted in English translation under the title 'Negation' in Frege, G. 1977, 31–53.

Frege, G. 1923/77. Gedankengefuge. *Beitrage zur Philosophie des deutschen Idealismus*; reprinted in English translation under the title 'Compound Thoughts' in Frege, G. 1977, 55–77.

Frege, G. 1977. *Logical Investigations*, ed. P. T. Geach. Oxford: Blackwell.

Fretheim, T. 1992. The effect of intonation on a type of scalar implicature. *Journal of Pragmatics* 18: 1–30.

Gazdar, G. 1979. *Pragmatics: Implicature, Presupposition, and Logical Form*. New York: Academic Press.

Gazdar, G. 1981. Speech act assignment. In Joshi, A., Webber, B. and Sag, I. (eds) *Elements of Discourse Understanding*, 64–83. Cambridge: Cambridge University Press.

Gentner, D. and Markman, A. 1997. Structure mapping in analogy and similarity. *American Psychologist* 52: 45–56.

Gentner, D., Bowdle, B., Wolff, P. and Boronat, C. 2001. Metaphor is like analogy. In Gentner, D., Holyoak, K. and Kokinov, B. (eds) 2001. *The Analogical Mind: Perspectives from Cognitive Science*, 199–253. Cambridge, MA: MIT Press.

Gerrig, R. 1989. Empirical constraints on computational theories of metaphor. *Cognitive Science* 13: 235–41.

Geurts, B. 1998a. The mechanisms of denial. *Language* 74: 274–307.

Geurts, B. 1998b. Scalars. In Ludewig, P. and Geurts, B. (eds) *Lexicalische Semantik aus Kognitiver Sicht*, 95–117. Tübingen: Gunter Narr Verlag.

Giaquinto, M. 1997. Propositionless thought. Unpublished MS, Philosophy Department, University College London.

Gibbs, R. 1989. Understanding and literal meaning. *Cognitive Science* 13: 243–51.

Gibbs, R. 1990. Comprehending figurative referential descriptions. *Journal of Experimental Psychology: Learning, Memory and Cognition* 16: 56–66.

Gibbs, R. 1994. *The Poetics of Mind*. Cambridge: Cambridge University Press.

Gibbs, R. and Moise, J. 1997. Pragmatics in understanding what is said. *Cognition* 62: 51–74.

Giora, R. 1997. Discourse coherence and theory of relevance: stumbling blocks in search of a unified theory. *Journal of Pragmatics* 27: 17–34.

Glucksberg, S. and Keysar, B. 1990. Understanding metaphorical comparisons: beyond similarity. *Psychological Review* 97: 3–18.

Glucksberg, S. and Keysar, B. 1993. How metaphors work. In Ortony, A. (ed.) 1993, 401–24.

Glucksberg, S., Manfredi, D. and McGlone, M. 1997. Metaphor comprehension: how metaphors create new categories. In Ward, T., Smith, S. and Vaid, J. (eds) 1997. *Creative Thought: An Investigation of Conceptual Structure and Processes*, 327–50. Washington, DC: American Psychological Association.

Glucksberg, S. 2001. *Understanding Figurative Language: From Metaphors to Idioms.* Oxford: Oxford University Press.

Glucksberg, S. and McGlone, M. 1999. When love is not a journey: what metaphors mean. *Journal of Pragmatics* 31: 1541–58.

Grandy, R. 1989. On Grice on language. *Journal of Philosophy* 86: 514–25.

Grandy, R. 1990a. On the foundations of conversational implicature. *Proceedings of the 16th Annual Meeting of the Berkeley Linguistics Society: Parasession on the Legacy of Grice*, 405–10. Berkeley, CA: Berkeley Linguistics Society.

Grandy, R. 1990b. Understanding and the principle of compositionality. In Tomberlin, J. (ed.) *Philosophical Perspectives 4: Action Theory and Philosophy of Mind*, 557–72. Atascadero, CA: Ridgeview Publishing.

Grandy, R. and Warner, R. 1986. Paul Grice: a view of his work. In Grandy, R. and Warner, R. *Philosophical Grounds of Rationality*, 1–44. Oxford: Oxford University Press.

Green, G. and Morgan, J. 1981. Pragmatics, grammar and discourse. In Cole, P. (ed.) 1981, 167–81.

Green, M. 1998. Direct reference and implicature. *Philosophical Studies* 91: 61–90.

Grice, H. P. 1957/89b. Meaning. *Philosophical Review* 66: 377–88; reprinted in Grice, H. P. 1989b, 213–23.

Grice, H. P. 1961/89b. The causal theory of perception. *Aristotelian Society Proceedings, Supplementary Volume* 35: 121–52; reprinted in Grice, H. P. 1989b, 224–47.

Grice, H. P. 1967. Logic and Conversation. William James lectures. Harvard University.

Grice, H. P. 1968/89b. Utterer's meaning, sentence meaning and word meaning. *Foundations of Language* 4: 225–42; reprinted in Grice, H. P. 1989b, 117–37.

Grice, H. P. 1969a. Vacuous names. In Davidson, D. and Hintikka, J. (eds) *Words and Objections*, 118–45. Dordrecht: Reidel.

Grice, H. P. 1969b/89b. Utterer's meaning and intentions. *Philosophical Review* 78: 147–77; reprinted in Grice, H. P. 1989b, 86–116.

Grice, H. P. 1975/89b. Logic and conversation. In Cole, P. and Morgan, J. (eds) *Syntax and Semantics 3: Speech Acts*, 41–58. New York: Academic Press; reprinted in Grice, H. P. 1989b, 22–40.

Grice, H. P. 1978/89b. Further notes on logic and conversation. In Cole, P. (ed.) 1978, 113–27; reprinted in Grice, H. P. 1989b, 41–57.

Grice, H. P. 1981/89b. Presupposition and conversational implicature. In Cole, P. (ed.) 1981, 183–98; reprinted in Grice, H. P. 1989b, 269–83.

Grice, H. P. 1986. Reply to Richards. In Grandy, R. and Warner, R. (eds) *Philosophical Grounds of Rationality*, 45–106. Oxford: Oxford University Press.

Grice, H. P. 1989a. Retrospective epilogue. In Grice, H. P. 1989b, 339–85.

Grice, H. P. 1989b. *Studies in the Way of Words.* Cambridge, MA: Harvard University Press.

Groefsema, M. 1995a. *Can, may, must* and *should*: a relevance-theoretic approach. *Journal of Linguistics* 31: 53–79.

Groefsema, M. 1995b. Understood arguments: a semantic/pragmatic approach. *Lingua* 96: 139–61.

Gross, S. 1998. *Essays on Linguistic Context-sensitivity and its Philosophical Significance.* Unpublished PhD thesis, Harvard University.

Gutt, E.-A. 1991. *Translation and Relevance: Cognition and Context.* Oxford: Blackwell.

Haegeman, L. 1991. Parenthetical adverbials: the radical orphanage approach. In Chiba, S. et al. (eds) *Aspects of Modern English Linguistics: Papers presented to Masamoto Ukaji on his 60th Birthday*, 232–54. Tokyo: Kaitakushi.

Haiman, J. 1983. Iconic and economic motivation. *Language* 59: 781–819.

Haiman, J. (ed.) 1985. *Natural Syntax*. Cambridge: Cambridge University Press.

Haiman, J. 1994. Iconicity. *Encyclopedia of Language and Linguistics*. Oxford: Pergamon Press and Aberdeen University Press.

Hale, B. and Wright, C. (eds) 1997. *A Companion to the Philosophy of Language*. Oxford: Blackwell.

Hand, M. 1993. Parataxis and parentheticals. *Linguistics and Philosophy* 16: 495–507.

Harman, G. 1974. Meaning and semantics. In Munitz, M. and Unger, P. (eds) *Semantics and Philosophy*, 1–16. New York: New York University Press.

Harnish, R. 1976. Logical form and implicature. In Bever, T., Katz, J. and Langendoen, T. (eds) *An Integrated Theory of Linguistic Ability*, 313–91. New York: Crowell; reprinted in Davis, S. (ed.) 1991, 316–64.

Haugeland, J. 1979. Understanding natural language. *Journal of Philosophy* 76: 619–32; reprinted in Lycan, W. (ed.) 1990. *Mind and Cognition*, 660–70. Oxford: Blackwell.

Heim, I. 1983. File change semantics and the familiarity theory of definiteness. In Bauerle, R., Egli, U. and von Stechow, A. (eds) *Semantics from Different Points of View*, 164–89. Berlin: Springer.

Hicks, D. 1990. Kinds of narratives: genre skills among first graders from two communities. In McCabe, A. and Peterson, C. (eds) *Developing Narrative Structure*. Hillsdale, NJ: Lawrence Erlbaum.

Higginbotham, J. 1986. Linguistic theory and Davidson's program in semantics. In Lepore, E. (ed.) *Truth and Interpretation: Perspectives on the Philosophy of Donald Davidson*, 29–48. Oxford: Blackwell.

Higginbotham, J. 1988. Contexts, models, and meanings: a note on the data of semantics. In Kempson, R. (ed.) 1988, 29–48.

Higginbotham, J. 1989. Knowledge of reference. In George, A. (ed.) *Reflections on Chomsky*, 153–74. Oxford: Blackwell.

Higginbotham, J. 1993a. Grammatical form and logical form. In Tomberlin, J. (ed.) *Philosophical Perspectives 7, Language and Logic*, 173–96. Atascadero, CA: Ridgeview Publishing.

Higginbotham, J. 1993b. Language, thought, and language. Abstract of talk given at the Third International Colloquium on Cognitive Science, San Sebastian, May.

Higginbotham, J. 1994. Priorities in the philosophy of thought. *Aristotelian Society Supplementary Volume* 68: 85–106.

Higginbotham, J. 1995. *Sense and Syntax*. Oxford: Clarendon Press.

Hintzman, D. 1986. Schema abstraction, in a multiple trace memory model. *Psychological Review* 93: 411–28.

Hirschberg, J. 1985/91. *A Theory of Scalar Implicature*. PhD thesis, University of Pennsylvania. Published 1991 in the series *Outstanding Dissertations in Linguistics*. New York: Garland.

Hobbs, J. 1979. Coherence and coreference. *Cognitive Science* 3: 67–90.

Hobbs, J. 1983. Why is discourse coherent? In Neubauer, F. (ed.) *Coherence in Natural Language Texts*, 29–70. Hamburg: Buske.

Hobbs, J. 1996. Monotone decreasing quantifiers in a scope-free logical form. In van Deemter, K. and Peters, S. (eds) *Semantic Ambiguity and Underspecification*, 55–76. Stanford, CA: CSLI Publications.

Holyoak, K. and Thagard, P. 1995. *Mental Leaps: Analogy in Creative Thought*. Cambridge, MA: MIT Press.

Hookway, C. 1997. Occasion sentences and eternal sentences. In Lamarque, P. (ed.) *Concise Encyclopedia of Philosophy of Language*, 286–87. Oxford: Elsevier Science.

Horn, L. 1972. *On the Semantic Properties of Logical Operators in English*. PhD thesis. Distributed by the Indiana University Linguistics Club, 1976.

Horn, L. 1981. A pragmatic approach to certain ambiguities. *Linguistics and Philosophy* 4: 321–58.

Horn, L. 1984a. Ambiguity, negation and the London School of Parsimony. *Proceedings of NELS* 14: 108–31.

Horn, L. 1984b. Towards a new taxonomy for pragmatic inference: Q-based and R-based implicature. In Schiffrin, D. (ed.) *Meaning, Form and Use in Context: Linguistic Applications (GURT '84)*, 11–42. Washington, DC: Georgetown University Press.

Horn, L. 1985. Metalinguistic negation and pragmatic ambiguity. *Language* 61: 121–74.

Horn, L. 1988. Pragmatic theory. In Newmeyer, F. (ed.) *Linguistics: The Cambridge Survey*, vol. 1, 113–45. Cambridge: Cambridge University Press.

Horn, L. 1989. *A Natural History of Negation*. Chicago: University of Chicago Press.

Horn, L. 1990. Showdown at truth-value gap: Burton-Roberts on presupposition. Review of Burton-Roberts 1989b. *Journal of Linguistics* 25: 483–503.

Horn, L. 1992a. Pragmatics, implicature, and presupposition. In Bright, W. (ed.) *International Encyclopaedia of Linguistics*, vol. 3, 260–6. New York: Oxford University Press.

Horn, L. 1992b. The said and the unsaid. *Ohio State University Working Papers in Linguistics (SALT II Proceedings)* 40: 163–92. Ohio State University.

Horn, L. 1996. Presupposition and implicature. In Lappin, S. (ed.) 1996, 299–320.

Hornstein, N. 1995. *Logical Form: From GB to Minimalism*. Oxford: Blackwell.

Horwich, P. 1997. The composition of meanings. *Philosophical Review* 106: 503–32.

Horwich, P. forthcoming. Meaning and its place in the language faculty. To appear in Anthony, L. and Hornstein, N. (eds) *Chomsky and his Critics*. Oxford: Blackwell.

Hovy, E. and Maier, E. 1994. Parsimonious or profligate: how many and which discourse structure relations? Unpublished ms.

Hugly, P. and Sayward, C. 1979. A problem about conversational implicature. *Linguistics and Philosophy* 3: 19–25.

Ifantidou, E. 1993. Parentheticals and relevance. *UCL Working Papers in Linguistics* 5: 193–210.

Ifantidou, E. 1994. *Evidentials and Relevance*. PhD thesis, University of London.

Ifantidou, E. 2001. *Evidentials and Relevance*. Amsterdam: John Benjamins. [Revised version of Ifantidou 1994.]

Ifantidou-Trouki, E. 1993. Sentential adverbs and relevance. *Lingua* 90: 69–90.

Iten, C. 1998. The meaning of *although*: a relevance theoretic account. *UCL Working Papers in Linguistics* 10: 81–108.

Iten, C. 2000. 'Non-truth-conditional' meaning, relevance and concessives. PhD thesis, University of London.

Iten, C. forthcoming. *Linguistic Meaning, Truth Conditions and Relevance*. Basingstoke: Palgrave.

Iwata, S. 1998. Some extensions of the echoic analysis of metalinguistic negation. *Lingua* 105: 49–65.

Jackendoff, R. 1983. *Semantics and Cognition*. Cambridge, MA: MIT Press.

Jackendoff, R. 1990. *Semantic Structures*. Cambridge, MA: MIT Press.

Jackendoff, R. 1997. *The Architecture of the Language Faculty*. Cambridge, MA: MIT Press.

Jacob, P. 1997. *What Minds Can Do*. Cambridge: Cambridge University Press.

Janssen, T. 1997a. Compositionality. In van Benthem, J. and ter Meulen, A. (eds) *Handbook of Logic and Language*, 417–73. Oxford: Elsevier Science.

Janssen, T. 1997b. Compositionality of meaning. In Lamarque, P. (ed.) *Concise Encyclopedia of Philosophy of Language*, 102–7. Oxford: Pergamon Press.

Kamp, H. 1981. A theory of truth and semantic representation, In Groenendijk, J., Janssen, T. and Stokhof, M. (eds) *Formal Methods in the Study of Language*, vol. 1, 277–321. Amsterdam: Mathematisch Centrum.

Kamp, H. and Reyle, U. 1993. *From Discourse to Logic*. Dordrecht: Kluwer.

Kaplan, D. 1977/89a. Demonstratives. In Almog, J., Perry, J. and Wettstein, H. (eds) 1989. *Themes from Kaplan*, 481–563. Oxford: Oxford University Press.

Kaplan, D. 1989b. Afterthoughts. In Almog, J., Perry, J. and Wettstein, H. (eds) *Themes from Kaplan*, 564–614. Oxford: Oxford University Press.

Karttunen, L. and Peters, S. 1979. Conventional implicature. In Oh, C. and Dineen, D. (eds) *Syntax and Semantics 11: Presupposition*, 1–56. New York: Academic Press.

Kasher, A. 1991a. Pragmatics and Chomsky's research program. In Kasher, A. (ed.) *The Chomskyan Turn*, 122–49. Oxford: Blackwell.

Kasher, A. 1991b. On the pragmatic modules: a lecture. *Journal of Pragmatics* 16: 381–97.

Kasher, A. 1991c. Pragmatics and the modularity of mind. In Davis, S. (ed.) 1991, 567–82.

Katz, J. J. 1972. *Semantic Theory*. New York: Harper and Row.

Katz, J. J. 1977. *Propositional Structure and Illocutionary Force*. New York: Thomas Crowell.

Katz, J. J. 1978. Effability and translation. In Guenthner, F. and Guenthner-Reutter, M. (eds) *Meaning and Translation: Philosophical and Linguistic Approaches*, 191–234. London: Duckworth.

Katz, J. J. 1981. *Language and Other Abstract Objects*. Oxford: Basil Blackwell.

Katz, J. and Postal, P. 1964. *An Integrated Theory of Linguistic Description*. Cambridge, MA: MIT Press.

Keenan, J., Baillet, S. and Brown, P. 1984. The effects of causal cohesion on comprehension and memory. *Journal of Verbal Learning and Verbal Behavior* 23: 115–26.

Kelley, H. 1972. Causal schemata and the attribution process. In Jones, E. et al. (eds) *Attribution: Perceiving the Causes of Behavior*, 151–74. Morristown, NJ: General Learning Press.

Kempson, R. 1975. *Presupposition and the Delimitation of Semantics*. Cambridge: Cambridge University Press.

Kempson, R. 1979. Presupposition, opacity, and ambiguity. In Oh, C. and Dineen, D. (eds) *Syntax and Semantics 11: Presupposition*, 283–97. New York: Academic Press.

Kempson, R. 1986a. Ambiguity and the semantics–pragmatics distinction. In Travis, C. (ed.) *Meaning and Interpretation*, 77–104. Oxford: Blackwell.

Kempson, R. 1986b. Definite NPs and context-dependence: a unified theory of anaphora. In Myers, T. et al. (eds) *Reasoning and Discourse Processes*. New York: Academic Press.

Kempson, R. (ed.) 1988. *Mental Representations: The Interface between Language and Reality*. Cambridge: Cambridge University Press.

Kempson, R. 1996. Semantics, pragmatics and natural-language interpretation. In Lappin, S. (ed.) 1996, 561–98.

Kempson, R. and Cormack, A. 1981. Ambiguity and quantification. *Linguistics and Philosophy* 4: 259–309.

Kempson, R. and Cormack, A. 1982. Quantification and pragmatics. *Linguistics and Philosophy* 4: 607–18.

Keysar, B., Shen, Y., Glucksberg, S. and Horton, W. 2000. Conventional language: how metaphorical is it? *Journal of Memory and Language* 43: 576–93.

Kintsch, W. 2000. Metaphor comprehension: a computational theory. *Psychonomic Bulletin and Review* 7: 257–66.

Kitis, E. 1995. Connectives and ideology. Paper presented at the 4th International Symposium on Critical Discourse Analysis. University of Athens.

Kittay, E. 1987. *Metaphor: Its Cognitive Force and Linguistic Structure.* Oxford: Oxford University Press.

Knott, A. and Dale, R. 1994. Using linguistic phenomena to motivate a set of coherence relations. *Discourse Processes* 18: 35–62.

Koenig, J. 1991. Scalar predicates and negation: punctual semantics and interval interpretations. *Chicago Linguistic Society 27*, Part 2: *Parasession on Negation*, 140–55. Chicago: Chicago University Press.

Kripke, S. 1977/79. Speaker reference and semantic reference. *Midwest Studies in Philosophy* 2: 255–76; reprinted in French, P., Uehling, T. and Wettstein, H. (eds) 1979. *Contemporary Perspectives in the Philosophy of Language*, 6–27. Minneapolis: University of Minnesota Press.

Lahav, R. 1989. Against compositionality: the case of adjectives. *Philosophical Studies* 55: 111–29.

Lahav, R. 1993. The combinatorial–connectionist debate and the pragmatics of adjectives. *Pragmatics and Cognition* 1: 71–88.

Lakoff, G. 1993. The contemporary theory of metaphor. In Ortony, A. (ed.) 1993, 202–51.

Lappin, S. (ed.) 1996. *The Handbook of Contemporary Semantic Theory.* Oxford: Blackwell.

Larson, R. and Segal, G. 1995. *Knowledge of Meaning: An Introduction to Semantic Theory.* Cambridge, MA: MIT Press.

Lascarides, A. and Asher, N. 1993. Temporal interpretation, discourse relations and commonsense entailment. *Linguistics and Philosophy* 16: 437–93.

Laurence, S. and Margolis, E. 1999. Concepts and cognitive science. In Margolis, E. and Laurence, S. (eds) 1999, 3–81.

Lepore, E. 1983. What model theoretic semantics cannot do. *Synthese* 54: 167–87.

Lepore, E. 1996. Conditions on language understanding. *Proceedings of the Aristotelian Society* 96: 41–60.

Lepore, E. and Loewer, B. 1981. Translational semantics. *Synthese* 48: 121–33.

Lepore, E. and Loewer, B. 1989. You can say that again. *Midwest Studies in Philosophy* 14: 338–56. Notre Dame, IN: University of Notre Dame Press.

Leslie, A. 1987a. Pretence and representation: the origins of 'theory of mind'. *Psychological Review* 94: 412–26.

Leslie, A. 1987b. Children's understanding of the mental world. In Gregory, R. (ed.) *The Oxford Companion to the Mind*, 139–42. Oxford: Oxford University Press.

Leslie, A. and Keeble, S. 1987. Do six-month-old infants perceive causality? *Cognition* 25: 265–88.

Levine, J. 1988. Demonstrating in mentalese. *Pacific Philosophical Quarterly* 69: 222–40.

Levinson, S. 1983. *Pragmatics.* Cambridge: Cambridge University Press.

Levinson, S. 1987a. Minimization and conversational inference. In Verschueren, J. and Bertuccelli-Papi, M. (eds) *The Pragmatic Perspective*, 61–129. Amsterdam: John Benjamins.

Levinson, S. 1987b. Implicature explicated. *Behavioral and Brain Sciences* 10: 722–3.

Levinson, S. 1988. Generalized conversational implicatures and the semantics/pragmatics interface. Ms. University of Cambridge.

Levinson, S. 1989. Review of *Relevance: Communication and Cognition* by D. Sperber and D. Wilson. *Journal of Linguistics* 25: 455–72.

Levinson, S. 1995. Three levels of meaning. In Palmer, F. (ed.) *Grammar and Meaning*, 90–115. Cambridge: Cambridge University Press.

Levinson, S. 2000. *Presumptive Meanings: The Theory of Generalized Conversational Implicature*. Cambridge, MA: MIT Press.

Lewis, D. 1970/83. General semantics. *Synthese* 22: 18–67; reprinted in Lewis, D. 1983, 189–229.

Lewis, D. 1975/83. Languages and language. In Gunderson, K. (ed.) *Language, Mind and Knowledge. Minnesota Studies in the Philosophy of Language*, 7: 3–35. Minneapolis, MN: University of Minneapolis Press; reprinted in Lewis, D. 1983, 163–88.

Lewis, D. 1979/83. Scorekeeping in a language game. *Journal of Philosophical Logic* 8: 339–59; reprinted in Lewis, D. 1983, 233–49.

Lewis, D. 1983. *Philosophical Papers*, vol. 1. Oxford: Oxford University Press.

Lloyd, D. 1989. *Simple Minds*. Cambridge, MA: MIT Press.

Lycan, W. 1984. *Logical Form in Natural Language*. Cambridge, MA: MIT Press.

Lycan, W. 1986. Thoughts about things. In Brand, M. and Harnish, R. (eds) 1986, 160–87.

Lycan, W. 1990. Mental content in linguistic form. *Philosophical Studies* 58: 147–54.

McGinn, C. 1982. The structure of content. In Woodfield, A. (ed.) *Thought and Object*, 207–58. Oxford: Oxford University Press.

Malcolm, N. 1949. Defending common sense. *Philosophical Review* 58: 201–20.

Mann, W. and Thompson, S. 1985. Assertions from discourse structure. *Proceedings of the Eleventh Annual Meeting of the Berkeley Linguistics Society*, 245–57. Berkeley: Berkeley Linguistics Society.

Mann, W. and Thompson, S. 1986. Relational propositions in discourse. *Discourse Processes* 9: 57–90.

Mann, W. and Thompson, S. 1988. Rhetorical structure theory: towards a functional theory of text organisation. *Text* 8: 243–81.

Margolis, E. and Laurence, S. (eds) 1999. *Concepts: Core Readings*. Cambridge, MA: MIT Press.

Marr, D. 1982. *Vision*. San Francisco: Freeman.

Martin, J. 1979. Some misconceptions in the critique of semantic presupposition. *Theoretical Linguistics* 6: 235–82.

Martin, J. 1982. Negation, ambiguity, and the identity test. *Journal of Semantics* 1: 251–74.

Martin, R. 1992. Irony and the universe of belief. *Lingua* 87: 77–90.

Martinich, A. 1984/91. A theory for metaphor. *Journal of Literary Semantics* 13: 35–56; reprinted in Davis, S. (ed.) 1991, 507–18.

Matsui, T. 1995. *Bridging and Relevance*. PhD thesis, University of London.

Matsui, T. 1998. Assessing a scenario-based account of bridging reference assignment. In Carston, R. and Uchida, S. (eds) *Relevance Theory: Applications and Implications*, 123–59. Amsterdam: John Benjamins.

Matsui, T. 2000. *Bridging and Relevance*. Revised version of Matsui (1995). Amsterdam: John Benjamins.

Michotte, A. 1963. *The Perception of Causality*. Andover: Methuen.

Millican, P. 1990. Contents, thoughts, and definite descriptions. *Aristotelian Society*, suppl. vol. 64: 167–203.

Moeschler, J. 1992a. The pragmatic aspects of linguistic negation: speech act, argumentation and pragmatic inference. *Argumentation* 6: 51–76.

Moeschler, J. 1992b. Une, deux ou trois négations? *Langue Française* 94: 8–25.

Moeschler, J. 1997. La négation comme expression procédurale. In Forget, D. et al. (eds) *Current Issues in Linguistic Theory 155: Negation and Polarity*, 231–49. Amsterdam: John Benjamins.

Montague, R. 1974. *Formal Philosophy: Selected Papers of Richard Montague*, ed. R. Thomason. New Haven, CT: Yale University Press.

Moran, R. 1989. Seeing and believing: metaphor, image and force. *Critical Inquiry* 16: 87–112.

Moran, R. 1997. Metaphor. In Hale, B. and Wright, C. (eds) 1997, 248–68.

Morrow, D. and Clark, H. 1988. Interpreting words in spatial descriptions. *Language and Cognitive Processes* 3(4): 275–91.

Murphy, G. 1996. On metaphorical representation. *Cognition* 60: 173–204.

Myers, J., Shinjo, M. and Duffy, S. 1987. Degree of causal relatedness and memory. *Journal of Memory and Language* 26: 453–65.

Nagel, T. 1993. The mind wins: a review of John Searle's *The Rediscovery of the Mind*. *New York Review of Books*, 4 March.

Neale, S. 1990. *Descriptions*. Cambridge, MA: MIT Press.

Neale, S. 1992. Paul Grice and the philosophy of language. *Linguistics and Philosophy* 15: 509–59.

Neale, S. 1994. Logical form and LF. In Otero, C. (ed.) *Noam Chomsky: Critical Assessments*, 788–838. London: Routledge.

Neale, S. 1999. Coloring and composition. In Murasugi, K. and Stainton, R. (eds) *Philosophy and Linguistics*, 35–82. Boulder, CO: Westview.

Neale, S. 2000. On being explicit. *Mind and Language* 15: 284–94.

Newmeyer, F. 1986. *Linguistic Theory in America*. 2nd edn. New York: Academic Press.

Newmeyer, F. 1998. *Language Form and Language Function*. Cambridge, MA: MIT Press.

Nicolle, S. and Clark, W. 1999. Experimental pragmatics and what is said: a response to Gibbs and Moise. *Cognition* 69: 337–54.

Nogales, P. 1999. *Metaphorically Speaking*. Stanford, CA: CSLI/Cambridge University Press.

Noh, E.-J. 1995. A pragmatic approach to echo questions. *UCL Working Papers in Linguistics* 7: 107–40.

Noh, E.-J. 1996/98a. A relevance-theoretic account of metarepresentative uses in conditionals. *UCL Working Papers in Linguistics* 8: 125–63. Reprinted in Rouchota, V. and Jucker, A. (eds) 1998, 271–304.

Noh, E.-J. 1998b. *The Semantics and Pragmatics of Metarepresentations in English: A Relevance-theoretic Approach*. PhD dissertation, University of London.

Noh, E.-J. 1998c. Echo questions: metarepresentation and pragmatic enrichment. *Linguistics and Philosophy* 21: 603–28. [Revised version of Noh 1995.]

Noh, E.-J. 2000. *Metarepresentation: A Relevance Theory Approach*. Amsterdam: John Benjamins. [Revised version of Noh 1998b.]

Noordman, L. and Vonk, W. 1998. Memory-based processing in understanding causal information. *Discourse Processes* 26: 191–212.

Noveck, I. A., Bianco, M. and Castry, A. 2001. The costs and benefits of metaphor. *Metaphor and Symbol* 16: 109–21.

Nunberg, G. 1990. *The Linguistics of Punctuation*. CSLI Lecture Notes 18. Stanford, CA: CSLI.

Nunberg, G. 1993. Indexicality and deixis. *Linguistics and Philosophy* 16: 1–43.

Nunberg, G. and Pan, C. 1975. Inferring quantification in generic sentences. *Papers from the Eleventh Regional Meeting, Chicago Linguistic Society*: 412–22. Chicago: University of Chicago Press.

Onishi, K. and Murphy, G. 1993. Metaphoric reference: when metaphors are not understood as easily as literal expressions. *Memory and Cognition* 21: 763–72.

Origgi, G. and Sperber, D. 2000. Evolution, communication and the proper function of language. In Carruthers, P. and Chamberlain, A. (eds) *Evolution and the Human Mind: Language, Modularity and Social Cognition*, 140–69. Cambridge: Cambridge University Press.

Ortony, A. (ed.) 1993. *Metaphor and Thought*, 2nd edn. New York: Cambridge University Press.

Oversteegen, E. 1997. On the pragmatic nature of causal and contrastive connectives. *Discourse Processes* 24: 51–85.

Papafragou, A. 1995. Metonymy and relevance. *UCL Working Papers in Linguistics* 7: 141–75.

Papafragou, A. 1996. Figurative language and the semantics/pragmatics distinction. *Language and Literature* 5: 179–93.

Papafragou, A. 1997. Remarks on epistemic and 'speech act' modality. Unpublished ms., University College London.

Papafragou, A. 1998a. Modality and semantic underdeterminacy. In Rouchota, V. and Jucker, A. (eds) 1998, 237–70.

Papafragou, A. 1998b. *Modality and the Semantics/Pragmatics Interface*. PhD thesis, University of London.

Papafragou, A. 1998c. Inference and word meaning: the case of modal auxiliaries. *Lingua* 105: 1–47.

Papafragou, A. 2000. *Modality: Issues in the Semantics–Pragmatics Interface*. Oxford: Elsevier Science.

Parsons, K. 1973. Ambiguity and the truth definition. *Noûs* 7: 379–94.

Partee, B. 1993. Semantic structures and semantic properties. In Reuland, E. and Abraham, W. (eds) *Knowledge and Language*, vol. II: *Lexical and Conceptual Structure*, 7–29. Dordrecht: Kluwer.

Partee, B. 1995. Lexical semantics and compositionality. In Gleitman, L. and Liberman, M. (eds) *An Invitation to Cognitive Science*, 2nd edn: *Language*, 311–60. Cambridge MA: MIT Press.

Patterson, S. 1996. Competence, performance, and levels of explanation. Poster presented at the fifth annual meeting of the European Society for Philosophy and Psychology, Barcelona, July.

Patterson, S. 1998. Competence and the classical cascade: a reply to Franks. *British Journal for the Philosophy of Science* 49: 625–36.

Pelletier, F. 1994. The principle of semantic compositionality. *Topoi* 13: 11–24.

Perry, J. 1977. Frege on demonstratives. *Philosophical Review* 86: 474–97; reprinted in Davis, S. (ed.) 1991, 146–59, and in Perry, J. 1993, 3–26.

Perry, J. 1979. The problem of the essential indexical. *Noûs* 13: 3–21; reprinted in Perry, J. 1993, 33–50.

Perry, J. 1986. Thought without representation. *Aristotelian Society Supplementary Volume* 60: 137–51; reprinted in Perry, J. 1993, 205–26.

Perry, J. 1988. Cognitive significance and new theories of reference. *Noûs* 22: 1–18; reprinted in Perry, J. 1993, 227–48.

Perry, J. 1993. *The Problem of the Essential Indexical and Other Essays*. New York: Oxford University Press.

Perry, J. 1997. Indexicals and demonstratives. In Hale, B. and Wright, C. (eds) 1997, 586–612.

Perry, J. 1998. Indexicals, contexts and unarticulated constituents. In Aliseda-Llera, A., van

Glabbeek, R. and Westerstahl, D. (eds) *Computing Natural Language*, Stanford, CA: CSLI Publications.

Pilkington, A. 1992. Poetic effects. *Lingua* 87: 29–51.

Pilkington, A. 1994. *Poetic Thoughts and Poetic Effects: A Relevance Theory Account of the Literary Use of Rhetorical Tropes and Schemes*. PhD thesis, University of London.

Pilkington, A. 2000. *Poetic Effects: A Relevance Theory Perspective*. Amsterdam: John Benjamins.

Pinkal, M. 1995. *Logic and Lexicon*. Dordrecht: Kluwer.

Posner, R. 1980. Semantics and pragmatics of sentence connectives in natural language. In Searle, J., Keifer, F. and Bierwisch, M. (eds) *Speech Act Theory and Pragmatics*, 168–203. Dordrecht: Reidel.

Powell, G. 1999. The referential–attributive distinction – a cognitive account. *UCL Working Papers in Linguistics* 11: 101–25. Revised version 2001 printed in *Pragmatics and Cognition* 9, 69–98.

Powell, G. 2000. Compositionality, innocence and the interpretation of NPs. *UCL Working Papers in Linguistics* 12: 123–44.

Powell, G. 2002. Underdetermination and the principles of semantic theory. *Proceedings of the Aristotelian Society* 102(3): 271–8.

Predelli, S. 1998. I am not here now. *Analysis* 58: 107–15.

Premack, D. 1988. 'Does the chimpanzee have a theory of mind?' revisited. In Byrne, R. and Whiten, A. (eds) *Machiavellian Intelligence*, 160–79. Oxford: Clarendon Press.

Premack, D. 1990. On the coevolution of language and social competence. *Behavioral and Brain Sciences* 13(4): 754–6.

Prince, E. 1988. Discourse analysis: a part of the study of linguistic competence. In Newmeyer, F. (ed.) *Linguistics: The Cambridge Survey*, vol. 2, 164–82. Cambridge: Cambridge University Press.

Pugmire, D. 1998. *Rediscovering Emotion*. Edinburgh: Edinburgh University Press.

Pustejovsky, J. 1995. *The Generative Lexicon*. Cambridge, MA: MIT Press.

Pylyshyn, Z. (ed.) 1987. *The Robot's Dilemma*. Norwood, NJ: Ablex.

Quine, W. V. 1960. *Word and Object*. Cambridge, MA: MIT Press.

Reboul, A. 1989. Relevance and argumentation: how bald can you get? *Argumentation* 3: 285–302.

Recanati, F. 1987a. *Meaning and Force*. Cambridge: Cambridge University Press.

Recanati, F. 1987b. Contextual dependence and definite descriptions. *Proceedings of the Aristotelian Society* 87: 57–73.

Recanati, F. 1989a. Referential/attributive: a contextualist proposal. *Philosophical Studies* 56: 217–49.

Recanati, F. 1989b/91. The pragmatics of what is said. *Mind and Language* 4: 295–329; reprinted in Davis, S. (ed.) 1991, 97–120.

Recanati, F. 1990. Direct reference, meaning, and thought. *Noûs* 24: 697–722.

Recanati, F. 1993. *Direct Reference: From Language to Thought*. Oxford: Blackwell.

Recanati, F. 1994. Contextualism and anti-contextualism in the philosophy of language. In Tsohatzidis, S. (ed.) *Foundations of Speech Act Theory*, 156–66. London and New York: Routledge.

Recanati, F. 1995. The alleged priority of literal interpretation. *Cognitive Science* 19: 207–32.

Recanati, F. 1996. Domains of discourse. *Linguistics and Philosophy* 19: 445–75.

Recanati, F. 1997. La polysémie contre le fixisme. *Langue Française* 113: 107–23.

Recanati, F. 1998. Pragmatics. *Routledge Encyclopedia of Philosophy*, vol. 7, 620–33. London: Routledge.

Recanati, F. 2000. Open quotation. Unpublished typescript, CREA.

Recanati, F. 2001a. What is said. *Synthese* 128: 75–91.

Recanati, F. 2001b. Déstabiliser le sens. *Revue Internationale de Philosophie* 55: 197–208.

Recanati, F. 2002. Does linguistic communication rest on inference? *Mind and Language* 17: 105–26.

Recanati, F. forthcoming a. The limits of expressibility. To appear in Smith, B. (ed.) *John Searle*. Cambridge: Cambridge University Press.

Recanati, F. forthcoming b. Unarticulated constituents. *Linguistics and Philosophy*.

Reimer, M. 1997. 'Competing' semantic theories. *Noûs* 31: 457–77.

Reimer, M. 1998. What is meant by 'what is said'?: a reply to Cappelen and Lepore. *Mind and Language* 13: 598–604.

Richard, M. 1990. *Propositional Attitudes*. Cambridge: Cambridge University Press.

Richard, M. 1993. Attitudes in context. *Linguistics and Philosophy* 16: 123–48.

Rieber, S. 1997. Conventional implicatures as tacit performatives. *Linguistics and Philosophy* 20: 51–72.

Rock, I. 1983. *The Logic of Perception*. Cambridge, MA: MIT Press.

Rouchota, V. 1992. On the referential/attributive distinction. *Lingua* 87: 137–67.

Rouchota, V. 1994a. The subjunctive in Modern Greek: dividing the labour between semantics and pragmatics. *Journal of Modern Greek Studies* 12: 185–201.

Rouchota, V. 1994b. *The Semantics and Pragmatics of the Subjunctive in Modern Greek: A Relevance Theoretic Approach*. PhD dissertation, University of London.

Rouchota, V. 1994c. On indefinite descriptions. *Journal of Linguistics* 30: 441–75.

Rouchota, V. 1996. Discourse connectives: what do they link? *UCL Working Papers in Linguistics* 8: 199–211.

Rouchota, V. 1998a. Procedural meaning and parenthetical discourse markers. In Jucker, A. and Ziv, Y. (eds) *Discourse Markers*, 97–126. Amsterdam: John Benjamins.

Rouchota, V. 1998b. Connectives, coherence and relevance. In Rouchota, V. and Jucker, A. (eds) 1998, 11–57.

Rouchota, V. and Jucker, A. (eds) 1998. *Current Issues in Relevance Theory*. Amsterdam: John Benjamins.

Ruhl, C. 1989. *On Monosemy: A Study in Linguistic Semantics*. Albany: State University of New York Press.

Russell, B. 1905. On denoting. *Mind* 14: 479–93.

Ryle, G. 1949. *The Concept of Mind*. London: Hutchinson.

Sadock, J. 1978. On testing for conversational implicature. In Cole, P. (ed.) 1978, 281–98.

Sainsbury, M. and Williamson, T. 1997. Sorites. In Hale, B. and Wright, C. (eds) 1997, 458–84.

Salmon, N. 1982. Assertion and incomplete definite descriptions. *Philosophical Studies* 42: 37–45.

Salmon, N. 1991. The pragmatic fallacy. *Philosophical Studies* 63: 83–97.

Sanders, T., Spooren, W. and Noordman, L. 1992. Towards a taxonomy of coherence relations. *Discourse Processes* 15: 1–35.

Sanders, T., Spooren, W. and Noordman, L. 1993. Coherence relations in a cognitive theory of discourse representation. *Cognitive Linguistics* 4(2): 93–133.

Sayward, C. 1968. Propositions and eternal sentences. *Mind* 77: 537–42.

Schank, R. 1975. The structure of episodes in memory. In Bobrow, D. and Collins, A. (eds) *Representation and Understanding*. New York: Academic Press.

Schiffrin, D. 1986. Functions of *and* in discourse. *Journal of Pragmatics* 10: 41–66.

Schiffrin, D. 1987. *Discourse Markers*. Cambridge: Cambridge University Press.

Schmerling, S. 1975. Asymmetric conjunction and rules of conversation. In Cole, P. and Morgan, J. (eds) *Syntax and Semantics 3: Speech Acts*, 211–32. New York: Academic Press.

Scholl, B. and Leslie, A. 1999. Modularity, development and 'theory of mind'. *Mind and Language* 14: 131–53.

Searle, J. 1968. Austin on locutionary and illocutionary acts. *Philosophical Review* 77: 405–24.

Searle, J. 1969. *Speech Acts*. Cambridge: Cambridge University Press.

Searle, J. 1978/79. Literal meaning. *Erkenntnis* 13: 207–24; reprinted in Searle, J. 1979. *Expression and Meaning*, 117–36. Cambridge: Cambridge University Press.

Searle, J. 1979/91. Metaphor. In Searle, J. 1979. *Expression and Meaning*, 76–116. Cambridge: Cambridge University Press; reprinted in Davis, S. (ed.) 1991, 519–37.

Searle, J. 1980. The background of meaning. In Searle, J., Keifer, F. and Bierwisch, M. (eds) *Speech Act Theory and Pragmatics*, 221–32. Dordrecht: Reidel.

Searle, J. 1983. *Intentionality*. Cambridge: Cambridge University Press.

Searle, J. 1991. Response: the Background of intentionality and action. In Lepore, E. and Van Gulick, R. (eds) *John Searle and his Critics*, 289–99. Oxford: Blackwell.

Searle, J. 1992. *The Rediscovery of the Mind*. Cambridge, MA: MIT Press.

Searle, J. 1996. *The Construction of Social Reality*. Oxford: Blackwell.

Segal, G. 1994. Priorities in the philosophy of thought. *Aristotelian Society Supplementary Volume* 68: 107–30.

Segal, G. 1996. The modularity of theory of mind. In Carruthers, P. and Smith, P. (eds) *Theories of Theories of Mind*, 141–57. Cambridge: Cambridge University Press.

Segal, G. and Speas, M. 1986. On saying ðət. *Mind and Language* 1: 124–32.

Seto, K. 1998. On non-echoic irony. In Carston, R. and Uchida, S. (eds) 1998, 239–55.

Seuren, P. 1985. *Discourse Semantics*. Oxford: Blackwell.

Seuren, P. 1988. Presupposition and negation. *Journal of Semantics* 6: 175–226.

Seuren, P. 1990. Burton-Roberts on presupposition and negation. *Journal of Linguistics* 26: 425–53.

Seuren, P. 1993. Why does 2 mean '2'? Grist to the anti-Grice mill. In Hajicova, E. (ed.) *Functional Description of Language*, 225–35. Conference proceedings, Charles University, Prague.

Seuren, P. 1994. Discourse semantics. In *The Encyclopedia of Language and Linguistics*, 982–93. Oxford: Pergamon Press.

Seuren, P. 1995. Reflections on negation. In de Swart, H. and Bergman, L. (eds) *Perspectives on Negation*, 153–76. Tilburg University Press.

Seuren, P. 2000. Presupposition, negation and trivalence. *Journal of Linguistics* 36: 1–37.

Sinclair, M. 1995. Fitting pragmatics into the mind: some issues in mentalist pragmatics. *Journal of Pragmatics* 23: 509–39.

Singer, M. 1994. Discourse inference processes. In Gernsbacher, M. A. (ed.) *Handbook of Psycholinguistics*, 479–516. New York: Academic Press.

Smith, N. 1999. *Chomsky: Ideas and Ideals*. Cambridge: Cambridge University Press.

Smith, N. and Tsimpli, I.-M. 1995. *The Mind of a Savant*. Oxford: Blackwell.

Smith, N. and Tsimpli, I.-M. 1996. Modules and quasi-modules: language and theory of mind in a polygot savant. *UCL Working Papers in Linguistics* 8: 1–17.

Sorenson, R. 1991. Vagueness within the language of thought. *Philosophical Quarterly* 41: 389–413.

Sperber, D. 1982/85. Apparently irrational beliefs. In Lukes, S. and Hollis, M. (eds) *Rationality and Relativism*. Oxford: Blackwell. Revised version in Sperber, D. 1985. *On Anthropological Knowledge*, 35–63. Cambridge: Cambridge University Press.

Sperber, D. 1990. The evolution of the language faculty: a paradox and its solution. *Behavioral and Brain Sciences* 13(4): 756–8.

Sperber, D. 1994a. Understanding verbal understanding. In Khalfa, J. (ed.) *What is Intelligence?*, 179–98. Cambridge: Cambridge University Press.

Sperber, D. 1994b. The modularity of thought and the epidemiology of representations. In Hirschfeld, L. and Gelman, S. (eds) *Mapping the Mind: Domain Specificity in Cognition and Culture*, 39–67. Cambridge: Cambridge University Press.

Sperber, D. 1996. *Explaining Culture: A Naturalistic Approach*. Oxford: Blackwell.

Sperber, D. 1997a. Intuitive and reflective beliefs. *Mind and Language* 12: 67–83.

Sperber, D. 1997b. Individualisme méthodologique et cognitivisme. In Boudon, R., Chazel, F. and Bouvier, A. (eds) *Cognition et Sciences Sociales*, 123–236. Paris: Presses Universitaires de France. [English version unpublished but available at *www.dan.sperber.com*.]

Sperber, D. 2000. Metarepresentations in an evolutionary perspective. In Sperber D. (ed.) *Metarepresentations: A Multidisciplinary Perspective*, 117–37. Oxford: Oxford University Press.

Sperber, D., Premack, D. and Premack, A. 1995. *Causal Cognition: A Multidisciplinary Debate*. Oxford: Clarendon Press.

Sperber, D. and Wilson, D. 1981. Irony and the use–mention distinction. In Cole, P. (ed.) 1981, 295–318.

Sperber, D. and Wilson, D. 1983. Early draft of *Relevance: Communication and Cognition*. Unpublished ms., University College London.

Sperber, D. and Wilson, D. 1986a/95b. *Relevance: Communication and Cognition*. Oxford: Blackwell; Cambridge, MA: Harvard University Press. 2nd edn (with postface) 1995.

Sperber, D. and Wilson, D. 1986b. Loose talk. *Proceedings of the Aristotelian Society* 86: 153–71. Reprinted in Davis, S. (ed.) 1991, 540–9.

Sperber, D. and Wilson, D. 1987a. Precis of *Relevance*. *Behavioral and Brain Sciences* 10(4): 697–710.

Sperber, D. and Wilson, D. 1987b. Presumptions of relevance. *Behavioral and Brain Sciences*. 10(4): 736–54.

Sperber, D. and Wilson, D. 1990. Rhetoric and relevance. In Bender, J. and Wellbery, D. (eds) *The Ends of Rhetoric: History, Theory, Practice*, 140–56. Stanford, CA: Stanford University Press.

Sperber, D. and Wilson, D. 1995a. Postface. In Sperber, D. and Wilson, D. 1995. *Relevance: Communication and Cognition*, 2nd edn, 255–79. Oxford: Blackwell.

Sperber, D. and Wilson, D. 1996. Fodor's frame problem and relevance theory. *Behavioral and Brain Sciences* 19: 530–2.

Sperber, D. and Wilson, D. 1997/98a. The mapping between the mental and the public lexicon. *UCL Working Papers in Linguistics* 9: 107–25; reprinted in Carruthers, P. and Boucher, J. (eds) 1998. *Language and Thought: Interdisciplinary Themes*, 184–200. Cambridge: Cambridge University Press.

Sperber, D. and Wilson, D. 1998b. Irony and relevance: a reply to Seto, Hamamoto and Yamanashi. In Carston, R. and Uchida, S. (eds) 1998, 283–93.

Sperber, D. and Wilson, D. 2002. Pragmatics, modularity and mindreading. *Mind and Language* 17: 3–23.

Stainton, R. 1994. Using non-sentences: an application of relevance theory. *Pragmatics and Cognition* 2: 269–84.

Stainton, R. 1997. Utterance meaning and syntactic ellipsis. *Pragmatics and Cognition* 5: 51–78.

Stainton, R. 1998. Unembedded definite descriptions and relevance. *Revista Alicantina de Estudios Ingleses* (special issue on relevance theory) 11: 231–9.

Stalnaker, R. 1970. Pragmatics. *Synthese* 22: 272–89.

Stalnaker, R. 1978. Assertion. In Cole, P. (ed.) 1978, 315–32.

Stalnaker, R. 1980. Review of G. Gazdar 1979, *Pragmatics: Implicature, Presupposition, and Logical Form. Language* 56: 902–5.

Stalnaker, R. 1981. Indexical belief. *Synthese* 49: 129–51.

Stalnaker, R. 1989. On Grandy on Grice on Language. Unpublished paper, MIT. Abstract in *Journal of Philosophy* 86: 526–7.

Stanley, J. 2000. Context and logical form. *Linguistics and Philosophy* 23: 391–434.

Stanley, J. and Szabo, Z. G. 2000a. On quantifier domain restriction. *Mind and Language* 15: 219–61.

Stanley, J. and Szabo, Z. G. 2000b. Reply to Bach and Neale. *Mind and Language* 15: 295–8.

Strawson, P. F. 1950. On referring. *Mind* 59: 320–44; reprinted in Strawson, P. F. 1971, 1–27.

Strawson, P. F. 1952. *Introduction to Logical Theory.* London: Methuen.

Strawson, P. F. 1964. Identifying reference and truth-values. *Theoria* 30: 96–118. Reprinted in Strawson, P. F. 1971, 75–95.

Strawson, P. F. 1971. *Logico-Linguistic Papers.* London: Methuen.

Strawson, P. F. 1974. *Subject and Predicate in Logic and Grammar.* London: Methuen.

Sweetser, E. 1986. Polysemy versus abstraction: mutually exclusive or complementary? *Berkeley Linguistic Society* 12: 528–38.

Sweetser, E. 1990. *From Etymology to Pragmatics: Metaphorical and Cultural Aspects of Semantic Structure.* Cambridge: Cambridge University Press.

Szabo, Z. G. 2001. Adjectives in context. In Kenesei, I. and Harnish, R. (eds) *Perspectives on Semantics, Pragmatics, and Discourse*, 119–46. Amsterdam: John Benjamins.

Tarski, A. 1956. The semantical conception of truth. In Linsky, L. (ed.) *Semantics and the Philosophy of Language.* Urbana: University of Illinois Press.

Taschek, W. 1990. Review of K. Bach, *Thought and Reference. Journal of Philosophy* 87: 38–45.

Taylor K   ist, and descriptus interruptus. *Synthese* 128: 45–61.

          cs, pragmatics and presupposition. Unpublished ms., University
) Thomason, R. 1990.)

          nodation, meaning, and implicature: interdisciplinary founda-
          hen, P., Morgan, J. and Pollack, M. (eds) *Intentions in Com-
          ridge, MA: MIT Press.

          the False: The Domain of the Pragmatic. Amsterdam: John

          trictly speaking true. *Canadian Journal of Philosophy* 15:

          Dan Sperber and Deirdre Wilson, *Relevance: Communica-
          Journal of Philosophy* 20: 277–304.

          ais: *Studies in the Way of Words*, by H. P. Grice. *Mind* 100:

          ale, B. and Wright, C. (eds) 1997, 87–107.

          atic presupposition. *Journal of Pragmatics* 18: 345–71.

          onsiderations in semantic analyses'. *Pragmatics and Cog-

          82. Causal schemas in judgements under uncertainty. In
          r. and Tversky, A. (eds) *Judgements under Uncertainty: Heuristics
and Biases*, 117–28. Cambridge: Cambridge University Press.

Urmson, J. 1956. Parenthetical verbs. In Flew, A. (ed.) *Essays in Conceptual Analysis.* Basingstoke: Macmillan; reprinted in Caton, C. (ed.) 1963. *Philosophy and Ordinary Language*, 220–40. Urbana: University of Illinois Press.

Van der Sandt, R. 1988. *Context and Presupposition*. London: Croom Helm.

Van der Sandt, R. 1991. Denial. *Chicago Linguistic Society* 27: Part 2: *The Parasession on Negation*, 331–44.

Van der Sandt, R. 1994. Denial and negation. Unpublished ms., University of Nijmegen.

Vicente, B. 1998. Against blurring the explicit/implicit distinction. In Mateo Martinez, J. and Yus, F. (eds) *Revista Alicantina de Estudios Ingleses* (special issue on relevance theory) 11: 241–58.

Walker, R. 1975. Conversational implicatures. In Blackburn, S. (ed.) *Meaning, Reference and Necessity*, 133–81. Cambridge: Cambridge University Press.

Welker, K. 1994. *Plans in the Common Ground: Toward a Generative Account of Implicature*. PhD thesis, Linguistics department, Ohio State University.

Welsh, C. 1986. Is the compositionality principle a semantic universal? *Berkeley Linguistics Society* 12: 551–63.

Westerstahl, D. 1985. Determiners and context sets. In van Benthem, J. and ter Menlen, A. (eds) *Generalised Quantifiers and Natural Language*. Dordrecht: Foris.

Wettstein, H. 1979. Indexical reference and propositional content. *Philosophical Studies* 36: 91–100; reprinted in Wettstein, H. 1991, 20–8.

Wettstein, H. 1981. Demonstrative reference and definite descriptions. *Philosophical Studies* 40: 241–57; reprinted in Wettstein, H. 1991, 35–49.

Wettstein, H. 1991. *'Has Semantics Rested on a Mistake?' and Other Essays*. Stanford, CA: Stanford University Press.

Wharton, T. 2000. Interjections, language and the *showing/telling* continuum. *UCL Working Papers in Linguistics* 12: 173–213.

Wilson, D. 1975. *Presupposition and non-Truth-Conditional Semantics*. New York: Academic Press.

Wilson, D. 1991. Types of non-truth-conditional meaning. Unpublished ms., University College London.

Wilson, D. 1994. Relevance and understanding. In Brown, G. et al. (eds) *Language and Understanding*, 35–58. Oxford: Oxford University Press.

Wilson, D. 1995. Is there a maxim of truthfulness? *UCL Working Papers in Linguistics* 7: 197–212.

Wilson, D. 1996. Grammar, pragmatics and knowledge. Paper presented at conference on 'The interface between language and cognition', Keio, Tokyo, March.

Wilson, D. 1998a. Discourse, coherence and relevance: a reply to Rachel Giora. *Journal of Pragmatics* 29: 57–74.

Wilson, D. 1998b. Linguistic structure and inferential communication. In Caron, B. (ed.) *Proceedings of the 16th International Congress of Linguists*, Paris, July 1997.

Wilson, D. 1999a. Relevance and relevance theory. In Wilson, R. and Chierchia, G. (eds) *MITECS Encyclopedia of Cognitive Science*. Cambridge, MA: MIT Press.

Wilson, D. 1999b/2000. Metarepresentation in linguistic communication. *UCL Working Papers in Linguistics* 11: 127–61; reprinted in Sperber, D. (ed.) 2000. *Metarepresentations: A Multidisciplinary Perspective*, 411–48. Oxford: Oxford University Press.

Wilson, D. and Sperber, D. 1981. On Grice's theory of conversation. In Werth, P. (ed.) *Conversation and Discourse*, 155–78. London: Croom Helm.

Wilson, D. and Sperber, D. 1986a. Inference and implicature. In Travis, C. (ed.) *Meaning and Interpretation*, 45–75. Oxford: Blackwell; reprinted in Davis, S. (ed.) 1991, 377–93.

Wilson, D. and Sperber, D. 1986b. Pragmatics and modularity. *Chicago Linguistic Society: Parasession on Pragmatics and Grammatical Theory*, 67–84. Chicago: University of Chicago Press; reprinted in Davis, S. (ed.) 1991, 583–95.

Wilson, D. and Sperber, D. 1986c. An outline of relevance theory. In Alves, H. O. (ed.)

Encontro de Linguistas: Acta, 19–42. Minho, Portugal: Universidade do Minho; reprinted 1987 in *Notes on Linguistics* 39: 5–24.

Wilson, D. and Sperber, D. 1988a. Mood and the analysis of non-declarative sentences. In Dancy, J., Moravcsik, J. and Taylor, C. (eds) *Human Agency: Language, Duty and Value*, 77–101. Stanford, CA: Stanford University Press.

Wilson, D. and Sperber, D. 1988b. Representation and relevance. In Kempson, R. (ed.) 1988, 133–53.

Wilson, D. and Sperber, D. 1992. On verbal irony. *Lingua* 87: 53–76.

Wilson, D. and Sperber, D. 1993a. Linguistic form and relevance. *Lingua* 90: 1–25.

Wilson, D. and Sperber, D. 1993b/98. Pragmatics and time. *UCL Working Papers in Linguistics* 5: 277–98; reprinted in Carston, R. and Uchida, S. (eds) 1998, 1–22.

Wilson, D. and Sperber, D. 1994. Varieties of non-truth-conditional meaning. Ms., University College London.

Wilson, D. and Sperber, D. 2000. Truthfulness and relevance. *UCL Working Papers in Linguistics* 12: 215–54.

Wittgenstein, L. 1931/80. *Culture and Value*. 1980, Oxford: Blackwell.

Wittgenstein, L. 1953. *Philosophical Investigations*. New York: Macmillan.

Woodfield, A. 1999. The semantic principle of compositionality. Unpublished paper, University of Bristol.

Yoshimura, A. 1995. A procedural view of metalinguistic negation. In Kawakami, S. et al. (eds) *Osaka University Papers in English Linguistics* 2: 223–40.

Yoshimura, A. 1998. Procedural semantics and metalinguistic negation. In Carston, R. and Uchida, S. (eds) 1998, 105–22.

Žegarac, V. 1991. *Tense, Aspect and Relevance*. PhD thesis, University of London.

Žegarac, V. 1993. Some observations on the pragmatics of the progressive. *Lingua* 90: 201–20.

Žegarac, V. 1998. What is phatic communication? In Rouchota, V. and Jucker, A. (eds) 1998, 327–61.

Žegarac, V. and Clark, B. 1999. Phatic interpretations and phatic communication. *Journal of Linguistics* 35: 321–46.

Ziff, P. 1972. What is said. In Davidson, D. and Harman, G. (eds) *Semantics of Natural Language*, 709–21. Dordrecht: Reidel.

Zwicky, A. and Sadock, J. 1975. Ambiguity tests and how to fail them. In Kimball, J. (ed.) *Syntax and Semantics* 4, 1–35. New York: Academic Press.

Index

Page numbers in bold indicate definitions in the Relevance Theory glossary.